*For my parents*

# THE LOUDEST VOICE IN THE ROOM

HOW THE BRILLIANT, BOMBASTIC ROGER AILES BUILT FOX NEWS—AND DIVIDED A COUNTRY

GABRIEL SHERMAN

RANDOM HOUSE • NEW YORK

Published in the United States by Random House, an imprint
and division of Random House LLC, a
Penguin Random House Company, New York.

Random House and the House colophon are registered trademarks
of Random House LLC.

Grateful acknowledgment is made to St. Martin's Press for permission to reprint excerpts from *The Man Who Would Not Shut Up: The Rise of Bill O'Reilly* by Marvin Kitman, copyright © 2007 by Marvin Kitman. Reprinted by permission of St. Martin's Press. All rights reserved.

ISBN 978-0-8129-9285-4
eBook ISBN 978-0-679-64409-5

Printed in the United States of America on acid-free paper

www.atrandom.com

987654321

First Edition

# CONTENTS

*"An institution is the lengthened shadow of one man."*
—Ralph Waldo Emerson

*"Television rarely, if ever, tells the whole story."*
—Roger Ailes

# PROLOGUE
## "The Most Powerful Man in the World"

On the evening of December 7, 2011, Roger Ailes found himself in enemy territory: mingling with journalists in the East Room of the White House at a holiday party hosted by the Obama administration. As the chairman and CEO of Fox News, Ailes was effectively the most powerful opposition figure in the country, with a wide swath of the Republican establishment on his payroll. The reception was studded with East Coast news anchors, Ivy League journalists, and Democrats—the kinds of people Ailes had built his career by attacking, and the kinds of people who Ailes believed had it in for him, too. Though Ailes had spent more than four decades in Washington, D.C., and New York City, he still saw himself as a scrapper from a small town in a flyover state who'd had to fight for everything he had. When asked by one reporter what his antagonists thought of him, he replied, "I can pretty much pick the words for you: paranoid, right-wing, fat."

But Roger Ailes believed in the importance of American institutions, and in the sacredness of the presidency, which was why he'd brought his eleven-year-old son, Zachary, along to meet the president. And the White House was a place where Ailes had long been comfortable. He had been going there since he was a twenty-eight-year-old television adviser who'd helped Richard Nixon become president by making the famously stiff, dour man seem warmer and more human on screen.

Ailes and Nixon met in Philadelphia in January 1968. Nixon, about to embark on his second presidential campaign, was in town to appear on *The Mike Douglas Show*, an afternoon variety program watched by seven million housewives across America. Ailes, who was the show's executive producer, understood the revolutionary power of the medium in ways that the politician did not. "It's a shame a man has to use gimmicks like this to get elected," Nixon told Ailes off-camera. "Television is not a gimmick," Ailes shot back, "and if you think it is, you'll lose again." Ailes would help to re-create Nixon, and Nixon, in turn, re-created Ailes. "I never had a political thought," Ailes recalled, "until they asked me to join the Richard Nixon presidential campaign." He imbibed Nixon's worldview, learning how to connect to the many Americans who felt left behind by the upheavals of the 1960s, an insight Ailes would deploy for political advantage, and, later, at Fox News, for record ratings and profits.

"Roger was born for television. The growth of television paralleled his whole life," said the journalist Joe McGinniss, whose landmark book about the 1968 election, *The Selling of the President,* turned Ailes into a star political operative. As a pugnacious television adviser to Presidents Nixon, Ronald Reagan, and George H. W. Bush and then as the progenitor of Fox News, Ailes remade both American politics and media. More than anyone of his generation, he helped transform politics into mass entertainment—monetizing the politics while making entertainment a potent organizing force. "Politics is power, and communications is power," he said after the 1968 election. Through Fox, Ailes helped polarize the American electorate, drawing sharp, with-us-or-against-us lines, demonizing foes, preaching against compromise.

At the prescribed time, Ailes hobbled with Zachary to the rope line to see the president. At seventy-one, his body was failing him. The proximate problem was arthritis, but it was his hemophilia that had accelerated it. He had suffered from the debilitating condition since he was a little boy. Over time, the disease caused blood to pool in his knees, hips, and ankles. Though the swelling ravaged his joints, he was stoic about the problem—on occasion he'd sit through a meeting, his shoe filling up with blood from a cut. His pain became a kind of badge. "The difference between pros and amateurs is that pros play hurt," he once said. Ailes displayed a certain fatalism, perhaps a result of his medical history. A couple of weeks before his thirtieth birthday, he told a reporter, "Most people think I'll be dead before I'm 35."

As a young man, Ailes had the striking features of an actor, with dark eyebrows over wide-set eyes and a sly, confident smile. But these days he looked more like Alfred Hitchcock. He was resigned to his girth, rationalizing it as beyond his control. "It's not that I eat too much," Ailes would say. "It's that I can't move." Which wasn't strictly true. During the 1988 presidential campaign, when his weight was ballooning, colleagues observed Ailes inhaling Häagen-Dazs ice cream. At rare moments, Ailes expressed vulnerability about his body image. "Photo editors are sadistic bastards," he told a journalist around this time. "And photographers always make me look heavy."

Mainly, his appetite was in keeping with his no-bullshit attitude—you're hungry, you eat—but it could also be seen as a metaphor for his gargantuan ambition. "I'm never going to be one of those $25,000 a year guys," he'd vowed at the outset of his career. He also knew what this goal might cost him. "I think I'll lead an unhappy life, in terms of what most people consider personal happiness," he said. "Personal unhappiness causes you to work harder, and working harder causes more personal unhappiness." He married three times and did not become a father until an age when most people think about retirement. He denied himself the American ideal of happiness—"home, family, the 9-to-5 job, a good golf score, three weeks paid vacation, a new car"—in the service of his career.

Money and power were one thing, important measures of success especially to someone from middle America, and Ailes liked to keep score. But another reason he worked so hard was that he saw himself as a field marshal in an epic battle to defend the American dream against the counterculture. "Revolutionaries want to take away from people who have. They don't want to create. They get in gangs for support," he said. All of his tactical genius as a political consultant—dismembering Michael Dukakis as soft on crime in the service of George H. W. Bush, for one—was driven by his urge to defeat them. Fox News itself, immensely profitable business though it was, was a continuation of his politics by other means. "A lot of the time Roger sees himself as holding back the tide. And a lot of the hysteria around him is people thinking he might be able to," said David Rhodes, who spent twelve years working at Fox and in 2011 became the president of CBS News.

For Ailes, Obama's meteoric ascent onto the national stage was yet another triumph of the counterculture and the liberal news media. "People need to be reminded," Ailes told Fox News executives around the time Obama declared his candidacy, "this guy never had a job. He's a community organizer." A few days after Obama's historic election, Ailes remarked during his morning editorial meeting, "There's no reason to have a civil rights movement anymore, since there is a black man in the White House." Obama's victory changed the mission of Fox News. "When he started the channel, it was a campaign against CNN. But it is now less about the competition and more about the administration," a former senior Fox producer said. "He honestly thinks Obama has set back the country forever. He feels like he is the only one out there who can save the republic. He has said it."

Ailes's battle did not end when he left the office. At his weekend estate in Putnam County, some forty miles north of New York City, Ailes bought the local newspaper and used it to advance his agenda. He complained to neighbors that Obama refused to call Muslims "terrorists." He told them that Obama was using the stimulus as a "political tool" in order to buy his reelection in 2012. Obama pushed green energy, when in fact climate change was a "worldwide conspiracy" spun by "foreign nations" to gain control of America's resources.

Ailes even told his advisers that if Obama were reelected, he could be prosecuted and jailed, like a political prisoner. During a forty-five-minute meeting at Bill Clinton's foundation in Harlem, Ailes told the former president that he might emigrate to Ireland, and had explored acquiring an Irish passport.

And yet, in the halls of the White House, Ailes kept these feelings to himself. As he walked up to Obama to shake his hand and pose for a photo, he faced a very different politician than the one he'd first met in the summer of 2008. At the time, Obama was a candidate who believed in his ability to overcome the grievance politics of the past through the force of his personal narrative. He told his aides he thought he could win over Fox's audience—and even Ailes himself—by reasoning with them. Now, nearly three years into his first term, Obama had learned—often the hard way—that his vision of harmony was a pipe dream.

On the rope line, Obama greeted Ailes and his son.

"I see the most powerful man in the world is here," Obama said.

Ailes grinned. "Don't believe what you read, Mr. President. I started those rumors myself."

Whatever President Obama intended to convey, there is no denying an essential truth in the remark. Roger Ailes has the power, more than any single person in American public life, to define the president. For many Americans—admittedly and patently not the ones that voted for him—the Obama they know, the one they are raging against, is the one Ailes has played a large role creating.

All of Obama's efforts as a conciliator cannot change the fact that conflict is intrinsically more interesting than consensus. And political conflict has never been more compelling than on Ailes's Fox News. His channel is a self-contained universe, with distinctive laws—"fair and balanced"—and sometimes its own facts. Though marketed as an antidote to the epistemic closure of the mainstream media, Fox News is as closed off as the media world it proposes to balance—Ailes's audience seldom watches anything else. They have been conditioned by Fox's pundits to see the broadcast networks, CNN, and MSNBC as opponents in a grand partisan struggle.

On Fox News, the tedious personages of workaday politics are reborn as heroes and villains with triumphs and reverses—never-ending story lines. And the beauty of it is that Ailes's viewers—the voters—are the protagonists, victims of socialist overlords, or rebels coming to take the government back. The viewers, on their couches, are flattered as the most important participants, the foot soldiers in Ailes's army.

In the early years of Fox News, Ailes kept a healthy distance between his own worldview and the product that ultimately ended up on the air. The network's original blueprint was more tabloid and populist than baldly conservative. When the Australian media mogul Rupert Murdoch hired Ailes in 1996 to launch Fox News, the media establishment wrote the effort off as a joke. Ailes, never one to heed criticism, turned the channel into a powerhouse that would earn more money than any other division in Murdoch's News Corp. In 2002, Fox passed CNN as the number-one-rated cable news network; within seven years, its audience more than doubled that of CNN and MSNBC, and its profits were believed to exceed those of its cable news rivals and the broadcast evening newscasts *combined*. In 2012, a Wall Street analyst valued Fox News at $12.4 billion. With numbers like that came privileges, and Ailes wasn't afraid to press his advantage. "No one could rein Ailes in," said a former News Corp executive.

Even Rupert Murdoch. It did not matter that Murdoch's romance with Ailes, which had burned hot at the beginning of their collaboration, had begun to cool after a decade. "He's paranoid," Murdoch told Ailes's friend Liz Smith, the gossip columnist. For all his right-wing bona fides, Rupert Murdoch himself was a pragmatist whose political commitments changed according to the needs of his business. In 2008, Murdoch even contemplated supporting Obama in the pages of the *New York Post* instead of the Republican, John McCain. When Ailes caught wind of the possible endorsement, he threatened to quit. It was a game of brinkmanship that Ailes won. Murdoch promised Ailes complete editorial independence and gave him a new five-year contract to stay at News Corp. In September, the *Post* endorsed McCain.

At times, Murdoch even sided with Ailes against his children. In 2005, Murdoch's older son, Lachlan, left the company after clashing with Ailes, among others, over management decisions. In 2010, Murdoch cut off contact with Matthew Freud, the husband of his daughter Elisabeth, after Freud told *The New York Times,* "I am by no means alone within the family or the company in being ashamed and sickened by Roger Ailes's horrendous and sustained disregard of the journalistic standards that News Corporation, its founder and every other global media business aspires to." In 2011, during the height of the phone hacking scandal at News Corp's London tabloids, James, the younger of Rupert's sons and no fan of Fox News, saw his chances to succeed his father implode. "He's a fucking dope," Ailes told a friend over dinner.

The more the hacking crisis engulfed the company, the more Murdoch relied on Ailes's profits. "They all hate me, I make them a lot of money and they go and spend the money," Ailes said to Bill Shine, Fox's head of programming. Ailes took a certain pleasure in watching News Corp executives face lawsuits and criminal prosecution over the scandal. "He was delighted it was happening," an executive recalled. "He said, 'It's nice to not be the only bad guy in the company.' "

Ailes's ego and temper, of the sort that sidelined lesser players, were tolerated. He openly bad-mouthed News Corp board member John Thornton, a former president of Goldman Sachs, who suggested programming ideas to him. "I'm not going to have some fucking liberal tell me how to program my network," Ailes told Bill Shine.

But Ailes's true interest was national, not corporate, politics. "I *want* to elect the next president," he told Fox executives in a meeting in 2010. If there was anyone in America who could deliver on such a boast, it was Ailes. At Fox News, he had positioned himself as the closest thing to a party boss the country had. In the spring of 2011, Fox employed five prospective Republican presidential candidates, and no serious Republican could run for president without at least seeking Ailes's blessing. "Every single candidate has consulted with Roger," one top Republican said. The challenge was that the field of candidates Ailes had assembled in the Fox studios, excellent entertainers though many of them were, were not deemed up to the job of a successful White House run. Although Ailes told one Fox contributor that even his security guard would make a better president than Obama, Ailes did not see any winners among his pundits. "He finds flaws in everyone," said a confidant. Former House speaker Newt Gingrich was a prick; former senator Rick Santorum was a nobody; former governor Mike Huckabee couldn't raise a nickel; former Alaska governor Sarah Palin was an idiot. And the two adults in the room, unaffiliated with Fox, former governors Jon Huntsman and Mitt Romney, were less than impressive.

In a meeting at Fox News, Ailes flatly told Huntsman, "You're not of our orthodoxy," citing his stance on climate change. ("To be clear. I believe in evolution and trust scientists on global warming. Call me crazy," Huntsman had tweeted.) After finishing third in the New Hampshire primary, Huntsman dropped out of the race. Over the course of his candidacy, he had only banked four hours and thirty-two minutes of Fox face time. By comparison, pizza mogul Herman Cain, who was a candidate for a similar length of time, notched eleven hours and six minutes.

To win the White House, Ailes would have to harness the circus he'd created to a candidate with crossover appeal, and he worked assiduously to recruit one. Ailes twice encouraged the brash New Jersey governor, Chris Christie, to run. Ailes also sent an emissary to Kabul, Afghanistan, urging General David Petraeus to jump into the primary. Both decided to sit out the race.

So Ailes dealt with reality. From the start, he'd been lukewarm on the front-runner and eventual nominee, Mitt Romney. "Romney came for a meeting at Fox during the primaries and did his speech in the second-floor conference room," a person in the room said. "What was most telling was that Roger himself didn't ask too many questions. Roger never liked Romney." Ailes told Romney once over dinner, "You ought to be looser on the air." In another conversation, he told him, "Be more real. Look the camera in the eye. Stop being a preppy." Behind his back, he had sharper words. He told one Fox host that Romney was "like Chinese food—twenty minutes after you eat it, you can't remember what you had." In a conversation at his Fox office with *Weekly Standard* editor Bill Kristol, Ailes questioned Romney's spine. "Romney's gotta rip Obama's face off," Ailes said. "It's really hard to do."

If Romney would not rip Obama's face off, Fox would. "Roger was running a political campaign," a person close to Ailes said. "He felt, 'We're going to have to do a lot of things to get this guy elected.' Instead of propping up Romney, it was more, 'Let's go after Obama.'" Ailes personally directed and stage-managed his channel's campaign, using entertainment techniques to shape a political narrative that was presented as unbiased news, a hybrid that makes Ailes a unique American auteur.

On the morning of May 30, 2012, the day after Romney clinched the GOP nomination, Fox unofficially launched Romney's general election campaign with a *Fox & Friends* segment. "What sort of change have we really seen over the last four years from the Obama administration?" host Steve Doocy asked.

"Let's take a look back," his co-host Gretchen Carlson chirped.

A four-minute video began to play. After several seconds of inspiring images of Obama's victory night speech in Grant Park, an ominous orchestral score, as if from a horror film, drowned out the cheers of Obama's supporters. Throughout the segment, the voices of news anchors broadcasted dire headlines. Dissonant alarm sirens blared. An animated money bag made a mockery of the mounting national debt. Unemployment numbers ticked up on the screen like a doomsday clock in reverse. A cartoon image of farm animals on a spinning circular platform illustrated the rising cost of food. At the end, Obama was given the last word: "That's the power of hope. That's the change we seek. That's the change we can stand for."

The video was Ailes's brainchild. According to an executive with firsthand knowledge, Ailes "gave the overview" of the segment in a meeting with Bill Shine. Shine then handed off the instructions to *Fox & Friends* executive producer Lauren Petterson, who tasked associate producer Chris White with the project. Before it was televised, Shine played the clip for Ailes.

Not surprisingly, the segment sparked a media firestorm. A news channel had produced and aired what could only be classified as a political attack ad. Ailes, in classic fashion, took no responsibility. Fox pulled the clip off its website and released a statement with Shine's name attached that assigned blame to a junior staffer. "Roger was not aware of the video," a Fox spokeswoman told *The New York Times*.

Obama's camp was not persuaded. Senior adviser David Axelrod emailed Ailes that day. "I see you're back in the spot business," he wrote, alluding to the infamous attack ads Ailes produced in the 1980s.

As the campaign unfolded, Fox would serve as a crucial plank in Romney's media strategy. "Fox is watched by the true believers," Romney told guests at a private fundraiser in Florida. Romney, for the most part, shunned the Big Three networks and CNN in favor of Ailes's channel.

In the year after he announced he was running for president, Romney gave twenty-one separate interviews to *Fox & Friends*. The appearances gave Romney a pulpit to stoke his base's passions. So when Gretchen Carlson asked, "Would you go as far as Rush Limbaugh did yesterday in saying this is the first president in modern time who's going to run a campaign against capitalism?" Romney played along. "Well, it certainly sounds like that's what he's doing."

In August, when Romney introduced his vice presidential pick, Wisconsin congressman Paul Ryan, Fox anchor Megyn Kelly giddily compared Ryan to Ronald Reagan. On her program, a montage of video clips showed Ryan and the Gipper inveighing against government spending with similar language. Kelly then welcomed Reagan's son Michael to make the comparison himself on camera.

Behind the scenes, Ailes helped prep Ryan for the race. "Ryan met with Roger," a person close to Ailes said. Ailes told Ryan he needed to work on his television skills and referred him to speech coach Jon Kraushar, who had worked at his consulting company Ailes Communications in the 1980s and coauthored with Ailes the book *You Are the Message*. "I know a guy who can teach you to read off a prompter," Ailes said.

That a news executive was essentially running the Republican Party was a remarkable development in American politics. But it was an outcome Ailes foretold. After the 1968 campaign, Ailes spoke of a time when television would replace the political party, that other mass organizer of the twentieth century. With Fox News, that reality was arguably established.

Ailes owes his power to a long tradition. The media mobilizers of an earlier era—Father Charles Coughlin, Walter Winchell—paved the way for Fox News, building followings that, in their time, vectored the country toward their goals. But these firebrands were limited by the reach of their own voices. At Fox News, Ailes commands a whole platoon of firebrands, multiplying his force.

Ailes built Fox into an entire political universe. But ultimately, it's the expression of one man, with all his obsessions and idiosyncrasies, everything he'd absorbed. "Roger is Fox News, without him you don't have it," Christopher Ruddy, the editor in chief of *Newsmax*, the conservative monthly, said. Ed Rollins, Ronald Reagan's campaign director and Fox News contributor, agreed. "Every single element of the network is his design," he explained. "He's not just an executive, he understands how to drive a message."

Not long before the 2012 election, Ailes told a reporter, "If Richard Nixon was alive today, he'd be on the couch with Oprah, talking about how he was poor, his brother died, his mother didn't love him, and his father beat the shit out of him. And everybody would say, Oh, poor guy, he's doing the best he can. See, every human being has stuff—stuff they have to carry around, stuff they have to deal with. And Richard Nixon had a lot of stuff. He did the best he could with it, but it got him in the end."

Ailes's own stuff is what has transformed Fox News from a news channel into a national phenomenon. "I built this channel from my life experience," he told an interviewer. And it was true. At his daily 8:00 a.m. editorial meeting, Ailes regularly lectures his closest advisers, about a dozen men and women, on his experience of American postwar history, which they use to program the channel. As the producer of *The Mike Douglas Show,* he had soaked up the chatty commercialism of 1960s daytime television, learning countless techniques to hold viewers' attention. As a consultant to Nixon, he adopted a sense of political victimhood, and a paranoia about enemies that has marked his career ever since. In the 1970s, he honed his theatrical instincts as a Broadway producer and ran a fledgling conservative television news service bankrolled by the right-wing beer magnate Joseph Coors—in essence, a dry run for Fox News. And in the 1980s, Ailes mastered the dark art of attack politics as a mercenary campaign strategist, skills he would soon put to use in turning a television news network into an unprecedented political force. At Fox, Ailes speaks frequently of his father, a factory foreman who lived a frustrated life. Fox News launched on October 7, 1996, but it truly began a half century earlier, out of a small frame house on a shady street in Warren, Ohio.

# ACT I

# ONE

# "JUMP ROGER, *JUMP*"

THE RAW MATERIALS FOR ROGER AILES'S MYTH of an America in danger of being lost come from his hometown of Warren, in the northeastern corner of Ohio. In the late 1800s, Warren became a center of trade and manufacturing, a city that worked. The town of six thousand boasted five newspapers, seven churches, and three banks. In 1890, two sons of Warren founded the Packard Electric Company, which would one day employ Roger's father. They produced the first Packard motorcar in their Warren factory in 1899, and made Warren's streets the first in America to be illuminated by incandescent light. Through the twentieth century, the company's growth was spurred by deposits of coal and iron ore in the Mahoning Valley. The region became one of the largest steel manufacturers in the country.

In 1932, the General Motors Corporation acquired Packard Electric to manufacture cables for its automobiles. Roger's father, who had been working at the plant since around the time of the 1929 stock market crash, held on to his job under the new management. Packard continued to thrive, as did the rest of Warren. In 1936, Neil Armstrong, age five, went for his first airplane ride in Warren in a Ford Tri-Motor. After World War II, Warren's industries boomed, and throughout the middle part of the last century it was a seat of limitless American potential.

That was the world into which Roger Eugene Ailes was born, on May 15, 1940. Warren residents earned incomes that were nearly 30 percent above the national average, redefining the middle class in ways that still have painful resonance today. "There were no slums," recalled Ailes's childhood friend Launa Newman. Warren, like blue-collar towns across postwar America, had been built on a benevolent compact between management and labor, which spread prosperity widely, as long as profits were growing. Packard, which employed six thousand workers in 1953, was like a city unto itself. It had its own newspaper, the *Cablegram*, and sponsored annual picnics for tens of thousands, where kids competed in pie-eating contests and lucky penny scrambles. The career of Roger's father, Robert Sr., who rose to the rank of foreman in the maintenance department, benefited from this arrangement. He raised his children in a tidy home on Belmont Street, with enough yard for his prized tomato garden and the family beagle hound, Tip. He worked for forty years at the company, retired in 1969 in his early sixties, and lived the last years of his life on a company pension.

Warren was a labor stronghold, but there were conservative currents coursing through the city's politics. Growing up in the 1920s, Robert Ailes Sr. was drawn toward them. He recoiled from unions. To him, they were arbitrary, often rewarding people who were undeserving. At the Packard plant, Robert was considered management, and thus excluded from the benefits of joining the union. But without a college degree he had no chance to advance into the corporate hierarchy. "I never could understand why he'd ever be a Republican. Ninety-nine percent of the people who came up through the school of hard knocks were Democrats," his son Robert Jr. said. His conservatism was a reaction against those who got breaks he never did, and his resentments consumed him.

Robert Sr. came of age at a time in which Warren was engaged in a culture war brought on by increasing ethnic and racial discord. Rapid industrialization brought waves of immigrants—Hungarians, Romanians, Italians, Yugoslavians, Greeks—to northeast Ohio. They came in search of work in the mills. In Warren, the immigrants lived in the Flats, a scruffy neighborhood by the rail depot. It was the Prohibition era, and corruption bloomed. The foreigners operated betting parlors and speakeasies—"vice dens"—in the back rooms of social clubs in the Flats. The city's Protestants blamed the newcomers, many of whom were Catholics and Orthodox Christians, for subverting their efforts to curtail bootlegging. One minister complained to the Dry Enforcement League that the county was "rich enough to lock up every bootlegger," but refused to do so.

As an adult, Robert joined Freemasonry, a fraternal organization that also stood up against the city's changing character. Robert devoted himself to the Masons. He became a 32nd-degree master and served for twenty-five years as chaplain of the Carroll F. Clapp Lodge in Warren. As a Master Mason, he was given entrée into an affiliated body called the Mystic Order of Veiled Prophets, for which he served as Shriner and Past Monarch. The organizations were the pride of his career. They gave him the titles and the respect he was denied at Packard. His wife complained that he spent far too many hours at the lodge. "One of his disappointments in life was that Roger and I didn't become Masons," Robert Jr. recalled.

Robert Sr. and his wife, Donna, met at church. She was a famous beauty, lithe, nine years younger than he, with brown hair and wide-set eyes. She had come to Warren from Parkersburg, West Virginia, when she was less than a year old. Her father, James Arley Cunningham, who lacked a high school diploma, sought work in the local steel industry. He was a religious man, who took his family to the fervent Evangelical United Brethren Church every Sunday. "They didn't believe in movies or dancing," Roger said. Robert and Donna had a swift courtship, and less than a year into their marriage she became pregnant with Robert Jr.

When Roger Ailes spoke of Warren, he invoked a small-town idyll, a lost American dream, but those images were only part of his childhood story, one in which tenebrous parts were edited out. The difficulties started with his illness. At the age of two, not long after learning to walk, Roger fell and bit his tongue. His parents couldn't stop the bleeding. Terrified, they rushed him to Trumbull Memorial Hospital. A doctor diagnosed their child with hemophilia, a genetic disorder that hinders the ability of the body's blood to clot. There was no cure for the little-understood condition. "Well, you died. That's what you knew about it," Roger later recalled. "I was told many times I wasn't going to make it." "The treatment for hemophilia back then was terribly crude," remembered Robert Jr., who would become a doctor. Their parents did what they could to keep Roger out of trouble, protecting him from uneven stretches of sidewalk where he could trip and scrape his knee, and from getting into backyard scuffles. The average life expectancy of a severe hemophiliac at the time was eleven years.

Notwithstanding his hemophilia, or perhaps in angry defiance of it, Roger had an incongruous physical boldness, with sometimes dire consequences. In grade school, when his parents weren't looking, Roger sneaked up onto the roof of his family's garage. He jumped to the ground and bit his tongue on impact. His father rushed him to Trumbull Memorial. This time the doctors there were unable to help him. "I heard the doctor say—I wasn't sure what it meant, but I heard him say, 'We really can't do anything,'" Roger said. His father, a short, obstinate man, pugnacious by nature, refused to give up. Robert Jr. remembered the incident vividly: "My dad bundled Roger in a blanket and put him in the family Chevy and drove to the Cleveland Clinic." Driving eighty miles an hour down Route 422, they were soon stopped by a state police car.

"Look, my son's bleeding. We've got to get to the hospital," Robert pleaded to a man in a Mountie hat standing outside his window.

The trooper looked at the boy wrapped in a blood-stained blanket in the backseat. "Get behind me," he said and escorted them, his lights flashing the rest of the way to Cleveland.

A whole crew of Robert's work friends, who had names like "Dirty Neck Watson," went to the hospital to donate their blood. Many were so filthy that the doctors had to scrub them down before they gave Roger a direct blood transfusion from their arms to his. "Well, son," his father said after he pulled through. "You have a lot of blue-collar blood in you. Never forget that."

The hospital traumatized the young boy, and the threat of returning there denied him many of the pleasures of childhood. "Roger told me one time, when he was really young, he was suspended upside down for hours at the hospital to keep the blood from pooling in dangerous ways," Launa Newman said. During recess, Roger often sat at his desk as the other kids played outside. But after school hours, his teacher could not stop him from playing touch football and sandlot baseball. "He participated until he got so black-and-blue he couldn't move," his brother said.

Simply walking to and from school was hazardous. A passing car clipped him once when he was in the second grade, an accident that landed him back in the hospital. "What saved me was a little square lunch box that I had," Roger said. "He hit the lunchbox and I flew into the air and into the curb." On another occasion, some neighborhood boys roughed him up on his walk home. "My dad, I saw tears in his eyes for the first time," Roger recalled. "I'd never seen it. And he said, 'That's never going to happen to you again.'"

Robert Sr. inculcated in his son a kind of Warren catechism, a blue-collar ethos summed up in epigrams: violence never solves anything, but the threat of violence can be very useful; if you have to take two, disarm one; if you have no options, then remember, son: for them, it's a fight. For you, it's life and death. "Roger and my dad were very, very close," Robert Jr. said. "It's all because of his handicap, his physical problem. He was very protective of Roger. He taught him a lot. My dad was a tough guy. He was built like a brick shithouse. He was quite the scrapper in his day. Sometimes, he had to fight. He was the low man on the totem pole. At work, you can't fight back. But his feeling was, don't take it if you don't have to." One time, Donna and Robert Sr. were out driving. She was behind the wheel and a man in a pickup truck yelled at her. Robert leapt out of the car and ran to the truck. "He stood on the running board and reached through the window and grabbed him and pulled him through the window, had him hanging out in the street," Roger recalled.

In spite of his protectiveness, Robert Sr. didn't believe his son's hemophilia should be an obstacle. "When I was thirteen, he allowed me to go to the Canadian north woods with the YMCA, a bunch of guys with an Indian guide," Roger said. "We were up there for three weeks. Now I remember my parents arguing about it but my dad said, 'Let him go, he'll be alright. He's a tough guy.' So they sent me. And I went up there and we went down the rapids of the Montreal River—we did a lot of stuff. And I got through it and it gave me a lot of confidence. And my dad said, 'You're going to lead a perfectly normal life, don't ever back out, don't ever back away. Don't ever be afraid.' So that set the course, and I think that had a big impact on me."

Robert Sr.'s lessons sometimes had a cruel edge. When Roger was recovering from the car accident, his father took him to a running track to help him practice walking again. One day, Roger fell into some manure that lay on the ground. "Don't fall down and you won't get that crap on you!" Robert snapped. The cruelest lesson Roger would speak of occurred in the bedroom Roger shared with his brother. Roger was standing on the top bunk. His father opened his arms wide and smiled.

"Jump Roger, *jump*," he told him.

Roger leapt off the bed into the air toward his arms. But Robert took a step back. His son fell flat onto the floor. As he looked up, Robert leaned down and picked him up. "Don't ever trust anybody," he said.

Stephen Rosenfield, who worked for Roger's consulting company in the 1970s, considered the episode "his Rosebud story," a moment that defined and haunted his boss. Ailes told it to him on several occasions with pain in his voice. "He was upset by it, but also felt his father was teaching him an important lesson," Rosenfield recalled. "Which is why I think you're describing a guy who doesn't have a lot of close friends. The people Roger works with become his close family. Roger feels way safer knowing he's in control."

Robert Sr. demanded quiet around the house. If the boys roughhoused in front of him, he warned them to stop. If they ignored him, he pulled out his belt, whipping them not until they began to cry, although they did wail, but until they fell silent. "He didn't scream, his voice never rose," Robert Jr. recalled. "He did like to beat the shit out of you with that belt. He continued to beat you, and he continued to beat you. . . . It was a pretty routine fixture of childhood." Over time, the boys learned to suppress their screams of pain. "If we stopped crying, he'd go away. He wanted it quiet," Robert Jr. said. "Roger definitely bruised, where I didn't. I got welts and things like that. He never hit us in the face. He always hit us in the leg or the butt." The boys had no perspective on their father's violence. "If this happened today, we'd be in a foster home, and he'd be in jail. In those days, we didn't know any better," Robert Jr. said. "I was terrified," Roger recalled, "but I loved my dad."

Years later the brothers learned that their father had had his own traumatic upbringing. Robert Sr. had always told the family that his father, Melville Darwin Ailes, had died in World War I, leaving his mother, Sadie, a schoolteacher, to raise him and his siblings alone. "There were two or three different stories," Robert Jr. remembered. "A war story made for a good one." Sadie kept up the fiction. On the 1930 census, she described herself as a "widow."

When Robert Jr. was a senior in high school, he received a shirt box from Grandma Cunningham. It was stuffed with newspaper clippings from the *Akron Beacon Journal*. They revealed that Melville Ailes was not dead, but was a respected public health official with a Harvard degree living forty-five miles away in Akron. He had married another woman.

Robert Jr. did not tell Roger about his discovery. Their mother told him that Roger was "too young" to know the truth, but Roger found out about it anyway. Donna pleaded with the boys to keep their knowledge from their father. "He would not tolerate *any* such discussion," Robert Jr. recalled. They never spoke of it to their father, and Roger would never meet his grandfather, who died, after suffering from Alzheimer's disease, in 1967.

Robert Sr.'s beatings stopped by the time his sons were teenagers, but high school brought different pressures. Donna was a competitive, overbearing mother who pushed her boys as hard as she had pushed herself.

In high school, she had been a star on the basketball court. She never went to college, but she wanted her sons to experience the world beyond Warren. "She was willing to do anything," Robert Jr. recalled. She enrolled the brothers in acting and music lessons and demanded perfection in the classroom. "She would want to know before she saw a test that I got an A," Robert Jr. remembered. "She wanted to know if I got 100 percent. And if I didn't get a 100, she'd want to know that I got the highest grade." Donna was also sparing in her display of affection. Roger remembered her hugging him only "once in a while." He speculated to a reporter that perhaps she was scared of his hemophilia.

Roger was proficient but uninspired in the classroom. There was not much use trying to compete academically with Robert Jr., who was class president at Warren G. Harding High before studying at Oberlin College on a scholarship and going on to medical school. "It was clear that my brother was sort of the favorite," Roger recalled. Donna's pressure worked for Robert, but backfired for Roger. "The more she'd hound him, the less he would do," Robert recalled. Roger would say, "I got a 'C,' and that's good enough!" To get through a Latin class, Roger cribbed the answers from his brother's homework assignments and exams.

The television screen was Roger's classroom. As a child, frequently homebound with bruises, he watched variety shows and westerns, lying on the living room couch for hours on end. "He analyzed it, and he figured it out," his brother said. Roger grew up as the medium did. In 1940, the year Roger was born, Herbert Hoover appeared on television for the first time, in an interview at the Republican National Convention. Seven years later, President Harry Truman staged the first telecast at the White House. Between 1950 and 1951, the number of households with sets doubled, to ten million. In 1952, Richard Nixon saved his political career delivering what became known as the "Checkers Speech" on television. Like his father, whose favorite program was *Gunsmoke,* Roger liked shows with strong male leads and simple plotlines.

Roger also loved acting. "I liked to get out of class and I wasn't a great athlete. That left the theater," he said. He put on plays with neighborhood kids. One of those fellow actors was Austin Pendleton, who grew up to be a noted stage and film actor. Pendleton's mother gave Roger acting lessons, and his father, the president of the Warren Tool Corporation, built a theater in the basement of their spacious home so that Pendleton and his friends could stage productions. Sometimes, Pendleton invited Roger to join them.

At Warren G. Harding High, Roger acted in several plays and MC'd *The Frolics,* the school's annual variety show. "He sat down and played the piano and sang," Kent Fusselman, a schoolmate, recalled. "He was very good. He was in his element." Launa Newman developed an instant connection with Roger at an audition for Ayn Rand's *Night of January 16th,* a courtroom drama of greed and moral decay. They had never spoken before reading a scene together. "It was a moment of kismet," she said. "He picked me. I picked him. The thing that crossed my mind was—*How did I miss this guy?* He was so good-looking. He was so intelligent." They won the parts of secretary and defense attorney. Before graduating, Roger also starred in a stage adaptation of *A Man Called Peter,* about the faith of a charismatic United States Senate chaplain.

Though Robert Sr. wanted his children to figure out a way to go to college, he had complicated feelings about academics. "Father did not encourage us," Robert Jr. recalled. His own Ivy League–educated father had abandoned him, and the condescension of college-educated managers at the Packard plant got under his skin. But he recognized that his path, going to work right out of high school, brought hardship. Once, when Roger saw those "college boys" give his father "orders in an inappropriate manner," he asked why he let them talk to him that way. "Son, because of you, your brother, and your sister," he answered. "I need the job, and you kids have got to go to college so you don't ever have to put up with this."

During his prime earning years at Packard Electric, he was paid $650 a month, the equivalent of a $60,000 annual salary in today's dollars. It was a decent wage, but after paying the bills for his wife, two boys, and younger daughter, Robert had little left over to spend on himself. To make some extra money, he took a second job painting houses in the evenings. Donna also worked outside the home, taking a clerical position at the local branch of the American Cancer Society, a further source of resentment for Robert Sr. "The poor guy never had a new suit. He had two pairs of shoes in the closet, one for Sunday and the other for the rest of the week," Roger recalled. When it came time to buy the family's 1957 Buick Special, Robert Sr. took out a home equity mortgage. For all his workingman bravado and his steady income, his life had the taint of failure. "He tried hard but never succeeded in anything," Robert Jr. recalled. "He didn't have the instinct to be a killer."

Roger learned enough about his father's blue-collar struggles to know he wanted no part of them. "All I wanted to do was to make enough money, so I'd never have to live the life my father lived," he once said. Roger also vowed never to let others dominate him. After landing a job on a highway crew digging ditches along Ohio Route 45 at the age of seventeen, Roger had his first try on the jackhammer. "He told me to put it against my belly and just pull the trigger," he recalled of the foreman. The jackhammer lurched, catapulting him onto his back. He lay in the mud, dazed. He wanted to attack the man, but recognized that "he'd kill me if I tried anything."

"Why'd you do that?" Roger yelled at him. He remembered the response for many years.

"I ain't your mama, boy," the man said.

One day, in the spring of Roger's senior year of high school, his father pulled him aside. "Where are you going?" he asked. Roger thought it was a strange question. He was sitting in the living room, not going anywhere. "You can't live here. You're eighteen. You're on your own. You have to make a life now. . . . If you get somebody pregnant, don't bring them home. I'm not paying for it."

Around this time, Roger had received an acceptance letter from Ohio University in Athens. He wanted to go, but there were no prospects for a scholarship, as his brother had to Oberlin. His father said he was not prepared to pay for his education. He suggested he join the military or get a job at Packard.

"I can put your name up at the shop, try to get you a job."

Roger was furious and did not speak to his dad for two months, but, looking back, Roger called it "the best thing he ever did for me."

Perhaps to spite his father, Roger enrolled in college. He may have been ambivalent about academics, but he would never allow himself to end up like his father.

Later that summer, Roger arrived in Athens, a small city tucked into the foothills of the Appalachian Mountains, for the beginning of his freshman year. The campus, with its stately redbrick buildings and manicured quads overlooking the Hocking River, a tributary of the Ohio, had the pastoral feel of an East Coast college. "It felt like a picture-perfect postcard of the Eisenhower years. You felt like there was a fort around the city," Arthur Nolletti, a classmate, recalled. Students went for hayrides in the fall and caroled at Christmas.

The Cold War was a campus preoccupation, while civil rights were viewed skeptically. During Ailes's sophomore year, the OU *Post* criticized a civil rights march down College Street, in which a mere eighty people participated. "If you are scared of the truth, don't read this editorial!" it read. "Equality is not a one-way proposition. With equality goes responsibility and obligation. There are negroes who have shown that they are not ready to accept this obligation. . . . Just remember one thing White Man—you're the minority in this here bigoted world of ours. And you're becoming a smaller minority with the passing of each day."

The handbook distributed to Roger's class encouraged students to conform to social convention. "The 'big man on campus' will want a dark suit and sport coats," the manual stated. "The co-ed will want sweaters and skirts, bobby sox and saddles, and Sunday ensembles." The guiding principle was modesty. "Individualism is encouraged at OU, so long as it is within University rules," it stated. "Put your best foot forward at OU. Leave your family skeletons in the closet." A caption in the 1959 yearbook below a photo of a boy and girl standing in a bowling lane noted, "he instructs and she listens." In December 1959, a group of three hundred students protested against the Beats.

When Ailes arrived on campus, he did not know what he wanted to study, but he was sure about one thing. He wanted to join the military, just as Doug Webster, his best friend from Warren, had done. Roger signed up for the Air Force ROTC and stayed with the program for two years, but his health was an issue. "What I really wanted to do was fly fighter planes. . . . But my eyesight and other physical problems made the government in their wisdom not allow me to have an expensive aircraft," he later said. In a certain sense, the closest he came was playing the bossy Private Irwin Blanchard in the university's stage production of *No Time for Sergeants*.

Just as in high school, Ailes had little interest in classes. "I was hammered all the time," he recalled. "I skipped a lot of classes, finally got an F. The dean brought me in, said 'We have to keep you because it's a state school, but we only have to keep you one more semester.'" But he found new direction when, on a lark, he applied for an on-air position at WOUB, the college radio station, during his freshman year. At the time, Ohio University was a pioneer in college broadcasting, one of only a handful of colleges in the country with a student-run radio and television station. Ailes's starting position was reading news headlines on a program called *Radio Digest*. He then hosted the *Yawn Patrol*, a morning variety show, with his friend Don Hylkema. Vincent Jukes, a stout, imperious man who ran the radio department, imposed rigid rules on his young broadcasters, insisting he approve all music played on air. Rock and roll records were expressly forbidden, but Ailes proved adept at skirting Jukes's authority. One day, he concocted a plan with Hylkema to slip a Bobby Darin record by him. "We took the record to him to get it okayed," Hylkema recalled. "The two of us talked and distracted him through the whole thing."

With his acting experience, Ailes was a natural broadcaster. Archie Greer, the thirty-seven-year-old faculty adviser for the station, spotted his talent. Unlike Jukes, Greer had a friendly disposition and was an enthusiastic mentor. "Archie was probably the first person to have confidence in me and say, 'You can do things,'" Ailes said. By the end of his sophomore year, Greer promoted Ailes to station manager, a position normally assigned to seniors. Ailes was soon selected to join the Alpha Epsilon Rho radio and television society for his performance in broadcasting. Even as an underclassman, Ailes seemed older and more imposing than the other students. "We were sort of afraid of him, because he was the boss," Mike Adams, who entered OU in 1960, recalled.

The radio studio became Ailes's home. To concentrate on broadcasting, Ailes decided to major in fine arts. When school was in session, he never seemed to leave the basement of the speech building, except to grab a bite to eat at Blackmore's up the street. He was often the first person to arrive at 6:00 a.m. to turn on the transmitter. During one summer, instead of going home, he took a job earning $1.10 an hour at the Athens commercial station WATH.

Despite the hours he spent in the tight-knit radio community, Ailes was an elusive figure. Without telling his classmates, he moonlighted as a rock and roll DJ under the pseudonym Dick Summers at WMPO, a radio station twenty-five miles south in Middleport, Ohio. "He didn't let anyone get close to him," Don Hylkema recalled. "He never talked about himself as an individual or things he felt or thought about. It was strange. . . . Everyone knew Roger, but they didn't know anything about him." His political convictions, if he had them, were unclear, even as he led the station during the 1960 election cycle. "He did not display any sign of extreme right-wing politics," Don Swaim, the WOUB special events director, recalled. Ailes refrained from discussing his hemophilia with most people. "I remember when he told me," said classmate Bill Klokow. "We were pulling music in the library. He said it was serious. At that time, he didn't know how long he was going to live."

Ailes's temper flared when he did not get what he wanted. "Control was extremely important to him," Hylkema recalled. Robert Jr. linked this trait to his medical condition. "The thing is about hemophiliacs, they're risk takers," he said. "They tend to deny their illness. They don't want to be special. They fight against it, and here's the thing: they become aggressive in their behavior."

Robert Sr. and Donna's marriage had been disintegrating throughout Roger's childhood, and after Roger went to college, it broke apart. During the fall of his sophomore year, Donna filed for divorce. Her amended divorce petition was painfully graphic, a window into the dark environment Roger grew up in. "Over the entire period of their marriage," her lawyer wrote, Robert Sr. "has screamed and yelled at her and inflicted physical abuse upon her all without valid provocation." She felt unloved. "Over the years the Defendant has failed to pay the Plaintiff the proper respect owing by a husband to a wife: has failed to evidence outwordly [*sic*] any affection or love for her, has never complimented her for any good or favorable action or conduct by her and thereby lost the affection and respect of the Plaintiff." She was lonely. "All during their marriage the Defendant has made his outside and social contacts largely with men and has not included the Plaintiff in any substantial amount of his social contacts." When Donna expressed her unhappiness in the marriage, she said Robert blamed her—among other ways, by writing down his complaints on a blackboard in the kitchen. He had a paranoid streak, telling his friends that she was unfaithful. "He has become repulsive and offensive to her so that she can no longer endure his presence and submit to continued abuse from him," read the complaint.

Donna worried that Robert might kill her. The original complaint, filed Wednesday, October 7, 1959, alleged, "he has threatened her life and to do her physical harm in the event an action similar to the one herein alleged is filed against him." She asked the court to bar him from coming to the house, calling her, or interfering with her job. "She fears that unless he is enjoined from molesting her that he will do her bodily injury," the document stated. Two days later, at 9:00 a.m., after the court granted her a temporary restraining order, Sheriff T. Herbert Thomas and his deputy Edwin James drove to the house on Belmont Street to serve Robert with court papers ordering him to leave the premises.

Nothing in the court records indicates that Robert contested the restraining order or the divorce filing. Roger recalled that he did not hear about the divorce from his parents until right before he was scheduled to come home from college for the Christmas break. "I got a call from them saying that I had to make arrangements to stay at my friend Doug's house," he said. "And then they told me they're getting a divorce." It was devastating news. "It affected Roger," his brother later recalled. "He had no place to go. . . . I sort of had a place to go more or less. Roger didn't."

On April 27, 1960, the court granted Donna a divorce, finding Robert "guilty of extreme cruelty." She was awarded custody of their daughter, Donna Jeanne, a senior in high school. Soon after the divorce was granted, Donna put the house up for sale. She had fallen in love with Joseph Urban, a fundraiser for the American Cancer Society and a former newspaper journalist, who lived in San Francisco. "He could speak German and French," Robert Jr. recalled. "He was the exact opposite of my dad. He was very gentle. He never got angry."

The next time Roger came back to Warren, the house on Belmont Street had been sold, a development for which he blamed his mother. "I never found my stamp collection," he said. "I never found anything. Everything was gone. . . . I learned from my grandmother, I guess, that my mother had gone to California. She gave me a phone number. . . . I've always been pissed off because I had great stuff in my closet. All your memorabilia from being a kid. I always missed that. I wondered, 'Where's my stuff?' "

As his parents' marriage was coming apart, Roger was beginning his own. As a freshman in college, he'd met Marjorie White, a pretty, brown-haired art major from Parkersburg, West Virginia—his mother's birthplace—who was two years older than Roger and engaged to the popular WOUB station manager David Chase. "Dave was a big man around WOUB. He was the key guy who was highly regarded," Chase's friend Frank Youngwerth recalled. A talented broadcaster, Chase would later move to New York to become program director of the NBC flagship television station WNBC. But after graduating, Chase was called into military duty with the Air Force, and Ailes moved in, winning White over. "Roger stole her away and married her," Hylkema said.

At 11:30 a.m. on August 27, 1960—four months to the day after his parents' divorce—Roger and Marjorie married at the Galbreath Chapel on campus. After the wedding, they moved into an apartment on Stewart Street, alongside a row of craftsman houses on the east side of campus. Marjorie taught art in Nelsonville, thirteen miles north of Athens, while Ailes stayed and finished his last two years. Their marriage sent a powerful signal to others. "Here's a guy, who's a freshman who steals a girl from a guy who's a big timer at WOUB and then in a year he marries her," Youngwerth said.

Making a home for himself was also a way for Ailes to find stability. The divorce left scars on all the Ailes children. For Roger, ambition would be a salve for early wounds. "Maybe that's why I kept going back to work," he once said. After graduation, he had the opportunity to work in radio in Columbus. But television was the future. He had applied for an entry-level position at a Westinghouse-owned television station in Cleveland. So he and Marjorie packed up and drove north.

## TWO

# "YOU CAN TALK YOUR WAY OUT OF ANYTHING"

WESTINGHOUSE'S CLEVELAND TV station, KYW, was a freewheeling enterprise, not exactly a start-up, but a node in a burgeoning new field. TV production was booming, and not only in New York and Los Angeles. After deciding to acquire the station from NBC in 1955, Westinghouse launched an ambitious slate of new programs in Cleveland, including *Eyewitness,* a one-and-a-half-hour local news block, and *Barnaby,* a popular children's program about an elf, starring the comedian Linn Sheldon.

Chet Collier, the program manager of KYW-TV, was walking with Ailes around the second-floor offices one day when a voice called out "Roger!" Ailes turned to see his high school friend Launa Newman sitting behind a desk in a room full of young producers. They had not seen each other since their performance in *Night of January 16th.* Newman was now a talent coordinator and producer for a new ninety-minute afternoon variety-talk program. Westinghouse was preparing to syndicate it in five metropolitan markets.

Forrest "Woody" Fraser, an excitable young producer from Chicago, had come up with the concept. A pioneer of daytime television, Fraser helped launch the short-lived afternoon variety shows *Hi, Ladies!, Club 60,* and *Adults Only.* Newman was the first person Fraser hired for the new show, for which he had come up with a novel format: a genial host paired each week with a different celebrity co-host. The two would spend more time interacting with each other than interviewing guests. Together, Fraser and Newman auditioned a half dozen candidates. The challenge was to find a permanent host who did not mind sharing the stage each week with names more famous than his own. "All they came up with was run-of-the-mill singers, out-of-work disk jockeys and a guy who could play 'Bye, Bye, Blackbird' on the piano," the eventual winner wrote in his memoir. Then, they found him.

One afternoon, Fraser was back in Chicago sitting in Henrici's bar at the Merchandise Mart Building, where NBC had a dozen studios. A small television monitor mounted on the wall played a game show on mute. "Mike Douglas!" Fraser shouted, pointing at the host on the screen. Douglas, an affable big band singer, had worked with Fraser on several shows and Fraser thought he'd be perfect for the job. "The bartender looked up, looked at the TV, then gently corrected him," Douglas recalled. "It was Merv Griffin on *Play Your Hunch*. Didn't matter. Woody didn't know Merv, he knew Mike. And he didn't have Merv's address, he had Mike's. A few days later, I was on my way to Cleveland."

At that point, Douglas was a faded talent on the verge of quitting show business. He had reached some measure of fame performing with Kay Kyser, the bandleader and radio personality (it was Kyser who told him to change his last name from "Dowd" to "Douglas"), and even recorded the singing voice of Prince Charming in Disney's *Cinderella,* but, far from hosting a game show, he was now buying and selling real estate in southern California to support his family and scraping together small gigs. Fraser's invitation seemed to be his last shot. "A million to one," Douglas told his wife, Genevieve.

Westinghouse signed him up for an initial three-month stint at $400 per week, and on December 11, 1961, *The Mike Douglas Show* had its debut. "His geniality, ready wit, personable appearance and pleasant singing voice all conspired to show him off as a nimble pro," the *Cleveland Press* television critic wrote the next day. The show's popularity grew steadily, and in a year's time it had become a smash hit.

"You're going to work on this show!" Launa Newman called out to Ailes as Collier led him down the hallway. "It's the only job at the station. Write down ten ideas and give them to Woody. *Please, please* do it. We'll have so much fun."

Starting out on *The Mike Douglas Show* as a $68-a-week prop boy, Ailes was rarely at home—just as he had in college, he devoted almost all his waking hours to the job, even though he was just a dogsbody, fetching whatever the show's senior producers needed. "He would usually be gone before I got up," recalled Marjorie's younger sister, Kay, who lived with them for a month in their apartment in Euclid-Green, nine miles northeast of downtown. "He was very intense. He was like a whirling dervish. He was always going. He was always talking," Debbie Miller, an associate producer who joined the show in 1965, said. "I was very tight with Roger. He and I were the low men on the totem pole." His disheveled appearance became a fixture of the studio. "I remember him having a pen leak in his pocket, and the whole front of his shirt was full of ink," Miller said. "His hair was always uncombed. His shirt tails were always hanging out, and his sleeves were always rolled up. He always wore black pants and a white shirt."

The hard work impressed his colleagues despite some initial mishaps. When Cleveland native Bob Hope first appeared on the show in 1963, Ailes held the cue cards, a job of significant responsibility. But when they were live on-air, Ailes dropped the cards. Hope had to ad-lib. After the cameras stopped rolling, Hope went over to talk to Ailes. Newman saw fear in the young producer's eyes. Hope, however, was gracious. "He gave him a pep talk. He thought it was adorable," she said. The mistake didn't hold Ailes back. He quickly developed the unassailable, blustering confidence that became his hallmark. One time a singer who was booked to perform noticed a rip in her stockings, just before going on air. Panicked, she fled to the bathroom and refused to come out. Ailes went in and dragged her into the studio and held her there until the camera's red light clicked on. She performed flawlessly.

For a young producer with limited experience, Ailes possessed formidable self-assurance. Not long after Ailes joined the staff in Cleveland, Douglas did a show with Sammy Davis Jr. Afterward, Douglas asked Ailes what he thought. "I didn't say anything, but I have a terrible problem. I tell people what I think," Ailes later said. "I've always had some natural tendency toward an aggressive posture." So when Douglas kept asking, Ailes snapped. "Mike, I thought it was terrible," he said. Ailes thought Douglas, who was in awe of Davis, had been dominated in the interview. "You've got to come back every day and be the star of the show, but you sat out there today and literally kissed his bottom. He took the whole show away from you. It's nice to show you're a nice guy, but you're the one who has to control things when the show goes to a commercial. You're the one who has to make it all happen." His words landed like a sucker punch. "There were tears in his eyes,"Ailes recalled. But as Ailes remembered, his truth telling sealed their relationship.

Though Ailes, with his bluff bonhomie, was a popular figure backstage, his colleagues sensed that, inside, other wheels were turning. "You didn't know what he was really thinking," Newman said. An emblem of his secrecy was his illness. "He used to come into work and he'd have these blood clots on his face," Larry Rosen, Woody Fraser's deputy, recalled. When he asked him what he had done to himself, Ailes would say, "I'm not supposed to shave with a razor." Another time, Ailes told Rosen that the only thing he was afraid of was surgery. "It would be the only time he wouldn't be able to control the bleeding," Rosen recalled.

Ailes's marathon work habits caused tensions at home with Marge. He rarely invited colleagues over to his place, which was not set up for entertaining anyway. Marje did not otherwise get to know the *Mike Douglas* team (although Roger did cast her in one episode that featured finger painting). He was among the few staffers who were married. They were all young, most just out of college, and flush with ambition and ideas. Douglas, at the ripe old age of thirty-six when he joined the show, liked to call them "kids."

The producers on the show all felt they were making history—if the old guard still thought of television as radio with pictures, they were fusing the words and images, supercharging the medium and connecting with the viewer on a visceral level. "I felt like I was one of those guys who are today part of Silicon Valley," Rift Fournier, a producer on the show, recalled. "All of us were part of something that could be compared today to doing Facebook."

After working grueling hours, they liked to blow off steam with pranks and antics, with Ailes often playing a central role. "He was always joking," Miller recalled. One of the staff's favorite activities was office chair basketball. As Ailes attempted to shoot the crumpled paper ball into the opposing team's wastepaper basket, he did not hold back. "He'd come in the next day with bruises all over, his whole arm would be black," Rosen recalled. One time, instead of playing basketball, the staff had a water balloon fight in the office. When they posed for a group photo, Ailes was soaked down to his white undershirt.

*The Mike Douglas Show* immersed Ailes in the world of professional entertainment. From Fraser, he learned that great TV had more to do with drama—conflict, surprise, spontaneity—than with expensive sets and cutting-edge broadcasting technology. Fraser created drama on the show by putting Douglas and his weekly co-host through what Douglas called "an intentional daily hurricane." Fraser said, "The most important ingredient for a daily show was to keep it fresh, and one way was to keep people off balance, not knowing what would happen, sitting on the edge of their seats. It's when people get bored that they switch channels." Producers brainstormed ways to throw in mystery guests or surprise songs and gags. Fraser insisted that every one of the show's segments had to end with a "payoff" for the viewer. "There were times when we would sit around the bullpen and think for thirty minutes, 'what's the payoff?' " recalled a former producer, Robert LaPorta.

Fraser had a clear vision for Douglas's television persona, conceiving him as the opposite of Jack Paar, Johnny Carson's predecessor on *The Tonight Show*. Paar opened with a monologue. Douglas opened with a song. The Ellie Frankel trio, a local jazz group, accompanied him in renditions of American standards. Fraser wanted Douglas to engage his celebrity guests in the manner of a wide-eyed fan, just as viewers at home would if given the opportunity. Where Paar was urbane and knowing, Mike Douglas was unaffected and enthusiastic, a mirror of his audience. "You can't ignore New York and Los Angeles," Douglas once told an interviewer, "but it's ridiculous not to realize there's a lot of real estate out there between them."

The show's promotional tone and loyal audience quickly made it a required stop for movie stars, singers, activists, and politicians. The occasional ambushes notwithstanding, it was a safe place. By giving his celebrity co-hosts five ninety-minute on-air appearances in a week, Douglas provided them far more exposure than they could receive on any other show on television. The show expanded to forty-seven markets by early 1965 and was on its way to becoming the number-one-ranked daytime program in America.

Like his audience, Douglas was curious but wary about the emerging culture. A good-natured conservative Catholic guide, Douglas helped to define for his viewers the boundary lines between the new culture and the old, as he introduced millions of American housewives to iconic figures including the Rolling Stones, Bill Cosby, and Martin Luther King. The show channeled Douglas's Eisenhower-era values. "We wrote him simple questions, not probing questions. They were everywoman's questions," Larry Rosen said.

The show was becoming a profit center, a major Westinghouse asset. But success changed the vibe among the tight-knit staff. Ailes and Fraser began to clash over production issues and tensions got so bad that Collier briefly reassigned Ailes to another job at KYW. The staff's relationship with Douglas also soured. According to Ailes, Douglas had "the attention span of a mosquito," and was a man who "never disciplined himself. He gave the impression of having been the kind of kid who always thought he could get around the teacher not by studying his homework, but by being funny or cute." "We had to write every damn thing for him," Larry Rosen said. "Usually, he didn't read the book and he didn't see the movies." For the first few years, Douglas sat in the bullpen with the producers, but with his rising star status, Douglas was granted his own office.

The ill feeling temporarily subsided when Westinghouse announced that KYW and the show would be relocating to Philadelphia. The company was gaining control of the NBC-owned station there. The staff was elated. Collier smoothed over the issues between Ailes and Fraser and agreed to bring Ailes back onto the Douglas staff.

In August 1965, *The Mike Douglas Show* began broadcasting from a 140-seat basement studio in a six-story building tucked between a furrier and a furniture store, two blocks east of Rittenhouse Square. The location made it easier for Douglas's producers to lure boldface names from New York, which was now just a limo's drive away. Within two years, the show was broadcast in 171 markets across the country, attracting six million viewers and generating $10.5 million in revenue—about $75 million in today's dollars. Douglas's agent soon negotiated a contract that made his client "the highest paid performer on television."

The longer the show dominated the ratings, the less inclined Douglas was to take Fraser's advice. Fraser was often an imperious producer, as volatile as he was visionary. "Mike was really controlled by Woody," Debbie Miller recalled. "Woody had a clipboard and would write out the questions, and Mike would read them. Hardly anything came out of Mike's mouth that was not read to him. That was Roger's training." After the move to Philadelphia, Douglas began to discuss more openly his unhappiness with Fraser's meddling manner. "The reason was very simple. Mike had become a star, but Woody had really created the show. Mike didn't like the fact that Fraser treated him the same way as when he first got there," Newman said.

In Douglas's memoir, *I'll Be Right Back,* he recounts an argument he had with Fraser when Don Ameche, the film actor, was on-set. Fraser had scripted a skit in which Douglas and Ameche would swap a series of funny hats. During the rehearsal, Ameche told Fraser he did not want to participate. Fraser kept walking them through the segment.

"You're not listening, Woody," Ameche told him. "I don't wear funny hats."

Fraser's temper flared. He appealed to Douglas for backup. Instead, Douglas shrugged his shoulders and said, "I don't wear funny hats either." Undermining Fraser publicly satisfied Douglas. "Yeah, I double-crossed him," he later recalled. "I had been waiting for that chance for years."

Douglas soon made an effort to have him sidelined—creating an opening for Ailes. One morning before a taping, Chet Collier called Larry Rosen into a meeting. "Give us the lowdown on what's going on with Woody Fraser," Rosen remembered Collier saying. Collier's question presented an opportunity: Rosen was in line to replace Fraser in the event of a shakeup. But Rosen was loyal to Fraser, who had given him his first job out of college. "They were trying to dig up enough dirt to get rid of him. I refused to talk to him at all about Woody," Rosen later said. It was a decision that would have consequences.

Unlike Rosen, Ailes had a skill for managing up, and he cultivated close working relationships with Collier and Douglas. "He became friends with Mike behind the scenes," Launa Newman said. "They had a simpatico relationship because they were at the core similar. They were Republicans. Roger kissed the Catholic ring of the show." Ailes had a sophisticated understanding of the unique needs of a star like Douglas. In public situations, Ailes would run cover for him. "It was a kind of game," Ailes recalled. "I'd say, 'Mike, you have to go now,' and he'd bawl me out—and go, as he wanted to do anyway."

In June 1966, a month after his twenty-sixth birthday, Ailes seized his moment during one of the show's regularly scheduled breaks. It had been a particularly cold spring in Philadelphia, so Debbie Miller and a friend hopped on a flight to Los Angeles for a last-minute vacation. They were joined shortly after by Launa Newman. Sitting one afternoon on the bed of their closet-sized room at the Beverly Hills Hotel, Launa noticed a piece of paper being slipped under the door. She picked it up and gasped. Ailes had called the hotel and left a message for Miller. "The deal is done," the note read. Fraser was leaving. Ailes was his replacement, not Larry Rosen.

Newman called Fraser to ask him what was going on. He confirmed that he had been ousted. Officially, Fraser had been moved into a corporate role overseeing "talent and program development" for WBC Productions in New York. But being kicked upstairs was Westinghouse's way of doing business. In 1967, Fraser left for a job at ABC producing *This Morning* with Dick Cavett. "That was a real palace coup," Newman recalled. "You would never have known it if you watched from the outside."

Larry Rosen was at home with his wife when he got the call. "Are you sitting down now?" Fraser asked. "I'm gone, and Roger is the executive producer."

Rosen was stunned. He was four years older than Ailes and had been on the show much longer.

"You gotta be kidding me."

"No, that's what they did."

The next day, Rosen drove to Douglas's home to confront him. "I was livid," Rosen recalled. "I was humiliated. Roger had been there nowhere as long as I had." Douglas told him it was *his* decision. "I hired Roger Ailes," Douglas later said.

How exactly Ailes leapfrogged Rosen to get Fraser's job remained a matter of debate. One producer heard that during the week off, Ailes had gone to Collier with an ultimatum: he was going to leave the show unless he got the job over Rosen. In his book, *You Are the Message,* Ailes casts himself as the triumphant victor who stood up to a senior producer's bullying. Fraser isn't named, but is clearly identified in other ways, and described as a "brutal, sadistic personality" who would "pick out a staff member and browbeat him or her all day long." Ailes writes that when it was his turn to face the producer's wrath, he snapped. "I went right up to him, looked him in the eyes, and said, 'That's it. Don't do that to me anymore.'" Fraser didn't stop. "So I took a swing at him. It turned into a regular brawl. We broke up some office equipment and finally two guys dragged me into the men's room to end the fiasco. I'd figured I just ruined my career. But actually it had quite the opposite effect." Ailes goes on to say that "the company president" (presumably Collier) promoted him because of the incident. According to Ailes's account, the executive told him, "Two years ago you proved that you're nobody's boy. You're the only one who fought back." When asked about the story, a half dozen staff members on *The Mike Douglas Show* could not recall such a brawl ever occurring.

As executive producer, Ailes acted quickly to consolidate his control. Within days of Fraser's ouster, Ailes moved into Fraser's large office, a spacious expanse on the first floor. On the wall, he hung a framed quotation from Theodore Roosevelt's 1910 speech "Citizenship in a Republic," one of his favorite sayings: "It is not the critic who counts; not the man who points out how the strong man stumbles, or where the doer of deeds could have done them better. The credit belongs to the man who is actually in the arena, whose face is marred by dust and sweat and blood, who strives valiantly; who errs, who comes short again and again; because there is no effort without error and shortcoming."

On his first day in charge, Ailes fired Debbie Miller. He claimed she spread the story of his involvement in Fraser's departure. Because of her, everyone on the staff believed that he had been promoted because of politics, not on the merits. "He was very blunt about it," Miller recalled. "He said, 'Somebody has to take the rap here.' Someone had to save his own skin." The experience stung, even years later after Miller had become a successful Hollywood agent. Larry Rosen and Launa Newman discussed quitting together in protest, but decided to delay a decision. "Roger always used to say to us, 'You can justify *anything.* You can have your back against the wall and you can talk your way out of anything,' " producer Bob LaPorta recalled.

In the hands of a less capable leader, the turmoil behind the camera could have derailed the show's run. But Ailes was completely comfortable in his new role. "Roger weighed 160 pounds. He looked like Bobby Darin. He was a handsome young kid," Bob LaPorta recalled. "He loved the sense of being an executive on the go. . . . During the show, he used to love to walk up the middle aisle and lean against the back wall and watch everything in front of him." Ailes made sure key members of his team, like the affable director, Ernie Sherry, stayed put, but he demanded loyality in return. "You can come in anytime and yell and scream 'Stupid!' behind closed doors," Ailes told Sherry. "But if you do it in front of the staff, I'll kill you." Unlike Fraser, he was not a micromanager. "He gave me a wide berth," Launa Newman said. "Roger had two buttons, stop and go all out. He trusted you if you were on his team. You knew you had someone in your corner no one else had. On the other hand, if you weren't, then God help you. You'd get the full measure of his wrath."

Ailes protected his staff. At one point, Mike Douglas's wife, Genevieve, complained to Ailes in front of Mike that she wanted to fire Ernie Sherry because, as Ailes remembered, "he was grumpy and disruptive."

"Gen, if you're going to run the show, try to make the meeting Monday at 8," he said.

Ailes impressed his staff with his resilience. During one production meeting in Ailes's office, Johnson observed Ailes turning sickly as the producers went around the room pitching stories. "As we're doing it I'm watching Roger get more and more pale," Johnson recalled. When the meeting concluded, Johnson shut the door.

"Are you okay?"

"I might need a little help here," Ailes said. His trousers from the waist down were soaked with blood.

"Why didn't you stop the meeting?" Johnson asked.

Ailes shrugged his shoulders. "It was important to get through."

"So many people would have given in to it," Johnson recalled. "It was clear that no way would he let himself be beaten by it."

Ailes dashed off memos to the staff like a seasoned boss. "I want everyone to be aware of the extra effort Larry Rosen put into the production," he wrote in a memo on August 10, 1966. "I know it took at least 15 hours of work above and beyond the call of duty to produce a better segment than what the other networks have turned out with a staff of 15 to 20 people. This example of a thorough job is to be congratulated."

No issue seemed too small or too great to become a target of his increasingly outsized personality. As executive producer, Ailes contacted classical music buff Gregor Benko, who had cofounded a New York–based nonprofit that preserved rare recordings, seeking a copy of the organization's newly released recording of Josef Hofmann performing a Chopin piano concerto. Benko wrote back explaining that he lacked the budget to send a free promotional copy, but could send one for $10. Ailes returned Benko's letter, with his handwriting over it: "I UNDERSTAND THAT YOU ARE A SMALL OUTFIT AND UNDERSTAND WHY YOU WILL REMAIN ONE."

The show had gone color eight months after Ailes's promotion, but did not otherwise deviate much from Fraser's original formula. Once, when Barbara Walters appeared on the show, Ailes had her perform with acrobats. "When NBC found out about it they were very angry. They felt it lessened the seriousness of my reputation," Walters recalled. "But the thing was, Roger was smart enough to know people are going to be interested."

In September 1967, producers planned a segment featuring *Peyton Place* star and *Mike Douglas* co-host Ryan O'Neal boxing with a famous fighter. They booked Joe Frazier, who would become heavyweight champion the next year, to spar with O'Neal in the ring. Floyd Patterson would referee and Muhammad Ali would do the announcing. But a day before the segment, Frazier canceled. "Roger got on the phone with him and just laid into him," LaPorta recalled. Kenny Johnson, another producer, said, "He just reamed his ass." Frazier relented, but he was angry. When he showed up at the set, he asked the producers "where's this Ralph guy? I got a bone to pick with this guy named Ralph." He had misheard Ailes's name over the phone. A quick-thinking producer told Frazier that Ralph was out of the office that day. "We called Roger 'Ralph' after that," LaPorta said.

In the fall of 1967, Ailes and Marje paid $41,500 for a house on a wooded cul-de-sac in the aptly named suburb of Media, Pennsylvania. Around this time, Ailes was making $60,000 a year (more than six times what his father earned at his peak salary at Packard). He even began inviting the producers to the house for dinner, which offered them a glimpse of the tensions at home. Bob LaPorta was a guest one evening when Marje's father was visiting. They were in the living room with the television on. Marje's father told Roger to turn it off. "You're not going to amount to anything," LaPorta overheard him telling Ailes. LaPorta sensed Ailes wanted to prove him wrong. "It was an obsession for him to succeed, to pass everybody," he said.

During this period Ailes met a twenty-four-year-old journalist named Joe McGinniss. A columnist for *The Philadelphia Inquirer*, McGinniss was the youngest writer to have a regular column printed in a major American daily. McGinniss called Ailes about writing a piece on Mike Douglas. "Roger and I, we found out right away that we shared the same sense of humor," he said. Ailes showed an instinct for how relationships with reporters could become valuable assets. He invited McGinniss and his wife, a quiet Catholic girl he'd met in Massachusetts at Holy Cross college, for dinner, and, not long afterward, they returned the invitation. "We always had a good time, my wife got along very well with Marje,"

McGinniss recalled. When Ailes would visit, he liked to play with McGinniss's two young children. "It was like Uncle Roger," McGinniss said. Their domestic lives had another parallel. By 1967, both men, who had married young, knew their marriages were not working out. They would occasionally get dinner after work in Philadelphia and discuss their woes.

Politically, Ailes seemed like a moderate to McGinniss, and on some issues, like civil rights, a progressive. "I would write columns that would get me called 'nigger lover' and Frank Rizzo, the police commissioner, would come after me," McGinniss said. "Roger was always sending me a note or making a phone call sympathizing and congratulating me and saying we need more of this. He had some incipient commitment to civil rights in Philadelphia." Ailes's views on race may have been shaped by an experience he had working on a roadside construction crew one summer in high school. When a crew member came after Ailes with a shovel and "literally almost took his head off," a friend recalled, "all of a sudden, this six-foot six-inch black dude stopped him in his tracks. Ailes and the guy had lunch together every day that summer. He said, 'The guy saved my life.' "

By 1968, Ailes and McGinniss saw each other less, as the frenzy of that year consumed them both. As if running the number one show in the country wasn't enough, Ailes was accelerating his television career. A year after being named Douglas's executive producer, he began pitching shows on the side. He formed two production companies called Bounty Enterprises and Project Five Productions with a group of Douglas producers. "I'm not sure Chet," Ailes's boss, "even knew about it," LaPorta remembered. "He had so much ambition. You just went along with him." Ailes filmed a couple of pilots—one with the mentalist the Amazing Kreskin in Camden, New Jersey, and another starring the singer Hal Frazier at the Hollywood Palace in Los Angeles. He also discussed doing a show with TV personality Dorothy Fuldheim, a onetime Douglas rival from Cleveland. LaPorta envisioned Fuldheim standing in the middle of a circular set in front of a large, glamorous photograph of the host in her twenties. He took as his inspiration the Man in the Arena quote, hanging in Ailes's office. The show never got off the ground, but Ailes held on to LaPorta's concept.

Although Ailes had managed to quell rebellion after he was promoted into Fraser's job, staff members eventually began to chafe at his imperiousness. For Larry Rosen, the trigger came in 1967 when the show was nominated for two Emmys in Program and Individual Achievements in

Daytime Television. The nomination for programming achievement cited Rosen, but Ailes wanted the accolade. "Roger wanted only his name on the nomination. He appealed to the Academy to do so," Rosen said. The citation did not change, but the day before the awards dinner in New York, Rosen found out that Ailes and Douglas would be the sole representatives of the show. Rosen took the train and showed up at the hotel where the dinner was taking place. "I walked right by the two of them," he said. As it happened, Rosen did not win. After the ceremony, Douglas offered Rosen a ride back to Philadelphia with himself and Ailes. In the limo, Rosen vented his anger about his exclusion from the Emmys and the way Fraser had been dumped. "I'm convinced to this day it was all political. I think Woody was put on the block. I think it was Roger who did it," Rosen recalled.

A few weeks later, Rosen resigned to take a job in Los Angeles as a producer on *The Outcasts,* starring Don Murray and Otis Young. "When Roger took over, a lot of the warmth and camaraderie that existed with Woody disappeared," Rosen told an interviewer after he left. "It was all politics and backstabbing. It became very uncomfortable." Launa Newman upheld her pact to follow him out the door.

# THREE
# THE PHILADELPHIA STORY

It was on *The Mike Douglas Show* that Ailes began to develop his ideas about politics as entertainment. Politicians were part of the show, a special subset of celebrity, and colleagues remembered Ailes closely observing the national figures who sat for interviews. During a 1968 segment with Bobby Kennedy in Washington, Ailes remarked that Kennedy, affable and confident off-camera, turned nervous and cold when the interview began. "Roger was just completely interested and intrigued by the mechanics of the ways these guys presented themselves and talked," producer Kenny Johnson recalled. "They had a common ability to convince you that you were the most important person in their life."

Ailes already had an instinct for the wedge issue, and how a clever question could exploit it. During George Wallace's appearance in 1967, Ailes prepped Douglas before the interview. He told Douglas to make sure to pin him down on the race issue. When the cameras started rolling, Ailes steered the conversation off camera. "I'd operate like a third base coach," Ailes said. "Roger was really gunning for him," Johnson recalled. "He really wanted to get Wallace on record in an interview saying he believed in segregation. I still remember Roger standing to one side with cue cards punching his fist and transmitting telepathically to Mike to have Wallace '*answer the fucking question.*' At that moment in time, if you asked me what Roger's politics were, I would have said he was a Democrat."

One morning in the summer of 1967, Ailes received an excited phone call from Launa Newman, shortly before she resigned. At the time, Newman was working out of an office in New York, and she had heard that Richard Nixon was going to be traveling to Philadelphia. After losing a run for U.S. president in 1960 and for California governor in 1962, he had moved to Manhattan and set up shop as a lawyer at Mudge, Rose. He was now laying the groundwork for a political comeback in the form of a presidential run, in the 1968 election.

Newman thought Nixon would be a prize get, but as she disliked Nixon, she did not want to call his people herself.

Newman urged Ailes to make the call. "Why don't you book him?" she recalled asking.

"I don't do bookings."

"I don't like him, you love him," she teased. "You're a Republican. I'm not. Why don't you call him up and invite him on the show?"

As it happened, Ailes had met Nixon briefly in Pittsburgh, but he didn't want to call. "That's *your* job."

"You know, one day you could work for him as his media adviser," she said and hung up. "There was no such thing as a media adviser," she later said. "I made it up because I didn't want to call him." Ailes took it from there.

By this point, Ailes was soaking up multiple influences. Kenny Johnson recalled one conversation in Ailes's office about the power of propaganda. Like Ailes, Johnson loved the theater. He had performed in high school plays and studied directing at Carnegie Tech, where he had become fascinated by the Nazi propaganda films of Leni Riefenstahl, especially *Triumph of the Will* and *Olympia*. "I was blown away," Johnson remembered. "I had an enormous hatred of Hitler, but when I saw *Triumph of the Will,* you find yourself thinking, 'Wow, he's pretty cool—no, wait, I hate these guys.'" Ailes told Johnson that he too was a big fan of Riefenstahl. "He thought her work was brilliant," Johnson said. They talked about "how she made different versions of the films for different countries not only to aggrandize the Nazis but to throw a bone to the other folks." Ailes was especially taken by Riefenstahl's use of camera angles. "There's so many subtle things you see in propaganda," Johnson said. "If you put the camera below a subject's eye height, it's the 'hero shot.' It gives him dominance. We talked about the psychological impact of the placement of the camera."

Nixon was scheduled to appear on October 31, 1967. But a few weeks before the taping, his team got cold feet. Philadelphia was becoming hostile terrain for Republicans, with Arlen Specter, the Republican candidate for mayor, locked in a tight race, so the meeting was postponed until January 9. The day before the interview, Clint Wheeler, an outside PR consultant to the campaign, went to Philadelphia to prep with Ailes. They discussed the topics for the interview, which included questions like "What's Bob Hope really like? Did David [Eisenhower] ask you for [your daughter] Julie's hand? What do you think of the demonstrators/LBJ situation? What about women in politics? Will you play the piano?"

At 9:45 the next morning, Nixon left his Fifth Avenue apartment and headed with his aide Dwight Chapin for LaGuardia Airport, where the *Reader's Digest* Gulfstream was waiting for the thirty-five-minute flight to Philadelphia. Ailes would retell the story of their conversation at the studio repeatedly. It was the moment that altered the trajectory of his career. The earliest account of their meeting was Joe McGinniss's, in *The Selling of the President*. McGinniss wrote that while waiting to go on-air, Nixon complained to Ailes about television, eliciting Ailes's retort that television was not a "gimmick."

In later years, Ailes would recast their first encounter, downplaying his ambition. In magazine profiles and speeches, Ailes said he spoke to Nixon about his campaign because he had booked him on the same show as a belly dancer and, wanting to spare Nixon an awkward encounter, let him wait in his office until the interview started. "I remember being 27 working for Mike Douglas," he told *The New York Times* in 2001. "The guests were Richard Nixon and a dancer called Little Egypt—with her boa constrictor. I didn't wanna scare Nixon and I didn't wanna scare the snake, so I stuck Nixon in my office for 15 minutes. If I'd put Little Egypt in there, I'd be managing belly dancers right now."

According to several of Ailes's colleagues who were present and the show logs, there was no belly dancer named Little Egypt booked that day. The guests during the Nixon taping were the singer Margaret Whiting, the actress Stella Stevens, the Philadelphia Brass Ensemble, and Tony Sandler's children. Mike Douglas later told an interviewer it was *his* idea to have Nixon wait in Ailes's office, and because Ailes wanted to get into politics, he seized the opportunity to have a private conversation with Nixon. "He wanted so to get into that area," Douglas recalled. Kenny Johnson was standing in the hallway and saw Ailes enter his office with Nixon and shut the door. The meeting lasted an hour. Afterward, Johnson saw Ailes emerge shaking his head and flashing a raffish grin. "I may have just shot myself in the foot or gotten myself another job," Ailes told Johnson, saying he repeated Launa Newman's advice:

"Mr. Nixon, you need a media adviser."

"What's a media adviser?"

"I am."

The taping began. As it happened, it was Nixon's fifty-fifth birthday, and the producers arranged for a cake. "We went to commercial," Douglas later recounted, "and he turned to me and said, 'Ask me anything you'd like, Mike.' "

After the broadcast, Nixon and Dwight Chapin headed to a luncheon with Philadelphia businessmen. Chapin could sense that Nixon had been impressed with Ailes. A few days later, Ailes got the call from Nixon headquarters. "The name of the game was to get Roger up to New York immediately," Chapin recalled.

Soon after, on an afternoon in January, Ailes was in New York City for lunch at the Plaza Hotel with Raymond Price, a thirty-seven-year-old speechwriter and Nixon aide with novel ideas about how television could be used to power Nixon's 1968 presidential campaign. Leonard Garment, who was heading up the campaign's media strategy, had arranged for Ailes to meet Price at Nixon's urging. Ailes and Price seemed to come from different realms. Ailes was a state school graduate immersed in the world of daytime television. Price was a Yale-educated writer who had once been the editorial page editor of the pro-Nixon *New York Herald Tribune*. A rare moderate in the Nixon orbit, Price had collaborated with Nixon on "Asia After Viet Nam," an essay that had been published in *Foreign Affairs* a few months before.

As it turned out, Ailes and Price had a kind of generational bond—they were the original TV babies, with an intuitive sense of the medium's potential to transform politics. Since the summer, Price had strategized how to revolutionize the emerging craft of image making. The campaign's television production was being headed up by Al Scott, a former NBC sound technician. But the fifty-three-year-old Scott was a product of the radio age. They needed someone young, who grasped the subtleties of modern television production and had the metabolism to get the job done. At twenty-seven, Ailes already seemed to have a career's experience handling talent. "Roger was not at all awed to be in the presence of power," Nixon adviser Fred Malek said. "He could look at the vice president and the rest of us and tell him he was full of baloney and he has to get his act together on something."

Ailes was hired as a part-time consultant in February 1968. The project of transforming Nixon, a political has-been, into a winner, was one for which Ailes had relevant experience. After all, he had helped transform Mike Douglas, whose career had been in a death spiral when the show debuted, into a national celebrity. Price wanted Ailes to do the same for Nixon, and for the same kind of audience. Nixon had a famously conflicted relationship with TV, having exploited the medium brilliantly with the Checkers speech, but having been destroyed by it in the 1960 Kennedy debates.

Ailes fit seamlessly into the culture of the Nixon campaign, partly because his life story had an uncanny symmetry with Nixon's: both grew up poor and both took from childhood an indefatigable drive to acquire power. "He's got guts, he's tough," Ailes later said of Nixon. "He picked himself up by the bootstraps two or three times and came back and won the prize." Perhaps more than anything else, Nixon and Ailes both thought of themselves as men who got things done. "Nixon's a doer, not a talker," Ailes said.

Ailes would later tell a *Washington Post* reporter that there was no other politician in the twentieth century he would have wanted to work for more than Nixon. When Price and Ailes met for lunch, the soft launch of Nixon's new media strategy had already begun. In New Hampshire, the campaign was airing five-minute television advertisements, in which Nixon conversed naturally with state voters in schoolrooms, firehouses, and community centers. The traveling press pool was barred from attending these staged events. When reporters howled, Garment and his team simply ignored them. Nixon crushed his opponents in New Hampshire, winning the primary with a seven-to-one margin over Nelson Rockefeller, then a write-in candidate.

Ailes's main assignment would begin in the fall and it would be far more audacious than the five-minute New Hampshire experiment. Garment and Price tasked him with producing a series of one-hour town halls in cities across the country—meetings designed to showcase Nixon engaging with a panel of citizen interviewers. They were also designed to blow the padlocks off the gates to the national media. To the viewer at home, it would seem like Nixon was risking it all by answering difficult questions on live television when in fact, as Garment later wrote, "the chances of a case-hardened politician like Nixon stumbling seriously over any question was near zero." The black and white world of newspapers was the past. And Nixon, with a much better makeup team, was going to be a man of his time.

It still stunned many that Nixon was attempting another run. Less than six years earlier, he had been left for dead, after an embarrassing failed run for governor of California, his home state. For this injustice Nixon blamed the national press. "For sixteen years, ever since the [Alger] Hiss case, you've had a lot of fun," the former vice president said in his self-pitying concession speech at the Beverly Hilton Hotel in November 1962. He concluded his remarks with a challenge to the assembled journalists: "If they're against a candidate, give him the shaft," he said, "but also recognize if they give him the shaft, put one lonely reporter on the campaign who will report what the candidate says now and then." Five days after the election, ABC broadcast a thirty-minute documentary titled *The Political Obituary of Richard M. Nixon.*

But Nixon—who joined Mudge, Rose as a consultant in February 1963, soon became a partner, and toyed with the notion of becoming commissioner of baseball—wasn't quite dead. The man who revived him was Len Garment. A Brooklyn-born trial lawyer, Democrat, and jazz saxophonist, Garment became Nixon's all-purpose adviser and fixer, and helped smooth Nixon's entry into the cloistered halls of Manhattan society. His main task was to assemble a crop of fresh faces for Nixon's new political team. "This game is all about youth," Dwight Chapin said. In addition to Ray Price, there was a fast-talking New York publicist named Bill Safire, and a young *Fortune* writer named Dick Whalen. Garment brought experienced hands on-deck, too, convincing municipal bond lawyer John Mitchell to sign on as campaign manager.

Nixon himself grasped how to channel his bitterness at his treatment by the media and the wider culture into the wellspring of his political strength. In the mid-1960s, many Americans believed that the culture was out of control, that it had lost touch with traditional values, that it had stopped listening to the wisest among them—men like Nixon himself. To counteract the excesses of the youth movement, the culture needed a dose of adulthood. Nixon called his sober prescription "law and order"—a triangulation between Lyndon Johnson's coddling liberalism and Barry Goldwater's reactionary conservatism. Nixon wagered that, having put ideological purity ahead of reason, the Republican Party would return to its senses and see value in his familiar visage. After he campaigned for eighty-six Republican candidates in thirty-five states during the 1966 election, nearly two thirds of them won.

Though Len Garment eagerly talked up a Nixon resurrection—"The man and the times have finally come together," he said—few believed him. In the wider public imagination, Dick Nixon was still a sad joke. A paradox struck Garment: in person, Nixon came across as confident and jocular. On television, Americans saw a diffident, humorless pol. Garment realized that all the talk about the "New Nixon" and the "Old Nixon" missed the point entirely. There was only one Nixon. But a hostile press establishment and the unforgiving lens of the television camera had prevented the voters from seeing the real man. His mission in 1968 was to highlight the positive aspects of Nixon's personality that had been obscured. Television, therefore, was not just a tactical consideration. It was a matter of strategic importance.

The hardest part of the job may have been convincing Nixon himself of this truth. Television was at the top of Nixon's list of resentments. To him, the Big Three networks were another tool the liberals on the East Coast had at their disposal to punish deserving men like himself. Nevertheless, he was determined to master the medium as he had mastered every other challenge in his life: with sedulous work and brute force. Harry Robbins Haldeman, the former J. Walter Thompson ad man with a famous buzz cut and athletic good looks, articulated the way forward. Bob, as he was known to friends, reasoned that one report on the nightly news would reach more people in an instant than the campaign could reach in ten months of stump speeches. "The time has come for political campaigning, its techniques and strategies, to move out of the dark ages and into the brave new world of the omnipresent eye," he wrote.

In the summer of 1967, Nixon sought out television advice from all over. Ed McMahon went to his office at 810 Fifth Avenue to help him prepare for his appearance on the Johnny Carson show, where the question of his presidential intentions was bound to be asked. In July, Nixon also took a meeting with Frank Shakespeare, the president of CBS Television. During a ninety-minute meeting at Nixon's office, Shakespeare evangelized for the new religion of television. An ardent conservative, Shakespeare first considered working for Ronald Reagan until deciding that Reagan was too inexperienced. After the meeting, Nixon told Garment to hire him.

Several weeks later, Garment ran into his summer neighbor Harry Treleaven, who would also become an important Ailes teacher, on the beach near his cottage in Amagansett, on Long Island. Treleaven had spent eighteen years at J. Walter Thompson and was the creative mind behind the campaigns for such mid-century icons as Ford, Pan Am, and Singer. In 1966, Treleaven took a leave from J. Walter Thompson to go to Texas, where he produced advertising for the long-shot campaign of George H. W. Bush, a forty-two-year-old Republican running for Congress in a Houston district that had only elected Democrats. Treleaven theorized that persuading voters depended more on a candidate's image than articulating positions on particular issues. "Political candidates are celebrities . . . and today with television taking them into everybody's home right along with Johnny Carson and Batman, they're more of a public attraction than ever," he wrote in a report. Interviewing Texas voters, Treleaven discovered that they liked Bush personally, even if they were vague on where he stood politically. So he created a character for Bush to inhabit: the hardworking underdog. In his TV spots, Treleaven presented Bush—the pedigreed product of Greenwich, Andover, and Yale—as a homespun Texan amiably strolling dusty streets with his blazer slung casually over his shoulder and his shirtsleeves rolled up. It worked. Bush won comfortably, and Treleaven came aboard the Nixon campaign.

Price acted as Garment's media theoretician, deepening and enriching his concepts. In late November 1967, Price circulated a strategy memo drawing on the ideas of Marshall McLuhan's 1964 book *Understanding Media: The Extensions of Man*. In his chapter "Television: The Timid Giant," McLuhan commented on Nixon's 1963 appearance on *The Jack Paar Show,* in which he performed a work he had composed for the piano. "Instead of the slick, glib, legal Nixon, we saw the doggedly creative and modest performer," McLuhan wrote. "A few timely touches like this would have quite altered the result of the Kennedy-Nixon campaign." Price's assumption was that in the age of television, humans inhabited multiple realities—the two most salient being the reality that actually existed and the reality burned onto a cathode ray tube. Since 99 percent of voters would never meet the candidate in person, Price was convinced that the only reality they would ever know was the one on their television screens. "It's not what's *there* that counts," Price wrote. "It's what's projected—and, carrying it one step further, it's not what *he* projects but rather what the voter receives." Television was the only reality that mattered to swaying the minds of millions of voters. "It's not the man we have to change, but rather the *received impression*."

Price argued that Nixon could win if the campaign made the audience *feel* differently about their candidate. "Politics is much more emotional than it is rational, and this is particularly true of presidential politics," Price wrote, adding, "Potential presidents are measured against an ideal that's a combination of leading man, God, father, hero, pope, king, with maybe just a touch of the avenging Furies thrown in." As Treleaven had done for Bush, Price drew up a character sketch for Nixon. The campaign would cast him as "the kind of man proud parents would ideally want their sons to grow up to be: a man who embodies the national ideal, its aspirations, its dreams, a man whose *image* the people want in their homes as a source of inspiration, and whose voice they want as the representative of their nation in the councils of the world, and of their generation in the pages of history." Pulling this off would require some deception. "The TV medium itself introduces an element of distortion, in terms both of its effect on the candidate and of the often subliminal ways in which the image is received," Price wrote. "And it inevitably is going to convey a partial image—thus ours is the task of finding how to control its use so the part that gets across is the part we want to have gotten across."

Roger Ailes would be responsible for executing this vision, transplanting his talk show techniques to the business of electing a president.

The legend of Roger Ailes has it that he almost single-handedly transformed Nixon from a schlump to a president with his talk-show alchemy. But the truth was more complicated. In many ways, Ailes was more student than teacher. Garment, Treleaven, and Price—and Nixon himself—had an incalculable influence on Ailes's thinking. Together, they provided a toolbox of concepts and linkages and techniques that Ailes would use throughout his career. But ironically, it was a member of what's now called the mainstream media—and a liberal—who provided the most crucial boost to Ailes's curriculum vitae. One morning in June 1968, a few months after Ailes signed on to the campaign, his friend from Philadelphia, Joe McGinniss, met with the ABC sportscaster Howard Cosell, about whom he was writing an article.

It turned out to be the biggest break of McGinniss's career. While shadowing Cosell, McGinniss shared a ride to the Stamford, Connecticut, train station with a friend of Cosell's, Edward Russell, an executive vice president at the Madison Avenue agency Doyle Dane Bernbach. McGinniss listened intently from the backseat of the car as Russell excitedly told Cosell that the agency had landed the account for Hubert Humphrey's presidential campaign. McGinniss possessed a reporter's antenna for news. The idea that presidential campaigns were being packaged and sold like cars and toothpaste to unsuspecting voters struck him as deeply cynical—and one hell of a story.

As it happened, McGinniss was scheduled to have lunch with Eugene Prakapas, an editor at Simon & Schuster, later that day. Over lunch, McGinniss related the conversation he had overheard. Prakapas agreed that political advertising was a potentially major unexplored subject. Theodore White, who had invented the modern campaign narrative with his landmark book *The Making of the President 1960,* was already under contract to write the definitive campaign book of 1968. McGinniss told Prakapas he wanted to focus strictly on the advertising efforts of the Humphrey and Nixon campaigns. "You wouldn't call it *The Making of the President,*" McGinniss told him. "You'd call it *The Selling of the President.*"

Prakapas liked his idea. "I'll have them cut you a check for five hundred dollars so you can pursue this a little further," he said.

After the lunch, McGinniss walked to a phone booth on Fifth Avenue, outside Rockefeller Center, and called Russell. His pitch was summarily rejected.

"No, no, that was off the record," Russell told McGinniss.

"So you won't cooperate?"

"Cooperate? What, you think we're crazy? No. And I don't want to hear from you again and I don't want to read anything about this."

Dispirited but undeterred, McGinniss called Harry Treleaven and delivered the same pitch he had presented to Humphrey's team. Astonishingly, Treleaven was receptive to McGinniss's idea. Treleaven's openness may have been due to the fact he had once been a writer himself, penning plays for radio shows in California. He told McGinniss to stop by his office at the agency Fuller & Smith & Ross. Len Garment professed no objections except to ensure that McGinniss would not publish the book until the campaign's conclusion in November, whatever the outcome. "We were intrigued with the idea of having him follow us," Garment later said. It was a decision he would later regret.

In late June, Nixon was in a New York television studio answering questions from Illinois voters, who had been flown in to film more advertising spots. The thirty-minute program was called *The Nixon Answer*. The campaign would air them in a half dozen markets in Illinois and Michigan and eight markets in Ohio. It was the latest experiment in the campaign's use of staged interviews. The campaign gave selected participants the full treatment, providing each with round-trip first-class airfare, two nights in a Manhattan hotel, and money for meals.

Ailes did not attend the broadcast, but he reviewed the sessions on tape. The show was a bust. The camera placements were off and the pacing was slow. Ailes noticed that the candidate continued to be stiff and unmodulated. There were no peaks and valleys, no surprises, little drama—no payoffs at the end of a segment. On July 6, he wrote Garment and Shakespeare a six-page memo that addressed his concerns about Nixon's performance. "If you were to time each of Mr. Nixon's answers, they probably would all fall within 45 seconds of each other," he wrote. "It gives the impression that his answers on all of the issues are 'pat' and thus he appears not to be responding to the specific question. The next logical step in the viewer's mind is maybe the questions are 'pat' or 'set up,' too."

Of course, the entire program was set up. The potential impact of the show was based on convincing the audience it was real.

Ailes echoed the concepts he had learned from Woody Fraser on the *Mike Douglas* set. Specifically, Nixon needed "more descriptive visual phrases" that would wrap his comments in memorable "kickers." "Television is a 'hit and run' medium," Ailes wrote. "The general public is just not sophisticated enough to wade through answers. Therefore, at least some of Mr. Nixon's answers should end with a . . . specific, graphic, succinct, memorable comment."

The memo showed early signs that Ailes wanted to influence not just television, but the underlying politics as well. Although he had no political experience and was just a part-time television adviser to the campaign, he offered some two dozen suggested responses for Nixon to deliver to questions—sound bites, as they're now called. Ailes's first efforts in this genre were catchy, but often too bombastic to be presidential, reflecting his father's gnomic voice. His memo offered answers on Vietnam ("This country is almost 200 years old—two hundred years from now we won't just be 200 years older—but 200 years greater!"), the United Nations ("The problem with war is that it is seldom discussed ahead of time. Too often one side is not clear why the other is fighting"), NATO ("outdated"), inflation ("If you make $10,000 a year and spend $15,000, it won't be long before you are in trouble"), taxes ("I sometimes hear people say 'America is going to the dogs.' These people pay their hard earned money to support a country and then spend their time running the country down"), poverty ("We cannot win these people by sharing government wealth.

Our healing gift is the capacity for self-help. They feel generosity as oppression"). The phrases represented Ailes's drive to simplify complex issues to emotionally resonant one-liners. The skills would find their flowering in cable news.

By the end of July, Ailes was realizing that balancing the Douglas show and the campaign was too much. A few days before the 1968 Republican National Convention opened in Miami Beach, Ailes asked Douglas for a leave of absence from his job. Douglas balked. "Mike turned me down. He was very upset, because we were about to go into the fall rating period," Ailes said. Politics was thrilling and he wanted more of it. "I said I would go anyway," Ailes said, "so permission was grudgingly granted." But it was a risk. "When I started out, I had my own personal career on the line," he later said. "It heightened the excitement. It's sort of like chicken-racing with yourself. If I hadn't, I'd probably be back in Ohio as a prop boy." Douglas felt betrayed. "I think Mike was hurt," Bob LaPorta said. "Mike wanted loyalty. That was one of Mike's big things." Ailes never returned to the show. He and Douglas did not speak for years afterward.

In the wake of Ailes's departure, the show struggled, partly because the culture had become much more complicated in the seven years since the show started, and it was near impossible for an essentially lighthearted show like *Mike Douglas* to strike the right tone in those chaotic times. The show limped along for another decade to declining ratings and assorted reinventions. In the early 1980s, the show was canceled and Douglas retired to Florida. He died on August 11, 2006—his eighty-first birthday. Ailes had drifted apart from his colleagues, but reconnected with many of them at Douglas's memorial service in North Hollywood. Ailes tried small talk with Debbie Miller and Larry Rosen, who had left television altogether and worked as a certified physician assistant, but it was evident the years had not eased the tensions.

"I have an admission to make," Ailes said to Rosen. "You were always a better producer than I was." Miller, standing next to Rosen, noticed how Ailes's remark stung Rosen.

Other colleagues retained fonder memories. When Douglas died, Bob LaPorta was on an Amtrak train in California when his son called and broke the news. LaPorta's first impulse was to call Ailes. "I just got his secretary. I said, 'Just ask the boss what he wants us to do.' "

Cheerleading gave him a capacity to sell himself [illegible] and gone only to [illegible] presents. The dramas he discovered [illegible] days [illegible] [illegible] interview [illegible] [illegible] were [illegible] the [illegible] on [illegible] shows.

By the end of July, Ailes was resenting that [illegible] of getting the Douglas show [illegible] guests normally. A few days before the 1968 Republican National Convention opened in Miami Beach, Ailes asked Dennis [illegible] for a leave of absence from the Mike Douglas Show. "Mike [illegible] me down [illegible] because we were about to go into the [illegible] period," Ailes said. [illegible] at finding [illegible] he wanted [illegible] more. "[illegible] asked I would go anyway," Ailes said. "[illegible] permission was [illegible] but it was a risk." When he returned, "I had my own personal [illegible]," Ailes later said. "[illegible] [illegible] of [illegible] racing with your [illegible] [illegible] back in Ohio [illegible]." Douglas [illegible] [illegible] Ailes was [illegible] in California and [illegible] [illegible] that it [illegible] [illegible] [illegible] Ailes [illegible] returned to [illegible] of the [illegible] Douglas didn't [illegible] [illegible] were [illegible].

In the wake of Ailes's departure, the show [illegible], partly because the [illegible] had become much more [illegible] during the seven years since the show started, and [illegible] was [illegible] [illegible] [illegible] broadcasts, [illegible] like NBC's [illegible] [illegible] [illegible] [illegible]. The show [illegible] for another decade [illegible] until 1980, and [illegible] [illegible], in [illegible] [illegible] [illegible] [illegible] [illegible] [illegible] Douglas [illegible] on [illegible] [illegible] [illegible] [illegible] Ailes [illegible] apart from [illegible] [illegible] [illegible] with many of [illegible] Douglas [illegible] [illegible] in [illegible] Ailes [illegible] [illegible] with [illegible] Larry Rosen, who had [illegible] together and worked [illegible] [illegible] [illegible] was evident [illegible] [illegible] [illegible].

There [illegible] [illegible] [illegible]," Ailes said. "[illegible] [illegible] [illegible] [illegible] [illegible] Mike [illegible] [illegible] [illegible] how Ailes [illegible] [illegible].

Their [illegible] [illegible] [illegible]. When Douglas [illegible] [illegible] [illegible] in California [illegible] [illegible] [illegible] [illegible] [illegible] [illegible] [illegible] [illegible] [illegible] [illegible] [illegible] [illegible] [illegible] Ailes said, [illegible] [illegible] [illegible] [illegible] [illegible].

# ACT II

# FOUR

# SELLING THE TRICK

THE 1968 REPUBLICAN NATIONAL CONVENTION was Roger Ailes's baptism in national politics, a chance to see the full spectacle of a presidential campaign—the media, the costumed delegates—at close range. On his first full day in town, he had an expensive dinner with Barbara Walters at the Fontainebleau Hotel. The rest of the week he was busy networking with some of the biggest names in broadcast journalism. Mainly, though, Ailes was a minor player among the heavy hitters, with few official responsibilities. Instead, he played campaign gofer, on one occasion taking a cab out to the airport to pick up Nixon's daughters. The candidate himself was not scheduled to arrive in Miami until the convention officially opened on Monday afternoon. Until then, he would be sequestered in a rented house on Long Island, furiously working on his acceptance speech.

After quelling a last-minute surge by Ronald Reagan, Nixon strode to the podium on August 8 to address the convention and accept the party's nomination. The speech would become a cornerstone of the campaign's television advertising. For the rest of the month, Harry Treleaven broadcast excerpts in thirty-second spots. "We are going to win because our cause is right," Nixon told the audience, to thunderous applause. "We see cities enveloped in smoke and flame. . . . We hear sirens in the night. We see Americans dying on distant battlefields abroad. We see Americans hating each other; fighting each other; killing each other at home. And as we see and hear these things, millions of Americans cry out in anguish. Did we come all this way for this?"

Ailes must have recognized the lament. Nixon was speaking of the everyday folks who tuned in to the Douglas show. They wanted to be entertained, not bludgeoned with daily reminders of the country's ills. "Did American boys die in Normandy, and Korea, and in Valley Forge for this?" Nixon asked. "Listen to the answer to those questions. It is another voice. It is the quiet voice in the tumult and the shouting. It is the voice of the great majority of Americans, the forgotten Americans—the non-shouters; the non-demonstrators. They are not racists or sick; they are not guilty of the crime that plagues the land." Nixon promised them absolution: "This I say to you tonight is the real voice of America. In this year 1968, this is the message it will broadcast to America and to the world."

Shortly after the convention, Ailes ran into Joe McGinniss at the Manhattan offices of Fuller & Smith & Ross. "Holy shit, what are you doing here?" McGinniss recalled saying.

"The question is, what are *you* doing here?" Ailes replied.

"I'm writing a book about this."

"The fuck you are? Who's letting you do that?"

"Well, Harry and Len—"

"—Jesus Christ. Don't they even *read*?"

McGinniss suddenly got nervous that Ailes could alert the campaign about his politics. "Every day I wrote columns, most of which appeared on the front page, saying, 'Boy, Nixon is an asshole. This is disgusting,'" McGinniss recalled. "All they had to do was to pick up the *Inquirer* and see, *holy shit, this guy is not a friend of ours*. But they didn't bother, because no one had ever heard of me." To write the book, McGinniss had quit his job at the newspaper. Without access to the Nixon campaign, the entire project would implode.

"Roger, don't rat me out."

"Don't worry about it," Ailes said. "But I can't believe this, Jesus. But hey, no one is asking me for approval."

A strategic alliance was forged—one that would make both young men into stars.

The first of the Nixon campaign's panel shows was scheduled for September 4, at the Chicago studios of WBBM, the local CBS affiliate, six days after the Democrats nominated Hubert Humphrey at their chaotic convention. For Richard Nixon, WBBM had painful history: it was the site of his disastrous 1960 presidential debate against Kennedy. McGinniss followed Ailes to Chicago to chronicle the production. A few hours before Nixon was due to arrive in the studio, McGinniss watched Ailes putting out fires. "Those stupid bastards on the set designing crew put turquoise curtains in the background. Nixon wouldn't look right unless he was carrying a pocketbook," Ailes said. He had the curtains pulled down and three wood-paneled columns with "clean, solid, masculine lines" wheeled onto the set. The stage was designed to engender sympathy: Nixon would face his inquisitors alone standing on a circular blue platform eight inches high and six feet in diameter, as *Mike Douglas* producer Bob LaPorta envisioned for the Dorothy Fuldheim pilot he had worked on with Ailes. "The subliminal message of the 'arena' works," Ailes wrote in a memo to Garment and Shakespeare. "Even if a viewer is not in favor of Richard Nixon, by 15 minutes into the program he almost subconsiously begins to root for him." In the audience, Nixon's family, political allies, and three hundred supporters recruited by local Republican groups would clap and cheer whenever Nixon delivered an answer.

The citizens on the panel were a part of the set, too. Garment, Shakespeare, and Treleaven combed through lists of names to come up with a "balanced" group. The program's authenticity depended on Nixon appearing to engage with a diverse cross-section of potential voters. The question of race was an especially delicate matter. It was decided that the panel should include exactly one black participant. "Two would be offensive to whites," McGinniss later wrote, describing their thinking, "perhaps to Negroes as well. Two would be trying too hard. One was necessary and safe." To that end, the campaign recruited a black former Chicago public schoolteacher named Warner Saunders. To represent Chicago's other major demographic blocs, there was a Jewish lawyer, a Polish community leader, a sandy-haired businessman, a round-cheeked farmer, a demure housewife, and two newspapermen.

The reporters covering the campaign would have no role whatsoever. "Let's face it, Nixon did not have good press," Ailes later said. "They were still playing, 'Would you buy a used car from this guy?' His only hope was to go around the press and go directly to the people." But Herb Klein, the campaign's press secretary, had been fielding complaints from journalists and warned that the campaign risked a backlash if they weren't invited. Treleaven was inclined to listen, but Shakespeare told him that under no circumstances would they be allowed in.

Ailes sided with Shakespeare. "I agree with Frank," he said. "*Fuck 'em*. It's not a press conference."

At *The Mike Douglas Show,* colleagues did not hear Ailes express antipathy toward the media. But in the crucible of the '68 campaign, Ailes adopted a new view: journalists were the enemy. Ailes warned Treleaven that reporters would point out all the crafty television techniques that went into the show. They might reveal for instance that the hopped-up studio audience had been primed by a jowly warm-up man named Jack Rourke. "The audience is part of the show," Ailes told him. McGinniss stood by listening. "And that's the whole point. It's a television show. Our television show." As McLuhan had theorized, the image on-screen was what mattered. Anything else was a distraction. "The press has no business on the set. . . . This is an electronic election. The first there's ever been. . . . TV has the power now," Ailes said. Like the voters at home, the press would watch the proceedings from a separate studio.

At 9:00 p.m., viewers tuning in to *The Dom DeLuise Show* were greeted instead with news footage of Richard Nixon receiving a hero's welcome on the streets of Chicago. Like a freak summer snow, confetti fluttered down on the thousands of smiling faces in the crowd. The title credits "NIXON IN ILLINOIS" flashed on the screen in bold yellow lettering. A baritone-voiced announcer intoned: "This afternoon, Richard Nixon arrived in Chicago and received one of the warmest and most enthusiastic welcomes in this city's history." It was Treleaven's idea to open the broadcast with clips of Nixon, standing in an open-air limousine, arms thrust victoriously in the air, making his trademark V. For the audience at home, the jubilant scene would contrast starkly with that of a week earlier, when Democrats had brought insurrection to the streets. When Richard Nixon came to town, there was a parade.

Ailes watched the introduction unfold on monitors in the control room as the director cued the next shot: Nixon bounding onto the stage. The studio audience jumped to their feet applauding vigorously, as Jack Rourke had coached them. The director cut back and forth between the candidate and the crowd. Nixon was beaming, seeming in that moment as warm and as human as Mike Douglas. He even had his own gag man onstage with him: former Oklahoma football coach turned ABC announcer Bud Wilkinson, one of the few celebrities backing Nixon in '68. Moments earlier, Wilkinson had greeted the audience and introduced the panel. "I'd like to stress the point that Mr. Nixon has absolutely no idea what questions will be asked," he said, sounding like a color commentator before a big game. "There could not have been any prior preparation."

Except Nixon had done nothing but prepare for this moment. And

Ailes had helped him. Before the broadcast, Nixon honed a series of stock answers that he could deploy at will, artfully tailoring the response to whatever question was posed. "If the material he is presenting can be made more succinct and memorable, there is no doubt that he can control this medium in the upcoming election," Ailes wrote in his July 1968 memo to Garment and Shakespeare. Because the broadcasts would be seen only in their local markets, Nixon could repeat his answers in one city after the next. He could also calibrate his response to the sensibilities of different audiences. Thus he would affirm civil rights in Chicago but hedge on school integration weeks later in Charlotte. (Years later, Ailes would advise his clients to use the same trick: "On an index card you can keep in your wallet, list the key phrases of ten stories that will entertain audiences for the next ten years," he wrote in his book, *You Are the Message,* "because you rarely speak to the same audience twice.")

Nixon followed Wilkinson's introduction with a monologue—it really was a talk show. "I'm not trying to filibuster before we go to the questions," he quipped, before turning sincere. "I would like to say a word about the pictures you saw a moment ago of the arrival in Chicago. Those pictures brought back many memories to me." The camera zoomed in tight: "Sixteen years ago in 1952, I was nominated for vice president in Chicago at the Republican National Convention. And then eight years ago, I was nominated for president of the United States in Chicago at the Republican National Convention. And today, as I begin this campaign tour, I would have to say I've received the greatest political reception that I've ever received in my life in Chicago." Over and over, a half dozen times, he repeated that code word for Democratic lawlessness: *Chicago*.

Jack Sundine, editor of the *Moline Dispatch,* asked the first question. "Yes, Mr. Nixon, George Wallace has said that, and others I suppose have said this, that there isn't a thin dime of difference between the two parties nor between the nominees of the two parties. Would you, sir, in specifics, recite what you think the differences are between you and the nominee of the Democratic Party?"

The camera flashed back to Nixon.

"How much time do I have?"

The audience provided the laugh track. Nixon picked up right where his monologue ended. "At the convention last week in *Chicago,* I think the American people received there a picture of the choice that they have, and I think it's probably the most decisive choice and the greatest difference you have between two candidates in this century." He went on for almost two minutes. He spoke of "new leadership" and a "new foreign policy" and "new policies to deal with the domestic economy." There wasn't a specific to be had.

The director switched to a camera positioned at the back of the studio. From this perspective, the room resembled an arena. Even though every member of the audience was on Nixon's team, the image suggested a candidate bravely facing threats from all sides without a podium or teleprompter to defend him. The viewers at home could sympathize with his position.

The director panned to the next questioner. It was Morris Leibman, the Jewish lawyer, and a Democrat to boot. The camera filmed Leibman from the front. Almost entirely bald and wearing thick plastic frame glasses, he had to tilt his head back to make eye contact with Nixon. It looked as if Leibman was gazing up in admiration.

"Mr. Nixon, would you comment on the accusation that's been made from time to time that your views have shifted, and that they're based on expediencies?"

Nixon showed no discomfort. The camera captured him looking down at Leibman, arms clasped loosely behind his back. More comedy: "Well, I suppose, Mr. Leibman, that what you're referring to in more the vernacular is, is there a 'New Nixon' or is there an 'Old Nixon'? I suppose I could counter by saying, which Humphrey should we listen to today?"

Nixon laughed. The audience laughed. Even Leibman was chuckling.

The game was fun for everyone except the panelists: set 'em up, knock 'em down. The cheers from the crowd revealed that the real prey was the panel, not Nixon. Every time the citizen questioners opened their mouths, they could surely feel the stares of six hundred Republican eyes on their backs.

Ailes had spent days perfecting it all. Treleaven, Shakespeare, and Price had come up with the controlled television concept but Ailes fine-tuned the camera placements and the staging. Filming Nixon below his eye level made him appear taller, a commanding leader.

Midway through the broadcast, Warner Saunders, the black community leader and former schoolteacher, sat at the microphone with his arms crossed, signaling confrontation. "I'd like to step out of the box of an educator and talk about communications. A communications gap that is basically a color gap," Saunders began in a voice steady with resolve. "I would like to explain to you that the black community feels the term 'law and order' means violence, destruction inside of our community on the part of a recalcitrant police department, on the part of recalcitrant mayors and other officials inside of our community. What does 'law and order' mean to *you*?"

If anyone at home had grown bored by the proceedings, they surely snapped to attention now.

Nixon leaned back and took a deep breath. "Well, first, Mr. Saunders," he said, "I'm quite aware of this fact that law and order, I think the term that I've heard used, is a code word, a code word for basically racism." Then he pivoted to one of his prepared points: past injustices never justified lawbreaking. "I have often said you cannot have order unless you have justice. You cannot have order unless you have progress. Because order without progress, if you just stifle the dissent, if you just stifle the progress, you're going to have an explosion, and you're going to have disorder. On the other hand, you can't have progress without order because when you have disorder—*revolution*—what you do is you destroy all the progress."

The director caught a reaction shot from Ed Brooke, the black Massachusetts senator, who was seated in the front row next to Pat Nixon. Then it was back to the candidate: "The greatness of America, with few exceptions, over the period of our history, is that we have had the combination of having a system in which we could have peaceful change, peaceful progress, with order. Now that's what I want for America."

The virtually all-white audience responded with ecstatic applause. This well-run talk show was a microcosm of the civil society Nixon and his team were trying to sell.

Nixon sailed through the rest of the broadcast. He spoke of ending the war and building "bridges to human dignity" and getting "this country on a sound basis again."

At the fifty-five-minute mark, Wilkinson spoke up. "I'm very sorry I have to interrupt this very interesting discussion, but our time is running short."

Nixon asked Wilkinson if Mary Frances Squires, the housewife, could have one more question.

"I never like to cut off a lady, you know," Nixon said. On cue: more laughs.

Squires wanted to know if Nixon favored releasing the names of POWs held in Vietnam. "If it doesn't involve the security of the country, there's no excuse whatever for that kind of retention of information," he said. "I will certainly look into it."

The final question of the night came from Wilkinson. "I wonder if definite plans have been set for Julie and David's wedding?"

The camera held on Julie Nixon and David Eisenhower grinning and squirming in their seats.

"That is confidential information," Nixon replied, with mock conspiracy.

The audience tittered. It was the payoff, just like one on *The Mike Douglas Show.*

The next morning, Ailes reviewed tape of Nixon's performance. On the Douglas set, Ailes's perfectionist streak would often cause him to feel down immediately after the taping. But watching the footage of Nixon in Chicago reassured him that Nixon had delivered. "Mr. Nixon is strong now on television and has good control of the situation," Ailes wrote in a memo to Garment and Shakespeare. "He looks good on his feet and shooting 'in the round' gives dimension to him. . . . The 'arena effect' is excellent and he plays well to all areas. The look has 'guts.' "

Nixon would tape three more panels that month. The next stops were Cleveland and Los Angeles, where Nixon made a four-second taped appearance on *Rowan & Martin's Laugh-In*. ("Sock it to *me?*" he deadpanned.) Ailes had already developed more than two dozen ideas to improve the Man in the Arena shows, which he delivered to Garment and Shakespeare. To play to the home audience, Nixon had to speak more directly into the camera. Because he would sweat under the hot studio lights, the air-conditioning needed to be turned up to the max at least four hours before his arrival. His deep-set eyes benefited from slightly whiter makeup applied to his upper eyelids. Ailes had timed all twenty of Nixon's answers: "Some . . . are still too long and over half tended to be the same length," he explained. Nixon needed "memorable phrases to use in wrapping up certain points." Ailes also recommended more applause and more music, perhaps a Connie Francis soundtrack. "It might give us a classy 'standard' opening to use," he wrote.

On September 18, McGinniss and Ailes arrived in Philadelphia two days ahead of the candidate. Ailes loved to ham it up for McGinniss's notebook. "He never forgot I was writing," McGinniss later said. Ailes's mordant one-liners about Nixon's running mate, Spiro Agnew, were especially bold: "We're doing all right," he told McGinniss. "If we could only get someone to play Hide The Greek."

Although his home in the suburbs was just ten miles from the studio, Ailes was staying at the Marriott Motor Hotel. Things were not going well with Marjorie. He had been on the road for six weeks working eighteen hours a day and the pace of the campaign was naturally pulling them apart. In Philadelphia, Ailes wanted to push the envelope. The previous taping in California had been flat—the panelists asked stale questions. Ailes wanted to scramble the cast. "Nixon gets bored by the same kind of people," he said. "We've got to screw around with this one a little bit." Dan Buser, an assistant from the local Republican Party, recommended the head of a black community group as a panelist.

"And he is black," Buser added.

"What do you mean, he's black?" Ailes asked.

"I mean he's dark. It will be obvious on television that he's not white."

"You mean we won't have to put a sign around him that says, 'This is our Negro'?"

Ailes booked him. McGinniss suggested the name of a political reporter, who Ailes found out was also black.

"Oh, shit, we can't have two. Even in Philadelphia."

The panel was almost complete. He had secured an Italian lawyer from Pittsburgh, a suburban housewife, a Wharton student, a Camden newsman, and a raspy-voiced radio and TV commentator named Jack McKinney. That left one open slot. As Ailes sat with McGinniss eating room service, Ailes told his friend just what he wanted. "A good, mean, Wallaceite cab driver. Wouldn't that be great? Some guy to sit there and say, 'Awright, mac, what about these niggers?'" Ailes went on: "A lot of people think Nixon is dull. They think he's a bore, a pain in the ass. They look at him as the kind of kid who always carried a bookbag. Who was forty-two years old the day he was born. . . . Now you put him on television, you've got a problem right away. He's a funny-looking guy. He looks like somebody hung him in a closet overnight and he jumps out in the morning with his suit all bunched up and starts running around saying, 'I want to be president.' I mean this is how he strikes some people. That's why these shows are important. To make them forget all that."

The Philadelphia taping was scheduled to begin at 7:30 the next evening. Ailes showed up at the studio at 2:00 in a fighting mood. "I'm going to fire this fucking director!" he snarled. The camera placements were all off. He needed close-ups of individual audience members. Having multiple people in every shot was dated 1940s direction. "I want to see faces," he said. "I want to see pores. That's what people are. That's what television is."

The director protested. "I don't want to hear that shit!" Ailes said. "I told you what I wanted, and it's your job to give it to me."

"He's crazy," the director later told McGinniss. "He says he wants close-ups, it's like saying he wants to go to the moon." (After the show, Ailes fired him.)

The evening show would be the fourth panel Nixon had done, on top of the thirty-minute "Nixon Answer" specials. But Roger Ailes was about to teach Nixon a lesson: the best television is unpredictable television.

Jack McKinney set the tone for the evening. His demeanor was decidedly unfriendly. He questioned why Nixon was being so evasive on his Vietnam position, noting that in 1952 the candidate had made partisan remarks about the political situation in Korea. Nixon winced.

"It was really a question, I think, of the timing," he replied defensively. "As a potential president of the United States, anything that I say would be interpreted by the enemy in Hanoi as an indication they would wait for me rather than discuss with the man we have as president."

The camera captured a woman wearing a gold dress glowering at McKinney.

Twenty minutes later, the floor returned to him. McKinney repeated a charge made by Humphrey: why had Nixon refused to appear on national political programs like *Face the Nation* where he would be interviewed by professionals and not by amateurs in a room full of Republicans ready to intimidate any questioner who sought to ask a tough question?

In the control room, Ailes's experiment was playing poorly. "The guy's making a speech!" Frank Shakespeare yelled. Ailes reached for the phone to tell Wilkinson to cut McKinney off, but he stopped before that was necessary.

Nixon stared down his accuser. "You talk about these quiz shows that take place on Sundays. I've done *Meet the Press* and *Face the Nation* until they were running out of my ears."

It was the exact image that Ailes wanted to create: Nixon was taking it and fighting back.

"That socks it to him, Dickie Baby!" Shakespeare said.

Later in the taping, another guest asked Nixon why, in 1965, he had called for the ouster of a Marxist professor at Rutgers. Insisting that he knew the facts, Nixon explained that on campus the professor had called for the victory of the Vietcong over American troops in Vietnam. When the questioning returned to McKinney, he went at Nixon one more time.

Referring to the Rutgers professor, he said, "When you said you knew the story, you did not give it in full context. He did not call for a victory of the Vietcong, he referred to what he recognized as the impending victory—"

Nixon cut him off abruptly. "And he said—and I quote him exactly—'I welcome that victory.' He used that word."

The crowd broke into applause.

McKinney replied, "I think there's a critical difference—"

And got cut off again by the candidate: "You think there's a difference between welcome or calling for?"

McKinney did not get it. That kind of nuance mattered in print journalism, not television. Television was about emotion. The audience did not care that Nixon had fudged a few words. What they saw was the candidate telling a sanctimonious newsman that some Commie professor had no right to say nice things about the enemy killing American teenagers.

After the taping, McKinney complained to reporters, "I don't think you can finalize a question with an applause-getting technique."

The Philadelphia panel was a step forward in political communication. "Mr. Nixon came off the undisputed winner in the McKinney questioning," Ailes later wrote in a memo to Garment and Shakespeare. "The audience sympathy was with him (McKinney was not likeable) . . . and when he 'turned it over to the television audience' to decide the semantics of 'call for' or 'welcome' victory by the Vietcong, it showed the strongest use of and confidence in television I've ever seen." In a way, Ailes had manipulated Nixon into delivering the performance he wanted. "Boy, is he going to be pissed," he told McGinniss. "He'll think we really tried to screw him."

On his way out that evening, Ailes bumped into Pat Nixon in the elevator. She greeted him with pursed lips.

"Everyone seems to think it was by far the best," Ailes declared. Mrs. Nixon did not say a word.

After Philadelphia, Ailes found himself working under a Nixon team that was increasingly reluctant to indulge his freewheeling vision. He was a television risk taker among political operatives who were becoming risk-averse. The ground was moving beneath their feet. On September 30, Humphrey called for a unilateral halt to bombing as "an acceptable risk for peace," and the antiwar tides flowed in his direction. Nixon's team responded to the tightening polls by blaming Ailes. Shakespeare in particular second-guessed Ailes's directing.

Ailes attributed Nixon's declining numbers to the fact that Nixon had been in front of television audiences nonstop since the primaries. "My honest opinion was that it did peak too early," Ailes later said. "It's such a highly sophisticated technical problem to keep a thing hyped for a whole bloody year." The press caught on to Ailes's frustration. During a stop in New York on October 8, where he was editing five hours of panel footage into a thirty-minute television special, Ailes gave a candid interview to *The New York Times*, which stated that his strength was growing up in an age of TV and that his "candidate's weakness might be that he didn't." Ailes noted: "Nixon is not a child of TV and he may be the last candidate who couldn't make it on the Johnny Carson show who could make it in an election. . . . He's a communicator and a personality on television, but not at his best when they say on the talk shows, 'Now here he is . . . Dick.'" If nothing else, Ailes would at least make a name for himself with these comments.

Ten days later, Nixon's political advisers pinned Nixon's poor performance at a Boston panel show on Ailes's choice of questioners. In truth, the campaign's only swing through Massachusetts was an all-around mess that had nothing to do with Ailes. But a week later, the campaign stripped Ailes of the task of selecting panelists. On October 25, the final taping at the CBS studio in New York was turned over in part to a young demographer named Kevin Phillips, who would later write a book about the campaign titled *The Emerging Republican Majority*. In the control booth shortly before the broadcast, Phillips proudly proclaimed that his panel was "perfectly ethnically weighted." Ailes groused that it was "the worst panel we've had," and complained to McGinniss that if Shakespeare knocked him again for his directing, he would walk out.

The Nixon campaign spent the final days of the race lurching from one self-inflicted crisis to the next. Ailes believed they were panicking. On Sunday, Nixon reversed himself and did what Jack McKinney had asked him to do: he appeared on CBS's *Face the Nation*. It was a middling performance. Nonetheless he agreed to do *Meet the Press* the next week.

On Sunday, November 3, Ailes met with Nixon to prep for his *Meet the Press* appearance. Still in a foul mood about being second-guessed, Ailes later told a reporter that "too many people were bugging" him. To blow off steam, he drove an hour and a half north to a rural airstrip and went skydiving. On the second jump, he took a hard landing. The impact shredded ligaments in his ankle.

The next morning, his ankle wrapped but hardly usable, he rode in a rented yellow Ford Thunderbird over to NBC's Burbank studios, where 125 telephones had been installed for a pre-election live telethon. He hobbled around the set on crutches, taking painkillers and barking orders to the staff. The injury seemed to draw out Ailes's cynicism. "It's going to be a dull fucking two hours," Ailes told McGinniss.

Indeed, the telethon was a polite and restrained affair—a celebration of square chic. Nixon trotted out a taped endorsement from Jackie Gleason. David Eisenhower earnestly read a letter from his grandfather that hoped for a Nixon victory.

The Humphrey telethon, by contrast, tacked hip. The candidate surrounded himself with celebrities including Paul Newman, fresh off his Oscar-nominated role in *Cool Hand Luke,* and the Brooklyn-born singer Abbe Lane, who offended many Americans with her frank sex talk.

"That's crazy," Al Scott said when he saw that Humphrey was taking live, unscripted phone calls. "They've got no control."

That was the point. Rick Rosner, Humphrey's television adviser and a former colleague of Ailes's from *Mike Douglas,* was counterprogramming against Nixon's controlled image. Throughout the evening, Humphrey roamed freely across the set, stepping over tangled electrical wires and discarded coffee cups, as he conversed with callers directly. The messy scene was deliberate: advisers wanted the stage to have an authentic feel. In its self-conscious messiness, the show attempted to tap into the deep vein of antiauthority running through America. To the millions of Americans tuning in, Hubert Humphrey's closing argument was that he was real; Richard Nixon was a television construct.

The next day, the country would issue its verdict. After breakfast, Ailes, McGinniss, and the rest of the campaign staff drove to the airport for the cross-country journey to New York. Ailes had arranged for Marje to meet him at his room at the New York Hilton, near Nixon campaign headquarters at the Waldorf Astoria. They would only see each other for a few hours, but a night in a luxury Manhattan hotel was a small gesture to make up for months of separation. Ailes spent the night watching the returns come in and talking to McGinniss, who had checked into a room four floors below. It was a long wait. A slew of eastern states went early for Humphrey. But California, Illinois, Ohio, and Texas were too close to call for most of the evening. Commentators proclaimed the race a toss-up.

Then, triumph: in the early hours of November 6, 1968, Ohio and Texas broke Nixon's way. At 12:30 p.m. that day, an hour after Humphrey had called to concede, Nixon addressed the nation from the Waldorf ballroom. Ailes watched the victory speech from the balcony as Nixon spoke of a desire to mend the country's divisions. "I saw many signs in this campaign, some of them were not friendly; some were very friendly," Nixon said. "But the one that touched me the most was one that I saw in Deshler, Ohio, at the end of a long day of whistle-stopping. A little town. I suppose five times the population was there in the dusk. It was almost impossible to see, but a teenager held up a sign, BRING US TOGETHER. And that will be the great objective of this administration at the outset, to bring the American people together."

Ailes surely knew Deshler. It was a farm town at the intersection of the B&O Railroad, less than a hundred miles from his grandfather Melville's birthplace in Shelby County. In 1948, Ailes's father had taken him to see Harry Truman wave from the back of a train that had brought him through towns like Deshler and Warren during his whistle-stop tour of the state. "I remember my dad holding me up and waving to the President," Ailes recalled. "Everybody went home and thought they knew Harry Truman."

Ailes had come a long way since then. The Nixon television experiment convinced him there was a vast new market to tap. "This is it. This is the way they'll be elected forevermore," he had told McGinniss the night before the election. "The next guys up will have to be performers." But he had doubts, too. "The interesting question is, how sincere is a TV set? If you take a cold guy and stage him warm, can you get away with it?"

The Nixon victory was evidence that you *could* get away with it. In his victory speech, Nixon projected himself as a humble conciliator pledging to heal a fractured electorate. It did not matter that Nixon's friend Dick Moore, who told the campaign about the Deshler girl with the sign, "may have made that up," as Bill Safire later wrote. The words were true in the sense that they were spoken by the president-elect of the United States and transmitted into living rooms across the country.

No matter what happened on Election Day, Ailes had made up his mind to strike out on his own. Going back to Philadelphia felt like the minor leagues. "I decided that after the campaign was over I didn't want to go back to the studio and figure out what to have a comedian talk about," Ailes said.

But politics, too, had its drawbacks. After watching Nixon's acceptance speech, Ailes and McGinniss went out to dinner. McGinniss asked Ailes about his plans.

"Are you going to move to Washington and become press secretary?"

"I wouldn't take that job with a million a year salary," Ailes said. "Whatever I do, and I haven't even discussed it, but it would be behind the scenes." Ailes told McGinniss he was burned out by politics. "TV is my business." Plus he was intrigued by his first passion—the theater. "I'm really interested in Broadway shows," he added.

He wanted to move to New York. Even before the campaign was over, he'd begun laying the groundwork, meeting with Ronald Kidd, a young associate at the Philadelphia law firm Duane Morris, to fill out paperwork to incorporate an entertainment company. He called it REA Productions. Then, shortly after Nixon's victory, Ailes looked for funding. At a Pennsylvania Society dinner at the Waldorf, he was introduced to a wealthy investment banker named Howard Butcher IV, who agreed to meet with him. In Philadelphia, Ailes pitched himself to a group of investors who asked him about his track record. "Well, my track record is actually pretty good," Ailes later recalled telling them. "I was the youngest producer of a national television show. . . . I took it to 182 markets. Tremendous success. And I took over a very difficult job when everybody said Richard Nixon couldn't win an election and he won it by television. So I think my track record is fine." They asked him about his business experience. "Let me tell you my business experience. My business experience is that you've got two columns. One's called 'in' and one's called 'out.' And if you've got more going out than you've got coming in, you're going to go belly-up."

Ailes cast it as yet another triumph of Midwest common sense over Ivy League frippery. One of the men asked Ailes to go outside for a few minutes. When he returned to the room, the men announced they were going to make an investment. "You know how many Harvard guys will get in here?" Ailes recalled one of the investors saying. "They've got charts, matrixes, and every other goddamn thing. . . . They don't know that if you got more going out than you got coming in, you can't make it."

It wasn't only Ailes's bottom-line approach that made an impression on Butcher. He could see his instincts as a campaigner. "Roger was very determined, very smart. He's the guy who understood the dark side better than I do," Butcher recalled. "When I say dark side, I mean the dark side of politics and human nature."

## FIVE

# REA PRODUCTIONS

AILES SOLD HIMSELF TO HIS NEW INVESTMENT PARTNERS as Nixon's indispensable image consultant, having played a role that had scarcely existed before, but the pitch was itself a form of image manipulation. From the moment of Nixon's election, Ailes found himself frozen out of Nixon's inner circle, and he would spend the next three years trying to fight his way back in.

In November 1968, Ailes sent a confidential report to the Nixon team on how the White House could use television as a propaganda tool. "To whatever extent possible, [the president's advisers] should make a conscious effort to control Mr. Nixon's image on TV," he wrote. "When it is necessary to run for re-election, it will be the public's composite impression of the President (formed over four years) that will influence them." The two-page document offered sixteen possible strategies the new administration could use to shape public opinion. His ideas dealt with logistics (making sure presidential television appearances were archived for later use) to questions of appearance (having Nixon talk directly into the camera to "give him a style of communication"). The memo also suggested creating a White House–produced program starring the president giving progress reports to the nation: "In effect, Mr. Nixon's own TV show giving the public something to look forward to and the feeling he is keeping them informed." As Nixon spoke publicly about bringing the country together, Ailes explained privately how TV could be a potent weapon for division. "Use TV as a political wedge with recalcitrant Congressmen for voting," he wrote.

The memo concluded with a sales pitch. "Any TV advisory group should include a TV production and direction specialist who is successfully working in the television industry. The person should also understand Mr. Nixon, his media history and problems, and the aims of the administration."

In the winter of 1969, Ailes moved into a Manhattan apartment on Eighth Avenue near 52nd Street, leaving Marjorie behind in Pennsylvania. That fall they had, for all practical purposes, separated. "Roger was going a lot of places in a hurry and Marje wasn't," Joe McGinniss said. Unburdened from the responsibilities of married life, Ailes focused on building his new production company. "At night, his office was his bedroom," his brother, who helped get the company off the ground, recalled. One of his first assignments after the campaign was for his old employer. Westinghouse tasked him with boosting ratings for ailing programs.

Ailes also looked for work in Los Angeles. Following the campaign, he cultivated his relationship with Jack Rourke, who hovered on the margins of Hollywood as a TV telethon host and member of the country club at Toluca Lake, where he socialized with Bing Crosby and Bob Hope. Two decades older than Ailes, Rourke was an industry insider who could help an upstart build his career. On January 8, 1969, Ailes wrote, "I think you know how much I enjoyed working with you, but I also want you to know that I have the greatest amount of professional respect for the job you do." Many of the twenty-eight-year-old's letters were signed "Roger E. Ailes, President/REA Productions, Inc."

In their correspondance, Rourke and Ailes enjoyed skewering politicians with towel-snapping one-liners reflective of a certain type of 1960s man. "I saw RN and several of the governors at the Governors' Conference a couple of weeks ago out here. Then I got the flu," Rourke wrote Ailes. Spiro Agnew was an especially easy target. Ailes wrote to Rourke shortly before the inauguration: "I requested that they send you an invitation. You are also invited to a very private party with Vice President Spiro T. Agnew. . . . Just you and him." In late January, after Ailes learned that Rourke was in the middle of a PR stunt—running for mayor of Los Angeles—he sent Rourke a typed letter on Westinghouse stationery: "I think it's time the minority groups had a representative. You faggots have been held down too long."

Rourke ribbed Ailes for a rumored dalliance with Lucy Winchester, the Kentucky socialite who became Nixon's social secretary. "I'm glad to see that no mention was made of your very special relationship with Mrs.

Lucy Winchester," he wrote after seeing Ailes's name in a *Los Angeles Times* article. "And you can count on my not mentioning it to anyone with the possible exception of Joe Gargan"—a Kennedy cousin who was on Chappaquiddick Island two weeks earlier, the night Ted Kennedy crashed his Oldsmobile Delmont, killing Mary Jo Kopechne—"and you know he won't say anything." ("I regret to report, he and I never held hands," Winchester later said when asked if she had a fling with Ailes. "It's like what Churchill once said, 'There's no truth to it at all, but thanks for the report.' ")

As he pursued new entertainment opportunities, Ailes continued to court the Nixon White House. He wrote a series of solicitous letters to top Nixon advisers trying to drum up business, making sure that his new production company had the imprimatur of Nixon's successful campaign. In early March, he asked Dwight Chapin, who had been named a special assistant to the president, for an autographed photo of Nixon for his Manhattan workspace. On March 14, Ailes picked up the picture at the White House and met with Nixon for ten minutes. A few days later, Ailes expressed to Haldeman his desire to consult for Republican politicians. To that end, Haldeman sent a letter on Ailes's behalf to Maryland congressman Rogers Morton, the chairman of the Republican National Committee: "The President was very pleased with the capable manner in which Roger carried out his responsibilities and the results, of course speak for themselves." Morton signed Ailes up for a $12,000 contract to offer television consulting to the RNC.

Although Haldeman was happy to praise Ailes to other GOP officials, he would not let Ailes into the tightening inner circle. Despite repeated efforts, Ailes could not get the administration to focus on the television pitch he had submitted after the election. Gone were the shambolic days of the campaign, in which Ailes had wide latitude to operate. Haldeman strictly controlled access to the president, policing which action memos made it to his attention. The centralized decision making reflected Nixon's obsession with control, and prevented movement on key initiatives including television strategy. Instead, Ailes was given piecemeal assignments. In May, he was not helped when one of his first productions—the televised introduction of Nixon's Supreme Court nominee Warren Burger—went awry. "He blew things pretty well," Haldeman wrote in his diaries. "Mistimed 'Hail to the Chief,' forgot the flags on the podium, etc. Probably would have done better without him, but CBS producer was a real nervous type."

Haldeman let the lapse slide, and in June, the White House paid Ailes $1,300 to review the presidential podium and suggest how to improve the lighting. The next month, Ailes helped produce the live broadcast of Nixon's dramatic phone call from the Oval Office to Neil Armstrong on the moon. On occasion, Ailes was brought in to provide basic sartorial advice. "He felt there was no problem with a dark suit but that it was crucial that the President should wear an off-white shirt and a tie with a non-busy pattern," Haldeman's aide, Lawrence Higby, wrote in a memo. "He felt that the President should have the barber take a look at his hair that day to make sure that there are no strands of hair or curls that are sticking out." Ailes also reminded Nixon's advisers to make use of the "hero shot" by positioning the camera at eye level and at a three-quarter angle to give the president dimension and depth. Ailes told Higby it was "crucial that when the President is on camera the camera be placed at eye level—not above him and shooting down at the President."

In August, Ailes was given his biggest assignment since the campaign: producing the first televised state dinner in presidential history, the star-studded gala to honor the Apollo 11 astronauts at the Century Plaza Hotel in Beverly Hills. Ailes was again pushing the boundaries of political communication. "The White House is concerned that it maintain the dinner's dignity," he told the *Los Angeles Times*. "On the other hand, we're concerned that the people at home enjoy it too." He cast Nixon as one of the heroes of the evening. Cameras captured the president, the first family, and the astronauts descending from the sky in a military helicopter to the parking lot of the hotel. As they emerged from the cabin, it seemed as if Nixon had also returned from space. The networks covered the occasion like the Oscars.

The astronaut dinner was essentially a one-off, which freed Ailes to take on entertainment projects. In the months since Election Day, Ailes looked to re-create *Mike Douglas* on his own. Living out of the Sheraton Gibson Hotel in downtown Cincinnati, he launched a new syndicated talk program, *The Dennis Wholey Show,* starring a thirty-one-year-old former game show host for Taft Broadcasting, the Ohio-based media conglomerate. For the debut on September 22, 1969, Muhammad Ali appeared alongside the old-time comic Irwin Corey, and an infantry officer back from Vietnam. The press panned the show. The problem was that the square Douglas style, with its roots in the placid American consensus, had fallen out of step. "Yesterday's premiere was embarrassingly ordinary," a *Washington Post* critic wrote, adding that it had a "total lack of novelty or entertainment or inspiration." It also lacked a fully dedicated producer. "Roger would say, 'I have to leave for a couple of days and go to Washington. Or I have to go to wherever Nixon is,'" Dennis Wholey recalled. "You could tell there was a little bit of a tug of war going on." Where possible, Ailes fused his two roles. "Early on, he booked Julie and David Eisenhower. That was a *huge* get," Wholey said.

As it turned out, the White House was more interested in Ailes's foothold in the world of celebrity than in his political ideas. "Your new show is most exciting, for lots of reasons," Lucy Winchester wrote Ailes. "One of them is that it is a real boon to the Administration having an intelligent intelligence agent in the talent field who can tell us who is a good performer-cum-Republican. I would welcome your suggestions and advice." She included a handwritten note at the bottom of the letter. "Will you even have time for D.C.? We hope so!"

Ailes proved a shrewd promoter of his own image. When Nixon addressed the United Nations General Assembly several days before the Wholey debut, Ailes detailed for *The New York Times* all the advice he provided (even though the extent of it was a two-minute briefing with Nixon). "He told the President to be careful not to touch the button on the lectern in the Assembly hall, because it activated a hydraulic lift that caused a platform behind the lectern to rise or descend," the paper reported.

At the time Ailes was still an obscure figure on the national stage, his work for Nixon known mainly to political and entertainment insiders. But Joe McGinniss's *Selling of the President,* which would be published in October 1969, was about to change all that. McGinniss had shared a prepublication copy of the book with Ailes, and he was all too happy to help promote it. In July, Ailes appeared on a radio show with McGinniss to hype a fifteen-page excerpt of the book in *Harper's Magazine*. Then, a few weeks before the title hit the stores, Ailes traveled to New York to join McGinniss for a panel discussion on presidential image making. McGinniss was critical of the Nixon effort, telling the audience that the Man in the Arena panelists were too timid to challenge Nixon on substance. Ailes contended that television revealed its own truth. "I don't think you can be dishonest for any length of time," he told the audience.

But by the time Ailes realized that his cutting and indiscreet remarks that McGinniss had recorded in the book might antagonize the White

House, it was too late. Four days before the book was released, he wrote a face-saving, back-pedaling letter to Nixon advisers John Ehrlichman and Bob Haldeman. "I am sending this letter to you and to Bob Haldeman to inform you of a situation which I just became aware of," he wrote. "Talking to a friend of mine in the newspaper business, I found out that the New York *Times* is publishing a book review of 'The Selling of The President 1968' in this weekend's book section. I'm sure you are aware of this book. My friend thought I should be aware of it since I was mentioned prominently, and I had it read to me over the phone. I was upset to find that quotes by me, which are inaccurate in the first place, have been lifted out and featured. I regret that the New York *Times* has decided to use me as a tool to embarrass the President. If you have any comments or suggestions on the handling of this, please advise."

Television critic Marvin Kitman concluded the *Times* review by raising the prospect that Ailes had irreparably damaged his relationship with Nixon. "When this book, filled with Ailes's colorful vocabulary, becomes a bestseller, Nixon-watchers will see a major test for the Administration," Kitman wrote. "It has been said that Nixon shares one attribute with the Kennedys and LBJ: ruthlessness. Ailes may become the John Peter Zenger of the Nixon administration," Zenger being the eighteenth-century German-American publisher who was a defendant in a legal case that helped establish printing the truth as a defense against libel. A few days later, Haldeman returned an icy, two-sentence reply: "Thank you for writing your note of October 2. I've been aware of McGinniss's book and statements for quite some time, and there's really nothing much that we can do about it at this point except hope that something like this doesn't happen again."

Despite the tensions caused by *The Selling of the President*, the book, which immediately shot to the top of the bestseller list, supercharged his reputation as a television impresario. McGinniss's contention that presidential politics was really the realm of hidden behind-the-camera forces seemed perfectly calibrated to the conspiratorial zeitgeist of the late 1960s—and in this universe, a wizard like Ailes was a crucial figure. McGinniss's ensemble cast of cynical characters were prime specimens of an altogether new archetype: the mercenary campaign operative. They constituted a vastly different breed from the public-spirited heroes who populated Theodore White's *Making of the President 1968*, which had been published earlier that year. White's elegant prose suddenly seemed dated.

Of all of McGinniss's characters, Ailes emerged as the most vivid—

the prime manipulator. He was the expletive-spouting antihero—the private dialogue was diametrically opposed to the public—who was willing to push himself to exhaustion to get the job done. Even those who despised Richard Nixon could find an alluring, likable quality to Ailes's roguish antics. "That was the thing. These other guys were ciphers and Roger was in Technicolor," McGinniss said. "Of course he's going to become the star of the book. All the quips and everything, that's the way he was all the time."

And, as a coup of image making, it far outdistanced anything he had done for Richard Nixon. Although he professed outrage to his bosses at the White House, Ailes lapped up the attention in other spheres. When McGinniss appeared on the *Today* show to promote the book, Barbara Walters berated him off-camera about how he portrayed her friend. "Roger isn't offended at all," McGinniss replied. "In fact, he likes the book."

Only a few weeks later, Ailes was back to joking about the whole thing. He sent a letter to Jack Rourke reveling in all the salty quotes McGinniss included in the book. "It's disgraceful," he wrote in mock indignation. "I don't know who the fuck he thinks he is."

The book was a boon for Ailes's consulting business. Republican politicians all over the country clamored for Ailes to do for them what McGinniss had shown him doing for Nixon. "His career was started not by Richard Nixon but by Joe McGinniss," Ailes's brother observed. And the upcoming midterm elections in 1970 would offer many opportunities. The week before McGinniss's book hit the stores, Ailes quit *The Dennis Wholey Show*. Ailes claimed that Taft Broadcasting had "breached" a deal to give him "creative control of the show and final decisions with regard to staff assignments."

And ultimately, even the White House was somewhat swayed by McGinniss's portrayal. Television was a strategic priority, and Ailes was a master of the medium. By the end of 1969, the administration finally turned its attention to developing a comprehensive TV plan at a time when Nixon was increasingly insecure about the public's perception of his leadership. The massing antiwar movement had heightened Nixon's paranoia that his adversaries were fomenting violent insurrection. Even the upsurge in support generated by his November 3 "Silent Majority" speech failed to erase his unshakable feeling that he lacked "mystique."

The renewed focus on television provided Ailes with another chance to secure an official place in the administration. A few days before Christmas, Haldeman wrote Ailes requesting a pitch for how Nixon could use television. Ailes worked through the holidays crafting a confidential seven-page proposal, which he sent to Haldeman on December 30. Ailes wanted to retain flexibility to build his business, so he proposed having the White House hire an assistant to work inside the administration, while Ailes remained on the outside, managing the staff person remotely. "I am proposing that you use me in this capacity because you know my work, I know your problems, I'm dedicated to the President on a personal and political basis, and I realize that in this type of work there is no margin for error," he wrote.

Access was important. Ailes explained to Haldeman that he wanted to report directly to him, "so television doesn't again slip to a secondary position of importance, given the President's feelings about it." He proposed that Nixon host a series of "fireside chats" and "person-to-person programs." He wanted Nixon's speechwriters to use language best suited to the medium. "Having spent a great deal of time studying audiences and writing introductions and interviews for TV, I know quite a bit about the 'effect' of words and phrases on people," he wrote. "My feeling is in keeping with the President's sincere style, sometimes more emotional words could be used to our advantage. 'Kickers' and memorable phrases need to be used more." The proposal reflected Ailes's earnest side, too. Under an idea he called the "Challenge of the 70s," Ailes advised Nixon to "make a major address on this and state publicly that poverty, air and water pollution will be eliminated in America totally by 1980." It was a strategy designed to burnish Nixon's legacy. "This is similar to Kennedy's challenge for the moon. It isn't met in his administration but when it's reached he gets the credit," Ailes wrote. "If done well it will markedly counterbalance his pragmatic image with that of an idealist and dreamer."

On January 7, Haldeman forwarded Ailes's memo to Nixon. "I think Ailes is probably the best man for this job, at least for the present time," he wrote. Nixon signed his initials in the box marked "Approve" and Ailes was hired at the consultant's rate of $100 per day, the equivalent of $600 in 2013.

Not everyone in the West Wing was on-board with the decision. "If he is hired," Dwight Chapin, who handled TV matters at the White House, wrote in a memo, "I think that the message should be made extremely clear that there is nothing permanent about the job." Ailes recognized that he faced bureaucratic rivals in the press office. Ailes told Chapin he wanted Haldeman to have a meeting with communications director Herb Klein and press secretary Ron Ziegler to "make sure everyone understands the setup."

A Nixon insider, Ziegler had known Chapin from their days together at the University of Southern California, and had been with Nixon since '62. After the failed gubernatorial campaign, he worked alongside Haldeman at J. Walter Thompson. At thirty, he was the youngest presidential press secretary in history and he wasn't going to cede ground easily to an outsider like Ailes.

On February 4, Ailes wrote an urgent memo to Haldeman raising concerns about the design of the new press briefing room that was being built in the space of the White House swimming pool. Ailes had spoken with a lighting designer who had told him that "the present plans seem to [be] lacking for TV." The comments must have embarrassed Ziegler, whom Ailes copied on the letter. That same day, Ziegler fired off a two-page memo defending the press room's design. "We have not looked at, nor do I think we should look at this facility as a television studio with highly sophisticated lighting capabilities," he wrote. Haldeman backed Ziegler and the press room blueprints remained unchanged. A few weeks later, when the press room was completed, Ziegler wrote a sarcastic memo to Chapin about Ailes. "I would like to test the lighting on the President in the new Press Room sometime in the very near future. . . . If you can give me an idea as to when we can do this, I will work it out with Roger Ailes. Of course, we would want to have our T.V. consultant Roger on the scene."

In late February, Ailes was subverted by Ziegler again. Haldeman had asked Ailes to recommend producers for the position of White House TV assistant. Ailes submitted three candidates, with Bob LaPorta, his former *Mike Douglas* colleague, at the top of his list. "Roger wanted me to be his eyes down there," LaPorta recalled. The White House brought LaPorta in for an interview, but he was passed over for the position.

After another candidate, a thirty-five-year-old news director named Bob Knott, was also resisted, Ailes vented about being frozen out. "I would very much like to get things arranged according to my original memo of some months ago since I cannot afford to drop everything for four days and lose large sums of money very frequently," Ailes wrote to Haldeman.

It may not have been the right message to convey. Nor did Nixon's advisers appreciate Ailes's bold self-promotion, even as he used interviews to spin the damage done by the McGinniss book. In mid-March, Ziegler wrote a terse memo to Haldeman titled "Roger Ailes appearance in CBS morning news show." Ziegler complained to Haldeman that Ailes was talking too much about his behind-the-scenes work for Nixon. "I have no objection to Ailes discussing from time to time the President's preparation for TV appearances. However, I think we should approach this extremely cautiously," he wrote.

Ailes's political work on behalf of Republican candidates caused problems, too. In Florida, drugstore magnate Jack Eckerd had hired Ailes to help him mount a challenge to incumbent governor Claude Kirk. Eckerd's move immediately prompted speculation that the Nixon administration was punishing Kirk for having supported Nelson Rockefeller at the 1968 GOP convention. "Ailes is involving himself professionally in Republican primary contests and too close of a public association between Ailes and the President could lead to problems," Ziegler wrote Haldeman.

Ziegler's concerns were well founded. In the spring of 1970, Ailes was in the middle of another contentious GOP primary race for an open Senate seat in Ohio, one that would have spillover effects for Nixon's presidency, and the country. Ailes was advising the Ohio congressman Robert Taft Jr. against the "law and order" candidate, Governor James Rhodes, who had been considered as a possible Nixon running mate in '68. The race was pushing Rhodes even further to the right.

When Taft debated Rhodes in Akron in late April, Ailes walked onstage thirty seconds before airtime and handed Taft a note with one word written on it: "*Kill.*"

"Rhodes got shook up," Ailes bragged afterward to a *Boston Globe* reporter. "I gave Taft the note, partly facetiously, partly for a laugh—just to try to get Bob to be a little tougher in his answers."

The gambit worked: the *Toledo Blade* noted that "the usually placid Mr. Taft accused the governor of lying about his record and told him he should be ashamed of himself." A few days after the debate, Rhodes flew to Kent State University, which was engulfed in student unrest. At a press conference on the morning of May 3, Rhodes lashed into protesters who had burned the ROTC building the previous night and declaimed that the demonstrators were "worse than the Brown Shirts and the Communist element."

Rhodes's inflammatory speech intensified the conflict in Kent. In the chaos, National Guardsmen fired into a group of marchers. The volley of more than sixty shots in thirteen seconds left four dead and nine wounded. Kent State, Bob Haldeman later wrote in his book *The Ends of Power,* "marked a turning point for Nixon, a beginning of his downward slide towards Watergate."

As the Nixon administration began to circle the wagons, Ailes was increasingly left on the outside—in hindsight, a fortunate development. Unable to get the White House to make a decision on his television memo, Ailes headed west, taking a room at the Knickerbocker Hotel in Hollywood. He was back into the zany world of daytime TV with a new variety program starring the game show host Tom Kennedy, who had a hit with *You Don't Say!* on NBC.

It was the type of producing work Ailes seemed to enjoy most—having the blank canvas, being in charge. He hired Kelly Garrett, a beautiful cabaret singer whom he had met on the set of *Mike Douglas*, to be Tom Kennedy's musical talent. Even though he was still married to Marjorie (they would not get divorced until 1977), he never spoke of his wife around the set. "All I knew was that he was single," Tom Kennedy said.

The taping of the premiere episode of *The Real Tom Kennedy Show,* as the new show was called, took place on March 31, 1970, at the KTLA studios in Hollywood. Ailes employed many of the *Douglas* elements, filling the episode with pranks and stunts. He was learning how television could harness the liberal culture even as it was critiquing it, a technique he would later apply to Fox News. Near the end of the debut, Kennedy interviewed the sexploitation movie director Russ Meyer, who was promoting his surprise hit *Vixen!* Kennedy chatted with Meyer about the controversy, then turned to the audience for their reaction, which was decidedly critical. When a middle-aged man in a dark suit vowed he would never watch one of Meyer's films, Kennedy called him on stage to appear in an improv skit with Edy Williams, the curvy star of a Meyer soft-core porn movie. Kennedy gave each of them cue cards to recite through a "scene." Williams playfully purred that her reading partner was "very sexy" and slowly positioned his right arm over her bare shoulder. His wife watched pensively from the audience as he stuttered and giggled, mangling his lines.

In late May, Ailes learned he was fired from the Republican National Committee. A White House memo later stated that Ailes had been "released by Jim Allison, Deputy Chairman of the Republican National Committee in February 1970, following statement made by Roger Ailes that REA would offer its services to Democrat as well as Republican candidates." There were competitive factors at play as well: Allison had a political consulting firm with his friend and former Ailes colleague Harry Treleaven. A *Boston Globe* profile noted that Ailes was aggressively signing up Republican clients, and was involved in half a dozen races that year. In the interview, Ailes boasted that one day television could *replace* the party itself: "The skeletons of political parties will remain. But television will accelerate the breaking down of mass registration by party. The figures show this already. Youth are independent."

After an unsuccessful attempt to get the White House to intervene to save his RNC contract, Ailes fired off an angry letter to Allison, copying Haldeman and Nixon hand Murray Chotiner:

> Once again it has been brought to my attention that you have been rapping me with certain campaign people around the country. Recently I have had two playbacks from states that I am involved in. There is always the possibility, of course, that these are erroneous reports and if they are, please ignore this letter and accept my apology. However, if they are not erroneous, please do not ignore this letter. If the reports are true, I can only assume that since you know nothing of my work, you are simply stating that our company is "over-priced" to protect your own financial game.
>
> Business is business, but I would hate to see you and me get into a shoving match since the only loser would be the GOP. Frankly, Jim, I am tired of being on defense in this matter. I'm instinctively better at offense.

Ailes, who had just turned thirty, was unafraid to step over men nearly twice his age. The letter revealed not only ferocious competitiveness, but also a palpable belief that enemies sought to harm him.

From the earliest days of the administration, Nixon had transformed the White House into a laboratory to incubate ideas that would strip the establishment media of its power, ideas that would inform Fox News decades later. New fault lines over civil rights, Vietnam, and the women's movement had cleaved the culture. Nixon intended to exploit this rift, turning his Silent Majority against the big-city newspapers and the broadcast networks, whom he saw as being on the side of liberals. "The press is the enemy," Nixon told his aides. "They are all against us."

On June 3, 1969, Haldeman had ordered Herb Klein to prepare a report on the political biases of the network anchors covering the White House. "The President is very concerned about the general attitude of a number of the television newscasters and commentators who are deliberately slanting their reports against the Administration's position," he wrote. A few hours later, Klein responded with a memo categorizing more than two dozen commentators and reporters. ("Bill Gill—a sensationalist who is more negative than positive. . . . Dan Rather—more favorable than he was prior to the election. . . . John Chancellor—sometimes negative. . . . The most vindictive is Sander Vanocur. You know him. He is in Saigon.")

The idea of "balance" took hold inside the White House. "I have discussed television balance with Reuven Frank, president of NBC News, and Dick Salant, president of CBS News," Klein told Nixon in a memo on October 17, 1969. "I have made them aware of the fact that we are watching this closely," he wrote, referring to the networks' perceived political bias. Klein mentioned that the White House could deploy the power of the FCC to revoke their broadcast licenses if they did not change.

Ailes volunteered for Nixon's war with the media, offering his services for some of the administration's most brazen propaganda campaigns. In June 1970, he participated in an aborted project to produce a covert White House–directed documentary, secretly financed by the Tell It to Hanoi Committee, to rebut a CBS program critical of the Vietnam War. The idea was abandoned when it became clear that any leak of the White House's involvement in the project would embarrass the administration. Ailes told Nixon aide Jeb Magruder to keep him in mind for such films in the future. "If you decide to go ahead with something like this at a later time," he wrote, "be sure to let me know as far in advance as you can and we'll try to put it together."

The White House had even bigger plans than one-off documentaries to try to influence the agenda of the national news media. It was developing a blueprint for its own television news service which would produce administration propaganda packaged as independent journalism. Ailes championed the project, titled "A Plan for Putting the GOP on TV News." In the summer of 1970, a highly detailed fourteen-page memo circulated around the White House outlining the plan, which Haldeman later named "The Capitol News Service." "For 200 years, the newspaper front page dominated public thinking," the memo began. "In the last 20 years that picture has changed. Today television news is watched more often—than people read newspapers—than people listen to the radio—than people read or gather any form of communication." The memo explained why: "People are lazy. With television you just sit—watch—listen. The thinking is done for you."

The plan's stated purpose was to "provide pro-Administration videotape, hard news actualities to the major cities of the United States." To pull it off, the White House would produce favorable political stories in Washington and rush the videotapes by airplane to local markets, thereby avoiding "the censorship, the priorities and the prejudices of network news selectors and disseminators." The top forty markets would have three same-day departures from Washington. A fleet of trucks traveling a total of 1,195 miles per week would pick up the footage from airports and deliver it to local broadcast stations. To illustrate the plan's effectiveness, the memo sketched out how it could work for four specific GOP senators, including Bob Dole. "Senator records statement between 8-9AM," which would result in a "Sample Arrival Time Home Market [of] 4PM . . . Makes the TV News Program At 6PM."

Ailes sent Haldeman a marked-up copy of the memo with his enthusiastic feedback. "Basically a very good idea," he wrote in the margin. What was striking was that, just a few months earlier, in his interview with *The Boston Globe,* he cast himself as an idealist, warning of the hidden dangers of propaganda. He had told the *Globe* that he wanted to work on a concept he called "Truth television . . . where people can distinguish between fact and fiction on television, where entertainment and life and opinion are separate." He noted that "twenty-nine percent of the nation relies on television as the only source of news. This is extremely dangerous, when the major news story of the day is done in 2½ minutes. Right after the printing press was invented, people believed everything they read. Television does the same thing. It can be lies and bull."

But in private, with the prospect of a lucrative assignment on the table, he was an eager propagandist, encouraging the White House to think even bigger. "It should be expanded to include other members of the administration such as Cabinet involved in activity with regional or local interest.—Also could involve GOP governors when in D.C.," Ailes wrote. He seemed unconcerned about the ethics. "Will get some flap about news management," he wrote. Though the plan struck some in the White House as too audacious and expensive to pull off, Ailes possessed none of these inhibitions. "If you decide to go ahead we would as a production company like to bid on packaging the entire project," he wrote Haldeman.

The Nixon White House never moved forward on the Capitol News Service plan. Instead, they studied long-term strategies to harness technology that would help build a counter–media establishment. One of the most promising was the one Ailes would later master: cable television. White House memos asserted that cable, with its capacity to carry an array of diverse channels, would be "the most effective and most lasting approach" to strip the broadcast news divisions of their power. A prescient 1973 document prepared for Haldeman noted that cable news was a development that was "ten years or so" away "for significant impact."

By November 1970, Bill Safire was advocating dumping Ailes for Bill Carruthers, an in-demand television producer who had recently opened his own production company. Even though Carruthers was "liberal compared to us," Safire encouraged hiring him. "He has much less emotion than Ailes does; he has more control," Dwight Chapin wrote, recounting Safire's thoughts. "He is probably a better producer than Ailes but he does not have as much flair as Roger. . . . You've got to consider the question of Flair versus ability and Safire buys ability."

Ailes would have one more chance to save his relationships. On November 19, he met with Haldeman at 10:45 in the morning to discuss his future. Ailes lobbied to be appointed television adviser. He said he would open an office in Washington and make the head of the office available to the White House full-time. He also stressed that he liked the Capitol News Service idea and thought the White House should move ahead on launching it. Haldeman asked Ailes to write another proposal outlining how Nixon should use television in the run-up to the '72 election.

The day before Thanksgiving, Ailes sent Haldeman a twelve-page proposal titled "White House Television—1971." It was written in his now characteristically blunt, dramatic tone and revealed the breadth of Ailes's understanding of how television could transmit a political message. "In my opinion," Ailes began, "Richard Nixon is in danger of becoming a one-term President. Further, he is in danger of leaving office, even if he is re-elected, with a stigma of leadership failure much as President Johnson did: not because of what he has done—his accomplishments are many—but because of what the people 'think' he has done, and because of the way he sounds and looks to them." Since *Selling of the President* had been published, Ailes had attacked McGinniss's thesis repeatedly in interviews, saying television couldn't artificially mold an image. Now he was arguing to do just that. "To follow a leader," he wrote, "people must feel that he is better than they are and not subject to anger or hatred quickly." Ailes said he knew what he was talking about because of his background. "It is important for you to know that I am not just echoing the eastern liberals when I express my concern and that I spent twenty five years in Ohio and know something about the silent majority."

Ailes also offered strategic advice: Wedge issues like busing and the war had banked much of the electorate. Now it was time to tack to the center. "The silent majority will automatically back the President because it has no place else to go," he wrote. "I think a good issue to drive a wedge between the Democratic leadership and the news commentators is Nixon's welfare plan. The only ones more frightened by the welfare plan than the conservatives are the liberals. If the President makes no major speeches but quietly visits Capitol Hill to press for this and at the same time calls in a group of 'liberal' reporters to discuss the plan, the commentators will be forced to applaud him and point out Democrat obstructionism." Ailes also demonstrated he was on-board with dirty tricks. "To guard our flank I would like to see us get one of our people inside the Wallace organization immediately," he wrote, an acknowledgment that George Wallace's candidacy could siphon off Nixon votes, especially in the South. "I'll discuss this in more detail in person."

As in 1968, Ailes recommended using television to soften Nixon's image and project cool confidence. "America's position can be compared to a teenager who is experimenting with trouble, tempted to really go bad, but still crying out for a father to step in and lead him home. Mr. Nixon must take on the father's role," he wrote. While he did not recommend reviving the Man in the Arena concepts for '72, a similar warming effect could be achieved through the right interview setting. Ailes suggested that David Frost interview the president "either at Camp David by the fireplace or walking around at the Western White House" because "he is recognized internationally as the best in-depth, humanizing interviewer." Ailes pitched himself in the role of packager: Westinghouse would fund the production and Frost would follow Ailes's directions. "I know him well and would approach him directly to set the ground rules and production controls." Ailes explained that Nixon could outline his intention to do future television broadcasts to communicate his plans to the American people, for which he included suggested scripts for the interview:

> FROST: "You mean, similar to Roosevelt's radio reports known as fireside chats."
> NIXON: "Well, yes, I think they were a good idea, but I may do some from California, so they might be more seaside chats than fireside chats."

In addition to the Frost interview, Ailes pitched a network film special "to air late in 1971 just prior to the 1972 election campaign, which would show a human, working President with an incredible schedule." If the networks balked at a White House–produced movie, Ailes suggested getting his friend, CBS correspondent Mike Wallace, on-board "and myself maintaining production control using the correspondent just to introduce the program and do a little narration where necessary, letting the film speak for itself."

The memo rattled off a list of ideas big and small. Better celebrity guests at White House events ("I know the talent business very well and can be useful here"). More physical contact between the president and Pat Nixon ("If he put his arm around her in public or held hands with her when walking once in a while, it would do much to endear him to women all over the country"). More religion at the Christmas tree lighting ceremony ("I suggested they drop Santa Claus and big name stars all together"). More jokes ("If a reporter keeps pressing him on something the President should smile and say something like, 'I believe I've answered that and if you ask me again I'm going to give your home phone number to Martha Mitchell' ").

Ailes concluded the memo by reiterating he wanted to remain an outside consultant. "By signing a large yearly PR contract with the RNC or a 'fat cat' firm, I can include the full time man from my DC office and produce the major things myself. . . . Per diem work doesn't allow the flexibility we both need."

Haldeman ultimately sided with those who felt Ailes brought too much baggage to the job. He hired Carruthers and a young assistant named Mark Goode instead. The White House worried that Ailes would react unpredictably to the news. "I have a gut feeling that we are bordering on disaster if we do not get Roger Ailes in and squared away soon," Dwight Chapin wrote to Haldeman two days before Christmas. "If we handle Roger in the proper way and quickly, I think we can avoid any bad feelings."

"Get Roger down," Haldeman scrawled on Chapin's memo. A meeting was scheduled for December 28, 1970.

A talking paper outlined scripts that Haldeman could use. "Roger," one suggestion read, "I want to be completely honest with you. As you know, we have felt the need for a full-time man here at the White House for a long time—to supervise our TV on a daily basis—and our efforts here have met with little success. I don't see anything developing on this need in the near future." Another script called for Haldeman to talk about Ailes's outside conflicts. "You and your operation have developed into a TV political consulting business. It is obviously successful, but it is a different animal than what we need here." It was also suggested he comment on Ailes's relationship with Nixon. "We have not been able to build the relationship between you and the President which we had hoped to see. It is no one's fault. We face this sort of thing every day. There are different directions that we can go which I think you can explore and which will continue to reap you rewards."

A few weeks later, Ailes sent Haldeman a confidential letter bragging about his performance advising campaigns in the 1970 midterms. He attached glowing notes from eight GOP politicians and operatives praising his performance. The White House clearly wasn't interested. "No need for H. to see FYI," an aide wrote to Haldeman's assistant, Larry Higby.

Ailes needed to retool his image. "I have been getting a lot of calls in the business about my being out at the White House," he wrote to Larry Higby in February 1971. "If I can say that I am working with the National Committee and am still with the White House, it will be very helpful to me professionally." Ailes's television career was sputtering, too. *The Real Tom Kennedy Show* had been canceled. In March, Ailes issued a press release announcing he was changing the name of his company from REA Productions to Roger Ailes & Associates, Incorporated. An article in *Backstage* headlined "Ailes Business Is Not Ailing" helped to quiet the rumors of his professional struggles. Ailes announced that his renamed company was launching "an expansion program" and would focus on "radio and TV production; TV counseling services to business and industry; and a division to handle personal management for talent."

On June 8, 1971, Ailes delivered a speech before Los Angeles business and civic leaders at the Town Hall of California. Ailes used the opportunity to offer a full-throated rebuttal to the criticisms that had dogged him since the publication of McGinniss's book. Principally, Ailes sought to put to rest the charge that shady media manipulators were distorting politics through television. "Like many technological advances, the impact of political television has preceded the understanding of its meaning or its uses," he wrote. "The natural human reaction to this lack of understanding is fear, and this single emotion—fear—overrides much of American life today and has brought about a national negativism which has wrapped around us like a shroud!"

Much of the speech, however, sounded like a sales pitch: "The biggest problem today, I believe, is communication on all levels," Ailes declared. It was corporate America's fault, Ailes said, for not marshaling a response to consumer advocates like Ralph Nader who spread the notion that "all large companies are greedy monolithic monsters determined to squash the little man." To the businessmen sitting in the crowd, who controlled their companies' marketing budgets, it would have been an incredibly seductive message. Ailes was declaring that slick public relations, the very kind he was selling, could reset the relationship of business to the American people. "America has a cancer. Cancer is usually fatal, but it doesn't have to be if it is discovered and treated in time," he wrote. "Our national life depends on our ability to use our technical knowledge to cure the ills in our country and upon our refusal to be caught up in this negative attitude about our system." His formulation was not unlike the words of his father about the struggle for survival. "We must exhibit and communicate an unbending will to live," Ailes stated. Unless the country changed its attitude, it might not make it out of the next thirty years. "Without these things," he asserted, "America will be nothing more than a history lesson in a student-run college of the twenty-first century."

That month, Ailes planned to move into a new office on Seventh Avenue, a few blocks south of Central Park. He told White House photographer Oliver Atkins that his interior designers were working up plans for the space, which he wanted to decorate with eleven-by-fourteen photographs of his memorable work for Nixon and other clients. "I would love to have a shot of that split screen to the moon," Ailes wrote to Atkins in mid-May 1971. Even as he projected the image of a rapidly expanding concern, the well-hidden truth was that Ailes was largely on his own. Cast out of the White House, Ailes would have to come up with a new act. "Roger got caught up in the politics he didn't yet understand," his brother later said. "In retrospect, he learned some lessons and he got out before the rest went to shit."

# SIX

# A NEW STAGE

Ailes was unmoored, both professionally and ideologically. Confidants observed in their friend a palpable sense of dislocation. "He was trying to figure out who he'd be when he grew up," his brother, Robert, recalled of that time. "He tried his hand at everything." Television and Republican politics had been the lodestars of Ailes's twenties. In an accelerated adulthood, Ailes approached them with single-minded determination, relishing the power and financial freedom of the grown-up world, even as he rebelled against the strictures of its institutions, such as marriage and corporate hierarchies. Now as his thirty-first birthday approached, Ailes, for the first time, began to pursue other paths.

Though far from a flower child, Roger Ailes was a product of the 1960s, who came of age in that era of cultural tumult. And after the Nixon administration severed ties with him, he began a four-year period of experimentation, one that in hindsight seems a quixotic professional detour. As he kept a toehold in politics, paying his bills by running media strategy for a few congressional and gubernatorial campaigns, Ailes ventured into the New York theater scene. In post-1960s New York, the counterculture itself had been institutionalized, made into a profit center. Reinventing himself as an all-purpose impresario and agent, Ailes befriended not merely Democrats, but activist members of the American left.

Paul Turnley, a liberal Democrat and civil rights activist from Detroit, Michigan, became an early assistant to Ailes. "Roger never let politics get in the way of good people," Turnley recalled. On May 15, 1971, Ailes was giving a speech at Indiana University, where Turnley, who was training to become a Jesuit priest, was taking graduate courses in communications.

He was so captivated by Ailes's lecture that he changed his mind about the priesthood and wrote Ailes a series of letters asking for a job. After Ailes hired him, they rarely discussed politics or Nixon, except in typically Ailesian terms. "He basically said that 'Man in the Arena' was his idea. Then, he'd say, 'I got Nixon to take his stupid ramrod out of his ass.'"

Politics in those days for Ailes was more about making money than ideology. He hinted that he would consider working for Democrats. "I don't have this burning thing to elect all Republicans," he told *The Washington Post* in the winter of 1972. And Ailes did discreetly advise Andrew Stein, a twenty-six-year-old Democratic candidate who was seeking reelection to the New York State Assembly. On one occasion, Ailes arranged for a barber to meet them in his office. "Andy called Roger aside and whispers to him, 'I have a hairpiece. You can't do this,'" Turnley recalled. "And Roger just says, 'we'll do a little bit around the sides.'"

Even when he worked for Republicans, Ailes did not kowtow to the party's handpicked candidates. His only statewide campaign work in 1972 that Turnley remembered was for Jim Holshouser, a thirty-seven-year-old moderate state representative in North Carolina, who owned a motel in his hometown of Boone. While he was considering whether to challenge James Gardner, the front-runner, in the Republican primary for governor, Holshouser flew to New York to consult with Ailes. At their first meeting, Turnley recalled, "Roger sat him down and said in no uncertain terms, 'You're gonna have to spend millions of dollars. I believe I can get you elected. But the downside is: you don't have the party's backing, you have to find your own funding, you're the underdog, and your name recognition is very poor. So we have a real uphill battle. Your opponent is going to find everything that you possibly ever did your entire life and drag it through the press. You have to realize all these things.'" Ailes's speech roused the young Republican. Right there in Ailes's office, Holshouser picked up the phone and instructed his real estate broker to sell the property to raise cash. After developing a set of devastatingly effective attack ads, Ailes propelled Holshouser into office, making him the first Republican governor elected in the state since 1901.

Despite the success, the political work seemed to be little more than a side project. "I don't think Roger had settled on a particular future at that juncture," Turnley recalled.

As he had done at earlier turning points in his career—at the college radio station, on the Douglas set, and during the Nixon campaign—Ailes reached out to more senior hands for help. On February 12, 1971, he wrote to Jack Rourke for help landing a new gig for Kelly Garrett. "Enclosed is a picture and biography of a gal that my company now manages. She is west coast based and a very talented gal," Ailes wrote. "I thought you might like to use her in one of your telethons." Ailes also asked Rourke to help book Garrett at the Hilton with the big band leader Horace Heidt Jr. In the black and white photograph, Garrett posed amid a stand of palm trees. Her wide movie star smile, plunging neckline, and long raven hair that spilled gently over her bare shoulders were striking.

Kelly Garrett, born Ellen Boulton, was four years younger than Ailes. One of ten children, she grew up in Santa Fe, New Mexico, in a house without a television. She started singing around town in small venues. At age twenty-two, she married an actor after running off with him to chase her show business dreams in California. As Garrett's cabaret career took off, her marriage foundered. She got a divorce in October 1970.

Rourke responded, offering to do whatever he could to help Garrett. "I'll put you in touch with Horace Heidt, Jr.," he wrote. But something more promising than a gig with Heidt was beckoning Kelly: Broadway. In 1972, Ailes raised money to mount his first theatrical production. Tapping into the 1960s cultural outwash, Ailes chose *Mother Earth,* a trippy, environmental-themed rock musical revue created by a group of social workers, academics, and antiwar protesters who founded the South Coast Repertory company in Costa Mesa, California. They were liberal outcasts in the heart of Richard Nixon country.

Costa Mesa, located about forty miles south of Los Angeles in the center of Orange County, was not exactly friendly territory for a progressive theater to open its doors in the summer of 1964. But the conservative spirit of the region did not deter the South Coast Repertory Company from attempting their experiment in an out-of-business marine supply store a few miles from John Wayne's home. Over several months in 1969, members of the company developed a rock revue about pollution and overpopulation. Toni Tennille, an aspiring Alabama-born pop singer, wrote the music, and Ron Thronson, a social worker with a master's degree in theater, wrote the script and the lyrics. Thronson also served as director. The musical, he wrote in the preface of the script, "has an element of mysticism." Many songs were written "to put humans into proper perspective with our universe."

The show opened the night of January 8, 1971, in front of a 150-person crowd. On a sparsely decorated stage, the cast performed their numbers in front of a projection of 35-millimeter slides showcasing photos taken by the theater's photographer, Ken Shearer. "I am one with the soil of my birth," they sang. What followed were dystopian scenes of overpopulated hellscapes ruined by pollution. One sketch, set on New Year's Eve in 1999, advocated unfettered access to birth control, abortion, and assisted suicides. Near the beginning of the first act, a woman, described by the stage directions as "the embodiment of all that is mediocre, middle-class, and narrow," tries to sow doubt. "Hello America! Who says pollution is bad for you? Who says it kills? Have YOU seen it kill?" But by the end of the play, she returns onstage having undergone a kind of spiritual transformation. "Brothers and sisters," she says, "these poisons in our environment are the omens of an angry God. Get down on your knees and beg forgiveness, that these things might be borne away on the wings of penance."

At curtain call, the actors knew the show was going to be a hit. "After we ended, it was dead silent. We were just standing there, and then all of a sudden, the audience erupted," South Coast cofounder and cast member Jim dePriest recalled. "They ran onto the stage, and everyone was hugging each other. They were just raving about the show." By the time *Mother Earth* closed five weeks later, bigger venues clamored to book the show. After successful runs in San Francisco and Los Angeles, veteran lyricist Ray Golden, a writer for the Marx Brothers whose credits included the Broadway revues *Catch a Star!* and *Alive and Kicking,* made a hard sell to Tennille and Thronson to sell him the rights to bring *Mother Earth* to Broadway's Belasco Theatre, a one-thousand-seat playhouse on West 44th Street.

Ailes was in on the deal. He knew Golden through the *Mike Douglas* world, and saw *Mother Earth,* at his urging, during its West Coast run. "Roger came back and said, we oughta do it on Broadway," Paul Turnley remembered. "I think he liked that it had that *Hair* quality." Over lunch at Musso & Frank, the iconic Hollywood restaurant, Ailes and Golden worked the young songwriters. They assured Thronson and Tennille they would not meddle in the musical when they brought it—and the show's cast—to Broadway. Thronson and Tennille agreed to sell the rights, but it soon became evident that Golden, who took over as director, in addition to being producer, had his own plans to modify the show for a mainstream audience.

A couple of months before the show was scheduled to open on October 19, 1972, Tennille refused to perform Golden's version. "It turned into a borscht belt musical," South Coast cofounder Martin Benson said. "We got bamboozled," Tennille later told the press. With Tennille out, Golden needed a new female lead and a serious cash infusion. Ailes, with connections to wealthy investors and a client looking for her Broadway star turn, could provide both.

As the Broadway debut of *Mother Earth* approached, Ailes recognized his need for an experienced guide to steer him through the unique folkways of the New York theater world. A year earlier, at Golden's suggestion, he met the Broadway producer Kermit Bloomgarden at a party in Bloomgarden's apartment on Central Park West. A decade had passed since the faded power broker's last hit, but Bloomgarden's career had taken him to the pinnacle of American theater. In the 1940s and 1950s, he collaborated closely with friends Arthur Miller and Lillian Hellman. His string of critical and commercial successes, in addition to Miller's *Death of a Salesman* and Hellman's *The Little Foxes,* included Meredith Willson's *The Music Man,* the original Broadway production of *The Diary of Anne Frank,* Frank Loesser's *The Most Happy Fella,* and Stephen Sondheim's musical *Anyone Can Whistle*. By the early 1970s, however, Bloomgarden had fallen on hard times. His right leg had been amputated, a consequence of arteriosclerosis, and his bills were piling up. When Ailes and Ray Golden went to him for advice on *Mother Earth*, Bloomgarden agreed to sign on as a consulting producer. "Given the circumstance he was in, the opportunity to create some income advising someone on a show was appealing," his son John Bloomgarden recalled.

Bloomgarden ushered Ailes into an entirely new artistic milieu. A first-generation Russian Jew, Bloomgarden produced plays in part as expressions of his deep belief in social justice. During the height of McCarthyism, Bloomgarden attended a meeting of the Freedom from Fear Committee to mobilize support for the blacklisted "Hollywood Ten." Though Bloomgarden was never called before the House Committee on Un-American Activities, his friends were. The experience left him with a conspiratorial view of politics and an acute suspicion of the American right.

"What the hell are you doing with people from Nixon?" Robert Cohen, Bloomgarden's assistant, asked after learning of his association with Ailes.

"Forget about that. Look, I got a script," Bloomgarden said.

Bloomgarden earned Ailes's admiration from his very first suggestion. Dump Ray Golden, Bloomgarden said. "Roger knew he had found a soul mate when Kermit told him that," Stephen Rosenfield, who worked for Ailes after Turnley, said. "His first suggestion is to fire the man who brought him in? That guy is only interested in success."

But Ailes couldn't dump Golden. He held the rights. What Ailes could contribute was money. To finance *Mother Earth,* Ailes reached out to Howard Butcher, the Philadelphia investment banker who had helped him launch REA Productions after the 1968 campaign. "The next thing I know, he calls me up and says, 'I wanna do this show. It's an ecology based show—a series of vignettes, put together by Kermit Bloomgarden,'" Butcher recalled. "I raised most of the money for the show. I should have known right there it wasn't a Broadway show."

Cast members struggled to muster enthusiasm for the production. The more Golden meddled, the worse the production became. Frank Coombs, a dancer who performed in the show, described Golden as an "old, bald and sporadic" director, who turned *Mother Earth* into something "pretty wretched." Cast member John Bennett Perry, the TV actor and father of *Friends* star Matthew Perry, said, "It needed a different staging. Ray was out of his element." The actors took their cues from Bloomgarden, who hobbled daily into the Belasco to observe the rehearsals. "He'd sit in the back room and look like he was looking at a big bottle of vinegar," the actor Rick Podell said. Ailes was less visible. "I think he was pushed around a bit by Ray," Podell said. "He didn't know how to bully his way in. Roger wasn't versed in how to do it. Kermit was, but, by that time, he was so fucking old, he'd just sit in the back and scowl at us."

By this point, Kelly Garrett was in rehearsals, having assumed Toni Tennille's starring role. "She was striking looking and a hell of a singer, but she had no Broadway experience that I knew of," Perry recalled. The actors started to wonder. "Roger made sure she had some solos," Podell said. "People go, '*Wait a minute. Is the producer fucking the leading lady?*'" Frank Coombs, who was asked to help Garrett learn the choreography, saw the show as a springboard for her ambitions: "It was horrifying to have to teach Kelly how to dance. I wasn't allowed to touch her. The only reason the show existed was Roger was dating Kelly Garrett, and Kelly needed Broadway work."

Ailes appeared to bask in playing the part of a big-shot producer. Inviting John Bennett Perry to his office one day, Ailes sat behind his expansive desk and doled out career advice. "What do you envision for yourself? If you get there, will you be happy?" Ailes asked him straight off. Looking back, Podell recognized "a lot of latent Donald Trump in Roger." Robert Cohen thought Ailes could pass for a Mississippi riverboat gambler. He talked a mile a minute. "I'm Roger Ailes, how do you do?" he said in their first encounter at the Belasco. "You were in the Joe McGinniss book, I read about you," Cohen replied. "Yeah, I sold The Trick to the American people," Ailes said, referring to Nixon, "now I'm going to sell this, and it's going to be *great*."

Ailes worked his political and media connections to promote the show. By staging a photo shoot of cast members riding bicycles around Manhattan wearing gas masks instead of helmets, Ailes got their picture in the newspaper. Ailes made another plug to Joe McGinniss, when he called up from the '72 Republican National Convention in Miami Beach. On assignment for *The New York Times Magazine,* McGinniss was hoping for a pithy quote from Ailes about Nixon, but instead got a mouthful about *Mother Earth*. "It's a great show. There's at least three songs in it that will become classics," Ailes boasted. "I don't know anything about Broadway, but I'm learning. It's much more exciting than politics. Nixon was O.K.—but all those state campaigns—wow! I mean, I finally got bored with South Dakota." Ailes also reached out to his White House contacts, having Len Garment spread word around the West Wing.

After the curtain came down on opening night, Ailes ran up to Cohen, gushing about the performance.

"What do you think?"

"What do I think about *what*?"

"Do you think we got a hit? I think we got a hit."

Cohen was incredulous. Based on disappointing advance ticket sales, he had already announced to the cast that the show might close.

"Forget it, Roger. You're opening with a closing notice up."

The next morning, *The New York Times* delivered its verdict. John Bennett Perry got a call from Ailes's office. "Don't read the paper," he was told. In a savage review, Clive Barnes called the music "at its worst characterless, and at its best—to use that chilling measure of air quality—acceptable."

The cast did not dispute Barnes's assessment. "The second night of the show, there were eight sailors and a doughnut," Podell recalled.

Ailes initially hoped that word-of-mouth marketing could overcome the harsh reviews. But Ailes soon confronted the embarrassing failure of the show, something the cast respected. Within a week, Ailes was in Perry's dressing room talking about the show's future. "The question was to close it or not. I told him, 'You might as well,'" Perry recalled. "He was resolved to do a good job even as it didn't work." After just a dozen performances, *Mother Earth* closed.

Ailes recognized he had overreached. "My eyes were too big for my stomach," he remarked years later. Before bringing the show to New York, Ailes considered a smaller venue. "The main discussion was whether we do it Off-Off Broadway or Broadway, but Roger never does things in halves," his assistant Paul Turnley recalled. Butcher's investors lost everything and Ailes's business suffered. "He had put a lot of his own money in," Turnley said. "When *Mother Earth* closed, he called me in and said, 'I'm sorry I have to let you go. I'll keep you on until you find a job. I'll write you a glowing reference, so don't worry about that.'"

Failure taught Ailes valuable lessons. He had agreed with Bloomgarden's directive at the outset to fire Golden, but was powerless to do so because Golden held the rights. It was confirmation that control was a precondition for success. Failure also taught Ailes not to listen to doubters. "Don't ever chase critics, and don't ever try to produce anything the critics are going to love," Ailes recalled Bloomgarden telling him.

The box office disappointment of *Mother Earth* did not diminish Ailes's appetite for the theater. In fact, in the months after *Mother Earth* closed, he pushed beyond the schmaltzy appeal of Broadway into the artistic swirl of New York's vibrant Off-Off-Broadway scene. As he would later tell it, Ailes often ventured, sometimes alone, into small playhouses at night to scout new productions—though the truth was less romantic. He hired Robert Cohen on a freelance basis to read scripts and attend openings.

One day in February 1973, Cohen received a phone call from Bloomgarden, who excitedly told him about a new play he had just seen at the Circle Repertory Company in its early home on the Upper West Side. The play had been written by Lanford Wilson, a cofounder of the company, and depicted a group of drifters who make their home near the Baltimore railway station in a crumbling nineteenth-century hotel slated for demolition. It's Memorial Day, but the characters are too far gone or strung-out to notice. The marquee identifies the hotel as *Hot l Baltimore*, the title of Wilson's play, as no one had bothered to replace the missing letter.

In the sinking fortunes of the hotel and its sad inhabitants, Wilson presented a wry meditation on American decline. Cohen, who attended the production the night Bloomgarden called, was impressed. "I thought, My God, it's like *The Iceman Cometh*. These are people on the margins of society. People you don't want to look at. But they're making you look at them. They're making you see them. And they're telling you truths about yourself and life and the society we live in."

After the show, Cohen hustled out to a pay phone on Broadway and called Bloomgarden.

"Do you really like it?" Bloomgarden asked.

"Not only do I really like it, more important, I understand why *you* like it. Kermit, this is the kind of show you would have put on twenty years ago."

"How much do you think it would cost to move the show to Broadway?"

"Don't do it on Broadway," Cohen said. "You're not exactly going to sell theater tickets to the Hadassah of Great Neck."

"Well, that's true."

"Do it big-time Off-Broadway."

"Do you think we could get the money from Roger?"

"You just might."

The next day at the office, Ailes reacted coolly to Cohen's idea like the dozen other shows he had brought to him. "Roger, take my word for it," Cohen said. "Kermit wants to do the play. He doesn't have any money, but he knows what's good. You want to do a play, you still want to juggle your other stuff, but you have the money. This is a marriage made in heaven, Roger. Take my word for it. If you don't like this deal, I will quit right now and you'll never see me again, I promise you."

Ailes reluctantly agreed and Cohen got him a ticket for that night. During the show, Cohen waited for Ailes on the sidewalk.

"You got a deal," Ailes declared when he saw Cohen on the street. Ailes called Bloomgarden from the pay phone and told him he would back the show.

Bloomgarden and Ailes soon secured the rights to stage the play at the Circle in the Square Theatre, a 299-seat venue in Greenwich Village. Ailes committed to raising $30,000 to finance the production. Once again he tapped Howard Butcher, who in turn leveraged his network of wealthy

Pennsylvania investors. "Roger called me up and he said, 'I have another one. This one is an Off-Broadway show.'" It was a bold pitch, as *Mother Earth* had vaporized the banker's investments just months earlier. But Ailes was a persuasive salesman: Butcher agreed to vouch for Ailes and raise the funds. "I called up a lot of clients and friends. It was a hard sell," Butcher remembered. "It was off the beaten track for all my clients."

But the investors stood to gain financially if the show was a success: the equity in the show was divided between Ailes, Bloomgarden, and their investors. Lanford Wilson and Marshall Mason, the show's director, were rebuffed. "We went to Kermit and we wanted to put in $5,000," Mason later said, "that way we'd realize a profit for it. But Kermit said, 'I can't let you do that because I've sold out the entire investment.' We said, 'How could this be? And he said, 'the money all came from Roger Ailes.'" Mason signed a paltry contract. "It was a slightly bitter point," Mason remembered. "Roger Ailes put us on the map, but he was taking money out of our mouths because we weren't invested in it."

Opening night came on March 22, 1973, six weeks after the premiere on the Upper West Side. "Everything that went onto the stage was real," recalled Conchata Ferrell, who played a foul-mouthed prostitute named April Green. "The champagne was real, the hot plate worked. It was Lanford's vision." Word spread across town about the new play. "The crazies are good to listen to! Wilson writes them with persuasive humor and dry accuracy," Walter Kerr wrote in *The New York Times*. A parade of notables, including New York mayor John Lindsay and Francis Ford Coppola, soon attended.

Ailes proved to be an imaginative marketer. He expressed keen interest in the design of the play's poster. Robert Cohen lobbied to hire the downtown graphic artist David Byrd, who had drawn the original poster for Woodstock. Bloomgarden balked at the budget of $1,000, but Ailes pushed for it. Byrd did a graphic of a neon sign with the title in hot pink type. Ailes's and Bloomgarden's names were below those of Mason and Wilson. "They both complained to me their names weren't big enough," Cohen said.

Ailes also struck deals with companies for product placement, including Benson & Hedges and Coca-Cola, long before the practice was publicly known. A few days after the play opened, Robert Cohen wrote to Malt-O-Meal in Minneapolis to sign up another deal. "We are the producers of the new off-Broadway play called The Hot l Baltimore which has just opened to marvelous reviews here in New York," the pitch stated.

"In the show two characters enjoy your product Soy Ahoy Barbequed Flavored Soybeans." (While the hotel residents drink champagne, one character pulls two large jars of snacks from his bag. The prostitute April, expecting nuts, tastes a handful and exclaims, "Jesus Christ, they're soybeans." The character counters, "They're great for you. And they're good.") The pitch continued: "Your jar and label are prominently displayed to a full house of 299 people every night of the week." Cohen proposed a deal to credit Malt-O-Meal in the program and offered as an incentive to "make tickets available to you and your distributors in this area for their own use on pre-determined occasions."

Ailes's behind-the-scenes role made him a mysterious and somewhat glamorous figure to the cast. "What a gorgeous looking guy he was," recalled Mari Gorman, who played the jean-jacket-wearing lesbian Jackie. "We hardly saw Roger at the beginning, Kermit was much more involved," the actress Stephanie Gordon said. Shortly after the show opened, Ailes summoned Gordon, who played the prostitute Suzy, to his Midtown office on a Sunday afternoon. He told her he wanted to photograph her in character wearing nothing but a towel. The promotional photo would highlight a pivotal scene at the end of Act One, in which Suzy appears on the stairs wearing only a towel and wails to everyone in the lobby that her client beat her and then locked her out of her room. When April starts laughing, Suzy slaps the towel at her and stands naked, while people laugh and stare.

Gordon, who was dating cast mate Jonathan Hogan, was unsettled by the invitation. She had grown up in a conservative family and could barely pull off the scene on stage. Making her way up to Ailes's office, Gordon started to panic. "It was dark. It wasn't my usual milieu. I remember thinking, 'What am I doing? Am I going to take off my clothes in front of Roger Ailes, whom I don't even know? Why am I by myself in a deserted office building with this guy?'" But her fears were not realized. "I got undressed in another room," she said. "He made me feel comfortable. He was lovely." After Ailes snapped the pictures, he called Gordon a cab and sent her home. Later, he framed a print for her and signed it. "Don't throw in the towel, you're a great actress. Roger Ailes."

*Hot l Baltimore* was the rarest type of hit—both artistically and commercially successful with a wide, middlebrow audience. In 1973, *Hot l Baltimore* earned three Obies and a New York Drama Critics' Circle Award for Best American Play. By the end of its run, the play generated a profit of nearly $400,000, a staggering sum for an Off-Broadway production. Agreements were signed to stage regional productions all over the country. ABC began developing the play into a sitcom starring James Cromwell. *Hot l Baltimore*'s success made the careers of Mason and Wilson, who in 1980 won the Pulitzer Prize for his comedy *Talley's Folly*. It was also the high-water mark of the odd Bloomgarden-Ailes partnership.

Mari Gorman recalled Roger Ailes fondly. Watching Fox News later on television, she said she "didn't think it was the same person for a long time." Stephanie Gordon struggled to reconcile the network's more brutish qualities with the empathy of Lanford Wilson's writing. "This play is about prostitutes, addicts, lesbians, and lost people, perennial losers, people who have given up on life. It's the end of the American dream. These are the last people in the world Roger Ailes is interested in. Why would he produce this play?" Marshall Mason, who lives in Mexico and has served as vice chair of a local chapter of Democrats Abroad, was also dumbfounded. "When he became the Roger Ailes we know and hate now, I thought, 'Oh my God, was this the same guy who was our producer?' " Conchata Ferrell, who went on to play the brassy housekeeper on the CBS sitcom *Two and a Half Men*, grasped for an answer. "Fundamentally, what the play is about is the American character. Even when they're losing, they don't lie down. It's about the idea that we didn't use to as a people just quit. I'm a liberal and I believe that. Roger is a conservative and he believes that. Everything Lanford wrote was deeply American."

Ailes was proud of *The Hot l Baltimore*. In his own telling, he was the one who discovered the play. He told a reporter in 2003 that he had been so taken with the show he ran backstage and paid the producers $500 on the spot to option the rights. At any rate, in the wake of the play's success, he had the funds to hire back a deputy.

His new employee, Stephen Rosenfield, had worked for Hubert Humphrey's chief speechwriter during the 1968 campaign before completing an MFA degree in directing at Stanford. When Rosenfield showed up for his first day of work he saw what a bare-bones operation the company really was. "At that point it was just Roger and his secretary," Rosenfield said. But Ailes presented a very different image in public. During one live television interview Ailes gave around this time, Rosenfield remembered him standing up and walking off the set before the segment was completed. "He said to the host, 'Great to talk to you, I gotta run.' He left. It looked like this guy had a schedule to keep. And he didn't have anything going on! I thought, *Man, what a great exit*. He thought about how to control the atmosphere."

Rosenfield labored, as Cohen had, to steer his boss's tastes in a modern direction. In December 1973, Ailes announced that he had acquired the rights to a script titled *Nice Girls*. "The premise was that 'nice girls' didn't talk about sexual things, and so the play was about nice girls who were sexually candid," Rosenfield recalled. "I told Roger women do talk about sex, and everyone knows it! This isn't going to be an oh-my-God thing." A decade had already passed since Mary McCarthy's bestselling novel *The Group* shattered the image of urban women as shy prudes.

As *Nice Girls* stalled, Ailes shifted his attention to a play that Bloomgarden discovered downtown. The quirky production, *Ionescopade,* a pastiche of short vaudevillian sketches based on the writings of the French-Romanian absurdist Eugène Ionesco, had received a favorable review in *The New York Times.* Ailes leaned on his investor list, a diverse mix of characters from his time in Philadelphia, Washington, and Hollywood. Tatnall Lea Hillman, an heir from the Main Line, went in for $2,400; Jack Calkins, the executive director of the National Republican Congressional Committee, contributed $1,200. Kelly Garrett gave $600. Ailes's company chipped in $400.

He was going full cylinder. Riding high with hopes for *Ionescopade* and flush with success from *Hot l Baltimore,* Ailes found a path back to television paved in the most glamorous and profitable brand of American liberalism: Camelot.

Robert Kennedy Jr. was in his sophomore year at Harvard in early 1974, when Lem Billings, Jack Kennedy's prep school roommate and Kennedy family confidant, came to him with an unorthodox proposition: Roger Ailes, Richard Nixon's former TV man, wanted to make him a television star. Ailes, he explained, had read an article by Bobby Jr. about the overthrow of Chile's Marxist president Salvador Allende. Kennedy had traveled to South America to report the story. On account of his interest in international affairs, Ailes was proposing that Kennedy travel with him to Africa to produce a wildlife television documentary.

The movie's origins involved the kind of creative and logistical challenges that Ailes thrived on. A wealthy American businessman had money tied up in Kenya after investing in a failed Nairobi life insurance company. The Kenyan government blocked him from taking his remaining assets out of the country. The businessman asked Ailes for his advice. "Roger's words were, 'we can bring the money out in a can,'" Kennedy recalled, meaning that funds could be used to finance a film that they could then sell in the United States. The documentary was Ailes's latest experiment intermingling celebrity and politics. Bobby Jr. represented America's closest approximation of a young royal, a bankable personality to take the television viewer to an exotic, wild land.

Naturally, Billings was wary about Bobby Jr.'s association with Ailes. "Lem Billings, I would say, vigorously disliked Richard Nixon," Kennedy said. But a three-hour meeting in New York with Ailes put the young Kennedy at ease. "We joked about Nixon," he recalled. After Kennedy signed on as a creative consultant and narrator for $1,500, Ailes promised him a spectacular summer vacation tracking wildebeest herds and hunting lions with spear-carrying Masai warriors. The pair traveled around the Rift Valley with a camera crew of Pakistani Muslims. "I had a lot of laughs with Roger," Kennedy said. "He was sensitive to other cultures and to conservation and not at all an ideologue."

But Ailes had a few headaches in store before he and Kennedy flew off to Africa. On April 25, *Ionescopade* opened at Theater Four on West 55th Street and bombed. Bloomgarden made the mistake he had sought to avoid with *The Hot l Baltimore:* he took a low-budget production that was a hit and changed it. After fourteen performances, the show closed.

Meanwhile, Ailes received what appeared like thrilling news. In April, Kelly Garrett got a call to read for the lead in David Merrick's $850,000 production of *Mack & Mabel,* a musical about the fiery romance between Hollywood director Mack Sennett and the actress Mabel Normand. Gower Champion, the musical's director, had cycled through two female leads, first Penny Fuller, then Marcia Rodd, and was looking for a replacement. After winning a Theatre World Award for her singing in *Mother Earth,* Garrett was performing in another musical revue, *Words and Music,* at the John Golden Theatre, which Champion saw and liked.

Ailes pushed Garrett to go for the part. The role would require substantial acting, crucial experience for Garrett. Ailes asked Rosenfield to coach Garrett over the weekend. "I don't think we should do this. Gower Champion isn't the type of person who's interested in nurturing some neophyte," Rosenfield cautioned. Ailes refused to back down.

"Are you seriously asking me to tell Kelly Garrett not to go to a callback to a David Merrick–Gower Champion musical?"

To please his boss, Rosenfield swallowed his reservations. "It was the one time Roger and I really disagreed with each other," he recalled. At the time, he was unaware that Ailes and Garrett were romantically involved.

"I didn't know anything, and it was just the two of us at the company. And I knew Kelly really well. And she kept it a secret. Roger felt it would not be in either of their best interests if it looked like he was promoting his girlfriend."

The next day, Garrett went to Rosenfield's studio apartment to rehearse two scenes over and over. Rosenfield's assistance paid off: Champion picked Garrett to star opposite Robert Preston at the Majestic Theatre. It was poised to be her breakout moment. Within days, however, Garrett was dismissed. "That one broke my heart," Champion told a reporter. "That face, that voice. But this role takes a lot of deep acting." The embarrassing public setback, as Rosenfield later put it, "ended her possibility as a Broadway star." A young actress named Bernadette Peters replaced her. "As far as I'm concerned, it was *their* loss," Ailes fired back. "I just don't have any respect for the way they handled it, it was really tacky."

Ailes's increasingly tough, angry public persona was accompanied by growing fears about his physical safety. He went to elaborate steps to protect himself. After he returned with Kennedy from Africa, Ailes was arrested in New York City for illegally possessing a handgun. When news of the arrest surfaced years later, colleagues of Ailes claimed that he had been using the weapon to protect a Kennedy. It felt like an excuse to Bobby Jr. "If I had known he was actually carrying a gun to protect me, I would have told him to get rid of it. It wasn't plausible," he recalled. (Ailes pleaded guilty to a misdemeanor and was given a conditional discharge.)

In truth, Ailes had a gun long before his association with Kennedy. After *Mother Earth,* Ailes called a young acquaintance into his office. "I wanna show you something," he said, flashing his gun. "I found him to be a scary guy," the acquaintance recalled. When Ailes moved to New York, the city was in the grip of a precipitous downslide, as residents fled for the suburbs, and crime spiked. The blocks around Times Square, where Ailes spent much of his time, were populated by peep shows and prostitutes, which turned the city into a national symbol of dysfunction. In response to the city's hostile environment, Ailes channeled the lessons of his father: *Violence never solves anything, but the threat of violence can be very useful.* It was advice he gave to his brother when he came to visit during this period. "I was walking across midtown when I see a pair of eyes staring out from behind an alley, the eyes are looking right at me," Robert recalled. "Roger had told me that if you put your head down and pretend not to notice, that's the victim's posture and you're in deep trouble." Robert put his hand in his pocket as if he had a gun. "I looked straight at the eyeballs and kept walking like I was an undercover cop. The guy stayed in the alley and never moved."

Ailes kept others at a distance, spending many nights at his Central Park South apartment with Kelly Garrett and her lapdog, Squeaker. Joe McGinniss was a rare close friend, possibly because McGinniss was in a similar situation, having left, but not yet divorced, his wife, and living with a beautiful young book editor, Nancy Doherty, whom he had met at a party for *The Selling of the President*.

At the time, Joe and Nancy made their home in a charming eighteenth-century house in rural Stockton, New Jersey. On weekends, Ailes and Garrett would often visit them. "We were people to whom he could bring Kelly for the weekend, and it wasn't going to be judgmental," McGinniss speculated. "We weren't going to say Roger Ailes is dating a client." Doherty, who bonded with Garrett over their experience growing up in large families, remembered Garrett being very affectionate with Ailes. In press interviews, Garrett swooned over him. "Do I ever get nervous about performing?" she told a reporter. "I used to, but not so much now. Principally because I have such faith in my manager Roger Ailes, who makes all the right decisions for me—about everything." Doherty found it telling that Marjorie never came up in conversation. McGinniss suspected that Ailes felt guilty about Marje. "Roger and I didn't talk about shared guilt a lot but I think it was an ongoing bond between us," he said. "With Roger and Kelly, the other complicating thing was, she was his big star-client, and he was her manager. And it wasn't *really* working the way they were hoping that it would. That's a complicated way to have a relationship."

Ailes's brooding moods seemed to consume him. "Roger was very unhappy at that time. He was physically sick," McGinniss said. Doherty recalled Ailes frequently coming down with strep throat. "After a visit from Roger, you'd count on getting sick, basically," she said. His whole body underwent a change. He gained weight and grew a beard. "He was eating to ease his pain," McGinniss said. It was hard for McGinniss to understand what, besides Kelly, was causing his friend so much agony. "He talked about his blue-collar father. He talked about hemophilia," McGinniss said. "But he wasn't telling terrible stories about being mistreated as a child or how he hated his father. He had a lot of respect for his father. His father had taught him these hard-core values."

McGinniss vividly recalled a conversation with Ailes around this time that would stay with him for years to come. "He told me he was worried about all this pent-up anger he had inside of him. He didn't know what was going to happen."

McGinniss tried to buck up his friend, reminding him of all the things that were going right in his life. *The Hot l Baltimore* was still running strong, and the Kennedy TV special was moving forward. "You should be feeling great right now," he said. "Look, it's not that way," Ailes replied. "I'm walking around, and I feel just all this anger. I can't figure out where it's coming from."

McGinniss told Ailes he was seeing a therapist and asked Ailes to consider going. "It's helping me," he said.

"I don't know," Ailes replied, his voice trailing off.

On August 9, 1974, Nixon resigned from the presidency. Watergate hit Ailes like a stomach punch. "He took Watergate really, really personally," Stephen Rosenfield said. At a party Rosenfield hosted not long after Nixon's resignation, Ailes fiercely defended the disgraced president when a guest expressed delight at his downfall.

"What should we do?" Ailes said, "be like some banana republic and drag him through the streets?"

Needing work, Ailes took on all manner of projects. In the fall of 1974, he went back to Pennsylvania to manage the gubernatorial campaign of Drew Lewis, a wealthy business executive. Lewis spent lavishly to oust the Democratic incumbent, Milton Shapp, but Nixon's disgrace had damaged Republican fortunes nationwide; Lewis lost by nearly 300,000 votes. After the defeat in Pennsylvania, Ailes confided in Rosenfield a rare expression of self-doubt. "Everything I touch turns to shit," he said.

Ailes was once again adrift. The prospects for signing up new candidates seemed grim. Nixon's undoing had scorched the national landscape for Republicans. It had been four years since Ailes had helmed a national television show, and the theater, which thrilled him for a while, was proving to be a hit-or-miss way to make a living, especially with so many misses. Indeed, the fall of 1974 was a fulcrum for Ailes, the moment the trajectory of his career might have vectored away from politics if his theatrical pursuits had panned out.

Years later at Fox News, Ailes would talk fondly about his theatrical experience. "Whenever he can, he gets into the conversation that he produced *Hot l Baltimore,*" a senior Fox executive said. Creating the Fox News afternoon show *The Five,* Ailes found his inspiration on the stage.

"He said, 'I've always wanted to do an ensemble concept,'" a close friend said. "He said, 'I wanted a Falstaff, and that's Bob Beckel. I need a leading man, and it's Eric Bolling. I need a serious lead and that's Dana Perino. I need a court jester and it's Greg [Gutfeld], and I need the leg. That's Andrea Tantaros.'"

As much as he loved New York—its loose, liberal culture seemed to bother him not a bit—the next opportunity came from a very different quarter, with very different values. The American right reached out and pulled him back in, and it marked his career ever since.

# SEVEN
# THOUGHT PATTERN REVOLUTION

In May 1974, Ailes received a call from a sandy-haired former Denver TV newsman named Jack Wilson, an emissary from a fledgling broadcasting start-up called Television News, Inc. At the time, TVN, as it was known, was beset by numerous problems, riven by staff struggles and failing to attract viewers and advertisers. But in essence, TVN was what Fox News became: a conservative news network, one that aspired to cut through the liberal cant of the Big Three to provide what even then was called a "fair" and "balanced" account of the news. It bridged Nixon's secret television propaganda efforts with the rise of right-wing media in the 1980s.

TVN was the brainchild of Robert Reinhold Pauley, a waspish broadcast executive with a Harvard MBA. As the president of ABC Radio, Pauley had given Ted Koppel and Howard Cosell their starts. Despite this success, or perhaps because of it, he had become a fierce critic of the network way of producing news. Pauley was an enthusiastic Goldwater supporter and a John Bircher. In his hometown of New Canaan, Connecticut, he denounced a local plan to fluoridate the water as a Communist plot to poison Americans. But in time, his vision would take hold. After being pushed out of ABC in 1967—for reasons he said he never understood—the forty-three-year-old Pauley gave up trying to reform the networks from within and set out to disrupt the existing media order.

Pauley had developed an innovative business plan to sell taped television news stories to local broadcast affiliates. At the time, United Press International Television News was the country's sole provider of nonnetwork TV news, air-shipping film clips to stations for their evening newscasts. The cumbersome, costly method forestalled competitors, including Nixon's scrapped Capitol News Service. Pauley instead wanted to send news stories to local affiliates over AT&T phone lines. In an era before cable television, Pauley's distribution system was a step forward.

In 1972, after four years searching for funding, Pauley heard from Joseph Coors, the ultraconservative beer magnate from Golden, Colorado. By the 1960s, Coors held a dark view of America. Inspired by books like Russell Kirk's *The Conservative Mind,* Coors was one of a handful of right-wing millionaires who sought to reverse the left's advances. Fearing the damage wrought by the counterculture, they believed the news media, as the transmitter of its pathogens, bore special responsibility. "All three networks slant the news with innuendos, accents, the sneers they make," Coors complained. Coors certainly shared Russell Kirk's lament that "radical thinkers have won the day. For a century and a half, conservatives have yielded ground in a manner, which, except for occasionally successful rearguard actions, must be described as a rout."

Coors represented a new breed of conservative philanthropist—ideologically rigid, religiously fervent, immensely wealthy—who poured millions into bringing about a right-wing revival that braided the strands of Christianity, nationalism, and free market economics into a political force. He committed $800,000 to Pauley's venture and pledged up to $2.4 million more. Coors was also funding such conservative causes as the Committee for the Survival of a Free Congress, the National Federation of Independent Business, the House of Representatives' Republican Study Committee, and a new think tank called the Heritage Foundation. Of all these investments, TVN was central to Coors's mission to save America. "We were discussing how we could tell the truth and have news that would not be so lopsided," Jack Wilson later said. Television had the power to spread conservative values unlike any policy paper. Their goal was to launch with upward of seventy employees in four domestic bureaus by April 1973.

Like Fox News, TVN presented an apolitical face. The press release announcing TVN's debut stated that it had "no philosophical axe to grind." Behind the scenes, however, Pauley, Coors, and Wilson maneuvered to exert a firm hand on TVN's journalism. Two weeks before TVN's launch, Pauley tasked Wilson and Coors to review tapes of each day's broadcast. Pauley also solicited the advice of leading conservatives, like William F. Buckley Jr. and Pat Buchanan. "I have suggested to Jack Wilson that he get in touch with you and that he keep you informed of the story line-ups," Pauley wrote Buchanan. But even these measures did not satisfy Pauley. He asked Wilson to make contact with Accuracy in Media, the conservative watchdog group, to provide feedback. "I would suggest that we hire them to look at our product every afternoon in Washington," Pauley wrote in a memo on May 2, 1973. He urged discretion. "I don't really think there is any need to broadcast the fact that we are seeking the opinion of the AIM Group."

When TVN finally launched in May 1973, a bedeviling problem immediately came into focus. While Coors wanted to control what was shown on the air, the journalists he'd hired, many of them network alumni, including a young Charles Gibson, insisted on nonpartisan newsroom standards. Dick Graf, TVN's news director, vowed to steer an independent line. "There will be days when I'll put pieces on the air that will make your flesh crawl because of your personal beliefs. But I'll be doing it because of my professional news judgment and I'll play them down the middle," Graf told Coors. "That's what we want you to do," Coors replied.

It was a false promise. Throughout the summer, Wilson fired off a series of histrionic memos to Pauley and Coors critiquing Graf's journalistic instincts. In one, he complained that a negative segment on the FBI left viewers with the impression that "the FBI and SS troops fit in the same picture." In another, he criticized the coverage of *Miller v. California,* in which the Supreme Court ruled that obscenity was not universally protected by the First Amendment. TVN's coverage of the decision made him want to "explode," he wrote. Instead of reporting on the dangers of "smut," the announcer "picks out a fellow that says that smut is OK and is allowed to give his reasons and that is the end of the story." In Wilson's view, "on this issue alone, several people should be fired!!"

Coors, too, was growing nervous. "Why are you covering Daniel Ellsberg? He's a traitor to this country," Coors barked at Graf during one board meeting. At another board meeting, he decried Graf's news instincts as "socialistic." Paul Weyrich, a cofounder of the Heritage Foundation and an unofficial TVN adviser, was also discouraged by TVN's lack of zeal. "I've had no influence," he told *The Washington Post*. "In fact, it's been the single most frustrating experience I've ever had." All of this heavy-handed political interference created dissension on TVN's board. Ronald Waldman, a board member and BBC executive, told Pauley that he objected to Wilson's written reports, warning that TVN's credibility could be ruined if the partisan memos leaked. As a compromise, Pauley applied some safeguards. On August 13, he outlined them to Wilson:

> Remove names from report such as "to," "from," and "cc."
>
> Number each page of the copies and keep a record of which went to whom. Mark them "Classified" although this is sometimes a red light to others.
>
> Mark envelope confidential.
>
> Remove "subject."
>
> If we observe these rules then any unauthorized use would have to be fictionalized to be believable and then it would be a forgery. I'm not going to ask you to stop. It's a Board matter. Thanks.

Pauley assured Waldman that the matter was under control "to help insure the classified nature of the critique." Deception was central to TVN's mission. "Let's not get labeled," Pauley later wrote in a memo. "This is the most dangerous thing which can happen to a journalistic institution."

In February 1974, Graf was finally let go, replaced by the Northeast bureau chief, who lasted all of two months. By the spring, Coors seized control, naming Jack Wilson president of TVN. "I hate all those network people. They're destroying the country," Wilson fumed around the office. "We have to unify the country. TVN is the moral cement." In short order, Wilson fired en masse most of the TVN network-trained journalists, replacing many of them with staffers more in sync with his conservative views.

It wasn't his television skills, or even his conservative ideas, that brought Roger Ailes into the world of television news. Rather, Ailes was recruited for his experience in public relations. After months of newsroom upheaval, TVN looked to buff up its image. In May 1974, Wilson hired Ailes as a PR consultant on a $1,500 retainer.

In July 1974, Ailes delivered a progress report to the directors, which was partly an exercise in managing up. The board minutes noted that Ailes had been "demonstrating the growth of TVN" to the press and "acquainting the trade with Mr. Wilson as its chief executive officer." To address TVN's minuscule distribution, Ailes sought creative ways to present a winning image. "He said that he would also hope to see TVN receive some awards and citations, as these would help establish TVN as an indispensable service in the eyes of the broadcasting community."

Ailes's bravado impressed the board so much that they named him news director four months later. His title was the latest identity change for Ailes. Given his responsibilities in the newsroom, there was a giant hole in his résumé. "He didn't know anything about news. He knew television," said Reese Schonfeld, a TVN executive. Still, Ailes eagerly played the part, moving into his spacious new office at TVN's New York bureau at 10 Columbus Circle. "He took on a role of a news guy," Stephen Rosenfield recalled. "But he *wasn't* a news guy. I remember seeing a typewriter in his office at TVN, which amused me. I don't think he knew how to type. He had a secretary from the time I could remember."

But Ailes's lack of a news background proved a selling point rather than a weakness. His partisan political work was what attracted his new employers. *"Ran 1968 Nixon campaign publicity,"* Pauley scribbled during a board meeting when Ailes's name was discussed. "Their politics were way further to the right than he was comfortable with," Rosenfield remembered. "They made Roger look like a New Deal Democrat." Ailes demonstrated he could translate their mission into management dictums. "Roger Ailes has quickly given needed leadership to his people while fully understanding the Board's policy statement regarding news coverage," Wilson wrote in an internal report. "We are now well on our way to the product we have dreamed of all along."

The week of Thanksgiving 1974, Ailes sent Wilson an ambitious analysis for an overhaul of TVN's newsroom. The document, an early road map that pointed toward the strategies he would apply at Fox News, called for an authoritarian management structure. He proposed crafting a "statement of news policy which outlines TVN's reason for being, self-image, goals and news philosophy." He would "get control of the news department and the daily feed so that the original vision of TVN can be carried out," adding, "it is my feeling that control of the TVN feed should be placed entirely in New York with the bureau chiefs primarily responsible for implementing the work of others in the bureau. . . . This will give us the opportunity to coordinate and achieve the goals and philosophy of TVN." He would also call out dissenters, naming one female employee for example. "I see her as negative to management and TVN. She is maintaining communications with former employees," he wrote. But he would reward loyalty and good ideas, "thereby reversing the trend of firings, insecurity and desperate searching for jobs presently going on."

In essence, Ailes treated journalism as he treated politics—it was another market to monetize. Shortly after being named news director, he suggested that TVN offer image consulting. "Roger Ailes has suggested offering a business communications advisory service," a memo to Jack Wilson noted. "Roger's reputation and expertise could turn this into a source of continuing contractual income as we coach corporate executives on how to improve their television performance." It seemed appropriate to Ailes that a news organization could offer PR advice to the very powerful people its journalists were covering.

As Rosenfield updated Ailes daily on his entertainment consulting projects and day-to-day speechwriting duties for clients such as Oregon Republican senator Bob Packwood, Ailes integrated the aims of his consulting firm and TVN. One of the first stories produced after Ailes arrived was a profile of Kelly Garrett. "She's been called the best new singer of 1974," the segment reported. TVN Enterprises, a division of TVN, would also distribute Ailes's documentary with Bobby Kennedy Jr.

Repeating the pattern of the *Mike Douglas* office dynamic, Ailes inspired young producers eager to advance, but clashed with senior employees who posed threats. Reese Schonfeld, TVN's vice president of operations, quickly became a rival. He represented a power center in the company, as Wilson had tasked him with studying the economics of satellite news delivery. "Roger and I were reasonably friendly for a while, then we were shouting at each other. He called me an asshole, I called him a fuckhead," Schonfeld said. Schonfeld sensed his rival's ambition. "From the day he walked in, he was looking for Wilson's job, it was my feeling," he said. "I'm sure he would have been better at it than Wilson."

Unfortunately for Ailes, he settled into the job at a perilous moment. In the winter of 1975, Stanhope Gould, a former CBS News producer, was putting the final touches on a cover story about TVN for the *Columbia Journalism Review*. Ailes did his best to parry Gould's inquiries. During an interview, Gould pressed Ailes hard about the Kelly Garrett segment, asking him why Ailes used TVN to promote his client. At first, Ailes blamed management, who, he said, had approved the story before he became news director. Gould did not let the matter drop. "There is definitely a question in some people's minds about conflict of interest," Ailes responded. "I take full responsibility. It may have been a bum decision—but I made it." Gould asked Ailes to comment on his lack of journalism training. "I've never run a newsroom, but I've been around them," he told Gould. "And 90 percent of what you do in any job is common sense." He stated that his consulting company stopped handling politicians (he could have meant political campaigns, as the '74 election cycle had just ended) and that he had turned the company over to subordinates (which was technically true, though Ailes and Rosenfield still spoke every day). Ailes also waffled when asked about TVN's politics. At one point, he said, "one thing is sure, the networks are not biased to the right." Just as at Fox, Ailes framed it as less a matter of ideology than of confronting the condescension of the media elites. The moralizing at the networks seemed to Ailes to be a pose, a front for their real agenda. He set himself up as the victim, creating a pretense to go on the attack.

There was one point that Ailes made completely clear: "No matter what has gone on here in the past two years, I'm not responsible," he told Gould, as he leaned back in his swivel chair.

Ailes was right to attempt to keep some distance between himself and TVN. Gould's fourteen-page article, which ran in the March/April 1975 issue of the *Columbia Journalism Review* and called Ailes "the only man in history to run a national news organization while owning an entertainment industry consulting firm," was a damaging one. The story, headlined "Coors Brews the News," crackled with embarrassing revelations detailing staff turmoil and allegations of political interference. TVN's image would never recover.

The negative press was only one problem. Pauley's original business plan was proving to be wildly optimistic. AT&T's exorbitant video transmission rates discouraged local television stations from buying TVN stories. In its first year, TVN was on track to lose more than $4 million. Losses ballooned to $6.2 million in 1974, and a similar amount was projected to be lost in 1975.

One of its last hopes was technological. In 1974, Western Union and NASA had launched Westar I, the first commercial geosynchronous communications satellite, which could beam television signals to receiver dishes on the ground. Jack Wilson put together a deal, and on January 9, 1975, TVN announced its plan to become America's first satellite news service. The theory was that the satellite would give TVN the opportunity to grow into a full-fledged network, with diverse programming, providing an alternative to the Big Three.

The broader mission put Ailes's TV skills to better use. He began to experiment with various news concepts, from longer documentary features, to ninety-second clips, which appealed to the "Action News" format in vogue with local stations. "I want to find out what they want and to give them what they want," Ailes said. In his first several months on the job, he had taken a series of meetings with producers to scout potential deals. His programming ideas reflected his middlebrow, Mike Douglas sensibility. He talked with Art Rush, the manager for Roy Rogers and Dale Evans, about producing a half-hour country-western show for TVN; explored adding ninety-second inserts with the advice columnist Joyce Brothers; and brainstormed specials ideas with the comedy writer Paul Keyes. Around this time, Ailes developed a new marketing tagline for TVN that previewed the cunning sloganeering he would apply to Fox News: "The Independent News Service."

As Ailes handled the content, Wilson worked on the business and political fronts. In the spring of 1975, he crisscrossed the country on a three-week trip to meet television executives. On his West Coast swing, Wilson spent an afternoon with Richard Nixon, newly in exile in San Clemente. The men enthusiastically discussed the mission to create a counterweight to the networks. It was what Nixon had been waiting for.

As Nixon's dream to dethrone the establishment media appeared within reach, Wilson hired Bruce Herschensohn, a forty-two-year-old former Nixon aide and film director, as a $200-per-day consultant, to develop more ambitious conservative news programming. Herschensohn was a true believer, with strong convictions about the role of the liberal media in politics. "It is not [Eric] Sevareid or [David] Brinkley that do the damage," Herschensohn told Wilson. "It is the reporting of the news."

From his apartment on Virginia Avenue, which overlooked the Watergate complex, Herschensohn went to work on his design. Projecting an annual budget for a fully staffed newsroom at $12.1 million, he scrawled the names of people who could execute his vision: "Ailes, Self . . . Jack, Coors." He sketched an organizational chart. At the top was a position marked "Philosophy," occupied by a senior executive who maintains the message and assigns "predictable and continuing stories," what TV executives would later call "flow." "The 'philosophy' man must know more than his subordinates know, or soon he is not top man," he wrote. It was vital that the "philosophy" enforcer operate as a macro thinker, shaping the news to help the cause. Disagreeing with Pauley, Herschensohn called on TVN to own its conservative bias. He believed that "the disguise of neutrality, and not bias itself, has been the great harm of CBS, NBC, and ABC." He proposed that TVN producers fill out paperwork "prior to the editing and narrative writing" for each broadcast to explain how the story would advance the conservative agenda.

Herschensohn viewed his television proposal as "a thought pattern revolution" as sweeping as the civil rights movement. "Though I disagreed with the civil rights leaders in asking for 'everything now,' I was wrong and they were right," he wrote in his private notebook. He went on, "What I would hope TVN will achieve is another 'thought pattern revolution,' this one to put faith and strength and humanity back into our country after a period of masochism, isolationism and selfishness. I believe the way to do [it] is to throw all the dice on the table and, in fact, ask for 'everything now.' . . . We are trying to create some balance within the media. That is a very noble enterprise. Few would disagree that the media needs some balance. . . . TVN was invented for a purpose."

On April 30, 1975, Herschensohn submitted his programming proposal to TVN for review. It would presage many aspects of Fox News's internal structure and programming tactics. The 179-page document, which detailed the evening newscast and other show ideas, identified twenty-eight techniques that TVN could deploy in its programming to "manipulate" the audience. Herschensohn explained terms like *Pretense Balancing,* the goal of which is "showing 'all sides' of a particular story when, in fact the balance is tilted." *The Hold Frame* holds a subject "in a flattering or unflattering position" (depending on the agenda) and gives "the impression of 'catching an event,' or 'catching a person.'" *Catch Phrases* are easily remembered words "which seem to be factual though they are, in fact, editorializations." *Repetition,* the last concept on the list, creates a news event through repeated assertion. "The creation of the most important story today" becomes "the truly most important story a week from today." ("We can send a newsman and a camera crew over to the Capitol and talk to a congressman or senator about 'the story.' If the congressman or senator is willing, we can create news in an instant. Most are willing," he wrote.) Repetition, Herschensohn wrote, is "the oldest and most effective propaganda technique."

Ailes would have read Herschensohn's memo when Wilson circulated it for review. "With a nightly news package we can create ongoing stories of importance," Herschensohn wrote. (Fox would do the same with sagas such as the "War on Christmas," "Obama's Czars," "Fast and Furious," and "Benghazi.") Herschensohn encouraged conservatives to identify whipping posts that played to their audience's resentments. "Whereas others selected the CIA and the FBI, we can take HEW and HUD," he wrote, referring to the Department of Health, Education, and Welfare, and the Department of Housing and Urban Development. (Fox would later take on the United Nations and the Environmental Protection

Agency.) Herschensohn proposed filling the network with a slate of former Nixon officials. "Staff Possibilities" included Frank Shakespeare, Ken Clawson, Bill Gavin, Dwight Chapin, Stephen Bull, and even Nixon's daughter Julie Nixon Eisenhower. (Fox News would become a way station for former Republican politicians and officials.) "Sex Appeal" needed to accompany the presentation of the news. "This is one of the most important elements which we should not ignore, and network news has ignored," Herschensohn wrote. (Fox would not make that mistake. Anchor Bob Sellers remembered Ailes once calling the control booth. "I was doing the weekend show with Kiran Chetry. He called up and said, 'Move that damn laptop, I can't see her legs!' ")

The ambitious programming slate, however, far outpaced where TVN was as an actual business. The dish to receive the network's satellite signal cost $100,000, more than stations were willing to pay. And at a choreographed rollout ceremony, the demonstration failed. With the project faltering, Herschensohn soon left to produce a bicentennial film for NASA and to write a book of media criticism he titled *The Gods of Antenna*.

Wilson had reached an impasse. By September 1975, TVN had lost $14.6 million, and Joe Coors was growing impatient. The scourge of big government was making Coors feel far less charitable. After his father died in 1970, the family had to pay a sizable estate tax. During a board meeting on September 25, Robert Pauley scribbled in his notes that management's mood of late was a "feeling of desperation." A few days later, the board decided to shut TVN down. On October 3, Wilson sent a letter to Nixon to inform him of the board's decision. "After the pleasant time we shared together in your office, you must know how distressed I am at this time. In spite of those emotions, however, none of us at TVN need have the slightest hesitation to hold our heads high. Every man and woman gave their utmost to this effort," he wrote. "Among those who worked the hardest and were most responsible were former associates of yours, Roger Ailes, Steve Bull and Bruce Herschensohn." The failure, Wilson explained, was actually confirmation that the free market had worked. "The Coors people believe so deeply in freedoms of the press that they were willing to take big risks. Although TVN was not able to survive and prosper at this time in history, it is still better to have tried under the free enterprise system than to have arbitrarily handed over the responsibility of news balance to existing agencies, or worse yet, to big government," he wrote.

Ailes did not wait for the inevitable—he quit in late September. His stated reason was outside meddling. The board had brought in consultants, including John McCarty, who had gotten Ailes the job. "Roger objected to their presence," Pauley wrote in his notes. He spent just under a year as news director, but absorbed many important precepts in that brief time. Bob Pauley, who died in 2009 at the age of eighty-five, lived long enough to see his vision of a right-wing network realized. "He believed all news should be fair and balanced. That was *his* phrase," Barbara Pauley said of her husband.

TVN, while largely forgotten, was a crucial breakthrough in the birth of cable news. After the company folded, Reese Schonfeld founded the Independent Television News Association, the first satellite-delivered TV news service. In 1976 at a television industry conference, Schonfeld ran into a profane thirty-something billboard magnate with a penchant for sailboat racing and beautiful women. A born dreamer, he was transforming his Atlanta-based outdoor advertising company into a pioneering television enterprise. In December 1976, he launched the first channel distributed nationally by satellite and soon hired Schonfeld to create a twenty-four-hour news channel. His name was Ted Turner, and the channel was CNN.

•

After TVN, Ailes had to regroup. Having wisely retained ownership of his consulting company, he glided back to the liberal world of the theater. In the spring of 1975, he teamed up with Bloomgarden on the production of *Bledsoe,* a drama about a self-absorbed American novelist in Rome who falls in love with a nun while being treated for cancer. Considering that the play was written by Arnaud d'Usseau, a blacklisted playwright and screenwriter who had moved to Europe after clashing with Joseph McCarthy, Ailes scooped up funding from an unlikely source: Joe Coors. In return for 18 percent of the net profits, Ailes persuaded Coors to invest $81,000. Coors insisted that his investment remain a secret. When Ailes sent the check to Bloomgarden, he laid down the terms. Coors requested that he not be publicly acknowledged as a backer, and "would appreciate all efforts we make to avoid unnecessary vulgarities in the script," Ailes wrote. "I'm sure you understand." Coors's investment came too late. The production of *Bledsoe*, which had been plagued by problems and cast changes for two years, was abandoned.

Though *Bledsoe* was called off, Ailes had another premiere that fall to look forward to. On the morning of September 4, 1975, a throng of reporters packed into Ailes's office on Central Park South to view *The Last Frontier,* his TV special with Bobby Kennedy Jr. In the run-up to the film's release, Ailes was a nervous wreck about Ethel Kennedy coming to the screening. "I hope his mom likes the movie," Rosenfield remembered Ailes saying. "What's not to like?" It went well enough that Ailes pitched Kennedy on making additional wildlife programs together.

Though Kennedy lost interest in the project, enrolling in law school, he stayed in contact with Ailes. In November 2005, Fox News aired *The Heat Is On,* Kennedy's one-hour documentary about climate change. Accompanied by a Fox camera crew to Glacier National Park, Kennedy showed the precipitous retreat of the ice pack in recent years. "Those guys were absolutely convinced," he recalled. A few months later, after Kennedy's documentary was widely criticized on the right, Fox aired another documentary, titled *Global Warming: The Debate Continues*.

In his private conversations with Ailes, Kennedy struggled to find traces of the adventurous young man he had shared a tent with decades earlier. "Roger believes that ends justify the means. Which was a Nixonian idea. It's the idea that everybody does it, that the world is really a struggle for power. That justifies a lot of the things he's done at Fox News," Kennedy said. "His views are sincere. He thinks he's preserving the American way of life. In his heart, he thinks America is probably better off being a white Christian nation. He's driven by his own paranoia and he knows how to get in touch with his own paranoia. He makes Americans comfortable with their bigotry, their paranoia and their xenophobia."

Even as he chased his show business dreams, Ailes never fully abandoned politics. In 1976, he took on multiple campaigns. He worked for moderate Republican congressman Alphonzo Bell Jr. in California. And in Maine, Ailes advised a wealthy lawyer named Robert Monks, who was running a long-shot Senate campaign against the popular incumbent and 1972 presidential candidate, Ed Muskie. A product of St. Paul's, Harvard College, and Harvard Law School, Monks was a conservative in the mold of Joe Coors, espousing hard-line positions against the social safety net. Ailes, not yet the archconservative he would become, recoiled at Monks's antigovernment fervor, which he saw as elitism of another stripe. "This guy has got to learn some empathy," Rosenfield remembered Ailes saying. "Roger said, 'You can't be against Social Security. If you want to run for public office in a position of responsibility, drop it!' "Ailes took it upon himself to teach his client a lesson.

When Monks was campaigning in Augusta, Maine, Ailes spotted some children playing on the lawn in front of the capitol. Because they appeared to be poor, he thought they would be useful for a commercial and he sent Rosenfield to go talk to them. "Roger said to me, 'see if those kids will take you home with them and ask whoever the parents are if they would agree to have a conversation about our candidate,' " Rosenfield recalled. "So I went back, and they lived in a kind of tenement, and they were white, and it was just a woman, there was no man in the picture. I knew I'd found what it was that Roger was looking for." The next day, Ailes brought Monks to the woman's house to film him explaining his anti-welfare positions. Monks "freaked out," Rosenfield remembered. "This woman explained her situation and she says she's disabled and she's alone and she has several children and she's unable to work because she's bedridden for six months of the year. And I'll never forget, she said the worst time is Christmas because I don't have enough money to buy them gifts. And Roger said to Monks, 'Go ahead, explain your position, go ahead and tell her how you're against any kind of help from the government.' He couldn't do it. I don't think he'd ever met anyone like that in his life. He was speechless. That was the kind of education Roger would give a candidate."

When crossed, Ailes was an unforgiving teacher. During one town hall meeting, Monks said again, according to Rosenfield, that "there is too much government and people should be able to take care of themselves." On the street afterward, Ailes had Monks by his lapels up against the wall. "He had him there saying, *'if you ever fucking do that again,'* " Rosenfield, who witnessed the scene, recalled. Monks later did not recall any dispute with Ailes over Social Security and welfare, but called Ailes a "genius." (Monks lost to Ed Muskie by more than a 20 percent margin.)

In these moments, Ailes was honing a reputation that would endure throughout his career as a political operative. He was a ruthless competitor who would lay himself down for his clients. His ads became known for incisively dissecting the opponent with biting wit. "Roger liked thirty-second spots, because he would say, 'are you for this or against this?'" Rosenfield said. "There's no time to nuance your way out of it."

In exchange for his determination to win, Ailes demanded that his clients give him ultimate control, reversing the client-consultant relationship. The candidates worked for *him*. One time Monks brought a Harvard friend to review a campaign commercial Ailes had cut.

"To be honest, I don't like it," the friend told Monks. Ailes turned to face the men.

"One of us—him or me—is *gone*. You have 10 minutes to decide which one it is," he said and walked out of the editing room.

"Is he kidding?" Monks asked Rosenfield, who was standing off to the side.

"No, he's not kidding."

Monks was silent for a moment. "I'm sorry," he said turning to his friend, "but you have to leave."

Ailes was also expanding his business into the emerging field of business communications. By the late 1970s, corporate America was shedding its fusty, paternalistic image. The greed-is-good ethos of the 1980s was just around the corner, and CEOs were beginning to become celebrities. Ailes said these businessmen needed a "psychological adjustment" to life in the spotlight and he wanted to get a foothold in this new market. He developed a $4,000 seminar that included twelve hours of coaching, or, for a $10,000 retainer, clients could get twenty-five to thirty hours of advice. In short order, his Central Park South studio became a boot camp for executives from companies such as Polaroid, Philip Morris, and Sperry Rand. In October 1983, he would incorporate Ailes Business Communications, Inc., which he merged two years later with his company.

Ailes's adventures in the world of show business—and liberals—were winding down. He traveled to Rome to produce a TV special on the Italian filmmaker Federico Fellini, one of his last attempts at packaging highbrow culture. When he came back, he told Rosenfield how he had to boss Fellini around on the set to get him to do what he wanted. "I remember thinking, *you told Fellini off*? You'd be the only person on the face of the earth who told Fellini off."

On September 20, 1976, Bloomgarden died of a brain tumor at his Central Park West apartment. About a year later, Rosenfield told Ailes he was leaving to make it as a director. Ailes took Rosenfield's decision hard.

During an interview to promote their final collaboration, *Present Tense,* a musical Rosenfield had directed and co-written, Ailes refused to acknowledge him. "He never mentioned my name," Rosenfield said. He only said "the director."

Ailes and Kelly Garrett were no longer a couple. After the setback of *Mack & Mabel,* Garrett experienced limited success singing that summer for a brief revival of *Your Hit Parade,* the 1950s television show, and performing the following year in the short-lived musical *The Night That Made America Famous,* for which she was nominated for a Tony Award. Garrett took her career swings hard. "When she didn't get a particular part, or when she hadn't had a booking in a week, she would get *down,*" Paul Turnley, Ailes's former assistant, recalled. "And when she had down times, he had down times." Garrett was devastated by her breakup with Ailes, according to a friend in whom she confided at the time. She eventually moved to Los Angeles and worked as a voice teacher, giving lessons from her home in North Hollywood. Ailes tried to help her with bookings in the early 1990s, but she failed to revive her career. In 2006, she moved back to New Mexico. She died of cancer in August 2013.

In 1977, Ailes began seeing a single mother of two named Norma Ferrer, whom he had met in Florida. His involvement was both romantic and professional. He named Norma a producer on *Present Tense.* "Roger made the people who worked with him his family," Rosenfield said. "But there's no question about it, he's the head of his household." In 1976, eight years after Ailes had moved to New York, Marjorie filed for divorce. It was finalized on April 22, 1977. She took possession of the Pennsylvania home, which she held on to for thirty years. She kept his last name and never remarried. "I've spent my life protecting Roger's privacy," she said before she died on April 20, 2013. "Roger is always in my heart and in my mind." In 1981, Ailes married Ferrer. She idolized her husband, once telling a reporter that even as an infant "he could see things in ways others couldn't."

Shortly before Rosenfield left Ailes's firm, Ailes asked about Garrett. "At sort of our parting, he asked me if I thought he'd been a good manager for Kelly. I said I thought he had been," Rosenfield recalled. "I was leaving, and he was looking for some substantiation."

# EIGHT
# RISKY STRATEGY

On January 31, 1986, the Sidney Lumet film *Power,* a dark examination of the lives of political consultants, opened at the Gotham Theatre in Manhattan. Richard Gere starred as Pete St. John, a hyperkinetic image maker, who represented clients of all stripes—from a right-wing Big Oil–backed Ohio Senate candidate to a Latin American president—so long as they paid his $25,000 a month retainer. Issues bored St. John. Profit fueled his ambition. When one client earnestly tried selling him on his campaign platform, St. John replied, "My job is to get you in. Once you're there, you do whatever your conscience tells you to do."

To prepare for the role, Gere shadowed Roger Ailes for several months. "Richard practically lived with him," recalled Gere's friend Joel McCleary, a Democratic media consultant who would face off against Ailes during the 1990 presidential election in Costa Rica. Ailes's charismatic influence was evident on the screen. Like Ailes, St. John was domineering. "You are paying me to give you a new life—politics," he said in one scene. "And in order for me to do that, I've gotta be in charge of all the elements. It's the only way I work."

*Power* hit theaters as Ailes was becoming the most successful political consultant of his generation. Between 1980 and 1986, Ailes propelled thirteen GOP senators and eight congressmen into office. During this period, he increasingly made use of wedge issues and marginal sideshow debates to bludgeon his clients' opponents. "He wasn't trying to win awards from *Vogue* magazine," recalled Republican pollster Lance Tarrance, who collaborated with Ailes on campaigns. "He just wanted to win elections." Ailes's candidates—Senators Dan Quayle, Phil Gramm, and Mitch McConnell, among them—would go on to play leading roles in shaping legislation for the next two decades.

Left on the sidelines of Ronald Reagan's 1980 presidential campaign, Ailes reemerged on the political stage that fall representing Alfonse D'Amato, the Republican town supervisor of a middle-class Long Island suburb, who was running for Senate from New York. D'Amato had stunned the political establishment by defeating liberal Republican senator Jacob Javits in the GOP primary, but he faced a tough general election campaign. Ailes arrived at a crucial moment. Javits was staying in the race on the Liberal Party ticket, and the Democrats were fielding a formidable candidate: Congresswoman Elizabeth Holtzman, a Harvard-educated lawyer who was the youngest woman elected to the House eight years earlier. During their initial meeting, Ailes diagnosed D'Amato's challenge. "Jesus, nobody likes you," Ailes said. "Your own mother wouldn't vote for you. Do you even have a mother?"

Both a putdown and an insight, Ailes's remark became the foundation for one of the most successful political ad campaigns of the 1980s. In Ailes's first commercial for the candidate, the star was his sixty-five-year-old mother. Ailes filmed Mama D'Amato walking home with a bag of groceries lamenting the middle-class bugbears of inflation and crime. At the end of the spot, she appealed to viewers to vote for her son.

Several weeks before the election, polls put Holtzman ahead by as much as fifteen points. (Javits had slipped into a distant third place.) But on election day, D'Amato beat the unmarried Holtzman by one percent. Ailes's shrewd messaging got the credit. "In a less obvious way," *The Washington Post* noted at the time, "Ailes mercilessly hammered away at Democrat Liz Holtzman for being single. Several of the D'Amato ads show pictures of the candidate in a variety of loving poses with his wife and kids, and end with a variant on the regular slogan: 'He's a *family man* fighting for the forgotten middle class.'" The *Post* dubbed the race "the complete rehabilitation of Roger Ailes." D'Amato said Ailes's ad starring Mama D'Amato "made my victory possible."

By the early 1980s, Ailes's politics had become more crisply ideological. He populated his office, which he renamed Ailes Communications, Inc., in April 1982, with true believers. They included Larry McCarthy, a twenty-nine-year-old former press secretary for Pennsylvania Republican senator John Heinz; Jon Kraushar, a speech coach who handled corporate clients; and operatives Kathy Ardleigh and Ken LaCorte.

In his 1980s campaigns, Ailes was a swaggering tough guy with an angry, at times megalomaniacal, edge to his leadership style. His rhetoric was violent, and he sometimes actually scuffled with colleagues. "Whatever it takes" was one of his office catchphrases.

This philosophy prevailed outside the political realm. After the D'Amato campaign, Ailes was appointed executive producer of NBC's struggling late-night talk show, *Tomorrow,* co-hosted by Tom Snyder and Rona Barrett, which aired after Johnny Carson. Because Snyder was barely on speaking terms with Barrett, NBC needed an aggressive producer to seize control—which is what NBC got. On one occasion, Ailes punched a hole through the wall of the control room. "If you have a reputation as a badass, you don't need to fight," he later said. But he *did* fight. During an office softball game, Ailes fought with *Tomorrow* producer John Huddy, whom Ailes met while working on the Fellini documentary. "He got into this screaming match," an eyewitness recalled. "It was so heated that they got into a fistfight. Everybody knew Roger had this blood disorder, and his hands swelled. Afterwards, he had ice around his hands. It was just crazy. This was his friend, and it was about *nothing*."

The ball field brawl rattled the staff. "Roger was not going to let someone tell him what to do. Never, never, *never,*" Barrett recalled. His approach to some young female staffers became a particular flashpoint. While interviewing Randi Harrison, a twenty-something out-of-work producer who had come in from Florida, Ailes steered the conversation onto uncomfortable terrain. According to Harrison, Ailes looked over at his NBC office couch and said, "I have helped a lot of women get ahead and advance their careers in the broadcast television industry." They were discussing her salary. Ailes offered $400 a week. Harrison told him it was a lowball figure. Ailes made a counteroffer: "If you agree to have sex with me whenever I want I will add an extra hundred dollars a week."

"I guess we'll be in touch," Harrison said, getting up to leave. Ailes maneuvered around his desk and gave her a hug. "I remember seeing all the windows in his office and wondering, 'Does he do it here?' " she later said. "I was in tears by the time I hit the street."

From a pay phone in front of NBC's offices at Rockefeller Center, she called her friend Chris Calhoun, who was hosting her while she was in town. He told her to call John Huddy, her original contact for the job, and withdraw her name from consideration. She reached Huddy's secretary and told her, without going into details, that she was no longer interested in the position. Over the next twenty-four hours, Huddy placed multiple calls to Calhoun's apartment. Each time Calhoun told Huddy she was not available. In one conversation, according to Calhoun, Huddy pressed him about her whereabouts.

"Do you know when she is expected?"

"—expected to do *what*?"

Finally, Harrison agreed to meet Huddy for a drink at Hurley's, a popular NBC watering hole on the corner of Sixth Avenue and 49th Street.

The first question he asked unnerved Harrison.

"Are you wired?" Huddy said.

"No, I'm not," she replied, crying. She proceeded to recount her interview with Ailes. "Huddy assured me that there would be no more sexual demands," Harrison recalled. "He said, 'You're the one we want.'" Harrison told Huddy she'd think about it. With no other employment alternatives, Harrison became a *Tomorrow* show researcher—at $400 a week. "This was the NBC network. It was New York City. And I needed the job," she later said. At work, she had few interactions with Ailes. "I remember once going into his office and he asked me to do research on Alzheimer's," Harrison said. Ailes did not explain the reason, but at the time, his father was suffering from advanced stages of the disease and would die within eighteen months. "Every woman who worked on the show I'd wonder about," she said.

Unbeknownst to Harrison, Shelley Ross, a former newspaper reporter turned television producer, experienced an interview in which Ailes posed romantically suggestive questions and made flirtatious comments about her appearance. "This is making me uncomfortable," Ross recalled telling Ailes. She had worked with Huddy at *The Miami Herald* and he had recommended her for the *Tomorrow* job. In a follow-up telephone interview, she told Ailes that she would never date a boss. Ailes's reaction was, according to Ross, "Don't you know I'm single?" When Ross said she was no longer interested in the position, Ailes began apologizing profusely. "This must be middle-aged crazy. I'm *so* sorry," he said. "If you come to work for me, you know, we're not going to have any problems." Ross eventually accepted the offer and had a positive experience working for Ailes. When asked by a reporter in the mid-1990s about the comments he made to Ross in the interview, Ailes called her "crazy" and a "militant feminist."

In fact, dominance was not only a crucial aspect of his self-image, but part of what he was selling. "He has worked at cultivating this Hemingway image over the years," Ailes's friend, the Democratic strategist Robert Squier, said. In the summer of 1981, Shelley Ross arranged for Ailes and Tom Snyder to conduct an interview with Charles Manson, the murderous cult leader, at a maximum-security prison hospital for the criminally insane. It was the first network interview Manson had granted in more than a decade. As Snyder prepared his questions, Ailes canvassed the holding cell where the interview was to take place. Rounding a corner, he bumped into Manson himself. "As our eyes locked, I at first said nothing. I realized that a very primitive confrontation and mutual assessment were taking place," Ailes recalled in his book, *You Are the Message*. "Then I said, 'Mr. Manson, I'm in charge of this interview. I'd like you to come with me.' For a split second more he stared at me. Then he lowered his head, backed away, and suddenly acted very obsequious." Shelley Ross, who attended the interview, did not find Manson intimidating. "Let me just tell you, it wan't hard to stare Manson down,"she said. "I hate to burst anybody's bubble."

The interview, which was widely criticized for providing Manson a public platform, was a ploy to juice ratings. It worked. The audience in key markets tripled. But it was not enough to revive *Tomorrow*'s fortunes. In November 1981, NBC announced that it was replacing the show with a new one called *Late Night with David Letterman*.

The metamorphosis of Ailes was evident in the difference in approach between the 1976 and 1982 Senate campaigns of New Mexico astronaut Harrison "Jack" Schmitt, a member of the final Apollo moon mission. In 1976, Ailes had run a respectable operation, impressing the first-time long-shot candidate with his artistic flair. One frigid winter morning before dawn, Ailes drove Schmitt out to the desert north of Albuquerque to film a campaign spot near a windmill. "We parked on the side of the freeway," Schmitt recalled. "Roger had scouted the location." Ailes filmed multiple takes of his client walking toward the camera introducing himself to the state's electorate. "He wanted to get a sunrise. My hands remained partially numb for six months," Schmitt said. He went on to win the race with 57 percent of the vote.

But in the fall of 1982, Senator Schmitt saw his reelection bid imperiled after Ailes produced a controversial attack ad about his opponent, state attorney general Jeff Bingaman. The spot claimed that Bingaman had freed "a convicted felon" who had been on the FBI's Most Wanted List. In reality, the FBI had requested his temporary release into its custody in order for him to testify as a key prosecution witness at a trial in Texas for the murder of a judge. "There is nothing false in those spots," Ailes told the press, explaining that his ad relied on an article in *The Albuquerque Tribune*. But the article had been retracted before the spot aired. In Ailes's view, it was the challenger's job to point out that fact. "My responsibility ends with the act. Maybe folks can say I'm an unethical guy. But it's not my job to make . . . Bingaman's case," Ailes said. Bingaman won the race 54–46 percent.

In the next election cycle, Ailes worked on behalf of Republican Mitch McConnell, a round-faced county judge from Kentucky. Ailes had been recruited by McConnell to devise a strategy against the two-term conservative Democratic senator Walter "Dee" Huddleston, a master of southern patronage politics. With two months to go before the election, McConnell was more than ten points down. "We were in a hopeless campaign," McConnell's campaign manager, Janet Mullins, recalled. "Roger lived it and breathed it and wanted to win as badly as Mitch did." As Ailes would tell it, he was watching television at home when a commercial came on that featured a pack of dogs chasing after a bag of kibble. A McConnell staffer had mentioned that Huddleston had missed several important votes while giving paid speeches around the country. Ailes jotted down the word "Dogs!" on a piece of paper. During a strategy meeting, Ailes presented his vision. Mullins remembered the moment: "There was Roger, sitting in a cloud of pipe smoke, and he said, 'This is Kentucky. I see hunting dogs. I see hound dogs on the scent looking for the lost member of Congress.' "

The McConnell campaign, desperate for a way forward, gave Ailes the go-ahead. Ailes dispatched Larry McCarthy to hire a dog trainer and a pack of bloodhounds. The script Ailes wrote included a goofy voice-over. *"My job was to find Dee Huddleston and get him back to work. Huddleston was skipping votes but making an extra fifty thousand dollars giving speeches. Let's go, boys!"* The ad concluded with the tagline "Switch to Mitch for Senator."

Ailes knew it might backfire. "He called me at home that night when they just finished the ad," McConnell's pollster, Lance Tarrance, said. "Roger said, 'This is either gonna blow us up or not. I'll send it to you. If you think it's too wild and crazy tell me.' "

When the campaign aired the commercial, subsequently known as the "Hound Dog" spot, the Huddleston campaign dismissed the attack as a carnival stunt. "They flicked us off like a piece of dandruff," Mullins said. But ignoring the deceptive power of humor was a strategic error—the ad was a hit. "All the local television stations and editorial cartoonists immediately picked up on it. It became the symbol of the race," Larry McCarthy later said. McConnell squeezed out a win by just five thousand votes out of 1.3 million cast. "We all know Roger can be deadly. When you combine Roger being deadly with Roger being clever, it's hard to beat," Mullins said.

The victory demonstrated yet again that attacks did not have to be fair to be effective. "The charge was baseless," *Newsweek* reported at the time. "Huddleston was present 94 percent of the time, but the lackluster campaigner failed to shake the scent of slacker that the ad sprayed over him." The ad, Mullins said, is "taught in every Republican campaign school about how to use humor as a deadly weapon."

Ailes leveraged the Hound Dog spot into bigger assignments. Not long after it aired, he talked it up to Tom Messner, a member of Ronald Reagan's advertising group, known as the Tuesday Team, over lunch at the '84 Republican National Convention in Dallas. "I got this spot, we were down forty points and after it ran we were only down six," Ailes told Messner. It was a classic Ailesian exaggeration, but his swagger paid off.

In early October, the Reagan brain trust summoned Ailes to Washington for an emergency meeting. A few days earlier, Reagan had bombed during the opening presidential debate against his opponent, Walter Mondale. The Gipper returned to Washington visibly rattled. His poll numbers declined sharply in several states. "It was a disaster," Tuesday Team member Wally Carey said.

"When I arrived at the White House," Ailes recalled, "the first thing Reagan's top aides, Jim Baker and Michael Deaver, told me was that I would not be talking to Mr. Reagan directly." After Ailes took his place at the table with Reagan's image makers, the president walked in. "Reagan said, 'I was just wondering, how'd I do in the debate?' " Wally Carey remembered. "Roger said, 'Mr. President, with all due respect, you were terrible.' And the President said, 'I really thought I was. It was all these numbers they made me memorize.' Roger said, 'You know Mr. President, the American people want you to be a leader and don't care whether you don't know a billion or a million and we'll ensure going forward you won't have those big cram sessions.' "

Ailes's blunt talk encouraged Reagan. Afterward, Ailes demanded that Deaver and Baker give him access. "If you give me that, he'll win. If you don't, he'll probably lose," Ailes said. The ultimatum worked: he was invited to help Reagan rehearse for the second debate. During a final run-through at the White House, Ailes ignored prior warnings about broaching the age issue. As Ailes walked with Reagan to the elevator, he said, "Mr. President, what are you going to do when they say you're too old for the job?" Reagan, according to Ailes, "stopped cold and blinked." Ailes went on: "It's critical that you get by that issue successfully."

It was the push Reagan needed. At the second debate, Reagan delivered the iconic one-liner: "I will not make age an issue of this campaign. I am not going to exploit, for political purposes, my opponent's youth and inexperience." Ailes observed Mondale's reaction. "Even he broke into a smile, but I could see in his eyes that he knew it was over," Ailes recalled. ". . . I could almost hear him thinking, 'Son of a gun, the old man got away with it!' "

When Democrats and even Republicans criticized Ailes, he played the victim. He claimed that attack politics was an issue of free speech. "It's a question of whether or not you have a right to discuss your opponent's record," he told *The New York Times*. "The essential thing is that you have to be fair. The public has a sense of when you're out of bounds."

But Ailes tested boundaries and sometimes crossed them. In 1986, he produced an incendiary thirty-second commercial for Wisconsin Republican senator Robert Kasten, who was locked in a tight reelection fight against Edward Garvey. Ailes's spot implied that Garvey, formerly the head of the National Football League Players Association, may have stolen $750,000 from the union fund. A few days before the election, Garvey named Kasten and Ailes in a $2 million libel suit. "There are limits to what you can say, even in a political campaign," Garvey told the press. But it was too late. Kasten won by three points. Seven months later, Kasten settled Garvey's suit out of court.

Ailes's behavior became legend in Republican circles. In October 1984, Ailes exploded when Ronald Reagan forgot to mention Mitch McConnell's name in his remarks at a rally for the Senate candidate. "We had to restrain him from trying to beat someone up," McConnell's campaign manager, Janet Mullins, recalled. On occasion, Ailes even made frightening jokes about killing his clients. During a strategy session in Manhattan with Al D'Amato for his 1986 reelection bid, Ailes stopped the conversation after D'Amato lit into one of Ailes's staffers. He turned to the candidate.

"Can you fly?"

"Why?" D'Amato returned.

"Because we're forty-two stories up, and you're going to go out that window if you say one more word."

Republicans tolerated his volcanic eruptions because Ailes won. "We used to joke that Roger always needed a crisis," a former Ailes Communications staffer said. "But it was not a joke. He actually did. He performed better when his back was against the wall."

Ailes's power became such that he could choose his clients. As the 1988 presidential campaign approached, Ailes was courted by every serious Republican candidate. Ailes saw a lot to like in Bob Dole and Jack Kemp. But in the end, after two private meetings, he settled on his man: Vice President George H. W. Bush.

Like Richard Nixon, George Bush was a candidate with heavy baggage, and who was bedeviled by the medium of television. "Everybody tells me there's a problem," Bush remarked to his chief of staff, Craig Fuller. The problem was that George Bush couldn't give a speech. He did not project the commanding stature of a White House occupant. His eyes had the distracting tendency to dart left and right. He mangled syntax with embarrassing frequency. When he wanted to stress a particular point, his voice climbed several octaves. Added to that, he was diminished by the nature of his office. Martin Van Buren was the last sitting vice president to ascend to the Oval Office through the ballot box, an achievement nearly 150 years in the past.

Bush envied Ronald Reagan's talent for performance "He didn't know how he could get as good as Reagan but he knew he had to," Fuller recalled. "But one of the things about George Bush was he didn't like handlers." Fuller played to Bush's self-image as an athlete. "If you were a professional tennis player, you would play a really good game of tennis a good part of the time. But sometimes you're off," Fuller told him. "A tennis coach would come in and improve your game so that the frequency of the outstanding games is up in the 90 percentile area. The same is true with your speaking."

Bush planned to officially declare his candidacy in October 1987, and Ailes used the year leading up to the announcement to whip him into fighting shape. He took an apartment across the Potomac River in Arlington, Virginia, and huddled with Bush up to ten times a week. Bush was a quiet man, but Ailes sussed out an inner intensity. After all, during World War II, he survived being shot down in the Pacific.

"Why didn't you bail out?" Ailes once asked.

"I hadn't completed my mission," Bush said without a pause.

Ailes suggested a character for Bush to play: Gary Cooper. The stoicism and grit that Cooper brought to his roles such as in *High Noon* would connect with wide swaths of the electorate. He taught Bush to slow down his speaking style and lower his voice. He instructed him how to focus his gaze into the camera and control his wild arm movements. He put him through so-called pepper drills, firing questions at him to sharpen his verbal reflexes. Ailes won Bush over even as he berated him. "Don't *ever* wear that shirt again! You look like a fucking clerk!" he roared when Bush sported a short-sleeved shirt during a speech. "Roger was the only guy strong enough to say to George Bush, 'Jesus Christ, you look like a pansy on TV,'" recalled political operative Roger Stone, who worked on the '88 campaign with Ailes.

As the Bush campaign structure took shape, Ailes joined an elite group of decision makers collectively known as the G-6. The team included longtime Bush loyalists Nicholas Brady, Robert Mosbacher, and the veteran pollster Bob Teeter. In this genteel bunch, Roger Ailes and campaign manager Lee Atwater, the motor-mouthed dark prince of attack politics from South Carolina, were outliers. Together, they formed the campaign's angry id.

Bush gave Ailes responsibility for media strategy. He would be crafting the message, overseeing the advertising, and running debate prep. In 1968, Ailes had focused exclusively on making his candidate likable. Twenty years later, Ailes trained his creative talents on the opponents. The campaign's ads would permanently tarnish Ailes's reputation but would make him rich. In addition to his Pete St. John–sized $25,000-a-month retainer, Ailes would earn more than $2 million during the primary alone. And he did not give up his outside commitments running other campaigns. "He had other business to attend to, so he wasn't there full time," Sig Rogich, a member of the Bush ad team, recalled.

The Bush campaign turbocharged Ailes's conviction that politics was war. This reality was confirmed on October 13, the day Bush was due to announce his candidacy. That morning, *Newsweek* put an unflattering image of Bush on its cover. The picture showed him in a banana yellow rain slicker steering his powerboat off the Maine coast and was accompanied by the headline "GEORGE BUSH: FIGHTING THE 'WIMP FACTOR.'"

The press response clouded over Bush's announcement. From that moment, Ailes locked into his mission, proving to the world that George Herbert Walker Bush was not a wimp.

He got his opportunity three months later when Dan Rather requested a taped interview with Bush for the *CBS Evening News*.

"Ab-so-lute-ly no!" Ailes said during a meeting at Bush headquarters in Washington.

CBS proposed a counteroffer: a live interview. The date was set for January 25, two weeks before the Iowa caucuses.

A few days before the interview, the campaign got a tip from a source at CBS: Rather was planning to sandbag Bush with pointed questions about Iran-Contra and even planned to lead the interview with a five-minute segment about the scandal. Bush was campaigning in New Hampshire the day of the interview and only had a brief window to prepare for the showdown. "I knew if we were gonna get through this we needed Roger," Craig Fuller recalled.

Ailes met with Bush and Fuller in Bush's office on Capitol Hill, where the interview would take place. He warned Bush that Rather was going to screw him. "All they have to do is press you on dates and bullshit that you haven't had time to review, and you're gonna look like you don't know what you're talking about," he said. "If somebody asked me what I had for lunch last Thursday, I wouldn't know, but I'd look guilty trying to think about it."

Bush downplayed the risk. "Dan Rather is a good newsman."

"Hey, his job is to get ratings," Ailes retorted. "His ass is on the line. He doesn't care about you. If he thought he could get away with it, he'd *shoot* you."

Ailes gave Bush a playbook. "Don't accept *anything* Rather says to you. Don't accept the premise of any question—I don't even care if it's *right*. Stay on the offense the whole time and wear him out."

Fuller proposed a zinger. "Look, if he really just trashes you on Iran-Contra, why don't you tell him, 'How would you like to be judged your whole career on the seven minutes you walked off the set?' " It was a reference to Rather's recent on-air meltdown over CBS's decision to interrupt his newscast to broadcast a tennis match. Because Rather had stalked off the set, CBS had to air a blank screen when the match ended.

Ailes loved Fuller's suggestion. He repeated it over and over. Later he would claim it was his idea, a fiction that Fuller never challenged publicly.

As he got wired up for the interview, Bush was uncertain about using Fuller's line. Ailes, reprising his role as a prop boy on the *Mike Douglas* set, directed Bush from the sidelines. He scrawled "WALKED OFF THE AIR" in block letters on a cue card and stood just off-camera.

Rather, who was in New York conducting the interview remotely, began on the attack. Bush countered, accusing CBS of luring him into a trap. "I find this to be a rehash and a little bit, if you'll excuse me, a misrepresentation on the part of CBS, who said you're doing political profiles on all the candidates," he said. The line landed like an uppercut.

Each time Rather asked a question, Bush cut him off. Neither were comfortable performers, and they had the awkward habit of talking at the same time. Rather, increasingly flustered by Bush's filibustering, raced through his questions as if producers might pull the plug at any moment.

"I don't want to be argumentative, Mr. Vice President," Rather said at one point.

"You do, Dan," Bush taunted.

*"Go! Go! Just kick his ass!"* Ailes mouthed and waved his cue card excitedly. It was time for the knockout. "It's not fair to judge my whole career by a rehash on Iran," Bush told Rather. "How would you like it if I judged your career by those seven minutes when you walked off the set in New York? Would you like *that*?"

He got the time and place wrong—Rather's tantrum had taken place during a broadcast from Miami and the screen was blank for six minutes—but details did not matter. The interview was over and Bush was euphoric. "Well, I had my say," he howled, yanking out his earpiece. "He makes Lesley Stahl look like a *pussy,*" he continued, referring to the CBS newswoman. Ailes desperately tried to remind Bush that his mic was still hot. "But it's going to help me. Because that bastard didn't lay a glove on me." (Bush later apologized to Stahl.)

The CBS switchboard lit up with calls from irate Republicans. On the campaign trail, Republicans began displaying anti-Rather signs and buttons. "Lee Atwater said, 'There are only a few defining moments in a campaign and this was one of them,'" recalled Craig Fuller. Though he had not meaningfully answered questions about Iran-Contra, George Bush answered the most important question of all: he was not a wimp.

Ailes had helped Bush slay the media, but to win, Bush would also need to slay his own kind. On February 8, 1988, Bush placed a dismal third in the Iowa caucuses. If he failed to win the Granite State on February 16, it was game over. On Tuesday morning—a week before the New Hampshire primary—Ailes was holed up in the Clarion Hotel, outside Nashua, with the Bush high command. He was racked with pneumonia and a temperature of 102, but Ailes refused to bow to his feverish state. Bush needed to hit Bob Dole, who was rising in the polls, hard. Ailes pitched the campaign on an attack ad that his friend Tom Messner had suggested. "I said, look, you gotta do something with taxes," Messner recalled. "That's what seemed to win or lose in New Hampshire. Even Reagan got beaten in New Hampshire because someone concocted an argument that the federal tax cuts he was proposing in '76 would result in higher state taxes in New Hampshire."

With laughably poor production values, Ailes's "Straddle Ad" would show two faces of Dole on a split screen as a voice-over stated that Dole "straddled" the issue of raising taxes. Bush rejected it, but Ailes ignored him. He called his wife, Norma, who worked at Ailes Communications, and told her to produce the ad.

"Do we have authorization?"

"They don't air it, I'll eat it. We're gonna need it."

Ailes read his script over the phone. "Bob Dole straddles, and he just won't promise not to raise taxes. And you know what that means," he told her. The tape arrived the following morning. By Thursday, five days before the primary, Dole was even with Bush in the polls. That night, Ailes played the Straddle Ad for the veep.

"God. That's awful," Bush said. The word "Straddle" flashed across the screen in garish type. The ad concluded with the tagline: "Taxes—He can't say no."

Over the next two days, the campaign lobbied Bush to go up with the Straddle Ad. "We gotta, uh, kick 'em in the nuts!" Atwater told Ailes. George W. Bush, campaigning for his father, also supported it. On Saturday morning, Atwater and Ailes went to Bush's suite to make a final pitch. New polls showed Bush *trailing* Dole by five points. "The press is gonna say we're desperate. Have we checked those facts?" Bush asked. He did not want to win dirty. Atwater said the campaign's opposition research guru, Jim Pinkerton, had the figures to back up the claims. "This is your business," Bush muttered in a resigned tone, "not mine."

It was the acquiescence they needed. The campaign put big money behind the spot. New Hampshire voters would see it an average of eighteen times over the next sixty hours. On Tuesday, February 16, Bush won

New Hampshire by nine points. The true impact of the Straddle Ad was not the doubt it sowed about Dole's tax policy; it exposed Dole's temper and mean-spiritedness, which had dogged his candidacy from the beginning. On primary night, Tom Brokaw hosted Bush and Dole for a joint appearance on NBC. Bush was on-set, Dole was on remote from his hotel. Brokaw asked Dole if he had a message for Bush. "Yeah," he sneered into the camera. "Stop lying about my record."

In an instant, Dole was laid bare on national television. "He responded with a Nixon-like scowl," recalled Janet Mullins, who was then on the Bush campaign. "There was always that talk of Dole not being a nice person, and of course that was opposite of George Bush's public persona." Five weeks later, Dole dropped out of the race.

On Thursday, May 26, the day before Memorial Day weekend, Ailes arrived at a nondescript office park in Paramus, New Jersey, to observe a focus group of likely voters. Massachusetts Democratic governor Michael Dukakis was all but certain to be Bush's opponent. Around the table sat white, middle-class Reagan Democrats who didn't know much about Dukakis but found his qualities attractive. The son of Greek immigrants, Dukakis was a Harvard-trained lawyer who had served in the military. His brand was technocratic and moderate. As governor, he had helped turn around his state—the "Massachusetts Miracle," as his campaign called it.

If Bush did not take back these voters, he would lose. Ailes watched from behind a one-way mirror, as a moderator asked the group questions based on Jim Pinkerton's oppo research. "If you learned the following things about Dukakis, would it change your mind about him?" the moderator asked. Willie Horton, a black convicted murderer from Massachusetts, had been given a "weekend pass" to get out of jail as part of a prison furlough program Governor Dukakis had approved. While on leave, Horton brutally raped a white woman and stabbed her boyfriend. Furthermore, Dukakis was also against the death penalty and prayer in school. "I didn't realize all these things when I said I was for Dukakis," one woman said. By the end of the session, half the room switched their support to George Bush.

Ailes maintained that focus groups were a waste of time and money. But the New Jersey session confirmed what he felt in his gut: Dukakis was impressive on paper but weak in person. Ailes had consulted a psychiatrist to get a read on Dukakis. Word came back that he was a narcissist. Ailes thought of him as the annoying kid in school who raised his hand at the end of class to remind the teacher she had forgotten to assign homework.

At a campaign retreat in Kennebunkport that weekend, Ailes and Atwater planned to tag-team Bush to convince him to go negative. "We're gonna have to destroy the littler fucker," one Bush official recalled Ailes saying. Polls showed Bush trailing Dukakis by as much as seventeen points. Before going to bed the first night, Atwater and Ailes left tapes of the New Jersey focus group with Bush. The next morning, they never had to make a sales pitch. "Well, you guys are the experts," Bush said quietly.

The assault started a week later. On June 9, in a speech at the Texas state GOP convention, Bush attacked Dukakis as a tax-hiking, U.N.-appeasing Cambridge hippie. "Michael Dukakis on crime is standard old-style sixties liberalism!" Bush crowed. "He has steadfastly opposed the death penalty . . . he supported the only state program in the whole country—the only one—that gives unsupervised weekend furloughs to first degree murderers!"

With Bush on board, Ailes got to work on his search-and-destroy battle plan for television. Ignoring the slick Madison Avenue creative types, he recruited lesser knowns who would be loyal to him. Dennis Frankenberry was one. He ran a small agency out of Milwaukee that produced commercials for Sentry Insurance and Leinenkugel Beer. He had done only one political race—a campaign for district attorney in Oshkosh, Wisconsin. Ailes also tapped some loyalists from the '84 Reagan campaign: Tom Messner and Sig Rogich.

In his multiple roles of grand strategist, speech coach, and television guru, Ailes set the creative tone of the campaign. While only fifteen of the campaign's forty spots were negative, such bald appeals to race, patriotism, and class had rarely been displayed on the national stage. To attack Dukakis on the furlough issue, Rogich came up with the idea to film actors dressed as prisoners walking through a revolving door. The ad's centerpiece was a black man who gazed menacingly at the camera the moment he walked through. To hammer Dukakis's reputation as an environmentalist, Rogich captured footage of the Boston Harbor on a drizzly, gray day, brazenly filming a bright orange sign that read "DANGER RADIATION HAZARD NO SWIMMING." The warning was an artifact from a decommissioned nuclear submarine base, and had nothing to do with Dukakis.

At least one of Ailes's own contributions was rejected for going out of bounds. The proposed ad, titled "Bestiality," featureed simple text scrolling across a black screen: "In 1970, Governor Michael Dukakis introduced legislation in Massachusetts to repeal the ban on sodomy and bestiality." As the word "bestiality" appeared, a soundtrack of bleating barnyard animals would play. Ailes told his team that ads like "Bestiality" weren't actually "negative." They were "comparative."

As the fall campaign revved into high gear, Ailes was a constant presence at Bush's side. "He didn't give a significant speech without Roger," Sheila Tate, Bush's campaign spokesperson, recalled. "Roger had an uncanny ability to buck up a candidate," campaign chief James Baker recalled. "He made them feel good about themselves. He gave them some confidence, and some great zingers. He always had good zingers." Bush enjoyed Ailes's dirty jokes and mordant asides. He called Dukakis "Shorty," and "Grapeleaf," a dig at his Greek ancestry, as well as a "Heartless Little Robot," for spouting policy positions and arcane statistics. Bush played along. One day when his dog walked into a campaign meeting, he joked about Ailes's bestiality ad pitch. "You're the reason I'm running," he said. "We've got to keep *those* people away from you."

On September 21, four days before the first presidential debate, a shadowy outfit called Americans for Bush, an arm of the National Security Political Action Committee, aired an attack spot titled "Weekend Passes." The ad's centerpiece was a grainy mug shot of Willie Horton. As Horton's bearded, black visage hovered on the screen, a male narrator intoned: *"Bush and Dukakis on crime. Bush supports the death penalty for first degree murderers. Dukakis not only opposes the death penalty, he allowed first degree murderers to have weekend passes from prison. One was Willie Horton, who murdered a boy in a robbery, stabbing him nineteen times. Despite a life sentence, Horton received 10 weekend passes from prison. Horton fled, kidnapped a young couple, stabbing the man and repeatedly raping his girlfriend. Weekend prison passes. Dukakis on crime."* The words "Kidnapping . . . Stabbing . . . Raping" were displayed under Horton's picture, explicitly calibrated to stoke the racial fears of white Reagan Democrats.

The ad created blowback for Bush. Federal election law barred campaigns from coordinating their media strategy with independent groups. Ailes denied any involvement in the ad's creation, but there were suspicious signs. In August, Ailes had boasted to the press, "The only question is whether we depict Willie Horton with a knife in his hand or without it." And the Horton ad was created by two former employees of Ailes Communications: Larry McCarthy, who had left the company the previous year, and Jesse Raiford, a thirty-year-old director, who had spent six years at Ailes Communications.

Roger Stone said that, while he did not think Ailes was involved in the Horton spot, Lee Atwater was. Atwater played it for Stone before it aired, an act that Stone called "an admission of illegality." When Stone told him, "You don't need to do this. You got this issue," Atwater called him "a pussy." Whether or not Ailes had any direct role in putting Horton's picture on millions of television screens, his style had clearly inspired the ad. "I know Roger very well," Larry McCarthy told the press. "I just tried to [make] it as if I were Roger."

In the hours leading up to the debate, Bush studied an array of briefing books. "Roger detected that the most important thing for Bush was to be relaxed," Sheila Tate said. "Roger said to him, 'Now what are you going to do if Mike Dukakis rips off his microphone and walks over to you and says, 'Iran-Contra! Iran-Contra!' Bush goes to look at his briefing book. Roger slams it closed. He said, 'No! That's when you say, 'Get out of my face, you little shit!' And Bush started laughing. Roger was just trying to get him to loosen up. That's one of his techniques."

That night, Ailes kept up his guerrilla tactics. He stood with Bush offstage as Jim Lehrer, the moderator, prepared to call the candidates out. When Dukakis looked over at Ailes, he pointed down to a riser that was installed behind Dukakis's podium and started to laugh. "That was his idea of getting inside Dukakis's head," Tate said.

As Election Day approached, Ailes behaved like a defensive lineman preparing for a game, his aggression spilling over into all of his relationships. In August, he walked into Bush headquarters and flipped a conference table over. He was verbally abusive to Janet Mullins, who was in charge of the campaign's ad budgets. "He threatened to kill me—twice—because I had the audacity to question some of his expenditures," Mullins recalled. "He was getting paid in a lot of different ways and earned every bit of it. But if you're in charge of the media budget, you want to make sure you're not spending it on the Ritz or the Four Seasons when Roger came to town." Staffers noted that Lee Atwater seemed afraid of Ailes. He told the press that Ailes had two speeds: "attack and destroy."

Ailes's appetite seemed to be a barometer of his ego. His weight ballooned to 240 pounds. Craig Fuller recalled one hotel stop when Ailes declared, " 'Dammit, I'm hungry! Can't we get some room service?' We said, 'Sure.' Well, Roger grabs the room service menu. He was kind of agitated and he said, 'I want page three, I want page four and I want page five and I want it *now*.' " He was also known to inhale Häagen-Dazs ice cream and donuts. During one commercial shoot, Tom Messner recalled, Ailes was "sitting there with a donut, and there's this frosting on it, and the frosting is dripping down his shirt." Ailes could turn donuts into projectiles. "When he would have his emotional moments, he'd throw his donuts across the room," Sig Rogich said. "I'd ask him if it was a one or two donut day."

Leaks sent Ailes into fits. "A donut throwing moment" occurred, according to Rogich, when the trade journal *Advertising Age* sent a reporter to write about one of Ailes's commercials. After *The New York Times* wrote a column about Tom Messner's contributions to the campaign, he received a heated phone call from Ailes. "How *did* you get this Bush assignment?" Messner recalled Ailes saying. He did not appreciate his subordinate getting press.

Bush marched toward Election Day along the low road paved by Ailes. A week and a half after the debate, Rogich's "Revolving Door" ad aired. Although Horton's name never appeared in the spot, the linkage between it and Horton was obvious. Television news producers were mostly interested in pictures, attacks, and gaffes, which was why Ailes's attack spots were discussed so widely in the press. "It was a hard ad to do without appearing to be racist," Janet Mullins said.

By mid-October, Ailes green-lighted an ad that showed Dukakis wearing a helmet and grinning while he rode around in a tank as an announcer ticked off various weapons systems he opposed. The visual said it all. As Mike Douglas had once told Woody Fraser: never wear a funny hat.

From the time Dukakis clinched the nomination in early June, his unfavorability standing among voters doubled, from 20 percent to 43 percent. Meanwhile, Bush held steady at around 40 percent unfavorable. Even Bush's positive spots were devastating to Dukakis's image. In the campaign's most memorable ad, titled "Family/Children," Ailes filmed Bush on the lawn in Kennebunkport surrounded by his adorable, flaxen-haired grandchildren—a Kennedyesque tableau that made Dukakis seem foreign by comparison. The force of Bush's ad war was met by Dukakis's inept response. "I sat there mute, which is one of the dumbest decisions I've ever made," Dukakis said years later. "I made a decision early on that I was simply not gonna respond to this stuff. . . . I blew it."

Roger Stone—no stranger to dirty tricks—said he felt Ailes ran an insignificant campaign. "Wedge issues can still be about big ideas," he said. "My problem was that the wedge issues in '88 were all confections."

Even the candidate himself recoiled at trafficking in race baiting. "Here's a man who has an exemplary record on civil rights," Craig Fuller recalled. "The Bush family hated it. None of us liked it, we knew it was a problem." In late October, Bush called Ailes and complained about his slash-and-burn stump speeches.

"I want to get back on the issues and quit talking about *him,*" Bush said.

"We plan to do that November ninth"—the morning after election day—Ailes said. Bush won by a commanding eight-point margin. It was validation that Ailes's brand of divisive politics could win national majorities.

Despite the professional success, it had been a difficult few years. Ailes's marriage to Norma, strained by the stress of the Bush campaign, was on the verge of ending. "My wife has made the case that I will be destroyed eventually," he told *Newsweek* around this time. In 1983, Ailes's father had succumbed to complications from severe Alzheimer's. His decline was painful for Roger and his siblings. "It hit Roger hard, very hard," his brother said. "He broke down, he couldn't think of Dad being dead. He was sobbing on the way to the cemetery." And after Bush's victory, Ailes was forced to defend his reputation. As Democrats and journalists singled Ailes out for the divisive, racially charged tone of Bush's media message, calling him "New York's master of the slick and sleazy" and a practitioner of "political terrorism," he had his assistants at Ailes Communications release a survey showing that 80 percent of ads he produced in his career were, in fact, positive. He offered a $100,000 reward to anyone who could prove he created the Horton ad and told the press that he did not even know that two of his former employees made the Horton ad. In April 1989, he blasted out a press release that read: "TO IMPLY COLLUSION BETWEEN ROGER AILES OR THE BUSH ADVERTISING CAMPAIGN AND THE POLITICAL ACTION COMMITTEE INVOLVED IN THIS AD IS TO ACCUSE US OF A FELONY."

In July 1989, Ailes welcomed the journalist Donald Baer to his home in Westchester County for lunch with his wife, Norma, and his mother, Donna, who was in town visiting. Over hamburgers and hot dogs, Ailes's family provided Baer with glowing testimonials. They spoke of his childhood struggle with hemophilia and how he once slept on the floor to comfort a sick dog. "Underneath that exterior, he's really soft inside," Donna told Baer.

"Yeah," Ailes chimed in, "that's what Mrs. Manson said."

Baer's profile, which was published in the business magazine *Manhattan Inc.*, was an attempt to dispel what Baer described as Ailes's "Jabba the Hutt" image. But Ailes's campaign for absolution was complicated by the fact that he showed no signs of modulating his explosive style. If anything, he was giving freer rein to his impulses.

In the fall of 1989, he went to war for his friend, former federal prosecutor Rudolph Giuliani, who was locked in a struggling campaign for New York City mayor against the popular black Manhattan borough president, David Dinkins. Ailes continued to stoke racial fears, running a spot on television that linked Dinkins to black community organizer Robert "Sonny" Carson, who was convicted in 1974 of kidnapping. At another point in the campaign, Ailes ran a print ad in a Jewish newspaper that featured a photograph of Dinkins standing next to Jesse Jackson (five years earlier, Jackson had called New York "Hymietown"). Dinkins attacked Ailes's charges as "gutter politics."

On the night of October 23, 1989, Ailes displayed the violence his father once unleashed in Warren. He charged at a group of AIDS activists who had infiltrated a Giuliani fundraiser in the ballroom of the Sheraton in Midtown Manhattan. As security guards escorted the protesters out of the room, Ailes plunged into the melee. "We were screaming, and I'm being hit in the hands and in the head. That's when Ailes started hitting me," recalled Kathy Ottersten, one of the activists, who at the time was a man known as Kevin. "I recognized him. I'd seen him before in the papers with the Bush campaign with the Willie Horton stuff." Ottersten said that Ailes was in a group that dragged her down the hotel stairs as her head slammed against each step. "I wound up having to be taken to St. Vincent's," she said, recalling the incident years later. "I'm at the point now where I'm suffering from early stages of brain issues most likely related to all the concussions I got. I'm slowly losing nerve functions in my hands and legs."

At the time, Sergeant Raymond O'Donnell told reporters that Ailes could face a third-degree assault charge, a misdemeanor punishable by up to one year in jail. But in the end, no charges were filed. "I attempted to file charges," Ottersten said, "but was told by cops there wasn't enough evidence." On the Sunday before Election Day, Ailes got into another scuffle with a news photographer during the final debate at NBC's Manhattan studios.

No matter how hard Ailes tried, he could not get the yoke of Willie Horton off his neck. Giuliani lost by 47,000 votes. Ailes's candidate for New Jersey governor, James Courter, was also defeated handily that Election Day by Democrat James Florio. In the fall of 1989, Ohio Democrats protested outside a conference in Columbus where Ailes was giving a speech. Ailes responded in typical fashion: he hit back harder. "They're trying to make me the issue. Screw 'em!" he told a reporter around this time.

One thing was certain: Willie Horton was bad for business. Lee Atwater's sudden diagnosis of brain cancer in March 1990 left Ailes as the GOP's prime exemplar of scorched-earth politics. Sensing partisan advantage, Democrats turned Ailes's attack ad strategy on him. In May 1990, the Ohio Democratic Party filed a complaint with the Federal Election Commission calling for an investigation into Ailes's ties to the PAC that produced the Horton spot. The inquiry proved that Ailes did speak with Larry McCarthy during the campaign, but the FEC was deadlocked 3–3 along party lines on whether to bring formal charges against the Bush campaign and the National Security PAC. Ailes denied any wrongdoing. "I'm not the candidate," Ailes complained to a reporter. "If I wanted to run for public office, I would."

By the fall of 1990, his political career was confronting a branding crisis. The constant fire from Democrats had taken a toll. On Tuesday, October 9, Ailes reached his snapping point in Chicago, where he was trying to rescue his client, Congresswoman Lynn Martin, from an imploding Senate campaign against the incumbent, Democrat Paul Simon. In front of a pack of reporters, Ailes delivered a surly news conference, as self-pitying as Nixon's 1962 gubernatorial concession speech. "People like Paul 'Slimon' Simon are the ones who are hurting America," Ailes moaned. "The truth isn't getting out there, so now we're going to have to let people know about him," he said. "There won't be anything in our ads that's not true. It will all be there—but it will hurt." He went on to call Simon a "weenie."

The slew of schoolyard insults backfired. Martin lost by thirty points.

After a decade in politics, his brand sullied, Ailes was ready to change course again. In 1988, Ailes published the book *You Are the Message: Getting What You Want by Being Who You Are* with his business partner Jon Kraushar. Ailes filled the slim title with self-glorifying anecdotes from his adventures in television and politics. But it offered more than mere PR tips. It was a manifesto that revealed Ailes's view that communication was a kind of spiritual life force. "When you control the atmosphere, you're not operating on other people's time," he wrote. "You *can* learn to control the time and space you move through, if you really believe in yourself and understand what your mission is in every situation." *You Are the Message* was a seductive product, published at a time when middle managers all over the country were awakening to the notion of "personal branding."

But the real money was in the boardroom, not on the bookshelf. The cultural and class resentments that Ailes harnessed for his Republican candidates could also be channeled for corporations. In the summer of 1988, he had signed a contract with Big Tobacco, beginning a relationship that would last at least for five years. His first assignment was running media strategy for a lobbying group called Californians Against Unfair Tax Increases, which was opposing Proposition 99, a referendum on a 25-cent cigarette tax increase. At the time, it represented the largest cigarette tax increase in history. In one memo, Ailes wrote: "Usually, in a referendum, if people are confused, anxious, or doubtful, they will vote 'NO.' " Ailes noted how deception was central to his mission. "We have no obligation to tell the viewer anything not to our advantage," he wrote.

His ads were designed to stoke these emotions and spread misinformation about Prop 99. One ad portrayed Prop 99 supporters—which included the American Cancer Society and the American Heart Association—as out-of-touch elitists who wanted to fleece the little guy. "If you went to medical school . . . you'll probably love Proposition 99," one script read. "But if you didn't, make sure you don't get fooled. You see, 99 directs that hundreds of millions of our tax dollars will end up in the hands of doctors and the medical industry. And guess what? They sponsored Prop 99. Prop 99 is simply a smokescreen; it raises taxes and doctors get richer. Vote no on Proposition 99. Doctors are already rich enough."

Ailes played upon racial fears by linking the tax to inner-city crime. One commercial portrayed a man identified as an undercover cop warning that raising cigarette taxes would increase cigarette smuggling by gangs. The ad sparked outrage by Ailes's opponents. California's Democratic attorney general, John Van de Kamp, called the spot "a scare tactic of the worst and baldest kind." Prop 99 supporters' hackles were raised when they discovered that the man was not an undercover cop, but a deskbound Los Angeles Police Department officer named Jack Hoar who moonlighted as an actor. (His biggest role at the time was a bit part playing a cop-killing henchman in the film *To Live and Die in L.A.* starring Willem Dafoe.)

In November 1988, voters agreed to the new tax, passing Prop 99 57.8 percent to 42.2 percent. Even so, Ailes Communications earned $1 million off the campaign and Ailes was defiant. "The antismoking zealots tried first to throw water in everybody's face," Ailes told the press. "Now, they're throwing legislation."

Ailes's populist bluster echoed that of another corpulent conservative in New York: Rush Limbaugh. It was only a matter of time until the two joined forces. In 1987, Reagan's FCC repealed the so-called Fairness Doctrine, the rule that mandated broadcasters give equal time to opposing political viewpoints on the airwaves. The change spurred the growth of right-wing talk radio, with Limbaugh as the medium's most successful practitioner. More than seven million fans listened to his radio show each week. In 1991, after bumping into each other at the 21 Club, Ailes put together a deal to launch a syndicated television show.

But Ailes had not completely left politics. The GOP paid him a $9,500 retainer to consult on media strategy. In August 1990, a few days after the Iraqi dictator Saddam Hussein invaded Kuwait, Ailes sent an urgent memo to Bush's chief of staff, John Sununu. "I have had at least half a dozen calls very recently from the press trying to lead me into discussions like, 'fiddling while Rome burns,' 'golfing while Americans are being taken hostage,'" he wrote. "The only reason this is of concern to me is that I notice the networks beginning to show more and more footage of the president in the golf cart. . . . I know first hand what a megatonnage dose of media hammering the same message can do." He went on: "Do a little more fishing and less golfing." In November, as Bush planned to travel to the Middle East to meet with U.S. military commanders and Arab leaders, Ailes advised the president on his wardrobe. "In the field he should wear khaki slacks, open shirts, long sleeves with the sleeves rolled up," he wrote. "It is my judgment that he should not wear hats or helmets. A fatigue jacket would be fine in the field with soldiers on Thanksgiving Day."

Bushworld put out feelers to Ailes about running media for the 1992 campaign. This forced Ailes's hand. He told colleagues he'd had enough. A few nights before Thanksgiving, he took his aide, Scott Ehrlich, to dinner at Goldberg's Pizza on Manhattan's East Side to discuss his decision to quit politics. Ailes expressed concern about the harm it might cause to his reputation. "He was thinking about the press reaction, about the spin and what the message was," a person familiar with the conversation recalled.

On December 6, 1991, Ailes announced that he was walking away from politics to focus on entertainment ventures. To quell any suspicion his business was suffering, he projected a hyperactive image. He was busy launching Limbaugh's TV show and consulting for Paramount Television on tabloid shows like *Inside Edition*. At the 1992 Democratic convention, he ran into Bob LaPorta, his old friend from *The Mike Douglas Show*. LaPorta recalled Ailes saying, "I really miss show business, I love it." Around this time, Ailes was taking meetings in Hollywood. One writer who ran into Ailes at the Century Plaza hotel marveled at Ailes's snap judgments about television. "We were meeting in the lobby," he recalled, and "there was a TV running and *Wheel of Fortune* was on with no sound. Roger was staring at it, he said, 'Do you know why the show works?' I said, 'I don't watch the show.' And he said, 'It works because of Vanna White. You gotta look at this girl and her clothes. It just works!' "

Ailes was even branching out into board games. In 1992, he lined up the makers of Pictionary to market a $19.95 campaign-themed game called Risky Strategy. In August, he traveled to the GOP convention in Houston to promote the game, which was created by his thirty-year-old assistant, Judy Laterza, who had joined him in 1987. To advance around the board, players rolled dice and drew from cards that featured political punch lines. ("Your opponent accuses you of removing the tags from your mattresses. You counter that was done in the privacy of your own home: Win all the states in TOO CLOSE TO CALL," one card read.) His political career had come full circle. "Politics was a 20-year habit, but somehow I decided I would walk away from it and go back to the entertainment business," he told the press.

He maintained his ties to Bush and other prominent Republicans in a quieter way, serving as a go-to surrogate, image consultant, and source of media intelligence. "By that time, he was in the media business, so it was hard for him to be overtly political," Jim Baker said. "It's not to say he didn't help us where he could. We felt free to call him and talk to him. But he couldn't take a public role in the campaign."

Ailes gave interviews attacking Bill Clinton as a "saxophone player" and Ross Perot as "loony toons." On the night of June 2, 1992, Ailes orchestrated a crucial summit between Bush and Limbaugh. The right-wing talker had been a vocal Bush critic, and Bush needed to mollify him to shore up support from his populist base. That night, Ailes, Limbaugh, and Bush attended the musical *Buddy* at the Kennedy Center and then retired to the White House for the night. Bush personally carried Limbaugh's luggage up to his assigned quarters: the Lincoln Bedroom (Ailes got the Queen's Room across the hall). Ailes's backchannel diplomacy paid off. Five days later, Limbaugh appeared on the *Today* show and gushed to Katie Couric about his visit, calling the president a "genuinely nice guy."

But Limbaugh's blessing was not enough to save Bush's ailing reelection campaign, which was buffeted by the post–Gulf War recession and a hapless message. Bush also faced another challenge: an emboldened opposition. The Democrats, stung by Dukakis's defeat, had learned valuable lessons, an ironic legacy of Ailes's success. Bill Clinton's campaign was, in many ways, an Ailes-inspired operation, with its famous "War Room" staffed by operatives, chief among them the wily attack dog James Carville, who characterized Bush as an aloof elitist who did not feel America's pain.

Ailes was coming around to the breakthrough insight: the media industry was a much more powerful platform to spread a political message. During the 1988 GOP convention, he got into an argument with NBC executive producer Joe Angotti, who was producing the convention broadcast. Ailes wanted NBC to air the seventeen-minute documentary he had filmed in its entirety, but Angotti refused: "We weren't going to devote all this time to a propaganda video," he later said." Ailes called Angotti three times in a day to lobby him to air the movie. "He said, 'What if it were ten minutes, would you carry it then?' I said, 'I'm not going to negotiate over the phone.' "

Ailes discovered he could achieve his political goals by changing roles. Instead of being at the mercy of the networks that controlled the airtime, he could control the message by *joining* the media. In the spring of 1990, he had formed a company, Belmont Street Broadcasting—a reference to his childhood address in Warren—and made his first exploratory moves.

In May, Ailes spent $325,000 to buy WPSL, an AM radio station in Port St. Lucie, Florida, close to where he owned a condo. "It was an oldies station. Roger brought in a lot of talk," recalled Greg Wyatt, who would later buy the station from Ailes. Ailes came up with a new slogan, "The Talk of the Treasure Coast," and added Rush Limbaugh to the lineup. Publicly, Ailes downplayed any political agenda. "It's just a fun thing. It's just something I wanted to do," he told *The Miami Herald*.

But those who worked with Ailes knew he was looking ahead to the future. Cable news was a thriving new industry. CNN had exploded onto the scene with its twenty-four-hour coverage of the Gulf War. Sig Rogich, Ailes's colleague on the Bush campaign, recalled conversations: "He wanted to do a conservative news network forever. I heard him talk about it for a long time. He said, 'The networks were biased. We need to have balance in America and we're not getting it and all these others are anti-Republican and anti-anything that's conservative.' He talked about it constantly."

# ACT III

# NINE

# AMERICA'S TALKING

IN EARLY 1993, AILES PAID A VISIT TO Robert Wright, the raspy-voiced chairman and CEO of NBC. Ailes's friend Jack Welch, the CEO of General Electric, NBC's parent company, had set up the meeting. A client of Ailes was interested in purchasing a TV station and Ailes wanted to see if Wright would sell him an NBC affiliate. As the conversation progressed, Wright had a brainstorm. "We were talking a lot about his background. We spent a lot of time talking about *The Mike Douglas Show*," Wright recalled. "I got the sense that this was the romantic period of Roger's career. He was out in Cleveland as a native Ohioan. As I listened, I said to myself, 'This guy is a producer. The advertising stuff is production. The political stuff is about producing.' So I said to him, 'You could buy a TV station. But it's a rocky road. You sound like you like to program the shows on the air. At a local station, you won't produce entertainment shows. Why don't you come over here and run CNBC?' "

Al Barber, the head of NBC's struggling Consumer News and Business Channel, had recently told colleagues he wanted to resign, and Wright was quietly putting out feelers for his replacement. CNBC was deep in the red. After NBC launched the channel in 1989, it had been plagued by anemic ratings and weak distribution, available only in some 17 million homes, which was less than half of that of its rival, the Los Angeles–based Financial News Network. Two years after the launch, NBC gambled on a merger, paying $154.3 million to acquire FNN. CNBC's ratings remained stalled. The channel suffered from a confused, hybrid identity: uninterrupted blocks of bland stock market reports by day and middlebrow talk shows by night. Wright realized that CNBC needed an executive with programming instincts to fix the ratings problem. "Al was a great guy, but programming wasn't his long suit," Wright said. When Wright spoke to Ailes, he seemed intrigued.

It's an irony that Ailes came into his own as a television executive at the network that is most currently identified with liberal ideas. But at NBC, where his tenure would last just twenty-eight months, his talents as an executive and his personality—his bold impulsiveness, his paranoia and aggression, his conservative instincts, his megalomania, and his huge gift for television programming, reached their maturity. His ambition had never been to fit in, to be just another executive—he wanted to dominate. It was a credit to his television talents that his inflammatory conservative rhetoric did not derail his campaign to get the job. Though Ailes had never run a channel, he knew a thing or two more about television than Barber, a numbers guy who had spent most of his career at General Electric. Moreover, NBC was planning to launch an all-talk cable channel that would be called America's Talking, and Ailes, the guru of the talk genre, would be well suited to run it. Wright was especially intrigued by Ailes's relationship with Rush Limbaugh, the king of talk radio. "One of the things I hoped he was going to do was bring in Rush Limbaugh," Wright recalled.

But when Ailes's name circulated at NBC as a serious contender to run CNBC and America's Talking, producers were incredulous. It was inconceivable to them that a man who was living out his so-called retirement from politics as executive producer of Rush Limbaugh's television show would be put in charge of a nonpartisan business news channel. And political associations aside, they worried about the things that Ailes was spouting on national television. It wasn't just an occasional slip of the tongue. In interviews, he called Clinton a "hippie president," and White House spokesperson George Stephanopoulos "a sociopath," and played the role of full-on Republican battering ram even as he was interviewing with NBC.

Ailes wanted the CNBC job badly. "He always craved a big stage, and the move to CNBC was about moving to a bigger one," said a colleague of Ailes at the time. On July 8, Ailes sent a confidential letter to Tom Rogers, president of NBC's cable division, lobbying for the job. "I continue to be very interested in the CNBC situation," Ailes wrote. "I believe the opportunities and problems are neither easy nor simple. However, I do believe they are exciting and solvable and that my creative background in programming, marketing and communications strategy are suited to the challenge." Ailes copied Bob Wright on the letter—if Ailes was going to become a network suit, he would only report to the top.

Much as he had indicated to the Nixon White House twenty-five years earlier, Ailes signaled that he was not willing to give up his independence. He told Rogers that he needed to retain his role as executive producer of the Limbaugh television show. He had also just renewed a consulting contract with Paramount Pictures—where he advised on *The Maury Povich Show*, among other projects, and would continue to advise Paramount's syndicated television programs. Most important, Ailes stipulated that if he took the CNBC job, he would "need to maintain Ailes Communications Inc. as a viable entity."

Ailes saw in the position an opportunity to secure new business for his consulting firm with CNBC. "Obviously I want to avoid any conflict of interest or perception of conflict of interest, however, I trust Ailes Communications research and production capabilities so we need to discuss this," he told Rogers. Ailes hinted that he had designs to rise into senior management at the network. He wanted to know if the new president would "be included in all meetings, and have a voice in the future of NBC cable operations."

Despite his ardor for the job, he played it cool in public. Over the next few weeks, as negotiations with NBC continued, Ailes projected an image in the press of a very busy man. On July 25, he appeared on Comedy Central in the debut of Bill Maher's new series, *Politically Incorrect*. Later that week, he popped up in *USA Today* defending his friend Joe McGinniss and his controversial biography of Ted Kennedy, *The Last Brother*. "It's important to remember who the scoundrel is," Ailes said. "There's not a lot to be proud of in Ted Kennedy's life."

Ailes's bid to reinvent himself as a news executive was complicated on July 21 as news broke that Christine Todd Whitman, the moderate Republican running for governor in New Jersey against incumbent Democrat Jim Florio, had hired Larry McCarthy, Ailes's former colleague. McCarthy's presence on the campaign sparked an outcry from Democrats and black leaders, ultimately leading to his departure.

In an interview a few days later, Whitman defended the hire, saying that she believed it was Ailes who had created the Horton spot. Ailes, who had been trying to undo the stain of Willie Horton for five years, was outraged. He tried reaching Whitman, but found she was on vacation in Idaho. He then tracked down her brother, Webster Todd, who was helping manage her campaign. "Ailes went off like a Roman candle," said Whitman's press secretary, Carl Golden, who was subsequently dispatched to handle Ailes. "He was screaming into the phone at me. He was almost irrational, screaming 'My kids are seeing this!'" referring to the children of his wife, Norma, from a previous marriage. "He kept demanding an apology. He wanted a written apology released to newspapers."

On the afternoon of July 27, Ailes blasted out a press release attacking Whitman as "Slick Christie." "When Christie Whitman hired McCarthy she was fully aware that he had produced the 'Willie Horton' commercial," the statement quoted Ailes as saying. The quote went on: "If Christie Whitman can't get the facts straight, isn't courageous enough to admit when she's in error, tries to sneak her misjudgments past the press corps and can't tell the truth, she'll end up like Bill Clinton—a joke."

Whitman's apology, released July 28, made news for the next several days. "There was no intention to disparage Mr. Ailes or his reputation," her statement said.

After putting out the fires in New Jersey, Ailes was close to clinching the NBC deal. He flew to Nantucket to meet with Jack Welch. "Roger had a really good relationship with Jack," an Ailes colleague said. In turn, Welch championed Ailes. "I was all for it. I became Roger's biggest supporter. He's creative. He's crazy passionate. He gets in there and goes after it. He's exciting to be around—he's incredibly fun," he said.

In the last days of negotiations, Ailes downplayed his interest in the NBC job. "There have been some conversations, but nothing concrete," *USA Today* quoted him saying on August 16. "I have a top priority right now and that is to be the executive producer of *The Rush Limbaugh Show*." The article suggested that Ailes would need a bit more money. "Limbaugh is one of the hottest properties in syndication and Ailes might be hard-pressed to leave that lucrative field," it read.

A week later, Ailes signed a three-year contract with NBC that satisfied nearly all his demands. He was given the title of president and a base salary of $550,000 with a guaranteed $25,000 raise in the second year and a final year salary of "no less than $600,000." If ratings jumped, he could earn a bonus of up to $1.7 million annually. Remarkably, NBC allowed Ailes to continue as Limbaugh's executive producer and remain as a board member at Ailes Communications, but the contract stipulated that he not do any "formal" advising of, or consulting for, Ailes Communications clients. Significantly, in a move that would have future consequences, his contract stated that Bob Wright, not Tom Rogers, would be his direct boss.

In effect, Ailes had maneuvered Rogers into a corner. As the head of NBC Cable, Rogers had just lost control of his division's biggest asset. "Tom's role was pushed back, and he had to look out for stuff to do," Welch later said. Before setting foot on the job, Ailes had already cast aside a formidable rival. He also made sure he maintained powerful allies. "Roger had enemies and friends," Welch recalled. "Some of the guys who built the cable unit felt he was taking it over. I was well aware of it—I sided with Roger."

The impending arrival of Ailes put CNBC staff members on edge. When Wright made the announcement, he recalled that "blood drained" from the faces of his executives. Wright assured them that Ailes had abandoned politics, but Ailes did not inspire confidence when he displayed a picture of George Bush in his expansive office at CNBC's studios. "A lot of us were leery," Doug Ramsey, co-host of CNBC's *This Morning's Business,* said. "It never sat well with me that a political hatchet man was coming to run what is basically a down-the-middle business news network."

It turned out that Ailes's self-image as an outsider was an asset in his new job. As Ailes infused the struggling newsroom with his competitive zeal, his employees dwelled less on his political baggage. "Look, there's one way to do it, and that's to do it right," he'd tell his cable producers. These were still the days of broadcast dominance, in which cable was viewed as the minor leagues and CNBC, in particular, as a backwater. In a cost-cutting move to avoid union rules, the channel had been exiled since its 1989 launch to studios across the Hudson River in Fort Lee, New Jersey, about ten miles from the NBC headquarters in glittering Rockefeller Center.

Ailes convinced the staff they were winners. "We're going to knock down whatever walls we have to turn this into a first-class operation," he said. He recruited new makeup artists to improve the look of the anchors on camera. He beefed up security at the front desk. "It used to be anyone could walk in. He had construction done to keep people out," a former senior producer explained. "He was there on Saturdays and sat there in the control room talking to them about lighting, how to change scenes, and camera work," Wright recalled. Early on, Ailes summoned the channel's anchors to the office for a weekend communications seminar, where he handed out copies of his book, *You Are the Message,* and trained the broadcasters in skills that he had previously taught to political candidates and business titans for a hefty fee. "If I'm talking to you, and you don't understand what I'm saying, well, it's on me to change," he told them. His locker room humor was irresistible. "Some said it was vicious, but I thought he had one of the quickest wits I ever heard," a former CNBC executive said. "So, for a few weeks anyway, I thought he was a hero."

Ailes clearly relished his new role as a powerful news executive. As a campaign operative, Ailes had "looked like he was wearing someone else's suit—but one he'd borrowed years ago (now the guy didn't want it back)," the author Richard Ben Cramer observed during the 1988 campaign. Since then, Ailes slimmed down, shaved off his graying goatee, and acquired a wardrobe of suits, pocket squares, and ties paired with the presidential tie clip given to him by George H. W. Bush. Ailes became a regular at the NBC executive dining room at 30 Rock, swapping gossip and campaign war stories with Jack Welch and NBC Sports president Dick Ebersol. He attended parties hosted by wealthy Republicans from Henry Kissinger to cosmetics mogul Georgette Mosbacher. At the Four Seasons, he maintained a regular table and dined with media industry players such as Barbara Walters and gossip columnist Liz Smith.

Positioning himself at the center of CNBC's social orbit, Ailes launched what one CNBC host termed his "charm offensive." To celebrate the marriage of his friend and CNBC anchor Mary Matalin to Clinton adviser James Carville, Ailes co-hosted a private dinner at the 21 Club. NBC grandees in attendance included Wright, his wife, Suzanne, Tom Brokaw, and Tim Russert. To mark the fifth anniversary of CNBC, Ailes put on an evening of dinner and dancing in a ballroom at the Sheraton in Manhattan. "My wife called it 'The Prom,'" one CNBC anchor said. "I'll never forget the big suck-up toast that Roger gave to Bob Wright," said a CNBC executive. "He's a master of that game." Ailes presented the image that he was thriving in the hyper-competitive GE culture fostered by Jack Welch, even though it wasn't entirely true. At GE budget meetings, for example, executives watched as the master communicator kept his head down, nervously reading from a script of financial reports. "He was awkward and uncomfortable," one attendee said. "I saw that he wasn't interested in advertising and affiliate relations," Wright said. "His focus point was on the programming."

Still, to the outside world, his media profile was rising. Eight months into his run, one reporter speculated that Ailes "could become a contender" for Wright's job to oversee all of NBC.

Initially, Ailes made cautious programming decisions at CNBC, focusing more on stylistic elements than strategic restructuring, turning news into entertainment. He encouraged his staff to think of business news like a spectator sport. "Markets were becoming a huge story," one producer explained. "There was this natural liftoff happening in the world of finance and the media that would propel CNBC." Ailes thought CNBC "looked and sounded too deferential," so he added "closer shots, more emotion, bolder sound, voice-overs announcing breaks instead of just music." Jazzing up CNBC's image with new marketing slogans, Ailes introduced the tagline, "First in Business, First in Talk." He injected a campaign mentality to the ratings race and seized opportunities to tweak his cable rivals. After the markets plummeted 7 percent in one week during the spring of 1994, Ailes took out a full-page ad in *The Wall Street Journal* that read: "The Dow plummets in heavy trading. But first, today's weather. CNN tells you if your shirt will get wet. CNBC tells you if you've still got one."

Pushing CNBC to amp up its sex appeal and energy level, Ailes placed Maria Bartiromo, a new hire from CNN, on the floor of the New York Stock Exchange, like a sideline reporter at a football game. Testosterone-fueled traders swooned over her smoky eyes, dark hair, and Brooklynese. She soon picked up the nickname "Money Honey." Ailes would also approve the redesign of the morning business news show. "We talked about the feel of the NFL Sunday show, and how everything was a build up to the game," a senior producer said. They conceived a show that would be modeled on a Wall Street trading desk, where guys would swap stock tips and headlines in advance of the opening bell. It would be called *Squawk Box*.

His major focus was assembling a loyal team. Ailes brought in Judy Laterza, his assistant from Ailes Communications, and hired his Westinghouse mentor, Chet Collier, to help him launch the new talk channel. In the twenty-five years since Ailes left *The Mike Douglas Show* he had remained close with his former boss. "Chet was his father in a lot of ways," America's Talking producer Glenn Meehan said. "Chet was probably the only man who could say, 'Roger, cut the shit.'"

He also probed existing CNBC employees. Lingering over a scotch at a restaurant near the studios, Ailes asked Bob Berkowitz, the host of the late-night sex advice show *Real Personal,* "is there anyone in your staff, anyone you can think of, who you would want with you in a foxhole?" The in-house acolytes Ailes found were ambitious young men and women who were not senior enough to pose a threat to his place in the corporate hierarchy. Politics weren't a concern. He cultivated Paul Rittenberg, a newly hired thirty-nine-year-old advertising sales executive who had voted for Bill Clinton. Ailes promoted another Democrat, David Zaslav, an excitable thirty-three-year-old lawyer, to head affiliate relations, a position responsible for signing up cable companies to carry their channels. Brian Lewis, a thirty-five-year-old public relations executive, also won over Ailes's confidence. In many ways, he was a younger version of Ailes, aggressive and street-smart, the son of a cop from Brooklyn, who attended St. John's University in Queens before working at Howard J. Rubenstein Associates and another PR firm in Manhattan. In the fall of 1993, before Ailes had decided to keep Lewis in his job, he put him through an initiation rite. In his office, Ailes informed Lewis that a journalist at *The New York Observer* was working on an article about Ailes allegedly advising Jeanine Pirro, who was running for district attorney of Westchester County. "Kill the story," Ailes said, pointing to the telephone.

*"Here?"*

As Ailes looked on, Lewis browbeat the journalist into agreeing not to go with the story.

"Nice job," Ailes said.

A made man, Lewis could stay. On his first day on the job, Ailes gave him some advice. "Look, you're my PR guy, you have to learn one thing: keep your door open in case the bomb goes off, you won't be dead." Lewis was captivated by his new boss, who talked of PR as war.

Then there was CNBC producer Elizabeth Tilson. Blond, divorced, and thirty-two, Beth oversaw the daytime programming of the channel. "She lived and breathed CNBC," a colleague said. One weekend, Ailes came into the office and found her slogging away.

"Where is everybody?" he asked. "Come on, let's have lunch."

Tilson soon became a regular presence at Ailes's side. "Roger demanded loyalty, and Beth was someone who wanted to be loyal," a colleague said. Her boss, Peter Sturtevant, CNBC's vice president of business news, had recently told her she had risen as high as she could go at the channel, but Ailes believed he could take her further. In December, he made her vice president of programming for America's Talking. Producers would often see her going to lunch with Ailes and Chet Collier near the Fort Lee studios. "You could see them walking across the street going to the pizza joint. Everyone got a kick out of that," a former producer said. When she didn't eat with Ailes, she gushed to her colleagues about him over lunch. "I used to have lunch with her all the time, she was always so enamored of Roger," a close colleague remembered.

With his team in place, Ailes insisted that he run CNBC's affairs without any encroachments on his turf. The simmering rivalry with Tom Rogers showed no signs of cooling off. Within months, Ailes began clashing with CNBC's programming chiefs for daytime and prime time, Peter Sturtevant and Andy Friendly, who had been promoted by Rogers. Under Barber, Friendly was free to run his programs without interference. But Ailes signaled publicly he planned to intervene in Friendly's decisions. "As someone with a background in producing and writing, it's impossible for me to watch the screen and not see things that drive me nuts," Ailes told the *Los Angeles Times* a month into the job. "So, for better or worse, I'll be involved in all of the programming."

Although running CNBC was arguably a more visible platform, Ailes spent most of his time preparing America's Talking, the all-talk cable channel, for its summer 1994 launch. His concept for A-T, as the start-up became known around the office, was essentially talk radio translated into television. Eschewing the tabloid vulgarities of popular daytime television—with its chair throwing and messy paternity disputes—Ailes geared his dozen hours of daily talk shows to the staid tastes of the heartland—the long tail of the Mike Douglas audience. "I figure there are 18 shows for freaks," Ailes told a reporter. "If there's one network for normal people it'll balance out." "His idea was *Queen for a Day*," said Bob Wright. "He was looking for shows that had a happy ending and moments of excitement. It was supposed to be uplifting."

As producers interviewed for assignments, Ailes gave them few specifics. In May 1994, once his staff had been assembled, Ailes called his new employees into a meeting in a conference room where he unveiled the lineup with a flourish. "The first day we're sitting in a conference room in Fort Lee and music from *Mission: Impossible* starts playing. We all got an envelope of what our assignments were," former CNBC executive producer Renata Joy recalled.

The lineup began with a morning chat show, hosted by Steve Doocy, a former host of the syndicated show *House Party,* and former New Haven local television anchor Kai Kim. Afterward, a call-in program called *Am I Nuts?* adjudicated viewers' interpersonal conflicts. Another phone-in program, *Bugged!,* provided a comedic forum for viewers to discuss whatever was bothering them. *Have a Heart* showcased acts of random kindness from Good Samaritans. *Pork,* with an oversize pig mascot onstage, exposed government waste. Ailes planned a two-hour evening political show, *A-T in Depth,* hosted by Chris Matthews, then a columnist for the *San Francisco Chronicle*, and former CBS reporter Terry Anzur. In late June 1994, Ailes signed an additional $125,000-a-year contract to host his own celebrity interview show called *Straight Forward,* a sort of middlebrow *Charlie Rose*. "He very much believed in the lineup of America's Talking," Dennis Sullivan, an A-T executive producer, said. "He knew you had to have an evening news show, that was more or less an investment in Chris Matthews. The other stuff—*Am I Nuts? What's New? Break a Leg, Alive and Wellness*—it represented what he thought that every human being was concerned about: 'Am I nuts?,' 'What's new?,' 'How do I feel?' And 'What can I do for my fellow man? Who needs my help today?' *Pork* was not part of that scheme, *Pork* responded to his anger."

Much of A-T's staff had little experience in television. Ailes shaped the novice producers in his mold. "When you work with Roger, you quote Roger," one assistant producer said. "You say lines like, 'Don't get caught in your head, don't get caught in your ego.'" His passion inspired his charges. "He's very good relating to a group of people, which made him a popular boss," Dennis Sullivan said. "The kids who worked there didn't think of Roger being a right-wing, nefarious person. They thought of him as a father figure."

Large staff meetings were electric, with Ailes playing the role of the coach firing up his team. "They were like a pep rally," one producer recalled. "He would say, this is what's working, this is what isn't. It would be a Kool-Aid meeting. Everyone's eyes would be glazed over and they'd be cheering." Ailes made his staff feel like he'd run through fire for them, and in one instance, he did. At around 4:30 on the afternoon of May 10, 1994, batteries for A-T's backup power supply exploded and caused a studio fire. The fire department rushed to the scene and evacuated the Fort Lee building. "Roger went back into the building and got all the commercial reels," a producer said. "He was the last one out of the building, and he made sure everyone was out."

But Ailes's motivational rhetoric was not always literal. In one early session around the time of A-T's launch, he told his staff that his door was always open and he believed in transparency. After the meeting, a fresh-out-of-college production assistant named Aaron Spielberg wandered up to Ailes's office and knocked on the door. "He got in terrible trouble," a senior producer recalled. "Official orders came down: tell Aaron Spielberg not to come back. It was like 'what are you, an idiot?' "

The staff clearly knew Ailes's politics, but he refrained in the early days of A-T from pressing a discernible ideological agenda. He simply reminded A-T staffers to appeal to viewers beyond the East Coast. "He called it the NASCAR audience," one former producer said. "We'd get newspapers from all over the place," producer Glenn Meehan said. "*Let's remember the flyover states,* we'd say a lot." More than politics, A-T was supposed to tap into the spirit of the early 1990s, when the idea of the "Information Superhighway" was in vogue. The network signed a deal with Prodigy, the pioneering Internet service, to showcase viewer emails and chat room comments on-air in real time. In this regard, A-T was ahead of its time. The concept of social media was still in its infancy, and the idea for a cable news channel that would allow viewers to engage with one another on-air was novel.

The weeks leading up to the launch were a frenzy of preparation as studios were built out, and shows were thrown together. It was a dizzying feat to create a dozen hours of shows in just ten months. But the elation was tempered by the sense among the staff that when A-T launched on Independence Day 1994, Ailes's experiment had flopped. Many felt that the network had a downmarket, public access feel. In the ensuing months, most of Ailes's program concepts also fizzled or were revamped. "They were struggling with the programming," junior producer Tony Morelli said. "There were a lot of awkward silences. It was very *Wayne's World*–ish."

While A-T bumbled along, Ailes was well on his way to making a success of CNBC. During his first year on the job, CNBC's revenues climbed 50 percent and profits tripled. He was benefiting from the 1990s boom. But from the beginning, Ailes had refused to comport himself according to journalistic standards. Even after he arrived at NBC to run a business news network, he drew a $5,000-a-month consulting salary from Philip Morris to "be available," according to an internal email written by Philip

Morris's vice president of corporate affairs, Thomas Collamore. In 1994, a group of tobacco companies turned to Ailes to roll out a PR campaign to promote their efforts to curb youth smoking. The goal, according to an internal memo, was "to protect the ability of tobacco companies to continue to compete for the business of adult smokers." In a section of the memo titled "Roll Out, Day One," the memo stated: "Ask Ailes to try to prime Limbaugh to go after the antis for complaining."

Ailes also behaved as if he never left the campaign war room. He went after *Time* magazine writer Kurt Andersen, who was at work on a cover story about Rush Limbaugh and Howard Stern. Convinced the story was going to be a hatchet job about Limbaugh, Ailes called Andersen to brush him back.

"How would you like it if a CNBC camera crew followed your children home from school?" Ailes said.

"I wonder how Jack Welch would like it if he knew that GE resources were being used to stalk small children," Andersen fired back.

"Are you threatening me?" Ailes bellowed. He never sent the camera crew.

It wasn't the only instance of Ailes attempting to use CNBC's journalism to hustle his enemies. One day Peter Sturtevant got an irate phone call from Ailes about a "nasty" newspaper article. Ailes told Sturtevant that he had to "get back" at the reporter, an executive remembered. Sturtevant talked with Ailes for ten minutes until he cooled off and dropped it, but the episode was chilling. At home, Sturtevant's wife implored him to quit and take a job at the Columbia Journalism School, but Sturtevant, who had hired more than 150 people in the CNBC newsroom, wanted to stick it out.

Meanwhile, NBC executives were growing increasingly concerned about Ailes's overt partisanship. On the morning of Thursday, March 10, 1994, Ailes called in to Don Imus's radio show to banter about politics and triggered a controversy. He told Imus that Bill and Hillary Clinton's ongoing Whitewater corruption scandal involved "land fraud, illegal contributions, abuse of power . . . suicide cover-up—possible murder." He made a reference to the popular allegation among the right wing that deputy White House counsel Vince Foster's suicide in July 1993 was actually foul play. He also called Foster's boss, White House counsel Bernard Nussbaum, "that little Nussbaum, that little loser." Referring to the president's upcoming trip to New York City, Ailes chortled, "He's coming up to New York today . . . and he's up here because he heard [Olympic figure skater] Nancy Kerrigan's on *Saturday Night Live.* She's the only one he hasn't hit on." Ailes also went after the first lady, noting that of the three lawyers whom she brought to the White House—Webster Hubbell, Nussbaum, and Foster—one was under investigation by the Justice Department, "one was forced to resign . . . and one's dead. I wouldn't stand too close to her." Before it was over, Ailes skewered his own employees. He joked that Mary Matalin and Jane Wallace, hosts of CNBC's *Equal Time,* were like "girls who if you went into a bar around seven, you wouldn't pay a lot of attention, but [they] get to be tens around closing time."

The Imus interview occurred at a delicate moment for NBC News. Like all the networks, NBC was negotiating with the White House to land a sit-down interview with the Clintons to discuss Whitewater, and there was fear Ailes had just torpedoed their chances.

As Ailes did damage control, speaking with Wright and NBC News president Andy Lack, he remained silent on the matter in the press, instead dispatching Brian Lewis to handle it. Lewis launched a minor counteroffensive and told *The Washington Post* that Ailes's comments were "in the context of a comedy radio show, and that's the way it should be treated." He added: "You know freedom of speech? Two hundred and fifty million Americans have that right." (In private, executives knew better. "Ailes wasn't joking," one colleague said. "That really was what he thought of the Clintons.")

Jane Wallace didn't appear in any news stories defending Ailes. "He had no right to say something like that," she later said. "He was our boss. It was completely sexist. It was disgusting. It was outrageous. I thought it was a hideously awful thing to say." But she, too, didn't make it an issue with Ailes. "I didn't say so out loud, I was working for the guy." A few weeks later, however, Wallace quit to host her own show on FX, the start-up cable network owned by Rupert Murdoch's News Corporation.

Ailes succeeded in arresting the controversy before it metastasized into something bigger. After the weekend, NBC released a statement echoing Lewis's talking points. Ailes's comments "were said in the context of a comedy radio show," according to an NBC spokeswoman. But the Imus episode revealed that inside NBC Ailes was becoming a divisive personality. He had a crucial ally in Welch and NBC's executive vice president for human relations, Edward Scanlon, but his working relationship with Wright and Tom Rogers was deteriorating. Ailes treated Rogers like a lesser adversary and needled him in public. "Tom's had a little trouble letting go because he basically used to run CNBC," Ailes told a trade journal. "I think he likes to see his name in the paper . . . Every once in awhile, we send a disinformation press release to Tom's office just to keep him on his toes." Rogers was furious with Ailes's gibe and told Wright about it. Wright asked Ailes to apologize but he refused.

Ailes's conflict with Rogers cleaved NBC's cable division. "Roger has a very large ego," Bob Wright said. Giving off the impression he was untouchable, Ailes forced executives to choose sides and made it clear there would be a price to pay for divided allegiances.

"Who are you loyal to?" Ailes asked one senior NBC executive who worked for him and Rogers.

"Look, I report to you both," he said.

From that moment Ailes treated the executive like a threat. In another conversation, Ailes told him to stay out of his team's way or "I'm going to rip your fucking heart out!"

One day, the executive noticed David Zaslav, CNBC's head of affiliate sales, almost visibly shaking in an empty office at 30 Rock. He asked him what was wrong.

"I can't go to Fort Lee," Zaslav responded in a hushed tone.

Ailes had become convinced that Zaslav was plotting with Tom Rogers to undermine him. "Ailes didn't trust David, no question about it," an A-T staffer said. Ailes asked Scott Ehrlich, a young aide from Ailes Communications who had joined NBC, to keep tabs on Zaslav.

In the fall of 1994, Rogers and Ailes clashed over staffing decisions. Rogers approached Peter Sturtevant about Sturtevant taking a position with CNBC's international division, an internal transfer that would get him halfway around the globe from Ailes. Their relationship had broken down over ideology and personality. "Sturtevant, I don't want to hear about your politics," Ailes barked at him on several occasions. Their relationship was also complicated by Beth Tilson, Sturtevant's former deputy. She had cut off contact with him. When they passed in the office, she barely acknowledged his presence. He later became convinced she was saying negative things to Ailes about him. Sturtevant finally was transferred to the international division. While Ailes seemed happy to see Sturtevant go, he was furious that the decision was being made by Rogers at a time that didn't suit Ailes's purposes.

Ailes's relationship with Andy Friendly, who was running CNBC's prime time, also grew increasingly dysfunctional. Ailes openly criticized him in meetings with staff, sometimes viciously.

Meanwhile, Ailes experimented with ploys to keep the audience tuned in. Long before Fox would interweave political story lines throughout its news programming, Ailes was toying with the power of narrative to keep people watching. In late 1994, he green-lit an idea that his friend, the comedy writer Marvin Himelfarb, came up with for a soap opera called *Cable Crossings* that would play out in thirty-second installments at the top of the hour throughout the day. Modeled after the popular mid-1990s Taster's Choice coffee commercials that chronicled a couple's romance, A-T's series took place at a fictional cable network called Starnet. Ailes made a dozen telling cameos: he played a swaggering network executive.

As the months progressed, the climate at the A-T studios became increasingly suspicious. "Roger ran his life like a campaign," said former A-T producer Glenn Meehan. While A-T's programming was more populist than conservative, Ailes worried about liberals in the office undermining him. There was some truth to his concerns. A joke circulated at 30 Rock about Ailes's network. "America is talking, but no one is listening," it went. Dennis Sullivan, who was the co–executive producer of *Pork,* recalled how Ailes called him into a meeting to discuss the political leanings of Josanne Lopez, then a producer for *A-T in Depth*. "He described her as suspiciously dangerous because of her left-wing leanings," Sullivan said. When Lopez was preparing to produce a special on immigration, Chet Collier called to ask her about her political beliefs. Sullivan, too, attracted Ailes's skepticism after he showed up at the office one day wearing cowboy boots. "Roger thinks you look like an aging hippie," a producer told him. "I never wore cowboy boots again," Sullivan recalled.

Frequently, the staff would not see Ailes at the office. Between his duties for Rush Limbaugh, running CNBC, and attending meetings at 30 Rock, he was spread thin. "It was a little bit like *Charlie's Angels,*" said Dennis Sullivan. "Roger was running the place from his car phone."

In Ailes's absence, CNBC was essentially run by Collier and Tilson. A-T staffers began to gossip about Ailes and Tilson's closeness in the office. The two had a lot in common. She grew up in a modest household, one of five children in a Catholic family in Watertown, Connecticut. It was a strict upbringing marked by traditional values. One of Tilson's brothers would grow up to become a priest. And like Ailes, who battled hemophilia and his parents' fractious marriage, Tilson's childhood was interrupted by tragedy. Her father passed away when she was five. Her mother instilled in Tilson an up-from-your-bootstraps ethic and encouraged her to excel in school. Tilson also shared Ailes's childhood love of the stage. Her mom hoped she would one day perform on Broadway. But Tilson's dream was to become a network star. In her high school yearbook, she wrote that she hoped to one day take Barbara Walters's place. She was, like Ailes, a state school kid—she got a bachelor's degree in journalism at Southern Connecticut State College. What she lacked in connections, she made up for in hard work. "I remember coming in on a Saturday before the launch of the network, and the two of them were both there in casual clothes. I remember seeing some sort of personal space situation, and something in their body language. It was clear to me something was going on," one producer recalled. Others marveled at how Ailes's dog, Jeb, a toy Yorkshire terrier, treated Tilson like an old friend. "It would run around the office and jump all over her. I thought to myself, 'That dog knows her *really* well,'" a producer recalled. "Beth was always cleaning up the poop in the office." Glenn Meehan also noticed the dog's affection for Tilson. "I was in Beth's office and the dog came in and came right to her," he said. "I had always heard rumors, but I grew up with dogs, so I knew."

Despite the turbulence with Rogers and others at 30 Rock, Ailes was accomplishing the image makeover he had sought since he had bailed out of organized politics three years earlier. In the fall of 1994, the journalist Nancy Hass began working on a profile of Ailes for *The New York Times Magazine*. At first Ailes resisted her requests for an interview. But Brian Lewis convinced Ailes to cooperate. Ailes professed to Hass that he had abandoned politics for good. "People think I stayed in politics because I wanted conservatives to run the world," he told her. "Actually, it was the money." Besides, Ailes explained in remarks that would have future resonance, television was bigger than politics. "This is the most powerful force in the world," he said in his office, as he scanned a pair of monitors playing CNBC and A-T. "Politics is nothing compared with this."

The article presented Ailes with a major opportunity to position himself to a national audience as a media mogul, a fully formed CEO, and a future heir to Wright's job running NBC. Ailes's powerful allies in media and politics provided quotes to Hass that read like blurbs on a book jacket. "I wouldn't want to be in the voting booth with him," Dick Ebersol told her, "but there's no one else I'd rather be in the control room with." Former Fox Broadcasting CEO Barry Diller said, "The important thing about Roger Ailes is that he has an uncanny knack for knowing what works." The quotes from Jack Welch were the ones that later stood out the most to executives at NBC. Hass interviewed Welch by phone from Brian Lewis's office in Fort Lee. Welch told her that Ailes's performance at CNBC was "utterly astonishing" and added that Ailes's hiring "may well turn out to be the smartest thing Bob Wright has done in his career." Hass reported on the speculation inside NBC that Ailes was being positioned to succeed Wright. In an interview, she asked Wright about it. "If you had asked me five years ago whether Roger Ailes could run a network, I would have said no," he told her. "Back then, most people thought that we needed corporate types to maintain the franchise. Today, it's obvious that what we need are risk takers."

The feature story, headlined "Embracing the Enemy," was published on the second Sunday in 1995. "It was taken internally as Roger positioning himself not only to succeed Bob as CEO of NBC, but to cause it to happen sooner," an A-T staffer said. Ailes's tensions with Rogers and Zaslav were hinted at. "Roger sees everyone as either for him or against him," an anonymous NBC executive told Hass. The article's publication proved to be the turning point in Ailes's career at NBC. "You can paint the arc of Roger's Q-score at NBC," the A-T staffer said, referring to the measurement television executives use to assess popularity. "The apex was right before that article."

# TEN

# "A VERY, VERY DANGEROUS MAN"

AILES HAD CHOSEN AN INOPPORTUNE MOMENT to launch a campaign for Wright's job. While Ailes was talking himself up to *The New York Times,* Wright was pushing NBC in a direction that would ultimately freeze Ailes out of the NBC hierarchy. Five days after the profile hit newsstands, in January 1995, Bob Wright and Jack Welch flew on NBC's corporate jet to DeKalb Peachtree Airport, outside Atlanta. From there, they drove to Buckhead, the tony Atlanta suburb, for a secret meeting with CNN founder Ted Turner at the Ritz-Carlton. Since the early 1980s, Turner had held on-and-off talks with NBC about merging. This round was the second time in two years that the executives had discussed a deal. The more recent courtship began several weeks earlier, when Turner reached out to NBC. Ever since CNN's coverage of the Gulf War, CNN had swelled into a global mega brand. The network's operating income would hit $350 million in 1995, nearly double that of 1990. A deal with CNN would make NBC the most serious cable news contender in the business.

As the men talked, Turner paced the room. They argued over the valuation of Turner's company. Turner continued to flit back and forth, as Wright tried to break through to Turner. He was accustomed to Turner's manic behavior, as the two men had been close since the 1970s. But Welch, who barely knew Turner, found it disconcerting. Sensing Welch's hostility, Turner feared, as he later recalled, "if we ever were to do a deal I'd be just another employee of General Electric."

After ninety minutes, Turner abruptly ended the meeting. "You know what? I don't think I want to do this," he told them.

The breakdown of the negotiations with Turner only increased

NBC's interest in developing a real cable news channel. The talks set off a chain reaction, resulting in a radical transformation of the cable news industry. With CNN off the table, NBC was determined to start a cable news channel of its own. And Ailes's rivals inside NBC were moving to ensure that Andy Lack and NBC News would be in charge of it, not Roger Ailes.

The *Times Magazine* article had raised Ailes's profile in a dangerous way—just as had happened with *Selling of the President*. And shortly after it was published, Ailes's opponents mobilized. One afternoon, a Rogers loyalist, who had been subjected to Ailes's dress-downs in meetings, walked into Bob Wright's fifty-second-floor office and shocked Wright with anguished accounts of how Ailes verbally abused and threatened subordinates. Wright called Ed Scanlon, NBC's human resources chief, into his office right away. "Good God, Ed, you gotta hear what he has to say," Wright told him. Shortly afterward, Wright and Scanlon visited the Fort Lee offices to observe the situation. Others came forward. CNBC's prime-time chief Andy Friendly confided to Wright's wife, Suzanne, that Ailes was out of control. Suzanne Wright was a powerful presence inside the network. Executives dubbed her Madam Chairman for her well-known habit of interweaving her social and professional life at NBC.

Concerned that Ailes was out for her husband's job, Suzanne encouraged Friendly to brief her husband on Ailes's management issues. On Monday, March 13, 1995, Friendly sent Wright and Scanlon a confidential memorandum that leveled a litany of explosive charges against Ailes. The dramatic letter, typed in all capital letters with multiple grammar mistakes, appeared hastily prepared, a result of Friendly's poor computer skills. "The sensitive nature of this precludes my assistant typing it," Friendly wrote.

Friendly's allegations were chilling, detailing instances in which, he claimed, Ailes harangued him in meetings, encouraged him to lie to the press, and left Friendly with the distinct fear that Ailes might become physically violent.

Given their fractious relationship and Friendly's loyalty to Rogers, Friendly had clear motivation to challenge Ailes. But the provocative letter also reflected Ailes's increasingly erratic behavior. "He has repeatedly forced, or tried to force my colleagues and I to lie, cover-up and use the journalistic and programming power of CNBC to promote himself or attack his enemies," Friendly wrote. Friendly asserted that Ailes called him in a panic at home at seven in the morning and told him to lie about putting his show *Straight Forward* on CNBC, after a newspaper raised questions about it being "another Ailes ego trip."

Within the boundaries of corporate culture, Ailes reacted like a caged animal. "I along with several of my most talented colleagues have and continue to feel emotional and even physical fear dealing with this man every day," Friendly wrote. "From in my face spitting and screaming to verbal threats of 'blowing [my] brains out', to psycological [*sic*] mind games questioning my family relationships, my marriage and other highly personal, totally inappropriate topics."

Friendly, whose father was legendary CBS News president Fred Friendly, called Ailes "a living, breathing integrity crisis" and implored his bosses for a transfer to a position in Los Angeles. Wright and Scanlon did not take any major steps to address the allegations. "When you get into the details, it's always ugly," Wright later said. Six months later, Friendly quit. He took a job as executive vice president for programming at the television syndicator King World Productions, which distributed *Inside Edition* and game shows including *Wheel of Fortune, Jeopardy!,* and *Hollywood Squares.*

As Ailes battled for control within the company, he fought a second front against CNBC's competitors. In June 1995, a few months after rebuffing Wright and Welch, Ted Turner announced that CNN was planning to launch a financial news network headed up by the veteran business anchor Lou Dobbs. Ailes had tried to recruit Dobbs to join CNBC, and now felt that Dobbs had played him in a ruse to coax a better deal out of Turner. He contemplated running attack ads against CNN. One would show elderly wheelchair-bound viewers watching Dobbs's CNN show *Moneyline* on a television inside a nursing home, a gambit Ailes hoped would poke fun at CNN's aging audience. Ailes also played his hand in the press. "At this point there's nothing Ailes would like better than the opportunity to kick Dobbs' ass," a source close to Ailes told a reporter. Ailes told the press that if Turner came onto his turf, he would turn America's Talking into a twenty-four-hour news channel to compete with CNN.

Ailes tried to use the brewing competition with CNN to his advantage. The negotiating window to renew his contract was open until June 30, and CNBC's success gave him leverage. Despite Wright's growing reservations about Ailes, Jack Welch remained a vocal booster who wanted to keep Ailes in the fold. Once again, Ailes continued to use the press. Nine days before the contract deadline, *USA Today* reported that Ailes's "chances of bolting are 50-50." The negotiating maneuvers paid off. On June 30, 1995, Ailes signed a four-year contract to remain at NBC. It was significantly more lucrative than his existing deal. Ailes's base salary jumped to $725,000, with guaranteed increases to $800,000 in January 1997, and $900,000 in July 1998. The contract stipulated that Ailes would receive an annual incentive bonus of no less than $250,000. As before, Ailes reported to Wright and was allowed to retain his outside business interests. He remained a board member and principal of Ailes Communications, executive producer of the Limbaugh show, and retained the right to consult on two outside talk shows.

What the contract did not do is resolve the tangled lines of reporting between Ailes, Rogers, and Zaslav, a smoldering ember that would soon ignite. Ailes wanted complete control of CNBC, but Rogers and David Zaslav were still in the picture. The competition heightened Ailes's concern that his rivals were plotting a new push against him. "This is where the beautiful marriage cracked," Bob Wright said.

In May 1995, NBC had announced a joint venture with Microsoft to create a new interactive channel. Tom Rogers started negotiations with Bill Gates. Ailes was initially unaware of the plan. At 30 Rock, executives were hatching the channel, which would take the place of America's Talking, under the informal code name, "The Ohio Project." When Ailes got wind of it, he considered the name a snide reference to his upbringing. He lobbied to save America's Talking and became especially enraged after learning that Zaslav backed the new channel. "The reality of it was, Bill Gates didn't want it to be under anyone but the president of NBC News," Wright remembered. "That was a crushing blow to Roger. He hated it."

It was at this time that Ailes seemed to spin into "meltdown mode," as Bob Wright would later put it. His fourteen-year marriage to Norma was nearing its end. Norma had filed for divorce in September 1994. A State Supreme Court justice finally granted a judgment on September 5, 1995. The dissolution of his second marriage had significant financial consequences, unlike that of his first, eighteen years earlier. He was now a man of considerable wealth.

Ailes's conflict with Zaslav deepened when he learned that Zaslav had questioned his projections for CNBC. "The bubble broke in the fall," Wright said. At a company dinner one evening that September, Ailes declared war on his colleague. "Let's kill the S.O.B.," he told loyalists dining with him. Then, in a meeting with Zaslav, Ailes allegedly called him "a little fucking Jew prick."

On Saturday, September 30, Tom Rogers called NBC's HR chief, Ed Scanlon, to inform him that Zaslav had made a shocking charge against Ailes. The insult, Rogers said, had been made during a "tirade," where there was a witness present. In handwritten notes on the matter, Scanlon reported, "I told Tom if this was an accurate story, it represented a serious charge against Roger Ailes and cannot be dismissed by NBC."

Jack Welch prized Scanlon for his discretion and his ability to keep messy employment matters out of the press. The allegation that a high-profile executive had hurled an anti-Semitic insult against a Jewish employee was just the type of matter that needed to be handled with extreme sensitivity, especially in a media company full of gossipy journalists. That night, Scanlon briefed Wright on the situation. The next day, Wright conferred with Rogers, and Zaslav called Scanlon to provide his firsthand account of the episode. Zaslav said that he was not trying to discredit Ailes, and asked to report to someone else at 30 Rock while keeping his current position. "I'm only trying to do my job," Zaslav said. Before they got off the phone, Scanlon told Zaslav that Ailes's remark, if true, was a serious violation of NBC standards of conduct, and the matter would have to be investigated.

As it happened, Scanlon and Wright were scheduled to attend a meeting at the Management Development Institute, GE's famed leadership training center in Crotonville, New York, on Monday and Tuesday. In between sessions, the men conferred and decided to consult Howard Ganz, a partner at the law firm Proskauer Rose, whom NBC had retained to handle employment disputes. "Howard Ganz is a tough and fair investigator," Wright said. On Tuesday evening, October 3, Scanlon asked Ganz to conduct an inquiry—quietly. NBC gave Ganz, according to Ganz's notes, "free rein—no conditions attached; no limitations imposed."

Instead, Ailes moved to discredit Zaslav. A week into Ganz's inquiry, Ailes forwarded to Scanlon a scathing letter that Jim Greiner, CNBC's new chief financial officer, had written him about Zaslav. According to Greiner's pro-Ailes account, it was Zaslav, not Ailes, who posed the problem. He said Zaslav was a "control freak" who managed through "intimidation" and lacked "good business judgment." The sources, whom Greiner did not name in his letter to Ailes, were "employees in good standing," who "didn't seem to have an ax to grind," and who "spoke rationally and reasonably."

Scanlon seemed to consider the letter a transparent attempt by Ailes to damage Zaslav. He sent a copy of the letter to Ganz. "Roger is really working to get a 'big and long story' on David Zaslav," Scanlon wrote to Ganz in a note attached to the letter.

Within two weeks, Ganz detailed his initial findings to NBC. "I have reported to NBC that there is substantial credible evidence corroborating this allegation—that I believe the allegation to be true," he noted, regarding the anti-Semitic slur. He found that it occurred "in context of history of abusive, offensive, and intimidating statements/threats and personal attacks reportedly made to and upon a number of other people." Moreover, Ganz investigated allegations that Ailes had "intimidated and threatened individuals who might be interviewed or have relevant information in connection with matters related to investigation." It was Ganz's opinion that Ailes's remark to Zaslav could be grounds for "cause termination." It was a persuasive account. Bob Wright later said that he believed Ganz. "My conclusion was that he probably said it," Wright recalled, referring to Ailes's comment.

NBC asked Ganz to temporarily suspend his investigation and meet with representatives of Ailes to see if they could resolve the matter without proceeding further. Their interest was self-preservation. "So far have been able to keep lid on and avoid leaks. If resume investigation, will necessarily involve substantial number of additional people—run risk of leaks," Ganz noted.

On Monday, October 16, Scanlon spoke with Ailes. After being "warned about his behavior," and being told that it was "unacceptable and did not comport with GE/NBC standards," Ailes told Scanlon that he wanted to put an end to the matter within twenty-four hours.

Friday, October 13, had been a difficult day for Zaslav. Around midday, an NBC researcher told Zaslav about a conversation he had had with Ailes's ally Scott Ehrlich. Ehrlich instructed him not to talk to Zaslav. In a letter to Ganz detailing the incident, Zaslav also related that his employees reported to him that Ailes was speculating that he was improperly using company funds to strike deals with cable operators. "I am particularly troubled by statements he has apparently made, indicating that he thinks I may be paying off cable operators with CNBC/A-T marketing funds," he wrote. He also said that Ailes's camp was spreading a rumor that Zaslav would be forced out by the end of the week. Zaslav concluded his letter on an ominous note. "I view Ailes as a very, very dangerous man. I take his threats to do physical harm to me very, very seriously and [the threats] have caused, and will continue to cause, great concern for me and my family," he wrote. "I feel endangered both at work and at home. I plan to seek counsel from Ed Scanlon as to whether I should continue to go to Ft. Lee."

On October 17, the same day that Zaslav wrote about his latest bouts with Ailes, Howard Ganz was scheduled to meet with one of Ailes's attorneys, Milton Mollen, a retired judge whose specialties included workplace discrimination cases. Ganz planned to detail for Mollen the findings of his investigation. "You should know that I have approached this entirely on merits—as totally neutral outside, independent lawyer/investigator," he wrote. "I have called it as I see it—period." Ganz noted that Ailes "was offered opportunity to meet with me, but declined." Ganz wanted to know "what avenues of possible negotiation do you see?"

NBC was considering two options. One was for Ailes to resign. Ailes and NBC would negotiate the spin they would put on his departure in the press and the exact timing of it, as long as Ailes signed a resignation letter within twenty-four to forty-eight hours. They would negotiate a financial settlement, but given the circumstances NBC was not prepared to pay out his full contract or to provide the minimum for a no-cause termination. If he wanted to remain at NBC—"don't know if possible, but (speaking off top of head)," Ganz wrote—Ailes would have to apologize to Zaslav, agree to cease his pattern of intimidating verbal abuse, and allow Zaslav to report to someone else.

When later asked about the meeing, Mollen criticized the manner in which Ganz approached the investigation. "He had come to the conclusion that Ailes had made an anti-Semitic remark. I asked him, 'Well what's your evidence?' I was shocked by his answer. I asked if he had conducted a hearing with Ailes. He had not at all." Mollen noted that Ailes had worked with a number of Jews in his career. "In fact, his first partner in business was a Jewish person," Mollen said.

NBC drafted "stay" and "exit" alternatives for Ailes. Under the stay scenario, NBC stipulated the terms of Ailes's apology to Zaslav: "(a) Must formally apologize for and retract anti-Semitic reference and commit never to making any such reference in the future. (b) Must retract any and all statements that Zaslav reasonably understood as intimidation or threats related to alleged communications that Zaslav had with NBC corporate executives; and must express a commitment not to make any such statements in the future." Because of business realities, Zaslav would continue to work with Ailes, but NBC demanded that Ailes allow Zaslav to report to him and Tom Rogers.

The exit scenario would include confidentiality clauses, a nondisparagement clause, a noncompete provision with, for example, "CNN/Turner, CBS, ABC, Fox, any Business News Services." Ailes would agree in addition not to "solicit NBC/CNBC/AT employees for any competitive employment." Other deal points included "departure announcement by Thanksgiving weekend effective December 31, 1995. . . . No conduct by R.A. that a reasonable employee would perceive as offensive, intimidating or abusive during the period through 12/31/95." Ailes would be offered "a "consultancy agreement with NBC effective January 1, 1996 through December 31, 1997 with a monthly payment."

On October 20, Ailes had a letter hand-delivered to Wright and faxed to Scanlon and Welch. Fighting to save his job, Ailes played both the victim and the aggressor. "We have an opportunity to resolve this matter quickly and effectively," he began. His letter went on:

> The charges are false and despicable.
> I have not received a fair hearing.
> This is un-American.
> All the lawyering will provoke an untoward outcome.

Meanwhile, Zaslav had been doing his best to avoid Ailes at the office. But Ailes was getting reports that Zaslav was leaking to the press. "It has come to my attention that David Zaslav has conducted several off-the-record conversations recently with Justin Martin, a journalist with Fortune Magazine," Brian Lewis wrote in a memo on October 18. "I have not raised this with David yet, but as you know, we have a policy that all media calls must first go through media relations to ensure that one corporate message be distributed. . . . Please advise." On the afternoon of Wednesday, October 25, Ailes showed up at Zaslav's door and walked in. He reached over and shook Zaslav's hand in a friendly way. "I like you and I have always liked you," Ailes told him.

"Thank you," Zaslav replied.

Ailes seemed armed with talking points to deliver a message. "There's been nothing personal in this whole matter," he said. "At this point, we are just hurting each other's careers." Ailes said that if Zaslav reached out to him, the feud would end. "We can find peace," he said.

"I appreciate that," Zaslav offered.

"This has been a real war. I don't like wars, but I am good at them. The thing about wars is that there are casualties," Ailes said and laughed. "I have been through about twelve train wrecks in my career. Somehow, I always walk away."

It must have been unclear if Ailes was trying to apologize to him or threaten him.

"I am a deeply spiritual man," Ailes continued. "It is not for me to pull the noose tighter on your or anyone else's neck. Our Maker does that. You can get some sleep now. . . . You don't have anything to worry about from me."

"Thank you," Zaslav said.

Ailes walked out of the office. Zaslav quickly typed up the conversation and sent a transcript of the encounter to Scanlon.

NBC executives were at a crossroads. "It was a he-said, he-said situation," Wright said. "If they could come together, I would have been satisfied . . . but that didn't happen." Ailes did not take the exit alternative, and executives continued to worry about the episode leaking to the press. At a staff meeting on the morning of October 30, Ailes began by declaring, "I feel like General Patton. I'm afraid they will find out I love war."

On November 10, Ailes reached an agreement with NBC and kept his job. "Ailes agrees to work constructively and harmoniously with Zaslav in the best interests of NBC, CNBC and AT," the agreement stated. It added: "During his employment by NBC/CNBC, Ailes agrees that he will not engage in conduct that a reasonable employee would perceive as intimidating or abusive. If, as determined by Scanlon, Ailes engages in such conduct, that conduct shall . . . entitle NBC to terminate the June 30 Agreement and Ailes' employment thereunder." A separate agreement between Ailes and Zaslav, which both men signed, ended the battle, in which "certain disputes and disagreements have arisen between or among the parties."

"There was no apology. There was no admission of any wrongdoing," Milton Mollen said.

On November 21, NBC announced that Zaslav had been promoted to executive vice president for cable distribution and domestic business development. One Ailes loyalist remembered how, before long, Zaslav began showing up to work in a gray Porsche 911, which he parked in a handicapped parking spot so it did not get scratched. "Roger walks with a limp. Of course it pissed him off," the source said.

The agreement did little to ease the tensions. In late November 1995, Ailes and Zaslav traveled to Anaheim, California, to the Western Cable Show, a major industry conference. "It was very, very uncomfortable," one staffer later said. "Roger was not speaking to David, David was not speaking to Roger. And here they were, being the face of CNBC."

Though Ailes had stayed, it became clear that he had little future at NBC. Wright and Welch ruled out the possibility of Ailes running the new NBC-Microsoft cable news network, even though Ailes lobbied Wright to change his mind. "He said he would run it for Gates," Wright recalled Ailes telling him. "I said, 'It has to be NBC News.' " Wright tried unsuccessfully to convince Ailes to remain in charge of CNBC. Ailes could not accept the offer. In an instant, he was being demoted from Wright's heir apparent to essentially a cable news producer in charge of CNBC's programming.

Ailes, however, showed no signs of backing off in public. "I love competition," he told a *Newsday* reporter shortly after the Zaslav episode. "That's why I get up in the morning."

On December 14, 1995, Ailes paced his office in Fort Lee, watching his career implode on a television monitor. America's Talking, his baby, was being ripped from his hands, and it was all happening in public. Onscreen, Bob Wright walked to the podium at 30 Rock's Studio 8H, the iconic set of *Saturday Night Live,* to open a press conference, flanked by Jack Welch and Andy Lack. Bill Gates and Tom Brokaw participated by video linkup. Wright confirmed the talk of the media industry for weeks: NBC and Microsoft were launching a new cable news channel named MSNBC, and Andy Lack, the flashy president of NBC News, would be in charge of its programming. Microsoft was investing $220 million in the 50-50 joint venture, and would pay NBC a $20 million annual licensing fee to distribute its news programming online. MSNBC would take over the America's Talking slot on the cable dial—and Ailes's channel would be dead.

The press conference was a response to the Time Warner–Turner Broadcasting System merger, which had been announced on September 22. The staggering $7.5 billion deal spurred CNN's rivals to take aim at Turner's cable news monopoly, lest they get left behind. In early December, ABC's blustery news chief, Roone Arledge, announced that ABC was planning to launch a twenty-four-hour cable news channel. Speaking to a group of business leaders in Boston around the same time, News Corp chairman and CEO Rupert Murdoch also announced his intention to launch a twenty-four-hour news channel. For Murdoch, the rivalry with Turner was personal. Just a few months earlier, in August 1995, Murdoch had had his own backroom talks with Turner in hopes of acquiring CNN, and had gotten nowhere. A day after Murdoch's announcement that he would start a "really objective" channel, Turner declared at the opening session of the Western Cable Show that he looked forward to "squishing Rupert like a bug." The battle lines were drawn. Despite Turner's public bravado, he was unnerved by Murdoch's advance. "From CNN's earliest days, I was concerned that someone would come after us with a right-wing network," he later wrote in his memoir, *Call Me Ted*. "Now it was happening."

NBC was determined to beat ABC and Murdoch's News Corp into the market, but there was one thorny matter to resolve. Behind the choreographed rollout of its Microsoft partnership, the internal conflict around Ailes was never far from view. One reporter asked the executives how Ailes had reacted to America's Talking being replaced with MSNBC. "Roger's been involved in these discussions for some time," replied Microsoft executive Peter Neupert, convincing no one. Ailes, Neupert claimed, would "be actively involved in this as it goes forward."

*"Fuck them,"* Ailes said, pacing around his office as his assistant, Judy Laterza, and Brian Lewis looked on. "Fuck them."

Ever since his truce with Zaslav, Ailes continued to be unable to adapt himself to the constraints of his corporate environment. He persisted in offering political advice to his old Republican friends. "I remember Dan Quayle would call all the time," one A-T producer said. In December, Ailes's political ties burst into public view when *Vanity Fair* published a lengthy article on conservative magazine publisher Steve Forbes, who was mounting a 1996 presidential campaign and had turned to Ailes for informal media advice. When *The Washington Post* asked Ailes about it, he lashed out. "I'm a friend," he said. "It's like meeting a doctor at a cocktail party. If he asks me, 'What do I do if it hurts under my arm?' I give him an answer. . . . What I do in my private life is my business, period."

Ailes sought to put out other fires. On December 1, 1995, Ailes's divorce entered the public record. Ten days later, his friend Liz Smith put out word in her *Newsday* column that Ailes was officially a bachelor. "New York hostesses are forever searching for 'extra men' to fill out their tables. Ladies who aren't dead yet are forever saying that a good man is hard to find and there aren't enough to go around. Both types will be happy to hear that Roger Ailes is a free man—divorced from his wife of over a dozen years," Smith wrote. "Roger says he is looking for a fine woman who is not 'high maintenance.' (He is paying hefty alimony)."

Over the Christmas holiday, Ailes flew to his condo in Florida to strategize. During his stay, he drove over to Jack Welch's house in Palm Beach to talk about his future at NBC. Despite their friendship, Welch backed Wright's moves to give MSNBC to Lack, a decision he clearly understood might lead to Ailes's departure. "We both realized there were people who didn't want him there anymore," Welch remembered. "We talked a lot. This was a sad thing for both of us in a way." It was a decision Welch later regretted. "Losing Roger was tragic for the business," he said.

When Ailes returned, his lawyers and NBC drew up a separation agreement. On January 9, 1996, Ailes and Scanlon signed the extensive paperwork. NBC agreed to pay Ailes $1 million to walk away, as well as his $250,000 incentive compensation and $100,000 in lieu of his stock option benefits. They agreed to a mutual nondisparagement clause and to release an announcement no later than January 26 and "in principle . . . to have NBC say favorable things about Ailes and wish continued success and . . . to have Ailes say favorable things about CNBC, NBC, Bob Wright and Jack Welch and wish them continued success." The agreement barred Ailes from taking a job at CNN, Dow Jones, or Bloomberg while receiving his payout from NBC, but said nothing about Rupert Murdoch's News Corp—a detail that would have historic consequence.

A week later, dozens of CNBC and A-T staffers and producers packed a studio in Fort Lee for a surprise meeting. Speculation was rife that Ailes was departing. It was confirmed when Wright showed up in Fort Lee to introduce Ailes's replacement, Bill Bolster, the general manager of NBC's New York City affiliate, WNBC. To Ailes's backers, he was a rousing general and they feted him with a standing ovation when he emerged on stage. "Now look," he told them. "I told 'em you were well behaved. . . . I can't cover your asses anymore."

Bolster acted like a man walking into enemy territory. "When Roger came out here, I kind of felt like the guy who shot Bambi's mother," he told the audience.

Many of the producers in the room were understandably nervous. The loyalists in Ailes's camp at A-T and CNBC recognized that, with their patriarch and protector exiting, Tom Rogers and Zaslav would soon move to purge the ranks. "It's an awkward day for me," Wright said to the assembled crowd. "We obviously have a difficult situation with the transition of America's Talking to Microsoft-NBC. That's not a secret." He papered over the tumult of the preceding months. "Even in a business where people are getting along, sometimes you have problems, and decisions are made by one party or another, and you have to accommodate that," he said. What Wright did not say was that Zaslav's allegations of anti-Semitism played a role in Ailes's departure. "That was one reason," Wright later said. "The reality is that Roger left and David stayed."

Ailes's run at NBC would leave its mark on the company and on the careers of nearly everyone who found themselves on either side of the chasm. Tom Rogers left NBC in 1999 to become the CEO of the magazine publisher Primedia and later the CEO of TiVo. David Zaslav followed Rogers as president of NBC Cable and would remain at NBC until 2006, when he was named CEO of Discovery Communications, parent company of cable channels including Discovery Channel, Animal Planet, TLC, and later Oprah Winfrey's channel, OWN. In 2011, he earned $52 million, making him the country's second-highest-paid television executive.

In the weeks before his departure, Ailes tried to save Beth Tilson's job, but was unsuccessful. Tilson left the company. As for Ailes's next move after NBC, he was coy. Speculation was rampant in the press when news broke of his resignation. The New York *Daily News* reported on talk that Ailes was in discussions with GOP presidential hopefuls Bob Dole and Phil Gramm about the 1996 primary, chatter Ailes was quick to splash water on. "Not a chance," he told the paper. But the truth was that even as he was negotiating his exit, Ailes was already well on his way toward lining up his next leading role. Earlier that fall, having learned that Rupert Murdoch was gearing up to challenge CNN, Ailes called him. Murdoch's secretary told him that Murdoch was returning from a business trip and would see Ailes that very afternoon. After their meeting, Murdoch decided that Ailes was the one to get the job done.

# ELEVEN

# THE AUSSIE AND THE MIDWESTERNER

Less than two weeks after leaving NBC, Roger Ailes stood at a press conference alongside Rupert Murdoch in front of a crush of reporters and cameras at Murdoch's Midtown Manhattan headquarters and officially announced that News Corp would be the third entrant in the cable news sweepstakes. Ted Turner's cable news pioneer was struggling, having failed to find long-term solutions to its strategic programming challenges in the years after the 1991 Gulf War. The ongoing O. J. Simpson murder trial remained a boon to ratings. But the tabloid saga was a source of concern for CNN purists, who were frustrated that major international headlines—the downing of American Black Hawk helicopters in Somalia, genocide in Rwanda, and ethnic strife in the Balkans—failed to entice viewers. In a break from Turner's starless anchor philosophy, CNN president Tom Johnson tried several times in the mid-1990s to infuse the network with broadcast news glamour, extending feelers to Tom Brokaw, Dan Rather, and Peter Jennings. Each of them turned him down.

Murdoch certainly spotted a weakened prey. But the hunt was risky, involving huge capital outlays and intense competition to win slots with cable providers. News Corp had been exploring the possibility for the better part of a decade, with little success. But Murdoch, as always, was an optimist. "The appetite for news—particularly news that explains to people how it affects them—is expanding enormously," he told reporters at the press conference introducing Ailes. "We are moving very fast for our news channel to become a worldwide platform." The channel, Murdoch announced, would launch by the end of 1996 and be made available on cable and satellite, and its chairman and CEO would be Roger Ailes—a man of "entrepreneurial spirit." "We would expect that our running costs of Fox News, from doing magazine shows for the network to a full, 24-hour news service, will come in at less than one hundred million a year," Murdoch boasted.

When it was his turn to speak, Ailes expressed admiration for his new boss: "When everybody says you can't do it, you get up the next day and find that Rupert Murdoch has done it." Echoing Murdoch, he sketched a lofty vision for his news network even as he was self-consciously evasive about how he would pull it off. His first priority, he said, would be to "look at the resources, look at the dollars, look at the people, and try to figure out how to put it together in one dynamic news organization." It would appeal to the "younger demographic" of Fox stations. "We're not starting up a reactive news service in any way," he stressed.

Murdoch acknowledged his immediate challenge was finding room for the channel on the country's crowded cable dial. Nevertheless, he expressed confidence, hinting that if the cable systems didn't make room for it, he would retaliate by depriving them of his sports programming. "I don't think people will want to lose [NFL broadcasts]," he said in a not-so-veiled threat.

The channel was not only a business venture; though politics weren't mentioned in the press conference, the seeds of what Fox would become were present. Ailes said that it "would like to restore objectivity where we find it lacking." He hinted at the doublespeak that would so antagonize liberals in the years ahead. "I left politics a number of years ago," he said. In words that would hark back to TVN's hidden agenda, Ailes said: "We expect to do fine, balanced journalism."

Murdoch's grandiosity was of a kind he'd backed up many times before. By the time Roger Ailes arrived at News Corporation, Rupert Murdoch had become, on the eve of his sixty-fifth birthday, the most powerful media mogul of the century. From a single Australian afternoon tabloid of modest circulation, which he had inherited at age twenty-one, Murdoch built a publishing and entertainment company with revenues of $9 billion, controlling the distribution of newspapers, books, movies, and television programming consumed on six continents. He had owned at one time or another more than two dozen magazines and more than one hundred newspapers, from the *Daily Mirror* in Sydney to the *News of the World*, *Sun*, and the London *Times* in Britain, to the *New York Post*, *Boston Herald*, and *Chicago Sun-Times* in the United States. He owned and operated a dozen American television stations and held the exclusive rights to televise some of the most lucrative sports franchises in the world.

HarperCollins, the publishing house, and Zondervan, a large publisher of religious books, belonged to him. Among his holdings in Hollywood, he counted the 20th Century Fox Film Corporation and the Fox Broadcasting Company. Investing early in satellite television, Murdoch had amassed a 40 percent stake in the British Sky Broadcasting Group, a 50 percent share of VOX in Germany, and full ownership of Star TV in Hong Kong, his outpost at the doorstep of China's vast media frontier. What Murdoch had created at News Corp was not merely a company but a kingdom—a virtual state unto itself.

Where he reigned, Murdoch could seem more influential than the politicians who populated the pages of his papers, using his media as a weapon to promote allies and to punish enemies. In Britain, he had provided crucial backing to Margaret Thatcher; in Australia, he'd cashiered a prime minister, Gough Whitlam—whom he'd helped to elect only three years earlier. And in New York, he'd used the *New York Post* to help elect Mayor Ed Koch.

Outside New York, however, Murdoch was confronting the limits of his power in the United States. The three American newspapers of national influence—*The New York Times, The Washington Post,* and *The Wall Street Journal*—were, frustratingly, beyond his reach. The dynastic families who owned them had no interest in selling. Despite Murdoch's ambitions, his American papers were never going to elect a president. "If you are an arch-conservative, fighting a world of left-wing journalists, particularly in this country," said a News Corp executive at the time, "wouldn't you want to have another influence, another say?"

In America, television made presidents. With its deeply ingrained car culture and suburban sprawl, America lacked the concentrated newspaper readership that existed in Britain. Television, as Joe Coors and other conservatives had discovered, was the medium that reached the masses. In the spring of 1985, Murdoch made a deal to purchase the largest existing collection of independent broadcast stations from Metromedia for about $1.4 billion. The investment gave Murdoch control of seven television stations in America's biggest markets, which he planned to string together to form the country's fourth broadcast network. But for the deal to be approved by regulators, he would have to give up his Australian citizenship and become an American. In fact, for Murdoch, the more painful consequence of the television transaction may have been the forced sale of his charmed *New York Post,* which he sold in 1988, due to regulations that prevented a single owner from controlling both a newspaper and television station in a given market. (When the regulations were lifted a few years later, he bought it back.)

Having muscled onto the American airwaves, Murdoch set about building the Fox Broadcasting Company into a juggernaut. Industry executives dismissed his early effort. NBC Entertainment president Brandon Tartikoff once sniffed that Murdoch ran "the coathanger network" because of the number of second-tier stations he owned. Within five years, however, the network was profitable, fueled by surprise entertainment hits like *Married . . . with Children* and *The Simpsons*. But they lacked news coverage, the crucial lever Murdoch pulled to gain political influence. A year before launching the Fox broadcast network, Murdoch lobbied Ted Turner to sell him CNN, but Turner rebuffed his overture. In 1992, Murdoch began hiring an army of men and women to build a television news division. They waged battles on many fronts. Some worked on a newsfeed service, not unlike TVN, for Fox's local affiliates. Some developed programming proposals. One idea was a Sunday public affairs show in the style of *Meet the Press*. Another was a *60 Minutes*–style prime-time newsmagazine. Others discussed the feasibility of a cable news channel to take on CNN. In 1994, Murdoch secured distribution by acquiring a 20 percent stake of New World Communications, the media company controlled by financier Ronald Perelman. The deal made News Corp the country's biggest operator of local television stations. What Murdoch lacked by 1995 was a visionary collaborator, someone who could bring logic and order to his acquisitions. Ailes had spent the past three decades preparing for the role.

Though separated by class and culture, Ailes and Murdoch were men of the same mind. The self-appointed elites of journalism elicited their unbridled disgust. Watergate particularly stung, and Murdoch spoke of it in Ailesian terms, long before the two met. "The American press might get their pleasure in successfully crucifying Nixon," Murdoch told a friend, "but the last laugh could be on them. See how they like it when the Commies take over the West."

As Murdoch came of age, he, like Ailes, developed an antiauthoritarian streak. He cast off his father's conservative politics, adopting the self-conscious pose of a leftist—a limousine liberal before the term was coined. When he shipped off to Oxford, "Red Rupert" proudly displayed a bust of Lenin on a mantel in his room. Though uninspired in the classroom, Murdoch was a student of power. When he was nineteen, he accompanied his father, Sir Keith, a lauded war correspondent and newspaper executive, to the White House to meet Harry Truman. On the same trip abroad, he met *New York Times* publisher Arthur Hays Sulzberger at Hillandale, his family's estate in Connecticut. John F. Kennedy would later grant him a private audience. The printed word was Murdoch's gateway to power. In a world that was increasingly controlled by television, Ailes was the ideal partner.

As adults, Ailes and Murdoch let their work consume them, a habit that would weigh on their families. Both would marry three times. They showed little interest in hobbies or sports. But when they did play, they competed fiercely. Ailes jumped out of airplanes, endured bruises during office games; Murdoch, though modest in skill, "played his heart out" against his executives on the tennis court at Cavan, his forty-thousand-acre estate in the Australian countryside. On the ski slopes, he was "clumsy" but "had an obsession with finding the most difficult route down a slope," recalled Andrew Neil, the British journalist who edited Murdoch's London *Sunday Times* from 1983 to 1994.

Their desire to win drove their aggressive and at times ruthless approach to business. Ailes ran campaigns that others could not stomach. Murdoch did not ask for permission to buy things and blithely broke sacred promises. Their risk taking, at times, brought on near-career-ending disasters. Murdoch's brush with bankruptcy following a debt crisis in the early 1990s was as dire as the train wrecks in Ailes's career. But both men always managed to walk away.

The strongest bond between them was politics—the Australian's abiding passion. "Murdoch loved to be part of the political game. He couldn't help himself," John Menadue, a former general manager of Murdoch's Sydney papers, wrote in his memoir, *Things You Learn Along the Way*. Murdoch's ideology was reflexively more anti-establishment than Ailes's politics when the two met. Murdoch, for one, loathed Ailes's hero, George H. W. Bush. In 1988, Murdoch's preferred Republican was the televangelist Pat Robertson. "You can say what you like," Murdoch told Andrew Neil at the time, "he's right on all the issues." Four years later, Murdoch voted for billionaire third-party presidential candidate Ross Perot. On a deeper level, however, Murdoch and Ailes shared a more primitive ideology: *winning*. Which is why Murdoch could easily back a liberal like the Australian Gough Whitlam and a union buster like Margaret Thatcher; and Ailes could transform a country-club Republican like George Bush into a heartland populist.

As much as anything, the bond between Ailes and Murdoch was

sealed by the benefits each brought the other. Murdoch provided Ailes with a chance to rise from the tumult of NBC. Ailes could help Murdoch recover from something of a mid-career malaise. After Murdoch bought the 20th Century Fox film studio in 1985, he purchased a Tuscan-style mansion in Beverly Hills, and his wife, Anna, quickly adapted to the Los Angeles lifestyle. But Murdoch was miserable living on the West Coast. Rupert despised everything about Hollywood, except the profits. When one of his newspaper editors called to tell him about a great story, Murdoch seemed despondent. "They wouldn't recognize one in L.A. if it came round the corner and hit them," he said. Ten years later, and four years removed from News Corp's near bankruptcy, Murdoch was carrying himself like a man at the outset of his career. Teaming up with a fellow warrior like Ailes was thrilling, and provided an excuse to spend more time in New York, "the capital of the world," he called it.

Together, Murdoch and Ailes were embarking on a holy mission to lay waste to smug journalistic standards. "We will be the insurgents in a business of very strong incumbents," Murdoch said shortly after hiring Ailes. He spoke of "a growing disconnect between television news and its audience," and "an increasing gap between the values of those that deliver the news and those that receive it."

The grand plans of Ailes and Murdoch were not received in the spirit with which they were delivered. Never mind the politics—almost no one besides the two principals thought the channel made sense as a business. Critics savaged its programming (having not seen a minute of it). The most critical review, which noted "widespread doubts" about the channel's "long-term survival," appeared on the front page of *The New York Times*. Veteran television reporter Bill Carter cited anonymous "insiders" who scoffed at the unnamed twenty-four-hour news channel. A former Fox News executive told him, "there is no *there* there." Carter's own words were the harshest: "The idea, some suggested, was to give Mr. Ailes a toy to play with, though, given the current state of Fox News as described by some insiders, it may be less a toy than an imaginary friend." It was a devastating assessment from an authoritative voice. In the television industry, Carter was more than a news reporter. He was an information broker, whose articles, like Nielsen ratings, could make or break careers.

After reading the *Times* article, Bob Wright, Ailes's former boss, expressed relief. The next day he told NBC employees on an internal videoconference that he doubted Ailes's new job would amount to much, pointing to Murdoch's track record at Fox. "They have yet to air a program, as far as I know, in ten years," Wright told his team. "They don't have affiliates with news. They don't have any structure at all, nationally or internationally, really. . . . So it's a real reach." And it was true. Murdoch's talk was sometimes cheap. Where was his Sunday morning public affairs program? Where was the 11:00 p.m. newscast? Both had been announced, but had yet to come into being. *A Current Affair,* which debuted in 1986, was tabloid, and his attempts at creating a serious newsmagazine had failed.

In March 1995, Murdoch recruited CBS News executive Joe Peyronnin, who had overseen *48 Hours* and *60 Minutes,* to try building up Fox's hard news capabilities. Murdoch told Peyronnin he wanted what he called "proper news." Peyronnin hired a stable of broadcast news producers and correspondents and placed Emily Rooney, daughter of legendary CBS newsman Andy Rooney, in charge of covering national political campaigns for Fox affiliates. In the fall of 1995, Peyronnin hired *Today* show producer Marty Ryan to executive-produce a weekly public affairs show called *Fox News Sunday*. Murdoch was personally involved. His ideal host for a morning or prime-time news show was Brit Hume, the conservative ABC News White House correspondent. Murdoch and Hume talked, but Hume didn't want to leave his comfortable perch at ABC until his contract came up for renewal. When Peyronnin suggested *60 Minutes* correspondent Ed Bradley, Murdoch replied, "I hear he's lazy." NPR analyst Mara Liasson was rejected as well. (Liasson would join Fox News in 1997.) Eventually, Peyronnin hired a conservative, the affable former George H. W. Bush speechwriter Tony Snow, who was a regular fill-in for Rush Limbaugh's radio show.

Peyronnin fared no better than earlier Fox television news executives. In particular, Peyronnin and his team battled Mitchell Stern, the Fox Television Stations president, who was in charge of the News Corp–owned broadcast stations, to get network evening news coverage on the air. "Mitch Stern was the enemy of our group," Rooney recalled. "He was negative. He was a big bully." Stern, whose performance was judged by the local stations' profitability, was reluctant to make programming changes at a time when they were minting money. In the mid-1990s, Fox had developed a successful strategy of positioning itself as a broadcast network for younger viewers, which was especially appealing to advertisers. Executives worried that news programming would skew the audience older.

In the fall of 1995, Murdoch abandoned his piecemeal approach. Several executives were assigned to work in secret on a business plan for a twenty-four-hour network. In December, they presented Murdoch with a seventeen-page confidential memo. The highly detailed plan, which included line items for prime-time hosts ($500,000 a year) and studio decorations ($75 a week for flowers), contained three options. A basic newsfeed for Fox affiliates was projected to cost $60 million per year. A headline news service that was "wall-to-wall (similar to CNN/Headline News)" would require an annual investment of $147 million. And a full-service cable news network would cost an estimated $182 million total, a significantly higher figure than the one Murdoch would announce at the press conference in January. The Fox News Channel, according to their financial analysis, had to differentiate itself to win. They rightly stated that CNN's founding maxim, "The news is the star," and its workaday presentation of headlines had grown stale. CNN, on the one hand, was "breaking news driven, processed event coverage, big story dependent . . . reactive and slow and predictable." On the other hand, "FNC" must be about "personality and programming, produced information, appointment TV, news plus human interaction," that was both "convenient and interesting" with "attitude." In other words, Fox News should be conceived as "news talk-radio with video." According to their analysis, the cable news channel would require a long-term financial commitment. They anticipated losses that could reach $785 million within a decade. To reduce risk, they recommended exploring a possible joint venture with CBS News, which was seeking to compete against the cable news efforts of NBC and ABC. The memo acknowledged the obvious business challenges of such a partnership: "long-term day-to-day control of the venture, CBS ability and willingness to fund sustained early-year losses . . . availability of CBS talent to channel and at what price . . . and union issues." After some discussions between News Corp and CBS executives, the partnership never happened, and Murdoch pressed ahead alone.

Having developed a plan, Murdoch looked for someone to put it into motion. "I've been trying to get a news channel started," Murdoch told Ailes. "I've had a bunch of guys try."

One of the thorniest challenges would be securing distribution. In those days, cable was analog and as such, had limited space. Digital signals were on the verge of making a world of five hundred niche channels and on-demand entertainment possible. But until then, the operators had tremendous leverage and tended to favor ABC, NBC and CBS. In the early 1990s, legislation mandated that cable operators had to compensate broadcast networks for "retransmitting" their programming. Some paid cash, others reserved space on their cable systems for the Big Three to create their own cable channels. In this way, NBC struck a deal with cable operators to make room for America's Talking, and ABC negotiated space for ESPN2. With such competition, Ailes faced a nightmare scenario of musical chair negotiations in which his upstart network, with the weakest track record in news, could be left standing. In the 1970s, TVN was hobbled by broadcast stations' unwillingness to sign up for the expensive newsfeed. At America's Talking, limited distribution hamstrung Ailes's ability to attract an audience (the talk channel was only available in about twenty million homes when it was shut down, while CNN was available in 67 million at the time). "Distribution is the name of the game," Ailes said. Murdoch agreed. "If you look at successive larger battles he's waged against the unions or the BBC," a Murdoch family intimate said, "the battles tend to focus on controlling distribution."

Rumors circulated inside News Corp that Peyronnin's days were numbered. By hiring Ailes and installing him as Peyronnin's boss, Murdoch had broken Peyronnin's contract. But Peyronnin agreed to have lunch with Ailes to see if a working relationship could be forged. Ailes took Peyronnin out to the Manhattan Ocean Club a few blocks north of News Corp headquarters. Peyronnin told him about his struggles to get news on the air and warned him that rival News Corp executives like Mitch Stern were bent on blocking him. Peyronnin explained that Ailes would have to move quickly and be aggressive. Ailes tried to persuade him to stay on. "I need you," Ailes told him. "I don't know anything about news."

But as the conversation progressed, Peyronnin became convinced that Ailes was not someone he could work for. "Why are you a liberal?" Ailes snapped at one point. At another moment, he attacked CBS, Peyronnin's previous employer, as the "Communist Broadcasting System." Ailes told Peyronnin that he was going to create "an alternative news channel."

Peyronnin went home that night and told his wife he was going to resign. "This guy thinks I'm a liberal. He's a godawful person and I get paid no matter what, so I'd like to leave," he told her. Peyronnin asked his agent, Washington lawyer Bob Barnett, to negotiate an exit deal with

News Corp. Ailes soon moved into Peyronnin's corner office on the second floor, where he would remain.

The logistical and technical issues involved in building the channel were far more complex and difficult than those Ailes had had at America's Talking. In his previous endeavor, he benefited from the talent pool and existing studio infrastructure of NBC. This time around, he was on his own. "We had no news gathering operation," Ailes recalled in 2004. "We had no studios, no equipment, no employees, no stars, no talent and no confidence from anybody." They also had no time. MSNBC was set to debut in July 1996, less than six months from the time he joined News Corp. ABC's cable news channel was also moving forward. Ailes told Murdoch that they had to launch alongside their rivals or risk getting left behind. Though MSNBC would be first, News Corp would not be last—Ailes still had a chance to beat ABC.

But before launching an entire channel, Ailes needed to prove he could launch a single show. Given Murdoch's checkered history in TV news, Ailes had to demonstrate he could succeed where his predecessors failed. He immediately put in motion Peyronnin's plan to launch *Fox News Sunday,* the weekly public affairs show for Fox affiliate stations, which had stalled in development. It was not merely a matter of public relations—a move to prove the critics, especially Bill Carter, wrong—but one of business survival. The annual convention of the National Cable Television Association, NCTA '96, was less than three months away. It was a place where channel executives pitched cable operators on new programming. NBC and ABC had gilded news brands and famous anchors to make their case. Ailes would need something to show for himself.

In starting with *Fox News Sunday,* Ailes chose the worlds he understood best: politics and daytime television. Sketching out the show, he experimented with formats and personalities that would fuse news and politics into an entertaining mix. He considered as potential hosts former Democratic New York governor Mario Cuomo, former Republican congressman Jack Kemp, and *Weekly Standard* founder William Kristol. In the end, Ailes settled on Peyronnin's choice of Tony Snow, with whom Ailes had crossed paths in 1992, when Ailes and Peggy Noonan were brought into the White House to rewrite Snow's first draft of the State of the Union address. On April 3, Ailes announced that *Fox News Sunday* would debut on Fox affiliate stations on the morning of April 28. Notably, it was the same day that the cable convention began. "We hope to attract the traditional Sunday morning news viewer," Ailes said, "but at the same time, we want to appeal to a more diverse and younger audience who are not currently regular viewers."

The announcement did not lead to a smooth corporate rollout. On April 4, *Daily Variety* reported that Fox affiliates were "caught off-guard" by the "sudden" announcement. "The last-minute nature of the show was not taken well by many affiliates," one source told the trade magazine. Until the Telecommunications Act of 1996 went into effect in February of that year, media companies could not own more than a dozen stations. *Daily Variety* reported that the Fox-owned stations—twelve out of the network's nearly two hundred affiliates—were going to carry the news show, and thus it would reach roughly a quarter of the country. In effect, getting *Fox News Sunday* on the air would be the first test of Ailes's corporate power.

In the weeks leading up to the launch, Ailes was on a war footing, convinced his rivals were out to damage him and the show. He announced the debut, in part, to force the hand of Mitch Stern, the News Corp television executive who had blocked Peyronnin's previous efforts at news programming. "Roger is acutely aware how the rest of the company views him. He calls News Corp a pirate ship, where everyone tries to stab everyone else," a former senior Fox executive said.

As Stern remembered it, the conflict over *Fox News Sunday* had more to do with Ailes's personal style than underlying business disagreements. "Roger isn't the easiest guy to get along with. He sees enemies in a lot of places," Stern reflected. "If he thought he had to win a big battle over *Fox News Sunday,* maybe that got him all nutty."

Though Tony Snow leaned to the right—in addition to his time in the first Bush White House, he had been an editor at the conservative *Washington Times*—*Fox News Sunday* resembled on the morning of its debut a conventional network news broadcast. Live from the Decatur House, a neoclassical mansion steps from the White House, Snow tackled a mix of foreign affairs and domestic politics with senators and congressmen. Worried that other networks would pressure politicians not to appear on *Fox News Sunday,* Ailes did not advertise the guest list in advance. Only a quarter of Fox's affiliates agreed to broadcast the program. Very few people watched, but John Carmody, *The Washington Post*'s influential television writer, tuned in. In a tough write-up, he graded the debut a "C-plus (well, maybe a B-minus)." He called the opening graphic "unexciting" and noted that correspondent Jed Duvall was caught on camera "scratching himself."

Despite the uneven launch, *Fox News Sunday* fulfilled Murdoch's stifled ambitions to break into the television news business and secured for Ailes a tangible victory at a crucial moment as he faced off against his chief adversary at NBC. Two weeks before the cable convention, NBC promoted David Zaslav to president of cable distribution, putting him in charge of the effort to sell MSNBC to cable operators. The feud between Ailes and Zaslav, which had started as an office rivalry, was metastasizing into a corporate clash between News Corp and NBC.

In Los Angeles, as 26,000 cable industry executives circulated through the sprawling convention hall, Ailes and Zaslav shadowed each other. The two men shuttled to meetings, making their pitches and talking to reporters. Zaslav was confident a majority of the cable operators that carried America's Talking would take MSNBC. He bragged to *The Seattle Times* that he had had a productive meeting that morning with executives from Tele-Communications, Inc., the country's largest cable operator with its fourteen million subscribers. "We've begun a dialogue," Zaslav said. His comment was a shot across Ailes's bow. Murdoch was already courting TCI's conservative co-owner John Malone, the Denver, Colorado–based media investor. Malone held stakes not only in TCI, but in nearly a hundred companies—from Turner Broadcasting and Court TV to Black Entertainment Television and MacNeil/Lehrer Productions.

As the incumbent, NBC seemed to be taunting Ailes. "We are the only players doing this that are credible," Tom Rogers told the press. Andy Lack announced that *Today* show anchors Bryant Gumbel and Katie Couric would be regular hosts on MSNBC. He also trotted out NBC News stars to woo cable operators. Tom Brokaw anchored the *Nightly News* from NBC's Burbank studios so he could be on hand at the convention. "We're here persuading the cable people that [MSNBC] is the place to be," Brokaw told a reporter. At the MSNBC booth, computer monitors displayed prototypes of the MSNBC website. Microsoft brought techno-wizardry to the marketing push.

Unlike MSNBC, Ailes had very little to actually show the industry. He was secretive about Fox News's plans and combative in his dealings with cable operators. "I went into their booth, they weren't communicative about what kind of programming they were going to have," recalled Richard Aurelio, the former president of Time Warner Cable's New York City Group. With Fred Dressler, the executive vice president of programming at Time Warner Cable, Ailes was even more hostile. When Dressler asked Ailes about his plans for Fox News, he replied, "I'm not going to tell you. It's a news channel, that's all you need to know."

The truth was Ailes was not in Los Angeles to sell programming. By all appearances, he was there to make it clear that Fox News would not play the role of supplicant in the negotiations. "There's a ritual dance with cable operators," Ailes recalled. "They don't want you, they don't want your service, they don't want your phone call." He would later recall that getting onto the cable dial required a kind of forced entry, like "breaking into Fort Knox." To pry open the door, cash was a powerful crowbar. Inside the Los Angeles Convention Center, word circulated that News Corp would pay cable companies millions to carry Fox News. In the conventional arrangement, cable operators were the ones who paid channel owners. In 1996, for instance, cable operators paid CNN roughly 25 cents per subscriber. Murdoch flipped the equation: he was prepared to pay cable operators a stunning $10 per subscriber. For a large cable system, agreeing to carry Fox News would be worth upward of $100 million. Chase Carey, a Harvard MBA who was chairman of Fox Television, had devised the risky plan to reverse cable television economics. "We had to put something on the table to grab the attention of the cable operators," Carey said. As one former Ailes colleague put it, "we had Rupert's checkbook and balls."

It worked. Murdoch's preemptive strike spooked the industry. Less than a month after the convention, ABC's parent company, the Walt Disney Company, pulled the plug on the ABC cable news channel. "It became more and more apparent as we looked at the numbers that there was no light at the end of the tunnel," Roone Arledge, the president of ABC News, told Bill Carter. He did not hesitate to blame Murdoch in the pages of the *Times*. "We couldn't believe that offer of $10 a subscriber," he said. "It's the same thing he did in escalating the costs of football rights and station values."

Ailes gloated. "Now we'll be getting résumés from ABC as well as NBC," he boasted to *USA Today*. Dozens of CNBC and A-T executives, producers, and anchors had already joined Ailes at Fox News. Judy Laterza, his seasoned assistant, was there. So was his *Mike Douglas* mentor, Chet Collier. Ailes Communications staffers, including Kathy Ardleigh and Scott Ehrlich, who had followed him to CNBC, followed him to News Corp. CNBC pressman Brian Lewis became his spokesperson. In December, he'd completed a master's thesis in communications at Fairleigh

Dickinson University that had been inspired by Ailes. ("The News Media: The Modern Day Electoral College," he titled it.) CNBC CFO Jack Abernethy left to do the same job for the new cable channel. CNBC ad man Paul Rittenberg became head of Fox's advertising sales. And, after peppering Ailes with requests to join the new network, Steve Doocy got a job as a weatherman and "man on the street." In all, eighty-two former A-T and CNBC staffers would decamp to News Corp. That spring, NBC CEO Bob Wright called Ailes to complain about the staff defections. The conversation was brief.

"You've been poaching my people," Wright said.

"It isn't poaching; *it's a jailbreak*!" Ailes roared.

In the press, Zaslav continued to provoke Ailes. "Our view is we wish Rupert luck," he told *The Hollywood Reporter* in a story published on May 7. "We don't see his service as a competitor. . . . We're launching with a real news and information service. We already have deals for distribution with the top 100 multiple system operators." A few weeks later, Ailes struck back. On Friday, May 31, Justin Manus, an attorney representing Ailes, sent a letter to Ed Scanlon threatening legal action. In it, Ailes accused Zaslav of dirty tricks that were designed to damage Ailes's ability to sell Fox News to the cable industry. "It has come to our attention that David Zaslav of NBC has been showing Cable Operators a carefully edited video of the start-up problems of the A-T Network, and telling them that these problems were created by Roger Ailes." Several days later, NBC's general counsel, Rick Cotton, fired back in a letter, denying any wrongdoing.

While Ailes and NBC traded legal letters, the war was shifting to a strategic piece of terrain, as News Corp and NBC sought to win over Time Warner Cable, the most important cable distributor in the country. The system reached 11.5 million domestic cable viewers, but, more important, it was the gateway to Manhattan, the media capital of the world, inhabited by the Madison Avenue advertisers who controlled the flow of billions of marketing dollars. Time Warner Cable had a monopoly on New York City's one million cable subscribers. Adding complexity to the negotiations, because Time Warner had merged with CNN's parent company, Turner Broadcasting, in 1995, it was against the company's interest to introduce into their market a competitor to CNN.

In early June, Murdoch and Chase Carey lunched with Time Warner CEO Jerry Levin and Time Warner president Richard Parsons in Murdoch's private dining room. Murdoch and Carey explained that because

Manhattan was so important for Fox News's launch, News Corp would pay handsomely for access. Murdoch was offering Time Warner $125 million—more than $10 per subscriber—to carry Fox News. Levin and Parsons were noncommittal. After the lunch, Murdoch followed up with a confidential two-page letter to Levin. Murdoch portrayed Ailes's channel in lofty terms. It was a sales pitch that clearly oversold the middlebrow product Ailes was actually planning to roll out. Fox, Murdoch promised Levin, would be a "high quality" news channel "designed to provide more information to viewers than any current news on the air." Remarkably, Murdoch even promised Levin that Fox News would carry "more news than talk programming," a direct contradiction to the vision Ailes and Chet Collier had for the channel.

At the time Murdoch was pitching Levin on carrying Fox News, he was gaining an unlikely ally. Regulators at the Federal Trade Commission, reviewing the Time Warner–Turner deal, were coming to Murdoch's aid. FTC chairman Robert Pitofsky, an antitrust scholar at Georgetown University and a vocal opponent of media concentration, was planning to ask Time Warner to carry a competing cable news network, in exchange for agency approval of the deal. The move essentially guaranteed that either Fox News or MSNBC would find long-term space alongside CNN in the crucial New York market. Given the clash of conflicting agendas between NBC, News Corp, and Time Warner, the three-way negotiations were always going to be fraught. But no one could have predicted that the competition would become as nasty as any of Ailes's most contentious political campaigns.

Meanwhile, Murdoch notched a major victory that sparked fear in the executive suites at NBC. On the morning of June 24, News Corp sent out a press release announcing a distribution deal with John Malone. The two men were both allies and adversaries. Malone was the one media mogul Murdoch was said to fear. Politically, however, they were in sync. "There's a huge diversity of values in this country between what people in central Manhattan think of the values of our society and what people in Peoria think the values of our society are," Malone, a self-described libertarian, told *The New Yorker*. In agreeing to distribute Fox News, Malone extracted a steep price from Murdoch: News Corp agreed to pay a rumored $200 million in return for Malone's commitment to put Ailes's network in ten million homes by the time of its October launch. (Ailes denied that TCI was being paid $200 million, and a TCI spokesperson claimed that the so-called incentive payment was "nothing close" to that amount.) As part of the deal, Malone was given the option to buy a 20 percent stake in Fox News.

The concessions were simply the price of admission: no matter what happened with the Time Warner Cable talks, the Malone deal delivered enough subscribers to ensure that Ailes's network would achieve a viable audience when it debuted in the fall. As important, Malone guaranteed that he would offer Fox News to all of TCI's subscribers, but made no such commitment to MSNBC.

Murdoch's distribution coup put wind at Ailes's back and gave Murdoch confidence to double down on television. A few weeks after Murdoch inked the pact with Malone, he negotiated an even bigger transaction with Ronald Perelman to acquire the remaining 80 percent of his media company, New World Communications, for $2.5 billion. The deal increased News Corp's stable of corporate-owned stations from twelve to twenty-two, and ensured that Ailes would have access to the biggest chain of broadcast stations, in terms of ownership. But as Murdoch was finalizing the deal with Perelman, NBC tacked ahead on July 15, when MSNBC debuted to mixed but extensive reviews. The News Corp channel was still a chaotic mess. But Ailes always viewed long-shot odds and operational challenges as opportunities. At America's Talking, he used them as raw material to spin an inspiring David-and-Goliath narrative about his start-up. The contest retained, for Ailes, a deeply personal dimension. From his spacious second-floor corner office at News Corp, Ailes had a clear view of Sixth Avenue toward NBC's offices at Rockefeller Center, where David Zaslav, Tom Rogers, and Andy Lack were working against him on a channel that should have been his. It was a visual reminder that his war with NBC was far from over.

# TWELVE

# OCTOBER SURPRISE

In ways that only became apparent years later, MSNBC's debut on July 15, 1996, signified the moment when news on cable television forever changed. News was no longer just to be found in the day's headlines. It became ever more deeply embedded in the context of shared cultural and political ideas that made viewers feel welcome and safe, while widening the chasms that separated them from people who were not like them. From the very beginning, MSNBC spoke, very deliberately, to the coasts. MSNBC's specific concept was to re-create on camera the vibe of an espresso bar in downtown Seattle, the home of NBC's new corporate partner. "People are going to be on television, having coffee," Andy Lack told NBC anchor Brian Williams, courting him to the channel over dinner. Exposed faux redbrick walls and industrial lighting transformed the America's Talking studio in Fort Lee, New Jersey, into a loftlike space where urbane twenty- and thirty-somethings chattered about the news of the day, like characters from *Friends* or *Seinfeld*. With so much casual banter, the message to the audience was that big-city life in MSNBC's America was easy and fun, where successful people had plenty of free time to chat, and the conversation flowed from one venti latte to the next. But MSNBC's urbane and cheerful family inevitably left a lot of America on the outside.

At 9:00 a.m., after a televised countdown clock ticked to zero, MSNBC went live for the first time. Following the headlines, anchor Jodi Applegate, who also anchored the *Today* show on weekends, talked with fellow NBC News correspondents whose faces appeared on a sleek video monitor suspended from the ceiling. Tom Brokaw, speaking from the

North Lawn of the White House, hyped *InterNight,* an interview program airing weeknights at 8:00 p.m. with Brokaw and other NBC veterans as hosts. That evening, viewers would enjoy, he said, "a very important appointment" with President Bill Clinton, who would answer questions that had been submitted to MSNBC's new website. Katie Couric and Matt Lauer chatted from 30 Rock about MSNBC's coverage of the 1996 Atlanta Olympics, set to open in five days. "I want you to know that Matt and I are extremely jealous, and we're gonna demand a cappuccino machine in our next contract," Couric said to Applegate. Jane Pauley, the anchor of *Time & Again,* a history program on at 7:00 p.m., promoted a documentary about the Apollo 11 moon mission. Brian Williams, host of the 9:00 p.m. newscast, sat in front of an oversized glass map of the world that was like a prop from NASA Mission Control. "It's been a dream around here . . . to have a full hour in prime time to present the news," he told Applegate. Last to appear on the video monitor was Soledad O'Brien, live from San Francisco, where she introduced her 10:00 p.m. technology show, *The Site.* "Hi, Jodi," O'Brien said. "Tell Katie and Matt if they want to borrow my cappuccino machine I'd love to have them borrow it if they ever come out to San Francisco."

On the day of the launch, Ailes himself fired a salvo, delineating the battle lines. "They're basing 98% of their promotion on five of their stars," he told the *Los Angeles Times.* Broadcast news glamour was liberal bias by another name. "MSNBC," he had told *USA Today* the previous month, "believes in giving face time to anchors. We believe in fact time for viewers." His point was that NBC was applying to cable news Manhattan-centric knowingness, but star power did not necessarily translate to the world of cable news.

As NBC took out half-page ads in *TV Guide,* featuring pictures of Brokaw, Gumbel, and Couric, Ailes was exploring the contours and mind-set of his new audience. That winter, Ailes assigned Scott Ehrlich to commission a poll on viewer attitudes about the news media. Ehrlich hired Democratic pollster John Gorman, who had worked on the presidential campaigns of George McGovern and Jimmy Carter. Gorman's results confirmed Ailes's instincts: more than half the country did not trust the news media. "It was a no-brainer," Ailes's brother, Robert, said. "When Roger was starting Fox, he saw that the needs of sixty percent of Americans weren't being filled by the existing media."

The point of view MSNBC was selling at its launch, though not overtly political, was elitist. Its sensibility was reinforced two days later, when MSNBC announced a deal to simulcast Don Imus's radio show, a favorite of the Northeast corridor chattering class.

On Thursday, July 18, Ailes stood in a ballroom at the Ritz-Carlton Huntington Hotel in Pasadena, California, parrying questions from journalists like a candidate before a crowd of voters at a rally. The assembled reporters received printouts of Gorman's poll results—essentially opposition research. Only 14 percent of Americans viewed the press favorably, compared to 31 percent with respect to the Supreme Court and 47 percent with respect to the military. Furthermore, 67 percent of Americans believed television news was biased.

Ailes's description of his own channel focused mostly on what it was not, keeping the heat on MSNBC while avoiding being boxed in. "We're not going to consider ourselves in the business of having to sell computers every five minutes," he said. "Nor will we have to be in the business to tell people to turn off their television set and go to their computer to get more information." Gone was the hype on display during his debut press conference with Murdoch, when they promised "a worldwide platform" for the channel. In Pasadena, Ailes practiced the communications art of lowering expectations. "We have not claimed we're going to be revolutionary," he said, knocking MSNBC. "I believe in underpromising and overdelivering."

But, subtly, he began to introduce the trope that would become Fox's hallmark. "If you couldn't give me two sides to a major issue I wouldn't hire you because I think you might have an agenda for one side," he said. "What I've said to my people in the newsroom is don't have any fear of anybody's ideas just because they are not your ideas."

If reporters were hoping for more than a few specifics, they were disappointed. There was a name: the Fox News Channel. There was a launch date: October 7. There was a schedule: live shows from 6:00 a.m. until 11:00 p.m. on weekdays and, on weekends, six hours of original content. Otherwise, Ailes refrained from filling in any details of his October surprise. "It's a very competitive climate, and we want to keep that under wraps," he said. Unlike MSNBC, which had announced a lineup three months before its launch, Ailes did not reveal a single on-camera hire. "There is no status with Rush Limbaugh," Ailes said, addressing hearsay that he might ink a deal with his friend to host a Fox News show.

From the beginning, politics was more than a subject to cover. It suffused everything at Fox News. "Roger is a political animal," a former senior Fox News producer said. "That plays into how he manages the place." Decision making flowed from the top. Secrecy was paramount. A binary win-lose ethic governed the office. The channel's debut was less than twelve weeks away, and things at campaign headquarters were getting chaotic.

The construction of studio space at News Corp's headquarters at 1211 Sixth Avenue was taking longer than expected and blowing through budgets. Fox leased space on the north end of the building's lobby that had previously housed a Sam Goody record store. The street-level studio was designed to attract tourists, like the *Today* show's Rockefeller Center plaza. But his team of thirty architects and engineers quickly realized that the space was unworkable. Subways rumbling underneath the building disrupted sensitive satellite signals and made sounds that were difficult to cancel out in the studio. They also were running out of room. The street-level space could only accommodate two studios. Bahman Samiian, who became a senior director, was forced to design a rotating riser that could turn ninety degrees in less than five minutes for speedy studio backdrop changes. "We had to do more than eight shows and had to ping-pong between the studios," a staffer recalled.

Ailes probed the allegiances of potential staff over the summer, ascertaining their ideology, ferreting out dissidents. His interview with Douglas Kennedy, his friend Bobby Jr.'s younger brother, was rocky. It was not merely his last name. The twenty-nine-year-old scion and former *New York Post* reporter was working for the enemy. MSNBC had recently hired him, but he was considering his options.

"I know your background, Ailes," Kennedy said.

"Well I know your background, too," Ailes returned. "I respect what your father stood for even if he had a political agenda different from mine."

Kennedy asked if Ailes would inject his conservative views into the news. "I have no mission, I have no intention of even looking at your stories," Ailes said. "But I want you to look me in the eye and tell me you'll make the effort to be fair on anything you cover." Kennedy met his gaze and said he would. He was hired.

Refusing to answer was worse than professing liberal ideas. In another interview, Ailes and Chet Collier questioned the background of Bob Reichblum, whom they were considering for the executive producer opening on the 7:00 p.m. newscast. "I'm looking at your résumé," Ailes said. It stated that Reichblum had been the executive producer of *Good Morning America*. "I see here you've worked at a network. And you're Jewish, so I assume you're liberal."

Reichblum winced. "Two of the three things must be true," he replied. "I'm not going to tell you which ones."

Ailes chuckled at the retort, but did not offer him a job.

While Ailes turned away refuseniks, he surrounded himself with committed lieutenants who were either conservative or didn't care. Two of the most important advisers at the channel were Chet Collier, his old boss from *Mike Douglas,* and John Moody, a right-leaning print journalist from *Time*. They were two men who in almost every respect could not have been more different. Collier was a Massachusetts liberal who had little interest in current affairs or politics. "Chet's idea of a show is two chairs and a plant," Bill Bolster, Ailes's successor at CNBC, liked to joke. Collier, then sixty-nine, envisioned Fox News as a smorgasbord of talk shows, television personalities, and animals, a personal programming favorite. In addition to working with Ailes, Collier served as president of the Westminster Kennel Club and helped transform the dog show into a national televised spectacle that could sell out Madison Square Garden. The trade journal *Dog News* called his contribution to dog shows "without comparison."

Throughout the spring and summer, Collier personally reviewed hundreds of tapes of potential hosts to present to Ailes. To gauge the appeal of possible anchors, Collier watched the screen with the sound off. "I'm not hiring talent for their brain power," he said to an executive. While news costs were strictly policed, Collier made sure the makeup department was a $1 million line item in the budget. "I didn't understand why makeup was a big deal," one skeptical producer said. "Chet would say, 'You have to get this *right*.' He just knew that those women in the makeup department were like psychologists—they had the talent in their hands." Like Ailes and the Nixon ad men, Collier was a devoted student of Marshall McLuhan. "Viewers don't want to *be* informed; they want to *feel* informed," Collier often told producers. "He hated anything to do with the news," a Fox News executive recalled.

Collier regularly rebuked Emily Rooney and her team of former network producers, condescendingly referring to them as "newsies." A constant presence at Ailes's side, Collier, as much as anyone, shaped the emerging talk show culture of the network. "Chet told me every section has to have a payoff," one Fox producer said, echoing *Mike Douglas* creator Woody Fraser's adage. "The segment needs to be produced."

John Moody, on the contrary, was a cerebral conservative journalist with a chip on his shoulder. He had spent a decade climbing the masthead at *Time* as a foreign correspondent in Eastern Europe, Latin America, and Rome. But Moody, a devout Catholic who had written a Cold War thriller in his spare time, had topped out as New York bureau chief, and aspired to a more significant position. In the establishment clubhouse of Time Inc., where baby boomer values prevailed, he stuck out. A "first-class journalist," and a "real pro," according to two former colleagues, Moody could be a dissenting voice at *Time*, willing to indicate his displeasure about basic assumptions they made. In 1992, Moody spoke up as editors were discussing a speech in which Vice President Dan Quayle critiqued *Murphy Brown*, the CBS sitcom. "There are a lot of people out there who don't think the way we do," he said, according to Janice Simpson, a former assistant managing editor at *Time*. "I wish we would take that into consideration."

It was an attitude Ailes shared. During a job interview in the spring of 1996, Ailes told Moody, "One of the problems we have to work on here together when we are this network is that most journalists are liberals . . . and we've got to fight that." Speaking with a reporter later that year, the men discussed the unflattering stories about Christianity often published in national newsmagazines at Eastertime. Moody called certain covers for *Time* and *Newsweek* "sacrilegious." Ailes agreed. "It's always a story that beats up on Jesus," Ailes said. "They call him a cult figure of his time, some kind of crazy fool, and it's as if they go out and try to find evidence to trash him." As they spoke, Moody found himself "finishing Roger's sentences."

As a television neophyte, Moody could provide journalistic ballast to Collier's talk show instincts without getting in the way too much. Ailes appointed Moody vice president for news, editorial. Moody freely confessed his ignorance in his new role. "When he first came in, Moody joked he didn't know broadcasting," a former senior producer said. Emily Rooney could not believe her eyes when Moody showed her a script he had worked on. "It was like an 8,000-word newspaper article," she recalled. Moody did not subscribe to Collier's news-as-entertainment creed. Like clashing campaign advisers with opposing visions for the candidate, they gave rise to competing camps within Fox News. "Collier hated Moody passionately," a former executive said. And Moody "hated" Collier's talk show concepts, a founding producer recalled.

In a certain respect, the animosity was useful to Ailes—it safeguarded his authority. Nixon, Ailes recalled, played his deputies off each other. Instead of conspiring against him, they went after each other. In meetings, Ailes spoke about the Nixon administration. "There were five guys in the inner circle. We all hated each other. And Nixon made sure we all hated each other," he told his executives. Though grossly inflating his importance to Nixon—he had never been in the inner circle—Ailes was an astute student. "He made sure his executives had to fight for his loyalty," a person close to Ailes said. "It was the most cutthroat place to be. You constantly had to renew your vow." These clashing viewpoints also helped restrain Ailes's right-wing impulses at the beginning. "So much of the success of Fox can be traced to the early years when Chet and John would push back," a senior executive said.

As announced, Murdoch invested some $100 million to launch Fox News. A stable of twenty news anchors had been hired, including former *Current Affair* correspondents Louis Aguirre, Jon Scott, and Shepard Smith. Associated Press White House correspondent Wendell Goler had been recruited to report from Washington. Camera crews in Europe, Hong Kong, Jerusalem, and Moscow would cover foreign news. In addition, the network had a deal with Reuters and would make use of raw footage from News Corp's Sky Television in Europe as well as the staffing resources of Murdoch-owned papers around the globe.

But the network was, at this embryonic stage, an unfocused hodgepodge. Ailes's anchors had little ideological or stylistic relation to each other. Neil Cavuto, late of CNBC, would lead with *The Cavuto Business Report,* a financial news wrap-up, at 5:00 p.m. Bill O'Reilly, a network correspondent turned tabloid anchor, would host *The O'Reilly Report,* an interview show, at 6:00. Traditional news anchors would hold court the following two hours. Mike Schneider, a former NBC weekend *Today* co-anchor, would present *The Schneider Report,* Fox's 7:00 p.m. newscast. Catherine Crier, a former Dallas County prosecutor and Texas state judge turned television journalist, would interview newsmakers on *The Crier Report,* at 8:00, the channel's answer to CNN's *Larry King Live* and MSNBC's *InterNight*. Rounding out the weeknight schedule, Sean Hannity, an Atlanta-based conservative talk radio host, would host a *Crossfire*-style debate show at 9:00 provisionally titled *Hannity and LTBD*—in other words, a "Liberal to Be Determined." Ailes had not yet decided on a suitable sparring partner, but was in talks with three candidates, including the political writer Joe Conason, who was then executive editor of *The New York Observer*. He was also considering casting different liberals every week. The weeknight slate would include two newsbreaks of at least five minutes every hour. Starting at 10:00 p.m., the prime-time lineup, excluding Mike Schneider's newscast, would reair, interspersed by live newscasts. Weekend coverage would include a handful of original shows, curated reruns from the previous week, and *Fox News Now* updates every half hour.

It was, to be sure, a ragtag lineup, comprised of overlooked, over-the-hill, and passed-over personalities. Hannity had never held a full-time job in television. O'Reilly had flamed out of more jobs than people could remember. "He had been in the business twenty-five years, and he was never a star," Ailes later recalled. Cavuto, the most visible of the bunch, was hardly a face on which to build a network, despite being a mature interviewer and having anchored CNBC's popular program *Market Wrap*. Schneider, probably the biggest name, joked around the studio that they were using his name to convince cable operators to carry the channel.

Perhaps that was how Ailes wanted it. At a press conference in September 1996, Ailes criticized the famous correspondents of rival networks for being more into "hair spray" than fact finding. He claimed he could have landed big names, but considered it a waste of money. "There isn't a shred of evidence to suggest that star power has the kind of draw in cable that it does in broadcast news," he told one reporter a few weeks later. "If we weren't paying $10 per subscriber, we could have spent plenty on hiring talent." Established talent were difficult and could claim credit for their success. As Ailes once said, "most television people are idiots." Ailes valued authenticity over talent. He knew viewers made snap judgments about likability in the first seven seconds. Plus, besides relating to the audience, newcomers and rehabilitated personalities were more likely to be loyal. From his earliest days with Mike Douglas and Nixon, Ailes excelled when he created his own talent, molding and shaping them in his image. "If I have any ability," he later remarked, "it's probably to find talented people and set up a structure that they can work in."

With the rank and file in the newsroom, Ailes recruited men and women who preferably lacked news experience. "None of us were news people," one founding producer said. "We were entertainment people. I can't tell you how many people were on Xanax, trying to adapt." Those with more experience included young producers such as Sharri Berg of *A*

*Current Affair,* Janet Alshouse of News 12 Long Island, and Bill Shine, who had recently jumped from the PBS affiliate WLIW to NewsTalk Television, an early cable channel. Ailes especially favored young people, often irrespective of ideology. "I was not a fan of the right wing at all," Jordan Kurzweil recalled. Fox News hired him in the summer of 1996 to launch the network's website. "We need $5 million," Kurzweil told Ailes in a meeting in his office. It was a small figure relative to Fox's competition. "I don't know much about this web stuff, but it sounds fine. Go do it," Ailes replied. Thrilled by the responsibility he was given, Kurzweil poured all his energy into the website. "This was not the A-team. It really did look like kids were going out to the garage to put on a show," a Fox News producer, who was present for launch, recalled. Catherine Crier agreed. "All these kids were running the shop," she said. "It was hysterical."

Meanwhile, Ailes began to sideline executives and producers who had arrived before him. The tribalism he fostered at CNBC became just as fierce at Fox News. After triggering Joe Peyronnin's resignation in February 1996, Ailes targeted his rump core of loyalists. "We became the enemy of the news channel," Emily Rooney said. "For one, we were making a lot of money. I was making at least $250,000." In the second-floor executive suite, stark divisions emerged between the old regime and the new. "It became very clear, it was Roger's guys, and everyone else," one producer recalled. "Joe had an open-door policy," remembered Jay Ringelstein, a production accountant for Fox News at the time. "Roger went in with an idea, so no one's ideas were welcome or needed, unless they were solicited."

At CNBC, Ailes's ruthlessness had become a liability. At News Corp, with its piratical office culture, it turned out to be an asset. Long before the world would learn about News Corp's practice of phone hacking, Murdoch was encouraging his executives to push boundaries, and to carve out their terrain and defend it, ignoring reputational concerns that normally bred caution. "At most organizations, there's a lot of low-level people who want to take risks," a former News Corp executive explained. "The further up it gets, more people say, 'No, we can't do that.' News Corp is the opposite. People at the top are like, 'What are you doing? Go out there and start something.' "

As long as they produced profits or news scoops, Murdoch tolerated, even appreciated, volcanic personalities. Once at a News Corp seminar, Murdoch's Australian chairman Richard Searby described the company's management style as "one of extreme devolution punctuated by periods of episodic autocracy. Most company boards meet to make decisions. Ours meets to ratify yours." (Murdoch was in the audience.)

Ailes's legendary temper and gyrating moods made him stand out, even by News Corp standards. He said things that other executives just did not say. But Murdoch's company was proving to be the place where, finally, Ailes could be Ailes. The corporate Darwinism Murdoch fostered was in practice no different from the brutal environment of a political campaign. Campaigns did not have HR departments to police office behavior or middle managers to appease. Come Election Day, all that mattered was results. "If you're good, you get to live. If you're bad, you don't," Ailes explained to a reporter not long after he joined News Corp. "It's somewhat primitive, but that's the way life is. In a capitalistic society, success is determined by whether you can pay the bills."

At a September 4 news conference, just five weeks before the network's launch, Ailes introduced Fox's famous slogan "fair and balanced." All stories, Ailes insisted, would be "told in context" and everyone appearing on his network would be given a "fair shot." He proclaimed that "it's important to be first, but even more important to be fair." It was a play off an old slogan he had once developed for a hypothetical local news channel: "We may not always be first. But we will always be fair." He vowed Fox would "unblur" the "lines between opinion and news." Graphics on the screen would clearly label what was "commentary" and "opinion." In a feat of messaging jiujitsu, he was suggesting the idea that only his rival networks practiced partisan spin. In an interview that fall, Ailes wondered why reporters were so quick to label Republicans "right-wing" but never called Teddy Kennedy "the left-wing senator from Massachusetts." Ailes's own analysis echoed the theories of media bias advanced by Bruce Herschensohn at TVN. The networks, Ailes contended, had "a hundred ways to spin the news." Television reporters used "hot words, or code words." They could broadcast "shortened sound bites" and elevate a favorable quote to "the front of a piece" or give preferred sources "more time." They could also frame their quotes "with spin from one side or the other side." "Journalists are by and large intelligent, well-read individuals who come at every story with a bias," Ailes said. It was a brazen gambit. Roger Ailes, the highly partisan fighter, was proclaiming himself the referee.

Ailes delighted in the anger and confusion this line of argument produced in his interlocutors. "I have noticed that the words fair and balanced are terrorizing people in the news business," he told the journalists. "Somewhere between 56 and 82 percent of American people think news is biased, negative and boring. So let's take 60 percent as the number—it looks like a marketing niche to me."

All his talk of Fox News's hard news cred artfully shaded the reality that, as compared to its competitors, his network's newsgathering capabilities were minuscule. Fox's three foreign bureaus could not hold a candle to CNN's twenty. The projected staff of five hundred was half the size of Ailes's competitors. Although Ailes was positioning Fox News as a serious news network, the channel he was actually building was essentially a reboot of America's Talking. Two chairs and a plant were far cheaper than staffing dozens of foreign bureaus in far-flung capitals. Even O'Reilly was disappointed to find that none of his staff that Ailes had hired understood how to do news. And distribution remained a thorny problem. Talks with Time Warner Cable for access to the New York market had so far not yielded a deal. In the end, Fox would launch with 17 million subscribers, at a time when MSNBC reached 25 million and CNN reached 60.

With Murdoch spending hundreds of millions to buy distribution, not staff bureaus, Ailes rallied his journalists with outsider fervor. The indoctrination began in earnest on Tuesday morning, September 3, about a month before the launch. Hundreds of newly hired Fox News employees packed into a conference room at the New York Hilton on Sixth Avenue, six blocks north of News Corp's headquarters. They were told the meeting was a company-wide orientation, but the charged atmosphere in the room made them feel like attendees of a political rally. As they milled about, loud music blared. Ailes was nowhere in sight. When the lights finally dimmed, forty-five minutes after the scheduled start time, a pair of giant monitors on the stage played short videos, styled like the ones screened at presidential nominating conventions. One, which concluded with the tagline *Fox Can,* catalogued Murdoch's impressive broadcasting accomplishments to date. Another, a video montage, showcased the faces of Fox anchors while "Something's Coming" from *West Side Story* played.

Ailes took the stage. His absence had only heightened the sense of anticipation. "You guys are at the beginning of history here," Ailes said. "Fox News is gonna be around for *decades.*" The crowd cheered. "He put it out there that we were going to take down CNN," one former producer recalled. "I remember thinking, 'This guy is no joke, he's impressive.'" Ailes was in a riotous mood. He introduced a female lawyer with a gag. "You know the difference between lawyers and prostitutes?" Ailes asked. "Lawyers keep doing you even after you're dead." Some laughed, others cringed. Fox News was unlike any other place they had worked.

At the orientation, employees received copies of *You Are the Message,* which became the channel's sacred text. "He made sure we read his book, and he'd refer back to it," Jay Ringelstein recalled. "You learned how to be a better person." Ailes's teachings were filling his mind. *Negative people make positive people sick. . . . If you think you're a victim, you are a victim. But if you can stand on your own two feet, you're okay. . . . If you make a mistake, and you tell me you did the best you could, I know you didn't do the best you could.* Staffers, if they hadn't realized it already, were now fully aware of their status. They were charter members of a new movement. "There was almost a sense of a cause, a political cause," Mike Schneider recalled, "a fervor that we were going to go out and slowly but surely achieve our goals."

"Fair and balanced," a precept formally introduced at the orientation, was put forth as a kind of spiritual goal. "I don't expect you not to be biased in your lives; you'll be too damn boring at the dinner table if you don't have opinions," Ailes told his staffers. "But when you walk into this newsroom, recognize your position or your bias and be fair to people who don't share that position." To reinforce the message, Ailes had John Moody host seminars in the basement newsroom for new hires. In one early session, Moody passed around packets of *New York Times* articles he had marked up with a pen to highlight its liberal bias. Pointing to an article about a book fair in Zimbabwe with a gay and lesbian booth, Moody grumbled, "How is this news? Why does anyone care about this?" Adam Sank, a young producer who was gay, remembered being offended. It was an early sign that Ailes's channel would not always be an easy place for a gay man like him. "I was more bewildered than anything," he said. "There would be a lot more homophobia that'd come my way later on." (Sank would later switch careers, leaving Fox to become a stand-up comedian.)

Memos to the staff warned that reaching the state of "fair and balanced" was so arduous that no other organization had ever attempted it. "Maybe the words 'fair' and 'balanced' are more terrifying than we realize," Ailes said. Fox News, the memos stated, by "reporting stories that competitors don't cover," would become a "haven for viewers looking for relief from the one-sided reporting by competition."

Fox's other famous slogan—"We Report. You Decide"—was developed for the channel's original marketing campaign. Like "fair and balanced," it communicated a message on multiple levels, with vastly different meanings for people on either side of the Fox divide.

Though credit for the slogan was often attributed to Ailes, it was in fact the work of veteran Republican advertising consultants from the boutique ad agency Messner Vetere Berger McNamee Schmetterer. Ailes had hired Tom Messner and his partners to create a series of promotional television spots for Fox about wedge issues, pornography and Israel among them. The ads would make the case that Fox tackled controversial topics differently from the rest of the media and that other television networks were "not trustworthy at all." In one brainstorming session, Messner's colleague read through a sample script. The words "we report" and "you decide" jumped off the page to his colleague Bob Schmetterer. "Why don't you use that as a tagline?" Schmetterer said. Messner and his partners knew instantly it was what they were looking for. "We did no market research whatsoever," Messner recalled. It was a piercing message, and one of the stickiest slogans ever to come out of Madison Avenue, irrespective of truth value. To wit: Ailes had proclaimed to *The New York Times* that television was "the most powerful force in the world." And yet his network's slogan was built on the premise that "it was up to you to decide if we're fakers or if we're telling the truth," as Messner said. What Ailes was selling, at its heart, was not news, but empowerment. Fox was putting forth the notion that their audience could come to their own conclusions, while "feeling informed," as Chet Collier said. "Of all the lines our agency was responsible for, this was probably the longest lived," Messner said.

As the network hurtled toward its October debut, some staffers were detecting the menacing side to the culture Ailes was creating. Certain colleagues, despite their scant journalism experience, lorded over others and could not be crossed. These friends of Roger, or F.O.R.'s as they were called, were longtime loyalists including Collier, Collier's assistant, Suzanne Scott, Judy Laterza, and the cadre of political operatives from Ailes Communications.

The influx of Ailes's former political operatives rattled staffers. "I was creeped out. I thought it was a strange group," one senior producer, who left shortly after the launch, recalled. Many believed that Ailes was building a political operation within a television network. It was not the mere fact that people were calling the glass-walled conference space, where John Moody held editorial meetings, the "War Room." It was the way they were saying it, without irony. What they found even more unnerving was a command center of networked computer terminals behind a locked door in the basement. Entry required a special security badge, which Ailes permitted only a handful of executives to have. The "Brain Room," as it was dubbed, seemed ominous. After being told it was the "research arm" of Fox News, at least two staffers feared, in earnest, that Ailes had hired ex-CIA and Mossad agents to conduct covert political missions for him. "These guys were researching people Roger wanted to know about. It was like 'black ops,'" a former Fox News executive said. "It was very Nixonian," a senior producer explained. "There was nothing like it at a news channel." The fact that F.O.R. Scott Ehrlich oversaw the operation from a glassed-in office only added to staff suspicions that Ailes was planning dirty tricks. One source close to Ailes said the Brain Room provided him with public information—such as political affiliation and real estate records—of his enemies and rivals.

According to broadcast consultant George Case, who worked at Fox, "the Brain Room existed to keep providing information to the screen." Ailes wanted his producers to respect and make use of the Brain Room's research for their programs. It was his theory that information boxes, text banners, factoids, and statistics could fill up the screen without distracting the audience. In memos to staff, he called it taking stories to the "next level of information." Fox's creative team developed catchy graphics that would light up the screen like a video game. The flashing and whooshing icons would, in fact, keep the viewers hooked.

The entire setup—the excessive secrecy, the security tags—was devised to influence how Fox News producers viewed the information. "Power is best wielded by men who never have to use it, and Roger knew how to do that," Case recalled. "The fact that it was down in the bowels of the building, and no one had access to it, all of a sudden, it takes on a mythology of its own." Essentially, Ailes had conceived a sophisticated theater set, another living part of his show, that was meant to evoke a cloak-and-dagger underworld.

Scott Ehrlich confided to one friend that he took a certain thrill in duping his more senior colleagues who had no clue what his role was. As he imagined it, they suspected he was going through James Carville's garbage—when in fact he was usually ordering pizza. Over time, the mystique attached to the Brain Room diminished and staffers began to see it for what it was—professional researchers from diverse backgrounds who were given an ample budget to mine the Internet for information and to fact-check the network's news stories. Fox hosts now routinely refer to information obtained for them by "the geniuses" in the "Brain Room."

Ailes also made it clear that employees would be making a grave mistake if they spoke to the news media without authorization. It was left to Ailes's PR chief, Brian Lewis, to roll out the press strategy. Not everyone adjusted easily to it. Early on, Mike Schneider went to John Moody to complain after being told by Irena Briganti, Lewis's fresh out of college PR assistant, that all media requests had to be cleared through Lewis's office. Schneider was surprised when Moody, a fellow journalist, reiterated the policy. Schneider turned around and headed toward Ailes's office to take it up with the boss. "Don't do it," Moody cautioned. Schneider walked in and found Ailes in a meeting with Jack Abernethy and several top executives.

He told Ailes he did not like being muzzled in the press. "Why would you want to talk to them?" Ailes said. "They're the enemy."

"They're not the enemy. They're *us,*" Schneider returned. Ailes's next comment set him off.

"I'm glad I didn't serve in a foxhole with you in Vietnam," Ailes said.

"Fuck you, Ailes! I've been nothing but loyal to you," he said, walking out of the office. Later Schneider apologized.

Although Ailes never served in the military, he recognized that his new job would put him on the front lines of a culture war. Because he was an exponent of revolutionary ideas—"I consider myself a freedom fighter," he once declared—Ailes's concern about his physical safety accordingly became more acute. According to Dan Cooper, an early Fox executive, Ailes called him into a meeting one day before the launch and declared he wanted bombproof glass windows installed in his executive suite. When he asked why, Ailes told him that after the launch, "homosexual activists are going to be down there every day protesting. . . . And who knows what the hell they'll do." Rudy Nazath, the architect designing the studios, told Cooper that there was no such thing as "bombproof glass" and suggested using polycarbonate glass, the strongest version of which can stop a .357 bullet. Ailes selected the sturdiest grade for his office. The original windows stayed in place as a weather shield and a layer of bulletproof glass was installed behind it, supported with steel.

As the launch approached, they were still looking for the "Liberal to Be Determined" to partner with Sean Hannity. Ailes finally found Alan Colmes, a liberal talk radio host and onetime stand-up comic. "We hired Alan as a last resort," a former Fox producer said. Visually, Colmes, with his bony cheeks and beady eyes, presented producers with a challenge. They gave him cosmetic glasses to wear on set. "We thought he looked better," one producer recalled.

Bill O'Reilly was also causing problems. Three staffers quit after O'Reilly's fiery first meeting. "Look, Roger, this is like Marine boot camp here," O'Reilly told Ailes. "I can't have namby-pamby people getting their feelings hurt about this bullshit, all right?" A little while later, O'Reilly erupted again, this time at his executive producer, Amy Sohnen.

Ailes was not pleased. "Now your producer hates you," he told O'Reilly.

With the launch just days away, Ailes decided his troops needed a dose of fear, and he began issuing a series of directives about the network's visuals with a take-no-prisoners tone. "I arrived in the control room at 5:50 a.m. today," he wrote in a memo to his senior staff on Monday, September 30. Over four single-spaced pages, he harangued his employees for the "total chaos" he saw around him. "There is too much orange in our promos and graphics. I don't want to look like the Halloween network," he wrote. And in spite of "a million dollars" spent, "the set behind the anchors in studio A looks like a housing project." Ailes savaged the way his anchors looked. "Everybody on camera looks greasy and hot," he complained. He pressed his staff to work harder, at least twelve-hour days for the first month following launch. "If you wanted some other line of work, you could get a job across the street in a shoe store," he wrote. "I think they're on 8-hour shifts."

The next morning, things were still going terribly. Ailes was dismayed as technical glitches derailed a run-through of the opening day's schedule. That evening, the channel would host a glitzy launch party for the city's political and media elite under a soaring tent outside News Corp's headquarters. But Ailes was not ready to let his staff toast themselves. He called a meeting of fifteen senior executives the morning after the party at 4:00 a.m., when he knew they would be hungover and in need of sleep. After they filed into headquarters before dawn, they watched Ailes calmly reading a newspaper at the head of the conference table. When he finished reading, Ailes lit into his team for a litany of mistakes. "We can either drop the ball for Rupert and be embarrassed, or we can make history," he told them. They sat there quietly taking it.

The hazing ritual would get Ailes's team to October 7. But not without being dealt a major setback. Throughout the summer, Time Warner executives had led Murdoch to believe that they would distribute Fox News along with MSNBC in New York. The arrangement called for Time Warner to carry Fox News in millions of homes at the outset, including the 1.1 million homes in New York. In return, News Corp would pay Time Warner $125 million. The contract, according to one Fox executive, was "within a half hour" of being signed. (A Time Warner spokesperson later denied that CEO Gerald Levin had given his word.) But now, Time Warner's executives had decided to table the talks with News Corp and postpone deciding whether they would carry Fox News in the crucial New York market. What was worse, they had already agreed to carry MSNBC. David Zaslav negotiated the deal. Time Warner's chief negotiator, Fred Dressler, suggested to his boss, Levin, that he should break the news to Murdoch.

It was pouring rain on the afternoon of September 17, as Levin hustled across Sixth Avenue from Time Warner's headquarters at Rockefeller Center to News Corp. Ushered into Murdoch's office, Levin informed him that his cable division had decided not to distribute Fox News in New York City. He left open the possibility for a future deal but the news was devastating. Without New York, it was unlikely that Fox News could survive as a business long-term. Given the grave news he had just shared with the News Corp chief, Levin was surprised by Murdoch's calm response. Murdoch even managed to thank Levin for venturing out in such unpleasant weather.

Murdoch's mood changed immediately. He made numerous angry calls that night and the next day, including one to Ailes, raging against Levin's decision. "Murdoch thought he had been lied to," Ailes recalled. Talks with Time Warner had advanced far enough that in August, News Corp sent a draft of a written contract to Time Warner for final review. Murdoch insisted that Levin had promised him they had a "done deal." "If these guys want to go to war, let's go to war," Ailes told Murdoch.

# THIRTEEN

# THE RIGHT KIND OF FRIENDS

NEWS CORP'S ASSAULT began the next morning when Rupert Murdoch and Chase Carey placed calls to their counterparts at Time Warner. Picking up the phone, Gerald Levin listened to an Australian voice unrecognizable in timbre to the one he had heard the previous evening. Time Warner's decision not to carry Fox News on its New York system was an outrage, Murdoch told him. News Corp would "let loose the heavy artillery" if necessary. "You are *immoral*," Carey raged at Fred Dressler, Time Warner's cable programming chief. "You are unethical. How could you have done this?"

"He called me a lot of names I don't want to see in print," Dressler recalled.

"What the hell happened?" Levin asked Dressler later that day. "Everything was fine. Then Rupert called, and he went crazy on me." Dressler had tried unsuccessfully to reason with Carey. "Chase, calm down, we can still do a deal," he said, reminding him that Time Warner would be able to accommodate Fox News as soon as its cable systems went digital and expanded capacity. The barrage of insults blindsided the men, but was in keeping with Murdoch's well-earned reputation for ruthlessness in the face of intransigence.

Time Warner's rejection was a serious provocation. The launch of Fox News was just weeks away, and without a slot on Time Warner Cable, Ailes's fledgling network would only reach seventeen million homes—about two-thirds the number required to break even.

The first intimation of serious turbulence came on August 30, the day Time Warner lawyers advised Dressler to postpone the deal with Fox. In Washington, regulators at the Federal Trade Commission were wrapping up an eleven-month review of the Time Warner–Turner Broadcasting merger. All signs pointed to its approval, but Time Warner's lawyers decided to play a dubious Washington game. They directed Dressler to delay announcing a deal with Fox News until after the FTC announced that Time Warner Cable needed to make a competitor to CNN available to half of its subscribers within three to five years. It was a move designed to make it appear as though Time Warner was responding to the rigorous new regulation (even though the company had already decided on carrying *two* CNN rivals: MSNBC and Fox). In effect, Time Warner wanted to let the regulators look tough and claim credit for busting CNN's cable news monopoly.

On September 12, the FTC approved the merger as expected. But instead of moving ahead on the Fox News contract, Dressler suddenly reversed course. There were those inside the company who had been against a Fox deal from the beginning, and the postponement gave the anti-Fox faction momentum. Richard Aurelio, the president of Time Warner's New York City Cable Group, was among the naysayers. He harbored bad memories of Ailes's show on America's Talking, *Straight Forward.* "It was awful," Aurelio said. "It was produced badly. He had a terrible on-air personality. That was one of the factors when the decision had to be made." In a meeting with Levin in his office, Aurelio made the case against carrying Fox News at its launch.

Dressler had similar concerns. In his negotiations with Fox, Ailes refused to "discuss anything" about his programming plans even after Dressler explained it would influence whether they carried it or not. The financial terms of the deal were also problematic. While Murdoch's cash offer was enticing, the contract stipulated that Time Warner would begin paying News Corp some 20 cents per subscriber in the first year, a fee that would be subject to adjustment based on the Consumer Price Index. The unknown future cost of these so-called backend payments worried him. Of more immediate concern, Dressler feared a potential "public-relations disaster." He realized that Time Warner could only take Fox News if it turned down MSNBC or bumped an existing channel. After John Malone's TCI announced in August 1996 that it was dropping Lifetime, the channel programmed for women, from 300,000 homes in order to make room for Fox, the company received a deluge of angry phone calls and letters. Viewers even staged protests in Eugene, Oregon, and Houston, Texas.

Rejecting MSNBC would be worse. During Dressler's negotiations with Time Warner that summer, David Zaslav said he would sue if Time Warner did not replace America's Talking with MSNBC. He also threatened to pull NBC's highly rated broadcast programming off Time Warner cable. "Then we're in a war over whether your subscribers get to see *Seinfeld* and football," Zaslav warned, "and we're in a major pigfuck." Dressler lobbied Levin to postpone signing Fox for the time being.

On the day that Murdoch called Levin, Murdoch huddled with Ailes and his general counsel and longtime confidant, Arthur Siskind, to weigh his options. Time Warner's refusal to carry Fox News was not about prosaic business matters like "channel capacity" or "public relations." Their view, which was partly a theory of the case and partly a PR strategy, was that Ted Turner was a killer. In the mid-1980s, Turner successfully crushed an early effort by NBC to launch a cable news channel. Now, having sold CNN to Time Warner, Turner was trying to do the same to Fox. It was a compelling story line—Ted Turner was the villainous monopolist; News Corp was the justice seeker.

The rivalry between Murdoch and Turner had become entertainingly vituperative in the year since Murdoch announced his intention to compete in cable news. They were perfectly matched masters of insult. In the press, Turner called Murdoch a "schlockmeister." Murdoch publicly accused Turner of "brown-nosing foreign dictators" and turning "Fidel Castro" into a CNN bureau chief. When Turner agreed to merge with Time Warner, Murdoch, age sixty-five, sniffed that Turner, age fifty-seven, had "sold out to the Establishment in his declining years."

To win, News Corp would need a multifaceted campaign. Murdoch listened as Siskind presented possible strategies, which included suing Time Warner for breach of contract on the grounds that they had entered into a verbal agreement. But total war had high costs, Siskind advised. "We don't want to burn too many bridges here," he told Murdoch. News Corp had built valuable interlocking relationships with Time Warner through the years, and both companies distributed each other's content. Fox Broadcasting, for example, purchased popular shows such as *The Rosie O'Donnell Show, Living Single,* and *Party Girl* from Warner Bros. Television. Time Warner's HBO aired films from Murdoch's 20th Century Fox studio.

There was another option—in effect going over Time Warner's head, into the world of politics. Murdoch had a decisive political advantage. At the time, his Republican allies were ascendant in New York. Senator Al D'Amato was the state's most powerful politician. George Pataki, a one-term Republican state senator, defeated three-term Democratic governor Mario Cuomo in 1994, the year in which Murdoch donated $100,000 to the New York State Republican Party. And Mayor Rudy Giuliani was the first Republican in twenty-seven years to take City Hall. Giuliani, in particular, had significant leverage over Time Warner. The city regulated the license by which Time Warner operated its cable system. As it happened, the city's Franchise and Concession Review Committee was scheduled to hold a public hearing on the Time Warner merger on October 7, the day of Fox News's launch. If the committee did not approve, the city could choose not to renew Time Warner's exclusive contract to operate a cable system in the city. The New York cable franchise was the most valuable in the world, with estimated annual revenues of a half billion dollars.

Murdoch's investment in the *New York Post,* though it hadn't made money in years, paid dividends in the battle. The paper had endorsed the candidacies of Giuliani ("MAN OF THE HOUR") and Pataki ("TIME FOR A CHANGE") in front-page editorials. From the outset of Giuliani's first term, the *Post* cheered the mayor's aggressive anticrime policies. Murdoch even employed the mayor's then wife, Donna Hanover, as a feature reporter on the morning show *Good Day New York,* which aired on his flagship New York broadcast station, WNYW. It was also the same year in which News Corp, as part of a Giuliani program to stanch the emigration of television production across the Hudson River to New Jersey, negotiated more than $20 million of tax breaks with the city to subsidize the construction of Fox News studios in Manhattan. The subsidies signaled Giuliani's commitment to Fox News's success.

But in these political battles, Ailes himself was Murdoch's most potent weapon. Both D'Amato and Giuliani had been Ailes Communications clients. Though he officially renounced politics in 1991, Ailes continued to socialize with both men, especially Giuliani. On the evening of the 1992 presidential election, Giuliani watched the returns at Ailes Communications headquarters at an intimate gathering of seven people, including Ailes and Rush Limbaugh. Listening to Ailes and Giuliani banter, one attendee recalled, was "like watching Sunday morning football with guys on the set on Fox Sports." A month later, Ailes attended a fundraiser for Giuliani at the New York Sheraton, where he declared to a reporter that if Giuliani lost to incumbent David Dinkins, "this city is going to turn into Detroit." When Giuliani took office, Ailes continued to give him advice.

And so, two days after Murdoch warned Levin he was about to "let loose the heavy artillery," Murdoch told Ailes to pull the trigger.

On Friday, September 20, Ailes called Giuliani to ask for help. Giuliani immediately invited Ailes to Gracie Mansion to discuss Time Warner's decision not to carry Fox News. As the men shared pizza, the mayor pledged his unwavering support. He tasked his forty-two-year-old deputy mayor, Fran Reiter, to head up City Hall's rapid response. As a former television syndication executive, Reiter was well versed in media issues. She was also plugged into Murdoch's plans for Fox News. The previous spring, she had negotiated News Corp's tax relief package with Arthur Siskind.

"Time Warner informed us they would not be giving us a cable channel, which puts us in jeopardy," Ailes told Reiter in a phone call later that day. "Is there anything the administration can do to help us turn this around?" Ailes explained that Ted Turner must have scuttled the deal to damage Murdoch and Fox News. Reiter assured him that she would look into it.

Reiter placed a call to Ailes's colleague Arthur Siskind. He told her that News Corp might not be able to hire more New York–based employees if Time Warner did not relent. As part of its tax relief package, News Corp had pledged to retain some 2,200 jobs and create 1,475 new positions. By invoking the loss of potential jobs, Siskind was making a threat: any obstacle to the growth of News Corp would embarrass the Giuliani administration. The mayor had made job creation, especially in high-profile sectors like media, a plank in his economic program.

Privately, however, Reiter thought that getting involved was a terrible idea. "No one is going to remember this except for the fact that you intervened," she told Giuliani. Although Time Warner Cable operated with a city contract, the First Amendment gave the company's executives wide latitude to program the channel lineup as they saw fit. Though Reiter agreed with her boss that the city had an interest in Fox's success, she believed stepping in was "an effort doomed to failure under the law." She also saw tight channel capacity as a legitimate issue. A couple dozen cable channels were vying for the same spot on Time Warner's New York system.

Furthermore, the optics were reason enough to stay on the sidelines. Giuliani was facing reelection in the coming year. In 1993, he had won by fewer than fifty thousand votes. Reiter, who had served as his deputy campaign manager, could easily script the attack lines Giuliani's opponents would use: *Here is a Republican mayor intervening on behalf of a conservative media mogul who invested $100 million to launch a conservative news channel run by the mayor's former media adviser. And by the way, the mogul, who donated $100,000 to the New York State Republican Party in 1994, also just happens to employ the mayor's wife as a television personality.*

Giuliani ignored her advice. "I got attacked," Reiter recalled. "He was angry. He felt what Time Warner had done was wrong and was bad for the city." Her worries were prescient. The situation soon devolved into a baroque tabloid spectacle of swooping egos and petty grievances, in which each side pursued maximum ends by questionable means, one of the defining imbroglios of the Giuliani years. The battle to launch Fox News, aided by Giuliani's strong-arm tactics, became the quintessential example of Murdoch's brazen manipulation of political relationships to help expand his media empire. And Ailes was at the center of it, crafting Murdoch's message and battling his Time Warner opponents as ferociously as any political candidate.

The months-long campaign tarnished the reputation of everyone involved. "Rudy was walking into a snake pit," Reiter said. "It was the worst episode in my time in government."

On Thursday, September 26, just a few days after Ailes called Giuliani, News Corp executives Arthur Siskind and Bill Squadron arrived at City Hall in lower Manhattan to make their case before the city's corporation counsel, Reiter, and her senior aides. They argued that Time Warner was breaking antitrust laws to protect CNN. Would Reiter call Time Warner's CEO, Gerald Levin? Reiter was amenable, but directed Siskind to first send her a detailed letter laying out his case. Meanwhile, uptown at a Time Warner luncheon to celebrate the merger, Ted Turner was comparing Rupert Murdoch to Adolf Hitler. "Talking to Murdoch is like confronting the late Führer," he declared to journalists at the reception.

Given the messy public row, Reiter decided to take action even before receiving Siskind's letter. She left a message for Time Warner president Dick Parsons, saying she was "very concerned." Reiter hoped that Parsons, a longtime Giuliani ally, could serve as an influential back channel.

By Friday afternoon, Reiter and her aides devised a novel solution, essentially a one-for-one channel swap, to free up a spot for Fox News.

As part of Time Warner's franchise agreement with the city, the Giuliani administration controlled five public channels. Named "Crosswalks," the channels had to be programmed, according to law, for noncommercial public, education, or government programming. It was a leap, but perhaps Time Warner could move a cable channel with educational content—the Discovery Channel or History Channel, for example—to one of the Crosswalks channels. Reiter desperately wanted to avoid the protracted lawsuit that Siskind was now threatening.

With the broad contours of a potential accord in place, Reiter needed to get Time Warner on-board. Dick Parsons had not called her back, which worried her. Over the weekend, Reiter and her aides decided to call Parsons and Levin at home, but they could not find their numbers. On Sunday, she managed to get through to Derek Johnson, a Time Warner vice president. Johnson listened as Reiter explained her "deep concern" over Time Warner's refusal to carry Fox. She said the city wanted Time Warner to agree to carry Fox before October 7, when the city's franchise review committee had a hearing scheduled on the Time Warner merger. After hinting at her channel swap plan, Reiter insisted that she meet with Levin or Parsons in the next week to discuss it. It was important enough, she said, that if Levin and Parsons were out of town, she would get on a plane to meet them.

On Monday morning, Johnson sent a memo to Parsons and Levin offering his assessment of Reiter's proposal. "Although attractive . . . could spark grave reaction from programmers and politicians alike," he wrote. With the backlog of other cable channels waiting to get into the New York market, it was not fair to jump Fox News to the front of the line just because the mayor's office endorsed the idea. After reading Johnson's memo, Levin and Parsons decided to turn down the request for a meeting and Dick Aurelio, a man closer to Reiter's level, was dispatched to handle the negotiations. He even had political experience, beginning his career as an aide to Republican New York senator Jacob Javits and as a deputy mayor under Mayor John Lindsay.

Aurelio left a message for Reiter, but David Klasfeld, her chief of staff, returned the call, which insulted the Time Warner executive. Aurelio said he wanted to talk to Reiter. As they spoke by phone later that day, Reiter was in the middle of explaining the channel swap when Aurelio cut her off.

*"No fucking way,"* he snapped. The proposal was illegal.

"There's no point in us meeting, then," Reiter said.

"Let's do the meeting," he said, advising Reiter to bring city lawyers.

Aurelio was entering the talks with a history of conflict with Giuliani and Murdoch. The locus of their friction was Aurelio's close friendship with Giuliani's predecessor, David Dinkins. As a veteran of New York's bare-knuckle politics, Aurelio was ready to hold Time Warner's ground. He believed the city's jobs argument was "a phony issue" used to cover up political favor trading. "The *New York Post* helped make him mayor," Aurelio recalled. "In my memory, there was never a newspaper cheerleader in New York City in *any* mayoral contest more overwhelmingly supportive than the *New York Post* for Giuliani in 1993."

On Tuesday, October 1, Aurelio arrived at Reiter's office at City Hall flanked by a pair of lawyers: Robert Jacobs, the general counsel of Time Warner's New York City Cable Group, and Allan Arffa, a litigator at Paul, Weiss. Six City Hall representatives lined one side of the table, outnumbering the Time Warner contingent two to one. The meeting was a disaster, lasting less than an hour. At one point, Time Warner's lawyers accused the Giuliani negotiators of proposing a cover-up to avoid making the channel swap seem like a quid pro quo for the city agreeing to renew Time Warner's franchise. Before Aurelio and his colleagues stood to walk out, Norman Sinel, the city's outside attorney, issued a blunt warning. "The mayor's office is fully aware of the risks involved here," he said. "We're willing to take those risks. The question is, is Time Warner willing to take those risks?"

Aurelio returned to the office and briefed Parsons on the fireworks. Aurelio wagered that the saber rattling would soon subside. "I don't know," Parsons said, knowing Giuliani and Ailes well. "I'm not sure that's the end of it."

Parsons was right. Later that day, he called Fran Reiter. It was the first time the two had spoken since she had left him a message the previous week. Reiter expressed outrage at Aurelio's abrasiveness. "The bottom line is, Dick, we have a very, very serious concern. Your guys totally rejected our proposal today. They got up on a soapbox about the First Amendment. I don't want to get into that discussion. I've got a new approach that I'd like to lay before you."

Reiter explained that the city planned to air Fox News on one of its Crosswalks channels. In the morning, Time Warner would receive a letter from the city requesting a "waiver" to proceed. Reiter suggested that Levin call Murdoch and make amends. Time Warner's city franchises came up for renewal in 1998, and as Reiter put it, Time Warner wouldn't want the Fox News issue clouding up the franchise issue. The mayor controlled four of six seats on the franchise review committee.

Although the call ended without any firm commitments, Reiter was encouraged by Parsons's collegial tone. The thaw in relations, however, was fleeting. At News Corp, Murdoch and Ailes were plotting a new phase in the campaign. "When you're screwed over, you fight," Ailes would tell a reporter. "We're not going to quit until we're all dead. This'll be a blood war until we get clearance in New York City."

That evening, Reiter was one of the hundreds of guests toasting the launch of Fox News under a giant white tent outside News Corp headquarters. The mayor himself was on hand at the gala and posed for photos with Ailes and Murdoch, which the *New York Post* published. Murdoch gave a brief speech introducing the "fair and balanced" creed. Giuliani told guests that Fox News was of "incalculable value to the people of the city." Governor Pataki added that Ailes "used to teach me how to campaign, and now he'll teach me how to watch the news." An assistant guided Reiter to speak with Murdoch. A few moments later, she bumped into Ailes, who thanked her for the city's assistance. Reiter was not the only politico getting the full-court press. The party was a public stage on which to flex political muscle.

Within twenty-four hours after the party, Ailes's Republican Triumvirate confronted Time Warner's leadership. Giuliani called his onetime ally Parsons, while Pataki and Al D'Amato made calls to Levin and Aurelio. "Why aren't you carrying it?" D'Amato pointedly asked Aurelio. "It was unusual to get the mayor, senator, and governor all putting pressure on us the next day on behalf of Rupert," Aurelio recalled. "I found it a display of raw political power that was extremely inappropriate." On Thursday, October 3, Giuliani's office received a disappointing answer from Time Warner. "Your request that we waive our rights in order to carry [Fox News] on a dedicated municipal access channel, however innocent your intent, is in the circumstances a violation of Time Warner Cable's franchise rights with the City, the Federal Cable Act and other law, including our First Amendment rights," Time Warner's general counsel wrote. "It is therefore a request we cannot and will not consider."

Time Warner's defiance did not deter Giuliani. Norman Sinel, the city's outside counsel, immediately called Allan Arffa, Time Warner's lawyer at Paul, Weiss, and threatened to raise antitrust issues at the franchise review. Reiter's chief of staff, David Klasfeld, sent one final letter to Parsons. "The City makes its request to Time Warner as an appeal to its good corporate citizenship," Klasfeld wrote, further revealing the city's desperation. "New York City's successful economic revitalization depends on businesses cooperating with these efforts so the City can create new jobs at all income and skill levels."

Friday, October 4, ended without a response from Parsons. Time Warner's silence, which ensured that New Yorkers would not be able to view Fox News when it went live at 6:00 on Monday morning, moved the crisis toward a showdown in court.

As Time Warner dug in, Ailes found himself scrambling. The distribution battle had escalated at the moment when the demands on his time were reaching an apex. After the launch party, Ailes returned to work a few hours later for the 4:00 a.m. meeting with his senior staff. But presidential politics had accustomed him to little sleep. It also reinforced a truism about the press: journalists love to report conflict. If Ailes could gin up controversy, what political consultants called "free media," articles would follow.

On the eve of the launch, Ailes opened the press front. "People who are out there saying we'll be a bunch of sleazy bastards are the same ones who said we wouldn't be able to get on the air," he told the *Los Angeles Times*. His competitors at CNN and MSNBC took his bait. CNN president Tom Johnson rebuked Ailes for his nasty barbs. "I see no value whatsoever in one news organization firing shots at another," he said. Andy Lack told *The Dallas Morning News* that competition "doesn't mean we have to try to destroy each other in the process or trample all over each other. So good luck, and let's go at it."

It was a good thing Ailes made news. He needed all the PR he could get. The only way to see Fox News in Manhattan on the morning of its debut was, in essence, to walk by its street-facing studio on 48th Street.

Shortly before 6:00 on the morning of October 7, Ailes barreled into the newsroom, giving locker room pep talks. "You set?" he barked to a group of employees. "Too much laughter over there!" he hollered at another bunch. "Act nervous!" The staffers ignored his request. They could likely sense he was hamming it up for an Associated Press reporter scribbling notes nearby.

In the control room, producers huddled over monitors watching the morning show hosts, Louis Aguirre, a hunky Cuban-American from Miami, and Allison Costarene, a pretty blonde, running through final preparations sitting at glass-topped desks, in front of a pastel pink and blue backdrop. The teleprompter was loaded with the show's top stories: a recap of the previous night's presidential debate at the Bushnell theater in Hartford, Connecticut, and a live report from Rome by correspondent Gary Matsumoto on Pope John Paul II's hospitalization for appendicitis. For a network that would be defined by its decibel level, the premiere was surprisingly subdued. "Good morning. Welcome to Fox News," Aguirre said into the camera when the clock struck six.

For the opening day, Ailes had assembled a guest list of boldface names, the most notable of which served as a counterweight to MSNBC's prime-time debut with Bill Clinton: Republican presidential candidate Bob Dole, live in the studio for his first post-debate interview. Other gets, which firmly leaned to the right, included Israel's prime minister Benjamin Netanyahu, Utah Republican senator Orrin Hatch, Governor George Pataki, and Ailes's friend Henry Kissinger. When it came to booking liberals, Ailes's producers tended to recruit guests—Nation of Islam leader Louis Farrakhan, imprisoned Whitewater witness Susan McDougal, liberal California senator Henry Waxman, Clinton drug czar Barry McCaffrey—who could inject culture war conflict into the conversation.

In his second-floor office, Ailes wrote down the channel's mission statement. "Fox News is committed to providing viewers with more factual information and a balanced and fair presentation. Fox believes viewers should make their own judgment on important issues based on unbiased coverage. Our motto is 'we report, you decide.' Our job is to give the American people information they can use to lead their lives more effectively. And our job is to tell them the truth wherever the truth falls." Unlike the executives at other channels, Ailes was crafting his message, as one Fox News executive said, to "define the market opportunity in news." Ed Rollins, the GOP campaign consultant who would later become a Fox News contributor, believed that politics gave Ailes insight that his competitors lacked. "He knew there were a couple million conservatives who were a potential audience, and he built Fox to reach them," he said. And Ailes's motto, a cunning tautology, flattered their sense of possessing discernment.

Fox News's launch on the morning of October 7 was the biggest moment in Roger Ailes's television career. But because of the Time Warner battle, he was absent for a good part of it. Shortly after 10:00 a.m., Ailes was three miles south of the Fox News studios, sitting alongside Arthur Siskind at City Hall, ready to deliver a withering indictment of Time Warner before city officials on the Franchise and Concession Review Committee. Time Warner made it clear they would not capitulate to Giuliani's pressure campaign. Representatives of Michael Bloomberg, the billionaire financial information mogul, were also on hand to testify. Time Warner had previously agreed to carry a six-minute feed from Bloomberg Information Television several times a day on CNN, they explained, but as a result of the merger, the Bloomberg TV feed was being taken off the cable system.

"Good morning," Ailes said at the opening of his prepared remarks. "An hour and fifteen minutes ago, Prime Minister Benjamin Netanyahu came into our channel live from Israel and his opening words were 'Congratulations on the new channel in New York. We need more news. The more news, the more accuracy.' So we thanked him for that." (Conspicuously missing was any mention that Netanyahu's comments had been cut off after a satellite glitch silenced the audio.) Time Warner was standing in the way for two reasons: "one, direct competition; and, two, the well-publicized personal animosity Time Warner's Vice Chairman, Ted Turner, bears towards Rupert Murdoch."

According to Ailes, Fox News was the only channel that could break CNN's monopoly. MSNBC was "not a true competitor" and therefore Time Warner's decision to carry it did not inoculate the cable company against criticism. "It is not hard news coverage," Ailes said. Ailes capped his argument with a patriotic appeal, one that his heartland audience might find objectionable. "New York City is the heart of America, and now Time Warner is trying to stamp us in the heart," Ailes said. "New York City now has a cable systems czar who can control access and tell New Yorkers what they can and cannot see. Unfortunately, the New York City cable czar lives in Atlanta. His name is Ted Turner. Thank you." Committee members did not have any questions.

The story, like many colorful Roger Ailes yarns, relied on a string of selectively chosen facts. As evidence, Ailes marshaled a *Los Angeles Times* article, reporting that "sources close to Ted Turner say he was instrumental in Time Warner's decision." But the truth was that, at Time

Warner, Turner was essentially a gadfly, albeit a very loud and wealthy one, rather than a driver of strategy. Gerald Levin stacked Time Warner's board of directors with advocates, who guaranteed his primacy as CEO and ensured that Turner's post-merger status as vice chairman and largest shareholder was largely symbolic. The men were frequently at odds with one another. A couple of years later, Turner would effectively be fired from the company that bore his name.

After hearing about Ailes's performance before the franchise committee, Parsons made a last-ditch effort at détente. He called Deputy Mayor Randy Mastro, a confidant, and told him he was reaching out, not as Time Warner's president, but "friend to friend." Parsons had sent a stinging response to the city's second request for a waiver that morning, a response that was resolute. "Time Warner would have to go to war on these issues if they were not resolved amicably," Parsons said.

Privately, Parsons wanted peace. On multiple occasions, he advised Aurelio, whose confrontational posture unsettled him, to seek an accord with Murdoch. "We have to worry about our franchise," Parsons told him and Levin. Aurelio, in turn, worried about Parsons's divided loyalty. "I had to go through this with Parsons *every* time," he recalled. "He even told me at one point, 'I guess that's the end of my friendship with Giuliani.'" He was right. Soon after speaking to Mastro, Parsons publicly severed ties with the mayor, releasing a letter resigning as chairman of the city's Economic Development Corporation.

Thus began the shooting war, which Parsons and Reiter and seemingly everyone on both sides of the fight had wanted to avert. On October 9, two days after the franchise hearing, News Corp filed a $1.8 billion federal antitrust lawsuit against Time Warner in the Eastern District of New York. New York State attorney general Dennis Vacco, whom Arthur Siskind had lobbied at the launch gala, opened an investigation and subpoenaed internal Time Warner documents. Time Warner's outside attorneys at Cravath, Swaine and Moore continued work on a lawsuit against the City of New York.

At once, Manhattan borough president Ruth Messinger, who was preparing to challenge Giuliani in the upcoming mayoral election, filed a complaint to the city's Conflicts of Interest Board, citing Giuliani's wife's job at WNYW, the local Fox station.

The board would dismiss the complaint. Giuliani was defiant. "Disagree with me, fine, say you have a different philosophy," he told a reporter after marching in a Columbus Day parade in Queens. "But don't start demeaning me with the cheap kinds of things that are being done here because people are involved in business rivalries." Giuliani kept up his campaign against Time Warner. On October 9, the administration announced it would unilaterally air Fox News and Bloomberg TV, stripped of commercials, on Crosswalks, waiver or no waiver. After receiving a tip from a media executive that Giuliani was about to act on his threat, Time Warner's leadership gathered at Cravath headquarters in Worldwide Plaza to watch the conference room televisions tuned to Crosswalks. Time Warner had the technical ability to block the Crosswalks signal from their system, but thought they could benefit from allowing Giuliani to overplay his hand. "We decided what we'd rather do is seek an injunction," Aurelio recalled. At 10:48 p.m., Bloomberg TV appeared on the screen. It was clear to those gathered in the room that Giuliani aired Bloomberg before Fox News in order to blunt allegations that he was rewarding his friends Murdoch and Ailes. A few minutes later, a Cravath attorney left the building and raced downtown. Arriving at the federal courthouse at Foley Square, he deposited a copy of Time Warner's complaint in the mail slot.

Judge Denise Cote's eleventh-floor courtroom was thronged with reporters for a preliminary hearing on Friday, October 11. Though the case officially pitted Time Warner against New York City, partisan politics undergirded the proceeding. One of many amicus briefs in support of Time Warner was signed by a trio of prominent Democrats: Ruth Messinger, New York City public advocate Mark Green, and Bronx borough president Fernando Ferrer. Ailes suffered the first of several setbacks when Judge Cote issued a temporary restraining order barring the city from airing Fox News and other commercial programming until she could hear evidence.

Over the next two weeks, lawyers deposed key players in Time Warner's dispute with the city. The sworn statements intensified the conflict. Reiter told the lawyers that it was Ailes who personally called Giuliani, a disclosure the mayor was said to be upset about. *New York* magazine speculated that Reiter might lose her job because of the testimony. Her statements also caused turmoil inside Time Warner. In an affidavit, Reiter revealed that Parsons had told her that Aurelio was near the end of his term. Parsons was forced to do damage control. "You know you're my man," Parsons told Aurelio. "I was just trying to calm her down."

Meanwhile, during a three-hour deposition on the morning of Friday, October 18, Ted Turner called Murdoch "a pretty slimy character," a "dangerous person," and a "disgrace to journalism." "I was just appalled that he bought the government of New York City," he said. "I can understand him doing it in England, maybe Australia or China. But here, having it happen in New York, it really surprises me."

On Monday, October 21, the *New York Post* ran the headline "Is Ted Turner Nuts? You Decide," and published an illustration of Turner thrashing about in a straitjacket. The immature taunts even spilled over into professional sports. That week, when Turner's Atlanta Braves faced the Yankees in a World Series game, News Corp arranged for a plane to buzz over Yankee Stadium, flashing the message "Hey Ted. Be Brave. Don't Censor the Fox News Channel." During the broadcast, Fox cameras captured the footage of the plane as well as Turner at embarrassing moments, such as when he was dozing off or after a Yankee hit a home run.

A few days later, Turner joked about his feud with Murdoch. "I thought about killing him," he playfully told guests during a gala at the St. Regis hotel. "I figure that now that his own paper says I'm crazy, I can kill him and get off by reason of insanity!"

The three-day preliminary injunction hearing began on October 28, and a week later Judge Cote issued her ruling. The 106-page opinion upheld the injunction barring the city from airing Fox News. She flatly rejected the notion that the city was acting to encourage job creation and to ensure diverse programming. "Time Warner has a right under the First Amendment to be free from government interference with its programming decisions," the judge wrote. "The City's actions violate longstanding First Amendment principles that are the foundation of our democracy."

It was a blistering rebuke. The ruling meant that Fox News would remain unwatchable in Manhattan for the foreseeable future. Limited distribution had foiled the television dreams of conservatives since TVN in the 1970s. It appeared to be happening again. But Ailes would fight. "I used to say, you pull a .45 on Roger, he'll have a bazooka trained between your eyes," Catherine Crier said. "I say that as a compliment."

Politics were moving against Fox and Ailes as well. The day before Cote's ruling, Bill Clinton resoundingly defeated Bob Dole by almost 10 percent of the votes. Most Fox affiliates refused to interrupt their programming for the cable channel's election coverage. Executives considered their refusal a blessing in disguise. The coverage had been riddled with technical problems. Mike Schneider and Crier bickered off-camera and things got so tense that Schneider even threw a phone across the set.

The day after the election, Ailes purged the remaining Peyronnin employees. Only the most loyal troops would remain. "Chet Collier called us in one-by-one," Emily Rooney recalled years later. Ailes expressed no reservations about the mass layoffs. When Rooney's name came up a few days later, Ailes simply said, "She'll work again."

News Corp vowed to continue the campaign against Time Warner with its federal antitrust lawsuit. And Ailes was busy crafting new story lines. It turned out that Bill Clinton would hand him and Fox News the biggest gift the network could ask for in the form of a blue dress.

# ACT IV

# FOURTEEN

# ANTI-CLINTON NEWS NETWORK

ON A SUMMER AFTERNOON IN 1996, John Moody was sitting in his Fox News office when his phone rang. The caller said his name was David Shuster and he wanted a job at the new channel. Shuster was a twenty-nine-year-old television reporter for KATV, the ABC affiliate in Little Rock, Arkansas. Before moving to the South to take an on-camera job, he had spent a few years working as a producer in CNN's Washington bureau, covering the first Gulf War and the 1992 presidential election. Moody had never heard of him before, and Shuster was speaking so fast that it was difficult to make out exactly what he was talking about.

Shuster sensed that Moody, who had been deluged with résumés in advance of the launch, was considering brushing him off and hanging up. But then Shuster began to talk excitedly about the panoply of scandals that fell under the catchall rubric of "Whitewater." Shuster told Moody he had covered the story on the ground since January 1994, and knew all of its particulars in granular detail. In the KATV newsroom, there was a timeline of the investigation, which catalogued the failed real estate saga's murky origins in the 1970s, when the Clintons and their investment partners, Jim and Susan McDougal, purchased a 220-acre tract of land in the Ozark Mountains to subdivide into lots for summer homes. Shuster had the timeline pretty much memorized and all but lived at the United States District Court for the Eastern District of Arkansas during the McDougals' recent trial for bank fraud relating to the collapse of their savings and loan, Madison Guaranty.

Many of President Clinton's enemies on the right promoted the idea that his connection to the McDougals was only the tip of the iceberg. In 1994, the same year in which Clinton's attorney general, Janet Reno, appointed Robert Fiske special prosecutor to investigate Whitewater, Jerry Falwell helped distribute the documentary *The Clinton Chronicles: An Investigation into the Alleged Criminal Activities of Bill Clinton,* which with plentiful, grainy, black-and-white, attack-ad-style footage accused the president, in addition to sexual harassment and financial misdeeds, of being complicit in cocaine trafficking and murder. Three hundred thousand copies went into circulation.

The wider public initially showed little interest in the scandal; the details were too technical, the attacks too outrageous. But Shuster, who intimately knew the ensemble cast of Whitewater characters after nights cultivating sources at the Capitol Hotel bar in downtown Little Rock, was convinced that the Clinton scandals were more than a right-wing fever dream. In their phone conversation, Shuster reminded Moody that Special Prosecutor Kenneth Starr, Fiske's replacement, had subpoenaed Hillary Clinton at the beginning of the year to determine whether legal documents from her law firm had been criminally concealed from investigators.

"Why is this important?" Moody said.

"Because," Shuster replied, "there's a fifty-fifty chance that the first lady is going to get indicted."

Moody was intrigued. Fox News's coverage of Whitewater and other assorted controversies—Troopergate, Filegate, Travelgate, Paula Jones, Vince Foster—would depend on scrappy, well-sourced reporters like Shuster who could translate the investigations into easily digestible news reports.

"Send me a tape," Moody told him at the end of their conversation, which lasted an hour and a half.

Shuster was thrilled. He had submitted his résumé to both Fox and MSNBC, but had heard nothing until Moody took his cold call. Eager to get back to Washington, Shuster assembled his best clips. They showcased his hard-charging style—in one of them, he banged on the door of a Little Rock accounting firm that was being investigated by Starr's prosecutors.

Two weeks after mailing the tape, Shuster received a promising call from Moody. "Take me through again why you think there's a chance Hillary Clinton might get indicted," Moody said. Shuster repeated every angle. "There's a big chance the story could explode," Shuster recalled saying. Moody later confided to Shuster that the second phone call was really for Roger Ailes. "Hire the guy," Ailes said.

For the next three years, David Shuster would be constantly on camera as one of Fox News's most visible interpreters of the Whitewater spectacle. The forces at play as it transmogrified from questions about a money-losing land deal into an adolescent sex fantasy were as diverse as they were powerful, and Ailes's new channel was the most important outlet in weaving them into a coherent story. The unfinished business of the 1960s culture wars, the acceptance of prurient Internet gossip as legitimate news, and the rise of a mobilized Christian base became raw material for a singularly American tragicomedy.

A crucial theme of the plot, which Fox News and conservatives wasted no opportunity to emphasize, was the notion that elites in the media were covering up for their good-times president. "I remember Roger once referred to CNN as the 'Clinton News Network,'" former Fox producer Adam Sank said. "I remember thinking, 'That's a strange thing for the head of a news network to say. So the conclusion is, we're the *anti*-Clinton news network?'" But this idea had large elements of fiction. In fact, many of Clinton's most ardent pursuers—starting with *Newsweek*'s Michael Isikoff—were members of the very newsrooms and networks that Ailes tagged as bastions of Clinton-loving liberalism. It was *The New York Times,* after all, that published one of the first major investigations into Whitewater.

Whatever else it was, the scandal was a media bonanza, and no medium benefited from it more than cable news—and no cable channel more than Fox News. As online purveyors of tabloid rumors like the *Drudge Report* transformed political scandal into serial entertainment, broadcast news remained virtually flat, and, in some cases, declined. Meanwhile, the ratings of CNN and MSNBC grew 40 and 53 percent, respectively. Fox News's ratings, minuscule in its opening year, spiked 400 percent in prime time. "The Lewinsky story did for Fox News what Fox News couldn't do for itself," a former producer in the Washington bureau said. The combination of sex and schadenfreude generated massive ratings at a fraction of the cost of a foreign crisis. "Monica [Lewinsky] was a news channel's dream come true," John Moody said. "It was cheap in both senses." It was during this period that Fox's prime-time stars, Bill O'Reilly and Sean Hannity among them, were reborn as cultural bulwarks against a growing number of contemptible influences: Bill Clinton's libido, the media, environmentalists, gay activists, you name it. As a former senior Fox News executive put it, "when Bill started wagging his finger at the president and raising his voice, that was the genesis of the modern Fox News."

Before leaving Arkansas for Fox News, Shuster had heard enough stories about Ailes to know his politics. But he believed conservative ideology was only a minor factor at Fox. Although his personal opinions were vaguely Democratic, Shuster never thought about advancing the interests of one side or the other through his journalism. The fact was, Shuster thrived on the energy of Ailes's high-octane start-up. He thought he had the best of both worlds, shuttling between Washington and Little Rock. "I was having the time of my life," he recalled.

One of the things Shuster liked most about his job was working for Brit Hume, the network's chief Washington correspondent and managing editor of the Washington bureau. While Shuster worked at the Little Rock ABC affiliate, Hume was an Emmy Award–winning correspondent at ABC News. Ailes recruited Hume, who was ideologically on board with Ailes's mission, a few months after Shuster. "We believe we are eligible to pick up the audience of the disaffected," Hume told a reporter. "Those who are looking for news but whose sensibilities are continually assaulted when they watch the other news outlets." Though clearly a conservative, Hume was "at heart a journalist," Shuster said. He remembered Hume holding the view that "there was a whole constituency of people at the White House who were trying to protect Clinton." Shuster appreciated that his new boss wanted to give him the resources to find out the truth.

In the beginning, no matter how many stories Shuster reported, hardly anyone in the capital recognized him, since many of the suburban precincts in which Washington's political and media classes resided didn't carry the channel; even Fox's Washington affiliate didn't carry the Fox News election night broadcast. And with Ailes's political baggage, Fox had little to offer the Clinton administration. In the summer of 1996, Moody had gone to Washington to meet with George Stephanopoulos, a senior adviser to the president. When Moody asked if Clinton would be willing to appear on Fox News on the day of its October launch, Stephanopoulos started laughing. "Why wouldn't he?" Moody asked, pointing out that Clinton had done the same for MSNBC during its recent debut. "Well, for one thing," Stephanopoulos said, "MSNBC's not owned by Rupert Murdoch and run by Roger Ailes." Kim Hume, Brit's wife and a former producer at ABC, had to fight to get Fox News included in the White House press pool after she joined Fox's Washington bureau as news director and deputy bureau chief in August 1996.

When Defense Secretary William Cohen made a trip to Europe in late February 1997, MSNBC and CNN were granted room on the plane, while Fox was not. A few months later, Fox complained that it was not allowed on Secretary of State Madeleine Albright's plane during her Middle East tour. "We're trying to be as fair and balanced as possible. But Fox is the relatively new kid on the block," a State Department official told *The Washington Post.*

The distribution problem continued to be a wellspring of frustration in the spring of 1997. News Corp's federal lawsuit against Time Warner in the Eastern District of New York proved to be a dead end. And a federal appeals court upheld Judge Cote's original injunction. But in mid-July, despite the victories, Time Warner suddenly reversed course. Over lunch at the annual Allen & Company media summit in Sun Valley, Idaho, Murdoch, Parsons, and Levin hammered out a deal.

Most observers viewed the agreement as a weak-kneed capitulation on Time Warner's part, but Murdoch made the deal irresistible, agreeing to pay Time Warner upward of $200 million to gain access to eight million cable subscribers, which included the 1.1 million households in New York City. Ailes was triumphant. "I made it look too damn easy," he told a reporter. "I'm afraid they think I can launch a new network every six months."

It was a short-lived celebration. That summer, Ailes learned that David Brock, a thirty-four-year-old investigative journalist, who had once declared, "I kill liberals for a living," was writing what Ailes surmised to be an unflattering profile of him for *New York* magazine. In July 1997, Brock published a widely read essay in *Esquire,* "Confessions of a Right-Wing Hit Man," that detailed his spectacular break from the conservative cause. As a movement insider, Brock understood Ailes's intentions for Fox News in a way others didn't. In a bid to get Brock to abandon the story, Ailes told him he was "confused." "You shouldn't be wasting your time on this article when you could be on our air," Ailes said.

Brock demurred. Ailes responded with trademark bluster, "Three people in the world hate me. You're not going to get to them, and everyone else is too scared. Take your best shot at me, and I'll have the rest of my life to go after you," he said. The six-page profile, titled "Roger Ailes Is Mad as Hell," hit newsstands on November 17, 1997. It was the most damaging article about Ailes to date, rendering him as a political operative in a newsman's suit.

A month later, Ailes put positive topspin on his public image. His friend, gossip columnist Liz Smith, announced his impending marriage to

Beth Tilson on Valentine's Day 1998 in a ceremony at City Hall. The officiant was a loyal friend: Rudy Giuliani.

On Sunday morning, January 18, 1998, John Moody was at home in suburban New Jersey getting ready for Mass when Kim Hume called him from Washington with mind-blowing news. Just past midnight—12:32 a.m. EST to be exact—Matt Drudge posted an article on his website with a salaciously tantalizing headline: "NEWSWEEK KILLS STORY ON WHITE HOUSE INTERN/BLOCKBUSTER REPORT: 23-YEAR-OLD, FORMER WHITE HOUSE INTERN, SEX RELATIONSHIP WITH PRESIDENT ** WORLD EXCLUSIVE ** ** Must Credit The Drudge Report **" At the top of the page, Drudge affixed a flashing police siren—a comic book touch that would become his trademark. "At the last minute, at 6 p.m. on Saturday evening, *Newsweek* killed a story that was destined to shake official Washington to its foundation: A White House intern carried on a sexual affair with the President of the United States!" Drudge did not reveal the intern's name, but noted that word of the liaison "caused blind chaos in media circles."

What should Fox put on the air? Kim wanted to know. The producers of *Fox News Sunday* had coincidentally scheduled a live interview with Wesley Holmes, a lawyer for Paula Jones, the former Arkansas state employee who had filed a sexual harassment lawsuit against Bill Clinton. Could they ask him about the intern allegations? Moody told her to avoid the story. He was heading to Fox News headquarters to hold a special meeting in the War Room to manage the coverage. On his drive into the studio, he reached Ailes from his car phone.

Ailes knew Drudge. In December, he met with the Internet entrepreneur to discuss the possibility of his hosting a tabloid show on Fox News. The thirty-one-year-old fedora-wearing gossip hound, who idolized Walter Winchell, was an unlikely protagonist in a national drama. His website, an incongruous mix of headlines—extreme weather events and movie industry talk—had the feel of a 1950s scandal sheet, with a readership of Beltway and media elites. Drudge's abiding passion was politics. He relished beating the press pack on national political news, like the time he reported that Bob Dole was going to choose Jack Kemp as his running mate. But sometimes he was disastrously wrong. On August 11, 1997, he posted a rumor that Sidney Blumenthal, a newly appointed adviser to Bill Clinton and former *New Yorker* journalist, had "a spousal abuse past that has been effectively covered up." Though Drudge pulled down the story within hours and issued a retraction the following day, Blumenthal sued for $30 million. "I don't give a damn what the bureau chief's going to think. I don't have one," Drudge told *USA Today*.

Though Whitewater had the potential to become Watergate, Ailes urged caution. "You better have multiple sources on whatever we go with," he told Moody. Given Drudge's uneven track record, Ailes made an understandable decision to hedge on the intern story. Acting on Ailes's directive, Moody instructed Kim Hume to inform Marty Ryan, the producer of *Fox News Sunday,* that Tony Snow and his panelists should refrain from addressing the Drudge item on camera until Fox could independently confirm it. Snow's co-anchor Mara Liasson danced closest to the overnight bombshell. "Do you have evidence of other episodes of the president committing sexual harassment?" she asked Paula Jones's attorney, Wes Holmes. "I'm sorry. I'm probably going to be pretty boring in this interview," he replied.

David Shuster was not surprised to find the Fox News bureau buzzing when he arrived at work on Monday, January 19, Martin Luther King Day. On Saturday, he had covered Bill Clinton's historic six-hour deposition in the Jones case. But without access to the Internet at home, Shuster was not prepared for just how wild the story was about to become. Carl Cameron, a lanky political reporter from New Hampshire who had joined Fox at the launch, motioned at Shuster and pointed to one of the computer monitors in the newsroom. "Did you see this stuff?" he said. Drudge's latest "world exclusive" was on the screen.

The item revealed the name of the intern, Monica Lewinsky, and a few biographical details. Drudge also reported that Lewinsky had been deposed in the Jones case.

*"Holy shit,"* Shuster thought.

At 6:00 p.m., Drudge went on to report that Lewinsky had signed an affidavit in the Jones case in which she denied having a "sexual relationship" with the president. According to Drudge, NBC News had obtained a copy and was "reading portions of it to sources to provoke comment." The news ricocheted around Fox, but Ailes continued to order his correspondents to hold off.

His decision to keep Fox News at bay may have been as much politically as editorially motivated, part of a strategy to obscure his channel's perceived conservative bent. If Fox anchors reported on the intern affair before confirming it, the channel's liberal adversaries would surely pounce. "They didn't want to play into the whole right-wing idea," one Fox producer recalled. But in fact Fox personalities were playing a role behind the scenes to move the scandal along. In the summer of 1996, *Fox News Sunday* host Tony Snow connected his friend Linda Tripp, a disgruntled former White House secretary who wanted to write a tell-all book about Clinton, to Lucianne Goldberg, a big-haired, chain-smoking conservative consultant to the *New York Post* and occasional literary agent, who would advise Tripp to tape her conversations with Lewinsky. "You ought to talk to Lucianne Goldberg," Snow told Tripp. "We were all part of a rat pack," Goldberg later said.

On a conference call with members of Fox's Washington bureau, Moody said not to worry about breaking new ground. "His message was—given Ailes's reputation and because of his Republicanism—as a news channel, we don't want to be first unless we have it dead right. We have to be sure," one participant on the call remembered. David Shuster received additional guidance from Brit Hume. "We know you know the story backwards and forwards, but it's okay to lay off," Shuster recalled Hume advising him. The guideline applied to Fox's prime-time opinion pundits as well. "We don't need to be first," Hannity's producer, Bill Shine, told another staffer.

Instead, Ailes instructed his team to prepare for the story breaking. On Tuesday afternoon, Shuster wrote a memo outlining the latest developments in the Jones lawsuit and the Whitewater investigation, "background info so we're ready to go." Shortly after finishing his memo, he heard Cameron's voice call him over to his computer. "TONIGHT ON THE DRUDGE REPORT: CONTROVERSY SWIRLS AROUND TAPES OF FORMER WHITE HOUSE INTERN, AS STARR MOVES IN! . . ." were the words on the screen. Shuster immediately placed calls to his contacts in Starr's office, but no one picked up. Returning home, he continued to dial his sources. Finally, shortly before midnight, Shuster got confirmation.

A couple of hours later, a Fox producer called to tell him that *Washington Post* reporters Sue Schmidt and Peter Baker had published a story on the paper's website. The producer read the headline aloud to him. "CLINTON ACCUSED OF URGING AIDE TO LIE; STARR PROBES WHETHER PRESIDENT TOLD WOMAN TO DENY ALLEGED AFFAIR TO JONES LAWYERS." (Drudge linked to the article with his own triumphant headline: "WASH POST SCREAMS INTERN STORY!")

To a competitive reporter like Shuster, the article stung. "*Fuck,* they got the scoop," he thought. ABC News and the *Los Angeles Times* followed with reports of their own. He had little time for rumination. As soon as the scandal had been reported by mainstream media organizations, Ailes shifted the message from "slow down" to "full speed ahead."

On Monday morning, January 26, Clinton handed Ailes an invaluable wedge that would define the political battle in the months ahead. "I did not have sexual relations with that woman, Miss Lewinsky," he said in a surprise appearance in the Roosevelt Room at an event promoting after-school programs. "I never told anybody to lie, not a single time, never. These allegations are false. And I need to go back to work for the American people. Thank you." On a day when his presidency seemed imperiled, Clinton's head-shaking, finger-pointing denial signaled to his enemies that he would never back down.

For Ailes, who had watched the moment on a wall-mounted television screen in his second-floor office, the president's remarks were a godsend—and a chance to redress past wrongs. Shortly after Clinton's first inauguration, Ailes received an anguished phone call from George H.W. Bush, who said he had seen a photograph of Clinton in the Oval Office in a short-sleeved shirt. If Clinton's sartorial choices caused offense, then fellatio from an intern was sacrilege. "Roger saw Clinton thumbing his nose at the institution of the presidency," an Ailes friend recalled.

The audience to which Ailes appealed likely felt the same way. They deeply resented Clinton's moral relativism and his lawyerly "I didn't inhale" evasions. "Roger once said that people in Iowa don't care about what's happening abroad. He said the focus is on American values," a former Fox producer said. And what could be more American than the country's conflicted relationship with sex? "Roger thought it was amusing, and so did I," Lucianne Goldberg said. "What Fox wanted was the president having sex in a room Reagan wouldn't walk into without a jacket on." She continued: "Roger understands you must simplify, simplify, *simplify*."

Clinton's brazen denial dared his enemies to expose him as a liar. It was all eerily reminiscent of the challenge candidate Gary Hart had leveled to reporters who were chasing rumors of his infidelity during the campaign for the 1988 Democratic presidential nomination. Clinton's taunting comments had the same crystallizing effect. They focused the minds of the American public on one basic question: *Did he or didn't he?*

Until Clinton came clean, Fox News had a never-ending story. Within hours, Ailes made the first of several significant programming moves to capitalize on the scandal. When Brit Hume called from Washington that morning, Ailes told him he wanted him to launch a new show. *That night.* Hume was astonished. The channel was planning to launch a program helmed by him in March, and there was some talk of moving up the start date, but he didn't think that would mean going live in less than twenty-four hours. Ailes envisioned Hume's 6:00 p.m. program, which he called *Special Report,* as Fox News's own *Nightline,* the ABC newscast in which Ted Koppel updated the American public on the Iranian hostage crisis. What Koppel had done for the abduction of fifty-two Americans, Hume would do for the president's creative use of cigars.

Hume infused *Special Report* with the immediacy of breaking news even when there wasn't anything new to report. Five producers and correspondents covered the Starr investigation full-time. "We had a whole formula," Shuster, who was part of the team, recalled. "Every story had to lead with a 'today' picture." So if the grand jury wasn't in session, Hume could open the lead story with video of Starr taking out the trash at his home in Virginia that morning. To keep tabs on the Whitewater grand jury, the producers developed a surveillance system. A source gave them a telephone number that connected the caller, usually a lawyer, to a recorded message announcing whether or not the grand jury would be in session. It was a valuable shortcut. Other news organizations had to stake out the courthouse to find out when a new witness was testifying. "I think we were the only ones who had that," Shuster said.

In short order, *Special Report* established itself as a competitive player on the Lewinsky beat. The program had a strong record of breaking stories, including Lewinsky's decision to become a prosecution witness, Clinton's agreement to testify before the grand jury, and Clinton confidant Vernon Jordan's grand jury testimony about his controversial conversations with Lewinsky. The show's relentless reporting infuriated the Clinton White House. The president's personal lawyer, David Kendall, and adviser Bruce Lindsey complained to Fox News's White House correspondents Jim Angle and Wendell Goler about the show's scandal-obsessed coverage. "We're trying very hard to be fair," Hume said. He took their complaints as something of a badge of honor. "The Clinton administration—they hated us!" he later told *The New York Times*.

Launching Hume's newscast at 6:00 p.m. required Ailes to juggle. He shifted Bill O'Reilly to 8:00 and Catherine Crier to 10:00. Mike Schneider's 7:00 p.m. time slot was in flux. After clashing with Ailes, Schneider had left the channel a few months earlier. Ailes had Jon Scott and others fill in. Moving O'Reilly to prime time was an unexpectedly brilliant move.

At the opening of his inaugural 6:00 p.m. program, O'Reilly had stated the mission that he at first was unable to execute. "How did it happen? How did television news become so predictable and in some cases, so *boring*?" he asked. "Well, there are many theories, but the fact is, local and network news is basically a rehash of what most regular viewers already know." It was the breakthrough insight. The viewers Ailes was trying to attract did not want television to tell them what happened in the world. They wanted television to tell them how to *think* about what happened in the world—the news itself would be secondary. "Few broadcasts take any chances these days, and most are very politically correct," O'Reilly continued. "Well, we're going to try to be different, stimulating and a bit daring, but at the same time, responsible and fair."

He failed, initially. In those opening months, he attracted only a few audience members and the scorn of television critics. At forty-eight, O'Reilly was a journeyman long past his sell-by date. His career began in Scranton, Pennsylvania, and climbed the affiliate ladder: Dallas, Denver, Portland. In 1982, he was called up to the Bigs, landing a job at CBS News, where he covered the Falklands War. In 1986 he switched to ABC News. He declared to the network staffers there that he had the talent to sit behind the anchor desk. "He would say he should have Peter Jennings's job," Emily Rooney, who worked with O'Reilly at ABC, recalled. There was no doubt he had talent. At six-four and with piercing, glacier-blue eyes, he owned the screen. In interviews, he proved himself to be an effective interrogator.

But O'Reilly burned hot. He harbored petty slights and made a habit of self-destructing. In one five-year period, he blew through four different television stations. "He was always in trouble with management," Ailes said. In 1989, he bailed out of the networks altogether to anchor the syndicated tabloid program *Inside Edition*. There, he sensed a shift in the national media conversation. Loudmouths, from Howard Stern to Rush Limbaugh, were building massive audiences as the medium of talk radio exploded. O'Reilly, a notorious loudmouth himself, wanted a piece of the action. "I'm not sure where the business is going," he told a friend, "but my gut says it's going in the direction of Rush, and man, I'm going to be there." O'Reilly turned *Inside Edition* into a programming laboratory. Unshackled from the on-the-one-hand, on-the-other-hand relativity crossfire that mirrors the journalism school ideal of objectivity, he was able to incubate the bullying Irish street cop delivery he would later master at Fox News.

His failure at Fox's 6:00 p.m. slot turned out to be a matter of timing. At 8:00, when many people were settling in front of the tube after dinner, O'Reilly finally connected. Like any skilled actor, he subtly calibrated his delivery to engage the full range of his audience's emotions. With the Monica Lewinsky scandal now at his disposal, O'Reilly gave his viewers all the different reasons it was okay for them to despise the president. One evening he told Nixon White House counsel John Dean that sex with an intern was an "abuse of power." If questions about sex seemed off limits, Dan Quayle told O'Reilly's audience that lying shouldn't be. "It's important if the president of the United States committed perjury," the former vice president said. For those who worried that condemning Clinton made a person sound like a conservative kook, O'Reilly took partisanship off the table. "You guys wanted him out since Day One," he barked to Jerry Falwell. "Don't care that he's been a good president. How do you answer *that*?" O'Reilly heard from voices on the right and the left as he marshaled his interviews toward his unassailable conclusion: Bill Clinton was fibbing to get out of a jam. O'Reilly was there for the folks to make sure Clinton couldn't pull a fast one.

It made sense, on several levels, that O'Reilly would become Ailes's brightest star. O'Reilly once remarked that their meeting was "just perfect synergy." Like Ailes, O'Reilly had a talent for constructing a compelling personal narrative. Although O'Reilly's father worked in Manhattan as an accountant, he presented himself as a scrappy son of Levittown, Long Island, where the local parish and the New York Mets competed for the faithful's attentions. "It was very basic," O'Reilly told his biographer. "It was tuna. It was hot dogs and beans. It was steak on Saturday night. It was spaghetti. It was secondhand sports equipment, movies now and then."

Class antagonism formed the foundation of O'Reilly's carefully honed public image. At prep school, he was sneered at by the WASPs from Long Island's wealthy North Shore. At Marist College, then an all-male liberal arts college in Poughkeepsie, New York, eighty miles north of Manhattan on the Hudson River, O'Reilly hung with an Irish and Italian crowd that tried to crash parties at Vassar on the fancy side of town. "I could feel those rich girls and their Ivy League dates measuring me," he recalled.

O'Reilly also shared another significant Ailesian trait: he understood television news was nothing but a show. "Bill O'Reilly is one of the greatest bullshitters in the world," Ailes's brother, Robert, said. "He can talk about any subject, he can get the best out of his guest by taking the opposite point of view even if he doesn't believe it."

O'Reilly's sudden success at 8:00 p.m. showed Ailes that the audience was responding to the nightly melodrama. So Ailes added more supporting characters to his cast. Disgraced former Clinton adviser Dick Morris—who was exposed patronizing a $200-an-hour Washington prostitute—became a frequent on-air presence and fount of embarrassing Clinton gossip. "What do you want me to say?" he asked a producer in the green room before one Lewinsky segment. "What do you mean?" the producer asked. "Well, which side am I?" Morris said. Playing the Clinton apostate proved the most valuable role. In March 1998, Morris told the Fox audience that years earlier Bill had asked him to poll-test how a divorce would hurt his political future. "Hillary and I are having some problems and I think we may have to split up," Morris quoted Clinton saying. "Do you think that's going to hurt me politically?" In April, Ailes hired Morris as a political analyst.

Several weeks later, Ailes recruited the mysterious figure who had done much to catalyze the scandal: Matt Drudge. But Drudge's transition to television was not an easy one. Inside Fox News, he was as much an oddity to producers as he was to the outside world. "It'll be me, a hat, and the hippest stories on the block," he told one reporter. "I'm going to go wherever the stink is." Lucianne Goldberg was a regular companion on his set, which one reporter described as "Raymond Chandler detective's office," complete with teetering stacks of faded newspapers and 1950s-style furniture. To complete the picture, Ailes even let Goldberg smoke cigarettes on air.

In the summer of 1998, to feed his audience's obsession with Clinton headlines, Ailes added more political news to the lineup. It was a period that marked a subtle transfer of power to John Moody from Chet Collier, who would retire a little more than a year later. In July, Ailes hired *McLaughlin Group* regulars Mort Kondracke and Fred Barnes to host

*The Beltway Boys,* a weekly political roundtable. A few days later, he scrapped Collier's original lineup. Hours of hard news between 9:00 a.m. and 4:00 p.m. would replace Collier's twenty-minute talk show blocks. The new lineup premiered on July 27.

It was auspicious timing. On the evening of August 17, Clinton spoke to the country from the White House's Map Room a few hours after his videotaped Whitewater grand jury testimony. His four-and-a-half-minute address finally answered the American people's singular question: *he did.*

As Clinton's presidency spiraled toward its nadir, Ailes and Fox News were rocketing to new ratings highs. On the set of *Hannity & Colmes* that night, the mood was ebullient. Matt Drudge called into the studio from his cell phone to commemorate the momentous occasion. "It's all popping. Congratulations," Drudge said, sounding like a star player celebrating with a teammate in the end zone. "I think this has been the finest night of the network."

Fox's wall-to-wall coverage of Lewinsky showcased Ailes's unmatched ability to fuse politics and entertainment into a marketable product. His wit and theatrical flair were embedded into Fox's programs in ways both big and small. Sometimes the channel covered the scandal as a comedy. That's what its zany poll questions were for. "Which of the following do you think better describes Monica Lewinsky: An average girl who was taken advantage of, or a young tramp who went looking for adventure and thrills?" "What is President Clinton more thankful for this Thanksgiving? Still having a wife? Or still having a job?"

At other points, the scandal was covered as pure soap opera. In April 1998, Fox aired exclusive video of Clinton in a hotel in Dakar, Senegal, where he was traveling on an official trip, after a judge dismissed Paula Jones's sexual harassment lawsuit. "You see the president walking around in his suite, smoking a cigar, walking around the room, eventually beating on an African drum," correspondent Jim Angle reported. "And at one point, he is also playing the guitar. So I think it gives you a pretty clear indication of the mood." In another report, by correspondent Rita Cosby, Fox showed the cad getting his due: "Sources tell Fox News that the reason the couple's recent ski vacation in Utah was abruptly cut short and they returned one day early was because they had a shouting match which left Hillary storming out of the room saying she wanted her bags."

Some Fox viewers kept the channel on for so long that the static Fox

News logo displayed on the lower left corner of their TVs burned the pixels. Before a rotating one was introduced, even when they turned off their sets for the night, the outlines of the graphic remained tattooed to the dark screens.

David Shuster was no longer having the time of his life. His unhappiness was on one level surprising, because he was being lauded by management. Shortly before Clinton admitted to the affair, Moody called Shuster and told him that Ailes wanted to meet him in person in New York "to pat you on the back." But Shuster was becoming increasingly frustrated with O'Reilly, Hannity, and other talking heads, who took his reporting out of context to damage Clinton. In August, Shuster told producers that he learned Starr was investigating the possibility of a "second intern." He did not report it on-air and cautioned that Starr had found no direct evidence for it. But Mort Kondracke, co-host of *The Beltway Boys,* promoted the allegation on camera. After Shuster complained about Kondracke to Brit Hume, Moody had Shuster indicate which part of his reports could be used on-air. "There was initially this Maginot line between the news and the commentary," said Steve Hirsh, a member of the Washington bureau. "As they became more successful and more identified with the niche they sought out to get, that line was blurred more. You had some of the old-line news folks, whether they agreed with the politics, who didn't want to do that."

During the impeachment saga, Shuster and other Fox journalists learned that Ailes was telling Brit Hume to commission Clinton-bashing assignments. "We would hear that Roger would call Brit with a laundry list of five or six stories that he would want us to do," Shuster said. "It was something like either the Clintons pushing a particular nomination, or that they were buying off someone for a vote. It was stuff that Roger was picking up." He went on, "But Brit would say, 'I'm not going to have my White House correspondent ask this at a briefing.'" In a private conversation in the bureau, Shuster told Kim Hume he was uncomfortable with the direction of the channel. "Kim said to me, 'Look, Brit's on your side. You don't realize it, but he's fighting tooth and nail protecting you and the other reporters from what Roger wants you to do,'" he recalled.

Catherine Crier was also increasingly unhappy. As the host of the 10:00 p.m. *Crier Report* and the newsmagazine *Fox Files,* her sensibility was vastly different from Ailes's. "I'm very interested in conflict resolution," she had told a reporter when the channel launched. "The world really doesn't exist in black and white, wrong and right, liberal and conservative." Ailes disagreed, at least for the purposes of television. "Be more opinionated," he told Crier in one meeting. "The guests are there as a foil for you." He also disagreed with her dress. "He had admiration for her legs," a senior executive said. In one meeting, Ailes barked, "Tell Catherine I did not spend x-number of dollars on a glass desk for her to wear pant suits."

Crier found the editorial direction worrisome. "Over time, in the three years I was there, I began to feel more of a heavy hand," she said. Ailes, she said, was "paying more attention to what stories were being covered or not covered." After months of Lewinsky mania, she was bored. "Of course everyone covered it ad nauseam. But it was to the point I was stopping strangers on the street saying, is there *anything* about this you don't know? I can't do this anymore. There certainly was a take that was emerging, it wasn't there when I was starting," she said.

She was also disturbed by Murdoch's influence on Fox's coverage. In the summer of 1997, at a time when Murdoch was seeking to expand his media empire into China, Crier was told to soften her coverage of the British handover of Hong Kong to Beijing. "I would get comments through my production staff and my executive producer," she said. Months later, Crier decided to leave Fox News for a position at Court TV. "They offered me a lovely contract to stay. I felt uncomfortable. There were no hard feelings when I left," she said. "I was troubled when I left. I can't even imagine the situation today."

*Hannity & Colmes* was another management challenge. Despite its bipartisan billing, the show was a vehicle for Sean Hannity's right-wing politics. An Irish Catholic from Long Island, Hannity came of age as two revolutions, Reagan conservatism and right-wing talk radio, sent the country on a new course. He harbored dreams of becoming the next Bob Grant, the caustic New York City radio commentator who provided an outlet for incendiary views on blacks, Hispanics, and gays. Radio personalities like Grant, Hannity said, "taught me early on that a passionate argument could make a difference."

In his twenties, Hannity drifted. He tried college three times but dropped out. By the late 1980s, he was living in southern California working as a house painter. In his spare time, he called in to KCSB, the UC Santa Barbara college station, to inveigh against liberals and to defend the actions of his hero Colonel Oliver North in the Iran-Contra affair. His combative commentaries impressed the station management. Though he was not a student, Hannity was soon given an hour-long morning call-in show, which he titled *The Pursuit of Happiness,* a reference to Reagan's 1986 Independence Day speech.

In April 1989, Hannity invited the virulent anti-gay activist Gene Antonio on the air to promote his already widely discredited book, *The AIDS Cover-up? The Real and Alarming Facts About AIDS*. A Lutheran minister without scientific training, Antonio peddled paranoid fictions about the epidemic. He wrote that the virus could be transmitted by sneezes and mosquito bites and that the Centers for Disease Control and the American Medical Association conspired to cover up the "truth."

At the opening of his hour-long interview, Hannity said: "I'm sick and tired of the media and the homosexual community preventing us from getting the true, accurate information about AIDS in this day." He went on to describe *The AIDS Cover-up?* as an "excellent book" that was "so full of facts" and added, "if you want the real truth about this deadly, deadly disease, he's not afraid to say what the homosexuals don't want you to hear." He gave his audience Antonio's mailing address, where they could order "autographed copies" and write to find out about "places where homosexuals can go for help if they want to change."

Hannity's description of gay life on the show was just as venomous as Antonio's extreme rhetoric. He described San Francisco gay men as "disgusting people," gay sex as "against nature" and "tantamount to playing in a sewer," and gay adoptive parents as "really sick." Hannity said he would not allow a gay man to teach his son at school. "I don't care if you call me homophobic. I'll take it," he said. Strangely, given his avowed disapproval, Hannity expressed a prurient interest in Antonio's explicit descriptions of enemas, golden showers, and bestiality.

As the men talked, irate calls flooded the studio. Jody May, a lesbian station employee, told Hannity about her baby boy.

"Artificial insemination?" Hannity asked. "Aren't you married to a woman, by the way?"

"Yes, I am."

"*Yeah,* turkey baster babies," Antonio interjected.

"Yeah, isn't that beautiful?" Hannity added.

"That's also a really disgusting remark," May said.

"I feel sorry for your child," Hannity snapped. "You wanna make any more comments?"

Gay rights groups, calling for a boycott of the station, pressured management to yank Hannity off the air. In June the station canceled his show, citing his "multiple discriminatory statements based on sexual orientation," which were in "violation of the University of California Nondiscriminatory Policy." Hannity played the victim of overzealous PC enforcers. After Hannity launched a free speech campaign, enlisting the Santa Barbara and Los Angeles chapters of the American Civil Liberties Union, the university agreed in the summer of 1990 to reinstate his program. Hannity insisted that the university double the standard one-hour show and one-semester appointment to two hours and two semesters. When the university balked, Hannity walked away. In his telling, he was a target of liberal persecution.

After applying for radio gigs around the country, Hannity found work in the South, eventually landing a job at the Atlanta talk station WGST. His bio on the station's website declared that he made "a proud name for himself by insulting lesbians." In an interview with New York's *Newsday* several years after joining Fox, Hannity glossed over his time in Santa Barbara, speaking the powerful language of conservative resentment. "You work for free at a college station, where they spit on you and then they fire you," he said. "Then you pack up and move to a small station across the country. And if you work hard and you are talented, eventually you get a shot. Everybody has that story in America. That's why I love the capitalist system in America."

Though cast as a supporting character for Hannity, Alan Colmes did not want to be Hannity's punching bag. To indulge Colmes, producers tried to help him feel like more than a prop. Each morning, a producer would first call Hannity to get a rundown on what he wanted to cover that night. Then the producer would call Colmes to get his input. Unbeknownst to Colmes, this second call was largely a ruse. "There was a real tightrope walk we had to do to make Alan feel like he was an equal voice," one producer recalled. "Sean basically served as executive producer of the show."

While conservatives like Hannity thrived at Fox, rank-and-file staffers began to express apprehensions with Ailes's programming directives.

Some struggled with the channel's self-conscious anti-intellectualism. Others felt uncomfortable with the overt politics. "I had higher-ups wanting to see my scripts," said producer Rachel Katzman. "They needed to make sure I wasn't too liberal. I was told to change stories." Jordan Kurzweil, who was hired to launch Fox News's website, also got pressure to conform. "John Moody would call my editor and ask me to change a headline or the positioning of articles because it was damaging to Republicans. The phone calls got made, it was frank," Kurzweil said.

In hushed conversations around the halls, these young staffers wondered why the channel masked Ailes's conservative aims with the "fair and balanced" slogan. One former producer remembered exchanges like this: *"What is the crime in coming out and saying what we're doing? Everyone knows this is what we're doing. . . . Why do we have to keep it a secret? What's this 'fair and balanced' thing the producers keep talking about behind the scenes? I don't know why they don't just say what it is. It's so blatantly obvious."*

The answer involved a combination of politics, history, and psychology. The conservative dream of establishing a counter-media hinged, in large part, on convincing the viewers that what they were getting was *news,* not propaganda. "Fair and balanced" was a commercial necessity. "If you come out and you try to do right-wing news, you're gonna die. You can't get away with it," Ailes said to the *Hartford Courant*. "There'd been four failures at that," he told *The New York Times,* without citing examples. "This was a different mission entirely."

TVN's failure had many causes. But certainly its stigma as a Coors propaganda tool contributed to its demise. Two decades later, Paul Weyrich's National Empowerment Television was ghettoed to the far right because the channel uniformly displayed Weyrich's dogmatic conservatism—a turnoff to most viewers.

Keeping Fox News's staff in line was not a major concern for Ailes. Brian Lewis and the PR operation took care of that. Lewis's absolute no-leaks policy scared employees into silence, from highly paid anchors to low-level grunts, at least when reporters came calling. Blasting rap music in his office—"Gangsta Nation" was a favorite track—Lewis planted negative stories about disloyal employees. When successful he liked to say, "I shoved a Scud up his ass!" The harder challenge involved the one thing Ailes could not ultimately control—the news itself.

By the winter of 1999, Fox News's prime-time lineup was passing MSNBC for second place, even though MSNBC was distributed in nine million more homes. But in February, the Lewinsky saga finished its final act. The Senate voted to acquit Clinton. Ailes would need a new story line.

The options were unappealing. The news cycle was favoring his less partisan rivals and Ailes was turned off by the coverage of the NATO air campaign in Kosovo, which he saw as both boring and expensive. His audience did, too. During the conflict's opening days in late March, MSNBC doubled its daytime audience and zoomed past Fox to reclaim second place in the ratings wars. One afternoon, Ailes barged into John Moody's office to complain about Fox's war coverage. "You gotta stop this bullshit, how much are we spending?" he said. "Who the hell gives a shit? Is there even a story? What the hell are we doing there?" Moody, the former *Time* foreign correspondent, stared back. "Are we done?" he said.

The evening lineup was also a problem. In January 1999, Ailes poached the respected CBS anchor Paula Zahn to helm a 7:00 p.m. newscast, which had rotated through anchors since Mike Schneider's exit. But Zahn's seriousness and elegance were out of sync with the prime time partisans. O'Reilly was firing on all cylinders at 8:00, which boosted *Hannity & Colmes* at 9:00. So Ailes tried a different tack. He moved Zahn to 10:00 p.m. and put Shepard Smith, a thirty-five-year-old fast-talking field correspondent, in her slot.

The goal was to go tabloid. After his forceful performance covering the Columbine massacre, Smith convinced Ailes he could own the screen. "Put Shep in front of a live picture, and it's unbelievable," one former Fox producer said. A gregarious Mississippian who had joined Fox at the launch, Smith was part of a clique of young staffers. He rented a beach house in the Hamptons with fellow Fox correspondent Rick Leventhal and began dating Julia Rolle, a beautiful field producer. But Smith had a dark side. He was known to explode unexpectedly on his colleagues. "He Shepped Out" became a phrase around the halls.

Whatever turbulence he caused, Smith had an ineffable quality that Ailes prized and that he had an instinct to spot. To produce his show, Ailes hired a former tabloid producer named Jerry Burke, who had done a stint in Los Angeles at *Extra,* the syndicated celebrity news show. But Burke's sensibility was not welcome in all corners of the channel. On one of his early shows, Burke told Smith to lead with a live report on the drama between basketball star Dennis Rodman and Carmen Electra. The phone in the control room rang. Burke answered. It was Brit Hume, who had just signed off *Special Report* from Washington.

"Why are you calling me?" Burke said.

"You are single-handedly going to destroy this network," Hume seethed. He told Burke the Rodman story had no place at the channel. Burke slammed down the phone. The following morning, Ailes walked into Burke's office in the newsroom and told him he was backing Hume. "Jerry, you gotta be true to the brand," Ailes told him. "I'm willing to risk a tenth of a rating point if you protect the brand. Think about it, we're not *Extra*."

While Ailes refused to acknowledge it in public, the Fox News brand had been set: the channel programmed news to appeal to conservatives. Which is why it was not tabloid for Hume to talk about blow jobs and semen stains on the air. That was a serious matter of national consequence. One of Ailes's gifts was knowing where the taste line was and pushing right up to the limit of it. Matt Drudge did not. In November 1999, Drudge stormed off his set when John Moody refused to let him show a photograph from the *National Enquirer* of a twenty-one-week-old fetus undergoing surgery for spina bifida. Drudge wanted to use the photo to illustrate an antiabortion segment. Moody overruled him, saying it would be out of context. The messy episode spilled into the press. "I guess I can go on and talk about Lewinsky's dirty dress," Drudge complained to *The Washington Post,* in a burst of truth telling. "I have to wonder whether their motto of 'we report, you decide' isn't just some Madison Avenue slogan." "Matt's entitled to his opinion. It was an editorial decision," Brian Lewis said.

After a few days of sniping, both sides stood down. Drudge agreed to cancel his contract, which had more than a year to go. "The network cannot live by the standards of the Internet, where each person is his own writer, editor and publisher," Ailes told a reporter. Drudge's exit signaled that Ailes's Lewinsky train had reached the end of its line.

# FIFTEEN
# THE CALL

As Americans made their quadrennial pilgrimage to the voting booth on the afternoon of Tuesday, November 7, 2000, John Prescott Ellis, first cousin of George W. Bush and the chief of Fox News's "decision desk," hustled into a second-floor conference room to brief Roger Ailes, anchors, and producers on the state of the race. A confidant of his cousin's presidential campaign, Ellis was part of the story he was covering, managing the team of analysts responsible for how Fox News would call winners and losers. In an hour, Brit Hume would begin anchoring the channel's live election night coverage.

For the conservatives around the conference table—Ailes, John Moody, Brit Hume, Fred Barnes, *Weekly Standard* editor and Fox News contributor Bill Kristol, and Fox News analyst Michael Barone—Ellis painted a depressing picture. Exit polls showed Hillary Clinton coasting to victory in the New York Senate race. Democratic presidential candidate Al Gore was surging, winning so-called late deciders by a two-to-one margin. Michigan and Pennsylvania, key battleground states, were breaking his way. More ominously for the George W. Bush–Dick Cheney ticket, Gore was pulling ahead in Florida. For weeks, the consensus had been that the Sunshine State would be ground zero on election night. The best news Ellis could offer was that Gore would likely be denied an early victory. The electoral math was such that Gore could not get over the top until the polls closed in California at 8:00 p.m. Pacific Time.

After the briefing, Ellis slipped out of the building for a cigarette. At forty-seven, with wavy brown hair and a wry sense of humor, Ellis exuded privilege and confidence. It was not the first time he'd been a kind of double agent. In 1978, as his uncle Poppy Bush was mounting a run for the GOP presidential nomination, Ellis joined NBC News as a producer in the election unit. In 1993, Ellis landed a political column at *The Boston Globe*. Ellis's role as a Bush family surrogate eventually complicated his role as a *Globe* pundit. "Looking back over the last 6½ years, the collected lies of William Clinton test the hard drive of memory," he wrote in a column in May 1999. On July 3, Ellis recused himself from covering politics. "Loyalty supersedes candor," he wrote. "I am loyal to my cousin, Governor George Bush of Texas. I put that loyalty ahead of my loyalty to anyone else outside my immediate family. . . . There is no way for you to know if I am telling you the truth about George W. Bush's presidential campaign. . . . And there is no way for you to know whether I am telling you the truth about Al Gore's presidential campaign." Three weeks later, he gave up his column entirely.

Ailes expressed no reservations about bringing Ellis to Fox. In the early 1990s, Ellis worked for him at Ailes Communications. It was Ellis who helped secure his lucrative consulting contract with Paramount Television at a moment when Ailes was transitioning out of politics. In 1998, Ellis ran Fox's election unit, his first experience in such a role. "We at Fox News do not discriminate against people because of their family connections," Ailes later said.

As Ellis smoked his cigarette outside the Fox studios, he dialed Bush in Austin. Earlier that afternoon, he had told Bush, who sounded tense, "I wouldn't worry about early numbers. Your dad had bad early numbers in '88, and he wound up winning by seven."

Now that Gore's apparent advantage was widening, Bush wanted to know what his cousin thought.

"I have no idea," Ellis said.

Bush told Ellis to stay in regular contact throughout the night.

Ellis ended the call and stamped out his cigarette. There was one more meeting he had to attend. Ailes was waiting upstairs for a private briefing in his office before venturing over to the Fox Sports Suite, a reception space on the second floor where Murdoch and senior News Corp executives would watch the returns come in. Ailes wanted fresh intelligence.

"What's your gut say?" Ailes asked.

Ellis pantomimed a knife motion across his throat.

In the messy aftermath of the 2000 election night debacle, and Fox's central role in the recount drama, liberals would single out the presence of

John Ellis as evidence of a conspiracy to propel Bush into the White House. The truth was more complicated. But Ailes's decision to place a candidate's cousin in charge of calling an election, regardless of his conduct on election night, reflected a lack of concern about journalistic standards.

Ellis's Bush family ties were not the only factor that made him a controversial choice to direct Fox News's election night coverage. While Ellis certainly possessed a sophisticated understanding of national politics, he lacked the mathematical skill that was essential to understand the complex computer models that guided the on-air calls. "From what Ellis says, he does not know how to read the screens," said Warren Mitofsky, the longtime head of CBS News's election operation, who is credited with creating the modern exit poll. "I cannot, for the life of me, imagine what Ellis is doing when he makes calls."

Ellis's decision team was made up of three people. They included John Gorman, a longtime Democratic pollster who had worked for George McGovern and Jimmy Carter; Arnon Mishkin, a Boston Consulting Group partner and former NBC News analyst; and Cynthia Talkov, a Berkeley-educated statistician, who worked with Gorman at his polling firm, Opinion Dynamics. Fox News received its election night information from the Voter News Service, a consortium established in 1993 by the Associated Press and the five major television networks—ABC, NBC, CBS, CNN, and Fox—to cut costs by sharing the burden of conducting exit polls and tallying vote counts for Senate, congressional, and presidential races. The consolidated system would become one of the factors that led to the disastrous 2000 results. Although the networks all used the same raw data, each outlet fielded their own decision teams (except CBS and CNN, who shared a joint unit). On election night, when millions of viewers were up for grabs, the pressure to be first—or at least not be last—created perverse incentives inside the competing newsrooms to make premature calls.

Cynthia Talkov, who was mentored by Warren Mitofsky and whom Ellis would later describe as his "statistical wizard," knew immediately that something was off about Fox News when she joined the decision team for the primaries. To Talkov, Fox seemed like a seat-of-the-pants outfit. She observed Ellis and her colleagues struggle to grasp the Voter News Service computer models. "They didn't understand half the numbers on the screen. . . . I couldn't believe how unqualified they were," she later recalled. "They weren't listening to me. I thought maybe it was because I was a woman, I didn't know." As a last resort, she brought in the editorial director of the Voter News Service, Murray Edelman, to tutor them on the computer system. Edelman was equally unnerved. "My God, you were right!" he told her after the session. Ellis, Edelman later recalled, was "so arrogant, as though he knew it all. When I talked with him, I thought, 'Whoa!'—he was so confident, but knew so little."

And then there was the politics. Although she had worked for the Voter News Service and done opinion polling for Gorman, Talkov never paid much attention to the actual campaigns. She was a moderate Democrat, and had voted for Bill Clinton, but to her, candidates were names "all flagged either Democrat or Republican" on a screen. "I enjoy crunching numbers," she said. "I'm not in the world of media or politics in any shape or form. People say to me, 'what's going on?' I just tell them, 'ask my mother, she's home watching CNN. I don't know who the candidates are.' " So it was a shock to arrive at Fox News and find Ellis, Gorman, and Mishkin gossiping on the phone with political operatives from both parties. "I was brought up in the ranks that we do not talk to any campaigns on election night," Talkov said. But her initial surprise was nothing compared with the surreal experience she had during the New Hampshire primary. When Ellis stepped away from his desk, Talkov noticed his phone ringing and leaned over to pick it up.

"We're surging now!" the voice said.

"*Who is this?*" she asked.

"George Bush," the voice returned. "Is my cousin there?"

Talkov was incredulous. VNS numbers were supposed to be strictly confidential. If Ellis disclosed exit poll data to a campaign, he would be in violation of the consortium's ironclad contract.

When Ellis got back to his desk after his post-cigarette meeting with Ailes, Talkov was hunched over her screen reading the latest exit poll numbers. The new data stream only bolstered the prediction Ellis had just given Ailes. North Carolina and West Virginia were listed as "too close to call," and Bush was "flat in Ohio," the state that had elected every president since 1964. The worst news came from the state that mattered most. Shortly after the Florida polls closed at 7:00 p.m., the trend lines shifted in Gore's direction. At 7:50, the VNS computer showed Gore with a 99.5 percent chance of winning Florida. The "status" menu on the screen read: "Call."

Ellis's former colleagues at NBC News did not wait for the official VNS go-ahead. At 7:49, Tom Brokaw announced on air, "We're going to now project an important win for Vice President Al Gore." Thirty-one seconds later, Dan Rather declared Gore the Florida victor. CNN echoed Rather's call. John Moody needed an answer from Ellis. It was up to Moody to sign off on all the calls. He would relay the word to *Fox News Sunday* producer Marty Ryan in the control room, who would in turn speak the result into Brit Hume's earpiece. Ellis polled his team about calling Florida. "Any objections?" They all agreed it was Gore. At 7:52, Hume made the pronouncement.

In Bushworld, the Florida call rankled. The polls had yet to close in the Republican-dominated Panhandle. How could they call it for Gore when citizens were still voting? Bush's senior strategist Karl Rove directed aides to call news executives and complain. Moments after Fox's call, Ellis's phone rang. "Jeb, I'm sorry," Ellis said, speaking to W.'s younger brother, the governor of Florida. "I'm looking at a screenful of Gore." Jeb asked Ellis about the polls in the conservative Panhandle counties that had not yet been tallied. "I'm sorry. It's not going to help," he said.

Upstairs, in the Fox Sports Suite, the mood was funereal. Ten minutes after calling Florida, the networks named Michigan for Gore, another blow for Bush. Ailes sat in a plush armchair, phone glued to his ear, fielding updates from John Moody. "You could see Roger hanging on every word," one person in the room recalled. "It was like the old school. He wasn't even trusting what was going on the screen." His senior executives—Bill Shine, creative director Richard O'Brien, and director of newsgathering and operations Sharri Berg—stood nearby, gloomily watching the screens. At 9:00 p.m., Hume put Pennsylvania in the Gore column.

Ellis was now virtually certain that his cousin would lose. W., however, wasn't ready to concede. "I think Americans oughta wait until all the votes are counted," he told reporters in Austin. "I don't believe the projections. In states like Florida, I'm gonna wait for them to call all the votes."

On the Fox News decision desk, Ellis scanned the screens and saw the Florida numbers going haywire. "Can you guys take a look at Florida, please? I think we may have to pull down the call," he said. A message flashed on the VNS monitor. There were irregularities in Duval County, a Republican stronghold on the Atlantic coast, about twenty miles south of the Georgia state line. "We are canceling the vote. . . . Vote is strange," the message read. It turned out that a VNS employee had incorrectly entered data into the system, giving Gore 43,023 votes instead of the much lower actual total of 4,301. Ellis huddled with his team and Moody. The VNS screen showed the letters REV, short for "reversal." They agreed it was time to pull it down. Moody relayed the news to Ryan. Hume declared Florida back up for grabs, as did all the networks. At 10:23, Hume called Gore's home state of Tennessee for Bush.

In the Sports Suite upstairs, the vibe around Ailes improved considerably. "It had been kind of a somber mood. Then it became a lot more celebratory," one executive in the room recalled. "You sensed you could change history here."

Ellis later recalled that he became certain his cousin would win Florida—and the presidency—at 1:55 a.m. In a first-person account of his election night activity for *Inside* magazine, Ellis wrote that he scrutinized the VNS data, which showed Gore failing to win enough of the remaining votes to overtake Bush's several-thousand-vote lead. Ellis called Bush to give him the remarkable news.

"What do you think?" Bush asked.

"I think you've got it."

After hanging up, Ellis turned to his team. "Any reason not to call Bush in Florida? It's the whole deal, so if you're not sure, say so." The analysts still wanted more time. Ellis told Moody he had confidence in a Bush-Cheney victory. "John, based on these numbers . . . he can't lose Florida."

The minutes ticked by. Ailes, who had left Fox around midnight for a nearby hotel, received updates from Moody.

At 2:07 a.m., the VNS screen showed Bush ahead in Florida by 29,000 votes, with 96 percent of the votes counted. Ellis was eager to make the call. Cynthia Talkov, who was sitting next to Ellis, did not observe him studying the statistics on the screen, as Ellis would write for *Inside*. Nor did he discuss with her Gore's "need/get" ratios, the projections Ellis would cite as the basis for making the call. Around 2:10 a.m., Talkov observed Ellis conferring with his cousins in Austin. When he hung up the phone, his eyes lit up. "Jebbie says we got it! Jebbie says we got it," he said.

Ellis was ready to call it. No other network had done so. He went around the room again. This time, no one expressed objections. Fox would be announcing the new president-elect. Talkov would later be haunted by her decision not to disagree with Ellis. "At the time, if you were gonna pick a winner, you'd pick Bush. But you couldn't. It was too close," she later said. "I didn't stand in his way. I should have said, 'Hey, it's not a statistically sound call.'" She felt powerless to intervene. Even that night, she was chided for her cautious approach. "If you listen to me, you'll never make a call," she told Moody. "Let me introduce you to the concept of live television," Moody responded.

After conferring with Ellis, Moody called Ailes, who was already asleep.

"We're gonna call it Bush," Moody said. "Roger was like, uh, *okay,*" a person familiar with the conversation later recalled.

Moody passed the word along to Marty Ryan. At 2:16 a.m. EST on November 8, 2000, Brit Hume looked into the camera and said, "Fox News now projects George W. Bush the winner in Florida and thus, it appears, the winner of the presidency of the United States." Whooshing graphics filled the screen: "BUSH WINS PRESIDENCY."

The Fox call brought the political world to a halt. Confusion reigned at Bush campaign headquarters in downtown Austin. "It's just Fox," Karl Rove cautioned.

"Is this going to be a bandwagon?" another staffer ventured.

The networks waited. At NBC News, Sheldon Gawiser, director of elections, was on the phone with Murray Edelman of VNS, discussing the numbers. Gawiser had been under pressure to end the uncertainty. Around midnight, Jack Welch stalked into the newsroom and was overhead barking, "Okay, how much do I have to pay you assholes to call this thing for Bush!" Edelman was telling Gawiser to keep Florida undecided. But Gawiser cut him off. "Gotta go, Fox just called it." Tom Brokaw made the announcement moments later.

Twenty-two seconds after Brokaw, Dan Rather took to the air at CBS. "That's it. Sip it. Savor it. Cup it. Photostat it. Underline it in red. Press it in a book. Put it in an album. Hang it on a wall. George Bush is the next president of the United States." CNN called it at 2:18, and ABC followed at 2:20. Only the AP held back.

Bush reveled in the triumphal news with his cousin. "Gore called and conceded. He was good, very gracious. What a night for him."

"Congratulations," Ellis said into the phone, "when are you going to speak?"

The electoral reality beneath this cheerful picture was beyond chaotic. The VNS system was as erratic as a loose garden hose, spraying bad information in all directions. At 2:48 a.m., Gore's numbers in coastal Volusia County, home to Daytona Beach, shot up by nearly 25,000 votes. Twenty minutes later, the Florida secretary of state's website had Bush with a razor-thin lead of 569 votes, based on 99.8 percent of the votes counted.

Gore was already in the motorcade on his way to deliver his concession speech when AP political reporter Ron Fournier got Gore's spokesman Chris Lehane on the line in Nashville to tell him the race was actually a toss-up. Campaign aides frantically tried to head Gore off before he stepped onstage.

It took nearly an hour for the AP's conclusion to reach John Ellis at Fox News. At 3:27 a.m., an urgent message popped onto his VNS screen. "Florida—the Sec of State Web site has a much narrower margin for Bush. We are comparing county by county trying to determine discrepancies." The VNS alert indicated the service could not vouch for the accuracy of its results. Ellis called Moody over to tell him the numbers were shifting.

"You said they couldn't," Moody said.

"I was wrong," Ellis said.

Ellis quickly called Bush to relay the disappointing news. "You gotta be kidding me," Bush said.

A few minutes later, Bush called back. "Gore unconceded."

At 3:57 a.m., for the second time, the networks began reversing their Florida call. CBS/CNN went first, then ABC at 4:00 and NBC/MSNBC at 4:02. Fox News, the first to declare Bush president, was the last to walk it back. Brit Hume made the announcement at 4:05 a.m. Talkov was concerned about Ellis's conduct that night, and what role it played in shifting the dynamic in Bush's favor, but decided to remain silent. "I was afraid to speak," she later said. "The reality was, I felt intimidated. It was a big network. . . . I naively thought eventually they're going to count the vote and there will be a winner."

For the next thirty-three days, from the contested network calls to the Supreme Court's decision to halt a statewide recount, Fox News largely stuck to the story line the channel authored on election night: George Bush was the president; Al Gore and the Democrats were sore losers, trying to steal it from him. Millions of Americans on election night watched television news anchors declare Bush the victor. The media reality had created its own reality. The Democrats were left with a hopelessly confusing argument. Just what the hell was a butterfly ballot, anyway?

Not that it was an easy transition for Fox. "The day after the election, we woke up and it was like, 'Oh shit, what do we do now?' " a senior producer recalled. "Before Bush, there had been such an attack dog mentality toward Clinton. It went on for so long, it was kind of like getting a marathon runner to change strides." Fox's coverage, in both news programming and prime-time punditry, championed the Bush campaign's line. Only hours after declaring Florida too close to call, Hume was questioning Gore's motives. "It won't be easy to get the Democrats to accept the result if it goes against them," he told viewers on *Special Report*. On *The O'Reilly Factor* that night, the whole notion of screwy voting practices went out the window. "There is a minor brouhaha in Palm Beach County about a confusing ballot. Now I've seen this ballot. It's not very confusing," O'Reilly assured his audience. "There are little arrows everywhere. Come on. Nothing will happen there. There are reports of voting irregularities across the country. That always happens."

The theme of Democrats' duplicity popped up routinely. "I think what's going on is the Democratic lawyers have flooded Florida . . . they are afraid of George W. Bush becoming president and instituting tort reform and their gravy train will be over," anchor John Gibson declared in one segment, hammering the popular line that Democrats were bankrolled by rich trial lawyers who wanted to sue corporations freely. On November 26, Fox was the sole television news organization that took Florida secretary of state Katherine Harris's certification as gospel. "FLORIDA DECISION" blared the on-screen caption. Republicans were grateful. "If it hadn't been for Fox, I don't know what I'd have done for the news," Senate majority leader Trent Lott would tell *The Washington Post*. Ratings soared. In November 2000, Fox zoomed past MSNBC, with average daily viewership climbing to one million. CNN, which enjoyed a twenty-year monopoly on cable news, was now within target range. Those who wavered from the pro-Bush narrative at Fox quickly learned painful lessons.

David Shuster was one casualty. At dawn on November 8, shortly after Hume walked back Fox's call, he was on a flight to Tallahassee. Shuster was eager to cover the recount drama as aggressively as he had dug into Whitewater. But from the moment he landed in the Sunshine State, he was given strict marching orders from Moody and Hume. "It became clear early on what their agenda was," he said. Moody criticized

Shuster's coverage of press conferences with Jim Baker, the Bush campaign's chief negotiator. "We think you're being impolite to Baker," Moody would tell him. "Shuster, you gotta ratchet down your tone with Baker," he ventured on another occasion. Shuster told Moody he was putting the same questions to Baker that he was asking Warren Christopher, the Gore negotiator.

Moody's protectiveness of the Bush camp confirmed Shuster's earlier suspicions. During the primaries, when he was covering Arizona senator John McCain's run for the GOP presidential nomination, he was assigned to do reports on how McCain was "unstable" and how he was "a moderate in conservative clothing." Shuster saw Bush getting lighter treatment. It concerned him that the wife of Fox's Bush correspondent, Carl Cameron, was campaigning for Bush. Shuster complained about it during a meeting with Moody. "Isn't that an ethical problem?" Shuster asked.

"Mind your business," Moody said.

Shuster tried lobbying David Rhodes, a fast-rising young news executive who ran Fox's political desk. "He was like, 'Look, I hear you. I know it's not fair. Do your thing,'" Shuster recalled.

Two weekends before the general election, Shuster joined Cameron on the Bush beat. After he discussed on camera the fact that Bush had spoken at Bob Jones University, the South Carolina Christian school that did not enroll black students until 1971 and prohibited interracial dating until March 2000, Moody called him to complain. "You've reported it twice, don't mention it the rest of today," Moody said.

In the days leading up to the election, Shuster watched how Fox expertly managed a potential bombshell crisis for Bush. On Thursday, November 2, a young reporter for WPXT-TV, the Fox affiliate in Portland, Maine, received a tip that Bush had on his record an unreported arrest from 1976 for drunk driving near the Bush family compound in Kennebunkport. Carl Cameron broke it on *Special Report* that night. Later, Ailes would tout it as evidence of Fox's objectivity. "I knew it would hurt him," Ailes told *The New Yorker*. "They said we should hold it. We ran it. We're in the news business and we do what's news." But it was also true that the story was about to break whether Fox reported it or not. And by reporting it first, Fox successfully shifted the story from an embarrassing reminder of Bush's frat boy past to a case of dirty politics (the reporter's source was a Democrat). On air, Tony Snow told viewers that "questions are being raised about how the story came to light, and whether it was leaked to make a political point." The next day, Bush appeared on Fox

News and gave his only interview about the subject. "I don't know whether my opponent's campaign is involved, but I do know that the person who admitted doing this at the last minute is a Democrat in Maine, a partisan in Maine," he said.

The coverage reflected a broader trend Shuster observed in the three years since he joined Fox. When he pursued Clinton, Ailes personally congratulated him. When he pursued Bush, his bosses questioned not only his objectivity, but his loyalty. He tried commiserating with a colleague, White House correspondent Jim Angle, but it was no use. "Jim said to me, 'Look, I always start with an argument from the Republican side. If you do that, you'll be fine.' "

As the recount stalemated in Florida, Shuster's disillusionment intensified. He challenged Cameron and Hume on a conference call to cover the butterfly ballot controversy in Palm Beach County. "Carl was arguing, there's no way the butterfly ballot is a story," Shuster recalled. "Brit became convinced that Gore's people were trying to steal the election. I think he got conditioned to think like Roger."

Shuster also clashed with Bret Baier, a thirty-year-old reporter from the Fox News Atlanta bureau. Baier and a camera crew had gone to the Panhandle to interview Republican voters who felt disenfranchised when the networks called the state for Gore before the polls closed in the Central Time Zone. On Fox, Brit Hume had cited claims by the libertarian economist John Lott, who estimated Bush lost as many as "10,000 votes in Florida" because of it. But Baier said he could not find any such disenfranchised Republican voters. Moody let Baier know that Fox would not air a story that poked holes in the claim. Shuster recalled: "I was arguing with Bret at the time, 'This is a canard, it's bullshit. You should at least send an internal memo and get pundits to stop saying that.' He said, 'I'm not going to do that.' " During Bush's first term, Baier was promoted to cover the Pentagon in Washington.

Shuster's time was running out. He later realized he had done himself in shortly after the Supreme Court's 5–4 decision that gave Bush the presidency. Waiting for Bush to emerge at a press conference in Washington, Shuster chatted with CBS News correspondent Bill Plante, who told him Bush would not take questions. "This is crazy," Shuster told him. "Sure enough, Bush comes out. He talks for like a minute and a half," Shuster recalled. "I said, Mr. President why are you in such a rush to leave? He glared at me." As soon as he walked offstage, Bush turned to his press secretary, Ari Fleischer. "Who's that asshole?"

Afterward, Shuster was called into a meeting with Brit Hume. "Roger doesn't think you're loyal to him," Hume said. "It was never the same for me after that," Shuster recalled. He would leave the network in February 2002.

Bush's victory at the Supreme Court did not end Ailes's election night problems. On November 9, John Ellis invited *New Yorker* writer Jane Mayer to his home in Westchester County, and gave a wide-ranging interview in which he boasted about his frequent election night conversations with his cousins. "Jebbie'll be calling me like eight thousand times a day," Ellis said. Recounting what it was like after Fox called W. the winner, he said, "It was just the three of us guys handing the phone back and forth—me with the numbers, one of them a governor, the other the President-elect. Now *that* was cool."

Ellis had seemingly admitted sharing confidential Voter News Service exit poll numbers with a campaign. Gore's campaign manager later told a reporter that if Gore's first cousin had done what Ellis did, "they would indict him!" There were congressional hearings into the networks' botched calls scheduled for February, and members wanted to subpoena the decision desk employees. Ailes and the networks protested, citing First Amendment grounds. Instead, the networks offered to conduct their own investigations. Ailes dispatched Fox's general counsel, Dianne Brandi, to interview the Fox decision team.

Cynthia Talkov had become increasingly incensed at Ellis's election night behavior and the spin he put on it afterward. Not only was his article in *Inside* magazine a sanitized history that bore no relation to what actually happened inside Fox News, but Ellis described her in the article as a "passionate Democrat," a move that seemed designed to make her into a bipartisan prop to maintain the "fair and balanced" mantra.

With her lawyer at her side during a conference call with Brandi, she detailed for Brandi everything she observed on election night. "I told them my truth 100 percent," she said. Talkov's attorney remembered that when Talkov repeated Ellis's declaration "Jebbie says we got it!" Brandi responded with a "pregnant pause." Talkov never worked for Fox again.

As the attacks on Fox's election night conduct persisted, Ailes displayed his gifts as a crisis manager. On Valentine's Day 2001, Ailes was in Washington to testify alongside network news presidents before the House Committee on Energy and Commerce. Prior to the hearing, Ailes was furious that he would be forced to take an oath in front of the cameras. The visual of the network chiefs holding up their right hands would make them seem like criminals. When it was Ailes's turn to speak, he turned in a valiant performance. As only Ailes could do, he took his critics' fiercest attacks and appropriated them as strengths. Ellis's newsroom presence was not a conflict of interest. It was smart journalism. "Obviously, through his family connections, Mr. Ellis has very good sources," Ailes's prepared statement read. "I do not see this as a fault or shortcoming of Mr. Ellis. Quite the contrary, I see this as a good journalist talking to his very high level sources on election night." Ellis resigned around this time. (He rejoined the network as a vice president of programming at Fox Business News in 2013.)

It was not long before Ailes and his troops would see just how consequential the results of the 2000 election would be. "That one little moment actually determined not just the course of the news channel, but of the country," a senior Fox producer said. "God knows what would have happened if Al Gore was elected."

# SIXTEEN
# HOLY WAR

AILES ARRIVED AT WORK on the morning of September 11, 2001, ready for a crusade. In a few hours, he was scheduled to meet with Greta Van Susteren, the veteran CNN anchor and legal analyst, who was flying up from Washington to talk to Ailes about a job. The sit-down, however, had far greater significance than a job interview. It represented a counterstrike in Ailes's intensifying battle with CNN for ratings supremacy and control of the American news agenda. Six days before, CNN had poached Paula Zahn to host a revamped morning program. Her departure came at a critical juncture for Ailes. Before she left, he told her he saw it as part of a "holy war," one he intended not to lose. In the wake of the Florida recount drama, Fox News had pulled even with CNN in the ratings. Bill O'Reilly was turning into a national phenomenon. Fox was even beginning to turn a profit, several years ahead of initial projections. In June, Ailes had been the subject of a *New York Times Magazine* article for the second time in six years.

Meanwhile, CNN's ratings were slipping. In March 2001, seeking to reverse the trend, Time Warner CEO Jerry Levin put Jamie Kellner, a brash entertainment executive and onetime protégé of Fox Inc. CEO Barry Diller, in charge of Turner Broadcasting. Kellner's explicit assignment was to halt Fox's gains by injecting CNN with buzz. "Give us six months to a year. We will be ahead of Fox," Kellner told the press. Ailes used Kellner's boast as fuel to sustain his forward advance. "Roger printed that quote out on a twenty-foot-long banner, which he hung in the newsroom," a senior producer recalled. "We were neck and neck with CNN, and every day I walked under that banner." Ailes's competitive drive knit Fox employees together. "Who wouldn't want to be part of a family, even a dysfunctional family? I loved who I worked with. What I most look back on is the scrappiness," former Fox producer Anne Hartmayer said.

Kellner, whom *The New York Times* once dubbed "one of the great poachers in the television industry," offered Zahn $2 million per year—triple her Fox News salary—to leave for CNN. Like Catherine Crier and other Fox News journalists, Zahn had found herself increasingly turned off by Ailes's partisan agenda. "She thought her career would be ruined if she got tainted as a Fox person," an executive said. On Tuesday, August 28, Zahn's agent, the self-described "b.s. artist" Richard Leibner, faxed Ailes a letter informing him of CNN's terms. Ailes exploded. He had already complained to colleagues that Kellner and his handpicked news chief, former *Time* magazine managing editor Walter Isaacson, were copycats, stealing Fox's swooping graphics and bright, candy-colored set designs. Now they were stealing his people.

After getting Zahn's letter, Ailes called an emergency meeting of his top executives to inveigh against Zahn's disloyalty and CNN's underhanded hiring practices. "Why don't we fire her?" Brian Lewis mused.

Ailes stopped to consider it. Zahn's contract was set to expire in February 2002. Dianne Brandi, Fox's general counsel, gave her imprimatur, suggesting that Zahn could be dismissed for cause for negotiating with a competitor while under contract. Later that week, Lewis followed up with a memo to Ailes about the merits of his idea. Preemptively firing Zahn "looks sincere" and "sends message thru ranks and to industry," he wrote, noting an "outnumbered army must have surprise on its side."

Over the Labor Day weekend, Ailes called Lewis several times to hash out his options. "I can't look like a bully," he said more than once. On Tuesday, Ailes gave Zahn a chance to answer for herself. "I just want to look you in the eye and ask what you're doing," he said during a meeting in his office.

"You'll have to speak to my agent," Zahn replied, coolly.

The nonanswer sealed her fate. "He made it very clear to me that he was not going to make life easy for me," Zahn later recalled.

The following morning, Ailes plunked himself down in a chair across from Lewis's desk. "I hope you're right about this," Ailes said. "You know, the Japanese bombed Pearl Harbor, and they ended up losing. Isaacson controls a lot of the press. They all love him."

At 2:30, Lewis sent out a press release announcing Zahn's ouster. Around the same time, Fox filed a lawsuit against Zahn's agent alleging "intentional interference." (The suit was later dismissed by the New York

Supreme Court, whose decision was affirmed the following year by the Appellate Division.) In the press, Ailes savaged Zahn's reputation. "I don't pay for disloyalty. And I'm not worried about her going to CNN," he declared to the *Times*'s Bill Carter. Ailes said he was "the victim of a 'Pearl Harbor attack' " by Leibner, whom he called a "liar." During the interview, Ailes delivered one of his most viciously descriptive explanations for a television personality's success. "I could have put a dead raccoon on the air this year and got a better rating than last year. That's all just the growth of the network," he said, speaking of a woman who, until that morning, worked for him. "All our shows are up."

Stealing Van Susteren would be a way to settle the score. "The key to the whole thing was hiring Greta," a senior Fox executive said. Like Zahn, she was a household name with crossover appeal, someone who could balance the hard-right partisanship of Fox's prime-time male pundits. Van Susteren had become a star at CNN during the O. J. Simpson trial. Her constant on-air dissection of the case helped make her CNN show the second-highest rated behind Larry King's. Ailes heard she felt unappreciated by Kellner's regime and was exploring her options.

But, of course, the September 11 meeting never took place. Ailes would have to wait three and a half months to hire her. Shortly after 9:00 a.m., Van Susteren and her husband, John Coale, a prominent Washington attorney and her agent, were sitting on the tarmac at Ronald Reagan National Airport waiting for their US Air Shuttle flight to take off when Van Susteren's BlackBerry started lighting up with emails.

"Oh my God, turn on CNN," Sharon Fain, Fox's Atlanta bureau chief, gasped into the speakerphone. It was just after 8:49 in the morning, and Fain was calling in to John Moody's editorial meeting. As she listened to a colleague propose a segment about embattled Democratic congressman Gary Condit, an image on the monitor near her desk caught her eye. "There's a live shot of a plane that hit the tower."

Moody, sitting in the glass-walled War Room of the basement newsroom, looked at his screen, which seemed to be showing a scene from a Hollywood disaster epic. The North Tower of the World Trade Center was on fire, spewing thick plumes of smoke. The producers sitting around the table watched in stunned disbelief. *Why didn't the pilot ditch in the East River?* one thought. *Was it a tourist plane?* another wondered.

It took four minutes from the time CNN went live with the news for

Fox to mention it on the air. *Fox & Friends,* nearing the end of its three-hour slot, did not yet have live video of the unfolding calamity. "Welcome back to Fox News, we have a very tragic alert for you right now. An incredible plane crash into the World Trade Center here at the lower tip of Manhattan," E. D. Donahey, the blond host, gravely announced. Donahey's co-hosts, Steve Doocy and Brian Kilmeade, struggled to make sense of the calamity. Kilmeade, a former sportscaster from Long Island, had little hard news experience. He speculated that the plane was a 737 narrow-body jet and "at least three floors were taken out." Owen Moogan, a Fox producer who lived five blocks from the towers, narrated the scene by phone. His uneven voice crackled over the cell line.

Two minutes later, Fox aired its first visual. "That is it," Donahey said.

Jon Scott, a seasoned anchor with experience at NBC News, took over from the *Fox & Friends* trio. Over the phone, Scott interviewed Vernon Gross, a veteran former investigator with the National Transportation Safety Board. Scott raised the specter of terrorism as a dark object streaked into the frame, quickly followed by an orange fireball. "There was another one! We just saw," he said haltingly, as if his eyes had betrayed him. "We just saw another one apparently go—another plane just flew into the second tower. This raises—this has to be deliberate, folks."

"I would begin to say that," Gross replied.

Just thirty seconds after the second explosion, Scott introduced Fox viewers to their archvillain. "Now given what has been going on around the world," he said, "some of the key suspects come to mind: Osama bin Laden."

Ailes watched the horrifying scene from his office televisions. "That means the second tower is coming down," he said to an executive as the first smoldered and crumbled. Ailes descended to the basement War Room. He sat at the head of the conference table surrounded by his top deputies. There was Bill Shine from programming; Moody from the news department; Richard O'Brien from graphics. "The country is at war, but I want my people to be safe," he told them. "I don't want this building hurt or this newsroom harmed. We're going to meet every hour today in this War Room." Ailes's confidence was inspiring. "Roger rallied the troops," one person in the room recalled.

While CNN had broken the news, Fox's coverage in the opening hours of 9/11 demonstrated how Ailes would master the biggest story of the decade. He took personal charge of the programming. Barely twenty minutes after the towers' collapse, Ailes introduced an innovation, known as "the crawl," that would soon be copied by Fox's competitors. "Day of Terror in the United States . . . Two planes crashed into the World Trade Center in New York . . . wtc towers collapsed . . . manhattan is sealed off . . . all train and bus service halted." The line of text streamed across the bottom of the screen like a stock ticker.

"A lot of guidance came down from the second floor," one senior producer recalled, referring to Ailes's executive suite. "We wanted to know, what is an act of terror? Are we at war? The word came through Moody, 'Yeah, we're at war. And it's a religious war and it's a Muslim war and they want to bring back the Caliphate.' "

Fox News's programming aimed to amplify the intense emotions of the event. Graphics in blood-red and white declared: "TERRORISM HITS AMERICA." Fox anchors in the studio were rarely visible. Their voices played over the day's surreal images, which repeated on a constant loop, as if the towers fell and were resurrected, only to fall again. It was on Fox that day that viewers saw some of the first, haunting photos of the tower jumpers.

The anchors delivered not just dire news, but patriotic spirit. "Folks, it just bears repeating. This is a tremendous tragedy, yes. But we are still the most powerful nation on earth," Jon Scott said. "It bears repeating, America is still standing. We are united, we are strong, and we will find out who did this," he later said. At another moment, he promised, "There will be a great uniting of America." On Fox, the defining tenets of the Bush years were coming quickly into relief: the with-us-or-against-us defiance; the battering of political opponents as unpatriotic; and an unmistakable undercurrent of Christian messianism.

And the politics. Though the Bush administration was in power, blame was cast on the Democrats: E. D. Donahey criticized the Clinton administration for allowing Al Qaeda to flourish. "They had this problem with Warren Christopher and with Madeleine Albright," she told viewers. "You know what? You come after us, we come back . . . you attack us here at home, on our turf, and it changes things."

That afternoon, as images of Palestinian children dancing in the streets played on the screen, anchor John Gibson talked with Oklahoma's Republican senator James Inhofe. "So what happens? I mean, do we sit here and say, 'Okay, we got to investigate this, and figure out who it is, and then we'll send FBI agents around the world and gather up the suspects and have a two-year trial?' . . . Or do we launch our military might?"

"No, we launch immediately," Inhofe said. "I think you're gonna see that we have a president who's on his way back to Washington as we speak who is gonna be very decisive."

In the evening, Reverend Billy Graham's son Franklin Graham prepared Fox viewers for the long battle ahead. "We need to be strong," he said on camera. "This, I'm afraid, is the beginning of a long and difficult process. . . . I've seen for myself these terrorists, these Islamic militants. They hate the United States. They hate us because they see us as the defender of Israel. They hate us because they see us as a Christian nation. They see our faith in the Lord Jesus Christ, and there are these militants that want to do everything they can to bring down this nation."

"It's extraordinary to hear a man of God such as Franklin Graham speaking in that way," Brit Hume told the audience.

The voice of Newt Gingrich, who made three appearances on September 11, stood out vividly in Fox's chorus. "This is a twenty-first-century Pearl Harbor. This is a twenty-first-century kind of war . . . it deserves a complete and total American response to ensure that it never happens again," he said an hour after the second tower fell. He soon remarked, "The administration has to reach out around the world and make quite clear that we are going to go after whoever did this, and that people can decide either to be with the terrorists or be with Americans, but there will be no middle ground. There's not going to be any neutrality in the process of getting even."

On the night of September 13, Bill O'Reilly had an exchange with Sam Husseini, a former spokesperson for the American-Arab Anti-Discrimination Committee, that characterized Fox's position as it was developing. "Here's what we're going to do, and I'll let you react to it," O'Reilly said. "We're going to take out this Osama bin Laden. Now, whether we go in with air power or whether we go in with a Delta force, he's a dead man walking. He's through. He should have been through long before this. He's been wanted for eight years. Now, they're going to go in and they're going to get him. If the Taliban government of Afghanistan does not cooperate, then we will damage that government with air power, probably. All right? We will blast them, because . . ."

Husseini told O'Reilly that innocent Afghans would be killed by a protracted air strike.

"Doesn't make any difference," O'Reilly huffed.

"Bill—"

"They—it was an act of war."

"No, no. It *does* make a difference," Husseini said. "I don't want more civilians dead. We've had civilians dead in New York and now you're saying maybe it's okay to have civilians dead in Afghanistan."

"Mr. Husseini, this is *war*."

"Yeah, exactly. And in war you don't kill civilians. You don't kill women and children. Those are your words, Bill."

"Oh, stop it," O'Reilly said. "You just made the most absurd statement in the world. That means we wouldn't have bombed the Nazis or the Japanese. We wouldn't have done any of that, because you don't want somebody who has declared war on us to be punished. *Come on.*"

"Who declared war on us?"

"The terrorist states have declared war, Mr. Husseini!"

"Get them. Get the terrorists," Husseini said.

"Cut his mic," O'Reilly responded, waving his finger across the screen, the lower third of which was covered with Stars and Stripes graphics and a caption that read: "AMERICA UNITES."

Everyone, from politicians to news anchors, wrapped themselves in flags after 9/11. Not long after the attacks, "it was like a World War Two mentality and we were fighting an evil empire," said a senior producer. "I remember running to Times Square to buy a fistful of flag pins off a vendor." Anchors began wearing the pins on-set. Ailes's creative director, Richard O'Brien, came up with a design for a waving American flag to be displayed on the screen.

In those opening days, all of the networks necessarily adjusted their coverage to reflect the country's wounded, angry patriotism, but Fox's rhetoric was hotter and louder. The anchors referred to bin Laden as "a dirtbag," and "a monster" who ran a "web of hate" made up of "terror goons." "What we say is terrorists, terrorism, is evil, and America doesn't engage in it, and these guys do," Ailes told *The New York Times* in December. "We understand the enemy. They've made themselves clear: they want to murder us. . . . We don't sit around and get all gooey and wonder if these people have been misunderstood in their childhood."

Ailes expressed the self-justifying belief that Fox's approach was not only the right thing to do but also great television, bigger than any good-versus-evil Hollywood blockbuster. Ailes had once dreamed of producing a feature film. Now he had one. At first, it was *Batman*. Mayhem broke out in the heart of Gotham. Then, it was *High Noon*. A cowboy president vowed to "smoke out" the bad guys and to find them "dead or alive." "I don't believe that democracy and terrorism are relative things you can talk about, and I don't think there's any moral equivalence in those two positions," Ailes said. He went on: "If that makes me a bad guy, tough luck. I'm still getting the ratings." And it was true—Fox's voice was very much in keeping with the views of much of America. In January 2002, Fox passed CNN in the cable news race, and never turned back.

Ailes experienced the traumatic day of 9/11 as a new father. On New Year's Day 2000, Beth had given birth to a son, Zachary Joseph Jackson Ailes. "He told me having a kid changed his life completely," former Fox anchor Bob Sellers later recalled. Ailes took measures to protect himself and his family. At the time, Judith Regan, host of *That Regan Woman,* was having an affair with New York police commissioner Bernard Kerik. On the night of September 11, Kerik even made a stop at Regan's apartment. Seeking security advice in the days after 9/11, Ailes called Regan's producer, Joel Kaufman, to arrange a private meeting with Kerik for him and Murdoch. Later, an internal New York Police Department memo surfaced that revealed Ailes asked for police protection with "a request for counter surveillance from [the] Threats Desk." The memo also detailed his elaborate security protocol. "Mr. Ailes employs a retired Detective NYPD as a personal escort. He arrives via private Car and is dropped off in front of 1211 Avenue of the Americas [Fox News headquarters] daily. . . . He is escorted into the building by his security and is met by building security."

The sense of lockdown pervaded the office. "After 9/11, it got really fucked up," a senior staffer said. On the second floor, a glass door with a key code would be installed in the hallway leading to Ailes's executive suite. That was in addition to the locked door that stood before visitors outside the elevator bank.

His private statements about the conflict were shocking. About a year after the attacks, Bill Clinton went for lunch at News Corp with Murdoch and his top executives. Murdoch's communications chief, Gary Ginsberg, who was a former lawyer in the Clinton White House and a key Murdoch emissary to powerful Democrats, brokered the meeting. Talk turned to Ground Zero and plans for reconstruction. The executives around the room offered ideas. When it was Ailes's turn, the conversation halted. "Roger said this insane thing," one person in the room recalled. "He was talking about rebuilding the towers and he said, 'We should fill the last ten floors with Muslims so they never do it again.' "

Ailes's sense of the drama, and Fox's own role in it, brought him into conflict with powerful forces at News Corp. On the evening of October 18, 2001, Ailes was a guest at the annual Al Smith dinner at the Waldorf Astoria, where Dick Cheney was delivering the keynote address. As the evening wound down, Ailes got a tip from Mayor Giuliani's office: the *New York Post* was the latest media organization hit with an anthrax-laced letter. Earlier that day, a *Post* mailroom employee had come down with symptoms of anthrax exposure, but no one knew where the letter was. Ailes raced back to the office. On the tenth floor, in the newsroom of the *Post,* Murdoch's oldest son, Lachlan, the tabloid's spiky-haired publisher, was handling the response. Workers in hazmat suits from the Centers for Disease Control and Prevention scanned the office. Lachlan wanted to keep the incident under wraps. News Corp had thousands of employees who were possibly at risk. There were human resources protocols to follow and certainly questions about the company's legal exposure if more employees got sick. Lachlan and Ian Moore, News Corp's head of HR, huddled together, strategizing options for alerting the staff in the morning.

Suddenly, someone told Lachlan that Ailes had burst into the Fox News newsroom shouting, "We're under attack! We're under attack!" To Lachlan, that was precisely the wrong message to be sending at that moment, and he decided to do something about it. He took the elevator to the basement and found Ailes in his white-tie tuxedo giving directions to the crew of overnight producers. Lachlan told Ailes he needed to settle down. Ailes did not take his advice well. "You could see him getting aggravated. He'd been taken down in front of his people," one executive said. The producers watching the confrontation were startled at what they were witnessing—Ailes was openly challenging the chairman's kid, who was the deputy chief operating officer of the entire corporation.

The gravity of the situation was not lost on Ailes. Fate could be cruel to News Corp executives who crossed the Murdoch children. In London, Sam Chisholm, the profane, New Zealand–born CEO of BSkyB, was forced out in part because he tangled with Rupert's daughter Liz, who worked for him (he had called her a "management trainee"). "On one level, Roger was very scared. No one had had a conflict with the children and survived. He didn't want to be Sam Chisholm," one executive close to Ailes explained.

Ailes needed to do something to turn the situation to his advantage.

Several months earlier he had already come close to overstepping his bounds when he decided to get rid of Fox News executive and longtime Murdoch ally Ian Rae. "Don't ever fucking fire a mate of mine again," Murdoch told Ailes. Within days of his confrontation with Lachlan, Ailes made an appointment to see Rupert. In the meeting, Ailes threatened to resign as a preemptive strike. Ailes told Murdoch that his kids were aligned against him. "Rupert is not the hardest person to manipulate," a family intimate said. It was an effective move—Murdoch offered him a new contract. Ailes had secured his place at the company. Dealing with Lachlan could wait.

## SEVENTEEN

# QUAGMIRE DOESN'T RATE

PROGRAMMING WAS ONLY ONE ARM of Ailes's effort to shape events. Shortly after the 9/11 attacks, he sent a confidential memo to Karl Rove with advice for George Bush. "The only thing America won't forgive you for is under-reaching," Ailes wrote. His missive expressed his view that the country was facing an epochal conflict against a ruthless adversary. "I wrote that letter as an American," he told a Fox colleague. He knew that Americans craved revenge. That's why, he'd say, Americans still loved John Wayne, even though he had been dead for two decades. The country had some basic rules.

Rove made sure Bush received Ailes's letter. Copies were also circulated to senior White House staff, including National Security Adviser Condoleezza Rice, deputy national security adviser Stephen Hadley, communications director Dan Bartlett, and press secretary Ari Fleischer. Fox News was a crucial ally. In the wake of the divisive recount, the White House recognized Fox's power to drive the debate and rally the faithful. On a personal level, Rove was said to be intimidated by Ailes, who antedated him on the national stage. "Roger was the bigger figure," recalled Bush aides who observed the power dynamic between the men. When Ailes complained that Fox was not getting enough access to White House officials, Rove leaned on White House communications director Dan Bartlett to rectify the issue. "Ailes would call Karl and say, 'we're not getting enough guests during the daytime,'" a Bush official said. "Ailes's message was: '*You better fucking do something about it*.' So Karl would then call the press office and be like, 'Why isn't [Attorney General John] Ashcroft getting out there?'"

To help Bush build his image as a war president, Ailes continued to feed Rove strategic advice. "It focused on how to use the presidential role and rally morale," a senior Bush official said. "Roger's reference point was Reagan. He would point out where he saw similarities to use the presidential pulpit. He would say, 'The president has to be out there more.' It was macro level advice, as opposed to tactical."

Ailes also made it clear he would leapfrog Rove if he felt particularly displeased. Around the time he sent the military strategy memo, Ailes discovered that the administration was filling a crucial vacancy in the press office—the White House's liaison to the television networks—with a former MSNBC producer named Adam Levine. Levine had worked for Chris Matthews on the staff of *Hardball* and was once a registered Democrat who worked in the office of New York senator Daniel Patrick Moynihan. Ailes complained directly to Dick Cheney about the appointment. "Roger was afraid it would favor NBC. He wanted to make sure Brit Hume and Tony Snow got the interviews," another Bush official said. Cheney's aide Mary Matalin, Ailes's friend, instructed Levine to go to New York to clear the air. During a meeting in Ailes's office, Levine pledged his loyalty. "Mr. Ailes," he said, "having worked for MSNBC and having been a Democrat, I can tell you I have more reasons than you could imagine to hate both organizations."

Ailes's producers clearly understood Fox's role. "Someone has to speak for the White House," one said. Though much of the media credulously amplified the Bush administration's case for the Iraq War, Fox News was its chief cheerleader, stoking passions born in the collapse of the towers and turning them to a new end. Three days after 9/11, Bill O'Reilly hosted foreign policy analyst Laurie Mylroie to make the argument for hitting Saddam Hussein. A year earlier, Mylroie—whom terrorism expert Peter Bergen would dub "the Neocons' favorite conspiracy theorist"—had published the controversial book *Study of Revenge: Saddam Hussein's Unfinished War Against America,* which argued that Iraq was responsible for the 1993 World Trade Center bombing. O'Reilly wanted to know if she had "any evidence" that Saddam Hussein was involved with 9/11.

"No," she said. "But I think there are things that suggest it."

Later in the interview, O'Reilly surmised, "You sound like you're a person who says, 'Hey, Saddam Hussein should be on the destruction death card, along with Osama bin Laden.' He should be target number two, maybe."

"I'd even say target number one," she said. "The direction and the expertise for these attacks are coming from Iraq. It would be good to get rid of bin Laden, I agree completely, but it won't solve the problem. It wouldn't be as meaningful as getting rid of Saddam Hussein's regime."

Given the president's approval ratings—87 percent in November 2001, according to Gallup—cleaving closely to the Bush administration's views was smart programming. In Iraq's mustachioed dictator, Ailes had a perfectly cast enemy and a ready-made narrative of conflict. "Every story needs a beginning, a middle, and an end," a senior Fox producer said.

Television networks roll out new series in the fall. The Bush administration did the same with its war plan. "From a marketing point of view, you don't introduce new products in August," Bush's chief of staff, Andrew Card, told *The New York Times* on September 7, 2002. Fox helped close the deal with the public, with Ailes personally directing the effort. Twice each day—first at 8:00 a.m. and again at 2:30 p.m.—Ailes assembled his senior leadership for strategy sessions. The morning meeting took place in his office and focused on news; the afternoon gathering was held in a second-floor conference room and dealt with operations and financial issues. Ailes ran tough meetings. His authoritarian management style could terrorize his inner circle into silence. Executives sat around the table hoping he would not call on them. "It's not easy to be in that room. He looks around and points at people. If you talked, you're fucking dead," one executive recalled. "You're supposed to take it until your face turns bright red, and you're thinking, *if you move, will the* T. rex *see you?*"

The meetings were highly secretive, in keeping with Ailes's background in political campaigns. In the network's early days, Ailes created a secret group of senior executives—he called it the "G-8"—to centralize authority. (During George H. W. Bush's 1988 campaign, Ailes had been a member of the "G-6" along with Lee Atwater and others.) Like George H. W. Bush, Ailes did not attend these meetings; he expected his team to get along without him. "Fox never went corporate," one of Ailes's executives said. Ailes was determined to keep the inner workings of his operation shrouded in mystery. He rarely communicated by email with his coterie of advisers, and when he did he usually used a pseudonymous account, "James Arlie," a variant spelling of his maternal grandfather's name. "Roger is very good about giving himself plausible deniability for everything," a senior producer said. When emails went out under his official "Roger Ailes" account, they were "generally to announce company-wide things." Otherwise, the producer said, "he prefers face-to-face meetings in his office."

In the newsroom, producers would hear senior executives whisper the phrase *"the Second Floor says"* or *"the Second Floor wants."* "You can't say Roger's name," an executive explained. "It reminded me of the scene in *The Godfather II* where Al Pacino is talking to Johnny Ola, and they're talking about Hyman Roth, except they never say his name. He was just 'the Man in Miami.' That's Roger. He's 'the Man from Fox News.'"

Ailes policed leaks, especially those about his political agenda, with ruthless determination. Judy Laterza, Ailes's longtime assistant from his Ailes Communications days, sat in on every meeting, writing detailed notes on yellow legal pads. She developed a system to help Ailes speak freely. "When Roger said something controversial, she just rolled her eyes," a meeting-goer said. "But then she wrote it down. Then she wrote down everyone else who was in that room. So if it leaked, then Roger would know who was there." Laterza's mysteriousness made her powerful. Fox seemed to be her life, and she was said to be one of Ailes's highest-paid employees. One producer joked to people that he wanted to follow her home to see how she lived.

Bill Shine, who had been promoted to head of prime time after Chet Collier's retirement, became the main conduit for Ailes's directives. To low-level Fox producers, Shine was an intimidating presence. Across his cheek was a large scar of unknown provenance. After serving as Hannity's producer, Shine moved into Chet Collier's position because he was willing to be Ailes's mouthpiece. When Ailes had a message to get on the air, he often turned to Shine. Where Collier was gruff, Shine was cryptic. He rarely put anything in email. "Call me," he would write to his colleagues. Or he would pop into producers' offices unannounced to pass along instructions from Ailes, although he rarely dropped his name; "We're not doing that," he'd coyly explain. Because Shine could not challenge Ailes as Collier sometimes did, he complicated Brian Lewis's PR mission to uphold Fox as a "fair and balanced" news network. As payback, Lewis would attach Shine's name on statements to the press when Fox had to disown programming embarrassments. Lewis had a nickname for Shine: around the office he called him "Toadie."

Colleagues did not think of Shine as a deeply political person. They saw his devotion to Ailes and Fox in more pragmatic terms. Like Fox's prime-time stars O'Reilly and Hannity, Shine was from Long Island.

He was "a blue-collar kind of guy, not a Harvard-Columbia guy," a colleague said. From his modest roots as a son of a cop, he had become a well-compensated TV executive who bought his wife, Darla, a Land Rover and built a luxurious vacation home.

John Moody was another surrogate through whom Ailes expressed his agenda. He wrote a daily editorial note to the staff, which appeared in the newsroom's computer system, offering guidelines about major stories to cover. "We looked at them every day," a former senior Washington bureau staffer said. "They were supposed to be mandatory reading." In addition to story lineups, the memos crackled with partisan gibes that overtly signaled how Fox should frame the news. "When Ashcroft was being confirmed as Bush's attorney general, one of the issues that came up at the time was his opposition to abortion rights," recalled producer Adam Sank, who spent six years at the network. "Moody's memo that day said something like, 'As we cover the Ashcroft hearings and the subject about his beliefs on abortion, I want you all to remember what this issue is really about: it's about killing babies.'" In October 2003, a Fox News producer named Charles Reina publicized Moody's memos to the press. Media critics railed that the memos proved Ailes's "fair and balanced" mantra was a sham.

But Moody's missives were probably unnecessary. "People know who's running things. People know who the audience is. If you drink the Kool-Aid things can go very well," recalled former Fox anchor Bob Sellers. "When I interviewed for the job, I had a script in mind for how I would negotiate the interview. It was: 'I was liberal when I was younger, conservative as I got older, and after 9/11, how can you not be conservative?'" Ailes built a campaign culture that was defined by staffers' need to prove their loyalty. "Watch out for the enemy within," he told Fox's staff during a company-wide pep talk. Adam Sank remembered the "little things you could do to win favor with people in power." On the one-year anniversary of 9/11, he happened to wear a red, white, and blue tie to work. "Every single executive stopped me and said, 'I *really* like that tie,'" he said.

Ailes cultivated the idea that he was everywhere. "Look, I know everything I need to know about you," he told one producer. "I talk to the people above you. I talk to the people below you. And I talk to the people on either side of you." Executives never knew Ailes's schedule. Sometimes he showed up for the morning editorial meeting, sometimes he didn't. If he wasn't there, chances were he was listening in on the speakerphone, although he would not announce himself. Suddenly his voice would crackle over the line. Ailes also put eyes in every department. One executive called it "the invasion of the secretaries." When Suzanne Scott, Collier's former assistant, sent directions to producers, the staff knew whom she was speaking for. "She had rules of what you could wear," a female producer recalled. "No jeans. If you went out to the field, no dyed hair. The camera people couldn't wear shorts unless it was over 90 degrees. All of us understood it." Brigette Boyle was another secretary promoted into Fox's HR department. "She had no HR qualifications, except to screen people who would be fit for Fox," a senior producer said. "Roger every so often had her do a task that was bizarre. Once, he asked for a list of every employee who went to Brown. He said it was because he never knew a conservative who came from Brown." Another time, he asked her to check for any employees who had played field hockey.

Ailes's most powerful tool of control was Media Relations. Brian Lewis's department not only had veto power over which guests could appear on Fox shows, but the department made Fox employees feel like the channel was a surveillance state. Lewis and his assistants berated employees for speaking to the press without authorization. They also used laptops with untraceable IP addresses to leak embarrassing stories about wayward Fox hosts and executives ("No fingerprints" was a favorite Lewis-ism). Fox employees worried their conversations were being recorded. After one former producer joked to a friend he was thinking about writing a book about Fox, he got an accusatory phone call from a senior Fox executive about it. The producer stammered he was only kidding. Lewis became feared for the perceived pleasure he took in trafficking in smears. "Look, I know you can kill me," an employee said to him once, asking him to hold his fire. "I don't wanna wake up tomorrow to read I'm gay and fucking sheep."

And just to ensure that there was no confusion about Ailes's ultimate wishes, Ailes conducted "fair and balanced" seminars himself. "He would call a group of senior producers and make you watch the channel and he'd point out stuff, like a banner that's slightly liberal," a senior producer recalled. "He would say, 'The news is like a ship. If you take hands off the wheel, it pulls hard to the left.'"

Ailes maintained to his newsroom that "fair and balanced" had nothing to do with a partisan agenda. "Am I a Republican? Sure," he said in a staff meeting. "But does that mean that my news network is biased Republican? Of course not."

Beyond the politics, however, Fox's lodestar was Ailes himself. At the Fox News Christmas party in 2002, held at a Midtown Manhattan bar, Ailes was conspicuously absent, but at one point in the evening employees were instructed to watch a Fox News presentation on a large video monitor set up in the basement. The MSNBC and CNN logos appeared on the screen and elicited boos from the crowd. On the third slide, Ailes's picture popped up. The attendees went wild, chanting, "*Roger . . . Roger . . . Roger . . . Roger!*"

As the administration rolled out its sales pitch for the war, Ailes installed a new head of daytime programming to package the production, promoting Jerry Burke, the producer of Shepard Smith's nightly newscast. Burke expressed a tabloid editor's thrill for the biggest story of a generation. Not long after 9/11, John Moody offered him the position overseeing the 9:00 a.m.–4:00 p.m. news block.

"Will you keep the car on the road or will you crash it?" Moody said.

"I want to see how fast it can go," Burke told him.

Fox's raucous cheerleading disguised the fact that, on a complex story like international terrorism, the channel was at a distinct disadvantage against its rivals. At the time, Fox News had just 1,200 employees and six foreign bureaus. CNN, in contrast, employed 4,000 people and had thirty-one international bureaus. When the war in Afghanistan started, Fox had no one on the ground, while CNN had a correspondent in the country. Although MSNBC was struggling to develop an identity, it still had the robust newsgathering assets of NBC News to fall back on.

So Burke improvised. Shortly after receiving the promotion, he teamed up with two staffers on the assignment desk—David Rhodes and Eric Spinato—to develop a flanking maneuver designed to pick away viewers from their better-funded rivals. They called it "Operation Rolling Thunder." CNN may have been the entrenched opposition, but Fox News would cover the story in a way that would be irresistible to viewers. Terrorism would become serial entertainment. "Fox approached news differently," a staffer who had done time at other networks said. "It wasn't actual journalism where you say, 'Let's go see what's going on.' At Fox, it's 'This is what we're doing, so go do it.' "

Every morning, Burke got off the commuter train at Penn Station determined to inflict damage on the competition. He told people that producing news was like scanning a searchlight across the horizon to hunt for the right story. His first read of the day was the *Drudge Report*, not *The New York Times*. Whatever items seemed to be generating heat on the right were fodder for the air. Conflict was good. *Too* much conflict was bad. After an interview with a Muslim guest devolved into a shouting match, Burke hollered across the newsroom, "I need a better Muslim!" He was adept at convincing angry subjects to keep coming back. He cajoled another prominent Muslim guest to back off on his threat to boycott Fox after one particularly harsh interview. "Why would I come on to have someone say I'm a child murderer?" he told Burke.

"You're doing a service, you're getting your message across," Burke replied. He also told him that, at the end of the day, it was just television. "You need to lighten up."

Fox News promoted the buildup to war like a pregame show. Anchors played the role of announcers, championing the home team: America. George Bush was the star quarterback, carrying the hopes of an expectant fan base on his shoulders. On-air, troops were "heroes" and "warriors." Ailes developed a roster of opponents who sought to block America's drive down the field. Saddam Hussein was the principal foe, backed up by supporting players: the United Nations, France, Germany, and Al Jazeera. "If they're going to get us, it's going to be in a gunfight," Geraldo Rivera said in one segment from Afghanistan. In November 2001, Ailes lured Rivera away from CNBC to be Fox's war correspondent. Rivera could be embarrassingly thin on his facts. On December 5, 2001, he reported that he visited the site of a friendly fire bombing raid that left three American servicemen and several Afghan fighters dead. "We walked over what I consider hallowed ground today. . . . It was just—the whole place, just fried, really—and bits of uniforms and tattered clothing everywhere. I said the Lord's Prayer and really choked up." A week later, *Baltimore Sun* reporter David Folkenflik revealed that Rivera was actually hundreds of miles from the incident he cited. Rivera was indignant. He attributed the error to the "fog of war" and impugned Folkenflik's manhood. "Have *you* ever been shot at?" he asked him.

Ailes was constantly on the lookout for developments to keep the story moving. When Dan Rather sat down with Hussein on CBS News in February 2003, Ailes smelled a rat. "Did [the Iraqis] have pre-look at his questions?" he complained to his executives. "Was anybody in the room with a weapon? . . . I have less of a problem in getting in a room with Saddam Hussein with ground rules as long as those ground rules are disclosed." Similarly, *Time* magazine's interview with French president Jacques Chirac—a former Ailes Communications client—was a "total setup" and "anti-American." "Nowhere in the *Time* magazine interview," Ailes huffed, "do they say, 'Mr. Chirac, do you have any business dealings with Iraq? Mr. Chirac, is there a one-hundred-and-twenty-billion-dollar oil contract with Iraq? Mr. Chirac, weren't you the guy that went over and set up a nuclear reactor? . . . How about the seven million Muslims down the street that are going to blow up the Eiffel Tower? Does that bother you?' There are a few other questions that a few other *good* journalists would work into the interview."

People who questioned Bush's policies were put on notice. "Americans and, indeed, our allies who actively work against our military once the war is under way will be considered enemies of the state by me," Bill O'Reilly told his viewers. "Just fair warning to you, Barbra Streisand, and others who see the world as you do." You could even see it if you walked by Fox's Manhattan headquarters. When antiwar protesters staged a rally on Fifth Avenue in March 2003, Ailes allowed Marvin Himelfarb, the comedy writer who had worked with him at America's Talking, to use the ticker to taunt them. It read: "ATTENTION PROTESTERS: THE MICHAEL MOORE FAN CLUB MEETS THURSDAY AT A PHONE BOOTH AT SIXTH AVENUE AND 50TH STREET."

Five days before America began its Shock and Awe bombing campaign, Fox News's creative director, Richard O'Brien, hired a composer to write the network's theme music for the war. He titled it "Liberation Iraq Music." "The other networks, they always go for that John Williams, big, grand music, but our music is always pointedly more aggressive," O'Brien explained. After listening to the sample, O'Brien told the composer to ramp up the intensity and add "more tom-tom drums because they had more urgency. I wanted it to sound like, I don't want to say war drums, but . . ."

Fox also created high-octane advertisements to introduce war segments. In one, a fighter jet streaked across the screen and morphed into an American eagle as the words "War on Terror" flashed. The script for a thirty-second Fox promotion read like a campaign spot: "*Fox News Channel. The country at war. Stay with us for breaking news and live updates, fair and balanced, exclusively from the team you trust: Fox News Channel. On the ground. In the air. Reports from the front. Inside the conflict. War coverage, second to none. Fox News Channel. The political fallout. With eyes around the world, a commitment here at home. The first place to turn for the latest in news—Fox News Channel. Real Journalism. Fair and balanced."*

In other ways, Ailes muted the coverage to build suspense. Anchor Bob Sellers recalled how the whooshing "Fox News Alerts" were used less frequently before the invasion so they would pack more punch when the fighting began. For the viewers, Fox provided a fully immersive experience that made them feel like they were going into battle alongside the heroic American liberators. On March 20, shortly after the invasion commenced, an on-screen banner made the point explicitly. "Fox troops with U.S. troops heading into Iraq," it read.

Ailes's embrace of Bush's hawkish, neoconservative agenda had a potent political consequence for the Republican Party. Fox's support of the war successfully marginalized the antiwar voices that existed on the right. Republican war critics like former George H. W. Bush national security adviser Brent Scowcroft and Pat Buchanan found themselves drowned out by Fox's boisterous boosterism. "The conservatives were not going to go anywhere," a Bush official later said. "You didn't have an isolationist wing anymore. Once you had political will on the right for the war, you had a changing political environment." As a public relations matter, this changing political environment freed the White House to promote the invasion to a broader constituency. "We needed to sell the war to the middle," the official said. They succeeded. *The New York Times*'s Judith Miller was one of the most aggressive promoters of the claim made by the administration that Iraq had weapons of mass destruction, a chief justification of the war. Bush officials found welcome receptions on the Sunday talk show circuit.

Ailes's network was invaluable in this sales effort. And Fox's ratings dominance also played a significant role in the media's abdication of journalistic skepticism in the coverage of 9/11 and its aftermath. Fox's cable news rivals approached the 9/11 story already spooked by Fox's post-recount surge. Both CNN and MSNBC were under pressure from their corporate parents to catch up to Fox. An obvious strategy was to become more conservative. In the summer of 2001, CNN chief Walter Isaacson courted Republicans. He traveled to Washington for private meetings with Senate majority leader Trent Lott and House speaker Dennis Hastert. He also wooed Rush Limbaugh and offered him a show. In October 2001, Isaacson sent a memo to CNN producers chastising them for not being patriotic enough. "We must talk about how the Taliban are using civilian shields and how the Taliban have harbored the terrorists responsible for killing close to 5,000 innocent people," he wrote. "We must redouble our efforts to make sure we do not seem to be simply reporting from their vantage or perspective."

At MSNBC, Ailes's influence was even more pronounced. Microsoft and GE's cable news partnership was in deep trouble. As Ailes predicted, MSNBC's strategy to promote the channel with NBC News celebrities backfired. NBC's broadcast stars, accustomed to reaching millions, sniffed at cable news's comparatively tiny audiences. MSNBC assigned senior producer Phil Griffin to convince royalty like Katie Couric and Tom Brokaw to increase their appearances. "It was torture," Griffin recalled. Griffin was a good choice to finesse difficult egos. Prior to joining MSNBC at its launch, he worked with many of them as a producer for *NBC Nightly News* and the *Today* show.

But no amount of Griffin's diplomacy could obscure the fact that MSNBC was faltering. As the ratings sagged, MSNBC was riven by finger-pointing. After Bush's election, Jack Welch and senior GE executives began leaning on Griffin's boss, MSNBC's president Erik Sorenson, to catch up with Ailes. "Jack would say, I understand why Fox has more ratings, it's more interesting!" recalled a former executive. At management reviews with Welch and senior GE executives, Sorenson was peppered with questions that he experienced as political interference. "*Why is Fox beating us? Maybe we should also be a conservative channel? What if you try and cut their audience in half?*"

For years, the values of an older generation of news churchmen held considerable sway at MSNBC. Tim Russert watched Fox with unease. An Olympian figure inside NBC News, Russert acted as an information hub, a kingmaker, and the scorekeeper to official Washington. "Let's just do news," he told Sorenson in one meeting. "I see what Fox's ratings are. However, you have to understand, if you do news really well, you'll get ratings."

The ratings did not materialize. So Russert's resistance proved futile when Jeffrey Immelt succeeded Welch as GE's CEO four days before 9/11 and increased pressure on Sorenson and NBC News executives to tap into the nationalistic fervor. "MSNBC is a dot on the side of a pool ball," Immelt told NBC News president Neal Shapiro, "but it's embarrassing. I don't like being No. 3." Following 9/11, NBC CEO Bob Wright gave Shapiro a direct order: MSNBC should go right-wing, like Fox. "We have to be more conservative than they are," Wright said. Shapiro complied. MSNBC rebranded itself "America's News Channel" and splashed American flag graphics on the screen.

But MSNBC's message was mixed. In April 2002, Phil Griffin brought Phil Donahue, a passionate liberal who had been Griffin's childhood idol, out of retirement to anchor an 8:00 p.m. prime-time talk show that would challenge Bill O'Reilly. Donahue was a former major leaguer, with great name recognition, and the show debuted with the highest ratings ever for an MSNBC program, attracting more than a million viewers in its first night. But within a month, the audience was slashed in half. Donahue's tumultuous run at MSNBC revealed Ailes's power to shape the media culture. As Donahue's ratings stalled in the run-up to the war, MSNBC executives expressed increasing concern about his vocal antiwar views. At a time when red-meat patriotism prevailed, Donahue booked antiwar guests like Michael Moore, Rosie O'Donnell, Susan Sarandon, and Tim Robbins.

Donahue's problems only increased when Chris Matthews let it be known that he wanted Donahue off the air. Matthews saw himself as MSNBC's biggest star—he commanded a salary of $5 million—and he was upset that the network was pumping significant resources into Donahue's show. Shortly before the war started, Sorenson and Griffin took Donahue off the air to make way for 24/7 coverage. For Griffin, the firing of his childhood idol was a career low point. "The guy that got me into TV probably hates my guts, and I wish he didn't because I love the guy," he recalled.

As his rivals flailed, Ailes gleefully poked at them in the press, though he usually kept his hand hidden. On the day MSNBC announced it was canceling Donahue, Brian Lewis told him Fox had a press release ready that would mock their decision. "We're putting it out that Donahue's numbers were higher than Matthews'," he said.

Lewis's staff regularly fed reporters with embarrassing news and gossip about Fox's competitors. After Andy Lack was quoted in the *Times* declaring he was "America's news leader," a Fox PR person sent an email to reporters that featured the quote and a Photoshopped picture of Lack's face superimposed onto Napoleon's body. After MSNBC anchor Ashleigh Banfield generated positive headlines for her post-9/11 dispatches from Afghanistan and Pakistan—which featured her head wrapped in a shawl and her Clark Kent–style glasses peeking out—Lewis's deputy, Robert Zimmerman, wanted to embarrass her in *The Washington Post*. "Take her out," Brian Lewis told him. Zimmerman called *Post* reporter Paul Farhi and fed him a tip that foreign correspondents were laughing that Banfield, despite her intrepid image as a foreign correspondent, was scared to leave her hotel.

Ailes's search-and-destroy approach to journalism and public relations destabilized his cable news opponents. They complained he played by a different set of rules. The news business was supposed to operate by a different creed than politics. Ailes did not agree. He had people on his payroll, like former *Tomorrow* producer John Huddy, who helped him devise political strategy. "He was the oppo research guy," one executive said. Ailes deployed Fox programs in service of his goals. He ran a relentless campaign against CNN. One morning in late fall 2001, Ailes called *Fox & Friends* host Steve Doocy and narrated a script for him to read. "Steve, just say that [CNN news anchor] Aaron [Brown]'s your dentist. Then have your co-anchor say, 'He's not a dentist. He's on CNN!' . . . No matter what happens, even if they torture you, say he's your dentist!" Doocy obediently followed Ailes's stage direction. "You know who's really jealous about our merchandising?" Doocy said during a segment promoting Fox-branded mugs and T-shirts. "My dentist is so jealous. You've seen him on TV—Aaron Brown. You know, the guy on CNN—he does that show at night? He just works nights over there. But during the day he's our dentist. Do we have a picture?" Doocy's producers splashed Brown's photo on the screen along with a series of captions. "AARON BROWN DDS . . . MOLAR MAN . . . ARROGANT BROWN."

Both MSNBC and CNN were too constrained to respond in kind, which was frustrating. "You wake up aware of Roger," Walter Isaacson told a reporter. "He's always on the attack," he said. Bob Wright shared Isaacson's lament. During a staff meeting with CNBC employees around this time, Wright threw up his hands after CNBC anchor Ron Insana complained about Ailes. "Are we going to continue to let Roger and Brian Lewis nip at us constantly?" Insana said.

"Fighting with Roger Ailes is a full-time job, and I already have one," Wright said.

By early April, with American troops on the outskirts of Baghdad, it appeared the war's end was in reach. On the morning of April 9, Moody was running his 8:30 editorial meeting when a camera positioned on the roof of the Palestine Hotel—the base for the international press in Baghdad—showed a convoy of American tanks and Humvees surrounding a thirty-nine-foot-tall statue of Saddam Hussein in Firdos Square. A small crowd of mostly Iraqi men was milling around the statue's plaster pedestal. Some smacked it with shoes, trying to impress the nearby photographers.

As the scene on the ground unfolded, Jerry Burke quickly absorbed the symbolic potential of the image, a way of punctuating the narrative with a replay of the images of rapturous East Germans knocking down the Berlin Wall. He immediately alerted his producers to make the most of the cinematic scene in Firdos Square. CNN and the broadcast networks were also carrying the shot live. Fox needed to move fast.

"Rolling Thunder!" he shouted to producers in the newsroom. "No one take a break! Do *not* leave that fucking shot!" Although firefights were raging in other parts of the city, Fox would not break away from Firdos Square for much of the day.

Burke quickly got David Rhodes on the phone to gather more information from the assignment desk.

"What else is there?" he said.

"We're working on it," Rhodes calmly replied.

Luckily, David Chater, a correspondent for Murdoch's British network, Sky News, was in Firdos Square and also recognized the moment's television value. He saw that the Marine convoy included an M88 Hercules, a tracked vehicle that was essentially a giant tow truck for tanks. A large crane mounted on the M88's roof was tall enough to reach the top of the statue. "Get that flag going!" Chater said to one of the Marines.

The event was a collaboration between the military and the media, with both realizing the power of the image. The M88 had moved into position at the statue's rounded pedestal. The square was largely empty. But the images shown by Fox and the other networks zoomed in tight on the crowd around the statue.

By now, Burke was receiving a string of excited phone calls from senior executives. The Washington bureau called to say that Bret Baier and Brit Hume wanted to get on camera. As the operation in Firdos Square progressed, Fox personalities worked to build anticipation and imbue the images with revolutionary significance. "My goose bumps have never been higher than they are right now," anchor David Asman said. Brit Hume chimed in: "This transcends anything I've ever seen. . . . This speaks volumes, and with power that no words can really match."

Cameras focused on a Marine as he climbed the M88's crane to wrap a chain around Saddam's head. Someone tossed him an American flag.

The Fox newsroom was transfixed. "What better picture than having our fucking flag in Firdos Square," one producer later said. "It was the capper on 9/11. The towers went down but the flag went up on that statue. It was like, *fuck you, Saddam*." The reaction on air was equally euphoric. "Here we go! The American flag!" a Fox News reporter exclaimed. "There we go! Saddam Hussein is now under the Star Spangled Banner. That's all you're gonna see from now on!"

The Pentagon was far less enthusiastic. The image of the American flag covering the statue's head like an eerie hood threatened to turn the victorious visual into a symbol of American imperialism. The unit's superior, Major General James Mattis, received a frantic order from the Pentagon to have the flag taken down. Before word could make it up to the crane operator, someone by chance handed him an Iraqi flag.

It was time for the Marines to put the crane into service. As the chain pulled tight, the statue wobbled, and then buckled. It broke off at the waist and jerked forward off its base. A scrum of Iraqi men thronged around it. " 'Jubilance' seems too mild of a word for what you're seeing here," a Fox anchor gushed. At a press briefing in Washington, Defense Secretary Donald Rumsfeld embraced the media's artificial narrative. "The scenes of free Iraqis celebrating in the streets, riding American tanks, tearing down the statues of Saddam Hussein in the center of Baghdad are breathtaking," he told reporters. "Watching them, one cannot help but think of the fall of the Berlin Wall and the collapse of the Iron Curtain."

For both Fox News and the White House, the toppling was supposed to be the fulcrum that signaled the story's final act. Throughout the day, Fox aired clips of the toppling every four and a half minutes, nearly twice as much as CNN. America had exposed the invasion's doubters to be cowards. "Now that the war in Iraq is basically over, the antiwar crowd is demanding a role in reshaping Iraq's future. You would almost think the axis of weasels were responsible for winning the war," a Fox anchor said a few days later. Although thirteen American soldiers were killed in Iraq the week after the scene in Firdos Square, Fox's coverage of the war plunged by 70 percent. "They had their ending," a producer said. "For America and the cable news audience, the story began on 9/11 and finished in Firdos Square."

Except the war was only beginning. And after Firdos Square, Fox's programming options became much more complicated. The narrative of struggle and triumph had concluded—but what the new narrative should be was far from clear. While Fox personalities and George Bush were declaring mission accomplished, troubling portents of the bungled occupation and brutal sectarian insurgency were impossible to miss.

Increasingly, the administration had to defend what they'd announced they'd won. And Fox was the preferred platform. In September 2003, after no WMDs had turned up, Bush's communications chief Dan Bartlett worked out a deal for Bush to appear on Fox with Brit Hume to do damage control. It was Bush's first extended interview since the WMD issue was threatening to become a liability. "I think he hid them," Bush told Hume. "I think he is so adapted at deceiving the civilized world for a long period of time that it's going to take a while for the troops to unravel. But I firmly believe he had weapons of mass destruction."

In the fall of 2003, Fox correspondents looked for upbeat stories that showed "signs of a return to normal life." One October 1 segment highlighted a renovated school with "excited kids checking out the new teacher." When a Spanish diplomat was murdered on October 9, Fox aired a piece about a theater production as evidence "that some of the artistic pleasures of life are re-emerging with new freedoms in Iraq."

Hume and others told the audience that the war was going fine, and it was the media that was portraying it negatively. "For a huge part of the Iraqi population, life is returning to normal and has picked up enormously . . . why would one go over there only to cover the bad news?" Hume complained in one segment.

John Moody told producers not to give too much attention to the rising number of U.S. deaths. "Do not fall into the easy trap of mourning the loss of US lives and asking out loud why are we there?" Moody wrote in one newsroom memo. "The US is in Iraq to help a country brutalized for 30 years protect the gains made by Operation Iraqi Freedom and set it on the path to democracy. Some people in Iraq don't want that to happen.

That is why American GIs are dying. And what we should remind our viewers." Moody's contention was that in war, people die. "It was the same reason why he hated hurricanes and snowstorms," a colleague explained. "He would say, 'Why are you surprised it's snowing in the wintertime?' "

Not long after the Abu Ghraib scandal broke, Moody called the newsroom and told producers to refrain from putting the photographs of abused Iraqi prisoners on a continuous loop. "You know what? I've seen enough of these," he said. In a memo, he said Fox producers should also focus on grisly pictures of an American prisoner. "[T]he pictures from Abu Graeb [*sic*] prison are disturbing," he said. "They have rightly provoked outrage. Today we have a picture—aired on Al Arabiya—of an American hostage being held with a scarf over his eyes, clearly against his will. Who's outraged on his behalf? It is important that we keep the Abu Graeb [*sic*] situation in perspective. The story is beginning to live on its own momentum."

In 2004, Fox even considered hiring Dan Senor, the Pentagon's thirty-three-year-old spokesman for the Coalition Provisional Authority, to oversee Fox's war coverage. His rose-tinted briefings from the Green Zone became an exemplar of wishful thinking. Senor turned down the offer, but signed on as a paid contributor.

As it became increasingly evident that the war in Iraq was not the victory that Fox had helped to proclaim, Ailes began to turn his audience's attention in other directions. There was also turmoil in the executive suite. In the fall of 2003, Ailes and Brian Lewis entered into a contentious contract negotiation over Lewis's future at the network. On the surface, it was a dispute over money. Ailes told people that Lewis was asking for too much. "I'll just fire him and put Zimmerman in his place!" he fumed, referring to Lewis's deputy, Robert Zimmerman. In reality, the friction represented a struggle between mentor and protégé. For a decade, Lewis had worked in Ailes's shadow. At forty-six, he asserted himself more, but Ailes chafed at his independent streak, calling Lewis a "cowboy" and a "leaker." Feeling frustrated, Lewis explored other job offers. One day in November, as Lewis was negotiating with Ailes in his office, the conflict reached a head.

"You demand loyalty from people, but *you* never show it," Lewis told him.

Ailes grimaced. He grabbed a water bottle on his desk and hurled it in Lewis's direction. It thudded against the wall. "I missed you on purpose," he said.

After the meeting, Lewis told colleagues that his time at Fox might be over. When Judy Laterza walked into his office, he teared up. Six weeks later, in February 2004, Ailes relented and signed Lewis to a new deal. Ailes would need Lewis by his side.

# EIGHTEEN

# "WHAT ARE YOU GOING TO DO WITH ALL THIS POWER?"

At Fox, one of the meanings of "fair and balanced" was that an outspoken Democrat could play a key role in the prime-time dismantling of the Democratic nominee for president. On Wednesday, August 4, 2004, Bill Shine recruited Patrick Halpin, a Long Island politician and liberal television pundit, to fill in for Alan Colmes, who was on vacation. It was a side gig that the plainspoken fifty-one-year-old had been holding down for a few years. Halpin and Shine met at the Long Island PBS station WLIW in the early 1990s, where Shine was a producer and Halpin hosted a *Crossfire* knockoff. Despite their political differences, the two clicked. "He was very grounded. I wouldn't call Bill Shine an ideologue," Halpin said.

Halpin only met Ailes once. "You know I elected *two* presidents?" Ailes said when Shine brought Halpin around the offices. Although he was not a Fox regular, Halpin knew the drill. "It's show business, make no mistake about it," he said. It's why, even though he knew *Hannity & Colmes* was rigged to make the liberal lose, he welcomed Shine's invitations to joust on air. It was good sport. Still, Halpin was troubled by some of the subtle tricks Hannity's producers pulled to manipulate the audience, like making the liberal co-host say the slogan "fair and balanced" on air. Halpin tried several times over the years to get out of reading it, but to no avail. "You could never change the script," he said. "They know exactly who their audience is: white men," he said. "They give them a message that resonates." Shine had told him as much. "I remember asking him once, 'Bill, what's with all these hot blondes?' He just smiled and said, 'you know, I gotta tell you, the ratings go through the roof.'"

The August 4 edition of *Hannity & Colmes* would forever change the way Halpin saw Fox. About an hour before going on air, Halpin huddled with Hannity's producers reviewing the lineup. The final segment caught his eye. "Later in the show, we'll give you an exclusive look at a new campaign ad that could do some damage to Senator Kerry. We'll have it before anyone else, and we'll show it to you here," his line on the script read. Halpin asked a producer about it but got a vague reply, something about a new conservative ad that had to do with a then-unfamiliar term: Swift Boats. The ad arrived at Fox through Hannity's right-wing connections. "A new television ad released tomorrow is sure to drive the Kerry campaign crazy," Hannity said on the air. "It was paid for by Swift Boat Veterans for Truth, and it features Vietnam vets who are opposing Senator Kerry's candidacy. Now *Hannity & Colmes* has exclusively obtained a copy of this ad before anybody else. Let's take a peek."

The spot opened on a grainy black-and-white photograph of Kerry in his Vietnam uniform, standing in a group of young servicemen. Vice presidential candidate John Edwards's voice, pulled from a stump speech, narrated the opening frames: "If you ask any question about what John Kerry is made of, just spend three minutes with the men who served with him thirty years ago." Bold text replaced Kerry's photo on the screen: "Here's what those men think about John Kerry," it read. Testimonials from middle-aged men played in quick succession. *"I served with John Kerry. . . . I served with John Kerry. . . . John Kerry has not been honest about what happened in Vietnam. . . . He's lying about his record. . . . I know John Kerry is lying about his first Purple Heart, because I treated him for that injury. . . . John Kerry lied to get his Bronze Star. I know. I was there. I saw what happened."*

"That's a hard-hitting ad," Hannity remarked when it was over. He told his viewers that, in addition to airing the ad in its entirety the next night, he would talk live with the Swift Boat vets themselves before allowing the Kerry campaign to respond. "We'll get both sides," he promised.

Halpin first thought the effort was "preposterous." Smearing Kerry's military service smacked of desperation. Off-camera, Hannity assured Halpin he was wrong: "This is going to change the whole campaign."

Hannity was right. The next day, a $500,000 ad campaign hit the airwaves in Ohio, Wisconsin, and West Virginia, key swing states. It was a modest buy. But Fox News gave the ad the oxygen it needed to explode. Throughout the week, hosts and pundits hotly debated the charges from all sides. On August 5, Brit Hume's newscast ran two segments about the ad. That night, Bill O'Reilly, burnishing his no-spin bona fides, castigated Kerry's accusers. "I think this is awful," he complained to Dick Morris.

"I not only think it's awful, I think it's stupid and dangerous," Morris replied.

Pro or con, it did not matter. Just talking about the controversy gave it juice. "Cable news," Ailes said around this time, was "beginning to change the agenda of what is news." The Swift Boat controversy, driven by Fox, showed a clear evolution from the Clinton era. The scandal around Clinton and Monica Lewinsky was at its core a real story. But Swift Boat began as a campaign commercial, spurring a cable-ready argument over what the underlying facts might be—the controversy was primary. And for Ailes, it was an apotheosis: take-no-prisoners campaign politics and engrossing television in one indivisible package.

The ad was the capstone of an extensive Fox campaign effort. Since Kerry locked up the nomination, Fox had painted a portrait of him as an out-of-touch Francophone with a superrich, foreign wife. "There were subtle commands from the second floor, like he's French," one senior producer recalled. Fox anchors helped transform Kerry into a cartoon. "He may be a Boston aristocrat with an Ivy League education and cousins in France, but that did not make it fair to laugh when John Kerry said last week that he pays close attention to rap music because it says something important," Brit Hume quipped in one segment in April. It was a message reinforced in John Moody's newsroom memos. "Kerry, starting to feel the heat for his flip-flop voting record, is in West Virginia," the news chief wrote in March. The Swift Boat ad offered Fox's audience a chance to relive the old grudge matches of the Vietnam generation. "Ribbons or medals? Which did John Kerry throw away after he returned from Vietnam?" Moody wrote in April. "This may become an issue for him today. His perceived disrespect for the military could be more damaging to the candidate than questions about his actions in uniform."

Of all the Fox hosts, Hannity gave the story line momentum. The week after he debuted the ad with Halpin, Hannity aired the first television interview with John O'Neill, the Texas lawyer who founded the Swift Boat group, while he was promoting his anti-Kerry book, *Unfit for Command*. "I read the book," Hannity told O'Neill. "It's frankly devastating to Senator Kerry, what his fellow Vietnam guys are saying, what they experienced with him. They contradict just about every story he has told about his experience here."

"It's a pattern of total lying and exaggeration, much of it very demeaning to the other people that served with him," O'Neill replied.

*Unfit for Command* hit the top of the *Times* bestseller list, and CNN and MSNBC were compelled to cover the story, too. "Heck, I know our group did in the range of a thousand different television and radio interviews. They were on virtually every network," O'Neill later said. Looking back, he was thrilled with the results. "Giving the kidney to my wife was the best thing I ever did. The Swift Boat [ads] was the second best."

Many Democrats saw the controversy as so obviously contrived as to pose no danger to their candidate. But Kerry's supporters didn't understand the new dynamics of cable television. They ignored the warnings of liberals close to Ailes who knew his playbook. It proved a grave miscalculation.

Fox News contributor Susan Estrich was one. When she watched the Swift Boat story snowball, she recalled her experience running Dukakis's 1988 campaign. All the dynamics were repeating themselves. In '88, the Willie Horton ad was produced by an outside group with shadowy connections to the George H. W. Bush campaign. The Swift Boat attack was also funded by powerful Republicans with financial and personal ties to the George W. Bush campaign. In 2004, however, the authors of Kerry's demise had one crucial advantage: Fox News. The group behind the Willie Horton spot had to buy airtime and hope the broadcast media and newspapers would pick it up. With Fox News, conservatives had a twenty-four-hour network that allowed them to inject attack lines directly into the political bloodstream. The interplay between political advertising and journalism was an old campaign gambit. When he was a political consultant in the 1980s, Ailes said networks only cared about pictures, conflict, and mistakes. If an ad generated conflict, reporters were bound to cover it as "news." Fox News was a perpetual conflict machine.

It had already happened once during the 2004 campaign. In May, Estrich received a call from a Hannity producer who wanted to book her for a segment about an Internet ad produced by the Republican National Committee. The spot mockingly compared Kerry to a cicada, who was trying to shed his liberal shell in time for the general election. "We want you to respond to the merits of the ad," the producer told her. Estrich lit into him. "How many times has it been shown on television?" The producer stammered. Before hanging up, Estrich warned him she was calling Ailes to complain. When she reached Ailes that afternoon, he "burst out laughing," she recalled. "He said, 'I like to think I pioneered that technique.' "

Estrich was in a position to try to defend Kerry on Fox. As it happened, she was booked to fill in for Colmes on August 5, the night after Halpin. Hannity would be interviewing Van O'Dell, a Swift Boat veteran appearing in the ad. When Estrich called the Kerry-Edwards campaign headquarters to get talking points to use on camera, her concerns were confirmed: the campaign did not have any. Instead of cultivating Estrich and capitalizing on her ties to Fox News, Democrats shunned her—it was punishment for collaborating with Ailes. At the Democratic National Convention in Boston, she was ostracized. "Wherever I went, I was subjected to criticism," she said. She was even left off the guest list for a party hosted by Dukakis. "Even if it was a clerical error, that was very hurtful," she recalled.

Greta Van Susteren's husband, the lawyer John Coale, was another Democrat with ties to Ailes who wanted to stave off disaster for Kerry. A few days before Hannity hyped O'Neill's book on the air, Coale received a frantic phone call from his friend Douglas Brinkley, the Rice University historian, who had recently authored the lionizing Kerry biography *Tour of Duty*. Brinkley told Coale he had gotten his hands on O'Neill's book and was aghast at the distortions and falsehoods. "Shit, you gotta call Kerry," Brinkley told him. Coale quickly arranged a meeting with Kerry and implored him to sue O'Neill and the Swift Boat group for defamation. "He was all hopped up to do it," Coale remembered. But like Estrich, Coale was ignored by Kerry's advisers. Kerry's campaign manager, Bob Shrum, and others warned the candidate that launching a counterattack would only dignify the allegations and give the scandal legs. Kerry did not personally respond to the Swift Boat vets for nearly three weeks.

Around-the-clock cable news coverage provided the free promotion. By the time Kerry defended himself, one poll found nearly half the country had heard about the Swift Boat ad or had seen it. In the closing days of the race, Kerry's camp exploded when Fox painted Kerry as a terrorist favorite. After a tape of Osama bin Laden was released in late October, Fox anchor Neil Cavuto said on-camera that he thought he saw a Kerry "button" in bin Laden's cave. John Sasso, a veteran Kerry adviser and onetime Dukakis campaign manager, threatened to throw Fox producer Catherine Loper off the campaign plane.

"Is that the one? Is that her?" Sasso said as he looked at Loper. "I want her off the plane tomorrow. I'm not kidding."

On the night of November 2, Ailes and Murdoch watched the returns together at Fox News. Moody fed Ailes updates from the decision desk.

Fox called Ohio for Bush at 12:40 a.m. The battleground win put Bush a single electoral vote shy of 270, and all but guaranteed him a second term. But hoping to avoid a repeat of 2000, Fox refused to take any gambles. As the minutes ticked by, Bush aides became apoplectic that Fox and the networks refused to declare their man the winner based on the projections in western states that would definitively put him over the top. Rove called Fox analyst Michael Barone.

"I just got some spin from Rove on New Mexico," Barone told Moody and the decision team members shortly after 2:00 in the morning.

"Not yet," Moody cautioned.

Dan Bartlett, at Bush high command, frantically tried to reach Ailes, but could not get through. Ailes had been burned after his memo to Rove leaked, and he understandably did not want to be seen coordinating with Bushworld. "You know I wasn't going to take your call, Bartlett," Ailes told him a few weeks later. In the end, Kerry made the decision easy for Fox. On Wednesday morning, he conceded.

After Bush's victory, "Swift Boating" joined the American political lexicon. Kerry's failings as a candidate—his Brahmin reserve and deliberative mien—certainly contributed to his defeat. But according to Sean Hannity, Fox News deserved at least some credit. "Sean said he felt he played an important role in taking Kerry down," Pat Halpin later said, recalling a conversation he had with Hannity not long after the election. Halpin said he felt unsettled at his minor role in promoting the Swift Boaters. "I was one of the props, unfortunately," he said.

Months later, Halpin sat in for Colmes and decided to speak up. Before a segment about Bush's intervention in the Terri Schiavo end-of-life case, Hannity told him to lay off his guests Rick Santorum and Focus on the Family founder James Dobson. "Go easy on these guys, they get good ratings," Hannity said. Halpin ignored the directive. He pressed both men with tough questions. "Sean was pissed off. He was like, 'Why did you do that?'" Halpin remembered. "I never got invited on to guest host again. Bill Shine indicated that Sean didn't want me."

For Democrats, the trauma of losing consecutive presidential elections confirmed the political reality: post-9/11 America was a Republican country. Fox News got much of the credit for this development, of course. But the victory made Fox News and Ailes himself into something they had never been on such a scale: a target.

Fox News was now a juggernaut, earning more than $200 million per year, and its success changed the gravity of the cable TV world, and the wider culture, too. As MSNBC tried to siphon off Ailes's viewers by bulking up with conservative commentary, Comedy Central began to prosper with Fox News satire. In July 2004, the progressive documentary filmmaker Robert Greenwald released *Outfoxed: Rupert Murdoch's War on Journalism*. Liberal groups like MoveOn.org, which was a producer of the film, aggressively promoted the exposé and turned it into a surprise hit.

The passion of Roger Ailes's audience was something that had never before existed in TV news, a consequence of Fox's hybrid of politics and entertainment. Fox did not have viewers. It had fans. They watched on average 30 percent longer than CNN viewers in prime time. In journalism, it was an achievement without precedent. When Ailes later decided to launch a website to aggregate conservative headlines, it was aptly named *Fox Nation*. To watch Fox was to belong to a tribe.

Fox's gleeful dismembering of Kerry's campaign forced liberals to acknowledge that Fox had changed politics. "Before Fox News, a lot of stories never would have gotten attention," Bob Shrum later said. "Take the Swift Boat story: If you had had the old Huntley-Brinkley hour, it would not have appeared on the network." Conservative passions had exploded into the mainstream, repackaged as prime-time entertainment. The dream of Bob Pauley and Joe Coors had been realized.

Democrats were in general agreement that something needed to be done to counter Ailes's influence. Unsurprisingly, they argued bitterly over strategy. The debate over Fox News was, in reality, a proxy war in a much bigger conflict within the Democratic Party. On one side, moderates, led by Bill Clinton and his allies, championed engagement with Fox. They contended it was a matter of basic electoral math. Given Ailes's audience—which at that point had grown larger than CNN's and MSNBC's *combined*—it was folly to ignore him. When Ailes hired Dick Morris in 1998, Clinton told his former adviser that he was happy he would be embedding with the opposition. "It's stupid to avoid Fox," Van Susteren's husband, John Coale, said, echoing the Clinton argument. "What's the worst case scenario? You get yelled at by Bill O'Reilly or Sean Hannity? But your base is going to love you for getting yelled at so there's no downside."

But Clintonian pragmatism incited vocal opposition among the party's ascendant grassroots base. Connecting online through nascent social networks and progressive websites like Daily Kos and MoveOn.org, members of the so-called Netroots movement espoused a brand of liberal populism that viewed Fox as the enemy. Confrontation, not engagement, was their preferred strategy. The left's anti-Fox groundswell started in the wake of the 2000 recount. During a 2002 interview with *The New York Observer,* Al Gore declared that Fox News was "part and parcel of the Republican Party." Admittedly, it was a partisan analysis. But Gore's claims had resonance on the left. And throughout the contentious 2004 Democratic primary, his combative stance was picked up by former Vermont governor Howard Dean. Dean's implosion in the Iowa caucuses ended his insurgent campaign, but the base's zeal was unabated.

Dean's eventual ascension to chair of the Democratic National Committee propelled his confrontational style toward the mainstream. At a Democratic fundraiser held shortly after Bush's second inauguration, pro-Fox Democrats from Clinton's camp attempted to stage an intervention. Dean was the honored guest that night. John Coale was in attendance and decided to confront Dean during the cocktail hour. "Let me talk to you," he said, pulling him into an empty bedroom. *Why are Democrats boycotting Fox?*

"They're not a real news organization!" Dean snapped.

"Good, cede it to the goddamn right," Coale said, angrily. "Let them go on and say anything they want. They have more Democrats watching than CNN does!"

Both men began shouting over each other in a ten-minute free-for-all.

Coale's diplomatic reasoning had merit, along with a self-serving element, given that his wife was a prime-time Fox anchor. But it was a losing argument. The momentum had already shifted in Dean's favor. Increasingly, Democrats viewed the media as the central front in the country's ideological struggle.

One morning in the summer of 2003, David Brock arrived for a private meeting with a small group of liberal senators on Capitol Hill. Leo

Hindery, the Manhattan media entrepreneur and Democratic fundraiser, had set up a gathering in South Dakota senator Tom Daschle's office to discuss a shared goal: taking down Fox News and conservative radio. If there was one man who knew how the right-wing media machine worked from the inside, it was David Brock, the former conservative muckraker. In the 1990s, Brock wrote for the right-wing magazine *The American Spectator* and was hailed as the Bob Woodward of the Clinton scandals. In 2002, he published a caustic tell-all memoir, *Blinded by the Right,* that detailed his years as a member of the vast right-wing conspiracy.

Brock told Daschle and his colleagues that they needed to build a media arsenal of their own. Brock had helped draw up plans for a liberal talk radio network and proposed launching a watchdog organization that would expose right-wing media bias. It was a stratagem conservatives had pioneered. Over the years, the right established a phalanx of activist groups that tarred newspapers and broadcast news as liberal mouthpieces. The tactic became known as "working the refs." Brock wanted to do the same for the left. He named his group Media Matters.

Like the groundbreaking conservative organizations Accuracy in Media and the Media Research Center, Media Matters' base of operations would be a war room. Instead of hounding *The New York Times* and CBS News with press releases, its targets would be Fox News and talk radio. Brock's operatives would instantly post incendiary comments made by a Fox pundit or Rush Limbaugh on the Media Matters website. Peter Lewis, the billionaire owner of the Progressive Insurance Corporation, invested $1 million. Other liberals, including hedge fund manager George Soros, would chip in $1 million more.

Media Matters launched in May 2004. A few months earlier, Democracy Radio went on the air. Its debut program was *The Ed Schultz Show.* Both projects were the first salvos in the liberals' counteroffensive against Ailes. But to effectively match Ailes, the left needed to alchemize entertainment and politics. Since the 1980s, conservatives had created a parallel media culture that had ended the left's monopoly on comedy. Right-wing celebrities had vast followings. It was a remarkable achievement given that Ailes came of age during the fractious 1960s, a time when fame became synonymous with fashionable New Left politics. But with the rise of talk radio, Fox News, and conservative book publishers, Republicans were able to build a self-contained thought system that made mocking liberals fun. Comedy motivated people to vote. Liberals were finally realizing they needed personalities of their own who were capable of performing at the same decibel level as Rush Limbaugh, Ann Coulter, and Bill O'Reilly. Al Franken had been rehearsing for the part for almost a decade.

A member of the comedy elite from his time as a *Saturday Night Live* writer and performer, Franken was also a diligent student of the culture and a political junkie. He figured out there was an untapped market on the left for a style of argument that could simulate conservative outrage while at the same time delivering a sophisticated critique of it. In 1996, he published the bestselling *Rush Limbaugh Is a Big Fat Idiot*. For his follow-up, Franken set his sights on the entire conservative-media-industrial-complex itself. He assembled a team of fourteen Harvard students to research his new book, which he titled *Lies and the Lying Liars Who Tell Them: A Fair and Balanced Look at the Right*. The book, published in September 2003, featured chapters devoted to slaying conservative giants with titles such as "Ann Coulter: Nutcase." Fox News came in for particular scorn. And one Fox pundit in particular wound up in Franken's crosshairs. Chapter Thirteen was titled "Bill O'Reilly: Lying, Splotchy Bully." Unexpectedly, Franken's transformation from improv comedian to muckraking polemicist was about to trigger a chain reaction that threatened to destroy Ailes's most valuable star.

By the spring of 2003, Bill O'Reilly was a booming national industry. On camera, he aspired to be a kind of cultural vigilante. Every night he went out to defend the little guy against the depredations of corrupt elites. Often his targets were Democrats. Or Hollywood celebrities. But O'Reilly could also aim his weaponized commentaries at less expected marks. He hammered the Red Cross and United Way for mismanaging restitution for 9/11 victims. "We've changed the country," he proudly declared. "Bad guys get it. They'll pay a price for doing bad things." O'Reilly's ambition was seemingly bottomless, and he continually found new ways to monetize his brand. Through his various ventures, O'Reilly was earning roughly $10 million a year. Ailes grumbled to his executives that O'Reilly shamelessly plugged his wares on *his* network. In a sense, they were competitive with each other. "He sees O'Reilly and says, 'If he can write a shitty book that's a bestseller, I want to do my own,'" an executive recalled. But there was little Ailes could do about it. O'Reilly delivered the eyeballs night after night. He was the linchpin of Ailes's prime-time lineup.

As O'Reilly's fame grew, his fuse shortened. More powerful than ever, he increasingly found himself consumed with petty feuds. One night, he called *New York Times* columnist Frank Rich a "weasel." On another program, he commanded his audience to boycott Pepsi because the company had hired the rapper Ludacris as its celebrity pitchman. His worldview became increasingly conspiratorial even as his grandiosity reached new heights. "He's hyper-suspicious about things, one of the things he shares with Ailes," a former O'Reilly staffer said. O'Reilly declared to a reporter that the press "are going to try to destroy me." He saw himself as part of a struggle with historical sweep. "This has happened since the Founding Fathers," he explained. "It has to do with power. It has to do with jealousy. It has to do with ideology. It has to do with money. The more power I get, the more lawyers I have to deal with, the more insanity I have to deal with."

O'Reilly was becoming an acute management challenge for Ailes. On- and off-camera, his rages were becoming less theatrical and more vituperative. Some days, he seemed to be spiraling out of control. During a February 2003 segment on the Iraq War protest movement, he blew up at a young antiwar activist named Jeremy Glick, whose father, a Port Authority worker at the World Trade Center, had died on 9/11. "Shut up, shut up!" O'Reilly said. At one point, O'Reilly accused Glick of shaming his family. "Man, I hope your mom isn't watching this," he told him, shortly before ordering Glick's mic cut and going to commercial. The argument continued off-camera. "Get the fuck off my set before I tear your head off," one producer recalled O'Reilly saying.

Staff came in for equally harsh treatment. After one taping, he stormed toward his staff's cubicles and tore into a young female producer, whom he blamed for botching a segment. Staffers watched in shock as O'Reilly, easily a foot taller than the woman, started yelling and slamming his fist down on a shelf. "He got really close and in her face," an eyewitness said. "She was scared he was going to hit her," recalled another colleague. O'Reilly stalked off. A senior Fox executive was called in and escorted the woman, in tears, out of the building to calm her down. She was later given paid vacation from Fox. "Bill never apologized," a person close to the matter said.

O'Reilly was also frosty with Fox hosts. "I'm the big gun," he declared to Fox executives. His relationship with Sean Hannity was almost nonexistent. O'Reilly, who was trying to build up his talk radio career, was competitive with Hannity, a talk radio star. O'Reilly sniffed to colleagues that Hannity was a right-wing shill. Hannity, in turn, mocked O'Reilly's tabloid instincts. "Can you believe this garbage?" Hannity complained when he saw O'Reilly on the monitor interviewing a porn star. It made for a tense atmosphere since their offices were both located on the seventeenth floor of the News Corp building and Hannity's Fox show directly followed O'Reilly's.

Fox executives had few options to rein O'Reilly in. "His was the only show that Roger doesn't get the credit for developing," a senior executive said. Which led to his disastrous encounter with Franken. As Franken was putting the finishing touches on *Lies and the Lying Liars Who Tell Them,* O'Reilly was completing his own book, *Who's Looking Out for You?* On May 30, 2003, O'Reilly was invited to appear onstage with Franken and columnist Molly Ivins to promote their titles at Book Expo America in Los Angeles. Brian Lewis's deputy, Rob Zimmerman, who handled O'Reilly's PR, advised O'Reilly against making the trip. "You're just going to give Franken more ammunition," Zimmerman told him. O'Reilly ignored him.

The event, televised live on C-Span's *BookTV,* was a predictable fiasco for O'Reilly. Standing at the lectern, Franken launched into a humiliating—and hilarious—roast of O'Reilly, and when it was his turn to respond, O'Reilly was painfully defensive.

The moderator watched passively as the two men sniped at each other. "This is what he does," O'Reilly said. "He is a vicious—and that is with a capital V—person, who is blinded by ideology. And that's all I'll say."

After the story blew up in the media, O'Reilly demanded revenge. He told Fox he wanted to sue Franken. Fox executives thought it a terrible idea, but O'Reilly's ratings made him hard to ignore. On August 7, 2003, about a month before Franken's book was set to be released, Fox sued Franken and his publisher, Penguin Group USA, in the Southern District of New York. Fox's suit against Franken alleged that his book violated the network's trademark because the cover featured the words "fair and balanced." The argument was not what got the most attention, however. The complaint was as bellicose as anything O'Reilly said on camera. It described Franken as "a parasite," "shrill and unstable," and, worse, "increasingly unfunny." Penguin's outside counsel, the acclaimed First Amendment lawyer Floyd Abrams, recalled that "it was one of the most extraordinarily abrasive affidavits I've ever read."

A hearing was scheduled for August 25, 2003. The judge, Denny

Chin, essentially laughed Fox's attorneys out of the room. "Is Fox really claiming that it has a monopoly on the phrase 'fair and balanced'?" he said. After a five-minute recess, he issued his decision. "This is an easy case," he declared. Fox's suit was ruled to be "wholly without merit, both factually and legally." It was ironic, Chin concluded, "that a media company that should be seeking to protect the First Amendment is seeking to undermine it by claiming a monopoly on the phrase 'fair and balanced.'"

Penguin rushed *Lies* into bookstores early and it spent weeks on the *Times* bestseller list. Fox waved the white flag. "It's time to return Al Franken to the obscurity that he's normally accustomed to," a spokeswoman told the press. Except Franken was bigger than ever. He launched a show on Air America, the new liberal talk radio network, and called it *The O'Franken Factor*. He later parlayed his fame into a successful run for the United States Senate.

In public, Ailes backed O'Reilly. "When somebody calls you a liar to your face, you know, sooner or later, you either say 'shut up,' or pop him, or leave," he told a reporter. "I think Bill was restrained. I wouldn't have given a shit. In the old days I would have popped him one." But in private, Fox executives struggled to figure out how to contain O'Reilly. When Ailes recruited O'Reilly, it was clear there was a risk he could self-destruct, since it had happened a half dozen times earlier in his career.

And then it happened again. The letter was hand-delivered to Ailes's office on the morning of Wednesday, September 29, 2004. Although it was short, just six terse paragraphs, the words on the page left little doubt that Ailes had a serious problem on his hands. It was sent on letterhead from the law offices of Benedict P. Morelli & Associates, a boutique Manhattan firm specializing in high-profile personal injury and employment cases. Morelli wrote that he represented "a young woman employee of Fox." His unnamed client had endured "constant and relentless sexual harassment" from "one of Fox's most prominent on-air personalities." Morelli indicated that a settlement was the most favorable course of action. If not, he would sue, an outcome, he warned, that "would be extremely damaging to both Fox's reputation and the reputation of the individual involved."

Morelli was a virtuoso trial lawyer who needed to be taken seriously. He claimed to have lost only two cases in twenty years, and was a fixture on New York's tabloid stage. Dianne Brandi, Fox's legal chief, went to investigate. Brandi met Morelli at his office on the East Side of Manhattan and reported back. Morelli's client was a thirty-three-year-old associate Fox News producer named Andrea Mackris. The alleged perpetrator of the "constant and relentless sexual harassment" was her boss: Bill O'Reilly. Having handled employment matters for Ailes, Brandi had presumably seen a lot in her time at Fox. "Dianne would often say, 'Get out of this place, they don't treat anyone well here,' " a Fox colleague recalled. And she may herself have felt out of step at Fox. "Not my politics," she once told a TV agent. Sex was a fact of life at Fox. "The whole Fox culture, like the *New York Post* newsroom, had a whole sexualized nature to it," a former female Fox producer said. But the Mackris suit was something new.

In their meeting, Morelli showed Brandi a draft of the five-count lawsuit. The document stipulated that settling each count would cost O'Reilly $100 million—but Morelli explained that Mackris would be willing to take "10 cents on the dollar, but nothing less." The discounted settlement amounted to the staggering sum of $60 million.

Mackris was not saying that O'Reilly ever touched her. What was detailed in the draft complaint was perhaps more damaging. The complaint told a strange tale that started with inappropriate office banter and culminated two years later with a late-night phone call at the 2004 Republican National Convention, in which O'Reilly masturbated while telling Mackris his sex fantasies. In exacting detail, the suit portrayed O'Reilly as a hypersexualized misogynist with a romance novelist's imagination. In one infamous exchange, O'Reilly described taking Mackris on a Caribbean sexcapade. "You would basically be in the shower and then I would come in and I'd join you and you would have your back to me and I would take that little loofa thing and kinda' soap up your back . . . rub it all over you, get you to relax. . . . So anyway I'd be rubbing your big boobs and getting your nipples really hard, kinda' kissing your neck from behind . . . and then I would take the other hand with the falafel [*sic*] thing and I'd put it on your pussy but you'd have to do it really light, just kind of a tease business . . ."

It wasn't just Mackris's recollection—she'd recorded him. The audio, if released, would certainly humiliate him—and potentially blow up his whole career. "O'Reilly couldn't afford to let [the lawsuit] go forward," Morelli told Brandi in one meeting.

The trouble had started not long after O'Reilly hired Mackris away from NBC a few years earlier. In short order, she impressed him with her hustle. "She was a very strong booker," a colleague recalled. But professional boundaries were allegedly crossed after she began confiding in him about her breakup with her long-term boyfriend. O'Reilly responded by giving her a raise—and romantic advice. Over dinner one night in May 2002, he told her that she should get "manicures and pedicures" and "pick up 23-year-old men in bars." From there, according to the suit, things got weird. Mackris said it was during this dinner that O'Reilly broached the topic of phone sex. Mackris described another dinner in which O'Reilly regaled her and a female college friend about his carnal conquests and propositioned the women to have a threesome. He said he could teach them "lessons."

The saga's bizarre final act commenced in January 2004. Feeling underpaid at Fox, Mackris left for a position on Paula Zahn's CNN program, but soon found she was unhappy in the job, and asked O'Reilly if she could return. In mid-April, she joined O'Reilly for dinner at Milos, an upscale Greek restaurant a few blocks from the Fox studios. She told him she would return to Fox but only if he laid off the dirty talk. He agreed. "Of course," O'Reilly said, according to her account, "because then you'd be working for me and I'd have power over you, so that couldn't happen." O'Reilly had other fantasies on his mind that night. He launched into a rant about his nemesis, Al Franken. "If you cross Fox News Channel, it's not just me, it's Roger Ailes who will go after you," he assured Mackris. "I'm the street guy out front making the loud noises about the issues, but Ailes operates behind the scenes, strategizes and makes things happen so that one day BAM! The person gets what's coming to them but never sees it coming. Look at Al Franken, one day he's going to get a knock on his door and life as he's known it will change forever," O'Reilly said. "That day will happen, trust me. . . . Ailes knows very powerful people and this goes all the way to the top."

"Top of what?" Mackris asked.

"Top of the country. Just look at who's on the cover of his book," O'Reilly replied, referring to Bush and Cheney. "They're watching him and will be for years. He's finished, and he's going to be sorry he ever took Fox News Channel on."

Mackris rejoined O'Reilly's staff in July. A few weeks later, O'Reilly called her at her apartment on the Upper West Side after he had interviewed two porn stars and allegedly talked dirty to her while masturbating. Shortly after 11:00 p.m. on September 1, O'Reilly called Mackris on her cell phone. Mackris returned the call a few minutes later. She turned on a tape recorder. She later said she told O'Reilly she was not interested but he steamrolled ahead. He explained he was watching a "porn movie" and "babbled perversely" about having sex with her. Mackris alleged O'Reilly was pleasuring himself during the phone call.

As Brandi negotiated with Morelli, Ailes learned the tawdry details of the allegations. He faced no good options. The press would run wild if Mackris sued. The story line was a ready-made tabloid soap opera: here was one of Bill Clinton's fiercest pursuers entangled in his own sex scandal with a female employee twenty-two years his junior. Even worse, O'Reilly—whose wife had just given birth to their second child a year earlier—was scheduled to promote his new book, *The O'Reilly Factor for Kids*. In one passage, he wrote: "Guys, if you exploit a girl, it will come back to get you. That's called 'karma.'" Ailes was furious. So was Murdoch, who made it clear that O'Reilly—and not News Corp—would be responsible for any settlement. Ailes may have been livid at his star, but he needed to protect Fox's biggest brand. Morelli continued to play hardball and reject Fox's offers, which were said to approach $2 million. Morelli's refusal to descend out of the stratosphere of $60 million pushed Ailes into a corner.

He huddled with Brian Lewis to map out possible attack lines. There were unanswered questions that could pick apart Mackris's narrative. *Why did she return to work for O'Reilly if she had been harassed by him? Why didn't she file a complaint with Fox's HR department or anyone in management? Why was she dining out at expensive restaurants with O'Reilly and winding up alone in hotel rooms late at night? And just who was Andrea Mackris, really?*

Lewis worked his sources inside the newsroom to find out. He was pleased to learn Mackris was unpopular in some corners. A colleague revealed that Mackris was struggling financially. "When she was with her boyfriend, he made a lot of money, and she had a good life," a friend said. And Fox found evidence that complicated Mackris's claims of being distressed working for O'Reilly. Just three weeks before filing her lawsuit, she gushed about Fox in an email to a friend at CNN. "To answer your question, things are: wonderful, amazing, fun, creative, invigorating, secure, well-managed, challenging, interesting, fun and surrounded by really good, fun people. i'm home and i'll never leave again," she wrote.

The more Lewis learned, the better he felt about O'Reilly's chances to survive the tsunami of schadenfreude that would blow his way. Sure, the tapes, if released, would be humiliating. But ultimately, it was a he-said, she-said situation. There was enough raw material about Mackris that Fox could use to construct an image of her as an opportunist shaking down a celebrity. When O'Reilly asked Lewis at one point how bad things looked on a scale of one to ten, Lewis replied, "Personally, I think it's a nine. Professionally? It's a four."

On the evening of Tuesday, October 12, O'Reilly's personal lawyer, Ronald Green, joined the talks. He accompanied Brandi to Morelli's office to try to hammer out a deal. After a half dozen meetings, Morelli was still holding firm. "If you don't resolve this case for the $60 million tonight, we are going to go public with this tomorrow," he told Green and Brandi.

Green got back to O'Reilly. "This is indeed absolute extortion," Green said. O'Reilly agreed. He wanted to go to war. They launched the preemptive strike at 9:01 the next morning. Green filed a lawsuit against both Mackris and Morelli in Nassau County Supreme Court. Morelli filed Mackris's suit hours later. The dueling lawsuits set up competing narratives. Mackris was telling a story about sex. O'Reilly tapped an equally potent force: politics. It was the tactic Ailes had deployed in his PR campaign against Time Warner. O'Reilly's suit asserted that he was the victim of a plot to "extort 'blood money'" by liberals who wanted to destroy Fox News in the final weeks of the 2004 presidential race. The campaign had begun.

From the outset, Ailes and Brian Lewis sought to be in control of the message. Ailes made sure O'Reilly got the directive: if he opened his big mouth, he could eventually lose his show. Except for a few fleeting comments, O'Reilly remained silent about the headlines. But O'Reilly had loud voices speaking for him. Fox's PR department and his lawyer, Ronald Green, fed the pack of tabloid reporters a steady supply of nasty gossip about his accuser. To gather dirt, O'Reilly hired the celebrity private investigator Bo Dietl. Sources with damaging anecdotes were tracked down. "This could be a message to people," Dietl said on MSNBC on the evening of October 15. "When you file these frivolous lawsuits . . . we're going to investigate you and we're going to uncover things."

Fox had a crucial ally in the war over O'Reilly: Murdoch's *New York Post*. On October 15, the front-page headline blared "EXCLUSIVE: O'Reilly Accuser in Bar Blow Up." The article, the first in a series of personal attacks on Mackris, quoted a pastry chef named Bethenny Frankel accusing Mackris of provoking a fight with her at the bar of the Peninsula Hotel after Frankel asked to borrow a chair from her table. "She literally verbally attacked and abused and harassed us . . . like a raving lunatic," Frankel told the tabloid. A few days later, one of O'Reilly's private investigators convinced Matthew Paratore, the owner of a bar and restaurant on the Upper West Side that Mackris frequented, to talk to O'Reilly's lawyers. On October 19, the *Post* ran a story headlined "BOOZY BOAST," which quoted Paratore alleging that Mackris had recently dined with Al Franken and that a few months before returning to Fox, she bragged about writing a book to "take [O'Reilly] down." O'Reilly's lawyer also told the *Post* that Mackris once drunkenly started stripping off her clothes in front of Paratore. "If you think I'm going to fuck Bill O'Reilly, I'm going to fuck you even more," Green quoted her as saying.

Mackris's camp worked the *Post*'s archrival, the *Daily News*. On October 17, the paper reported Mackris had the upper hand. "FOR EXTORTION, O'REILLY'S SUIT MIGHT NOT FIT: Accuser May Have Outfoxed Network Star, Legal Experts Say," a headline declared. On October 20, Mackris and Morelli sat down with the *Daily News* for her first extended print interview.

In response, Fox News worked to inject its point of view into the *Daily News*'s coverage. Green went after Mackris viciously. He told the paper Mackris was "insolvent" and that when she was a White House intern in 1991, she gave herself the nickname "Andrea Mattress." "It speaks volumes to what was going on then," he said.

Brian Lewis told people he was thrilled with how the campaign was going, but O'Reilly was getting weak-kneed. Several days after filing the lawsuit, Morelli consented to allow O'Reilly's lawyers to listen to excerpts of Mackris's audio recording. By Friday, October 22—ten days into the scandal—settlement talks resumed. "Word came down Bill wanted to settle," one person who heard the tapes said. The following Thursday, it was over. The *Daily News* played it big. "CALL HIM OWE-REILLY!" the headline blared. O'Reilly, the tabloid reported, paid Mackris as much as $10 million to make the whole thing go away. "This brutal ordeal is now officially over, and I will never speak of it again," O'Reilly told *Factor* viewers that night. Lewis was disappointed. He told executives that Fox could have prevailed if he had been allowed to continue the PR campaign.

The success of Fox's PR offensive was validated by the most important measure: ratings. Like Bill Clinton, O'Reilly survived a sex scandal by retaining the support of his fans. Ratings for the *Factor* jumped 30 percent during the heat of the scandal. On Monday, October 25, the show pulled in 3.7 million viewers. After it was all over, Ailes recalled that he had been confident that O'Reilly would weather the worst of it. "About a week after we were in the middle of it, and I sent word down to the executive producer, 'How's Bill doing?' And he said the staff just says, 'It must be going well, because he's back to being a prick.' "

In the winter of 2005, a quieter but more consequential struggle was about to unfold within News Corp. For all his conservatism, Rupert Murdoch did not have an ideological litmus test, and a younger generation of executives, many of them Democrats, had moved into positions of influence at the highest reaches of the company, leaving Ailes encircled by executives who welcomed Fox's profits but chafed at the network's conservative message. The trigger for this shift was the departure of Chase Carey, Murdoch's co–chief operating officer, who left to become CEO of DirecTV, the satellite TV service News Corp controlled. Carey was a powerful Ailes ally and boardroom protector. He had backed Ailes during Fox's launch and gave Ailes wide latitude to run his affairs—as long as Ailes met his numbers. Carey's exit was accompanied by the rise of a competing power center inside the company: Peter Chernin.

Chernin, who held the president and COO title following Carey's departure, was already a Hollywood eminence, with all the cultural and political baggage—and ego—that implies. Chernin based himself on Fox's studio lot in Century City and devoted a considerable amount of his time to News Corp's entertainment assets. Chernin also fashioned himself as an operator—in the movie business, the players were in the political game—but his politics were considerably to the left of the News Corp norm.

Wall Street valued Chernin's polished mien, especially after Murdoch's brush with prostate cancer in 2000, but the management ranks at News Corp did not readily bow to his commands. Chernin promoted loyalists into key positions. The most visible casualty of Chernin's drive to consolidate power was the heir apparent. Lachlan Murdoch was thirty-two when Chernin took over, and held the title of deputy chief operating officer. Rupert had hoped that Lachlan would train under the experienced entertainment executive. Lachlan even bought a house in Los Angeles and took an office on the Fox studio lot. But Lachlan felt frozen out in California. Chernin did not see himself as a regent to chaperone the king's successor and left him out of management decisions. The mounting tension between Chernin and Lachlan created a polarizing dynamic. Ailes started out a bit player in this boardroom drama but ended up delivering a performance that many would remember long afterward.

Lachlan decided to give up on California to focus on his portfolio of businesses in New York. As deputy COO, he was responsible for the *New York Post,* HarperCollins, and the Fox Television Stations Group. But he could not fully escape Chernin's reach. Their relationship finally ruptured over internal arguments over retransmission rights to cable operators. Lachlan wanted cable systems to pay News Corp cash; Chernin wanted to negotiate channel slots to launch the Fox Reality channel. The debate came to a head during a tense conference call with senior executives. Rupert sided with Chernin. Feeling betrayed and lost, Lachlan began spending more time at the *Post,* a Murdoch pet that Chernin had no interest in caring for.

But in seeking to avoid Chernin, Lachlan confronted another formidable power: Ailes. Ailes wanted Lachlan to take his programming ideas for the Fox broadcast stations. He pitched Lachlan on giving Geraldo Rivera a syndicated broadcast show. He also pressed Lachlan to develop a procedural drama called *Crime Line*. Lachlan resisted. He told Ailes he would look at some pilots but did not make any promises. The truth was, he did not need Geraldo. In early 2005, he recruited Australian tabloid television pioneer Peter Brennan to relaunch *A Current Affair*. And *Crime Line,* Lachlan told his staff, would likely cost millions. Rejecting the show was the "100 percent right decision," he told News Corp executives.

So Ailes undercut Lachlan. He opened a back channel to Lachlan's deputy, Jack Abernethy, the CEO of the Stations Group and an Ailes loyalist going back to their CNBC days. Before being promoted by Lachlan in 2004, he worked alongside Ailes as Fox News's CFO. Ailes also went over Lachlan's head. Having been blocked by Lachlan on *Crime Line,* Ailes pitched the show directly to Rupert over the summer of 2005. "Do the show," Rupert told him. "Don't listen to Lachlan."

In late July, while in Sydney on a business trip, Lachlan received the news that Ailes had outmaneuvered him. The flap over *Crime Line* was, on the surface, a minor issue. But as Lachlan flew home to New York, Ailes's meddling came to symbolize much more. Lachlan's resentments festered. The pressure of satisfying his father's dynastic ambitions had taken its toll. He had sided with his mother, Anna, during her divorce from Rupert. And Lachlan resented that Rupert pushed to relocate the company from Australia to New York, a city he never felt at home in. He loved the laid-back Australian culture and rugged countryside. His Australian wife, Sarah, a swimsuit model, also yearned to return home, where they were celebrities, almost royalty. Rupert could not understand these feelings. "Rupert used to say to me, 'What kind of stupid person would give this up to go live there?'" former News Corp executive Mitch Stern recalled.

On Tuesday, July 26, 2005, Lachlan flew to Los Angeles to see his father for lunch. "I have to do my own thing," Lachlan told his dad. "I have to be my own man." Three days later, News Corp announced Lachlan's resignation.

Lachlan's departure created a power vacuum within News Corp—and Ailes wasted no time in filling it. It was an illustration of Ailes's gifts for bureaucratic infighting that he was able to transform his adversarial relationship with Lachlan into a strategic alliance. Lachlan, too, saw that he could position Ailes to damage Chernin, who was his true adversary. When it came time for Rupert to divvy up Lachlan's businesses, Lachlan lobbied Rupert to give Ailes control of the broadcast stations. In December, Rupert gave Ailes a new contract that added the unit to his Fox News portfolio. Rupert also named Ailes to the Office of the Chairman, an elite group of a half dozen executives who ran the company, and gave him Lachlan's vacant office on the eighth floor.

In the company, and in the wider culture, Ailes was at a peak. Fox News had conquered its cable rivals, revolutionized news, and helped secure Bush's reelection. It was profitable years ahead of schedule. Rupert was after Ailes to launch a cable business channel to take on CNBC, and Fox News Talk, its radio arm, struck lucrative deals to air on Sirius satellite radio. Moreover, Ailes had positioned himself as a hedge against Chernin's dominance. Chernin eyed Ailes warily. "There was a thinking from Peter, what is Roger going to do now?" an executive recalled. There was reason for concern: Ailes was throwing his weight around in Chernin's West Coast cable realm. In the winter of 2003, the News Corp cable channel FX released a docudrama about the Pentagon Papers. Ailes was not pleased. He called Peter Liguori, the president of FX.

"You making a movie about the Pentagon Papers?" Ailes said.

"Yeah," Liguori said.

"Why would *you* do that? It's bad for America," Ailes said, echoing the complaint Joe Coors had leveled when TVN covered Daniel Ellsberg. The FX film was already scheduled to air, so there was nothing Liguori could do. As a half measure, he told his team to cut the marketing budget in half.

Around this time, a Fox executive went to visit Ailes in his new office on the eighth floor, "the biggest I've ever seen," the executive thought, "like something out of *2001: A Space Odyssey*." The executive was startled to walk in and find Ailes with his back turned, scrolling through his email. It made the executive uncomfortable. "Roger talks about being in places people don't expect to keep them off guard," a Fox producer later said.

Ailes swiveled around. "Do you know whose chair I'm sitting in? I'm sitting in Lachlan Murdoch's chair." There was a cold pause. "Do you know who's sitting on the other side of that wall? Rupert Murdoch."

"What are you going to do with all this power now?" the executive ventured.

Ailes looked him in the eye. "We'll see where it goes," he said.

# ACT V

# NINETEEN

# SEARCHING FOR A NEW CAST

On the evening of April 26, 2006, the luminaries of George Bush's Washington—all but the president himself—gathered at Cafe Milano, the trendy Italian restaurant in Georgetown, to celebrate the tenth anniversary of *Fox News Sunday*. The party served a more important purpose—it was an opportunity to genuflect before the man who had altered the power equation in American politics. Roger Ailes's name was at the top of the invitations. No one, it seemed, turned him down. Shortly after 7:00, waiters circulated through the crowd passing out cocktails and cigars as attendees craned their necks to catch glimpses of Cheney, Rove, and the newest addition to the Bush administration's team, Fox host Tony Snow. Just that morning, Bush had introduced Snow as his new press secretary. "Congratulations on your promotion—or maybe it's a demotion," Rupert Murdoch said in front of the guests. Ailes explained that the appointment merely affirmed Fox's influence. "Ten years ago we could have never gotten the White House press secretary to come to this party," he said. For attuned observers, the party was a barometer of presidential ambition. John McCain and Hillary Clinton, with eyes on 2008, made sure to pay proper homage to Ailes.

The party represented a new high point. But the network's success was built on ground that appeared to be dangerously unstable. As the Bush administration's fortunes turned, so, too, would those of Fox. More than 2,300 troops had been killed in Iraq with no end in sight. Osama bin Laden remained at large, despite Bush's vow to "*smoke 'im out.*" Hurricane Katrina, the previous August, provided a visceral shorthand for the administration's shortcomings, and its failure to represent all Americans. The facts overwhelmed Ailes's abilities to find a story line that engaged his audience. In the 8:00 a.m. editorial meeting, the talk was getting desperate. "Look at these people," Fox executive Ken LaCorte said as pictures of bedraggled survivors standing on rooftops, many of them African American, flashed on screens on the wall. "What, do they think the government is supposed to come bail them out?" Executives shifted in their seats uncomfortably. "Everyone tries to out-Roger Roger," a senior producer recalled.

Fox lost about 15 percent of its total viewership in the year after Katrina. For the first time since 9/11, the polarities that powered Fox's ascendance had begun to shift. Sensing that the left's rage was to become almost as potent a media force as the right's had been, MSNBC tried a new tactic. In September 2005, Keith Olbermann, a former star of ESPN's *SportsCenter* who had transformed himself into a voluble MSNBC personality, emerged as an unlikely liberal icon. In one emotionally charged segment, he lashed the Bush administration's mismanaged response to Katrina. The commentary went viral. On August 30, 2006, Olbermann debuted a segment of his *Countdown* show called "Special Comment." The first target was Donald Rumsfeld. "The man who sees absolutes where all other men see nuances and shades of meaning is either a prophet or a quack," Olbermann began. "Donald H. Rumsfeld is not a prophet." That year, *Countdown*'s ratings jumped 67 percent. Even Ailes's boss, detecting the shifting landscape, contemplated a move to the middle. That summer, Murdoch hosted a fundraiser for Hillary Clinton at News Corp headquarters.

Ailes told executives this moment might come. Even as Fox had rolled over its rivals, Ailes tried to maintain an underdog mentality. He kept costs low. Fox's green rooms were notoriously grimy. Shows were programmed with a bare-bones staff. One senior executive even changed out the toner cartridges in the copy machine himself. Ailes told a reporter that acting like an underdog was "inspiration to people to try to get out there and do well." He said he wanted to guard against "complacency on the part of people who get to be successful, get to be stars, get too much money and get comfortable and start to think they are winning." It was easier in those early years to "fight from behind," he said.

The battles Ailes had waged to increase his power within News Corp had lingering repercussions. As Ailes approached the channel's ten-year mark in October 2006, Brian Lewis learned that Julia Angwin, an enterprising investigative reporter for *The Wall Street Journal,* was preparing a lengthy front-page article about Ailes. From what Lewis gleaned, the story could be damaging. Angwin had discovered that Ailes's takeover of the television stations that Lachlan Murdoch had run was plagued by mismanagement and mediocre ratings.

Fox's PR department had history with Angwin. The previous May, when Angwin was working on another story about Fox's advertising sales department, Lewis's deputy, Irena Briganti, screamed at Angwin, who was pregnant with her first child, that she was "acting hormonal." Angwin angrily told Lewis she would no longer deal with Briganti.

In mid-September, a few days before Angwin's front-page story went to press, Ailes agreed to an interview. He denied undercutting Lachlan. "If that's what happened, I don't know it," he told Angwin. "I don't think that's what happened because Lachlan and I get along great." He also brushed off questions about his sharp elbows. "There are lots of things that can be said about me—but not playing for the full team is not one of them," he declared. "If the only way to win is to damage someone else . . . you're no damn good." Angwin's article, headlined "After Riding High with Fox News, Murdoch Aide Has Harder Slog," appeared on Tuesday, October 3.

Later that day, Ailes and Murdoch gave a joint interview to the *Financial Times*. Murdoch called Angwin's article "a hit job," "cheap," and "completely wrong." Ailes was defiant. "I have no knowledge what they are talking about. *The Wall Street Journal* just flat out got it wrong," he told the interviewer. "They obviously went in with an agenda and Rupert and I were trying to figure out if he was the target or I was the target."

Ailes's campaign against Angwin was not over. At one point, Steve Doocy mocked Angwin during a segment on *Fox & Friends* while showing a distorted, grainy photo of her snapped from News Corp's front-desk security camera. Ailes approached Angwin at an event at the Waldorf Astoria. "You've had your chance," he blustered as he walked by her in the crowd. "Now I have the rest of my life to get back at *you*."

Even as Murdoch publicly defended Ailes, his attentions had moved beyond Fox to a trophy he had long coveted: *The Wall Street Journal*. Though Ailes was useful in this regard—Fox's profits would help finance Murdoch's $5 billion offer for the *Journal*—Murdoch realized that Ailes's role at News Corp, in the interest of corporate harmony, should not extend far beyond his news channel. Peter Chernin expressed concern to colleagues that Ailes might be given control of News Corp's cable assets, including the entertainment channel FX, which were run out of Chernin's domain in Los Angeles. Murdoch told a senior executive that Chernin had nothing to worry about. " 'We don't want to give cable to Roger,' " he said. "Rupert knew the schtick," a person close to Murdoch said. "He knew Roger was great fun, but it was great fun in small dosages." Executives began to see Ailes as akin to on-air talent—as a performer, whose stage was the Fox News offices. Like many of his anchors, Ailes could be temperamental and needy. Colleagues often remarked that the most entertaining show at Fox News was Ailes's daily editorial meeting, where he would monologue about his political enemies and cable news competitors. "He needs to know he's being appreciated," a former News Corp executive explained.

It did not help Ailes's corporate position that the Republicans' travails worsened through the 2006 midterms. On the morning of Election Day, the Democrats were poised to reclaim the House of Representatives and the Senate, an outcome Bush would call a "thumpin'." That afternoon, Ailes assembled his news team for a pre-coverage briefing in a second-floor conference room. No matter what the final score was, he told them to put on a winning face. "I was watching CNN in 2004 and saw some really unhappy people on camera," he said. "We don't want that to be on Fox tonight."

The next day, Nielsen reported that Fox News had beaten CNN by just 100,000 viewers.

For almost a decade, Ailes had played a role in driving the news; now he was captive to it, with few apparent options to reverse the ratings trend, and at Fox there were incipient signs of panic. "We had the concern that the slide could turn into a freefall," a producer said. Ailes's plans to turn the ship around were running aground. He made an aggressive bid to convince his old friend Rush Limbaugh to come to Fox. Limbaugh turned him down flat. "Rush was kind of laughing at the whole thing," a Limbaugh friend who spoke with him during the talks recalled. "He said, 'Roger is really trying to get me to come back.' And Rush was like, 'Why would I do this?' " Ailes acknowledged the problems. "We're in a challenging news cycle because of Hurricane Katrina," he explained to a reporter around this time. "You are sort of forced in the cable business to play even if you don't want to." Ailes sought to play a game he could win. The War on Christmas was a classic Fox ratings ploy. "Roger said, 'Let me think, 90 percent of the people like Christmas, so CBS, CNN, and

MSNBC, you can take the other 10 percent, we'll say, "Merry Christmas," and we'll make all the money,'" Ailes's brother, Robert, recalled. "Roger learned from an early age what you can quote unquote sell on television. He's looking for an audience. The bigger the audience, the more money the company makes, the more successful he will be."

Meanwhile, Ailes's relationship with his news chief, John Moody, was fraying. It was a tension that had existed from Fox's early days. Moody told executives that his role was "to be the antagonist" and "the conscience of news." "Roger is not a news guy," a producer said. "He will respect you for a period of time. After a while, you'll get on his nerves and he will kill you." A Fox contributor recalled that Moody "would try and impose some standards and Roger would override him." Ailes increasingly relied more on programming executives such as Bill Shine and Kevin Magee.

Although Moody shared Ailes's conservatism, friends and colleagues sensed Moody's growing discomfort with Ailes's rage and lack of journalistic rigor. "He was aghast from day one at shit that was going on there," a person close to Moody recalled. Adam Sank, who left Fox in 2002, said, "I look at John as a tortured soul."

For a while, Moody tried to downplay Ailes's crude view of journalism. "He insults me to my face but I don't want you to think it's a sign of disrespect," he told a colleague. But, in early 2006, Moody vented about his boss to a friend over lunch. As it happened, his friend knew Bob Wright and decided to give him a call.

"You should hire John Moody to run MSNBC. In one stroke you steal Roger's number two and he can run the network."

"That's a great idea," Wright said.

GE sent a helicopter to fly Moody to the corporation's headquarters in Fairfield, Connecticut. The courtship, however, was brief. Ailes offered Moody a raise to stay. The MSNBC job went to Phil Griffin instead. Moody's frustrations were left to simmer, and he would continue to keep an eye on the exit.

Moody was not the only veteran journalist looking to decamp. Kim Hume, the Washington bureau chief, had had enough. At the beginning of the year, she came under fire for Fox's coverage of the mining accident in Sago, West Virginia, that left a dozen men dead. Kim had been skiing in the Rockies at the time, and after CNN was first with the news, Fox and several other outlets reported a false rumor that the miners had been saved, prompting a barrage of criticism. After returning to work, Kim took her frustrations out on staff members. "You will never embarrass me again," she told them. In September, Kim resigned.

With the daily headlines no longer driving ratings, Ailes looked for other ways to regain his edge. In the fall of 2006, he brought in an old hand: Woody Fraser. They reconnected at the Los Angeles memorial for Mike Douglas, who had died that year. The following spring, Ailes hired Joel Cheatwood, a veteran television executive from CNN, to gin up programming concepts for Fox. "Roger would call him Helmet Head, because Joel has a very unique coif," a colleague said. More than for his hair, Cheatwood was known in the industry for being a tabloid-TV revolutionary. As head of a Fox affiliate in Miami in the early 1990s, he juiced ratings with gory, sensationalized crime stories and flashy graphics. And at CNN, Cheatwood and his deputy, Josanne Lopez, who had worked for Ailes at America's Talking, had discovered a charismatic Philadelphia talk radio host and put him on Headline News. His name was Glenn Beck.

Over the summer, Ailes tasked Cheatwood and a small group of executives—Bill Shine, Woody Fraser, and Suzanne Scott—to propose steps that would halt the ratings slide. "Roger likes things to be produced simply and overtly," a producer said. "For example, he likes words in graphics to be big. There is a story he tells all the time about the live bug"—the graphic in the lower corner of the screen. "He made his bigger than CNN's at the launch, then, when CNN made its bigger, Roger made his bigger still. He kept doing that until CNN gave up."

O'Reilly's was the only show that seemed to be working and Ailes expressed uneasiness about it. "One person should not be the identity of this network," he told executives. Ideas were thrown around about shuffling shows and hosts. One glaring weak spot was *Hannity & Colmes*. The show typically had higher ratings than its rival 9:00 p.m. offerings, but was far from meeting corporate expectations. While some observers said the format of left-and-right pundits was an anachronism, the consensus at Fox was that Colmes was the problem. After a decade, liberals were convinced he was a patsy; and conservatives simply did not want to listen to him. It was like a pro wrestling match where the result was scripted, the outcome the same every time. Hannity himself was one of Colmes's most vocal detractors. "Sean was bitter he had to do the show with Alan for many years," a senior producer said. Hannity also complained that Colmes did not hustle to book guests. As the Iraq War intensified, Hannity bombarded the White House with pushy personal appeals. "If you don't give me Powell for the TV show, I'm going to fuck you on the radio," he snapped to a press aide.

"We don't do debate shows," the aide said. Hannity repeated his threat.

"Listen," the aide replied. "There is a policy of this government that we don't negotiate with terrorists and those who harbor them."

In 2007, Hannity and Colmes's relationship continued to unravel. "There were times he'd freeze Alan out and be curt with him," said a former senior producer at Fox. "Sean became less close-mouthed about his feelings about Alan. They'd sit on set right before the show and Sean would say, 'What's it going to be like when you're gone?' "

One of the paradoxes of Ailes's management style was that, while he bulldozed through barriers, he could be excruciatingly cautious when it came to making talent decisions, which frustrated his executives. He wavered when they suggested dumping Colmes. "Roger wanted the counterpoint," the senior executive said. "They were a team. That's what Fox was—these people. The only thing that changed in the prime-time lineup were the women, from Catherine to Paula to Greta." As a stopgap, in January 2007, Ailes gave Hannity a Sunday night solo show. But Ailes still had doubts. While he shared Hannity's hard-right politics, he privately complained that he was too stiff. "I want you guys to slap him in his head," Ailes told Bill Shine. "There's entertainment value here and he doesn't get it. When he's on camera, it's like he expects Alan to have an epiphany on air and say, 'You know, Sean, you're right. I've been such a moron for fifty years. How did I not see it?' "

Hannity's pressure ate at Colmes. In the fall of 2008, Fox announced Colmes was leaving the show.

As usual for Fox, salvation was on the horizon, in the form of a presidential election, which was certain to provide the armature of a new narrative. For the first time in eight years, Democrats and Republicans would be choosing candidates for the general election. The jump ball for the nomination on both sides of the aisle gave Ailes an opportunity to reignite the passions of his weary audience, who could rally behind a Republican nominee and enjoy a compelling gladiator death match on the Democratic side.

The obvious priority was the Republican primary. In early 2007, Ailes dispatched senior executives to lock down the highest-profile GOP debates. Katon Dawson, the former chairman of the South Carolina Republican Party, recalled how Fox outmaneuvered CNN in the negotiations to air the primary debate on May 15, 2007, in Columbia. Although Wolf Blitzer personally lobbied Dawson on behalf of CNN, Fox was swifter with its official pitch, and had carrots CNN did not. "Fox had a specific South Carolina audience. A very Republican audience," Dawson said. Fox also had sticks. "I would never want to get on the wrong side of Roger Ailes," he added.

Those who crossed Ailes during his campaign to win the Republican primary telecasts faced his fury. On February 14, 2007, the Ronald Reagan Presidential Library Foundation announced that it was partnering with MSNBC and *Politico* to host a debate, which would be moderated by MSNBC's Chris Matthews. Ailes complained to Fox executives that NBC and *Politico* cut an inside deal with the library. Frederick Ryan Jr., the chairman of the Reagan foundation's board, was also the president and CEO of *Politico*. Ryan had recused himself from the selection process, but Ailes was not appeased. "Roger likes to win, not most games, but every game, every single day," Ryan said. Fox hosts began denouncing *Politico* as "far left wing."

The Republican debates took on more urgency after Democrats mobilized to freeze Fox out of their primaries. Ailes had triggered the backlash himself. On March 8, Ailes was in Washington to accept a First Amendment Leadership Award from a group of radio and television news directors. During his speech, he mixed up Barack Obama's name with Osama bin Laden, for humorous effect. "And it is true that Barack Obama is on the move," Ailes said. "I don't know if it's true that President Bush called [Pakistan president Pervez] Musharraf and said, 'Why can't we catch this guy?'" Ailes's impudence fed into a narrative about Fox's hysteria over Obama's candidacy. A couple of months earlier, Steve Doocy announced on *Fox & Friends* that Obama had attended a madrassa funded by "Saudis" in Indonesia. Obama advisers erupted, labeling the claim "completely ludicrous." Robert Gibbs, Obama's communications chief, called Moody to complain. Moody said he could not control *Fox & Friends*. "It's an entertainment show," Moody explained.

On March 9, a day after Ailes jokingly confused Obama with Osama, the Nevada Democratic Party canceled its Fox News debate. It was a move progressive groups like MoveOn.org had been calling for. Fox quickly fired back. David Rhodes, Moody's deputy for news, was put out front, to issue a statement. "News organizations will want to think twice before getting involved in the Nevada Democratic Caucus, which appears to be controlled by radical fringe, out-of-state interest groups, not the Nevada Democratic Party," Rhodes said.

Ailes triangulated. Around this time, he ran into Maryland congressman Elijah Cummings, a member of the Congressional Black Caucus, and suggested Fox could co-host a televised debate with the group in Detroit. It was a difficult sell, because many caucus members saw Fox as hostile to African Americans. Ailes met privately with former Michigan congresswoman Carolyn Kilpatrick. When she questioned him about his interest in civil rights, Ailes whipped out a photo of himself with Malcolm X on the set of *The Mike Douglas Show*. Kilpatrick was swayed. On March 29, Fox announced that the CBC would host a pair of debates on Fox News, the first taking place in Detroit in September. But the maneuver failed. One week later, the Democratic National Committee announced that Fox News would be shut out from hosting the six official DNC primary debates. The next day, John Edwards pulled out of the Detroit debate, and the following Monday, Clinton and Obama announced that they were aligning with Edwards on the Fox boycott. "CNN seemed like a more appropriate venue," Obama spokesman Bill Burton told the press.

The problem with the 2008 Republican primaries from an entertainment standpoint was that the talent was weak. Around the second floor, Ailes evinced little enthusiasm for his party's 2008 candidates, who included former Arkansas governor Mike Huckabee, John McCain, former Massachusetts governor Mitt Romney, and Kansas senator Sam Brownback. Ailes called them the "seven dwarves." He made an exception for an old friend: Rudy Giuliani. In April, Giuliani was a guest at News Corp's table at the White House Correspondents' Dinner. What's more, Fox gave the New York mayor an invaluable national platform to propel his candidacy. A study found that in the first six months of 2007, Fox gave Giuliani more interview time than any other candidate.

Which is why the news that broke on Tuesday afternoon, November 13, two weeks before the crucial GOP debate in St. Petersburg, Florida, threatened to derail Giuliani's campaign. Judith Regan, the flamboyantly abrasive HarperCollins book publisher, filed a $100 million defamation suit against News Corp. It was the latest chapter in a tabloid circus that followed Regan's abrupt firing the previous December, and would soon entangle Ailes and Giuliani in a web of competing agendas.

At the heart of it was television. Books had fueled Judith Regan's rise. A former *National Enquirer* reporter, she possessed a sixth tabloid sense, which she tapped to publish a string of salacious bestsellers—including Howard Stern's *Private Parts* and Jenna Jameson's *How to Make Love like a Porn Star*. But her desire was to be bigger, more famous, than her celebrity authors. In 2006, Regan got Murdoch's permission to pay O. J. Simpson $880,000 for the rights to publish *If I Did It,* Simpson's hypothetical "confession." The book was a centerpiece of Regan's plan to reinvent herself as a prime-time personality. (In 2002, when Ailes canceled her weekly Fox News show, Regan told the press it had been her decision.) To roll out Simpson's book, Regan would interview Simpson for a prime-time special to air on Fox TV. Regan had even relocated to Los Angeles in a quest to become a "multi-platform" media star—an Oprah for the *Sex and the City* Age.

The whole thing blew back massively at Regan and News Corp on November 14, 2006, when details of the Simpson book and television special first appeared in the press. As pundits moralized about Regan's morally suspect pursuit of profit, the flurry of headlines metastasized into a full-fledged corporate crisis. After days of withering criticism, News Corp pulled the plug. Although Murdoch and HarperCollins CEO Jane Friedman had supported the project, Regan took the brunt of the blame for the scandal. By this point, Regan had few allies left inside News Corp. In a company full of massive egos, she stood apart. Stories of her office rage and the way she tormented underlings were legend. "Judith would call them 'cunts' who only had a job because of her hard work," one former employee said. Things got so out of control that, in 2003, News Corp opened an HR investigation into her behavior. Jane Friedman, who had clashed with Regan for years, was running out of patience.

In December 2006, Friedman fired Regan. She got the news in Los Angeles when her work computer suddenly was shut off. The two-sentence press release went out on December 15. Accounts soon leaked to reporters that Regan had been dismissed after she made an anti-Semitic slur to Mark Jackson, a HarperCollins lawyer. During a heated phone conversation, Regan allegedly told Jackson, who was Jewish, that a "Jewish cabal" was out to get her. "Of all people, the Jews should know about ganging up, finding common enemies and telling the big lie," Regan allegedly said. Her lawyer, Bert Fields, strenuously denied the account, attributing the termination to Regan's long-running feud with Friedman. As crass as she sometimes was, Regan vehemently objected to being branded an anti-Semite. Striking back, she had leverage.

Like Ailes, Regan was a brilliant storyteller and mythmaker. Her November 2007 lawsuit was no exception. The complaint, filed in the New York State Supreme Court, read like a pitch for a pulp corporate whodunit she might have published. "This action arises from a deliberate smear campaign orchestrated by one of the world's largest media conglomerates for the sole purpose of destroying one woman's credibility and reputation," it began. "This smear campaign was necessary to advance News Corp's political agenda, which has long centered on protecting Rudy Giuliani's presidential ambitions." Regan's narrative sizzled with sex, power, and money. The media seized on an alluring nugget about Regan's affair with Giuliani's disgraced former police commissioner Bernard Kerik, who was indicted the previous week on multiple federal corruption charges. Her lawsuit alleged that a "senior executive at News Corp told Regan that he believed she had information about Kerik that, if disclosed, would harm Giuliani's presidential campaign. This executive told Regan to lie to, and withhold information from, investigators concerning Kerik." Regan would later allege that the unnamed executive was Roger Ailes.

The next week, the strength of Regan's hand became immediately apparent. Susan Estrich, a Fox News contributor and Regan friend, was at Thanksgiving dinner at a friend's home in Malibu when she got a tip that, like Andrea Mackris, Regan possessed a trump card. Regan claimed to have secretly captured Ailes on tape allegedly advising her to lie to the Feds. Estrich got a copy of Regan's complaint and called her friend Joel Kaufman, who had been Regan's producer at Fox. "We have to help Roger," she said. "We've got to strategize how we deal with this."

Ailes passed Estrich off to his personal lawyer, Peter Johnson Sr., a former street cop turned hard-nosed Manhattan litigator who had taken part in the battle at Iwo Jima in World War II. A meeting with Murdoch and News Corp's senior legal team was convened. In Murdoch's cold calculus, Ailes was the asset that needed to be protected. Murdoch had come to blame Jane Friedman for impatiently firing Regan, which had set off the unfortunate chain of events. "He's the talent. News Corp wants to make sure we helped him as much as we could in a way that was legal," an executive involved in the talks said.

The view inside News Corp was that Regan was capable of anything.

Estrich, who was dispatched to act as a backchannel intermediary between Ailes and Regan, advised her against releasing the tape. "Susan acted as Judith's shrink," one executive said, "making sure she did not self-destruct." Complicating matters, Regan's camp refused to allow Murdoch and his lieutenants to listen to her alleged tape of Ailes. Without knowing what was precisely said, News Corp's lawyers were flying blind. In meetings, Ailes denied he advised Regan to obstruct justice. "It's embarrassing," he told his lawyers, referring to his conversation with Regan. "I use salty language." Lon Jacobs, who was then News Corp's general counsel, pressed Johnson for hard facts. "I need to know what News Corp's exposure is," he said. Johnson backed his client up. He assured Jacobs that Ailes had said nothing illegal on the tape. Even if Regan relented, Jacobs did not want to hear the recording. News Corp's outside counsel advised him not to listen to it, in case Ailes had made incriminating remarks.

Regan's deft play pushed News Corp to fold. On January 25, 2008, four days before the Florida primary, News Corp settled the lawsuit for $10.75 million, with no admission of guilt by either party. As part of the deal, Regan signed a nondisclosure agreement and a letter stating that Ailes had not pressured her to lie to assist Giuliani (News Corp kept a copy of her letter on file, in case they needed to release it at some point). After the Mackris case, it was the second time in less than four years that a News Corp employee earned millions of dollars for keeping the secrets of Fox News out of the press.

The settlement did not reverse Giuliani's fortunes. He dropped out of the presidential race five days later, after placing third in Florida. Years later, Regan blamed Ailes for smearing her. "Connect the dots," she told a reporter.

The marathon battle between Hillary Clinton and Barack Obama for the Democratic nomination was the biggest story of 2008—and for most of the campaign, Fox struggled to grab a piece of it. CNN's prime-time audience was surging, up 42 percent in January from a year earlier, and up 68 percent in the third quarter of the year. Wolf Blitzer—a decidedly uncable personality—was somehow anchoring the highest-rated election night show. MSNBC was also finding success as a destination for an energized liberal audience. In the fall of 2007, Tim Russert called Phil Griffin into his office in the Washington bureau and said, "Griff, you're gonna have the greatest election of our lifetime. Own it." Griffin debuted a new tagline: "The Place for Politics"—a phrase Russert had happened to say on the air. "It gave us the focus that we never had," Griffin later said. "We once branded ourselves 'America's News Channel.' It was a lie! We weren't."

Watching CNN and MSNBC benefiting from the Obama phenomenon, Ailes found a way to counterprogram. "Roger felt that as Obama emerged as a candidate, the media was giving undue coverage to him," a person close to Ailes recalled. "At one point he said, 'We have to be the one to balance the Democratic side.'" Despite his partisan bluster, Ailes continued to triangulate. In early 2008, Fox News and Hillary Clinton, who was performing strongly with blue-collar white voters in the industrial heartland—Fox News country—forged one such surprising alliance.

Hillary needed all the allies she could get. Relations between the Clinton campaign and MSNBC had all but broken down. The day after Clinton roared back into the race winning the New Hampshire primary in January, Chris Matthews declared that her political career was made possible because "her husband messed around." MSNBC president Phil Griffin ordered Matthews to apologize, but it did little to mollify the Clinton camp. At Clinton campaign headquarters, an order went out that none of the twenty televisions in the press room were allowed to be tuned to MSNBC. On the evening of February 7—two days after Super Tuesday—David Shuster, MSNBC's political correspondent, speculated that Chelsea Clinton was being "pimped out" in a bid to win over superdelegates. After Hillary threatened to boycott future MSNBC debates, the network suspended Shuster. In early March, Chris Matthews again displayed MSNBC's Obama tilt when he gushed on air that Obama's oratory talents gave him a "thrill going up my leg."

Ailes helped out where he could. On March 19, he forwarded an email to John Moody, Bill O'Reilly, and Bill Shine containing an opposition research file on Obama's relationship with the controversial Illinois state senator and pastor James Meeks with the subject line "Maybe God is a Republican." "*Meeks has denounced 'Hollywood Jews,' blaming them for homosexuality; called Mayor [Richard] Daley as a 'slave master' and supporters of Daley 'house niggers'; and called gays 'evil,'*" the file read. That night, O'Reilly and Hannity did segments on Meeks. "Now we don't know the relationship between Reverend Meeks and Barack

Obama," O'Reilly announced. "We are working on that story and a number of other people are as well. But the question tonight is how will the Clinton and McCain campaigns handle all of this? It's a growing story."

News Corp was also populated with influential Clinton surrogates who could hit back against MSNBC and Obama. Susan Estrich lobbied behind the scenes to arrange a private meeting between Ailes and Hillary. "This would be a good thing for her," she told Bill Clinton. "No one has to know about it. Fox isn't looking for publicity, they understand the sensitivities on the Democratic side." Gary Ginsberg, Rupert Murdoch's director of communications, was another pro-Hillary voice. Earlier in the campaign, Ginsberg played a crucial role neutralizing an attack by John Edwards in which he criticized Hillary for accepting donations from Murdoch. Ginsberg called HarperCollins and found out that the company had paid Edwards a $500,000 advance to write a coffee-table book, *Home: The Blueprints of Our Lives.* (The Edwards campaign said the money went to charity.) Ginsberg promptly fed the information to Howard Wolfson, Clinton's communications chief, who leaked it to the press.

Fox's clubbiness with the Clintons created bad blood inside the Obama campaign. In May, Hillary gave a widely viewed sit-down interview to Bill O'Reilly. "Are you surprised that Fox News has been fairer to you than NBC News and a lot of the other liberal news networks?" he asked. "I wouldn't expect anything less than a fair and balanced coverage of my campaign," she replied. "She made some kind of compact with Murdoch," Obama's former communications director Anita Dunn later said. Another senior Obama adviser recalled, "Our campaign opened with Fox saying that Obama had gone to a madrassa as a child." "If you watched Fox, you would not have known there was a financial crisis and two wars going on. You would have thought the most important issues in America were Bill Ayers and Reverend Wright."

Not surprisingly, Obama harbored a deep distrust of Fox. After clinching the Democratic nomination, Obama agreed to meet Murdoch at the Waldorf while he was in town attending a fundraiser. Obama's senior adviser, David Axelrod, who had been talking secretly with Gary Ginsberg, had agreed to set up the meeting. For sport, Murdoch brought along Ailes. Obama told Ailes he would not deal with Fox if they continued to portray him and his wife as dangerous subversives. Ailes told Obama that he would get better treatment if he engaged, rather than opposed, Fox. At that, the meeting ended.

Afterward, Murdoch asked Ailes his impression of Obama. "He's like a middle manager," Ailes said. Murdoch was taken aback.

"I wasn't asking you to evaluate him for a position at Fox," Murdoch replied. "I'm asking what you thought of him as a presidential candidate."

"Well, that's what I think," Ailes said.

A few weeks later, Ailes told Axelrod that he was concerned that Obama wanted to create a national police force.

"You can't be serious," Axelrod replied. "What makes you think that?"

Ailes responded by emailing Axelrod a YouTube clip from a campaign speech Obama had given on national service, in which he called for the creation of a new civilian corps to work alongside the military on projects overseas.

Axelrod had a long history with Ailes, having defeated him in 1984 while running Paul Simon's Senate campaign in Illinois. He later said that the exchange was the moment he realized Ailes truly believed what he was programming.

Ailes eventually settled on McCain as his preferred candidate, though his campaign performance was far from ideal. "He doesn't have the charisma, the message isn't honed to the point where you know who he is," Ailes said of McCain. "He has this fantastic story, and he tends to minimize it." "Roger is a producer first and foremost," a former staffer said.

Some News Corp executives privately discussed whether Ailes would be out of sync with Murdoch's political allegiances. Murdoch notoriously blew with the political winds, and he began making noises that he would be open to endorsing Obama for president in the pages of the *New York Post*, lest he be left on the wrong side of history. (In January, the *Post* had endorsed Obama for the Democratic nomination.) Members of Murdoch's own family were also captivated by the candidate and lobbied Rupert, including his third wife, Wendi. As these tensions played out, the writer Michael Wolff was putting the finishing touches on his authorized biography of Murdoch. The book, based on hours of interviews with Murdoch and many of his lieutenants and family members, itself became a flashpoint within News Corp. Over nearly a decade, Gary Ginsberg had worked tirelessly to soften and massage Murdoch's image and had done a remarkable job of making News Corp, if not exactly admired, then palatable to a certain subset of Manhattan. Ginsberg, along with Murdoch's son-in-law Matthew Freud, a London public relations executive, was involved in dealing with Wolff on the book. But ultimately, much of what Wolff wrote in his book infuriated many camps inside News Corp. In a preview of the book in *Vanity Fair,* Wolff revealed how embarrassed Murdoch was by Ailes and Bill O'Reilly—a view Wolff says came from interviews with Rupert—and Ailes became enraged. "Is this true?" he demanded in a September 2008 meeting.

"No, it's not true," Murdoch replied.

Just as he had done after his confrontation with Lachlan over the anthrax attacks, Ailes forced Murdoch to demonstrate his loyalty. Murdoch assured Ailes he was happy with Fox News and offered him a new five-year contract, which was signed in November, that guaranteed him editorial independence. "That was the beginning of when the network went crazy," a Murdoch adviser said. Ailes made sure to capitalize on the moment. "As Ginsberg was blowing up because of the Murdoch book, Brian Lewis and Roger would huddle about the best way to leverage that to hurt Peter Chernin," a senior executive said.

Any speculation about whether Murdoch was becoming liberal ended on September 8, when the *New York Post* endorsed McCain. Within the next year, News Corp's top Democrats—Ginsberg and Chernin—would depart the company, leaving Murdoch with fewer checks on Ailes's power. Ailes savored the moment. "Roger took credit," an executive close to him recalled. "The day Ginsberg left, Roger walked into his afternoon editorial meeting, dropped the press release onto the conference table and said, 'In life, there are winners, and there are . . .' And just smiled as people passed around the note."

The promise of a new contract gave Ailes time to prepare for the effect of an Obama win on Fox ratings, but it turned out he didn't need the time. On September 3, a day after confronting Murdoch, Ailes, watching the Republican convention, was riveted by the appearance of an exotic political creature: Sarah Palin. "She hit a home run," he told executives the next day. Her gleeful establishment bashing made her a perfect heroine for a new Ailes story line—and Fox's ratings soared to a cable news record. During Palin's speech, Fox attracted more than nine million viewers, eclipsing every other news network, cable or broadcast. "At least people care now," Ailes told his team.

He was intensely interested in the Alaska governor. Palin had somehow managed to graft the old western myth of the self-reliant frontiersman onto a beauty-pageant face and a counterpunching, don't-tread-on-me verbal style—a new kind of character, and a remarkably compelling one. A few weeks after her convention speech, Ailes secretly met with Palin during her swing through New York, when she toured the U.N. and had a photo op with Henry Kissinger. That afternoon, Shushannah Walshe, a young Fox producer who was covering Palin's campaign for the network, had gone on-air and criticized McCain's staff, which had prevented reporters from asking Palin questions during her U.N. visit. "There's not one chance that Governor Palin would have to answer a question," Walshe said on camera. "They're eliminating even the chance of any kind of interaction with the candidate—it's just unprecedented."

Ailes didn't know Walshe, but he was angry when he heard her comments. Liberal media outlets like *The Huffington Post* were using her words to make it appear that Fox was turning on Palin. He called Suzanne Scott and demanded Walshe be taken off the air. "It's not fair-and-balanced coverage," an executive later told Walshe. Walshe was allowed to continue covering Palin but was barred from future on-camera appearances. She soon left Fox.

In October, Ailes found the other star of Fox's next era: CNN's Glenn Beck. Ratings for his CNN Headline News show had jumped by more than 200 percent since he joined the channel in 2006. He had a string of *New York Times* bestsellers, and ratings for his radio show were nearing Rush Limbaugh's. When Ailes met the forty-four-year-old for the first time that fall, he could tell he was born for television. Beck's performances, a mix of New Age self-help speak and right-wing fervor, gave him the lineaments of Lonesome Rhodes, the drifter played by Andy Griffith in Elia Kazan's *A Face in the Crowd*. With his neat, alabaster hair and doughy cheeks, he was a prophet of a nascent political movement that was rising up in tandem with Obama's candidacy.

As they spoke, Ailes and Beck bonded over their shared triumphal version of American history. Ailes wanted Beck for the 5:00 p.m. hour, which had continually failed to attract an audience and delivered a weak lead-in to the shows that followed. Fox executives dubbed it the "black hole." This was especially problematic because Brit Hume was telling executives he wanted to step down from his nightly newscast at 6:00 p.m. His departure would further imperil the lineup. On Thursday, October 16, Fox announced that Beck was jumping from CNN to Fox.

Ailes was assembling his cast for television in the age of Obama. While he was unimpressed with Mike Huckabee as a candidate, he recognized he had a following among social conservatives. In addition to snapping up Huckabee, Ailes signed Karl Rove and John Bolton as pundits. Still, as Election Day approached, Ailes seemed to be in a dour mood. In late September, McCain had suspended his campaign in hopes of negotiating a congressional accord on a proposed financial bailout in the wake of Lehman Brothers' bankruptcy. "He was so angry when McCain suspended his campaign," an executive recalled. "He said, 'The only people who suspend campaigns are the ones who are losing.' "

Ailes told executives Obama's election would be "the worst thing for America," but others sensed opportunity. Brian Lewis, a savvy operator and pragmatist—"Everything is a situation" was his mantra—felt that an Obama victory would be better for business than a McCain presidency. A few days before the election, Lewis scheduled a meeting to tell Ailes he was voting for Obama.

Before heading to Ailes's office, he called Gary Ginsberg. "If Obama wins, it's good for us," Lewis said. "I wanted to tell you that before I go into the lion's den."

# TWENTY
# COMEBACK

THE WEEK AFTER OBAMA'S 2008 ELECTION NIGHT VICTORY SPEECH in Grant Park, Chicago, Ailes took his son, Zachary, and Beth back to Warren, Ohio, for Veterans Day. Members of the community had asked Ailes to give the keynote address at the dedication ceremony for the Trumbull County Veterans' Memorial. Since leaving for college fifty years earlier, Ailes had returned home only a handful of times—he had few remaining ties to the community. Ailes decided it was time for his son, who was then eight years old, to see where his father came from. In the plush seats of News Corp's corporate jet, the Ailes family descended through the clouds over the flat landscape of northeast Ohio. It was unseasonably cold for early November, barely above freezing in the afternoon. From the air, the fallow farmland was a quilt of brown and gray patchwork.

The Aileses were in town for just one night and had a lot of ground to cover. There was a gathering of Roger's high school friends at the Avalon Inn, the hotel where they were staying on Warren's East Side, followed by a downtown reception for civic leaders and memorial donors at the Huntington National Bank and an interview with a reporter from the Warren *Tribune Chronicle*. The morning would bring the monument unveiling and a celebratory luncheon at the Trumbull Country Club. But before all that, Ailes had a promise to keep. He had told Zachary that they would eat at the Hot Dog Shoppe, a favored watering hole for high school kids in his father's time.

On the drive from the airport, Roger could see how Warren was now a very different city from the one he had grown up in. The giant aluminum hot dog that blinked as it rotated on a fifteen-foot red pole mounted on the Shoppe's roof was still in working order, but many of the restaurants from his day were gone. Warren's decline was no less precipitous than that of Rust Belt emblems like Detroit or Flint, Michigan. The financial crisis of 2008 visited its own kind of apocalypse. During one eighteen-day period after Lehman filed for bankruptcy, Warren's then-mayor, Michael O'Brien, received ten letters from local companies announcing mass layoffs or closures. Severstal Steel, one of Warren's few remaining employers, announced it was cutting its workforce from one thousand to thirty-five. Packard's employment fell to nine hundred, about 5 percent of its peak.

Once a city that worked, Warren had become a city that was broken, sick with the all-too-familiar symptoms. Drug addicts robbed homes in broad daylight, running off with flat-screen TVs or video game consoles to pawn. Prostitutes leaning against shady oak trees worked the streets. Scavengers stripped foreclosed houses of their guts—copper plumbing and electrical wiring—to sell to local scrap dealers. The municipal government cut social services and laid off 30 percent of its police force. To keep cops on the street, Mayor O'Brien—himself a former officer—dismantled the department's detective bureau and put a dozen veteran detectives back into uniform.

After checking into the Avalon Hotel, Ailes went to a private room with a dozen former schoolmates from Warren G. Harding High School's class of 1958. They chatted for an hour about their youth, with Ailes speaking warmly about his time acting in high school plays. But when the conversation moved toward current events, the mood darkened. Ailes had a specific diagnosis for his hometown's decline. "We have fed more people and freed more people than any country in history. Obama needs to focus Americans on personal responsibility," Ailes said. He recounted his summertime encounter with the president-elect at the Waldorf Astoria. "If he wants to bring the nation together, as he says, now is the time to reach out," Ailes explained. He told his classmates that he had hoped McCain would win, but that the "unbelievable" financial crisis had eliminated the Republicans' chance.

Then Ailes talked about his own role in the struggle, and the stakes. "I defend the United States, Israel, and the Constitution. That's when I get my death threats," he told them. "I stand up for what I believe. I don't back off. I've been that way for forty years. That's the secret to my success. I have thick skin. I don't care what people say about me. . . . We're not a perfect nation. But the question is, if the U.S. is destroyed, what would the world be like?" Later that afternoon, he told a local newspaper reporter that his hometown could learn a thing or two from the lesson his father had taught him as a boy. "If you want a helping hand, look at the end of your arm," Ailes said. It was the same lesson he imparted at Fox News. He liked to tell people how, several years earlier, he launched a job-training program for minorities called "The Ailes Apprentice Program." It was one of his genuine sources of pride. "If every company did this, could you imagine what they'd do to minority unemployment?" he later said.

It was cold and damp the next morning when Ailes and his family arrived at the dedication ceremony in Monument Park. Hundreds of people had gathered. It was the largest crowd Warren had seen downtown in many years.

As Ailes took to the microphone, he saw visions of his past. "You see that fountain pool right around there?" he told the audience, pointing toward a Victorian-era sculpture of a crane in flight with water shooting from its beak. "My mother and grandmother would bring me there, and I used to feed the squirrels." He motioned at the YMCA across the street from the courthouse. "I used to go there every Saturday and take swim lessons."

He told the audience that he was moved to speak at the dedication ceremony because his best childhood friend, Doug Webster, was killed in the Vietnam War. Webster was a grade behind Roger in school, but they were like brothers. Webster grew up on Edgewood Street, a mile away from the Ailes house.

Webster's life exerted a palpable pull on Roger. In many ways, he was the man Ailes wanted to be: a star athlete, vice president of his high school class, co-captain of the Ohio State gymnastics team, and a Navy fighter pilot. Ailes went to the military recruiting office with Webster to enlist together. "He got in, I didn't," Ailes said. But Webster died in a freak accident three months into his first deployment to the Pacific, when his Navy A-4 Skyhawk slid off the deck of the aircraft carrier USS *Ticonderoga*. His body was never recovered. "I guess there is a certain amount of survivor guilt there," Ailes said.

After the crowd dispersed, Ailes headed to the Trumbull Country Club for lunch. An hour later, he motioned to his wife.

"Hurry up, we gotta go."

"What do you mean?" Beth said.

"We gotta go back to the Hot Dog Shoppe so we can load up."

On the way, Ailes made a detour onto Belmont Street. He wanted to show Zachary the house he grew up in. The two-story home had not changed much since his parents had sold it following their divorce. Ailes would have noticed only slight alterations to it. Now it had gray siding and navy blue shutters on the upstairs windows. The other houses on the block were in varying states of disrepair. Ailes knocked on the door. A young man named Chris Monsman answered. He was not yet thirty, a former high school baseball star, and now worked at a cabinet manufacturer.

"I grew up in this house," Ailes said. "My son is here today, and I wonder if I could just show him the living room. Do you mind?"

"No, come on in."

The house had one bath and five other low-ceilinged rooms. Roger pointed upstairs toward the cramped bedroom that he shared with his brother. Zachary looked around the small interior. "Dad, this living room is only as big as our car."

"Well, three of us grew up in here, son," Ailes said.

Ailes told the Monsmans that he ran Fox News. Did they ever watch it? Chris did not, but his wife, Danella, a home health aide, liked the channel. Danella thought the hosts seemed friendlier and were having more fun than those on the other news channels. Ailes complimented them on the condition of their home. They visited for ten minutes. Before Ailes left, he gave Chris his Fox business card. What he could offer the young man was not clear.

Three years later, the Warren *Tribune Chronicle* publisher Charles Jarvis invited Ailes to return to Warren to deliver a speech. Ailes would not commit to a date and did not return. Although he wrapped his identity in his hometown's blue-collar history, there was only so much of Warren that Ailes likely wanted to see. "I left there in 1958," Ailes said in 2012. "Anything that anyone says there about me is *wrong*. They don't *know* me." Everywhere he looked, he was confronted with the vanishing America he had known as a boy. He had come to fear it might not return. "We are in a storm, our mast is broken, our compass is off, and there is a damned big hole in the boat," he often said. For Ailes, Fox News had a purpose higher than profits and ratings.

Ailes found the key to ratings in the Obama era shortly after 8:00 on the morning of February 19, 2009. About halfway through his morning editorial meeting, a remarkable television moment was unfolding on CNBC. Rick Santelli, a loudmouthed former hedge fund trader turned financial correspondent, uncorked a Howard Beale rant during a genial discussion of Obama's stimulus bill and the housing crisis. "The government is promoting bad behavior!" Santelli yelled from his position on the floor of the Chicago Board of Trade. "How about this, president and new administration? Why don't you put up a website to have people vote on the Internet as a referendum to see if we really want to subsidize the losers' mortgages?" Traders standing nearby nodded and chanted their approval. "President Obama, are you *listening*?" Santelli bellowed into the camera. "We're thinking of having a Chicago Tea Party in July."

The phrase and the sentiment were irresistible. As Tea Party groups sprang up around the country in the winter and spring of 2009, Ailes capitalized on the wave of excitement, making their protests, with their tricorn hat wardrobes and creative if sometimes over-the-top signage, a significant fraction of his news programming. The conflict between the president and his detractors was great for business; prime-time ratings jumped 25 percent in the opening months of the Obama presidency. Fox personalities more than ever before blurred the line between reporter and activist, often taking a direct role in creating the story they were covering. One reporter donned colonial costume for a segment on the movement's history. Another producer helped whoop up crowds before a live shot. Fox built anticipation in the run-up to the tax day protests. On the morning of April 15, Fox hosts fanned out across the country to broadcast live from the barricades. "It's Tea Party time, from sea to shining sea," anchor Megyn Kelly giddily announced. The new movement was often written off by left-leaning pundits as artificial grass roots, but Fox helped them grow into an enduring force. "There would not have been a Tea Party without Fox," Sal Russo, a former Reagan gubernatorial aide and the cofounder of the national Tea Party Express tour, said.

But amidst the journalism-as-advocacy, some of the network's journalistic ballast was disappearing. In July 2008, news broke that Brit Hume would step down from anchoring *Special Report* after the election. Then, two weeks after the election, David Rhodes, Fox's vice president for news, quit to work for Bloomberg Television. Rhodes's brother, Ben, was a senior national security adviser to Obama, and David told staffers that Ailes had expressed concern about this closeness to the White House. David, for his part, felt uncomfortable with where Fox was going in the Obama era. He cringed when Fox sent a camera crew to interview Philip

Berg, a Philadelphia attorney who had filed a lawsuit challenging Obama's birth certificate. (The suit was thrown out later that month.) The network's coverage of fringe groups like the New Black Panther Party made him concerned that Fox was stoking racial fears. Finally, a few months after Rhodes's departure, John Moody left. (Murdoch put him in charge of launching News Corp's wire service.) "They used to tell Roger no," a senior executive said. "They could also filter his demands and make him think he was getting what he wanted on air."

The turnover revealed that loyalty to Ailes had its limits. Although the culture he built at Fox had its rollicking appeal, its fear-inducing dark side pushed some toward the exits. One Christmas season, Brian Lewis and his staff went to the second floor to hand out gifts to senior Fox executives, a tradition Lewis had started. "Ho ho ho, Merry Christmas from Media Relations!" Lewis bellowed as he pushed a mail cart full of gifts down the hall. Sitting in his office, one executive heard the holiday greetings, followed by screams. "*What the fuck are you doing! What the fuck! What the fuck!*" Lewis yelled. His young female assistant had handed out the wrong present to the wrong person.

The executive sat there shaken. A moment later, Lewis popped his head into his doorway wearing a Santa Claus hat and handed him his gift. "Merry Christmas," Lewis said cheerfully. He continued wheeling his cart down the hall.

The staff replacements tended to be either weak or ideologically driven. Bill Sammon, a former *Washington Times* correspondent, was appointed managing editor of the Washington bureau, and angered Fox's political reporters, who saw him pushing coverage further to the right than they were comfortable with. Days after Obama's inauguration, an ice storm caused major damage throughout the Midwest. At an editorial meeting in the D.C. bureau, Sammon told producers that Fox should compare Obama's response to Bush's handling of Katrina. "Bush got grief for Katrina," Sammon said.

"It's too early; give him some time to respond," a producer shot back. "This ice storm isn't Katrina."

Later, Sammon caused problems internally when David Brock's Media Matters obtained a series of controversial emails about Fox's coverage of climate change and health care. "We should refrain from asserting that the planet has warmed (or cooled) in any given period without *immediately* pointing out that such theories are based upon data that critics have called into question," he wrote in one December 2009 email.

Media Matters also revealed that Sammon admitted in a speech to conservatives aboard a private cruise that he had knowingly misled Fox viewers in the closing days of the 2008 campaign by calling Obama a socialist. It was a notion he privately found "far-fetched."

Moody's replacement was an ABC News producer named Michael Clemente. Early in his tenure, Clemente tried to fire F.O.R. Ken LaCorte because he had a vague brief. "What he does officially is a mystery," one executive said. Many believed he was Ailes's eyes and ears in the newsroom, who engaged in, as another executive put it, "black helicopter shit." When Clemente told LaCorte he was out, a screaming match erupted. LaCorte immediately went to Ailes, who rescinded the firing. By undercutting Clemente, Ailes sent a powerful message to the entire organization that Clemente lacked influence. "Clemente fucked up with LaCorte. He never should have taken that on," a senior producer said.

The most potent force in Fox's reinvention of Obama was Glenn Beck, who debuted in the 5:00 p.m. time slot the day before Obama's inauguration. Within weeks, he was pulling in more than two million viewers a day, a 50 percent increase. Only Bill O'Reilly and Sean Hannity put up better numbers, and that was in prime time, when the television audience was vastly larger. Although Ailes was often unsparing in his praise of hosts, he told Beck in one meeting, "You are probably the most uniquely talented person on television I've seen."

When Ailes hired Beck, he imagined him hosting a conventional cable news talk show. "I see your show being more of a Jack Paar show," he told him. "Jack delivered a monologue, but you also have guests and it has a variety component." Beck had a different idea. He conceived his program an anti-television show—partly because Beck said he didn't like television—which would feature Beck roaming his set in plain view of the cameramen and cables. There would be few guests. Instead, his studio was like a one-room prairie schoolhouse where he delivered daily sermon-like lectures before a chalkboard, on which he traced a web connecting his progressive enemies, George Soros central among them, though Obama senior adviser Valerie Jarrett was a supporting player. With the Dow plunging from its peak of 14,000 toward 6,000, Beck's dire scenarios—FEMA concentration camps, societal collapse—were fears that became imaginable.

Beck broke the mold at Fox. Unlike most of the unknowns and has-beens Ailes recruited, Beck joined Fox at a time when he was well on his way to becoming a star. He was also a driven businessman. He founded his own company, Mercury Radio Arts (a play off Orson Welles's radio broadcasts of the 1930s), and brought in executives to run it. In a break from Fox tradition, Beck had his own team of aggressive public relations counselors who had worked with Katie Couric and film mogul Harvey Weinstein.

But Beck's show built on Ailes's playbook, making the culture wars personal. He seemed to many to be Fox News's id made visible, saying things—Obama is a racist, Nazi tactics are progressive tactics—dredged from the right-wing subconscious. Beck crossed lines that weren't supposed to be crossed, even at Fox, and the presentation—childlike, angry, often tearful—was as remarkable as the content. Some at Fox were alarmed by Beck's rhetoric but Ailes was fully on-board. Privately, Ailes said Beck was telling the truth. The day after Beck said on air that the president has a "deep-seated hatred for white people," Ailes told his executives, "I think he's right." The only question was how to manage the fallout. It was decided Bill Shine would release a statement. "Glenn Beck expressed a personal opinion which represented his own views, not those of the Fox News Channel," it read. "And as with all commentators in the cable news arena, he is given the freedom to express his opinions."

The White House failed to recognize Beck's growing influence, until he dug up and publicized White House green jobs czar Van Jones's collegiate flirtation with black nationalism and communism. At the time, Jones was something of a media darling, and the subject of a recent *New Yorker* profile. One day in the summer of 2009, Jones received a Google alert on his BlackBerry about one of Beck's commentaries. When he checked it out, he remembered thinking it was "almost clownish." "The general attitude in the White House was this guy is a jokester and they didn't want to give it a lot of oxygen," he said. But as Beck kept up the barrage, Jones grew concerned. "I started to feel besieged. Because the guy's ratings exploded and he's using my face for a springboard," he said. Jones began asking White House aides to defend him.

Obama officials, consumed over the summer with selling the health care bill and other crises, did not consider Jones a high priority. Dan Pfeiffer, a senior communications staffer, did not even know who Jones was before Beck sparked heat around his posting. Jones asked his chief of staff for security after receiving a death threat, but was told that he did not qualify for Secret Service protection. "I've got children," he said. "I'm just a regular civilian walking around here, and you had someone telling a couple million people every night that I'm a Communist and a felon."

On September 1, Jones was sitting in his office across from the White House in a townhouse off Lafayette Park when his intern asked, "Did you ever say Republicans are 'assholes'?"

"Probably," Jones said.

"That's what they're reporting on now." Jones looked at the screen. A YouTube video of him was going viral on conservative websites. "Somebody found the videotape where I was yukking it up with students at Berkeley," Jones recalled. Under pressure, he released a statement to *Politico* apologizing, calling his remarks "offensive" and "clearly inappropriate." The same week, news broke that Jones had signed a so-called Truther petition that claimed the 9/11 attacks were in fact carried out by the Bush administration. White House officials confronted Jones. "They said, 'Why did you sign this?' And I said, 'I didn't sign this. I've never seen this. In my most wild left-wing days I wasn't a conspiracy theorist. This wasn't anything I've seen.'" Jones investigated and discovered a group had approached him at a conference and gotten him to sign his name under false pretenses. "Now other people besides Beck were covering it. That was the beginning of the end," Jones said. On September 6, Beck got his scalp: Jones resigned. Jones's ouster was a symbolic victory for Ailes that proved Fox was again driving the news.

Four days later, Ailes dealt another blow. On the morning of September 10, Fox aired the undercover video of conservative activist James O'Keefe's sting of the Baltimore branch of ACORN, the community organizing group. In the edited clips, O'Keefe captured ACORN employees allegedly showing him how to hide income earned from a brothel. Andrew Breitbart, the conservative provocateur turned Internet publisher, worked with O'Keefe to get the video exclusively to Fox after other media outlets turned him down. One reporter told Breitbart it was "too political." Breitbart thought it was a bombshell, "the Abu Ghraib of the Great Society," he called it.

Inside the White House, a debate unfolded over how to deal with Fox. Michelle Obama particularly loathed the network. That summer Obama himself had lashed out at Fox in an interview with John Harwood on CNBC. "I've got one television station that is entirely devoted to attacking my administration," he told him. "That's a pretty big megaphone. And you'd be hard-pressed, if you watched the entire day, to find a positive story about me on that front." Now Obama advisers were getting word that Fox was actively manipulating the coverage of the health care debate, which at the time was being played out in a national series of town halls. "We had anecdotal reports that where there was no screaming, they would not report it," said Anita Dunn. In meetings, Ailes told producers that health care reform was a disaster. "He claimed there was nothing wrong with the current system," one producer said. What most alarmed the White House was that the rest of the media was suddenly following Fox News's lead. In an interview posted on the *New York Times* website after Van Jones's resignation, the paper's managing editor, Jill Abramson, acknowledged that they would need to follow Fox's reporting in the future. "The narrative was being hijacked by Fox," Dunn said. "Fox had taken over a thought-leader role in the national press corps. What we could influence was the way everyone else looks at Fox. Frankly, that's the real problem."

As the White House hashed out their strategy, Dunn reached out to David Rhodes at his new perch at Bloomberg Television. He told Dunn the White House was making a mistake. "You guys have this all wrong. Everything you're doing is anticipating that they're somewhere having a meeting which is like, 'What if Beck says something that embarrasses us?' That's an NBC meeting. Now, let me tell you what a Fox meeting is: A Fox meeting is, 'Boy, he's really emotional. Now he's tearing up. What if he gets really emotional and doesn't do the show and we don't get the ratings, what are we going to do?' "

After conferring with Obama, his aides decided that the White House would go to war with Fox. The White House first attempted to isolate the channel. In mid-September, when Obama agreed to appear on the Sunday political shows, he skipped *Fox News Sunday,* leaving Chris Wallace to complain on *The O'Reilly Factor,* "They are the biggest bunch of crybabies I have dealt with in my thirty years in Washington." In early October, Dunn went on CNN and declared Fox the "research arm of the Republican Party." Then, in late October, a Treasury Department official tried to deny Fox an interview with Ken Feinberg, the compensation regulator for the Troubled Asset Relief Program. The move backfired when journalists from other networks, angered that the White House was picking on a member of the press, rallied behind Fox. David Axelrod called Ailes and blamed the decision on a low-level Treasury employee.

For the White House, Axelrod was a valuable back channel, who willingly played the good cop. "He's a fierce competitor. He lives on the line. Occasionally, he waddles over it," Axelrod once told a reporter, referring to Ailes. About a week before Dunn's CNN appearance in the fall of 2009, Axelrod sat down with Ailes at the Palm in Midtown Manhattan before the restaurant opened to avoid drawing attention. Axelrod told Ailes they should try to defuse things and work together.

But Ailes saw no benefit to laying down arms. Ratings were ticking up. "He relished it," an executive said. In editorial meetings, he told his lieutenants to return fire. One executive recalled Ailes saying, "They hate America. They hate capitalism." Another recalled, "He would say, beat the shit out of them." "To use Roger's vocabulary, he said, '*Fuck these guys. Kick them as hard as you can.*'" Some executives agreed. One told news chief Michael Clemente that the White House's attacks were like "a hanging curveball" for Fox. But the war was hard on Fox's more dedicated journalists. For all the larger-than-life talking heads who dominated its airtime, Fox still had a substantial Washington bureau made up of many nonpartisan journalists, and they were already beleaguered watching Glenn Beck become the network's mascot. "The D.C. bureau's job was being made much more difficult," said one producer, "but Roger loved it."

On Friday, October 23, Obama's press secretary, Robert Gibbs, called Clemente to work out a truce. Clemente didn't take the call. Gibbs complained to Fox's well-regarded White House correspondent, Major Garrett, that Clemente had blown him off. On Monday, Garrett told Ailes and Clemente on a conference call that the White House was looking to make peace.

Clemente finally called Gibbs on October 27 and traveled to Washington the next day to try to ease the tensions. In November, on a trip to Asia, Obama granted an interview to Garrett, his first since the war with Fox began. Both sides walked away claiming victory. But Major Garrett had had enough. Months later, he quit Fox to become a correspondent for *National Journal*.

Garrett's departure reflected a larger truth. "Roger's thinking about 'fair and balanced' changed," a senior executive said. "He decided MSNBC and CNN had gone so far to the left in response to him that he needed to go further right. So you didn't need to hear both sides of the story at Fox. You were getting the other side by coming to Fox."

But Ailes *was* the catalyst that politicized the media. By hiring every conservative media personality of significance, he prevented his rival networks from airing prominent voices on the right. "The way the business works is, they control conservative commentary the way ESPN controls the market for sports rights," a person close to Ailes said. "If you have a league, you have a meeting with ESPN, you find out how much they're willing to pay, and then everyone else agrees to pay the same amount if they want it. . . . It's sort of the same at Fox. I was surprised at some of what was being paid until I processed it that way. If you're ABC and you don't have Newt Gingrich on a particular morning, you can put someone else on. But if you're Fox, and Newt is moving and talking today, you got to have him. Otherwise, your people are like, 'Where's Newt? Why isn't he on my channel?' "

By 2009, Ailes had fundamentally altered the basic idea of news on television as it was historically understood. While millions continued to watch the Big Three nightly newscasts, partisan cable news drove politics. And CNN, lacking a partisan brand, was left out of the conversation. In the months since the 2008 election, CNN's prime-time ratings dived nearly 25 percent. The down-spiral dashed any hope that the network's 2008 surge might usher in a post-ideological media moment. Jonathan Klein, the swaggering president of CNN/U.S., grasped for a solution to reverse the trend line.

Meanwhile, CNN's rivals were happily trading blows, and eating away at CNN's audience. The main event took place nightly at 8:00 p.m. Olbermann operatically savaged "Bill-O the Clown" O'Reilly. The attacks were successful enough that Murdoch took notice. "Keith Olbermann is trying to make a business out of destroying Bill O'Reilly," Murdoch complained to an interviewer. O'Reilly was regularly crowned "Worst Person in the World" and at one point Olbermann tastelessly invoked O'Reilly's family in a segment about a transgendered man who became pregnant. "Kind of like life at home for Bill's kids," he said.

O'Reilly fired back, although he never mentioned Olbermann by name ("a vicious smear merchant," he called him). Raising the stakes, he went after Olbermann's boss and his boss's boss, airing a series of segments on General Electric CEO Jeffrey Immelt and Bob Wright's successor, NBC CEO Jeff Zucker. O'Reilly slagged Immelt for GE's business deals with Iran, claiming the company had blood on its hands. "If my child were killed in Iraq, I would blame the likes of Jeffrey Immelt," O'Reilly said. At other points, he called Immelt a "pinhead," "a despicable human being," and featured GE's logo alongside a photograph of Iran's president, Mahmoud Ahmadinejad, with the caption "Business Partners." Zucker came in for similar treatment. O'Reilly railed that

Zucker's network "spews out far-left propaganda" and was "the most aggressive anti-Bush network." Ailes had warned Zucker that Olbermann was playing with fire. In the summer of 2007, Ailes called Zucker's cell phone and vowed that if Olbermann did not stand down, he would tell the *New York Post* to go after Zucker.

Both sides realized the collateral damage threatened to outpace the feud's ratings gains. Beth Comstock, Immelt's marketing chief, reached out to Brian Lewis to arrange a private sit-down with Ailes. One afternoon in April 2009, Ailes was spirited into a private entrance at 30 Rock and ascended to Immelt's fifty-third-floor dining room for lunch.

Both men had talking points ready. Ailes said MSNBC was to blame, not Fox. I can control my nutcases, but you can't control yours, he said.

Immelt responded that his mother in Cincinnati was a loyal O'Reilly viewer. How did she feel when O'Reilly blamed her son for killing U.S. troops?

What about O'Reilly's wife? Ailes shot back. Olbermann constantly brought up the Andrea Mackris sex harassment suit. After clearing the air, both executives agreed to talk to their stars and try to calm the waters. The following month, Immelt and Murdoch were guests at a Microsoft corporate retreat in Redmond, Washington. During an off-the-record panel discussion moderated by Charlie Rose, Murdoch and Immelt shook hands and agreed to a truce against personal attacks.

It took a few weeks, but by June, Olbermann and O'Reilly were staying quiet.

The whole deal got blowtorched in July after *New York Times* media reporter Brian Stelter began calling around to confirm the Immelt-Murdoch summit. Stelter's front-page article, published on Friday, July 31, shattered the uneasy peace. Olbermann defiantly told Stelter he was "party to no deal." Three days later, he proved it. During his "Worst Persons" segment, Olbermann denounced Stelter, O'Reilly, and Murdoch. O'Reilly answered two nights later. He reported that GE was forced to pay $50 million to settle SEC charges of misleading investors. The feud appeared to be back on. But it died down just as quickly as it flared.

Shut out of the partisan cage match, CNN flailed, and Ailes pressed his advantage. He set up an anonymous blog called *The Cable Game* that took shots at his rivals. Ailes assigned Fox News contributor Jim Pinkerton to write the entries. "*The Cable Game* was Roger's creation," one person close to Ailes said. "Is CNN on the Side of the Killers and Terrorists in Iraq?" one headline read. "David Brock Gets Caught! (Although

Secretly, He Probably Loves Being Naughty and Nasty)," blared another. The item's text was accompanied by a photo of Brock posing in a skin-tight tank top with Congressman Barney Frank. "Media Matters, of course, is the *notoriously* left-wing hit group, founded by that *flamboyantly* self-hating conservative apostate, David Brock," it said. "Brock has that rare distinction of being accused of being dishonest by both liberals and conservatives alike. But don't take my word for it: Here's what you get if you type 'David Brock liar' on Google: 168,000 hits." CNN chief Jon Klein saw Ailes's hand behind the articles. He called Ailes and blamed Fox for posting anonymous online gossip that outed the sexual orientation of CNN's star prime-time anchor, Anderson Cooper. Ailes denied any role. (Cooper wouldn't announce he was gay until July 2012.)

Klein did not last long enough to get his retribution. In September 2010, he was fired.

For Sarah Palin, the months since Election Day had been a letdown even bigger than the loss to Barack Obama and Joe Biden. Being governor, she found, was drudgery compared to her media stardom. "Her life was terrible," one adviser said. "She was never home, her [Juneau] office was four hours from her house. You gotta drive an hour from Wasilla to Anchorage. And she was going broke." Her sky-high approval ratings in Alaska—which had topped 80 percent before McCain picked her—had withered to the low 50s. She faced a hostile legislature, a barrage of ethics complaints, and frothing local bloggers who reveled in her misfortune. All this for a salary of only $125,000? The worst was that she had racked up $500,000 in legal bills to fend off allegations that she had dismissed Alaska's public safety commissioner because he refused to fire a state trooper who was her ex-brother-in-law. She needed money and worried about it constantly.

Partly because of her embarrassing campaign interview with Katie Couric, and partly because of her outlandish family life and moose-shooting habits, Palin was a massive American celebrity. In November 2008, John Coale tagged along with his wife, Greta Van Susteren, on a trip to Alaska to tape an interview with Palin for Fox News. Later, the Fox camera crew, Van Susteren, and Coale gathered around the Palins' kitchen table for some moose chili. After dinner, Coale and Palin retreated to the pantry and sat on stacks of boxes and talked for the next hour about her

Troopergate dilemma. Palin confessed she didn't know what to do about her legal bills. Coale assured Palin he would figure something out.

Whatever one thought of her intelligence, she was more than shrewd enough to see that there was money to be made on her newfound national profile, and she hadn't been the one making it. Planning quickly got under way for a book. Conservative pundit Mary Matalin introduced Palin to Washington superlawyer Robert Barnett, who helped Palin land a reported $7 million book contract with HarperCollins. Two former Palin campaign aides were hired to plan a book tour with all the trappings of a national political campaign. But there was a hitch: with Alaska's strict ethics rules, Palin worried that her day job would get in the way. In March, she petitioned the Alaska attorney general's office, which responded with a lengthy list of conditions. "There was no way she could go on a book tour while being governor" is how one member of her Alaska staff put it.

On the morning of July 3, 2009, in front of a throng of national reporters, Palin announced that she was stepping down as governor. To many, it seemed a mysterious move, defying the logic of a potential presidential candidate, and possibly reflecting some hidden scandal—but in fact the choice may have been as easy as balancing a checkbook.

Once she resigned from the governorship in July, the race was on to sign her up on television. Producers had already put out feelers. Weeks after the 2008 election, reality show producer Mark Burnett, the creator of *Survivor,* called Palin and pitched her on starring in her own show. Then, in September 2009, Ailes arranged for Palin to fly on a private jet when she needed to travel from San Diego to New York to meet with her editors at HarperCollins. During the visit, Murdoch met Palin at a charity dinner hosted by his wife, Wendi, at Cipriani 42nd Street, and that only increased the network's appetite. Ailes deputized Bill Shine to land her.

Negotiations dragged out over the next six months. Palin made it clear to Fox that she wouldn't be willing to move to New York or Washington. Fox offered to build a remote camera hookup in her Wasilla home. Palin also told Fox that she didn't want producers hounding her for interviews. She wanted all her appearances to have to go through Shine personally. In January 2010, Palin finally had her $1 million–a–year deal. Shine was responsible for making sure the various Fox personalities got equal booking time, to maximize her ratings appeal across the network. "Obviously, there needs to be a sense of fairness," Shine explained.

Hiring Palin brought the number of prospective presidential candidates on Ailes's payroll to five: Mike Huckabee, Rick Santorum, Newt Gingrich, and John Bolton. Presidential politics were what brought in viewers, and in the Obama age, Ailes was dominating both politics and business. Fox was on track to generate nearly a billion-dollar profit. A Wall Street analyst valued the network at more than $12.4 billion. In 2009, Ailes earned $23 million. The Obama era turnaround plan was firing on all cylinders. Ailes "predicted that the Democrats would lose the House," one senior producer said. Ailes was right. In the midterms, Republicans would retake the House in the biggest electoral gain since 1948.

But Ailes's biggest stars—Glenn Beck and Sarah Palin—were burning hot—too hot—which posed new problems. Beck's numbers were moving toward three million a day, a stunning achievement. "I've never seen anyone build an audience this fast," Ailes told executives. The concern was that Beck was almost engulfing Fox itself. He did not follow Ailes's directives, and some of Fox's other big names seemed diminished by comparison—and were speaking up about it. Sean Hannity complained to Bill Shine about Beck. And it didn't help matters that O'Reilly, who had become friends with Beck, scheduled him as a regular guest, a move that only annoyed Hannity further. In March, *The Washington Post* ran an article that reported on grievances Fox employees had about Beck's inflammatory rhetoric and his self-promotion.

Palin also ruffled Fox executives' feathers. In the winter of 2010, tensions between Palin's camp and Fox arose over a prime-time special that the network wanted her to star in. Nancy Duffy, a senior Fox producer, wanted Palin to host the show in front of a live studio audience. Duffy hoped to call the program *Sarah Palin's Real American Stories*. Palin hated the idea. She complained to her advisers that she didn't want to be a talk show host. She wanted to just do voice-overs. More important, she didn't want Fox to promote her name in the title of the program. Not that it mattered: Palin's ratings were starting to disappoint Ailes anyway. Fox did not schedule any additional specials.

In the control room, the Palins entertained producers with their private reality show. Fox staffers chuckled watching Sarah and husband Todd on the video link Fox had installed in her Wasilla office. "On the internal feed you see everything. Someone should tell her that. Todd does the camerawork. She barks at him big time, 'Todd, what are you doing!' It's embarrassing," one person explained. Fox producers came up with names for their characters: "The Bitch" and "The Eskimo."

Ailes began to doubt Palin's political instincts. He thought she was getting bad advice from her kitchen cabinet and saw her erratic behavior as a sign that she was a "loose cannon." A turning point in their relationship came in the midst of the national debate over the Tucson shooting massacre, which left Congresswoman Gabrielle Giffords almost fatally wounded. As the media pounced on Palin's violent rhetoric—her website had put the image of a target on Giffords's congressional district months earlier to mobilize her voters to defeat Giffords at the polls—Palin wanted to fight back, angry that commentators were singling her out. Ailes agreed but told her to stay out of it. He thought if she stayed quiet, she would score a victory.

"Lie low," he told her. "If you want to respond later, fine, but do not interfere with the memorial service."

Palin ignored Ailes's advice and went ahead and released her controversial "blood libel" video the morning Obama traveled to Tucson. For Ailes, her decision was further evidence that she was flailing around off-message. "Why did you call me for advice?" he wondered aloud to colleagues. "He thinks Palin is an idiot," a Republican close to Ailes said. "He thinks she's stupid. He helped boost her up. People like Sarah Palin haven't elevated the conservative movement."

What had been an effort to boost ratings became a complication. Employing potential presidential candidates and Glenn Beck opened the network up to criticism that it was too politicized. Ailes also got an earful from leaders in the GOP establishment who were apoplectic that Beck, Palin, and Christine "I'm not a witch" O'Donnell, the Tea Party–backed candidate running for the Senate in Delaware, were becoming the face of Fox News and, by extension, the Republican party. "Why are you letting Palin have the profile?" Karl Rove said to Ailes in one meeting. "Why are you letting her go on your network and say the things she's saying? And Glenn Beck? These are alternative people who will never be elected, and they'll kill us."

Ailes was inclined to listen. After Fox News gave the inaugural Tea Party rallies wall-to-wall coverage in the spring of 2009, Ailes told executives to dial back the promotion. His message, according to one executive, was: "Let's not abandon them, because their audience is driving the ratings, but we're not going to have that umbilical cord connection to them. They're on their own. So the next big iconic event that happened, there was no planned coverage. It was just planned news coverage."

Although Ailes valued the ratings, he had a grander goal. One afternoon not long before the midterms, Ailes told executives who sat in his office, "the network's a success. We're making a lot of money—that's fine. But I want to elect the next president."

# TWENTY-ONE
# TROUBLE ON MAIN STREET

As Ailes told Fox executives of his desire to install a Republican in the White House, he found himself caught up in a conflict of a much more personal sort: small-town politics. It was an imbroglio that Ailes would later say he did not want. At Fox News, the steel security doors, the public relations apparatus, and the discretion of generously paid confidants kept the full measure of Roger Ailes's paranoia and rage from the world. In his hometown, Roger Ailes was exposed.

From the outset, Ailes spoke of his residence in Garrison, forty-six miles north of Manhattan in Putnam County, New York, as an escape from the partisan front lines at Fox News. "All I ever wanted was a nice place to live, a great family, and to die peacefully in my sleep," he said around the time of his move. Garrison, a few other hamlets, and the neighboring villages Nelsonville and Cold Spring formed the larger town of Philipstown, although it was not very large at all: fewer than ten thousand citizens. It seemed, on the surface at least, to be an ideal place to instill in Zachary the Eisenhower values Ailes had known as a boy. Putnam County even had a Republican bent: while voters tended to vote Democratic at the state level, the last Democratic presidential candidates to carry the county were Woodrow Wilson and Lyndon B. Johnson.

Cold Spring's downtown held on to everything Warren, Ohio, had let go. It was a vibrant civic space, dotted with well-maintained Victorian homes, quaint storefronts, and stately churches. The area appealed to Ailes's sentimental ideas about America. From his mountaintop aerie, an impressive nine-thousand-square-foot mansion constructed of Adirondack river stone, he overlooked triumphal reminders of the country's might. To the west was the spot where Continental Army troops strung a

185-ton iron chain across the Hudson to block British ships advancing upriver. To the north were shuttered ironworks that had produced vital armaments and steam engines in the nineteenth century. Across the river stood West Point military academy. The grand interior of his house also bore witness to American greatness. Photographs of Generals George Patton, Ulysses Grant, Robert E. Lee, and Dwight Eisenhower lined the walls.

Roger and Beth were good neighbors. They attended the local Catholic church, Our Lady of Loretto, where on Sundays, Beth sometimes played the organ. They got to know the contractors who built their house, hosted a cookout for members of the volunteer fire department, and bought locally. Leonora Burton, the proprietor of the Country Goose, a gift shop on Cold Spring's Main Street, considered Beth "a first-rate customer who spent freely." "I liked her and, being a hugger, sometimes gave her one," the chatty Brit recalled. Stories circulated of Roger's generosity. One was that, upon hearing about a store owner who had fallen on hard times, he extended a personal loan.

Buying *The Putnam County News & Recorder,* in the summer of 2008, was Roger and Beth's first public endeavor in their adopted town. Founded in the mid-nineteenth century as the Cold Spring *Recorder,* the weekly newspaper was like the community itself: an artifact from a bygone age. The previous owner and publisher, Brian O'Donnell, kept production methods antique. In a one-room office, housed in a former barbershop on Main Street, staffers laid out the paper with scissors and glue. Under O'Donnell's steady ownership, the *PCN&R,* or simply "the paper," as it was affectionately known by residents, was a quirky, if reserved, information source. "It covered the 4-H Club and the kids' activities at the school," said Elizabeth Anderson, the founder and managing director of the investment firm Beekman Wealth Advisory, and a part-time resident of Philipstown. Letters to the editor—the paper's liveliest section by far—were welcomed, but there were no editorials. When citizens complained that the paper ignored divergent points of view, O'Donnell responded that it was *their* job to express them at public meetings, not for him to stir them up.

Ailes described Philipstown as a bastion of traditional America. In a certain sense, he was right. Many of the town's contractors and restaurant owners were the descendants of nineteenth-century Irish and Italian immigrants who had found work in the local foundries. Other residents had ancestors living in the area since before the nation's birth. But that was only part of the town. In the second half of the twentieth century, a different kind of settler had arrived: the college-educated urbanite who idealized country life.

In the 1960s, when Consolidated Edison, the electric utility, proposed building a power station on the face of Storm King, a 1,340-foot domed mountain that rose like a carapace above the banks of the Hudson River, a coalition of newcomers filed a lawsuit, forming a counterweight against local businesses that supported the development. The ensuing legal battle played out in the courts until Con Ed settled and abandoned the project in 1980. The landmark victory, coming at a time when the Reagan administration was seeking to dismantle environmental regulation, emboldened citizens across the country to speak up in local development matters and helped spawn the modern environmental movement. In Philipstown, a host of preservation groups took root. They fought to preserve the community's bucolic character and acquired land in trust from Gilded Era estates that had fallen into disrepair.

After 9/11, residents saw a new wave of city dwellers moving in. Along with their politics, they brought their own back-to-the-land ethic with all the predictable signifiers. The number of Priuses and Subarus parked in the lot at Foodtown increased, as did the variety of heirloom produce at the weekend farmers' market. It was this growing population that sustained local groups like the Garrison Institute, a nonprofit dedicated to applying "the transformative power of contemplation to today's pressing social and environmental concerns."

It all added up to a rich brew of clashing sensibilities that bred resentments. The contours of the conflict traced the same lines that had defined the old battles of the Nixon years. For a long time, these passions bubbled at a low simmer. With the pages of the *PCN&R* now at their disposal, the Aileses were about to turn the temperature up.

One morning in July 2008, Brian O'Donnell called the employees of the *PCN&R* to the newsroom to meet Roger Ailes and his wife. The staff was on edge. "Has he even *seen* this place?" one employee asked O'Donnell. Although Beth was taking the title of publisher, Roger did most of the talking that day. They could keep their jobs, he said, but there would be "new" rules. "The first one was, 'Don't badmouth your employer,'" reporter Michael Turton, an affable Canadian, recalled. "In all the places I've worked, including on farms, I've never been told not to." Roger's second proviso was to "get both sides of the story." "He was talking about the name the *News & Recorder,*" Turton remembered, "and he said the 'Recording' part was fine, but he didn't think the 'News' part was up to snuff."

In public, Roger and Beth maintained that the *PCN&R* would not become Fox News. But Roger communicated other intentions privately. "He said the community needed more of a speaking to," said local journalist Kevin Foley, who was once a campaign volunteer for Democratic governor Mario Cuomo and a deputy superintendent of the New York State Insurance Department. Shortly after buying the paper, Roger invited the fifty-seven-year-old Foley up to the mountain several times to interview for the top editing job. He spent much of the time monologuing about the ills afflicting his adopted home. He said he would never send Zachary to the public school because it was overrun with liberalism. At his window, he pointed at an outdoor sculpture exhibit at Boscobel House and Gardens, a half mile in the distance. "Do you think they have the right to block my view?" Roger asked. "Isn't it their property?" Foley asked. "It's not their property! It's a nonprofit! They get tax breaks!" Roger replied. He spoke of his security more than once. "He worried about his kid and his wife and said he wouldn't want anything to happen to them because of what he was," Foley recalled. Roger told him his German shepherd, Champ, helped protect them. "He said, 'I let the dog out of the car when we come here. The dog gets out first. He's trained to patrol the whole grounds and report back before we get out.' "

Foley quickly lost interest in the job, and Ailes lost interest in him. Later that summer, Ailes hired Maureen Hunt, a Fox News human resources employee and Philipstown resident, to edit the paper, but she didn't last long.

As summer turned to fall, political issues began to arise. Alison Rooney, the copy editor, at first found reasons to be optimistic about the ownership change. She liked using the new computers to put out the paper and looked forward to the newsroom moving into a renovated two-story building on Main Street. But that honeymoon ended when Rooney laid out a press release from the Garrison Art Center that described a work invoking the "mythological story" of the virgin birth. After the release was published, the priest of Our Lady of Loretto wrote a letter to the editor, and Beth Ailes lit into Rooney. A few weeks later, Rooney got another dressing-down as she formatted a promotion of the high school's upcoming production of *Urinetown*, this time from an editor who found the language offensive and removed the title of the show from the headline.

Michael Turton failed to impress. He was assigned to cover Haldane Middle School's mock presidential election. After the event, Turton filed a report headlined "Mock Election Generated Excitement at Haldane; Obama Defeats McCain by 2–1 Margin." He went on, "The 2008 U.S. presidential election is now history. And when the votes were tallied, Barack Obama had defeated John McCain by more than a two to one margin. The final vote count was 128 to 53." Reading the published version a few days later, Turton was shocked. The headline had been changed: "Mock Presidential Election Held at Haldane; Middle School Students Vote to Learn Civic Responsibility." So had the opening paragraph: "Haldane students in grades 6 through 8 were entitled to vote for president and they did so with great enthusiasm." Obama's margin of victory was struck from the article. His win was buried in the last paragraph.

Turton was upset. "I've been mulling over the changes made to my article and need to voice my concern," he wrote in an email to Hunt. "I'm also sure the article left students, parents, teachers, administration and trustees wondering how a reporter can omit the actual results when covering an election. . . . I know editing is part of the process, but the rationale for the omission escapes me."

He never heard back from Hunt, but soon received a series of accusatory emails from the Aileses. Turton had disregarded "specific instructions" for the piece, Beth wrote. Accordingly, the piece had been edited. Headline changes occur all the time, she noted. "Do you anticipate this becoming an ongoing problem for you?" A short while later, Roger weighed in. Maureen Hunt's instructions to focus on the school's process for teaching about elections had been "very clear," he wrote, and Turton's "desire to change the story into a big Obama win" should have taken a backseat. Ailes described himself as "disappointed" by Turton's failure "to follow the agreed upon direction."

Turton defended himself. "I would not disregard clear direction," he replied in an email. "Had the results been exactly opposite I would have written the story in the same manner, including the results." Beth responded cryptically, thanking Turton for his "thoughtful explanation," which she said she would "pass on to Roger." Soon afterward, Turton learned that Maureen Hunt had resigned.

Ailes had seen similar newsroom turbulence at TVN and during the early days at Fox. To bring "fair and balanced" to the people of Philipstown, he continued his search for someone who understood in which direction the paper was meant to take the community.

In February 2009, Ailes met Joe Lindsley, a twenty-five-year-old journalist, for lunch in his private third-floor dining room at Fox News. A fast-rising star in the conservative movement, Lindsley came on the recommendation of Martin Singerman, a former News Corp executive who had worked with Lindsley at the Intercollegiate Studies Institute, an organization that funds right-leaning student newspapers on college campuses. When he was a student at Notre Dame, Lindsley completed the rigorous Great Books program and launched *The Irish Rover* to combat the liberal bias of the *Notre Dame News*. A fervent Catholic with a low, booming voice and a certain likeness to Ailes, Lindsley inspired his classmates with his earnest sense of mission, once leading a pilgrimage to northern Michigan to visit the home of conservative historian Russell Kirk. After graduating, he worked for *The Weekly Standard,* assisting executive editor (and Fox News contributor) Fred Barnes, before moving over to the magazine's culture section.

After they spoke, Ailes offered Lindsley the position of editor in chief, asking him to start right away. Ailes was in the process of buying a second paper, *The Putnam County Courier,* out of bankruptcy and needed a committed journalist to run the newsrooms of his budding publishing enterprise. Lindsley jumped at the opportunity to work directly for an icon of the cause. Without time to line up an apartment, Lindsley moved into the pool house on the north end of Roger and Beth's property. It was silent and near freezing the day he stepped out of his Jeep Wrangler on the circular driveway atop the mountain. It was an isolated environment for a recent college grad. He later told friends that he drifted off to sleep that night full of doubt. "*What am I doing here?*" he thought.

When Lindsley moved to Philipstown in the winter of 2009, Ailes's mountain was a topic of intense conversation on Cold Spring's Main Street. "[Ailes] was said to have ordered the removal of all trees around his house so that he . . . had a 360-degree view of any leftist assault teams preparing to rush the house," Leonora Burton recalled. Roger and Beth also bought up as many surrounding houses as they could. "I don't think he has all of them yet," Roger's brother said. "He probably only has 80 percent of them. He is a strong believer in the security of real estate. He thinks they don't make any more of it." Security cameras were installed throughout the property. "A team of landscapers was, in the absence of the Ailes family, working on the grounds of the compound," Burton later recounted. "They were planting a tree when the boss's cell phone rang. It was the absent Beth. 'No, no,' she said. 'That's not where I want the tree. I insist that you move it.' She directed them to the correct site. The landscapers were puzzled until they realized that the many security cameras on the grounds had captured them at work. Beth had been watching them from wherever she was and called to correct the tree planting." Other local contractors helped install a bunker that could weather a terrorist attack underneath their mansion. "He can live in there for more than six months," a friend who has visited it said. "There are bedrooms, a couple of TVs, water and freeze-dried food." "I'm not allowed to talk about it," Robert Ailes said. "I think the proper term is a 'panic room.' "

Most of all, it was the *PCN&R* that inspired a deepening sense of panic among the town's liberals. The signs were impossible to miss. As Lindsley began to redesign the papers, his bosses suggested that he place the Cold Spring *Recorder*'s original motto—"By the grace of God, free and independent"—on the masthead. Articles were sharper-edged. Overt religiosity crept into the pages, evidence, they suspected, of the growing influence of Father McSweeney, the priest of Our Lady of Loretto. Patriotic paeans, including to Medal of Honor recipients, and excerpts from the Federalist Papers filled the weekly.

In May 2009, readers opened the paper to find something they had never seen before: an editorial. The unsigned attack on Obama's stimulus titled "Debt, Decisions, and Destiny" called the plan "reckless" and said "rich people should be shown some respect." Lindsley was the editorial's author, and he quoted from *Atlas Shrugged:* "We either see ourselves as a nation of people who want to achieve, produce, succeed, and contribute to society or else we see ourselves as a people who want to rely on the producers to create 'free money' and support us with grants and federal spending."

This was too much for some. Leonora Burton stopped selling the paper in the Country Goose. "After Beth learned of my decision, she boycotted the store," she recalled. Individual subscribers also expressed their outrage. Elizabeth Anderson later decided not to renew her subscription. In an email to the paper, she questioned the relevance of publishing the names of Medal of Honor recipients who did not live in the area. A few minutes after sending the note, she received a phone call. It was Lindsley. Why was she canceling her paper?

"I think I said so in my email," she said.

"Aren't you an *American*?" Lindsley shot back.

A few days later, she opened the paper to find her comments mocked in an editorial. In response, she wrote a letter detailing her family's long involvement with the Navy. "I do not require lectures from the *PCN&R* on patriotism, nor on the valor and bravery of the military, nor on the sacrifices made by military families," she wrote. Lindsley and Beth declined to publish the letter.

Lindsley relished the partisan combat. With the intensity of a bulldozer, he devoted upward of eighty hours a week to the Aileses' papers. He moved into a nearby apartment on the Hudson River so he could be close to the newsroom. He had no time to meet anyone his own age in town or to pursue outside interests. A state-ranked track star in high school, Lindsley gave up running. He put on weight, forty pounds at the peak, adding to his resemblance of Ailes. During the first part of the week, he worked out of the *PCN&R*'s newsroom editing articles and handling production. On Thursdays and Fridays, he often accompanied Ailes to Fox News, where he wrote speeches for him and attended to other personal matters. On Sunday mornings, Lindsley sat with Roger and Beth at Mass. He was up on the mountain at all hours, watching the Fighting Irish games with Ailes or joining the family for dinner with the likes of John Bolton and Glenn Beck. He joined Ailes in the News Corp box at Yankee Stadium and he traveled with the family on News Corp's private plane to visit prominent Republicans across the country. "You know you can't tell anyone about this, right?" Beth said to him before their first trip on the jet.

With his trusted editor in place, Ailes used the paper to muscle local pols. James Borkowski, a lawyer and town justice in Putnam County from 1998 to 2009, learned the danger of crossing the *PCN&R* when he decided to run for Putnam County sheriff in the 2009 election, challenging Ailes's close ally, the incumbent Don Smith. A few months before the Republican primary election, Lindsley invited Borkowski to meet with him and Beth for breakfast at a restaurant across the street from the *PCN&R* offices. At one point in the conversation, Beth turned to Borkowski.

"*So,*" Beth said, leaning in close, "you are pro-life, aren't you?"

Borkowski hesitated. “Personally I am pro-life. But I’m of the position that reasonable people with genuine belief can disagree.”

Wrong answer. “It cast a pall over the whole meeting,” Borkowski said later. “I remembered thinking, what does that have to do with running for sheriff?”

A few weeks later, Borkowski got another call from Lindsley. Roger wanted to see him this time. They met in the *PCN&R*’s conference room.

“Why are you running against him?” Ailes asked, referring to his friend Smith. “This guy is a West Point grad, a religious guy, a family guy.”

“He might be a nice guy, but he’s not doing a good job,” Borkowski countered. Ailes was unswayed.

Ailes spent an hour pumping Borkowski for information about local political players, in particular New York state senator Vincent Leibell III. “What do you know about charitable organizations? Does Vinnie Leibell make money off of them?” “It kept coming back to Leibell,” Borkowski recalled. At the end of the conversation, Lindsley and Beth escorted Borkowski to the front door. Borkowski lost to Smith several months later.

Richard Shea was also one of the politicians Roger asked about. A moderate Democrat who served on the town board, Shea was running in the 2009 election for Philipstown supervisor, the title given to the town’s senior elected official. He was a fifth-generation Cold Springer. He owned a successful local contracting business and fashioned himself as a fiscal conservative and a social moderate. There was one issue, however, on which he was progressive: the environment. Shea was campaigning on reforming the town’s decades-old zoning codes to preserve open space. This brought him into conflict with Ailes.

The notion of zoning was abhorrent to Ailes. The more he studied the issue, the more he disliked what he found. “Jesus, wait a minute,” he told a reporter, describing his thought process. “They’re starting to try and tell you how much glass you can have in your window, what color you can paint your house, and they’re saying, well, you can’t cut down any trees.” He added, “God made trees so you can build houses and have baseball bats.” He felt that he had a right to chop down any tree, and that the legal implications were obvious: “They’re going around to old ladies and telling them if they have a mud puddle they’re in a wetland and stealing their farm and stuff.”

It was a risk for Shea to take Ailes on over zoning. For decades, ever since the Storm King saga, it had been the third rail of Philipstown politics, the one issue that brought all the various cultural and economic resentments into stark relief. The first time Shea met Ailes was at a town forum, sponsored by the *PCN&R* and moderated by Joe Lindsley, in October 2009. Afterward, Ailes went up to Shea and told him that he was dodging Lindsley's questions about zoning. "What are you trying to hide from me?" Ailes said. "I *own* the newspaper." (Ailes claimed that he simply asked for Shea's phone number and complained about the local environmentalist "zealots.")

The next month, Shea won the election. Immediately, he set about making good on his campaign promise to push through a rezoning plan. A few weeks later, Shea discovered just what life with Roger Ailes as a constituent would mean. On Sunday morning, January 10, he received a string of frantic phone calls from friends in town. Ailes had been calling around ranting about a front-page *New York Times* profile of him that appeared in that morning's paper. "My takeaway was that this guy is pretty much threatening me," Shea was quoted saying about the town forum. Friends told Shea he had made a big mistake. "You can't mention Ailes's name in the press," they said. Later that day, his phone rang.

"*You have no fucking idea what you've done!*" Shea immediately recognized the voice. "You have no idea what you're up against. If you want a war you'll have a battle, but it won't be a long battle."

"It was an accurate portrayal of the exchange," Shea said calmly. "If you're offended I'm sorry about that, but it was accurate."

"Listen," Ailes seethed, "don't be naive about these things. I will destroy your life."

Throughout the winter, the *PCN&R* filled with stories and editorials questioning Shea's zoning plan as avidly as Fox attacked Obama's policies. According to the *PCN&R,* an out-of-control band of tree-huggers and Manhattan elites was overrunning the town, dictating to the little guy how he could use his land. The paper framed the debate as a skirmish on a much wider battlefield. It was another case of government trampling the rights of the individual. Readers chose sides and hardened their positions. Jeannette Yannitelli, a Fox News fan whose son ran a liquor store near Main Street, saw linkages to forces threatening her way of life. Half the town did not pay property taxes just as she heard on Fox that half of all Americans didn't pay any federal income tax. "Thomas Edison wasn't told to invent the lightbulb. It was *his* idea. You can't take things and give it to others," she told her grandkids. "Look at what is happening to Greece. They give everything away. It's just not right!"

The emotions stirred up in part by the *PCN&R*'s crusade drew extreme elements into the debate. Anti-zoning factions had begun making posters displaying photos of guns and the slogan "They're Taking Away Your Property Rights." To lower the temperature, Shea decided to call a town-wide meeting at Haldane High School. It would be a chance for all the citizens to get in a room together and clear the air.

Shortly before 7:30 p.m. on Wednesday, April 7, 2010, Ailes walked across the parking lot of the high school with a white-haired lawyer from Poughkeepsie named Scott Volkman. Hundreds of townspeople were streaming into the school's gymnasium. Joe Lindsley arrived and readied himself to write up the proceedings for the next edition of the paper. That morning, the *PCN&R* ran a front-page article by Lindsley, headlined "Residential Re-Zoning: Will Property Owners Weigh In?" Mimicking Fox's wall-to-wall promotion of the Tea Party rallies, the article noted that special interest groups on both sides of the debate had "strongly encouraged attendance" at the event.

And the locals turned out in force. Inside the gym, the mood had the electric energy of a political rally. Ailes and Volkman, seemingly the only two men in suits, sat in the middle of the main floor as Shea brought the meeting to order. "Let us observe civility above all," he said, instructing citizens to keep their remarks to two minutes.

It was a futile request. Jeannette Yannitelli took to the mic. "Fifty-two percent of this town is now tax exempt!" she said, sounding like a Fox pundit.

"Stop right there, that's not true," Shea said.

Facts did not sway Yannitelli. "If you were stealing from me, I'd call 911!"

An hour into the contentious meeting, Ailes's lawyer got up from his seat and took the microphone. After he tangled with Shea for a few minutes, demanding a one-on-one meeting, Shea jokingly asked if Volkman wanted him to burn the zoning proposal on the spot. At that, Ailes stood up and intervened. Without giving his name—he was a man who acted as if he needed no introduction—Ailes began to lecture the supervisor.

"Civility above everything, please, Mr. Shea," Ailes said, pointing the fingers of his right hand at him. "Civility above everything, Mr. Shea. Sarcasm is not useful here, Mr. Shea."

Ailes buttoned his suit jacket, lowered the microphone, and plunged his left hand into his pants pocket. He had the floor now.

"Apparently this process has been going on since before the Civil War," he said. "This is, as you explained to me, the first night that private property owners were going to have a workshop."

"Can I ask you why Mr. Volkman is here?" asked Democratic town board member Nancy Montgomery, who was sitting next to Shea. "He's not a private property owner in this town."

"In America you are allowed to have an attorney represent you who understands the law!" Ailes replied. Cheers, whoops, and whistles rang out from the balcony and the sides of the parquet. "But this is Philipstown," Montgomery said. "This is a civil meeting where our community has come together to discuss—"

"Oh, this is not part of *America*?" Ailes said, waving his right hand through the air dismissively. "No. *No*. The private citizens of this thing have been overlooked. This isn't even about me."

Ailes turned to face the board. "Is it true that this document puts institutional interests above businesses and private citizens?"

Shea explained that the plan was designed to help nonprofits keep their open space out of the hands of real estate developers.

Ailes did not appear to be listening. "Why would everybody not be equal under the law: Businesses? Private— There's probably no greater position to hold than to be a citizen of the United States. Why would their interests be subverted?"

Shea told him that no one was getting special treatment.

"So, they won't be above the law and private interests?"

"No, they're not going to be."

"Fine. End of story," Ailes said. He wanted to know if the law would regulate the size of his windows or the color of his house.

"No," Shea said.

Ailes used the opening. After thanking the board and the citizens for their turnout, he had a lecture about American history to deliver. "George Washington said, 'A violation of my land is a violation of my being,'" he intoned. "That is in our core for two hundred thirty years." Ailes loved to quote Washington, but this saying does not appear in any archive of Washington's writings or speeches.

Ailes sat down and unbuttoned his suit jacket, then noticed that a woman had been shooting a video of him with her iPhone. "*Take it off,*" Roger growled. He leaned forward and grabbed a chair, shaking it menacingly.

"What are you doing to the chair, sir?" she asked. Roger sat back and folded his hands in his lap.

The meeting continued for more than an hour as residents debated the pros and the cons of the zoning law. Ailes stayed until the bitter end. After the meeting concluded, he approached Nancy Montgomery, who was cleaning up her papers at the white table.

"You're the only one I haven't met yet," he said, by way of introduction. "You know, I'm just here for the little guy."

"Do you even know what I do for a living?" Montgomery asked. Ailes had already turned around and was walking away.

"I'm a bartender, Mr. Ailes," she said, calling after him.

Ailes stopped and looked back at her. "You're just a *liberal Democrat,*" he said.

It was not Ailes's politics that bothered Montgomery, although she was no fan of Fox. She didn't like how he showed up in town one day and started throwing his weight around.

Later, Ailes had his own version of his exchange with Montgomery. "I made the mistake of saying, 'I think Philipstown's in America,' and now she's mad at me and goes against everything I'm for and hates me and wants to kill me," he said.

The debate on the zoning reforms dragged on for another year while Shea met with citizens one-on-one to address their concerns. In the fall of 2010, Ailes succeeded in getting a private sit-down with Shea and Joel Russell, a land-use attorney who had been consulting Philipstown on the zoning issue for years. On the day of the meeting, Ailes arrived at Town Hall with his bodyguard and Scott Volkman in tow. Ailes slapped a set of color charts down on Shea's desk.

"What do you think of *that*?"

Shea looked down at the printouts. They showed ratings figures for Fox News and its rivals.

"Fox is outperforming any other cable news network!" Ailes said.

"Well, there are a lot of stupid people out there," Shea deadpanned.

Ailes guffawed. "Ha! A friend of mine said that, too."

The bluff pleasantries were brief. Ailes let out a blast about zoning bureaucrats depriving him of his property rights. "It was ninety percent inaccurate," Russell later said. "That rhetoric was over the top and basically was straight out of Fox News. He kept talking about how he had a young son and his son wouldn't be able to live in the America he knew."

Shea told Ailes that he was misinformed about the zoning restrictions, which triggered another eruption.

"I'll see you out of office!" Ailes snapped. "I've never lost a campaign I've been involved with!"

Shea looked at Russell. "Are you hearing this stuff? There are laws against this sort of thing."

Volkman shifted uncomfortably in his seat. "I'm not hearing any of this," he muttered. "I'm here to talk about zoning."

For two hours, Shea and Russell attempted to calm Ailes down. It turned out that Ailes's concerns were not totally unfounded: a zoning map had incorrectly marked his mountaintop property with a scenic designation, which could have limited some development. Shea and Russell immediately assured Ailes they would make the change. As the conversation wound down, Ailes told the men that he would spend millions if necessary to keep dangerous elements out of the town. To that end, he was thinking about buying Mystery Point, a 129-acre plot of land with a nineteenth-century brick mansion that overlooks the Hudson, to turn into a corporate retreat for Fox. "That's up for sale," Ailes said. "I could buy it in a heartbeat. You know why I'm interested?"

The men stared back at him.

"I hear a group of Chinese investors are looking. I'm not going to have some Chinese investors set up a missile silo right across from West Point." Shea and Russell waited for the punch line that never came.

Getting to know Ailes changed Shea's mind about Fox News. "I used to think it was showmanship, or theater," he later said. "I was really naive. I was awakened to the reality it's not made up. The profit is part of it, but it is ideology-driven."

Putnam County resident Gordon Stewart did not attend the town hall at Haldane, but he heard postmortems the next morning. It provided one more data point that the "Ailes problem," as a friend called it, would not be going away. Unlike many in Philipstown's progressive set, Stewart did not immediately begin to fret about Ailes's increasing power in the community. Although Stewart and Ailes had crossed paths only a handful of times, they had shared history. Born on the South Side of Chicago in 1939, Stewart was originally, like Ailes, a midwesterner of modest means.

He moved to Ohio for college, studying history and music at Oberlin, and in a remarkable coincidence roomed there with Roger's brother. ("He was an easy guy to get along with," Robert Ailes recalled.) Stewart's peripatetic career, like that of Ailes, intermingled the worlds of politics, entertainment, and business: Stewart had worked as a theater director, as a presidential speechwriter, and as a vice president of the American Stock Exchange. Though a Democrat—he had served as Jimmy Carter's deputy chief speechwriter and helped craft what came to be known as the "malaise" speech—he respected his conservative neighbor's formidable talent. In the late 1980s, while working as an executive at an insurance industry trade association, Stewart had invited Ailes to address a group of corporate chieftains. "He talked about how television is the Enrico Fermi nuclear reactor of contemporary society, and how it shapes everything," Stewart recalled.

In 2005, after living many years on the Upper West Side of Manhattan, Stewart and his wife bought a place in Garrison. They looked forward to watching their young adopted daughter run in the backyard and swim in their pool. Stewart often dropped by Pete's Hometown Grocery on Main Street to pick up a copy of the *PCN&R*. Reading the articles each week, he did not at first see glaring signs of right-wing agitprop. He especially liked the paper's tough coverage of a contract dispute at the local school board. Shortly after Stewart gave a quote to the *PCN&R* criticizing the Garrison school, he bumped into Ailes in Manhattan at lunchtime at Michael's, a restaurant frequented by media executives.

"We gotta get together on this, that school sucks!" Ailes said to him.

"What's your problem with it?" Stewart said.

"There's no Christ child on the lawn at Christmastime!" Ailes said. "They have all this fucking Kwanzaa stuff, they have this Hanukkah shit, and you can't even get Jesus! They think it's illegal. You can't show any flags. So I'm *not* sending our kid there." As Stewart turned to leave, Ailes told him to stay in touch. "Call me," he said.

In the fall of 2009, Stephen Ives, a documentary filmmaker, invited Stewart over to his house in Garrison. A group of neighbors were gathering there to brainstorm ways to confront Ailes. They called themselves the Full Moon Project, but Stewart liked to call them "the Cold Spring Village Commune." The folk singer Dar Williams was the gravitational center of this constellation of politically active residents. As the conversations unfolded over several weeks, an idea took shape. The Full Moon Project would launch an online publication to rival the *PCN&R*. There was even a plan to start a Media Matters–like watchdog group to police right-wing bias in the *PCN&R*. They called it the Rapid Response Team.

When Ailes got wind of the meetings, he called Stewart and asked him whether he was a member of the "Full Moon conspiracy." Stewart laughed.

But by the time of the zoning town hall at Haldane in April 2010, Stewart's benign view of the *PCN&R* was changing. Under Joe Lindsley's editorship, Stewart saw undeniable evidence that the paper was taking on a partisan tack. He also heard a string of troubling stories of Ailes threatening locals who stood in his way. "You want to see a Fox News truck parked outside your place? I can have one up here *tomorrow,*" he said to one.

It struck Stewart how disconnected Ailes's simplified vision of the town was from the diverse reality Stewart had come to know. "Until Roger showed up, no one much cared what your party affiliation was," Stewart said. "With nine thousand people it doesn't work too well. It's hard to demonize people for party affiliation when they all know each other. Scaling Rogerism and Foxism down is a disaster." A canny businessman, Stewart sensed opportunity. The Full Moon meetings had produced a lot of talk, but Stewart was ready for action. He set out in secret to launch a local news website to take on Ailes directly.

On Tuesday morning, July 6, 2010, Lindsley was at his desk at the *PCN&R* working on the coverage of the Independence Day parade, which Roger and Beth had revived in 2009 after a thirty-year absence, when he let out a grunt. While searching the Internet, he came across the bylines of two *PCN&R* writers, Michael Turton and Liz Schevtchuk Armstrong, writing about Putnam County news on a site called Philipstown.info, which he had never heard of before, the proprietor of which was none other than Gordon Stewart. Alison Rooney, the copy editor, had also defected. Lindsley pushed his chair back from his computer and called Ailes. "What does this mean? Are we going to have trouble getting the paper out?" Ailes asked in light of the staff walkout. "Absolutely not," Lindsley replied. The lineup was already settled with a July Fourth recap and Federalist Paper no. 78.

The following day Ailes called Stewart and screamed at him for stealing *his* people. Stewart returned the bluster. "You're a big United States Constitution guy," he said. "The last time I checked, indentured servitude is illegal in the United States. I didn't steal them. They *left*. They don't want to work for you."

"I can give them all health insurance and they will quit and come back!" Ailes replied.

"Good. At least then I will have reformed your miserable labor practices."

Stewart's newsroom, set up across the street from the *PCN&R* in a former aromatherapy shop, posed a significant problem for Ailes. Despite the small-town stakes, it was a rivalry freighted with larger symbolism: for the first time since launching Fox News, the media business was changing in ways Ailes did not fully understand. The Internet was a wave washing over every corner of the communications industry. Newspapers and magazines had been the first casualties. It was only a matter of time until cable television began to suffer, too. "There was no push to innovate technologically," a former senior Fox executive said. CNN invested millions in the latest gadgetry such as touch screens and holograms. Fox didn't. Ailes, the executive added, felt "his core audience of older, white viewers preferred the simplicity of a traditional television newscast."

Ailes decided to sit down with Stewart in New York to gauge his intentions. Over the course of a two-and-a-half-hour meal at Fox News, Ailes was surprisingly open about his lack of knowledge of new media. "I don't know what to do with you," he told Stewart. "I have the same problem with you that I have at Fox News. I don't do a lot of web at Fox News." Ailes indicated if he gave away content for free on the web, his viewers might not pay for cable bills. "I'd be eating my own lunch," he said. The best Ailes could hope for was a war of attrition. "I'm going to run you out of money," Ailes assured Stewart. "What he didn't know is, I don't have any money," Stewart later said. "My deal with my wife was, if you want to spend the money you earn on the website, it's better than a blonde and a red sportscar."

In the days after the reporters defected, a cloud of suspicion enveloped the *PCN&R* newsroom. "They thought everyone was a traitor," reporter Liz Schevtchuk Armstrong said. Alison Rooney noticed strange activity on her *PCN&R* laptop: her email box had been opened remotely. Later, Roger and Beth accused her of all manner of conspiracies. "It was weird," one person familiar with the events said. "There was this whole James Bond spy type of stuff, like we were dealing with national security here, but all her emails were like, 'Dammit I hate my job!'"

As a final measure, just in case the reporters did not fully grasp what

Roger and Beth thought of their decision to leave, the *PCN&R* printed a reminder the week after they jumped ship. Tucked between the articles, readers came across a small cartoon of a rat.

The exodus of reporters created an opening on the staff. A few days after the Philipstown.info walkout, T. J. Haley, the *PCN&R*'s paperboy, mentioned to Lindsley that he was a good writer. Lindsley said he would give him a tryout. In June, Fox News HR had placed Haley, a twenty-three-year-old former Marine and *O'Reilly Factor* intern, with the paper. In his interview, the HR rep told Haley, who was eager for a full-time job at Fox, that working upstate was a way to get a leg up and impress Ailes. And so, after a month delivering papers for ten bucks an hour, Haley began contributing articles.

The commute to Cold Spring was soul-crushing. Haley was spending almost three hours in the car each day driving to and from his parents' house on Long Island, paying out what little he earned on gas. Beth offered to let him crash upstairs on an office couch next to the conference room where Roger addressed local politicians. "When you are here at the office, you're at home. This is a family," Beth told him. He slept there for three months. In the mornings, Haley cleaned himself up in the paper's bathroom. The decor in the bathroom unsettled him: on one wall hung a decorative artwork with a small photo of Beth's face, and on another, a drawing of Roger. Although Lindsley was a contemporary, Haley at first found his secretive manner off-putting. When Haley quoted lines from his favorite movies to Lindsley, the references did not register. Lindsley's touchstones were confined to conservative politics, journalism, and Notre Dame football. He seemed more like a factotum for the Ailes family than a newspaper editor. "Don't talk about them," he would say. Haley got along far better with Carli-Rae Panny, a bubbly Catholic twentysomething from east Putnam County, who joined the paper around the same time he did. Like Haley, Panny had been a Fox News intern, and they often had lunch together.

Ailes made zoning the litmus test by which politicians would be judged, even Republicans. Vincent Leibell, Putnam County's long-serving state senator, soon learned this painful lesson. A successful estate lawyer, Leibell was the godfather of the Putnam County GOP. His wide shoulders, jowly cheeks, and bald pate contributed to his bosslike persona. "Uncle Vinnie," locals called him. "Anytime that anyone new would come on the scene he'd want to know everything about them. *Everything,*" a local politician recalled. "Vinnie would co-opt them or if they wouldn't do what he'd say, he'd kill them in the cradle. He called it a 'crib death.'" Ailes, for a time, was a welcome presence. "Vinnie thought it was great Ailes was buying the newspaper and it'd be a Republican propaganda machine," Sam Oliverio, a Democrat on the Putnam County legislature, said.

Ailes heard the stories about Uncle Vinnie's sway. They ran into each other for the first time on the eve of the 2008 presidential election at a dinner sponsored by the Philipstown Community Council. A local politico in attendance told Uncle Vinnie that Ailes wanted to meet him.

"You're the guy that runs everything around here," Ailes said.

"No, I am actually not."

Roger did not buy the modest schtick. "I *know* you run everything in this county."

Ailes spent months trying to butter Uncle Vinnie up with dinner invitations and phone calls. In one conversation, he asked Uncle Vinnie if he wanted to run for governor. In another, he suggested that Uncle Vinnie build "a panic room" like he had. Ailes also liked to give his take on the national conversation or dole out bits of inside information. He said Obama did not have an American birth certificate and Murdoch was telling him to lie low on the Chinese because of his then wife, Wendi. But after Uncle Vinnie showed his independence by backing Shea for Philipstown supervisor, the relationship soured. "You endorsed a Democrat!" Ailes howled into the phone.

The zoning debate was the final rupture. Ailes reached Uncle Vinnie at the office. "Well, what are you going to do about it?"

"I am not going to do anything about it," Uncle Vinnie said. "That's a local issue. I wouldn't want the town trying to tell *me* what to do."

In the spring of 2010, Uncle Vinnie decided to downshift from the state senate and run for Putnam County executive. Some weeks after declaring his candidacy, Uncle Vinnie was invited to stop by the *PCN&R* to see Ailes, who accused him of "being behind" several new papers that were starting up in the county.

"You are trying to destroy these papers I got!"

"Roger, I don't even know who owns these papers!"

"*No,* you are behind them. You are involved with them."

"Roger, I don't know anything about them. I wish you well."

But Uncle Vinnie had liabilities. For years, there had been talk of kickbacks and shakedowns. People wondered how Leibell, a country lawyer, could afford a sprawling home on horse pastures once owned by the television actress and *Bewitched* star Elizabeth Montgomery. Ailes knew the talk, and he had a lever to pull: connections to law enforcement. Sheriff Don Smith called the FBI and fed the bureau information about Uncle Vinnie. In June 2010, the *PCN&R*'s sister paper, the Putnam County *Courier,* broke the news that the FBI had subpoenaed his financial records. Not long after the *Courier* report, Uncle Vinnie received a call.

"Has the FBI been by to see you lately?" Ailes said.

"No," Uncle Vinnie replied, trying to hide the panic in his voice.

"I know more about you than you think I do."

"Well, that's great you know stuff about me."

The line went dead.

Uncle Vinnie told people Ailes was out to bring him down. He claimed mysterious cars were tailing him around the county, and they were not the FBI's. One night at home, someone aimed flashlights into his back windows. He told friends he could not report the unsettling activity to Sheriff Smith because of Smith's loyalty to Ailes. "This was an ego fight about who was going to control the Republican Party in the county. And then Vinnie was stupid enough to do something illegal that Roger got wind of," Sam Oliverio said.

Although Uncle Vinnie handily won the election, it was a Pyrrhic victory. The Feds were closing in. Just four weeks later, Uncle Vinnie revealed he would not take office as county executive. Then, on Monday morning, December 6, Ailes got his man. Uncle Vinnie admitted to taking kickbacks from lawyers in his district. At the federal court in White Plains, New York, Leibell pleaded guilty to one count of obstruction of justice and one count of tax evasion, for which he would later be sentenced to twenty-one months in federal prison.

The Uncle Vinnie saga was a crucible that helped Lindsley finally bond with Haley and Panny. The three young reporters began to lunch together, and during these outings Lindsley let his guard down. Haley and Panny were beginning to realize that the unusual things they saw around the office—like the bathroom pictures of Roger and Beth—were only surface elements.

The story Lindsley told was deeply strange.

Roger and Beth were trying to inculcate in Lindsley their conspiratorial worldview. There were little things. At a restaurant, Lindsley once remarked on a cute waitress. "She's probably a spy," Beth said. And there were larger issues. They repeatedly told Lindsley they did not want him spending time with Haley. "They don't trust you," Lindsley told him. "They think you're trying to use them." Roger, in particular, was suspicious of Haley's background. He claimed Haley might be an unmarried father because of an incident when Haley joined the family for Mass on Father's Day. When the priest asked the fathers in the pews to rise, Haley, who was not paying attention, stood by mistake. But then Ailes would also tell Lindsley on multiple occasions that Haley was gay and that was the reason he had left the Marines. (Haley, who is straight, was given an honorable discharge for health reasons.) Beth and Roger also told Lindsley that Haley and Panny might be plants for MSNBC, or even Obama. Lindsley knew their claims were ludicrous, but confessed that the isolation was getting to him. When he went for pints at McGuire's pub on Main Street, Lindsley found himself sitting in silence while eyeing the doorway, afraid that someone was trailing him. He feared no one would believe him. "It's lonely at the top," Beth told him once.

Initially, the proximity to power had been intoxicating to Lindsley. Roger called him Ailes Junior and intimated that he had big plans in store for him. He suggested his protégé could write his memoirs or perhaps become the youngest editor of *The Wall Street Journal*. Roger introduced him to George H. W. Bush and Rush Limbaugh. Beth joked morbidly about his future. "When Roger dies, you're going to have some special responsibilities around here," she said. According to two senior Fox executives, Ailes spoke often about Lindsley at the office. "We thought he would be brought in to run the Fox News newsroom," one executive said. "Roger would talk about how great he was, and how he had the best news instinct." Ailes bragged about his papers' role in bringing Uncle Vinnie down. "He talked about these local politicians like it was national news. He said we should be doing more stories like this ourselves, more *investigations*," the executive said.

But Lindsley began to feel unnerved by Roger and Beth's attentions. Instead of letting Lindsley go home to visit his family in North Carolina, Roger invited his sisters for an extended stay at the mountain. When Lindsley said he wanted to go on vacation to visit relatives in Ireland, Roger and Beth said they would go with him. They flew together on News

Corp's private jet. Some days Lindsley felt that Champ, Roger's German shepherd, was his only friend.

Haley and Panny tried to convince Lindsley to leave. "No, it's disloyal," Lindsley would say. When Haley threatened to leave, Lindsley warned him, "Don't quit. You don't know what they will do to you."

At his apartment one night, Lindsley turned on Martin Scorsese's noir thriller *Shutter Island*. He felt an unsettling resonance watching Teddy Daniels, the anguished U.S. marshal played by Leonardo DiCaprio, lose his moorings inside a sinister mental facility. Lindsley wanted to spring for the exit, but didn't know how to get out.

Joe Lindsley's awakening came at a delicate moment for Roger and Beth. Ailes had learned that *New Yorker* journalist Peter Boyer was interviewing locals for an article about the contretemps surrounding the *PCN&R*. As was his custom, Ailes expressed wariness about his intentions. "You going to talk to that guy? It's going to be a hatchet job!" Ailes told Gordon Stewart. But as Boyer was a serious reporter who had published an acclaimed book about CBS News in the late 1980s, Roger and Beth eventually agreed to speak with him. Although Boyer wrote for a magazine that Ailes labeled a liberal rag, he had reason to trust him. Boyer was a southern gentleman and a conservative.

When Boyer showed up at the *PCN&R* one morning in December to interview Beth and Lindsley together, the mood in the newsroom was tense. Despite the rift emerging between Lindsley and the Ailes family, Lindsley played the good soldier in front of the journalist. But Roger was wary. He began peppering Lindsley with phone calls about the impending article. "So how's your friend Boyer doing? What's your friend Boyer doing today? Hey man, what's up with Boyer?"

"I'm not talking to the guy," Lindsley would tell him. "When he calls, I tell you he calls."

The *New Yorker* article hit newsstands on January 24, 2011. Headlined "Fox Among the Chickens" and written along the lines of Dr. Seuss's *The Butter Battle Book*, Boyer's story portrayed Roger and his liberal antagonists, like the Yooks and the Zooks, as destined to destroy any hope for peaceful coexistence. But unlike the Seuss book, which ends without any resolution of the conflict, by the end of Boyer's tidy fable, mutual understanding ensued. "Many places a thousand times larger are served by only a single newspaper; Philipstown now has two, each distinctly better than what was there before," he wrote.

Ailes was pleased with the result. "He called me the day after the story ran," Stewart recalled, "and said he liked it and thought Boyer was really good, and Beth loved her picture." Stewart and other townsfolk had a much dimmer view. They felt Boyer got spun.

As Boyer was completing his article over the Christmas holiday, Lindsley finally decided to resign. He told Roger and Beth about it in early January, a couple of weeks before the article was published. He said he would keep the information confidential and stay on for several months until they found a new editor in chief.

Roger and Beth did not take the news well, and it seemed to draw out Roger's paranoid nature even more. One day, Roger called Lindsley with instructions for Haley: "Tell him not to wear a hoodie. It's creepy." Lindsley realized that Roger must have watched Haley leave the office on the security cameras, which were installed after a vandalism incident. Surveillance became a fact of life for the three reporters. During their lunch breaks to Panera Bread, a more discreet location in the next town, they wondered if they were being tailed by Ailes's security detail. They wanted to leave, but had no place to go. Aware it was a gamble, Haley decided to call Boyer for help. He agreed to meet him, Panny, and Lindsley for a beer. "They made it clear that they were unhappy—which, frankly, quite surprised me," Boyer later said. Boyer told them that, unfortunately, he did not have any promising leads.

Roger's demands on Lindsley grew more controlling. One night, Lindsley got a call on his cell phone. Roger told him that the security alarms in the compound had been tripped. Roger, who was out of town and couldn't make it to the house, told Lindsley to race up to the mountain and stop the intruders.

"What if they're armed?"

"Doesn't matter," Ailes said. "Go up there!"

Lindsley arrived at the Ailes compound before the police did. Ailes stayed on the cell phone with Lindsley as he walked through the dark and empty mansion. He told Lindsley to flip on different lights to scare off any burglars. It turned out to be a false alarm.

In early March, Ailes arrived at the *PCN&R* office to stage an intervention of sorts and quell another staff rebellion. He met with Haley and Panny one-on-one. "I have two thousand employees at Fox, yet this small newspaper is the cause of all my headaches," Ailes said. "I'm sick of the drama in this office." He doled out to the young journalists kernels of self-help wisdom, iterations of lines from his book, *You Are the Message*.

The last week of March, Beth showed up on the warpath. She told Haley to stop coming in to the office and work from home, filing cover stories as usual. He did not know if he was being fired or not. She criticized Lindsley and Panny as well. It was the final push that the three needed. While Beth stepped out, Haley looked to his friends and nodded. They gathered up their things and walked out of the newsroom. Lindsley wanted to get the hell out of Cold Spring. Haley agreed to drive him to Washington, D.C., that night to see friends. As they drove out of town, they saw a dark Lexus SUV heading in the opposite direction. Beth was behind the wheel. Haley floored it and did not stop for miles.

The young journalists had reason to fear Ailes. When Panny went back to the office a few days later to offer her resignation in person, Roger and Beth screamed at her for an hour. They accused her of spreading dirt about them and asked her to sign a nondisparagement agreement that they had already prepared. Panny refused to look at the document and left. After a few days in D.C., Lindsley returned to his apartment in Cold Spring and noticed strange cars parked out front. As he drove to lunch that day, he saw a black Lincoln Navigator in his rearview mirror. He stopped his Jeep at a red light. When he saw the Lincoln swerve off the road into a construction site, he floored the gas as soon as the light turned green and headed back toward his apartment. Back in Cold Spring, Lindsley spotted the SUV on a side street and decided to turn the tables. He drove straight toward it. The Lincoln sped off. After a few blocks, his pursuer pulled over. Lindsley drove up alongside the driver and recognized him as a News Corp security officer. Later, Lindsley called the agent and asked if he was sent to follow him. He said Ailes told him to.

Peter Johnson Jr., who was taking over for his father as Ailes's lawyer, sent the reporters a flurry of threatening emails and certified letters. They contained a nondisparagement agreement and a list of potential charges Roger and Beth were considering filing. Lindsley barraged Haley with panicked text messages. "The world's fucking ending!" he wrote in one.

In April 2011, a few weeks after the walkout, *Gawker* reported a detailed account of the spying episode. Brian Lewis refused to comment for the story. "I hate everything that goes on up there," he told people. None of the former *PCN&R* staffers were quoted by name in the article. But Beth blamed Lindsley. As soon as *Gawker* posted its story, Beth released a nasty statement attacking Lindsley as if he were the source: "These rambling allegations are untrue and in fact not even reality based."

When Ailes walked into a meeting at Fox that week, he told his executives, "Lots of stuff is out there. None of it is true." In future meetings, Ailes did not utter Joe Lindsley's name.

The saga provided another example of how Ailes wielded power. The fear that swept through the *PCN&R* office was every bit as visceral as the panic experienced by CNBC executives during Ailes's tenure.

In the spring of 2011, after moving out of his apartment in Cold Spring, Lindsley traveled around the East Coast staying with friends. He began running again and got back down to his high school weight, eventually taking a job as a writer for Foster Friess, the conservative billionaire. He helped Haley get a job with Friess as well. Panny went on to work as an editor at *The Daily Voice,* which serves Connecticut, New York, and western Massachusetts. Lindsley's uncle, a lawyer in Ohio, handled Peter Johnson, and the threatened legal action never materialized.

Roger and Beth did their best to disappear the three journalists. Shortly after Lindsley left, he discovered that their bylines had been erased from the *PCN&R* archives. On the online version of dozens of articles they had written, the author field stated simply: "Staff Reports."

On January 31, 2011, a week after Boyer's Cold Spring article was published in *The New Yorker,* Tina Brown announced that she was hiring Boyer as a senior correspondent for *Newsweek* and *The Daily Beast*. It was an inauspicious move for Boyer. On October 18, 2012, the same day *Newsweek* announced it would fold its print edition by year-end, Boyer found a new job. "I have followed Peter's work throughout his storied career," Roger Ailes said in a statement to the press. "He's a talented and insightful journalist who will add weight and depth to our investigative reporting." Boyer, Fox's newest editor-at-large, was welcomed to the family.

# TWENTY-TWO
# THE LAST CAMPAIGN

March 2011 was a turbulent month for Roger Ailes. Joe Lindsley had just walked away. He was also losing his biggest star of the Obama era. On Monday afternoon, March 28, Ailes called Glenn Beck to his office to discuss his future at the network. He had spent the better part of the weekend in Garrison strategizing how to stage-manage Beck's departure from Fox, which at that point was all but inevitable. But, as with everything concerning Beck, the situation was exhausting, simultaneously a negotiation and a therapy session. Beck had already indicated his willingness to leave.

"You've got to be crazy. No one walks away from television," Ailes said.

"I may be," Beck replied.

Ailes asked Beck's producer, Joel Cheatwood, to translate. "What the fuck is he doing? Does he want a raise? Tell me how much." Beck's people held firm.

Moving him out the door without collateral damage was proving difficult.

"Let's make a deal," Ailes told Beck flatly.

During a forty-five-minute conversation, the two men agreed on the terms: Beck would give up his daily 5:00 p.m. program and appear in occasional network "specials"—but even that didn't solve their problem. They haggled over how many specials he would appear in. Fox wanted six a year, Beck's advisers wanted four. At another sit-down, Beck choked up as he talked about his bond with Ailes over right-wing politics and history. But Ailes threatened to blow up the talks, saying that Beck's advisers were jerking him around. "I'm just going to fire him and issue a press release," he snapped to a Fox executive.

The relationship had been strained since Beck joined Fox. In early 2009, Fox News executives denied a request from Beck's production team to allow Beck's head writer and close friend, Pat Gray, to accompany Beck to the Fox News studio for his daily program. At CNN, it had never been an issue for Gray to join Beck at the studio; in fact, Beck leased space for his entire staff at the Time Warner Center. Beck wrote an email to Ailes stressing that Gray was a key writer for the show and that his presence in the studio was important. Ailes responded that he did some checking and it was against the "policy" to give out a building pass. In private, Ailes expressed wariness about Beck's staff. "I don't want too many of his people here," he told an executive.

Things took a turn for the worse as Beck gathered 300,000 of his devoted followers in front of the Lincoln Memorial for a "Restoring Honor" rally—scheduled for the August 2010 anniversary of Martin Luther King's "I Have a Dream" speech. Fox executives showed little enthusiasm. "I'm going to D.C. in case something happens, and we have to react," Bill Shine told a colleague the day before. "We'll probably do a cut-in during the news." In the end, Fox gave the event scant coverage; CNN actually seemed to cover it more. Ailes praised Beck in a meeting with his executives afterward—"I don't know anyone else in the country who could have done that"—but Beck could not understand why Ailes did not actively promote an event that drew so many potential Fox viewers. Brian Lewis was selling Ailes on the idea that Beck, who had graced the covers of *Forbes, Time,* and *The New York Times Magazine,* was amassing a power base independent of Fox. "Beck had his own PR apparatus and Brian resented that," a colleague said, "so Brian one day explained to Roger during a meeting called on a completely other topic, that Glenn's problem was that he felt he was bigger than Fox." Ailes agreed: talent should never eclipse the brand. "From that day on, that was Roger's theme with Glenn: he didn't appreciate the platform Fox had given him and needed to be pushed out," the colleague said.

Tensions continued to escalate when, a few days after the rally, Beck launched *The Blaze,* a conservative news website. Fox executives told Beck he couldn't promote his new venture on air. At times, *The Blaze* undermined stories that Fox pushed, like its piece debunking conservative provocateur James O'Keefe's NPR sting, which had received wall-to-wall coverage on the channel. After the New Year, the cold war turned hot. Beck's company, Mercury Radio Arts, hired an executive from *The Huffington Post* to run *The Blaze,* and later poached Joel Cheatwood from

Fox. The moves signaled Beck's ambition to build a conservative media empire of his own—a clear encroachment on Ailes's turf. Brian Lewis retaliated by having his department tell the entertainment news website *Deadline Hollywood* that Cheatwood had earned $700,000 a year at Fox, a low-ball figure that was designed to damage his earning potential at future jobs. "Joel lost Roger's respect and trust a long time ago," an unnamed Fox "insider" told the website. Reporters began highlighting that Beck's ratings had been slipping and that progressive groups had orchestrated an advertising boycott of his show. But ratings for his time slot were still nearly double those from before he joined the network, and Fox simply shifted the advertising inventory to other programs.

On April 6, Fox and Beck announced the breakup. Both were careful to squelch the anonymous backbiting that had been going on for weeks in the press. Ailes did not want a public meltdown to alienate Beck's legions of fans who had become loyal Fox viewers. Most of all, he didn't want Beck's departure to be seen as a victory for the liberal media; that would ruin the most important story line of all.

By the time of Beck's departure, Ailes had been spending considerable energy discussing the consequences of an Obama reelection. For the past two and a half years, he had committed himself to blocking the Obama agenda. When the Affordable Care Act passed the previous March, "he went apeshit," a senior producer said. Ailes instructed his producers to book former New York lieutenant governor Betsy McCaughey, a conservative health care advocate who popularized the notion of "death panels." "He said she was the best person to talk about this," the senior producer recalled. "He even gave her a prop: a giant stack of papers of the law itself."

And so Ailes set out to recruit a viable Republican candidate. In the summer of 2010, he invited Chris Christie to dinner at his home in Garrison with Rush Limbaugh. Like much of the GOP establishment, Ailes fell hard for the New Jersey governor. They talked about pension reform and getting tough with the unions. Ailes saw in Christie a great candidate: an ordinary guy, someone you'd be comfortable talking to over your back fence. But Ailes may have seen something else. Christie had Fox News television values with a ready-made reel. And, of course, Obama versus Christie was a producer's dream: black versus white, thin versus fat, professor versus prosecutor. Maybe, just maybe, Ailes could laugh all the way to the White House *and* the bank. Nevertheless, Christie politely turned down Ailes's calls to run. Christie joked at dinner that his weight was an issue. "I still like to go to Burger King," he told the three rotund conservatives.

In April 2011, Ailes sent Fox News contributor Kathleen T. McFarland to Kabul to make a pitch to then-General David Petraeus. "He adored Petraeus," a senior producer said. "When Moveon.org put the 'General Betray Us' ad in the newspapers in 2007, Roger said it was treasonous and we reported it as such." Ailes had already told Petraeus that if he ran for president, he would quit Fox News to run the campaign. War hero presidents were especially impressive to Ailes. It was why he spoke almost daily to George H. W. Bush. "The big boss is bankrolling it," McFarland told Petraeus, referring to Murdoch. "Roger's going to run it. And the rest of us are going to be your in-house." But Petraeus also turned Ailes down. "It's never going to happen," he told McFarland. "My wife would divorce me."

Around this time, Ailes set up a meeting with David and Charles Koch, the billionaire industrialists who were financing a phalanx of right-wing groups to defeat Obama. Ailes had never met the brothers, and both sides expressed that it would be a good moment to sit down. Charles Koch flew to New York for the meeting. But Ailes, for unclear reasons, canceled. "Charles was miffed," one conservative familiar with the meeting explained. Perhaps Ailes recognized that if details of the gathering leaked it would further cement his image as a conservative kingmaker, a fact he was working overtime to dispel. "Listen, the premise that I want to elect the next president is just bullshit," Ailes told a reporter. "The idea that I'm grooming these Republicans is just wrong." Though the meeting was called off, Ailes's interests were aligned with those of the Kochs. In the winter of 2011, Ailes had called Chris Christie, the Kochs' preferred candidate, and implored him for a second time to run. Christie turned him down again.

The first Fox primary debate proceeded on May 5, 2011, in Greenville, South Carolina, without an A-list candidate. The aspirants on the stage were a bunch of also-rans: pizza mogul Herman Cain; former governors Gary Johnson and Tim Pawlenty; former senator Rick Santorum; and Congressman Ron Paul. Ailes's Washington managing editor, Bill Sammon, had assured Fox executives that bigger names would show up, but Sammon proved to be misinformed. The debate confirmed what a mess the field was—a mess partly created by the loudmouths Ailes had given airtime to and a Tea Party he had nurtured.

Meanwhile, Ailes had his hands all over the campaign in his backyard. It was also a mess. Democratic town supervisor Richard Shea was up for reelection in November 2011. Ailes wanted him out. "I still owe you one for that article," he told Shea, referring to his comments in *The New York Times.* Since the volatile town hall meeting on zoning, their relationship had settled into a stalemate. But a few months before the election, Ailes asked Shea to meet him at the *PCN&R* office on Main Street. "What you should do is hire an opponent to run against you and then you win," Ailes said. Shea later told others he wondered if Ailes was secretly taping him to set him up.

The campaign season was unlike any the community had seen. The Ailes-backed conservative candidate, Lee Erickson, who owned a well-drilling business in town, sent out nearly a dozen high-gloss mailers to voters and conducted telephone push polls against Shea. Then, in October, Erickson refused to attend a debate that Gordon Stewart and Philipstown .info were organizing at the Haldane School. Stewart even promised to publish the website's questions in advance, but Erickson was unswayed.

On the day of the *PCN&R* debate, Ailes engaged in a bit of psychological warfare. The latest issue of *Newsmax* magazine had a cover story about Ailes, calling him "The Most Powerful Man in News." That day, several local politicians, including Shea, received hand-delivered copies of the issue, with candy-colored tabs affixed to the pages of the glowing profile. "Using his instincts about on-air talent and the assault on American values, Roger Ailes has set the new agenda for TV journalism. But he's decidedly not the kind of media mogul described by his liberal critics," the article read. The text seemed tailor-made to rebut a series of articles about Ailes that had recently appeared in national magazines. Ailes had included personal notes with the magazine, at least one of which read, "Be careful what you say about my wife." That night at the Haldane cafeteria, Shea was overheard asking Ailes about the *Newsmax* story and his note: "What's up with that?"

"Oh, I sent that out to everyone," Roger said, and smirked.

After Beth gave opening remarks to the crowd of 150, Joe Lindsley's replacement, Doug Cunningham, moderated. Over the course of the debate, Erickson hurled Ailesian putdowns. He called Shea "King Richard" and criticized his "disappointing level of arrogance." Erickson, who had cofounded the property rights group Citizens of Philipstown, mainly went after Shea's zoning legislation. Shea remained unflappable. "One of the things I'm most proud of is the zoning," he said. Instead, Shea accused Erickson of distorting his positions. He said his opponent "went up and down [Route] 9 spreading a campaign of disinformation to business owners, riling people up."

The consensus in town was that Shea dominated Erickson that night. On Election Day, after an Erickson supporter went up and down Main Street in colonial garb stumping for his candidate, Shea won decisively by 518 votes, or 58.8 percent of the vote to 41.2 percent for Erickson. It should have been an augur of things to come. The *PCN&R* succeeded in monopolizing access to Philipstown Republicans, but failed to get Erickson into office. The same dynamic was about to play out on the national stage.

Republicans referred to the 2012 campaign as the "Fox News Primary." "It's like a town hall every day on Fox News," Kansas governor Sam Brownback told *The New York Times* not long before the Iowa caucuses. "I like Fox, and I'm glad we have an outlet, but it is having a major, major effect on what happens." For both the candidates and Ailes, the Fox Primary was a ratings boon but a branding challenge. In the last eight months of 2011, GOP presidential candidates made more than six hundred appearances on Fox News and Fox Business while largely ignoring non-Fox media. ("I'm sorry, we're only going to be doing Fox," Gingrich's spokesperson, R. C. Hammond, told a CNN producer on the eve of the Iowa caucuses in Des Moines.) Their face time on Fox during this period totaled seventy-seven hours and twenty-four minutes. But as Fox's pundits and anchors pushed the candidates into the conspiracy swamps of Fast and Furious, the gun-running debacle, and Solyndra, the bankrupt solar panel company, Fox risked alienating independent viewers—and voters.

It was a case of Ailes being unable to put his party's goal of winning independents ahead of his personal views. "He doesn't like green energy—period," a senior producer said. "He says all the time that no one in America has died from nuclear power, but fifteen people have been chopped up by those damn windmills." For Ailes, Fast and Furious was a passionate cause. "He wants indictments. He thinks [Attorney General Eric] Holder should resign and go to jail for the death of a federal agent. He won't be happy until he gets it," the producer said.

Branding issues aside, the Fox Primary was a cunning programming ploy. It gave Ailes's audience a new reality TV show with a revolving cast of characters to follow. In May 2011, Mike Huckabee ginned up interest in his weekly Fox show by promising to reveal his presidential ambitions live. "Governor Huckabee will announce tomorrow night on his program whether or not he intends to explore a presidential bid," his producer, Woody Fraser, teased in a press release. "He has not told anyone at Fox News Channel his decision." On the night of May 14, when Huckabee announced he was not running, ratings soared to 2.2 million.

But when the action took place off his set, Ailes, like any director, went wild. In October, Sarah Palin made the mistake of breaking the news that she would not be running for president on Mark Levin's talk radio show. "I paid her for two years to make this announcement on my network," Ailes told Bill Shine in a meeting. Fox was left with sloppy seconds: a follow-up interview with Palin on Greta Van Susteren's 10:00 p.m. show, after news of Palin's decision had been drowned out by Apple Inc. founder Steve Jobs's death. Ailes was so furious that he considered pulling Palin off Fox entirely until her $1 million annual contract expired in 2013. Shine told Palin's agent, Bob Barnett, that Palin was at risk of being "benched." After conferring with Palin, Barnett called Shine back and told him that Palin recognized the misstep. But tensions between Palin and Fox did not subside.

Ailes questioned the spine of the eventual nominee, Mitt Romney. In a private conversation with Bill Kristol, Ailes said, "Romney's gotta rip Obama's face off. It's really hard to do. I did this with Bush Sr. He was uncomfortable with ripping Dukakis's face off. George had to tell Barbara, 'Look, this is Roger's thing.' It made Barbara uncomfortable that George was going so negative, but I had to rip off Dukakis's face."

Romney's shaky interview with Bret Baier on the afternoon of November 29 proved Ailes's point. For days, Romney had been declining invitations to appear with a roundtable of "All-Star" pundits. Romney's campaign did not think it would look "presidential" for the candidate to be surrounded by Fox News commentators lobbing questions at him. Finally, they reached a compromise. Bret Baier would interview Romney at a Conchita Foods warehouse in Miami, where the candidate was on the trail. But just because Baier agreed to travel to Florida did not mean he was going to go soft. After rattling off a list of Romney's flip-flops on climate change, gay marriage, abortion, and immigration, Baier confronted Romney about his position on universal health care. "Do you believe that that was the right thing for Massachusetts?"

"Bret, I don't know how many hundred times I've said this—" Romney stammered. "This is an unusual interview." The back-and-forth continued for several excruciating minutes.

When the cameras cut out, Romney complained to Baier about the exchange. Not coming prepared had been Romney's first mistake. Insulting Baier was his second. The following night, Baier appeared on *The O'Reilly Factor* and reported Romney's off-camera tantrum.

At times, it seemed that Ailes was using Fox to manufacture moments of excitement around alternative candidates. After receiving just 9.4 percent of the vote in the New Hampshire primary, Newt Gingrich bounced back in South Carolina. His springboard was a fiery on-air exchange with Fox analyst Juan Williams at a debate in Myrtle Beach held on Martin Luther King Day. Williams, who is black, asked Gingrich about his campaign trail comments that inner city children lacked a "work ethic" and should work as "janitors" in schools. Weren't these remarks "insulting to all Americans but particularly to black Americans?" "No," Gingrich shot back. His answer was greeted with rapturous applause. "Only the elites despise earning money," he said. Gingrich carried the state's primary five days later.

Some in Romney's camp blamed the outcome on Ailes. Stuart Stevens, Romney's media strategist, later told Romney's advisers that he thought Ailes put a black newsman onstage as a way of symbolically putting Obama in a room filled mainly with white conservatives. Gingrich's defiant retort, red meat in the cradle of Dixie, was a symbolic smackdown of the president.

In one editorial meeting, Fox News executive Suzanne Scott wondered aloud if Ailes was damaging the party by stoking on-air death matches. "You can create a Reagan through an intra-party fight," Ailes responded. "If there's a fight, we should be the one doing the shooting."

By any measure, 2012 was shaping up to be a phenomenal year for Ailes: Fox News was on track to make $1 billion in profit, the network was in the driver's seat during the fractious Republican primary, and it still was crushing its cable news rivals. And yet, to some who knew him, Ailes seemed to be consumed by increasingly paranoid and morbid thoughts.

"Listen, one out of every twenty-five people in America is a psychopath," he told his executives. Petty grievances and past battles triggered outsized responses.

In the fall of 2011, Ailes found himself in a row with Google after the company co-sponsored a GOP debate with Fox at the Orlando Convention Center in Florida. Michael Clemente had worked hard to develop the relationship with the Internet search giant, but the relationship did not last long. Ailes was furious that the third hit in search results for his name was a liberal blog called rogerailes.blogspot.com ("Not affiliated with the fat FOX fuck," the blog informed readers at the top of its homepage). Ailes told Fox executives that he wanted Google to push the blog's ranking down. Google told Fox that they did not intervene in such matters. Afterward, Fox canceled the partnership and did not co-host future debates with Google.

Ailes spoke frequently about death. "I'd give anything for another ten years," Ailes would say. Having a child amplified these sentiments. "I don't want the kid growin' up in a fouled-up world," he told a reporter. "He has common feelings of a parent who wants to protect a son," a close colleague said. "The thing is, most parents don't run a television network." To prepare Zachary for his absence, he gave him an accelerated education. When Zachary was twelve, Roger set up a summer internship for him at the Manhattan-based PR firm the Dilenschneider Group, whose founder, Robert Dilenschneider, was Ailes's personal PR consultant. Each morning, Zachary would put on a coat and tie and get driven in Roger's News Corp SUV to the office. Around this time, Roger told a journalist that he set aside boxes filled with keepsakes. Besides family photographs and letters, the contents included a pocket-size copy of the Constitution ("The founders believed it and so should you," he wrote on it), press clippings lionizing his accomplishments, some gold coins ("in case everything goes to hell"), and Sun Tzu's *The Art of War,* with a note inscribed on the opening page:

> *Avoid war if at all possible but never give up your freedom—or your honor. Always stand for what is right.*
>
> *If absolutely FORCED to fight, then fight with courage and win. Don't try to win . . . win!*
>
> *Love,*
> *Dad*

But there was more on his mind than his own mortality. He sometimes feared the worst for Zachary. In February 2012, Gordon Stewart received an unexpected, hysterical call from Ailes.

"You're putting a target on my son's back!" he screamed. "You'll be responsible if something happens!"

Stewart, who had to hold the phone away from his ear, asked Ailes what on earth he was talking about.

That week, Philipstown.info published a brief item about recent hearings of the local planning board. The final paragraph reported that Ailes and his neighbor were seeking approval to adjust the line between their properties, which were owned by "Hudson Valley 2009, formed by Roger Ailes; Viewsave LLC; and Gerald Morris."

"I'll sue you!" Ailes yelled into the phone.

The article, he said, put Zachary in danger because it disclosed the existence of a trust. He began fulminating about unrelated disputes, including the old charge that Stewart encouraged his employees to quit without giving notice. "You must know I did no such thing," Stewart said.

"You're a liar!"

"Roger, since you called and I said hello, you have insulted my integrity, called me a liar to my face, have threatened me with a lawsuit, accused me of potentially being an accomplice to the murder of your son," Stewart said. "Can you explain to me how you can expect that approach will advance the purpose of your calling?"

Ailes paused. "You need to get help!" he blurted out and hung up.

An hour later, Ailes called back. This time, he calmly asked Stewart to take down the article from the website. Stewart told him he would get back to him. After discussing his concerns with his editor, Kevin Foley, and the reporter on the story, Stewart called Ailes and informed him that he would not be removing it.

"You don't know how people are out to get me! I asked you for a favor and you're turning me down."

"First of all," Stewart said, "there's no mention of your son. There's nothing in this article that would jeopardize you and your family. You're asking me to remove what happened at a public meeting, and I can't do that."

Ailes repeated his claim that Stewart needed mental help. The conversation ended there. At home that night, Stewart's cell phone rang. It was Ailes calling for the third time that day. Stewart didn't pick up.

Later that month, Ailes's old nemesis David Brock coauthored a new book, *The Fox Effect: How Roger Ailes Turned a Network into a Propaganda Machine,* which synthesized the most damaging research that Media Matters had published over the past decade on its website. "He was obsessed with Brock's book," one Fox contributor recalled. In one meeting, Ailes said he couldn't "do anything" until it was published. Highlighting leaked emails from Fox executives, which expressed overt right-wing bias, and detailing wild on-air claims about Obama's religion, background, and policies, the text provided Fox's detractors with rounds of ammunition to deploy in their battle to define Ailes as a master propagandist. In retaliation, Fox aired segments claiming Brock was mentally unstable.

Google, Media Matters, and Philipstown.info were new media antagonists. Ailes's threats did not have the same effect on them that they did on legacy media outlets. This was especially the case with *Gawker.* On April 10, the gossip website introduced a new series. "What follows is the inaugural column of a person we are calling The Fox Mole—a longstanding, current employee of Fox News Channel who will be providing *Gawker* with regular dispatches from inside the organization," the editors wrote. The columns brought about a minor media convulsion, but the show had a short run. Within twenty-four hours, Fox executives successfully identified the Mole as Joe Muto, a thirty-year-old associate producer who'd worked at the network for eight years, and fired him.

When Muto quickly landed a low-six-figure book deal in early May to write about his exploits, Ailes decided to send a message. Jimmy Gildea, Ailes's security guard, told the boss he could press charges. "If this *Gawker* paid for stolen goods, it could be part of the crime, same as if somebody hires a hit man," the former cop said. Brian Lewis wanted Ailes to let it go, but was overruled. "I told them," Lewis said, "but I was told that legal would be handling this from here forward. I'm like, *Okay.*"

At 6:30 in the morning on April 25, officers from the New York district attorney's office arrived at Muto's apartment with a warrant charging him with grand larceny and conspiracy, among other charges. They seized his iPhone, laptop, and old notebooks. A year later, a month before his book was published, Muto appeared in handcuffs at the Manhattan Criminal Court, where he pleaded guilty to a pair of misdemeanor charges: attempted unlawful duplication and criminal possession of computer-related material. The judge fined Muto $1,000, ordered him to forfeit a $5,000 fee he earned from *Gawker* for reporting on Fox, confiscated his Mac, and ordered him to do ten days of community service and two hundred hours of private service.

In the closing weeks of the 2012 presidential campaign, Ailes's worldview radiated from his daily editorial meetings onto the screen. "He likes to raise questions in chyrons," a senior producer said, referring to the graphics and the text that appear at the bottom of the screen. "Is Obama a socialist? He tells producers that such an approach is better than simply saying Obama is a socialist." Ailes's anchors and pundits breathlessly inflated a panoply of administration blunders into full-blown conspiracies. While Fox reporters did some enterprising coverage of the deadly attack on the American consulate in Benghazi on September 11, 2012, the journalism was undermined by one host claiming it was "the biggest news story since Watergate." A few days before the election, the mother of Sean Patrick Smith, a State Department employee killed in Benghazi, said that Fox's reports had caused her to believe that "Obama murdered my son." Fox hyped the influence of fringe groups like the New Black Panther Party and pushed fears of stolen elections. "ELECTION OFFICIALS IN BATTLEGROUND STATE OF OHIO FEAR WIDESPREAD VOTER FRAUD," one on-screen banner read.

Ailes's executives flattered him with suggestions that he go on camera and deliver the attack lines himself or even run for president. (Michael Clemente had "Ailes 2012" bumper stickers printed and distributed around the second floor.) At some moments, Ailes demurred. "Those days are gone," he told his team. At other moments, he indulged them. That summer, he told his inner circle at the afternoon strategy meeting that he wanted to host a talk show. His PR deputy, Irena Briganti, who was sitting in the room, advised him against it. "The media will go after you," she warned.

So when Ailes wanted to get his message out, he often turned to his lawyer, Peter Johnson Jr., who took to *Fox & Friends* to spread it. In private, Johnson spoke of Ailes like a father. Johnson told a Fox colleague Ailes thought of him as a son. Owing to his special status, Johnson was allowed to use the teleprompter to read from scripts, a perk that was normally reserved for Fox hosts. "He can load a script directly into the teleprompter. So it's not even Ailes unplugged. It's Ailes plugged in," one person familiar with the matter said. Johnson served up frightening scenarios filled with Muslim extremists and Occupy Wall Street anarchists and overreaching government bureaucrats, lacing his commentary with Nixonian bogeymen. On the day before Obama and Romney squared off in their final debate on foreign policy, Johnson discussed the situation in Benghazi. He speculated about whether Obama had known about the attack early enough to have ordered military action to save the Americans who were killed. "If he did nothing, then that is the shame of America," Johnson said. "I have no evidence for this," he mused, but "were these people expendable as part of a Mideast foreign policy?"

On the afternoon of November 6—Election Day—Ailes had lunch with Karl Rove, who still believed in a Romney win. Few Fox pundits had stumped as hard as Rove had for the candidate. Rove's Super PAC, American Crossroads, and its affiliate, Crossroads GPS, had vowed to spend up to $300 million to back conservatives in the 2012 political campaigns. "Hell, maybe Karl's right," Ailes said later that day.

At 5:00 p.m., Ailes assembled his network's election team in the second-floor conference room to discuss the night's coverage. "Guys," he told them, "no matter how it goes, don't go out there looking like someone ran over your dog." But as Fox's exit poll team presented the numbers, Ailes came undone. "They weren't good for Romney," a person in the room said. "Roger started arguing about how the sample skewed toward liberals." Ailes said, "Liberals like to share their feelings, and conservatives work, so they don't vote until later." Arnon Mishkin, the head of Fox's decision desk team, told Ailes that the data accounted for a sample skew. It appeared that Romney was going to be trounced. Worse, so-called late deciders were breaking for Obama.

"Thank you, Chris Christie," Ailes grumbled. He was still furious that Christie had given Obama a bipartisan photo op on the New Jersey coastline after Hurricane Sandy.

"Actually, that's not true," Mishkin said. "We asked people that. There's no data in the polling to suggest that Sandy hurt Romney."

"Well, hugging the guy couldn't help people feel good about Romney either," Ailes countered.

Data was no substitute for what his gut told him. "Everyone left that room with the knowledge that Roger didn't believe the polls," a participant said. His opinion would be channeled on-air later that night, with embarrassing consequences.

About an hour later, Ailes settled into a plush chair in the Fox Sports

Suite. A couple hundred people, including Rupert Murdoch, mingled in the room snacking on sushi and lamb kabobs. One Fox executive recalled he made sure to avoid eating the raw fish in front of Ailes. "Sushi is liberal food," he explained. The election coverage played out on eight flat-screen televisions mounted on the wall. Around 8:00, Beth arrived. The *PCN&R* was going to press that night. She sat beside Ailes reviewing the week's edition on her iPad. Shortly before 11:00, with Romney's chances fading, Roger and Beth called it a night. "I want to kiss Zac good night before he goes to sleep," Ailes told a journalist, trying to put the best spin on the outcome. "If Romney wins, it's good for the taxpayers. If Obama wins, it's great for our ratings."

Downstairs, Arnon Mishkin and Fox's number crunchers were preparing to call Ohio for Obama. "Let's remember this is Fox News calling Ohio. This will say something beyond Ohio going for Obama," Mishkin told Fox brass. Fox executives told Mishkin to get the numbers right and ignore the politics: "If we think Ohio has gone Obama, we call Ohio," said a Fox News executive.

Bret Baier announced the call on set. "That's the presidency, essentially," he said. Instantly, Fox phones lit up with angry phone calls and emails from the Romney campaign, who believed that the call was premature. After Baier's Ohio call, Rove took their complaints public, echoing Ailes's earlier comments, and conducting an on-air primer on Ohio's electoral math to dispute the outcome. With the network divided against itself, senior producers held a meeting to adjudicate. The decision desk stood their ground. They knew how momentous the call was. In the end, producers had to find a way to split the difference. Megyn Kelly walked through the newsroom to interview the decision desk. "This is Fox News," a person in the room said, "so anytime there's a chance to show off Megyn Kelly's legs they'll go for it."

By midnight, Rove reluctantly seemed to concede. The moment became a symbol of the denialism that had taken hold on the right in the closing days of the election. On air, Dick Morris had predicted a Romney landslide, putting Romney's odds of winning at 90 percent. In private, some Fox staffers thought the network's boosterism had become a joke. At a rehearsal on the Saturday before the election, Megyn Kelly chuckled when she relayed to colleagues what someone had told her: "I really like Dick Morris. He's always wrong, but he makes me feel good."

Only half of Roger Ailes's grand plan had come to pass. While Fox's ratings were still unchallenged, the channel had failed to elect the next president—the circus on Fox had complicated the effort as well as assisted it. By giving airtime to the most outlandish voices on the right, Fox had helped distort the debate over the country's future, making it easier for voters to dismiss Republican arguments. Ailes's personal political impulses—to enlist Chris Christie, or David Petraeus—were at odds with the vivid political comedy Fox often programmed. It turned out that television and politics were different disciplines. In pursuit of ratings, Fox had sharpened national divisions—and the division had favored the Democrats. Since the Nixon administration and TVN, the right had dreamed of a television channel that could make its case with the American public, to balance the debate. "You're a hero to our people," one prominent conservative told Ailes at a gala at the Kennedy Center. But in 2012, by this measure, Fox had been a failure.

After Mitt Romney's 2012 defeat, Mark Rozell, the acting dean of the George Mason University School of Public Policy, and Paul Goldman, a former chairman of Virginia's Democratic Party, wrote an essay noting the inverse relationship between the rise of conservative media and the Republican Party's ability to win national majorities. "When the mainstream media reigned supreme, between 1952 and 1988, Republicans won seven out of the ten presidential elections," they reported. "Conservative talk show hosts and Fox News blame the 'lamestream' national media's 'liberal bias' for the GOP's poor showing since 1992. Yet the rise of the conservative-dominated media defines the era when the fortunes of GOP presidential hopefuls dropped to the worst levels since the party's founding in 1856." Perhaps the freak show had become too freakish.

The post-election soul searching that consumed the Republican Party took place inside Fox News as well. Ailes, like other GOP heavyweights, took orchestrated steps to reposition his channel in the post-election media environment, freshening story lines—and, in some cases, changing the characters. Bill Shine sent out a directive mandating that producers needed permission from senior executives before booking Karl Rove or Dick Morris. In February, Fox declined to renew Morris's contract. Rove made the cut. Palin didn't. The previous month, the news broke that she and Fox had parted ways.

In meetings, Ailes told producers that viewers were tired of politics. Between Election Day and the inauguration, Fox toned down its coverage. In mid-December, in the immediate aftermath of the horrific school shooting in Newtown, Connecticut, that left twenty children dead, Ailes told producers not to program segments heavily debating the politics of the Second Amendment. A day after the shooting, David Clark, the executive producer in charge of Fox's weekend coverage, sent producers instructions. "This network is not going there," Clark wrote one producer on Saturday night. Fox also spiked a pro–assault weapon column by Foxnews.com contributor John Lott, one of the country's most vocal Second Amendment absolutists. "They didn't send me an e-mail. I got a call," Lott explained. "They said, 'This is just too sensitive.'" The policy wasn't ironclad. Some pundits and anchors did discuss the politics of the tragedy. But Fox hosts would let the audience's emotions cool before cranking up the volume of the gun rights debate.

The reprieve ended on the morning of January 21, 2013—inauguration day. The hosts of *Fox & Friends* signaled how the network felt about the opening of Obama's second term. "As if a cold Monday in January wasn't dreary enough, today has been dubbed—they figured this out about five years ago—'Blue Monday,' the most depressing day of the year," Steve Doocy said. To help viewers cope, they welcomed to the set self-help guru Larry Winget, the "Pitbull of Personal Development." Throughout the morning, the mood on-screen was melancholy. "This was an unyielding, uncompromising espousal of a liberal agenda," Chris Wallace said, following Obama's speech.

The post-election tweaks at Fox were just that—minor programming adjustments. Ailes was staying the course, taking little responsibility for the loss. He blamed his party for Romney's defeat. "The GOP couldn't organize a one-car funeral," he told executives. At a speech to journalism students the previous spring, Ailes said, "Sarah Palin had no chance, right?" He went on, "Did anybody think she had a chance to be president? Anybody in here? Okay. *Oops*. Newt Gingrich couldn't get anybody he worked with in Congress to support him, remember? A *little* bit of a problem. Rick Santorum, anybody ever hear of him until about six weeks ago? He lost his own state by 17 points."

When Ailes re-signed a contract through 2016, Fox seemed as if it were frozen in time. He brought back John Moody as executive editor and executive vice president. Hannity, O'Reilly, Van Susteren, and Megyn Kelly all signed new multiyear deals. Even Sarah Palin was rehired in June 2013. In October 2013, Ailes shuffled his prime-time schedule for the first time in years. It was a modest update: Megyn Kelly took over the 9:00 p.m. hour, Hannity shifted to 10:00 p.m., and Van Susteren took over

Shepard Smith's 7:00 p.m. newscast. O'Reilly, the bedrock of the lineup, remained at 8:00 p.m.

At the senior reaches of News Corp, Ailes's static vision for Fox was concerning. Obama's reelection coincided with the time News Corp was reorganizing its business. In June 2013, the company split into 21st Century Fox (its film and TV assets) and News Corp (its scandalized newspaper division). Fox News had been a rocketship but now some board members wondered if Ailes's fuel was spent. Although the company's cable assets remained phenomenally profitable—for the quarter ending June 2013, cable revenue was up 16 percent over a year earlier, to $3 billion—the Fox News channel was not viewed as a growth asset. The ratings in the wake of Obama's reelection were down markedly. All of cable news took a hit, but Fox's drop-off among twenty-five- to fifty-four-year-olds—the key advertising demographic—was steeper than its rivals'. In February 2013, Hannity's audience was down by 35 percent from the same period in 2012, while O'Reilly's audience had decreased by 26 percent. Ad revenue was also down in the first quarter, because it was no longer an election year.

After a News Corp board meeting in Manhattan in April 2013, some directors privately questioned whether Ailes had a programming strategy to reverse the slide. They also voiced concern over the issue of succession. Ailes's grip on power was so firm that some Fox executives described fearing *Lord of the Flies*–type chaos. Ailes at times seemed unaware of the worrying trend lines at his network. When one sales executive pointed out in a meeting that Fox's audience demographics skewed older than those of its cable news rivals, Ailes did not believe him. "Our demos suck," the executive said. "No they don't!" Ailes barked. When Ailes was shown the numbers, he seemed genuinely surprised. "Why didn't I know about this?" he asked. The truth was, over the years, executives, fearing Ailes's wrath, had shielded him from bad news. One executive recalled how Bill Shine would conveniently engage Ailes in partisan banter whenever his prime-time ratings dipped. "Did you see what Olbermann said last night?" Shine would venture. The question would cause Ailes to launch into a five-minute monologue about the former MSNBC host, and Fox's ratings were left unmentioned.

The Fox Business Network was also a ratings disappointment to some News Corp executives. Ailes had never wanted the channel in the first place. When Murdoch tapped Ailes to launch it in 2007, Ailes told the five executives hired to run the channel, "the world doesn't need another business network." Because the boss had signaled his lack of enthusiasm, executives took concerted steps to undermine the spinoff's success. "Welcome aboard. You're set up for failure," Ailes's loyalist Ken LaCorte told Ray Hennessey, the new director of business news, not long after he was hired. Neil Cavuto, who was named managing editor of the channel, followed Ailes's lead. "Cavuto wasn't involved," an executive said.

Kevin Magee, a trusted Fox News executive in charge of the day-to-day operations of the business channel, struggled to craft an identity for it. Ailes told Magee and his team that he did not want politics on-air—"we do that on the news channel," he said—but in the next breath he'd say that politics was what affected business. In the summer of 2010, Magee and his team sought to carve out a niche by giving airtime to libertarians like Judge Andrew Napolitano, the host of the prime-time show *Freedom Watch*. But this clashed with Ailes's efforts to steer Fox away from the Tea Party. One night, the judge ranted against U.S. drone strikes against American citizens who were labeled terrorists. "Roger the next day was really furious," an executive recalled. "He said, 'If the Russians shot missiles at us, the Judge would want us to consult Congress to get their permission to respond.' And then Ailes said he wanted the show off the air. A few weeks later, it was gone. The whole show. He kept the Judge, who is popular, but not the show." Libertarians flooded Facebook and other websites with complaints. Ailes ignored them. "If all the people who emailed Fox on the Judge's behalf had a Nielsen box, I would have kept him on the air," Ailes said.

More than politics, the business channel had a fundamental programming flaw: the entertainment values of Fox News produced comical results when applied to business journalism. Shortly before the business channel launched, a young female Fox Business anchor went to meet with the staff of the *New York Post*'s business desk to brainstorm story ideas.

"What do you know about business?" asked Roddy Boyd, a brash financial reporter who was then on staff at the *Post*. She told them her experience was in weather, but "I'm reading a lot. I know the Dow is up. I'm reading the blogs."

"Why'd they hire you?" Boyd asked. She smiled and shook her breasts.

Ailes sought to infuse Fox Business with well-known talent. In September 2009, he hired disgraced radio host Don Imus—whose show had been dropped by MSNBC two years earlier, after he said on air that the

Rutgers women's basketball team were "nappy-headed hos"—to anchor a morning show. Around this time, he also considered poaching CNBC star Maria Bartiromo. "Roger passed on her," one executive involved in the talks said. "He wished she hadn't gained so much weight. He said she went from looking like Sophia Loren to Mamma Leone. He felt he was being used to get more money from CNBC. He told us her agent should give him part of the commission, because the talks were worth another million dollars." (In November 2013, Bartiromo jumped from CNBC to Fox Business.)

The business network's failure to catch on was all the more glaring given that Murdoch had acquired *The Wall Street Journal* in 2007. But Ailes spoke of the *Journal* as a threat. The paper had no synergy with Fox. Executives noticed that Ailes resented Murdoch's lavish support of the *Journal*'s parent company, Dow Jones, and his friendship with Robert Thomson, the former editor of *The Times* of London whom Murdoch tapped to be publisher of the *Journal*. As Les Hinton, then president of Dow Jones, accompanied Ailes on a tour of the *Journal*'s gleaming new newsroom a few floors above Fox News, Ailes said, "So, you're showing me what I paid for."

In the fall of 2012, Ailes held a meeting with Fox Business executives to discuss whether Fox should sign a content arrangement with Dow Jones. That year, Dow Jones was exiting a long-term partnership with CNBC and was free to sign up with Fox. "Why would I pay them anything?" Ailes said. Neil Cavuto stoked Ailes's fears of a corporate rivalry. "*The Wall Street Journal* is a Trojan horse. They want the business channel," he told Ailes.

Then Ailes largely banned *Journal* reporters from his air. It happened after Ailes learned that *Journal* deputy managing editor Alan Murray, who was steering the *Journal*'s expansion into video production, made a snide comment about Fox. "Alan made the mistake of telling folks how he could make FBN better," the executive said. A few months later, a junior Fox Business staffer mistakenly disclosed the ban to a *Journal* employee. "We had to deny that there ever was a ban. It was so silly," the Fox executive said.

The feeling at the newspaper was mutual. Some *Journal* reporters, whenever they had to bring important sources up to the office, intentionally positioned themselves in front of the screens in the elevators that broadcast Fox News.

After the election debacle, Ailes's position in the company seemed to weaken. By the spring of 2013, Murdoch and senior executives viewed Ailes as a caricature of himself. On issues like gun control and immigration, Murdoch was moving away from Ailes. "Rupert doesn't have a worldview, Roger does," a senior executive said. "Roger said Rupert doesn't understand the threat of China," a senior producer recalled. "Roger doesn't think Rupert understands the threat about the Middle East." In one meeting, Ailes told his team that Murdoch asked him to meet with Saudi prince Alwaleed bin Talal, who was at the time News Corp's second-largest voting shareholder after Murdoch. "Roger said he wouldn't do it," the producer said. "He said it was the only time he told Rupert 'No.' "

Top News Corp brass traded stories of Ailes's paranoia. "He was convinced that the Democratic National Committee had targeted him for assassination," one Murdoch family intimate remarked. "Michelle Obama had come up to him at a dinner and smiled and said, 'I'm surprised to see *you* here.' He took that to mean it was a real threat." Other executives spoke of Ailes's tangles with Joel Klein, the former New York City school chancellor, whom Murdoch hired in November 2010 to launch a for-profit education business. "Roger said, 'The education business is a big mistake. The teachers' unions will *never* let Rupert Murdoch educate their children,' " an executive said. About a year after Klein joined the company, News Corp hired Klein's former spokeswoman, Natalie Ravitz, to serve as Murdoch's chief of staff. Ravitz went to Fox News to introduce herself to Ailes. She reported back to colleagues that her conversation with Ailes went well. Ailes had a different take. "I've just seen that spy!" he later told Chase Carey. "I know she's a Clinton spy and Joel's spy!"

Ailes was more isolated than ever. "Roger doesn't trust anyone around him anymore," an executive said after the election. No one was spared from Ailes's eruptions. He vented constantly about his talent. He complained about *The Five* co-host Andrea Tantaros, who was a former political consultant. "She's pretty, but did she ever get anyone elected, even a dog catcher?" When Gretchen Carlson's name came up, Ailes pointed out she was once Miss America, then added, "It must not have been a good year." Her co-host, Brian Kilmeade, was a "soccer coach from Long Island." Bill O'Reilly was a "book salesman with a TV show."

No one seemed safe, even his longest-serving confidants. On the afternoon of Júly 25, 2013, Ailes called Brian Lewis to his office. News Corp's outside counsel Ronald Green was sitting in the room. Ailes told Lewis to take "a vacation."

"A paid vacation?" Lewis asked.

"*Yeah,*" Ailes said.

Before Lewis walked out of his office, Ailes said to him, "You're one of the best I've *ever* seen. But I'm still better."

Over the next several weeks, Lewis negotiated a separation agreement. On August 20, after talks derailed, Fox released a statement saying that Lewis was terminated for cause, due to "issues relating to financial irregularities" as well as "multiple, material and significant breaches of his employment contract." Ailes cut off Lewis's salary and dispatched Fox executives and personalities to trash Lewis publicly as a turncoat and a nonperson.

Lewis retained powerhouse lawyer Judd Burstein. "People hire Burstein not because they're guilty. They hire him because they're pissed-off!" Lewis told people. On August 27, Burstein fired off a statement to *Gawker,* a move designed to tweak Ailes. "Roger Ailes and Newscorp have a lot more to fear from Brian Lewis telling the truth about them than Brian Lewis has to fear from Roger Ailes and his toadies telling lies about Brian Lewis," it read. "The toadie" was Lewis's well-known nickname for Shine. It was Lewis's way to send a message to Shine that he knew Shine had carried out Ailes's press attacks against him.

The veiled threat brought Ailes to heel. In September, Burstein met with Ronald Green and Peter Johnson Jr. A year earlier, Johnson tried to salvage Lewis's relationship with Ailes. "Brian, you've got to show him some respect," Johnson said. "You and I are like the sons he never had." Later that fall, Fox settled with Lewis for millions. To friends, Lewis expressed relief to be on the outside. He talked about opening a Subway franchise in New Jersey. Lewis had been in the game long enough not to fear the end. "I got whacked," he told a friend.

Even as Lewis and Ailes's longtime relationship collapsed, others close to Ailes continued to profess adulation. When Beth Ailes received an honorary doctorate from Mount Saint Mary College in May 2012, she said in her remarks, "I am the wife of a great man, Roger Ailes." "Roger Ailes is like my second father," Shepard Smith told a journalist that January. "He's one of the greatest men I've ever known. I respect and admire him infinitely." "He changed my life," Sean Hannity said on camera in

March 2013. "I would not be known in American households to whatever extent I might be if he didn't take a chance on me." "Who has been your biggest career influence?" a man asked Megyn Kelly in October 2013 over Twitter. "My boss Roger Ailes," she responded.

A month before the 2012 election, Joe McGinniss thought a lot about Roger. It was a tough time. McGinniss, who had turned seventy, had recently been diagnosed with prostate cancer. Roger was treating him like family. "He said, 'You never have to worry about money. If you get to the point where you can't work anymore, just let me know, I'll write a check.'" Roger made some calls and put him in touch with Dr. Eugene Kwon, one of the country's preeminent specialists for his particular condition. McGinniss was touched by Roger's warm generosity, but also felt sad for his old friend, recalling an episode of *The Sopranos,* the HBO mob drama. "It was the one where Carmela says to Tony: You don't have friends. All those people? They laugh at your jokes, but that's just because you're the boss and they're afraid of you. And he says: What are you talking about?" McGinniss went on, "Then they have a scene later in the show where Tony says a really stupid joke, and all of a sudden, all these guys are going *'Hah hah hah.'* And then it slows down to real slow motion, and you just see Tony looking at their faces with this fake laughter. And he's realizing that, of course, she's absolutely right."

A few days after the 2013 Independence Day parade in Cold Spring, Ailes called Richard Shea to a meeting at *PCN&R* headquarters. He had business to discuss. In June, the conservative Bradley Foundation had awarded Ailes a $250,000 prize for being a "visionary of American journalism" at a gala at the Kennedy Center in Washington. His acceptance speech electrified the faithful with gibes at Obama and the shadowy forces who sought to harm the country. Armed IRS agents, he said, would enforce Obama's health care law at gunpoint. "We must stop waving our extended arms in an effort to balance ourselves as we tiptoe along the edges of the Constitution, in an effort not to upset weak-kneed appeasers with our unflinching belief in the ideas and principles that made our country different and, yes, *better,*" Ailes said. Onstage later that evening, he sang "God Bless America" with a shiny gold medal around his neck and danced.

Ailes told Shea he would donate the prize money to build a senior center in Philipstown. In the conference room at the *PCN&R,* Shea quickly realized that Ailes had other things on his mind besides charitable giving. Shea listened as Roger unloaded a stream-of-consciousness speech about the troubled state of the world, a kind of life reckoning. Ailes said that if he were president, he would solve the immigration problem by sitting the president of Mexico down and giving him a stern talking-to: "Your country is corrupt. You can now only take thirty percent of what the people earn instead of seventy percent. If you don't do that, I'll send the CIA down there to kill you." He had been careful to moderate his immigration position in public. "If I'm going to risk my life to run over the fence to get into America, I want to win. I think Fox News will articulate that," he told *The New Republic* a few months earlier. But Ailes told Shea that as president he would send Navy SEAL trainees to the border as part of a certification program: "I would make it a requirement that you would have to personally kill an illegal immigrant coming into the country. They would have to bring home a dead body."

When Shea brought up Ailes's past, he erupted. "I had nothing to do with Richard Nixon!" Ailes claimed it was Ronald Reagan whom he had been close to.

"Why don't people like me?" Ailes asked Shea. The Navy SEALs loved him. Couldn't people in Philipstown see all that he and Beth had done? Throughout his career, Ailes had wielded generosity as a form of power—he recently said he gave away 10 percent of his annual income—and yet it failed him in his community.

His strongest venom was reserved for Gordon Stewart. "Why do people like him?" Ailes complained to Shea. "He's trying to drive me out of town!" Since Stewart had launched Philipstown.info on July 4, 2010, their feud had escalated. In June 2012, Stewart started a weekly print newspaper, which he slyly called *The Philipstown Paper.* The new *PCN&R* editor asked Stewart if there was a liberal conspiracy behind the venture involving the Hudson Highlands Land Trust or "the Facebook guys," referring to Facebook cofounder Chris Hughes and his husband, Sean Eldridge, who owned an estate in the area. Stewart said no one was backing the paper but himself.

In March 2013, Beth rejected a "Business Person of the Year" award from the Cold Spring Chamber of Commerce because the group asked her to share it with Stewart. "Due to scheduling conflicts and the fact that Gordon Stewart has behaved in an unethical manner toward me, my family and my business, I decided to decline," she said. A few months later, Roger and Beth paid $30,000 to the village of Cold Spring to sponsor the July Fourth fireworks exclusively for three years, outbidding Stewart, who had sponsored them the previous year. Stewart instead funded the music. When the *PCN&R* published a town advertisement thanking the sponsors of the day's festivities, the paper failed to credit Stewart for his contribution. "He's trying to drive my wife's paper out of business!" Ailes told Shea. (As turmoil inside the newsroom intensified, Ailes had transferred ownership of the paper to Beth.) What about competition? Shea asked. Ailes waved off the question. He was engaged in a zero-sum game. "Stewart is doing everything!" Ailes said, even claiming that Stewart was behind a parody website *The Pretend Putnam County News & Recorder*. ("I have nothing to do with it," Stewart later said.) Shea was shaken by Ailes's state. "I have never experienced such expressions of spitting hate," Shea told Stewart a few days later. "I have to tell you that if Roger could kill you, he would do that. The hatred is that deep."

As the conversation ebbed, Ailes warned Shea that there could be consequences if he continued to associate with Stewart. Shea was up for reelection in November. He was popular in town. Republicans had yet to field a challenger. Ailes was running out of patience. "The last time I backed that half-wit," he said, referring to Lee Erickson. "If I go after you this time, I'll knock you out. I'll run for supervisor myself."

Roger Ailes did not jump into the race. Richard Shea won the November election handily, running unopposed. But while Ailes sat it out, he was still stumping to be remembered as a friendly civic father of Philipstown, which was a microcosm, however currently imperfect, of the America he loved. For a man in his business, Ailes is surprisingly sensitive. "He doesn't want to be hated," said a Republican who knows him well. "It really bothers him."

Ailes's campaign to be liked was at odds with his uncompromising vision. "All progress is made by irrational people," he told a journalist in 1989. The statement could well be turned back on Ailes, because he embodied a number of contradictions. He accommodated naive idealism about American life and history alongside profound cynicism about many Americans, from presidents on down. He justified the use of smash-mouth political tactics in the service of protecting his sentimentalized notion of picket-fenced America. He bullied real and perceived enemies, but played the victim when criticized. He could be the most menacing or the funniest, most engaging conversationalist. He decried Manhattan elites, but was one. He entered the journalistic trade, whose practitioners he regularly expresses contempt for. And the starkest contradiction, the one of lasting consequence, is his creation of a "fair and balanced" news network that effectively functioned as an arm of one political party.

In interviews in recent years, Ailes reflected a politician's sense of winning and losing, that the moment is today, and that tomorrow may belong to another. "I don't care about my legacy. It's too late. My enemies will create it and they'll push it," he said a week after the 2012 election. "Right now, everybody thinks I'm the greatest guy in the world," he told another journalist. "The eulogies will be great, but people will be stepping over my body before it gets cold. Within a day or two, everybody will be complaining about what a prick I was and all the things I didn't do for them."

It's a surprisingly open-eyed assessment, both humble and grandiose, but it omits a larger truth. Ailes made his career in a winner-take-all world of 50.1 percent majorities measured by the pull of levers and click of remotes: thumbs up, thumbs down; in or out; like him or hate him. But his career, unlike a campaign, will be judged by both the good and the bad. There are no referenda on a man's legacy.

For four and a half decades, Roger Ailes had directed his candidates from the wings, even if they were half-wits. He played tougher and said the inconvenient truths that no one wanted to hear. He knew it made him hated. "Most of the media in this country would prefer Roger went away," his brother, Robert, said. "Fox News is the beacon of conservatism in the American media. There are an awful lot of people who would like to see Fox News collapse." But it was Ailes's burden to carry, and he was never going to quit: "I can't walk away until I think enough people understand how valuable and how important being an American is."

Near the end of his book, *You Are the Message,* Ailes described an encounter he had with Judy Garland shortly before she died, in 1969. Ailes was not yet thirty. "In her twilight days, Judy was so ill that she often couldn't complete a show. . . . Her voice was almost gone, and she had trouble controlling her vibrato. When I met her, I was so shaken by her voice in rehearsal and her appearance that I couldn't understand why she had such a loyal following," he wrote. "But anyone who saw her in concert understood her magic. The audience identified with her 'humanness.' They identified with her frailties. They understood her vulnerability. When she sang at Carnegie Hall and tried to hit the high notes in 'Over the Rainbow,' twenty-eight hundred people were praying for her to make it."

It was a lesson that applied to his own life. "If you can get the audience to pull for you, you'll always win," Ailes wrote. "After all, audiences are just like you. They're human. They care. They're sympathetic. They're supportive. The audience wants you to succeed. . . . An awareness of your own vulnerability and the vulnerability of others will make you a better and more human communicator. And only a human communicator can become a master communicator."

Roger Ailes was still out on the stage. He had two million Americans rooting for his network. They grew older every day, as he did. Fox News was his best show on his biggest stage yet, but every show has its run.

# ACKNOWLEDGMENTS

One of the paradoxes of publishing a book is that while my byline is on the cover, every word on the page is the product of many hands. Without the generosity of my sources, editors, fact-checkers, family, and friends, I would not be writing this expression of gratitude now.

My principal collaborator was my wife, Jennifer Stahl. In the winter of 2012, after spending five years in the fact-checking department of *The New Yorker,* she left the magazine to work with me full-time on the book. She played a variety of roles as the manuscript took shape, all of which were crucial. As a researcher, she helped track down important interview subjects and documents, and studied thousands of pages of primary source material that detailed formative periods of Roger Ailes's life. She was my closest editor, who helped me conceive the story and the structure of the book. She line-edited the first and subsequent drafts. This book is as much hers as it is mine.

John Homans, my editor at *New York* magazine, did a sophisticated and generous edit to the manuscript over eighteen months, refining the ideas and sharpening the narrative. His gifts as a writer have improved my writing immeasurably, and I can't thank him enough for all his hard work and forbearance. I am also grateful to Adam Moss, *New York*'s editor in chief, for giving me a journalistic home for the past six years and for publishing four cover stories that became the foundation of several chapters of this book. I've learned a lot about reporting and writing from my colleagues at the magazine, who continually inspire me with their journalism.

During the three years it took to report and write this book, my agent, Gail Ross, provided me with intelligent counsel and support. Years before that, she encouraged me to move beyond long-form magazine journalism and pursue book writing. One of her best decisions was steering me to Jonathan Jao, my editor at Random House, who has shared my enthusiasm for the project from the moment he acquired it to the hours we spent working together on the final edits. His incisive notes and cuts were invaluable. I also want to thank Jonathan's colleagues at Random House for their contributions: president Gina Centrello; publisher Susan Kamil; deputy publisher Tom Perry; London King and Barbara Fillon in Publicity; associate general counsel Laura Goldin; production editor Steve Messina; and Jonathan's assistant, Molly Turpin.

Without my team of fact-checkers, Cynthia Cotts and Rob Liguori, this book would not have moved through Random House's publishing system on such a tight deadline. They brought their top credentials to the project, having worked at publications including *The New Yorker, Vanity Fair,* and *The New York Times Magazine*. Cynthia and Rob were dogged reporters in their own right, adding nuance and context to every piece of text they handled.

This book builds on the groundbreaking journalism about Roger Ailes and the News Corporation produced by writers including Kurt Andersen, Julia Angwin, Tim Arango, Ken Auletta, Donald Baer, David Bauder, David Brock, Bryan Burrough, Michael Calderone, John Carmody, David Carr, Bill Carter, John Cassidy, Scott Collins, John Cook, Rebecca Dana, Sarah Ellison, James Ellroy, Steve Fishman, David Folkenflik, Jason Gay, Vanessa Grigoriadis, Lloyd Grove, Joe Hagan, Nancy Hass, Tom Junod, Andrew Neil, Frank Rich, Marshall Sella, Brian Stelter, and Michael Wolff. Tom Junod, of *Esquire,* deserves special thanks for publishing an extended transcript of his 2011 interview with Roger Ailes, which informed the chapter on Ailes's childhood experience. I also want to thank my mentor, Peter Kaplan, the longtime editor in chief of *The New York Observer* who passed away in November 2013 at age fifty-nine. When I was a young reporter covering media at the *Observer,* Peter told me to approach the beat as a *New York Times* reporter would cover the State Department. It's a message I will hold on to. I wrote this book imagining Peter as my reader and I will miss him very much.

Since September 2012, I have been fortunate to be a fellow at the New America Foundation in Washington, D.C. Steve Coll, Anne-Marie Slaughter, Rachel White, Andrés Martinez, Becky Shafer, Kirsten Berg, and Casey Scharf provided generous support and institutional backing for this book.

I am grateful to my friends and family for their patience as I worked to complete this project, including my brother Todd and his wife, Claire, and my sister-in-law Christine and her husband, David. My in-laws, Kermit and Deborah Stahl, were a wellspring of comfort and support, reminding me once again that they have welcomed me into their family like a son. More than anything, this book is a product of the love of my parents, Leonard and Raechelle Sherman. The sacrifices they have made on my behalf, which continued through the writing of this book, have left me with debts I will never repay.

# A NOTE ON SOURCES

This book is based on interviews with 614 people who have worked with Roger Ailes and observed him at close range at various points in his five decades in public life. In addition, I have relied on contemporaneous notes, emails, calendars, letters, court filings, deposition transcripts, corporate documents, White House memoranda, and secondary sources, including videotapes, newspaper clippings, magazine articles, and books. Wherever possible, I have confirmed the facts with a minimum of two sources. Dialogue, as the Pulitzer Prize–winning investigative journalist James B. Stewart has written, is a type of fact, like the color of a wall or the make of a shirt. Where I have detailed the emotional states or thoughts of characters, the descriptions are based on interviews with either the principals themselves or people who had conversations with them about what they thought or felt. Before this book went to press, a team of two fact-checkers, Cynthia Cotts and Rob Liguori, spent a combined 2,098 hours vetting the manuscript for accuracy and context. They did a phenomenal job. Any errors or omissions that remain are my responsibility alone.

Roger Ailes did not participate in this book, notwithstanding my numerous attempts over two and a half years to arrange a sit-down interview. He discouraged sources close to him from speaking with me and went to elaborate lengths to obstruct my reporting. Through surrogates, Ailes attempted to create a counter-narrative about my journalism. "From what I understand, you're preparing a personal dossier about Roger," his attorney, Peter Johnson Jr., told me in December 2011. When I asked to interview Johnson two months later, he threatened legal action. "What the hell am I going to talk to you about? I may wind up suing you, for Christ's sake."

Around the office, Ailes spread odd, inaccurate stories about this book, telling his executives, for instance, that I was being secretly paid by George Soros to write it. "There's a lot of liberal, George Soros money behind him," Ailes told his brother, Robert, who relayed the conversation to me. In 2012 I received a fellowship at the New America Foundation, a nonpartisan think tank based in Washington, D.C., that received .5 percent of its funding from Soros that year. James Pinkerton, a Fox News contributor and former Republican operative, was for years a New America fellow.

Fox News's head of programming, Bill Shine, encouraged Fox personalities to post derogatory comments about me on Twitter. Andrea Tantaros, co-host of *The Five,* tweeted that I was a "harasser" and a "Soros puppet." Sean Hannity called me a "phoney journalist" [*sic*]. Karl Rove wrote about my "disturbing habit of misinterpreting anything Fox News related." In a Foxnews.com column, Fox political analyst Patrick Caddell called me an "embarrassment to the journalistic trade."

Conservative websites also participated in Ailes's campaign. From December 2012 to May 2013, the website *Breitbart News* posted a series of columns, many of them anonymously written, totaling more than 9,250 words that described me as a "Soros-backed attack dog," a "harasser," and a "stalker." On December 21, a *Breitbart* column quoted a "Fox source" saying "Gabe Sherman is Jayson Blair on steroids," a reference to the disgraced former *New York Times* reporter who fabricated articles and abused drugs. As it happened, two days earlier, Bill Shine told Ailes in a meeting that I was like "Jayson Blair." When I asked Shine if he was behind the *Breitbart* smear, he declined to comment.

Another way Ailes sought to shape his narrative was to release his own book. In December 2011, I learned that Ailes was moving forward with his memoir. He wanted to title the book *Fluke,* a riff on his improbable, Horatio Alger career. But shortly after the New Year, Ailes unexpectedly put the memoir on hold. Instead, he invited Zev Chafets, an Israeli-American journalist in his mid-sixties who had recently published a glowing biography of Rush Limbaugh, to write an authorized biography.

Ailes's decision to collaborate with Chafets was at odds with what his PR department told me when I first approached Fox News the previous January about writing this book. I had been covering media full-time for almost a decade, first at *The New York Observer* and then for *The New Republic* and *New York* magazine. In a meeting at the News Corporation cafeteria in January 2011, Brian Lewis and Irena Briganti informed me that Ailes had turned down multiple interview requests from book authors over the years. "You might get a few disgruntled former employees to talk, but that's it," Lewis said. I replied that I would press ahead with my research, and that I remained hopeful that Ailes would eventually speak with me. A few weeks later, Lewis contacted me with good news. Ailes would meet for an off-the-record conversation to discuss the book. But twenty-four hours before our sit-down, Ailes canceled and did not offer an alternative date.

In the spring, Lewis presented me with a condition. Before Ailes even agreed to "think" about speaking with me, Lewis said, I must agree to refrain from using any background quotes or anecdotes that Ailes could consider "negative." I told Lewis that while I agreed that on-the-record sources should be the bedrock of reporting, I could not agree to such a blanket deal, as Ailes might retaliate against people whom he deemed to be disloyal.

In the course of my reporting, I spoke to Ailes twice at public events, both of which encounters were illuminating of his character. On the evening of April 11, 2012, I attended a party hosted by *The Hollywood Reporter* at the Four Seasons restaurant in Midtown Manhattan, where Ailes was being honored along with media industry luminaries such as CBS CEO Les Moonves and *Today* anchor Matt Lauer. As Ailes and his wife, Beth, entered the restaurant's Grill Room, I approached them and introduced myself.

"I don't want to be rude, but you know what? I don't want to talk to you," he said.

"I understand," I replied.

"I don't think you *do* understand," Beth added over his shoulder.

"No, you don't," Roger said. "Look, leave her paper alone. You're harassing her. I don't care what you do to me."

I was taken aback. The subject of my book was Roger, not Beth.

"I'm just a reporter, Mr. Ailes."

"No, no, no. You're a *harasser,*" he shot back.

"Roger, he's got his recorder on," Beth interjected, then looked at me. "You're trying to make a *buck* off my husband."

"Your entire premise is *wrong,*" Roger added, referring to a cover story I wrote for *New York* magazine in May 2011 that revealed Ailes's efforts to shape the 2012 GOP field. "I'm not going to go into it. But I am going to tell you—leave her alone. Leave her *alone*."

They walked off, and I ventured to the other side of the room. Half an hour passed. I didn't think I'd see Ailes again that evening and began to make my way toward the exit. A bottleneck around the bar prevented me from moving very far. Then, out of the corner of my eye, I saw Ailes barreling toward me. At first, I thought he must be walking to see someone else, but his eyes locked on mine. "Listen, your entire premise is wrong. It is just flat wrong," he said, shaking his arms.

"What do you mean, Roger?"

"I'm not going to get into it. I'm just not." He was speaking loudly now and people began to look our way. In front of us, CBS president David Rhodes was talking with Moonves and *60 Minutes* correspondent Steve Kroft. Rhodes excused himself from his conversation and approached us.

"David, how ya doing?" Ailes said, then addressed me. "You know, I have a present for you. Barbara Walters is back there. She says she'll talk to you for your book."

"Great, I'd love to speak with her. I've been trying to for months," I said.

"But you won't want to talk with her because she'll only say *nice* things about me," Ailes said.

"Listen, I don't want to get in the middle of any of this," Rhodes said.

"No, stay here," Ailes barked.

"Well," Rhodes said, "you know what Mike Wallace said once"—the veteran *60 Minutes* anchor had passed away earlier that week—"'You know when people say nice things about you? When you die.'"

Rhodes's stab at humor did not lift Ailes's mood. Ailes took a step back. It was unclear now who he was addressing. "Let's look at this for a minute: Sarah Palin? She couldn't get elected to *anything*. Huckabee? He says to me, 'I couldn't raise a nickel.' Santorum? When we hired him, no one, I mean *no one*, knew who this guy was. And Gingrich has been working here for a long time. So the idea that I'm somehow propping up these candidates is just absurd."

"Roger, I want to incorporate your point of view," I replied.

"No!" Ailes snapped. He pointed to Rhodes. "You're witnessing this! You're a witness! This is *not* an interview."

Ailes spun around and headed off toward his table. "You don't think if I wanted to I couldn't get back into politics?" he said, looking back. He stopped in the middle of the room, where I caught up with him. "And what's it with you going to Warren? I left there in 1958. Anything that anyone says there about me is *wrong*. They don't know me."

"I went to Warren because I wanted to figure out where you came from. You talk a lot about how you program Fox for all the small towns that have been left behind by the media."

"That's right. Well, you can write whatever you want. It's because of people like me that you have the freedom to do what you do. You have freedom of the press because I defend it every day."

He took a few more steps. "Okay, kid, that's all I got. You're a good reporter, but you're wrong. You don't get me."

I decided to leave. Bill O'Reilly was standing alone near the way out. I walked up to him. His air was as frosty as his boss's. "I know who you are. I have *nothing* to say to you," he said.

At the coat check, I bumped into Roger and Beth. "Mr. Ailes, thank you for speaking with me. I'll see you down in North Carolina." As it happened, I was flying there the next morning to see Ailes give a speech at the University of North Carolina. "Yeah, I know," he said. "I've been trying to figure out a way to have you barred. But it's a public event."

Ailes did not speak to me in North Carolina, but I encountered him briefly fourteen months later, on the evening of June 12, 2013, in Washington, D.C. I was invited as a member of the press to attend a ceremony at the Kennedy Center, where Ailes was being celebrated by the conservative Bradley Foundation. When I arrived, a young man wearing a blue blazer and a bow tie offered to show me into the reception. He asked me my name as we walked down a long corridor. When I answered, his demeanor changed. "I know who you are," he said. I asked him his, but he did not respond. Instead, he quickened his pace.

In the reception hall, I saw the young man slalom through the crowd to the far side of the room. He approached Ailes, who was standing with his bodyguard. Ailes's face tightened. His head turned left and right as he scanned his surroundings.

After a few moments, Ailes, the young man, and the bodyguard walked in my direction. I asked Ailes if he would have time to speak. His bodyguard pushed me aside. Ailes was several steps ahead of me when I regained my balance. He spun around and said, "I don't mean to be rude, but this is a family night!" He turned to the young man in the bow tie. "Zachary, where's your mother?"

Despite Ailes's concerted efforts at obstruction, many of his closest colleagues, friends, family members, and business rivals did speak to me at length and offered candid accounts of their firsthand experiences with Ailes. A large number of these people spoke on the record. Many others, however, asked to speak with me on a not-for-attribution background basis. I granted sources anonymity in instances where they expressed credible fear for their professional livelihood. It was not an uncommon occurrence for me to hear things from sources like the following remark one prominent Fox personality made: "It would totally destroy my life if it gets out that I'm talking to you. If he even thought I *knew* you, he'd see it as a personal betrayal." Other sources expressed concern that Ailes might be having me followed by private investigators and that my phone might be bugged and my computer hacked.

While Roger Ailes did not grant me a sit-down interview, I strove to reflect his point of view throughout this book. I relied on the thousands of quotes he has given to the press over the years on a wide array of subjects, from his childhood to his thoughts on religion, politics, and culture. Although he may not have intended it, Ailes's confrontational response to the reporting of this book was as revealing as any comment he would have made in the course of an extended interview. It confirmed one of the defining aspects of his career: he had amassed power by harnessing television to control the images of politicians and media personalities. And so it made sense that he would seek the same degree of influence over the story he cared about most: his own.

# NOTES

## EPIGRAMS

ix *"An institution"* Ralph Waldo Emerson in his essay "Self-Reliance."

ix *"Television rarely, if ever"* Roger Ailes, "Candidate + Money + Media = Votes" (transcript of speech), Town Hall of California, June 8, 1971, Nixon Presidential Library and Museum.

## PROLOGUE: "THE MOST POWERFUL MAN IN THE WORLD"

xi **On the evening of December 7** A government official familiar with the guest list. See also http://www.whitehouse.gov/files/docs/Holidays-at-the-White-House-2011.pdf.

xi **When asked by** Tom Junod, "Why Does Roger Ailes Hate America?," *Esquire,* Feb. 2011.

xii **"It's a shame a man"** Joe McGinniss, *The Selling of the President: The Classic Account of the Packaging of a Candidate,* reprint edition (New York: Penguin, 1988), 63. See also Tim Dickinson, "How Roger Ailes Built the Fox News Fear Factory," *Rolling Stone,* May 25, 2011.

xii **"I never had"** Hoover Institution, "Fox and More with Roger Ailes" (video interview), *Uncommon Knowledge with Peter Robinson,* Feb. 5, 2010, http://www.hoover.org/multimedia/uncommon-knowledge/26681.

xii **"Roger was born for television"** Author interview with author Joe McGinniss.

xii **More than anyone** In his interview on *Uncommon Knowledge,* Ailes said that he spotted this trend early in his career, as he worked for a wildly popular television variety program. At the 5:07 mark, he notes, "I produced *The Mike Douglas Show* back in the sixties, so I had a sense of audience. In fact, we began in that show to use politicians' wives. We filmed in Hubert Humphrey's home. We had his wife, Muriel, on as a co-host. So I had a sense of what was going to happen in television. That there would be a mixture of entertainment, information, politics. It's all one now."

xii **"Politics is power"** David Nyhan, "Roger Ailes: He Doctors a Politician's TV Image," *Boston Globe,* May 3, 1970.

xii **"The difference between"** Lloyd Grove, "The Image Shaker; Roger Ailes, the Bush Team's Wily Media Man," *Washington Post,* June 20, 1988.

xii **"A couple of weeks"** Nyhan, "Roger Ailes: He Doctors a Politician's TV Image."
xii **"It's not that I eat"** Junod, "Why Does Roger Ailes Hate America?"
xii **During the 1988** Tom Mathews and Peter Goldman, *The Quest for the Presidency: The 1988 Campaign* (New York: Simon & Schuster, 1989), 191.
xiii **"Photo editors are sadistic"** Grove, "The Image Shaker; Roger Ailes, the Bush Team's Wily Media Man."
xiii **"I'm never going"** Author interview with former Ailes deputy and comedy teacher Stephen Rosenfield.
xiii **"I think I'll lead"** Nyhan, "Roger Ailes: He Doctors a Politician's TV Image."
xiii **"Revolutionaries"** Ibid.
xiii **"A lot of the time"** Email comment from CBS News president David Rhodes.
xiii **"People need to be reminded"** Author interview with a person familiar with the matter.
xiii **A few days after** Author interview with a person familiar with the matter.
xiii **Obama's victory** Author interview with a person familiar with the matter.
xiii **"When he started the channel"** Author interview with a former senior executive at Fox News.
xiv **Ailes's battle did not end** Author interviews with residents of Philipstown, New York.
xiv **Ailes even told his advisers** Author interview with a person familiar with the matter.
xiv **During a forty-five-minute** Author interview with a person familiar with the matter.
xiv **"I see the most powerful man"** Author interview with a person familiar with the matter. On the same night Ailes was meeting Obama, Sean Hannity was turning the White House Christmas party into another data point in Fox's narrative about Obama. He talked with two Fox personalities about the party: Sandra Smith, a young anchor for the Fox Business Channel, and Monica Crowley, the conservative radio host who was once an assistant to Richard Nixon in the 1990s.

"You're saying that there was a party for the media people at the White House tonight?" Hannity said to the women.

"Yes, and I can't believe none of us got invited," Crowley commented. "It's so lame—"

"Why aren't we there?" Smith said.

"Wait a minute. Did *anyone* get to go?" Hannity asked.

"Uh, well, *certain* media organizations—" Crowley said.

"No, but, did anyone from *Fox* go?" Hannity said.

"I don't know, but none of *us* are there. Cuz we're workin', tellin' the truth about Obama," she said.

"I didn't get an invitation. I have *never* gotten an invitation," Hannity complained. "And I saw all the liberal media at Bush's—I went to *one* party in eight years when Bush was there and all the liberals showed up."

"Yes, and us conservatives continue to get nixed by this White House," Crowley said.

"Did *anybody* from Fox get an invitation?" Hannity repeated.

"*Tsss*, you know, I don't know—" Smith said.

"We don't know, either," Hannity added.

"Maybe we will hear about it tomorrow, though," Smith continued.

"It will be interesting," Hannity said. "We will see."

xv **In 2002, Fox passed CNN** Jim Rutenberg, "MEDIA: Gazing into 2003: The Balance of Media Power Is Poised to Change—Cable News; At CNN, Hoping for Restored Glory," *New York Times*, Dec. 30, 2002. See also Carr and Arango, "A Fox Chief at the Pinnacle of Media and Politics."
xv **In 2012, a Wall Street analyst** Merrill Knox, "Estimated Fair-Market Value of

Fox News at $12.4B," *TVNewser*, Feb. 6, 2012, http://www.mediabistro.com/tvnewser/estimated-fair-market-value-of-fox-news-12-4_b110790.

xv **"No one could rein Ailes in"** Author interview with a person familiar with the matter.

xv **"He's paranoid"** Author interview with a person familiar with the matter.

xv **In 2008, Murdoch even contemplated** Gabriel Sherman, "The Elephant in the Green Room," *New York*, May 22, 2011.

xv **Murdoch promised Ailes** Matea Gold, "Roger Ailes Extends Fox Deal," *Los Angeles Times*, Nov. 21, 2008.

xvi **In September, the *Post*** "Post Endorses John McCain," *New York Post*, Sept. 8, 2008.

xvi **In 2010, Murdoch cut off** Carr and Arango, "A Fox Chief at the Pinnacle of Media and Politics." Freud released the quotation after getting into a dispute with Murdoch. Freud lobbied Murdoch to kill a story in the *New York Post* about a client of his PR firm, Pepsi CEO Indra Nooyi. Murdoch dismissed Freud's requests. On the morning of January 10, 2010, Freud sent an email to Murdoch's BlackBerry informing him of his payback: "I've given a quote to the New York Times, and you're probably not going to like it."

xvi **"He's a fucking dope"** Author interview with a person familiar with the matter.

xvi **"They all hate me"** Author interview with a person familiar with the matter.

xvi **"He was delighted it was happening"** Author interview with a person familiar with the matter.

xvi **He openly bad-mouthed** Author interview with a person familiar with the matter.

xvi **"I *want* to elect the next"** Author interview with a person familiar with the matter.

xvi **"Every single candidate"** Author interview with a national Republican official.

xvi **Although Ailes told one Fox contributor** Sherman, "The Elephant in the Green Room."

xvii **"He finds flaws"** Author interview with a person close to Roger Ailes.

xvii **In a meeting at Fox News** Author interview with a person familiar with the matter.

xvii **"To be clear"** Darren Samuelsohn, "Huntsman on Evolution, Warming: 'Call Me Crazy,'" *Politico*, Aug. 18, 2011, http://www.politico.com/news/stories/0811/61656.html.

xvii **After finishing third** Jim Rutenberg and Jeff Zeleny, "Huntsman Says He's Quitting G.O.P. Race," "The Caucus" (blog), *New York Times*, Jan. 15, 2012, http://thecaucus.blogs.nytimes.com/2012/01/15/huntsman-says-hes-quitting-g-o-p-race/.

xvii **Over the course of his candidacy** "The Fox Primary: 8 Months, 12 Candidates, 604 Appearances, 4644 Minutes," *Media Matters for America*, Feb. 27, 2012, http://mediamatters.org/blog/2012/02/27/the-fox-primary-8-months-12-candidates-604-appe/185876.

xvii **pizza mogul Herman Cain** "The Fox Primary: 8 Months, 12 Candidates, 604 Appearances, 4644 Minutes."

xvii **Ailes twice encouraged the brash New Jersey** Sherman, "The Elephant in the Green Room."

xvii **Ailes also sent an emissary** Bob Woodward, "Fox Chief Proposed Petraeus Campaign," *Washington Post*, Dec. 4, 2012. See also "Petraeus in 2011 Fox News Interview: 'I'm Not Running for President' " (audio), *Washington Post*, Dec. 3, 2012, http://www.washingtonpost.com/posttv/lifestyle/style/petraeus-in-2011-fox-news-interview-im-not-running-for-president/2012/12/03/c0aa0c72-3d6d-11e2-a2d9-822f58ac9fd5_video.html.

xvii **From the start, he'd been lukewarm** Author interviews with Fox news executives.

xvii **Ailes told Romney once** Howard Kurtz, "Roger's Reality Show," *Newsweek*, Sept. 25, 2011.

xvii **In another conversation** Author interview with a person familiar with the matter.

xvii **He told one Fox host** Author interview with a person familiar with the matter.

xvii **"Romney's gotta rip"** Author interview with a person familiar with the matter.

xvii **"Roger was running a political campaign"** Author interview with a person close to Roger Ailes.

xviii **On the morning** Excerpts from the *Fox & Friends* retrospective can be found on YouTube. See http://www.youtube.com/watch?v=Cq26qtY8Muo and http://www.youtube.com/watch?v=tmVXmO7RomI.

xviii **The video was Ailes's brainchild** Author interview with a person familiar with the matter.

xviii **Fox pulled the clip** "What the Fox," *Hotline,* May 31, 2012.

xviii **"Roger was not aware"** Brian Stelter, "Obama Video on Fox Criticized as Attack Ad," "Media Decoder" (blog), *New York Times,* May 30, 2012, http://mediadecoder.blogs.nytimes.com/2012/05/30/obama-video-on-fox-news-criticized-as-attack-ad/.

xviii **Senior adviser David Axelrod** Author interview with a person familiar with the matter.

xviii **"Fox is watched"** Michael D. Shear, "Aides Play Down Romney's Talk on Taxes for Wealthy," *New York Times,* April 17, 2012.

xix **In the year after** Jeremy W. Peters, "Enemies and Allies for 'Friends,'" *New York Times,* June 21, 2012.

xix **So when Gretchen Carlson** Fox News interview with Mitt Romney (transcript), Federal News Service, May 24, 2012.

xix **In August** Solange Uwimana, "Fox Runs Montage Splicing Together Quotes from Paul Ryan and Ronald Reagan," *Media Matters for America,* Aug. 14, 2012, http://mediamatters.org/blog/2012/08/14/fox-runs-montage-splicing-together-quotes-from/189345.

xix **Behind the scenes** Author interview with a person familiar with the matter. In an email, a spokesperson for Ryan said, "Congressman Ryan has known Jon Kraushar for a couple of years but he didn't recall Mr. Ailes introducing the two of them."

xix **After the 1968 campaign** Nyan, "Roger Ailes: He Doctors a Politician's TV Image."

xix **"Roger is Fox News"** Author interview with *Newsmax* editor in chief Christopher Ruddy.

xix **"Every single element"** Author interview with consultant Ed Rollins.

xx **Not long before the 2012** Junod, "Why Does Roger Ailes Hate America?"

xx **"I built this channel"** Carr and Arango, "A Fox Chief at the Pinnacle of Media and Politics."

xx **"At his daily 8:00 a.m."** Author interview with an executive who has attended the meetings.

# ACT I

## ONE: "JUMP ROGER, *JUMP*"

3 **The town** Henry Howe, *Historical Collections of Ohio: An Encyclopedia of the State,* Vol. 2, (Cincinnati: C. J. Krehbiel and Company, 1908), 669–70.

3 **In 1890, two sons** Dennis Adler, *Packard* (St. Paul, Minn.: Motorbooks International, 2004), 11–15. Also: http://packardmuseum.org/ed1.aspx.

3 **In 1932, the General Motors** "A. Wolcott Dies, Auto Parts Maker; Head of Packard Electric Co., Manufacturers of Cables," *New York Times,* Oct. 14, 1933.

3 **Roger's father, who had been** Entry for Robert Eugene Ailes, created by his son, Robert Ailes Jr., on Findagrave.com.

4 **In 1936, Neil Armstrong** James R. Hansen, *First Man: The Life of Neil A. Armstrong* (New York: Simon & Schuster, 2012), 45–46.

4 **That was the world** Roger's birth date is given in his parents' divorce papers: *Donna M. Ailes v. Robert E. Ailes,* Trumbull County (Ohio) Court of Common Pleas, Division of Domestic Relations, Case 5396, Oct. 7, 1959.

4 **Warren residents** *Warren* (Ohio) *Tribune Chronicle,* April 20, 1954.

4 **"There were no slums"** Author interview with television executive Launa Newman-Minson. At the time she went to school and worked with Ailes, she went by her maiden name, Launa Newman.

4 **Packard** "Employment Hits New High of 6000: All-Time Mark Exceeds Both War-Time and Post-War Peaks, Further Growth Expected," *Cablegram,* March 23, 1953, National Packard Museum.

4 **sponsored annual picnics** See, for instance, "Packard Family Picnic Program" and "18,000 Attend Picnic; Ruth Drenski Wins Top Prize," *Cablegram,* July 1955, National Packard Museum.

4 **The career of Roger's father** Author interview with Robert Ailes Jr. *Cablegram* also identifies Robert Ailes as "foreman, Maintenance Dept" in an article mentioning Roger Ailes, "Employes' [*sic*] Sons Get Collegiate Honors," ca. 1959–1960.

4 **He raised his children** Author interview with Robert Ailes Jr.

4 **He worked for forty years** Entry for Robert Eugene Ailes, created by his son, Robert Ailes Jr., on Findagrave.com.

4 **Growing up in the 1920s** Author interview with Robert Ailes Jr.

4 **"I never could understand"** Ibid.

4 **Rapid industrialization** William D. Jenkins, *Steel Valley Klan: The Ku Klux Klan in Ohio's Mahoning Valley* (Kent, Ohio: Kent State University Press, 1990), 57–58.

4 **One minister** Ibid., 58.

4 **As an adult** Entry for Robert Eugene Ailes, created by his son Robert Ailes Jr., on Findagrave.com.

5 **As a Master Mason** The full title of the affiliated body is Mystic Order of Veiled Prophets of Enchanted Realm, Ali Baba Grotto.

5 **His wife complained** *Donna M. Ailes v. Robert E. Ailes,* Trumbull County (Ohio) Court of Common Pleas, Division of Domestic Relations, Case 5396, March 18, 1960.

5 **"One of his disappointments"** Author interview with Robert Ailes Jr.

5 **Robert Sr. and his wife** Ibid.

5 **She had come to Warren** Entry for Donna Marie Cunningham [Ailes] Urban, created by her son, Robert Ailes Jr., on Findagrave.com.

5 **Her father** Entry for James Arley Cunningham, created by his grandson Robert Ailes Jr., on Findagrave.com.

5 **He was a religious man** Author interview with Robert Ailes Jr.

5 **"They didn't believe in movies or dancing"** Deroy Murdock, "This Is the Most Powerful Man in News," *Newsmax,* Nov. 2011.

5 **Robert and Donna had a swift** Author interview with Robert Ailes Jr.

5 **At the age of two** Ibid.

5 **"Well, you died"** Junod, "Why Does Roger Ailes Hate America?"

5 **"The treatment"** Author interview with Robert Ailes Jr.

5 **The average life** Robert A. Zaiden, MD, "Hemophilia A," http://emedicine.medscape.com/article/779322-overview#aw2aab6b2b6aa.

5 **In grade school** Tom Junod, "Roger Ailes on Roger Ailes: The Interview Transcripts, Part 2," The Politics Blog, *Esquire,* Jan. 27, 2011, http://www.esquire.com/blogs/politics/roger-ailes-quotes-5072437.

6 **His father rushed him** Author interview with Robert Ailes Jr.

6 **"I heard the doctor say"** Ibid.

6 **Robert Jr.** Author interview with Robert Ailes Jr.

6 **"Look, my son's bleeding"** Junod, "Roger Ailes on Roger Ailes: The Interview Transcripts, Part 2."

6 **"Get behind me"** Ibid.

6 **Dirty Neck Watson** Ibid.

6 **"Well, son"** Ibid.

6 **"Roger told me"** Author interview with Launa Newman-Minson.

6 **During recess** Junod, "Why Does Roger Ailes Hate America?"

6 **"He participated"** Author interview with Robert Ailes Jr.

6 **"What saved me"** Junod, "Roger Ailes on Roger Ailes: The Interview Transcripts, Part 2."

6 **"My dad, I saw"** Ibid.

6 **"violence never solves"** Lloyd Grove, "The Image Shaker; Roger Ailes, the Bush Team's Wily Media Man," *Washington Post,* June 20, 1988.

6 **"if you have to"** Ibid.

6 **if you have no options** Junod, "Why Does Roger Ailes Hate America?"

7 **"Roger and my dad"** Author interview with Robert Ailes Jr.

7 **One time** Junod, "Roger Ailes on Roger Ailes: The Interview Transcripts, Part 2."

7 **"When I was thirteen"** Ibid.

7 **When Roger was recovering** Ken Auletta, "Vox Fox: How Roger Ailes and Fox News Are Changing Cable News," *New Yorker,* May 26, 2003.

7 **The cruelest lesson** Author interview with Stephen Rosenfield.

8 **Robert Sr. demanded quiet** Author interview with Robert Ailes Jr.

8 **"I was terrified"** Junod, "Roger Ailes on Roger Ailes: The Interview Transcripts, Part 2."

8 **Years later the brothers learned** Author interview with Robert Ailes Jr.

8 **On the 1930 census** "United States Census, 1930," index and images, Sadie H. Ailes (Warren, Trumbull, Ohio), FamilySearch. In reality, her husband, Melville, had married another woman on July 24, 1922. See "Michigan Marriages, 1868–1925," index and images, Melville Ailes (1922), FamilySearch.

8 **When Robert Jr.** In college, Robert Ailes Jr. went by himself to meet his grandfather for the first time. Melville was living in Sidney, Ohio, suffering from Alzheimer's. "We had dinner," Robert recalled. "He wasn't alert then. When I met him, he didn't realize who I was." After the meal, Robert went to the house of his great-aunt Helen, a history teacher, who told him family stories at the kitchen table late into the night. The experience instilled in Robert a lifelong interest in genealogy. He would go on to write an unpublished family history. "The first Ailes came to this country in 1700. Brothers William and Stephen Ailes. They were the first Ailes in America," Robert said. "They settled in Pennsylvania. They were farmers, and the funny part was, they married two sisters by the name of Underwood. William's first child was William Underwood Jr. Roger and I are descended from him." The Aileses participated in many of the founding myths of America: escaping religious persecution in Europe, living the frontier log cabin life in the Midwest, serving valorously in the military, helping to build the country. William Jr.'s son, Moses Hoffman Ailes, was the first Ailes in Ohio. A veteran of the War of 1812, Moses brought his family to Shelby County, Ohio, forty miles from the Indiana border in 1842. There they bought a farm from a hunchbacked man named Daniel Baldwin. (Neighbors gave him the nickname Sassafras because, according to a local history, he carried a basket of the medicinal root from house to house to "purify and thin the blood of our people grown thick and sluggish by too substantial food and lack of exercise.") They lived on the farm for seven years before Montra, the nearest settlement, was surveyed. In August 1862, Moses's youngest surviving son, Hezekiah, went off to fight for the Union. Two years later, he was shot in the shoulder

at the Battle of Resaca, Georgia, where 112 out of 220 men in his regiment were killed or wounded in a five-minute salvo. Because of his bravery in the battle, he was promoted from the rank of sergeant to sergeant major. After the war, he returned to Shelby County and lived out his years teaching and holding political offices. He was a justice of the peace, a county auditor, and a three-term mayor of Sidney, Ohio. A history of the area remarked that "few can look back upon a busier and more blissful domestic and public life replete with honors." His older brother Alfred Ailes—Roger's great-great-grandfather—was a successful farmer and businessman. In April 1852, Alfred married Melissa Jane Young, the daughter of a Methodist Episcopal revivalist, a month before her seventeenth birthday. They worked on a farm for fifteen years—the dirt lane that winds by it is still known as Ailes Road. In 1868, they moved into Montra, where Alfred bought a half interest in a steam sawmill. By this time, Montra was a growing frontier outpost. It had a hotel, a liquor store, and a blacksmith shop. Like Hezekiah, Alfred was a civic leader and a member of the Democratic Party. From 1870 until his death in 1882, he served as a justice of the peace. A chronicle of the area noted that Alfred "was a man of importance." On May 19, 1858, Alfred's oldest son, John Forsythe Ailes, was born in Franklin Township, in the center of Shelby County. John continued the upward trajectory of the Ailes family in America. A bright man, he was the first in his family to attend college. He enrolled at Southern Ohio University. He married a schoolteacher named Rebecca Lovina Drumm who hailed from Hardin County. John taught school for thirty-two years and oversaw the remaining eighty acres of his family's farm. John, like his father, was a prominent, politically active member of his community. "In politics he is democrat," an area history noted, "of that school which prefers the doctrines of the fathers, based on the experience of the ages, to the untried theories of innovators." John served for three years as deputy auditor for the county and for one year as deputy probate judge. For eight years, he was clerk of Jackson Township and also served as a board member of the county school examiners. For two decades, John frequented the local Odd Fellows hall and rose to leadership in the fraternal organization. He represented Ohio's thirty-seventh district for four years. John and Rebecca raised three boys and a girl. Two became teachers, and two became doctors. Their first son, Melville Darwin Ailes—Roger's grandfather—was born on April 17, 1883. Melville earned three advanced degrees, the highest level of education of any member of the Ailes family. He first studied at Ohio Northern University, graduating around 1905 with a bachelor's degree and a law degree. Around this time, Melville married Sarah Hortense McMurray, a schoolteacher and Ohio Northern graduate, whom friends called Sadie. She was seven years his senior. Melville and Sadie had three children in quick succession. Roger's father, Robert Eugene, was the middle child. He was born in 1907 in Springfield, Ohio. The primary sources for this genealogy are interviews with Robert Ailes Jr., A. B. C. Hitchcock's *History of Shelby County, Ohio, and Representative Citizens* (Chicago: Richmond-Arnold Publishing, 1913), *History of Shelby County, Ohio with Illustrations and Biographical Sketches of Some of Its Prominent Men and Pioneers* (Philadelphia: R. Sutton & Co., 1883), as well as birth, death, and marriage records on Ancestry.com.

8 **Robert Jr. did not tell** Author interview with Robert Ailes Jr.

8 **died, after suffering** Entry for Melville Darwin Ailes, created by his grandson Robert Ailes Jr., on Findagrave.com.

8 **Donna was a competitive** Author interview with Robert Ailes Jr.

9 **Roger remembered her hugging him** Junod, "Roger Ailes on Roger Ailes: The Interview Transcripts, Part 2."

9 **There was not much** Author interview with Robert Ailes Jr.

9 **"It was clear"** Junod, "Roger Ailes on Roger Ailes: The Interview Transcripts, Part 2."

9 **"The more she'd hound"** Author interview with Robert Ailes Jr.
9 **"He analyzed it"** Ibid.
9 **In 1940, the year Roger** O.E.D. Jr., "Mr. Hoover Televiewed," *New York Times,* June 30, 1940.
9 **Seven years later** Samuel A. Tower, "Truman Calls on Nation to Forego Meat Tuesdays, Poultry, Eggs Thursdays," *New York Times,* Oct. 6, 1947.
9 **Between 1950 and 1951** Richard Sutch and Susan B. Carter, eds., *Historical Statistics of the United States: Millennial Edition* (Cambridge, U.K.: Cambridge University Press, 2006), Vol. 4, 977–98. The statistic appears in "Communications," a contribution by economist Alexander J. Field.
9 ***Gunsmoke*** Nancy Hass, "Embracing the Enemy," *New York Times Magazine,* Jan. 8, 1995.
9 **"I liked to get"** William Alcorn, "Fox News Chairman Ailes Comes Home, Discusses Obama's Tasks," *Vindicator,* Nov. 11, 2008.
9 **One of those fellow actors** Author interview with Robert Ailes, Jr.
10 **"He sat down"** Author interview with Warren resident Kent Fusselman.
10 **Launa Newman developed an instant connection** Author interview with Launa Newman-Minson.
10 **Before graduating, Roger** Author interview with Warren resident Bernice Marino.
10 **"Father did not encourage"** Ibid.
10 **Once, when Roger** Auletta, "Vox Fox."
10 **During his prime earning years** *Donna M. Ailes v. Robert E. Ailes,* Trumbull County (Ohio) Court of Common Pleas, Division of Domestic Relations, Case 5396, Oct. 7, 1959.
10 **To make some extra money** Author interview with Robert Ailes Jr.
10 **"The poor guy"** Grove, "The Image Shaker; Roger Ailes, the Bush Team's Wily Media Man."
10 **When it came time to buy** *Donna M. Ailes v. Robert E. Ailes,* Trumbull County (Ohio) Court of Common Pleas, Division of Domestic Relations, Case 5396, March 18, 1960.
10 **"He tried hard"** Author interview with Robert Ailes Jr.
10 **"All I wanted to do"** Grove, "The Image Shaker; Roger Ailes, the Bush Team's Wily Media Man."
11 **After landing a job** Donald Baer, "Roger Rabid," *Manhattan, Inc.,* Sept. 1989.
11 **One day, in the spring** Junod, "Roger Ailes on Roger Ailes: The Interview Transcripts, Part 2."
11 **"It felt like a picture-perfect"** Author interview with Ohio University alumnus Arthur Nolletti.
11 **Students went for hayrides** See, for instance, *Athena,* 1959 (Ohio University yearbook), 32.
12 **During Ailes's sophomore year** *The Post* (Ohio University), May 19, 1960.
12 **The handbook** 1958–1959 Student Handbook, Ohio University, Athens, Ohio.
12 **A caption** *Athena,* 1959 (Ohio University yearbook), 9.
12 **In December 1959** Wesley M. Stevens, "Beatniks Protested at Fireside Group," *Athens Messenger,* Dec. 30, 1959.
12 **He wanted to join the military** Tom Hodson, *Conversations from Studio B* (interview with Roger Ailes at 4:18), WOUB Public Media, Ohio University, May 20, 2012. http://woub.org/2012/05/20/fox-news-chairman-and-ceo-roger-ailes.
12 **In a certain sense** Playbill, Ohio University, Athens, Ohio.
12 **"I was hammered all the time"** Marshall Sella, "The Red-State Network," *New York Times,* June 24, 2001.
12 **"I skipped a lot of classes"** Roger Ailes interview with Brian Lamb on C-Span, Dec. 19, 2004.

12 **Ailes's starting position** Hodson, *Conversations from Studio B* (interview with Roger Ailes, at 4:40).

12 **He then hosted** Author interview with Ohio University alumnus Donald Hylkema. (On-air, Hylkema used the pseudonym Don Mathews.) See also Hodson, *Conversations from Studio B* (interview with Roger Ailes, at 7:42, 8:10).

12 **Vincent Jukes, a stout** Author interview with former WOUB station manager Frank Youngwerth.

13 **One day, he concocted** Author interview with Donald Hylkema.

13 **Archie Greer** Jaine Wyatt, "Archie Greer," *Athens* (Ohio) *News*, Jan. 4, 2010.

13 **Unlike Jukes** Author interviews with WOUB students.

13 **"Archie was probably the first person"** Roger Ailes remarks at dedication of Roger E. Ailes Newsroom, Ohio University, April 24, 2008.

13 **By the end** Author interviews with WOUB students. *Cablegram* noted in an article titled "Employes' [*sic*] Sons Get Collegiate Honors" that "Roger Ailes, a sophomore at Ohio University, Athens, Ohio, was named station manager of WOUB, the university's radio station. It was reported that this is the first time a sophomore student has been named to the position."

13 **Ailes was soon selected** *Cablegram* reported that Ailes was also "named the outstanding sophomore in radio-television by the local chapter of Alpha Epsilon Rho." See also *Athena*, 1962 (Ohio University yearbook), 215.

13 **"We were sort of afraid"** Author interview with Ohio University alumnus Mike Adams.

13 **When school was in session** Hodson, *Conversations from Studio B* (interview with Roger Ailes, at 5:40).

13 **He was often** Ibid., at 11:30.

13 **During one summer** Author interview with Donald Hylkema.

13 **Without telling his classmates** Hodson, *Conversations from Studio B* (interview with Roger Ailes, at 10:12). According to *Broadcasting*, Ailes was also the program director for WMPO in 1962. ("Week's Profile: How to Change Debate Loser to Arena Winner," *Broadcasting*, Nov. 11, 1968, 101). For the pseudonym "Dick Summers," see Nadine Brozan, "Chronicle," *New York Times*, April 2, 1993.

13 **"He didn't let anyone"** Author interview with Donald Hylkema.

13 **"He did not display"** Author interview with Don Swaim.

13 **"I remember when he told me"** Author interview with Ohio University alumnus Bill Klokow.

13 **"Control was extremely important"** Author interview with Donald Hylkema.

14 **"The thing is about hemophiliacs"** Author interview with Robert Ailes Jr.

14 **Her amended divorce petition** Amended Petition, *Donna M. Ailes v. Robert E. Ailes*, Trumbull County (Ohio) Court of Common Pleas, Division of Domestic Relations, Case 5396, March 18, 1960.

14 **The original complaint** Petition, *Donna M. Ailes v. Robert E. Ailes*, Trumbull County (Ohio) Court of Common Pleas, Division of Domestic Relations, Case 5396, Oct. 7, 1959.

14 **temporary restraining order** Journal entry, Judge Bruce Henderson, Trumbull County (Ohio) Court of Common Pleas, Division of Domestic Relations, Oct. 8, 1959.

15 **"I got a call"** Junod, "Roger Ailes on Roger Ailes: The Interview Transcripts, Part 2."

15 **"It affected Roger"** Author interview with Robert Ailes Jr.

15 **On April 27** Journal entry (decree of divorce), Judge Bruce Henderson, April 27, 1960. That Donna J. Ailes was a senior in high school, see the amended petition.

15 **Joseph Urban** Entry for Joseph Urban, created by his stepson Robert Ailes Jr., on Findagrave.com.

15 **"He could speak German"** Author interview with Robert Ailes Jr.

15 **"I never found my stamp collection"** Junod, "Roger Ailes on Roger Ailes: The Interview Transcripts, Part 2."

15 **As a freshman** Author interview with Frank Youngwerth. See also Chafets, *Roger Ailes,* 22. That Ailes's mother was born in Parkersburg, see entry for Donna Marie Cunningham (Ailes) Urban, created by her son, Robert Ailes Jr., on Findagrave .com. Lisa Chase, daughter of the late David R. Chase, confirmed that Marjorie was engaged to her father.

15 **"Dave was a big man"** Author interview with Frank Youngwerth.

15 **A talented broadcaster** Author interview with Lisa Chase, daughter of David R. Chase. See also "Fates and Fortunes," *Broadcasting,* Feb. 20, 1978, 64.

15 **"Roger stole her away"** Author interview with Donald Hylkema.

15 **At 11:30 a.m. on August 27, 1960** Original logs of Galbreath Chapel, Ohio University Archives.

15 **After the wedding** According to the 1960–1961 student directory, they lived at 49 Stewart Street. Ohio University Archives.

15 **Marjorie taught** Author interview with Robert Ailes Jr.

16 **"Here's a guy"** Author interview with Frank Youngwerth.

16 **"Maybe that's why"** Junod, "Roger Ailes on Roger Ailes: The Interview Transcripts, Part 2."

16 **After graduation** Ailes mentions the Columbus radio job in his interview with Hodson at 17:20.

16 **He had applied** *Cablegram* reported in 1962 that "Roger E. Ailes, son of Robert E. Ailes, Depart. 551, will be graduated this June from Ohio University where he majored in radio-television. Upon graduation, he will assume a position as an associate director at KYW-TV in Cleveland and will work in the program department and assist in the production and direction of television shows."

## TWO: "YOU CAN TALK YOUR WAY OUT OF ANYTHING"

17 **After deciding to acquire** For 1955, see Val Adams, "TV Variety Show Faces Time Cut," *New York Times,* May 18, 1955. For *Eyewitness,* see archive.wkyc .com/company/about_us; for *Barnaby,* see Tim Hollis, *Hi There, Boys and Girls! America's Local Children's TV Programs* (Jackson: University Press of Mississippi, 2001), 217–18.

17 **Chet Collier** *Radio Annual and Television Yearbook 1962* (New York: Radio Daily Corp., 1962), 803. Author interview with Launa Newman-Minson. Collier died in 2007.

17 **"Roger!"** Author interview with Launa Newman-Minson.

17 **Westinghouse was preparing** Author interview with Launa Newman-Minson. For date of syndication, see Gil Faggen, "Cleveland Local Show Begins Syndication," *Billboard,* Aug. 17, 1963.

17 **Forrest "Woody" Fraser** Mike Douglas, *Mike Douglas: My Story* (New York: Ballantine, 1979), 209. For *Hi Ladies!,* see Mike Douglas, Thomas Kelly, and Michael Heaton, *I'll Be Right Back: Memories of TV's Greatest Talk Show* (New York: Simon & Schuster, 2000), 17. For *Club 60* and *Adults Only,* see Douglas, *Mike Douglas,* 202–3.

17 **Newman was the first** Ibid.

17 **Together, Fraser and Newman** Mike Douglas, *Mike Douglas,* 211. Author interview with Launa Newman-Minson.

17 **"All they came up with"** Ibid.

18 **One afternoon** Mike Douglas, *I'll Be Right Back,* 21, 203. Douglas tells a different version of the anecdote in *My Story,* 212.

18 **it was Kyser** Douglas, *My Story,* 6. There are many variations on the story of how Douglas got his stage name. Page 82 of the Harry Harris biography, *Mike Douglas:The Private Life of the Public Legend* (New York: Award Books, 1976), has two: Douglas says that "Mike Dowd" sounded too much like one of Kyser's friends. Kyser says that "Douglas" had a softer sound and more rhythm than "Dowd." Page 168 of Douglas's *My Story* has another: Douglas says that Kyser changed the name from "Michael D. Dowd Jr." to "Michael Douglas" because the former sounded too "fancy," like the name of a Supreme Court justice.

18 **buying and selling real estate** Douglas, Kelly, and Heaton, *I'll Be Right Back,* 16.

18 **"A million to one"** Ibid., 23.

18 **Westinghouse signed him** Ibid., 18, 23.

18 **"His geniality"** Harris, *Mike Douglas,* 100.

18 **"You're going to work"** Author interview with Launa Newman-Minson. Ailes joined *The Mike Douglas Show* circa 1962–63. On March 11, 1963, *Broadcasting* reported that "Roger Ailes, associate director of Mike Douglas Show on KYW-TV Cleveland, [was] promoted to staff producer-director."

18 **Starting out** Harris, *Mike Douglas,* 122.

18 **"He would usually be gone"** Author interview with Marjorie's sister Kay Luckhardt. She lived with them for a month in 1964. According to the 1964 Cleveland City Directory, they lived at 17400 Euclid Avenue, Apartment 221. It was a commercial street, predominantly developed in the 1920s, a short walk to the train tracks. For Euclid-Green neighborhood boundaries and facts, see http://planning.city.cleveland.oh.us/cwp/districts.php?dt=dist6&dn=green.

19 **"He was very intense"** Author interview with former *Mike Douglas* producer Deborah Miller. At the time she went by the name Debbie Miller.

19 **When Cleveland native** Author interview with Launa Newman-Minson. See also Faggen, "Cleveland Local Show Begins Syndication."

19 **One time a singer** Author interview with a former colleague of Roger Ailes.

19 **For a young producer** Harris, *Mike Douglas,* 108. See also Faggen, "Cleveland Local Show Begins Syndication."

20 **"You didn't know"** Author interview with Launa Newman-Minson.

20 **"He used to come into work"** Author interview with former *Mike Douglas* producer Larry Rosen.

20 **He rarely invited** Author interviews with *Mike Douglas* colleagues.

20 **Roger did cast her** Author interview with Marjorie's sister Kay Luckhardt.

20 **"I felt like"** Author interview with former *Mike Douglas* producer Rift Fournier. He died on October 6, 2013.

20 **"He was always joking"** Author interview with Deborah Miller.

20 **"He'd come in"** Author interview with Larry Rosen.

20 **One time, instead of** Ibid.

20 **Fraser created drama** Douglas, *I'll Be Right Back,* 28.

20 **Fraser said, "The most"** Harris, *Mike Douglas,* 108.

21 **Fraser insisted** Ibid.

21 **"There were times"** Author interview with former *Mike Douglas* producer Robert LaPorta.

21 **Fraser had a clear vision** Douglas, *I'll Be Right Back,* 26–27.

21 **"You can't ignore New York"** Harris, *Mike Douglas,* 114.

21 **The show expanded** Harris, *Mike Douglas,* 104, 109. See also Mike Douglas Archive of American Television Interview: http://www.youtube.com/watch?v=8QPooRay9eY&list=PL065FoDF2B108C359.

21 **A good-natured** For the Rolling Stones, Cosby, and King, see Douglas, *I'll Be Right Back,* 56–57, 97–98, 187–89.

21 **"We wrote him simple questions"** Author interview with Larry Rosen.

21 **Ailes and Fraser began** Harris, *Mike Douglas,* 121.
22 **According to Ailes** Harris, *Mike Douglas,* 60, 105.
22 **"We had to write"** Author interview with Larry Rosen.
22 **For the first few years** Harris, *Mike Douglas,* 105.
22 **The company was gaining** "NBC to Make Trade with Westinghouse," United Press International, June 3, 1965.
22 **Collier smoothed over** Harris, *Mike Douglas,* 121.
22 **In August 1965** Harris, *Mike Douglas,* 110, 112, 116; Inga Saffron, "Channeling TV History," *Philadelphia Inquirer,* Feb. 4, 2011.
22 **Within two years** "Television: Mommy's Boy," *Time,* Oct. 6, 1967.
22 **Douglas's agent soon** Douglas, *I'll Be Right Back,* 36.
22 **"Mike was really controlled by Woody"** Author interview with Deborah Miller.
22 **"The reason was very simple"** Author interview with Launa Newman-Minson.
22 **In Douglas's memoir** Douglas, *I'll Be Right Back,* 217–19. (Woody Fraser, who now works for Fox News, declined to be interviewed for this book.)
23 **"Give us the lowdown"** Author interview with Larry Rosen.
23 **"He became friends"** Author interview with Launa Newman-Minson.
23 **"It was a kind of game"** Harris, *Mike Douglas,* 66.
23 **Debbie Miller and a friend** Author interview with Deborah Miller.
23 **Ailes was his replacement** On July 18, 1966, *Broadcasting* announced that "Roger E. Ailes, associate producer of *The Mike Douglas Show,* named executive producer, replacing Forrest L. Fraser, who becomes manager of talent and program development of WBC productions, New York."
24 **Officially, Fraser had been moved** Harris, *Mike Douglas,* 120–21. Fraser told Harris, "Westinghouse did move me upstairs, because they were trying to hold on to me, but it didn't last long. I only stayed to kind of cover myself monetarily. Westinghouse is very fair in one respect. When they let someone go, it's in a much nicer fashion than many other big corporations." Fraser returned to *The Mike Douglas Show* in 1973.
24 **In 1967, Fraser left** Author interview with Kenny Johnson; "New Morning TV Show in March," The Record Newspapers, Troy, New York, Jan. 20, 1968; "Upbeat in Variety Talk Syndication," *Broadcasting,* Feb. 26, 1968, 19–20.
24 **"That was a real palace coup"** Author interview with Launa Newman-Minson.
24 **Larry Rosen was** Author interview with Larry Rosen.
24 **One producer** Author interview with a former *Mike Douglas* producer.
24 **In his book** Roger Ailes and Jon Kraushar, *You Are the Message: Getting What You Want by Being Who You Are* (New York: Crown Business, 1988), 128–29.
25 **Within days of Fraser's ouster** Author interview with Larry Rosen.
25 **On the wall, he hung** Author interview with Robert LaPorta. In an interview with *Broadcasting,* Ailes refers to putting the quote on his office wall: "Week's Profile: How to Change Debate Loser to Arena Winner," *Broadcasting,* Nov. 11, 1968, 101. See also McGinniss, *The Selling of the President,* 67.
25 **Theodore Roosevelt's** Theodore Roosevelt, "Citizen in a Republic" (speech, Sorbonne, Paris, April 23, 1910), http://www.theodore-roosevelt.com/trsorbonnespeech.html.
25 **Ailes fired Debbie Miller** Author interview with Deborah Miller.
25 **Larry Rosen and Launa Newman** Author interview with Launa Newman-Minson.
25 **"Roger always used to say"** Author interview with Robert LaPorta.
25 **"Roger weighed 160 pounds"** Author interview with Robert LaPorta.
25 **Ailes made sure** Harris, *Mike Douglas,* 54.
25 **"He gave me a wide berth"** Author interview with Launa Newman-Minson.
26 **At one point** Harris, *Mike Douglas,* 53–54.
26 **During one production** Author interview with Kenny Johnson. Later in his ca-

reer, Johnson broke into Hollywood and co-wrote and directed the CBS television movie *Senior Trip,* about a small-town class trip to Manhattan, which featured a hugely ambitious hemophiliac character named Roger Ellis, played by Scott Baio. "I'm gonna make it. Big—and in New York . . . where it counts," Ellis declares in one scene.

26 **"I want everyone"** Roger Ailes memo, Aug. 10, 1966.

26 **Ailes contacted classical music buff** Author interview with International Piano Library cofounder Gregor Benko.

26 **The show had gone color** "Douglas Show to Make Color Debut," *Billboard,* Feb. 11, 1967. The article notes that the show would begin taping in color on February 20 in Cypress Gardens, Florida, and would be made available on March 6.

26 **Once, when Barbara** Author interview with Barbara Walters.

27 **In September 1967** "People," *Sports Illustrated,* Sept. 18, 1967, 86.

27 **"Roger got on the phone"** Author interview with Robert LaPorta.

27 **Kenny Johnson** Author interview with former *Mike Douglas* producer Kenny Johnson.

27 **"We called Roger 'Ralph'"** Author interview with Robert LaPorta.

27 **In the fall of 1967** Indenture filed in the Deed Book in the Recorder of Deeds Office, Media, Pennsylvania, Book 2287, 560–61. They took out a $31,000 mortgage for the house (see Book 2786, page 411). The cul-du-sac is Oak Valley Road.

27 **Ailes was making $60,000** "Nixon's Roger Ailes," *Washington Post* (Q&A), Feb. 13, 1972, http://www.scribd.com/doc/53543922/Roger-Ailes-I-Dont-Try-to-Fool-Voters. In an author interview, Kenny Johnson, who followed Ailes as executive producer, said that the figure was commensurate with his own salary as executive producer.

27 **Bob LaPorta was** Author interview with Robert LaPorta.

27 **During this period** McGinniss, *The Selling of the President,* xi.

27 **"Roger and I"** Author interview with Joe McGinniss.

28 **Politically, Ailes** Ibid.

28 **When a crew member** Author interview with a friend of Roger Ailes.

28 **A year after** Author interviews with Bob LaPorta and Kenny Johnson.

28 **He formed** Author interviews with Robert LaPorta and Kenny Johnson. According to Pennsylvania state filings, Bounty Enterprises was created on July 8, 1968. Project Five Productions, Inc. was created on August 12, 1968. Roger Ailes's profile in *Broadcasting* on November 11, 1968, mentions Bounty Enterprises.

28 **"He had so much"** Author interview with Robert LaPorta.

28 **Ailes filmed a couple** Author interviews with Robert LaPorta and Kenny Johnson.

28 **For Larry Rosen, the trigger came** Author interview with Larry Rosen.

28 **nominated for two Emmys** "The Complete Emmy List: Over 160 Nominations Are Made in 33 Categories with CBS Leading," *Broadcasting,* May 8, 1967, 82–83. Alyssa McGovern of PMK*BNC confirmed on behalf of the National Academy of Television Arts & Sciences that Larry Rosen was listed as the producer on the nomination for the program achievement award. Mike Douglas was also nominated for an Emmy in Individual Achievements in Daytime Television.

29 **"Roger wanted only"** Author interview with Larry Rosen.

29 **As it happened** Robert E. Dallos, "'Death of a Salesman' Wins Emmy as Best Drama," *New York Times,* June 5, 1967. Mike Douglas took the prize for Individual Achievement.

29 **A few weeks later** Author interview with Larry Rosen. His departure was noted on page 68 of the October 2, 1967, issue of *Broadcasting.* "Larry Rosen, producer of *Mike Douglas Show,* appointed producer for *Screen Gems* in Hollywood," the magazine reported. Screen Gems produced *The Outcasts.*

29 **"When Roger took over"** Harris, *Mike Douglas,* 121.

## THREE: THE PHILADELPHIA STORY

30 **During a 1968 segment** Author interview with Kenny Johnson.
30 **During George Wallace's appearance** Ibid.
30 **"I'd operate like a third base coach"** Harris, *Mike Douglas*, 60.
30 **"Roger was really gunning for him"** Author interview with Kenny Johnson.
30 **One morning in the summer** Author interview with Launa Newman-Minson.
30 **After losing a run** Peter Kihss, "Nixon, Happy as New Yorker, Says Job Is Law, Not Politics," *New York Times*, Dec. 29, 1963.
31 **Newman thought Nixon** Author interview with Launa Newman-Minson.
31 **Kenny Johnson recalled one conversation** Author interview with Kenny Johnson.
31 **Nixon was scheduled** Memo from Nixon aide Dwight Chapin, Oct. 6, 1967.
32 **The day before the interview** Memo from Clint Wheeler, Feeley & Wheeler advertising agency, Jan. 8, 1968.
32 **At 9:45** Daily agenda for Richard Nixon, Jan. 9, 1968.
32 **The earliest account** McGinniss, *The Selling of the President*, 63.
32 **"I remember being 27"** Marshall Sella, "The Red-State Network," *New York Times Magazine*, June 24, 2001. Ailes also repeated this account to the journalist Zev Chafets, who wrote his 2012 authorized biography, *Roger Ailes: Off Camera*. On page 32, Chafets quotes Ailes: "We had Little Egypt on the show that day. She was an exotic dancer who performed with a boa constrictor. I figured I better not put her and Nixon in the same greenroom."
32 **The guests during** *Mike Douglas Show* talent log for the week of Jan. 8, 1968. The dance duo John Brascia and Tybee Arfa, who were regulars on the talk show circuit and opened for the likes of Frank Sinatra and Lena Horne, had been scheduled to come into the studio on January 9, but were bumped back a day according to a talent log for that week's shoots. Tybee, as she was known, was certainly exotic. But she never performed under the name Little Egypt. And the snake? "No one has any recollection of Tybee ever dancing with a boa," recalled John Brascia's daughter, Christina, in an author interview.
32 **Mike Douglas later told an interviewer** Archive of American Television interview with Mike Douglas conducted by Karen Herman on March 31, 2005, Part 1 of 7, 30:47 mark.
32 **Kenny Johnson was standing** Author interview with Kenny Johnson.
32 **The meeting lasted** See also "Nixon's Roger Ailes," *Washington Post*. Ailes told the interviewer: "I spent an hour with him personally."
33 **As it happened** In a note to Mike Douglas on January 16, 1968, Nixon writes "my sincerest thanks to you and your staff for the birthday cake."
33 **"We went to commercial"** Archive of American Television interview with Mike Douglas conducted by Karen Herman on March 31, 2005, Part 3 of 7, 16:00 mark.
33 **After the broadcast** Daily agenda for Richard Nixon, Jan. 9, 1968.
33 **A few days later** "Week's Profile: How to Change Debate Loser to Arena Winner," *Broadcasting*, Nov. 11, 1968, 101.
33 **"The name of the game"** Author interview with Dwight Chapin, a former aide to Richard Nixon.
33 **Soon after, on an afternoon** Author interview with Raymond Price, a former speechwriter for Richard Nixon.
33 **A rare moderate** Leonard Garment, *Crazy Rhythm: From Brooklyn and Jazz to Nixon's White House, Watergate, and Beyond* (Cambridge, Mass.: Da Capo, 1997), 106.

33 **"Asia After Viet Nam"** Richard M. Nixon, "Asia After Viet Nam," *Foreign Affairs,* Oct. 1967, Vol. 46, No. 1.

33 **The campaign's television production** Alfred M. Scott was born on Oct. 6, 1914. "Cornell Alumni News" (Feb. 17, 1938, Vol. 4, No. 18, page 259) mentions his early work as an NBC sound technician. In the 1960s, he became head of the international broadcasting division of J. Walter Thompson (see *Broadcasting,* June 25, 1965, page 39). He worked as a television adviser under Harry Treleaven on the 1968 campaign. "Al Scott was a terrific guy," said Dwight Chapin. "He was a guy of the old television age. He was shuttled to the side as I recall. What happened was Roger." After the election, Scott continued to work with the Nixon administration. He died in 1989.

33 **"Roger was not at all awed"** Author interview with Fred Malek, a former adviser to Richard Nixon.

33 **Ailes was hired** Robert Windeler, "Nixon's Television Aide Says Candidate 'Is Not a Child of TV,'" *New York Times,* Oct. 9, 1968.

34 **"He's got guts"** Nyhan, "Roger Ailes: He Doctors a Politician's TV Image."

34 **"Nixon's a doer"** Nyhan, "Roger Ailes: He Doctors a Politician's TV Image."

34 **Ailes would later tell** "Nixon's Roger Ailes," *Washington Post.*

34 **In New Hampshire** Theodore H. White, *The Making of the President 1968* (New York: HarperCollins, 1969), 155.

34 **winning the primary** "Nixon in New Hampshire: Granite State Saved Nixon's Political Life," *Manchester* (New Hampshire) *Union Leader,* April 23, 1994.

34 **as Garment later wrote** Garment, *Crazy Rhythm,* 133.

35 **"For sixteen years"** Garry Wills, *Nixon Agonistes: The Crisis of the Self-Made Man* (New York: Houghton Mifflin, 1969), 414–15. See also Gladwin Hill, "Nixon Denounces Press as Biased," *New York Times,* Nov. 8, 1962.

35 **Five days after the election** Peter Kihss, "Nixon Aide Says TV Program Twisted 'Life of Great American,'" *New York Times,* Nov. 13, 1962.

35 **The man who revived him** Garment, *Crazy Rhythm,* 65–69, 126, 128.

35 **"This game"** Author interview with Dwight Chapin.

35 **After he campaigned** Donald Richard Deskins, *Presidential Elections, 1789–2008* (Ann Arbor: University of Michigan Press, 2010), 439.

36 **"The man and his times"** Garment, *Crazy Rhythm,* 121.

36 **Harry Robbins Haldeman** J. Y. Smith, "H. R. Haldeman Dies, Was Nixon Chief of Staff; Watergate Role Led to 18 Months in Prison," *Washington Post,* Nov. 11, 1993.

36 **"The time has come"** Christopher Matthews, *Kennedy & Nixon: The Rivalry That Shaped Postwar America* (New York: Touchstone, 1996), 257.

36 **In the summer of 1967** Ed McMahon and David Fisher, *Laughing Out Loud: My Life and Good Times* (New York: Warner, 1998), e-book.

36 **In July, Nixon also took a meeting** Garment, *Crazy Rhythm,* 129–31.

36 **An ardent conservative** "Reagan Chooses Ex-U.S.I.A. Head," *New York Times,* May 16, 1981.

36 **Several weeks later** Garment, *Crazy Rhythm,* 131. See also McGinniss, *The Selling of the President,* 45.

37 **In 1966** McGinniss, *The Selling of the President,* 43–45.

37 **"Political candidates are celebrities"** Harry Treleaven, "Upset: The Story of a Modern Political Campaign" (unpublished).

37 **In his TV spots** Rick Perlstein, *Nixonland: The Rise of a President and the Fracturing of America* (New York: Scribner, 2008), 234.

37 **Marshall McLuhan's** McGinniss, *The Selling of the President,* 181, quoting from McLuhan's *Understanding Media.*

37 **Price's assumption** McGinniss, *The Selling of the President,* 193–94, citing Price memo.

38 **One morning in June** Ibid., xii–xvi.
39 **"No, no"** Author interview with Joe McGinniss.
39 **Treleaven's openness** Irvin Molotsky, "H. W. Treleaven, Nixon Consultant, Dies at 76," *New York Times,* Dec. 20, 1998.
39 **He told McGinniss** McGinniss, *The Selling of the President,* xvi.
39 **"We were intrigued"** Author interview with Leonard Garment. He died on July 13, 2013.
39 **The thirty-minute program** "Nixon and TV: Changing a '60 Weak Suit into a '68 Trump," *Broadcasting,* July 22, 1968, 53. See also video of a Nixon television special shot in Michigan during the 1968 presidential campaign, YouTube, http://www.youtube.com/watch?v=yFeWFjbeEQ8.
40 **On July 6** Memo from Roger Ailes to Leonard Garment and Frank Shakespeare, July 6, 1968.
41 **A few days before** Harris, *Mike Douglas,* 52, 122; "Week's Profile: How to Change Debate Loser to Arena Winner," *Broadcasting.*
41 **"When I started out"** "Nixon's Roger Ailes," *Washington Post.*
41 **"I think Mike was hurt"** Author interview with Robert LaPorta.
41 **He and Douglas** Harris, *Mike Douglas,* 47; see also page 122. Ailes told Harris, "When I told Mike I was going to do the thing with Nixon anyway, he granted me the leave of absence, but by then our relations—after six and a half years of being so close—were not so good."
41 **In the early 1980s** "TV Personality/Singer Mike Douglas Dies at 81," *Billboard,* Aug. 11, 2006.
41 **Ailes had drifted** "Mike Douglas Tribute Scheduled Saturday," *Los Angeles Times,* Oct. 19, 2006.
41 **Ailes tried small talk** Author interviews with Larry Rosen and Deborah Miller.
41 **When Douglas died** Author interview with Robert LaPorta.

# ACT II

## FOUR: SELLING THE TRICK

45 **On his first full day** Roger Ailes expense report filed with the Richard Nixon presidential campaign, Aug. 21, 1968.
45 **Until then, he would be** Stephen E. Ambrose, *Nixon, Vol. 2: The Triumph of a Politician, 1962–1972* (Los Angeles: Premier Digital Publishing, 2013), ebook.
45 **"We are going to win"** The American Presidency Project, Richard Nixon acceptance speech (transcript), Aug. 8, 1968, http://www.presidency.ucsb.edu/ws/?pid=25968.
46 **Shortly after the convention** Author interview with Joe McGinniss.
46 **McGinniss followed Ailes to Chicago** McGinniss, *The Selling of the President,* 64–67.
47 **"The subliminal message"** Memo from Roger Ailes to Leonard Garment and Frank Shakespeare, Sept. 27, 1968.
47 **a "balanced" group** McGinniss, *The Selling of the President,* 64.
47 **"Two would be offensive"** Ibid.
47 **"Let's face it"** "Nixon's Roger Ailes," *Washington Post.*
47 **"I agree with Frank"** McGinniss, *The Selling of the President,* 66.
47 **At *The Mike Douglas Show*** Author interviews with *Mike Douglas* producers.
48 **"The audience"** McGinniss, *The Selling of the President,* 66.

48 **At 9:00 p.m.** "Nixon in Illinois" (DVD of Chicago campaign broadcast), Richard Nixon Presidential Library and Museum.

48 **It was Treleaven's idea** McGinniss, *The Selling of the President*, 68.

49 **"If the material"** Memo from Roger Ailes to Leonard Garment and Frank Shakespeare, July 6, 1968.

49 **Thus he** Perlstein, *Nixonland*, 331.

49 **Years later** Ailes and Kraushar, *You Are the Message*, 82.

52 **"Mr. Nixon is strong now"** McGinniss, *The Selling of the President*, 73.

52 **Nixon would tape** E. W. Kenworthy, "'The Richard Nixon Show,'" *New York Times*, Sept. 22, 1968.

52 **Nixon made a four-second taped appearance** Diane Werts, "You Bet Your Bippy That 'Laugh-In' Is Back," *Newsday*, Feb. 7, 1993.

52 **Ailes had already developed** McGinniss, *The Selling of the President*, 72–76.

52 **On September 18** Ibid., 97.

52 **"He never forgot I was writing"** Author interview with Joe McGinniss.

53 **"We're doing all right"** McGinniss, *The Selling of the President*, 97.

53 **"Nixon gets bored"** Ibid., 98–103.

53 **The Philadelphia taping** Ibid., 103–5; "Nixon in Pennsylvania" (DVD of Philadelphia campaign broadcast), Richard Nixon Presidential Library and Museum.

54 **He questioned** McGinniss, *The Selling of the President*, 106–11.

55 **After the taping** Kenworthy, "'The Richard Nixon Show' on TV Lets Candidate Answer Panel's Questions."

55 **"Mr. Nixon came off"** Memo from Roger Ailes to Leonard Garment and Frank Shakespeare, Sept. 27, 1968.

55 **"Boy, is he going"** McGinniss, *The Selling of the President*, 111.

55 **On September 30** R. W. Apple Jr., "Humphrey Vows Halt in Bombing if Hanoi Reacts; a 'Risk for Peace,'" *New York Times*, Oct. 1, 1968.

56 **Shakespeare** McGinniss, *The Selling of the President*, 134.

56 **"My honest opinion was"** "Nixon's Roger Ailes," *Washington Post*.

56 **Ailes gave a candid interview** Robert Windeler, "Nixon's Television Aide Says Candidate 'Is Not a Child of TV,'" *New York Times*, Oct. 9, 1968.

56 **Ten days later** Crocker Snow Jr., "Nixon in Boston Tonight," *Boston Globe*, Oct. 17, 1968. See also McGinniss, *The Selling of the President*, 129.

56 **On October 25** McGinniss, *The Selling of the President*, 133.

56 **Kevin Phillips** Kevin P. Phillips, "The Emerging Republican Majority" (New Rochelle, NY: Arlington House, 1969).

56 **On Sunday, Nixon reversed** McGinniss, *The Selling of the President*, 136–37.

56 **To blow off steam** Ibid., 148. See also Garment, *Crazy Rhythm*, 135.

57 **"It's going to be a dull"** McGinniss, *The Selling of the President*, 149.

57 **The Humphrey telethon** White, *The Making of the President 1968*, 456, McGinniss, *The Selling of the President*, 136–37.

57 **"That's crazy"** McGinniss, *The Selling of the President*, 156.

57 **Rick Rosner** Author interview with former *Mike Douglas* producer Rick Rosner.

57 **Throughout the evening** Arlen J. Large, "Mr. Nixon on TV: 'Man in the Arena,'" *Wall Street Journal*, Oct. 1, 1969.

57 **After breakfast** McGinniss, *The Selling of the President*, 160–61; author interview with Joe McGinniss.

57 **Ailes had arranged for Marje** McGinniss, *The Selling of the President*, 162.

57 **A slew of** White, *The Making of the President 1968*, 456, 458.

58 **Then, triumph** Ibid., 459–61.

58 **Ailes watched** McGinniss, *The Selling of the President*, 164.

58 **"I saw many signs"** Rowland Evans and Robert Novak, *Nixon in the White House: The Frustration of Power* (New York: Random House, 1971), 33–34.

58 **"I remember my dad"** E. G. Marshall, "Television & the Presidency," Part 13, 1984, http://www.youtube.com/watch?v=ky30KChtz_Y.

58 **"This is it"** McGinniss, *The Selling of the President,* 162.

58 **"may have made that up"** William Safire, "The Way Forward," *New York Times Magazine,* Sept. 2, 2007. In November 1968, a *New York Times* reporter tracked down a Deshler girl with such a sign and the paper ran a story about her, accompanied by an Associated Press photo of her holding the sign. See Anthony Ripley, "Ohio Girl, 13, Recalls 'Bring Us Together' Placard," *New York Times,* Nov. 7, 1968. Safire later wrote, "When I asked Dick Moore years later if he had really spotted that girl or whether he had imagined the sign that day, his eyes took on a faraway look." William Safire, *Safire's Political Dictionary* (New York: Oxford University Press, 2008), 83.

58 **"I decided that after the campaign"** Harris, *Mike Douglas,* 122.

59 **Ailes and McGinniss** Author interview with Joe McGinniss.

59 **Even before the campaign was over** Author interview with Philadelphia lawyer Ronald Kidd.

59 **He called it REA Productions** Articles of Incorporation filed with the Commonwealth of Pennsylvania, Department of State, Corporation Bureau, Oct. 28, 1968.

59 **At a Pennsylvania Society dinner** Author interview with Howard Butcher IV.

59 **In Philadelphia** Junod, "Roger Ailes on Roger Ailes: The Interview Transcripts, Part 2."

59 **"Roger was very determined"** Author interview with Howard Butcher IV.

## FIVE: REA PRODUCTIONS

60 **In November 1968** Memo from Roger Ailes to unnamed Nixon advisers, Nov. 1968.

61 **In the winter of 1969** Roger Ailes letterhead from the time. Ailes told Chafets that he drove up to New York in a snowstorm. Chafets, *Roger Ailes,* 37.

61 **"Roger was going"** Author interview with Joe McGinniss.

61 **"At night"** Author interview with Robert Ailes Jr.

61 **One of his first assignments** Roger Ailes letter to Jack Rourke, Jan. 8, 1969.

61 **Jack Rourke** "Passings: Jack Rourke, 86; Producer of Sam Yorty's Show," *Los Angeles Times,* Oct. 21, 2004.

61 **On January 8** Letter from Roger Ailes to Jack Rourke, Jan. 8, 1969.

61 **"I saw RN"** Letter from Jack Rourke to Roger Ailes, Dec. 30, 1968.

61 **Spiro Agnew** Letter from Roger Ailes to Jack Rourke, Jan. 8, 1969.

61 **In late January** Letter from Roger Ailes to Jack Rourke, Jan. 29, 1969.

61 **Lucy Winchester** Biographical note on Nixon social secretary Lucy Winchester, Nixon Presidential Library and Museum, http://www.nixonlibrary.gov/for researchers/find/textual/central/smof/winchester.php.

61 **"I'm glad"** Letter from Jack Rourke to Roger Ailes, Aug. 1, 1969.

62 **"I regret to report"** Author interview with Lucy Winchester.

62 **In early March** Letter from Dwight Chapin to Roger Ailes, March 10, 1969; letter from Dwight Chapin to Nixon secretary Rose Mary Woods, March 10, 1969.

62 **On March 14** President Richard Nixon's Daily Diary, March 14, 1969. They met from 12:55 to 1:05 p.m.

62 **A few days later** Letter from H. R. Haldeman to Roger Ailes, March 27, 1969. "This is just a note to acknowledge your March 18 letter," Haldeman wrote Ailes. "I have contacted Rogers Morton and informed him of your interest in being of assistance to any Congressmen or Senators seeking guidance on arrangements for television appearances."

62 **To that end** Letter from H. R. Haldeman to Rogers Morton, March 26, 1969. On

April 3, 1969, Haldeman wrote Ailes, "I have received word from the Honorable Rogers Morton the other day that he had discussed your participation in future events with Herb Klein and Harry Treleaven. Congressman Morton requests that you be in contact with Harry Treleaven at the Republican National Committee after April 15 to try and develop fully your future relationship with the RNC."

62 **Morton signed Ailes up** Letter from Roger Ailes to H. R. Haldeman, June 8, 1970. "For the past year my company has had a small consultancy contract of $12,000.00 with the Republican National Committee," Ailes wrote. "Can you advise me if there is any chance of getting it renewed?"

62 **In May** H. R. Haldeman, *The Haldeman Diaries: Inside the Nixon White House* (New York: Putnam, 1994), 75.

63 **in June** Memo from Nixon aide Stephen Bull to Carson Howell, June 30, 1969.

63 **The next month** http://nixonfoundation.org/2012/09/roger-ailes-recalls-the-moon-landing/. "I was watching the feed from the moon and I realized we could have the first inter-planetary split screen," Ailes told Bill Hemmer in a 2012 interview. "The problem was that there was no way to predict which way Armstrong would be standing and facing." After having monitors placed on both sides of the president's desk, Ailes cued Nixon which way to look. On the screen, it appeared as if Nixon and Armstrong were facing each other. "That was my contribution," Ailes recalled.

63 **"He felt"** Memo from Haldeman aide Larry Higby to H. R. Haldeman, Aug. 6, 1969.

63 **"The White House"** Mary Wiegel, "Apollo 11 to Star on Earth," *Los Angeles Times,* Aug. 13, 1969.

63 **Sheraton Gibson Hotel** Jack Rourke letter to Roger Ailes, Aug. 1, 1969. The letter was mailed to the hotel. See also Fred Ferretti, "Nixon TV Adviser on Standby Call; Roger Ailes Flew in from Ohio for Briefing at U.N.," *New York Times,* Sept. 21, 1969. Ferretti writes of Ailes, "He maintains an apartment here as well as others in Washington and Philadelphia, has a hotel room in Cincinnati, and a house in New Jersey."

63 **"Yesterday's premiere"** Lawrence Laurent, "Wholey Does His Thing," *Washington Post,* Aug. 19, 1969.

64 **"Roger would say"** Author interview with liberal TV personality Dennis Wholey. Despite their political differences, Wholey and Ailes got along well. "I didn't see eye-to-eye with him," Wholey said, "but I recall him having a presence, having a strong sense of humor, and having a great sense of confidence." Wholey was also struck by Ailes's bluntness. In one conversation, Ailes confronted Wholey about his excessive drinking. "Only two people I can recall ever called me on my drinking. Roger was the first," Wholey said. "As I recall, he said, 'You certainly like to drink, don't you?' And I replied, 'Yes, I like to drink!'" Ailes stared back at him. "He said, and this was the point that scored with me, 'That's a good way to lose a career.' I said, 'What do you mean by that?' He said, 'If you get caught in any kind of an incident, disorderly conduct'—specifically he mentioned drinking and driving—'that's a way to totally lose a career.'" Ailes's advice stayed with him even as his alcohol problems worsened. It was not until the early 1980s when Wholey thought he had run another car off the road, that he got himself into rehab. "It's amazing how few people step up to the plate to say you have a problem," he says. "Roger recognized it way back."

64 **"Your new show"** Letter from Lucy Winchester to Roger Ailes, Sept. 23, 1969.

64 **When Nixon addressed** Ferretti, "Nixon TV Adviser on Standby Call."

64 **In July** Joe McGinniss, "The Selling of 'Selling of the President,'" *Los Angeles Times,* Jan. 4, 1970. McGinniss's excerpt appeared in the August 1969 issue of *Harper's.*

64 **Then, a few weeks before** Large, "Mr. Nixon on TV: 'Man in the Arena.'"

65 **Four days** Letter from Roger Ailes to H. R. Haldeman and John Ehrlichman, Oct. 2, 1969.

65 **Marvin Kitman** Marvin Kitman, "The Selling of the President 1968," *New York Times,* Oct. 5, 1969.

65 **A few days later, Haldeman** Letter from H. R. Haldeman to Roger Ailes, Oct. 1969.

66 **"That was the thing"** Author interview with Joe McGinniss.

66 **When McGinniss appeared** McGinniss, "The Selling of 'Selling of the President.'"

66 **Only a few** Roger Ailes letter to Jack Rourke, Oct. 23, 1969.

66 **"His career was started"** Author interview with Robert Ailes Jr.

66 **The week before** Lawrence Laurent, "Virginia TV Gets School Film Contract," *Washington Post,* Oct. 4, 1969. "Ailes Leaves 'Wholey' in Contract Dispute," *Broadcasting,* Sept. 29, 1969.

66 **By the end of 1969** Memo from Richard Nixon to H. R. Haldeman, Dec. 1, 1969.

66 **A few days before Christmas** Letter from H. R. Haldeman to Roger Ailes, Dec. 19, 1969.

67 **confidential seven-page proposal** Letter from Roger Ailes to H. R. Haldeman, Dec. 1969. In a Jan. 7 letter to Roger Ailes, Haldeman thanks him "for the material you sent me on December 30."

67 **On January 7** Memo from H. R. Haldeman to Richard Nixon, Jan. 7, 1970.

67 **Ailes was hired** Memo from Nixon aide Lawrence Higby to John Brown, Jan. 22, 1970.

67 **"If he is hired"** Memo from Dwight Chapin to H. R. Haldeman, Jan. 10, 1970.

67 **Ailes told Chapin** Memo from Dwight Chapin to Lawrence Higby, Jan. 27, 1970.

68 **A Nixon insider, Ziegler** Jessica Garrison, "Ron Ziegler, 63; Press Secretary Remained Loyal to Nixon Throughout Watergate," *Los Angeles Times,* Feb. 11, 2003.

68 **On February 4** Memo from Roger Ailes to H. R. Haldeman, Feb. 4, 1970.

68 **new press briefing room** James S. Brady Briefing Room, White House Museum (historical note), http://www.whitehousemuseum.org/west-wing/press-briefing-room.htm.

68 **That same day, Ziegler** Memo from Ron Ziegler to H. R. Haldeman, Feb. 4, 1970.

68 **A few weeks later** Memo from Ronald Ziegler to Dwight Chapin, April 7, 1970.

68 **Ailes submitted three candidates** Memo from Roger Ailes to White House, undated.

68 **"Roger wanted me"** Author interview with Robert LaPorta.

68 **The White House brought LaPorta in** Memo from Ronald Ziegler to H. R. Haldeman, Feb. 26, 1970. In an author interview, LaPorta recalled, "Ziegler was very cold to me. It was not a very long interview."

68 **After another candidate** Memo from Roger Ailes to Lawrence Higby, March 3, 1970; memo from Roger Ailes to H. R. Haldeman, April 29, 1970.

68 **In mid-March** Memo from Ronald Ziegler to H. R. Haldeman, March 14, 1970.

69 **drugstore magnate** *St. Petersburg Times,* Times Wire Services, "Eckerd's Moves Hint Nixon's Fighting Kirk," Feb. 28, 1970, http://news.google.com/newspapers?nid=888&dat=19700228&id=uM5aAAAAIBAJ&sjid=InwDAAAAIBAJ&pg=3405,6023454.

69 **"Ailes is involving himself"** Memo from Ronald Ziegler to H. R. Haldeman, March 14, 1970.

69 **When Taft debated** Nyhan, "Roger Ailes: He Doctors a Politician's TV Image."

69 **the *Toledo Blade*** George Jenks, "Heat Level Rises as Rhodes, Taft Engage in Third Debate," *Toledo* (Ohio) *Blade,* April 28, 1970.

69 **A few days after the debate** Kent State University's May 4 Task Force, chronology of events that took place May 1–4, 1970, http://dept.kent.edu/may4/chrono.html. See also Richard Reeves, *President Nixon: Alone in the White House* (New York: Simon & Schuster, 2001), 213.

69 **At a press conference** Perlstein, *Nixonland,* 486.

69 **Kent State, Bob Haldeman later wrote** David Butler, "The Case Against 'Operation Menu,'" *Newsweek,* April 30, 1979, citing H. R. Haldeman, *The Ends of Power* (New York: Times Books, 1978).

70 **Knickerbocker** Letter from Robert Ailes Jr. to H. R. Haldeman, June 11, 1970. "Roger is staying at the Knickerbocker Hotel for an indefinite period," his brother wrote. "When Roger is not at the hotel he can be reached via The Real Tom Kennedy Show at KTLA-TV in Los Angeles."

70 **Even though he was still married** Marjorie Ailes divorce filing, "Lunatics, Drunkards, Divorces: 1977–1978," Delaware County Courthouse, Media, Pennsylvania.

70 **"All I knew"** Author interview with TV personality Tom Kennedy.

70 **The taping of the premiere** Recap of premiere episode of *The Real Tom Kennedy Show,* http://www.game-show-utopia.net/realtomkennedy/realtomkennedy.htm.

70 **In late May** Letter from Republican National Committee deputy chairman Jim Allison Jr. to Roger Ailes, May 25, 1970.

70 **A White House memo** Memo from Nixon aide Gordon Strachan to H. R Haldeman and Herbert Klein, Nov. 13. 1970.

71 **A *Boston Globe* profile** Nyhan, "Roger Ailes: He Doctors a Politician's Image."

71 **After an unsuccessful attempt** Letter from Roger Ailes to H. R. Haldeman, June 8, 1970.

71 **Ailes fired off an angry letter** Letter from Roger Ailes to Jim Allison, Aug. 26, 1970.

71 **"The press is the enemy"** Jonathan Aitken, *Charles W. Colson: A Life Redeemed* (New York: Random House, 2010), 143.

72 **On June 3, 1969** Memo from H. R. Haldeman to Herbert Klein, June 3, 1969.

72 **A few hours later** Memo from Herbert Klein to H. R. Haldeman, June 3, 1969.

72 **"I have discussed television balance"** Memo from Herbert Klein to Richard Nixon, Oct. 17, 1969.

72 **In June 1970** Letter from James Cordes of WordCraft Productions to Roger Ailes, June 16, 1970.

72 **Ailes told Nixon aide** Letter from Roger Ailes to Nixon aide Jeb Magruder, July 3, 1970.

72 **In the summer** Memo from Nixon aide Gregg Petersmeyer to Herbert Klein, Aug. 13, 1970.

73 **Ailes sent Haldeman** Roger Ailes's marked-up, signed copy of the memo proposing a White House news service.

73 **just a few months earlier** Nyhan, "Roger Ailes: He Doctors a Politician's TV Image."

73 **"It should be expanded"** Roger Ailes's marked-up, signed copy of the memo proposing a White House news service.

74 **A prescient 1973 document** Memo from T. O'Donnell to H. R. Haldeman, March 12, 1973.

74 **By November 1970** "Memorandum for Bill Carruthers File," by Dwight Chapin, Nov. 16, 1970.

74 **On November 19** Unsigned White House memo, Nov. 19, 1970.

74 **The day before Thanksgiving** Ailes proposal to Haldeman, Nov. 25, 1970.
76 **He hired Carruthers** The announcement was made in *The Hollywood Reporter*. "President Nixon Names Carruthers Consultant," *Hollywood Reporter,* Feb. 1, 1970. On December 29, 1970, Chapin wrote to Carruthers, "Bob Haldeman has talked to Roger Ailes and Roger is fully aware of your coming aboard here as well as Mark Goode's." See also Haldeman, *The Haldeman Diaries,* 266.
76 **The White House worried** Chapin memo to Haldeman, Dec. 23, 1970.
77 **A meeting was scheduled** Haldeman, *The Haldeman Diaries,* 270.
77 **A talking paper** Undated document, "Re: Roger Ailes' Meeting," Nixon Presidential Library Archives.
77 **A few weeks later** Letter from Roger Ailes to H. R. Haldeman, Feb. 9, 1971.
77 **"No need for H."** Memo from Nixon aide Bruce Kehrli to Lawrence Higby (undated).
77 **"I have been getting a lot"** Letter from Roger Ailes to Lawrence Higby, Feb. 12, 1971.
77 ***The Real Tom Kennedy Show*** Author interview with Tom Kennedy.
77 **An article in *Backstage*** "Ailes, Business Is Not Ailing," *Backstage,* March 5, 1971.
77 **a speech** Roger Ailes, "Candidate + Money + Media = Votes" (transcript of speech), Town Hall of California, June 8, 1971. The speech was mentioned in the pages of *Broadcasting* on June 14, 1971, in an article titled "Nixon's Specialist on TV Defends Its Political Use."
78 **He told White House photographer** Letter from Roger Ailes to Nixon photographer Oliver Atkins, May 14, 1971.
78 **"Roger got caught up"** Author interview with Robert Ailes Jr.

## SIX: A NEW STAGE

79 **"He was trying to figure out"** Author interview with Robert Ailes Jr.
79 **Paul Turnley, a liberal Democrat** Author interview with former Ailes assistant Paul Turnley.
79 **On May 15** Letter from Roger Ailes to H. R. Haldeman, May 19, 1971. Even though Ailes lost out on the White House television position, he continued to cultivate a relationship with the administration. In this letter, Ailes told Haldeman that when he traveled to Indiana, he learned that Gene Pulliam, the publisher of *The Indianapolis Star,* was turning against Nixon. "He has gone as far as to say he is going to back Scoop Jackson for 1972," Ailes wrote, advising Nixon not to attend the Indianapolis 500 car race. "I think it would be a very bad idea. The situation in Indiana is just too volatile at the moment and I can't see anything that the president could gain from it politically." On May 21, Jon M. Huntsman, special assistant to the president, wrote Ailes that he would make office space available for him "during your consultation visits to the White House, as a White House Consultant." On May 28, Ailes wrote to Haldeman, thanking him for the offer of office space. "I am very happy to know that our relationship is to continue," Ailes wrote. "As you know, my personal and professional loyalty is with the President and I want to do everything I can to help get him re-elected in 1972. As you pointed out, Bob, I have become somewhat of a political animal now as well as a media adviser and I think this does give me some added strength and in some ways makes me a double-threat man. I was used by Westinghouse Broadcasting as a trouble-shooter in trouble program areas and I think I could serve the same role politically in some of the states where we have problems. . . . Thank you for your confidence in me." On June 2, Haldeman replied, "I wish you the best of luck in

your new political trouble shooter role. I am sure you will do an excellent job." Documents available at the Nixon Presidential Library and Museum do not indicate that the administration used Ailes in any substantive way. On July 1, Ailes wrote Haldeman's assistant, Larry Higby, suggesting that Nixon attend a Washington Senators baseball game, at a time when the team was considering relocating to Texas. "We have done nothing recently to build up his 'sports enthusiast' image," Ailes wrote, "and it might be worth a trip during his 'private hours' over to the ballpark to see the Senators or to talk to their management about their problems—not as the President but as a sports fan trying to keep the Senators in Washington." Ailes told Higby that the stunt would "give the President a down-to-earth look."

80 **"I don't have this burning thing"** "Nixon's Roger Ailes," *Washington Post.*

80 **Ailes arranged for a barber** Author interview with Paul Turnley. In an interview, Andrew Stein confirmed that he wore a hairpiece but said he could not recall Ailes calling in a barber. Stein praised Ailes's talents for communication. "He was a force of nature then too. It was a terrific experience. . . . I remember him saying something once: 'Sometimes it's important to say nothing, to have a pause. Some people always think they have to be talking, but that's not true.'"

80 **Jim Holshouser** "Holshouser Releases Promised Tax Records," United Press International (printed in Lexington, North Carolina's *The Dispatch*), Aug. 12, 1974. See also http://www.wral.com/former-gov-jim-holshouser-dies/4369405/, http://www.unctv.org/content/biocon/jamesholshouser/installments.

80 **Holshouser flew to New York** Author interview with Paul Turnley.

80 **"I don't think"** Author interview with Paul Turnley.

81 **On February 12** Letter from Roger Ailes to Jack Rourke, Feb. 12, 1971.

81 **born Ellen Boulton** Earl Wilson, "Snakes Alive! Patrice Munsel Has Pet Boa," *Milwaukee Sentinel,* June 24, 1974, http://news.google.com/newspapers?id=EmlRAAAAIBAJ&sjid=rBEEAAAAIBAJ&pg=6410,1719404&dq=kelly-garrett&hl=en.

81 **four years younger** Tom Sharpe, "Kelly Garrett 1944–2013: Acclaimed Singer Had Roots in New Mexico," *New Mexican,* Aug. 12, 2013.

81 **she grew up in Santa Fe** Jay Sharbutt, "Kelly Garrett Isn't 'Overnight' Success," Associated Press, published in *Pittsburgh Post-Gazette,* July 1, 1974, http://news.google.com/newspapers?nid=1129&dat=19740710&id=e2QwAAAAIBAJ&sjid=YW0DAAAAIBAJ&pg=3300,1401941.

81 **At age twenty-two** Author interview with Kelly Garrett's sister, Georgia Pearson. See also "California, Marriage Index, 1960–1985," index, Michael T. Mikler and Ellen M. Boulton (1966), FamilySearch.

81 **She got a divorce** "California, Divorce Index, 1966–1984," index, Ellen M. Boulton and Michael T. Mikler (1970), FamilySearch.

81 **Rourke responded** Letter from Jack Rourke to Roger Ailes, Feb. 24, 1971.

81 **Ailes chose *Mother Earth*** Entry for *Mother Earth* on Internet Broadway Database, http://ibdb.com/production.php?id=2966.

81 **But the conservative spirit** South Coast Repertory (historical account on the company's website), http://www.scr.org/about/scrstory.aspx#.UYp1YYLuf30.

81 **Toni Tennille** Bob Thomas, "Both Critics and Audience Like 'Mother Earth,' Stage Musical," Associated Press, published in *Daytona Beach Morning Journal,* Aug. 25, 1971.

81 **The musical, he wrote** Script of original production of *Mother Earth.*

82 **The show opened** "Repertory Show Will Start Jan. 8," *Los Angeles Times,* Dec. 27, 1970.

82 **"I am one"** Script of original production of *Mother Earth.*

82 **"After we ended"** Author interview with South Coast cofounder Jim dePriest.

82 **After successful runs** Margaret Harford, " 'Mother Earth' to Move to Bay Area," *Los Angeles Times,* May 23, 1971; Gregg Kilday, " 'Mother Earth' Set at Hartford," *Los Angeles Times,* July 25, 1971.

82 **Ray Golden** "Screen News Here and in Hollywood," *New York Times,* Feb. 22, 1941; "The Theatre: New Revue in Manhattan," *Time,* Sept. 19, 1955; "Openings of the Week," *New York Times,* Jan. 15, 1950.

82 **"Roger came back"** Author interview with Paul Turnley.

82 **Over lunch** Author interview with April Garrett, Ron Thronson's widow.

82 **A couple of months before** Louis Calta, "2 Musicals Set Their Premieres," *New York Times,* Sept. 7, 1972; author interview with April Garrett.

83 **"It turned into"** Author interview with Martin Benson.

83 **"We got bamboozled"** Jan Herman, "Toni Tennille: No Hits but 'Always Sold Out,' " *Los Angeles Times,* April 10, 1988.

83 **he met the Broadway producer** Scott Collins, *Crazy Like a Fox: The Inside Story of How Fox News Beat CNN* (New York: Penguin, 2004), 29.

83 **His string** Albin Krebs, "Kermit Bloomgarden, Producer of Many Outstanding Plays, Dead," *New York Times,* Sept. 21, 1976.

83 **"Given the circumstance"** Author interview with Kermit Bloomgarden's son John Bloomgarden.

83 **During the height of McCarthyism** California Senate, *Report of the Senate Fact-Finding Committee on Un-American Activities, 1948: Communist Front Organizations,* 1948, http://archive.org/stream/reportofsenatefaoocalirich/reportofsenatefaoocalirich_djvu.txt.

83 **Though Bloomgarden was never called** See, for instance, Elia Kazan, *A Life* (New York: Da Capo, 1997), 440, 461, 592.

83 **"What the hell"** Author interview with Robert Cohen. Bloomgarden was not a Nixon supporter. During the 1968 campaign, he helped produce a "Garden Rally for McCarthy" hosted by Tony Randall at the Waldorf-Astoria. The A-list crowd of attendees included Mike Nichols, Dustin Hoffman, Leonard Bernstein, Alan Arkin, Neil Simon, Barbra Streisand, and Arthur Miller. (Private Papers of Kermit Bloomgarden obtained from the Wisconsin Historical Society.) When Robert Cohen went to work for Ailes, Bloomgarden would ask Cohen about Ailes's politics. "Every now and then Kermit would ask, 'Do you talk about politics with Roger?' " Cohen recalled. "And I said, 'As little as possible to be very honest with you. It's not my politics, you know that.' He goes, 'Yeah.' "

84 **Bloomgarden earned** Author interview with Stephen Rosenfield.

84 **To finance *Mother Earth*** Author interview with Howard Butcher IV.

84 **Frank Coombs** Author interview with dancer Frank Coombs.

84 **Cast member John Bennett Perry** Author interview with actor John Bennett Perry.

84 **"He'd sit in the back room"** Author interview with actor Rick Podell.

84 **"She was striking looking"** Author interview with John Bennett Perry.

84 **"Roger made sure"** Author interview with Rick Podell.

84 **Frank Coombs, who was asked** Author interview with Frank Coombs.

85 **Inviting John Bennett Perry** Author interview with John Bennett Perry.

85 **Looking back, Podell recognized** Author interview with actor Rick Podell.

85 **Robert Cohen thought Ailes** Author interview with Robert Cohen.

85 **By staging a photo shoot** Author interview with Frank Coombs.

85 **Ailes made another plug** Joe McGinniss, "The Resale of the President," *New York Times Magazine,* Sept. 3, 1972.

85 **Ailes also reached out** Memo from Peter Flanigan to Starke Meyer, Oct. 11, 1972. "Leonard Garment has asked me to let you know about a new musical being produced by Roger Ailes, called 'Mother Earth,' " Flanigan wrote. "Please let me know if you are interested."

85 **After the curtain** Author interview with Robert Cohen.

85 **John Bennett Perry got a call** Author interview with John Bennett Perry.
85 **In a savage review** Clive Barnes, "Stage: 'Mother Earth,' a Rock Revue," *New York Times,* Oct. 20, 1972.
85 **"The second night"** Author interview with Rick Podell.
86 **Within a week** Author interview with John Bennett Perry.
86 **After just a dozen performances** Clara Rotter (compiler), "Closing the Record Book on 1972–1973," *New York Times,* July 1, 1973.
86 **"My eyes"** Collins, *Crazy Like a Fox,* 30.
86 **"The main discussion"** Author interview with Paul Turnley.
86 **"Don't ever chase critics"** Collins, *Crazy Like a Fox,* 30.
86 **As he would later tell it** Collins, *Crazy Like a Fox,* 30. When asked if Ailes scouted productions himself, Robert Cohen said: "Not that I know of. He depended on me. I was the guy who had to go find these things." He went on: "The fact of the matter is, Roger wasn't in the club. . . . Roger subscribed to every trade publication on earth and I would sit with a razor blade and I would be clipping out articles. You can do that forever but by the time it's in the trade, it's been picked up." Cohen said that Ailes usually rejected his ideas. "There was Roger with his big Roger office. There was me in my little office, and I would get ahold of every agent in New York and read every play they would send to me," Cohen recalled. "But the problem was the stuff I was interested in Roger wouldn't go for at all. All this left-wing stuff about hippies and banning the war. I'd go, 'Read this,' and he'd go, 'I don't want to do things like this. I want to do American things.' "
86 **He hired** Author interview with Robert Cohen.
86 **One day in February 1973** Author interview with Robert Cohen.
86 **Lanford Wilson, a cofounder** Circle Repertory Company Records, New York Public Library, http://archives.nypl.org/the/21737.
86 **depicted a group** Lanford Wilson, *The Hot l Baltimore* (New York: Dramatists Play Service, 1973), 7.
87 **"I thought, My God"** Author interview with Robert Cohen.
87 **After the show** Ibid.
87 **The next day at the office** Ibid.
87 **a 299-seat venue** Letter from Robert Cohen to Malt-O-Meal public relations, March 26, 1973.
87 **Ailes committed to raising** Certificate of Limited Partnership of Hot l Baltimore Company, March 16, 1973, Kermit Bloomgarden papers, Wisconsin Historical Society.
87 **he tapped** Author interview with Howard Butcher IV.
88 **Lanford Wilson and Marshall Mason** Author interview with Marshall Mason.
88 **Opening night came** Wilson, *The Hot l Baltimore,* 4.
88 **"Everything that went onto the stage"** Author interview with actress Conchata Ferrell.
88 **"The crazies"** Walter Kerr, "The Crazies Are Good to Listen To," *New York Times,* March 4, 1973.
88 **A parade of notables** Author interview with Robert Cohen.
88 **He expressed keen interest** Author interview with Robert Cohen.
88 **graphic artist David Byrd** Biography on David Edward Byrd official website, http://www.david-edward-byrd.com/biocontact-1.html.
88 **Byrd did a graphic** Image of the poster for Circle on the Square production of *Hot l Baltimore* on Byrd official website, http://www.david-edward-byrd.com/theatre7-4.html.
88 **"They both complained"** Author interview with Robert Cohen.
88 **A few days after** Letter from Robert Cohen to Malt-O-Meal public relations, March 26, 1973. Cohen mentions the Benson & Hedges and Coca-Cola arrangements in this letter.

89 **While the hotel residents** Wilson, *The Hot l Baltimore,* 32, 33.
89 **"What a gorgeous"** Author interview with actress Mari Gorman.
89 **"We hardly saw Roger"** Author interview with Stephanie Gordon.
89 **Shortly after the show opened** Ibid.
89 **a pivotal scene** Wilson, *The Hot l Baltimore,* 32, 33.
89 **Making her way** Author interview with Stephanie Gordon.
89 **In 1973, *Hot l Baltimore*** www.villagevoice.com/obies/index/1973/, http://www.dramacritics.org/dc_pastawards.html.
89 **generated a profit** *Hot l Baltimore* balance sheet, Jan. 4, 1976, Kermit Bloomgarden papers, Wisconsin Historical Society.
90 **ABC** Wesley Hyatt, *Short-Lived Television Series, 1948–1978: Thirty Years of More Than 1,000 Flops* (Jefferson, NC: McFarland, 2003), 232.
90 **Mari Gorman recalled Roger Ailes fondly** Author interview with Mari Gorman.
90 **Stephanie Gordon struggled** Author interview with Stephanie Gordon.
90 **Marshall Mason, who lives** Author interview with Marshall Mason.
90 **Conchata Ferrell, who went on** Author interview with Conchata Ferrell.
90 **In his own telling** Collins, *Crazy Like a Fox,* 30.
90 **His new employee** Author interview with Stephen Rosenfield.
91 **In December 1973** Louis Calta, "News of the Stage," *New York Times,* Dec. 9, 1973. "It's a women's show," Ailes told Calta, "and deals with the sexual freedoms of today."
91 **favorable review** Howard Thompson, " 'Ionescopade' Shifts to the Cherry Lane," *New York Times,* July 28, 1973.
91 **Ailes leaned on** Kermit Bloomgarden papers, Wisconsin Historical Society (finance notes for *Ionescopade*).
91 **Robert Kennedy Jr.** Author interview with Robert Kennedy Jr.
91 **A wealthy American businessman** Ibid.
92 **But a three-hour meeting** Kiki Levathes, "Robert Kennedy Jr. at 21," New York *Daily News,* printed in *The Evening Independent* (St. Petersburg, Florida), Sept. 9, 1975.
92 **"We joked about Nixon"** Author interview with Robert Kennedy Jr.
92 **After Kennedy signed** Levathes, "Robert Kennedy Jr. at 21." See also "A Kennedy in Africa," *Broadcasting,* April 1, 1974. *Broadcasting* reported that Kennedy agreed to do an untitled wildlife series of twenty-six half hour episodes with Ailes, but only one TV special was made.
92 **The pair traveled** Author interview with *Last Frontier* writer and producer Tom Shachtman.
92 **"I had a lot of laughs"** Author interview with Robert Kennedy Jr.
92 **On April 25** Mel Gussow, "Theater—'Ionescopade,' " *New York Times,* April 26, 1974.
92 **After fourteen performances** Dan Dietz, *Off Broadway Musicals, 1910–2007: Casts, Credits, Songs, Critical Reception and Performance Data of More Than 1,800 Shows* (Jefferson, NC: McFarland, 2010), Entry 773.
92 **In April** Author interview with Stephen Rosenfield. Garrett's appointment was announced in May. See Louis Calta, "News of the Stage" ("Kelly Garrett in 'Mack & Mabel' "), *New York Times,* May 12, 1974.
92 **David Merrick's $850,000 production** Ellen Stock, "Mack & Mabel: Getting the Show off the Road," *New York,* Oct. 7, 1974.
92 **two female leads** Ibid.
92 **Garrett was performing** Ibid.
92 **Ailes pushed Garrett** Author interview with Stephen Rosenfield.
93 **"That one broke my heart"** Stock, "Mack & Mabel: Getting the Show off the Road."
93 **The embarrassing public setback** Author interview with Stephen Rosenfield.

93 **"As far as I'm concerned"** Ellen Stock, "Mack & Mabel: Getting the Show Off the Road."

93 **After he returned** Richard Esposito, "Giuliani Adviser's '74 Gun Charge," *Newsday,* Oct. 23, 1989. According to Esposito, the date of the arrest was November 10, 1974. See also Chafets, *Roger Ailes,* 31.

93 **When news of the arrest surfaced** Esposito, "Giuliani Adviser's '74 Gun Charge." "My understanding is that Ailes was over in Africa doing a documentary with Bobby Kennedy Jr. and was carrying a gun over there for protection," Giuliani's deputy campaign manager Ken Caruso told Esposito. "He came back to the United States and had this gun in his film equipment, and went out in Central Park." Esposito reported, "Caruso said Ailes took the equipment belt out and strapped it around his waist, unaware that the gun was still in it." See also Todd Purdum, "Amid the Shouts, Dinkins Remains Calm," *New York Times,* Oct. 26, 1989.

93 **It felt like an excuse** Author interview with Robert Kennedy Jr.

93 **Ailes pleaded guilty** Esposito reported that after being charged with a felony, Ailes pled guilty to a misdemeanor and was given a conditional discharge.

93 **Ailes called a young acquaintance** Author interview with an acquaintance of Roger Ailes in the 1970s.

93 ***Violence never solves*** Grove, "The Image Shaker; Roger Ailes, the Bush Team's Wily Media Man."

94 **It was advice** Author interview with Robert Ailes Jr.

94 **Ailes kept others at a distance** Author interviews with friends of Roger Ailes in the 1970s.

94 **her lapdog, Squeaker** Jack O'Brian, "Gal from Santa Fe," *Spartanburg* (South Carolina) *Herald,* July 26, 1974, http://news.google.com/newspapers?nid=1876&dat=19740726&id=yXosAAAAIBAJ&sjid=TcwEAAAAIBAJ&pg=4122,4508433.

94 **McGinniss was in a similar situation** Joe McGinniss, *Heroes* (New York: Simon & Schuster, 1976), 152 and passim.

94 **Joe and Nancy made their home** Author interviews with Joe McGinniss and Nancy Doherty.

94 **"Do I ever get nervous"** O'Brien, "Gal from Santa Fe."

94 **"Roger and I didn't talk"** Author interview with Joe McGinniss.

94 **"After a visit from Roger"** Author interview with Nancy Doherty.

94 **"He was eating"** Author interview with Joe McGinniss.

95 **"He took Watergate"** Author interview with Stephen Rosenfield.

95 **In the fall of 1974** Author interview with Stephen Rosenfield. Charles M. Madigan, "Governor Candidates Will Take to the Air," United Press International (printed in *The News-Dispatch,* Jeannette, Pennsylvania), Aug. 12, 1974. See also John J. Kennedy, *Pennsylvania Elections: Statewide Contests from 1950–2004* (Lanham, Md.: University Press of America, 2006), 100–101.

95 **Lewis lost** Pennsylvania Historical & Museum Commission website (biographical entry for Milton Shapp), http://www.portal.state.pa.us/portal/server.pt/community/1951-present/4285/milton_j__shapp/471867.

95 **After the defeat** Author interview with Stephen Rosenfield.

95 **"Whenever he can"** Author interview with a senior Fox executive.

95 **Creating the Fox News** Author interview with a friend of Roger Ailes.

## SEVEN: THOUGHT PATTERN REVOLUTION

97 **In May 1974** Minutes of TVN board meeting of May 21, 1974.

97 **Harvard MBA** Robert Reinhold Pauley résumé, recorded in Robert Reinhold Pauley papers.

97 **As the president** Jeff Byrd, "Robert Pauley '42 Remembers Radio Days," *Tryon Daily Bulletin,* Sept. 10, 2004.

97 **Goldwater supporter and a John Bircher** Author interview with a person close to the late Robert Pauley.

97 **a local plan** Ibid. See also Drew Pearson, "Fluoridation Battle Dividing New Canaan; DAR Leading Foe," *Sunday Herald,* April 2, 1948, http://news.google.com/newspapers?nid=2229&dat=19580420&id=h2MmAAAAIBAJ&sjid=KQAGAAAAIBAJ&pg=2395,2064825.

97 **After being pushed out** Brian Stelter, "Robert Pauley, Former Head of ABC Radio, Dies at 85," *New York Times,* May 13, 2009.

97 **United Press International** "TVN Inc. to Weaken Networks' Hold on Television News," *Gallagher Report,* March 19, 1973.

98 **In 1972** Robert Pauley memo to John Shad, April 9, 1973. "I disclosed the existence of News, Inc., which company I founded in early 1968. . . . In January of 1972, Joseph Coors of Adolph Coors Company called me and said that he had learned of News, Inc. and its objectives," Pauley wrote to Shad.

98 **"All three networks slant the news"** Testimony of Joseph Coors, U.S. Congress, Senate, Committee on Commerce, hearings on nomination of Joseph Coors, 84th Congr., 1st session, 104.

98 **Coors certainly shared Russell Kirk's lament** Russell Kirk, *The Conservative Mind* (Washington, D.C.: Regnery, 1953), 4.

98 **He committed** Memo from Robert Pauley to John Shad, April 19, 1973.

98 **Coors was also funding** Stephen Isaacs, "Coors Beer—and Politics—Move East," *Washington Post,* May 4, 1975.

98 **"We were discussing"** Author interview with Jack Wilson.

98 **Their goal was to launch** John O. Gilbert, "The Story Behind Television News Inc.," *Backstage,* March 23, 1973.

98 **The press release** "New Television News Service for U.S. Broadcasters Announced," Shaw Elliott Public Relations (press release), Jan. 22, 1975.

98 **Two weeks before** Robert Pauley memo to Jack Wilson, May 2, 1973. "That is one reason why I am happy you are going to be in Washington and that I insisted that Joe have a line in or cassettes on a daily basis. We are dealing here with some what of a vertical situation, that is, the product of Network training. It is up to us to shape changes as time goes by."

98 **William F. Buckley Jr.** Letter from Robert Pauley to William Buckley, Oct. 10, 1973.

98 **"I have suggested"** Undated letter from Robert Pauley to Pat Buchanan.

99 **He asked Wilson** Confidential memo from Robert Pauley to Jack Wilson, May 2, 1973.

99 **When TVN finally launched** Memo from Dick Perkin to Jack Wilson, May 11, 1973. "As you know, most of our activity this week is tied into the start-up on May 14," Perkin wrote.

99 **"There will be days"** Dan Baum, *Citizen Coors: An American Dynasty* (New York: HarperCollins, 2000), 112.

99 **In one, he complained** Memo from Jack Wilson to Joseph Coors and Robert Pauley, June 27, 1973.

99 **In another** Memo from Jack Wilson to Joseph Coors and Robert Pauley, June 28, 1973.

99 **"Why are you covering"** Stanhope Gould, "Coors Brews the News," *Columbia Journalism Review,* March/April 1975.

99 **At another board meeting** Robert Pauley's notes from TVN board meeting of Dec. 18, 1973.

99 **Paul Weyrich** Jack Shafer, "Fox News 1.0," *Slate,* June 5, 2008.

99 **"I've had no influence"** Stephen Isaacs, "Coors Bucks Network 'Bias'—Sets Up Alternative TV News to Offset Liberals," *Washington Post,* May 5, 1975.
99 **Ronald Waldman** Letter from Robert Pauley to TVN board member Ronald Waldman, reiterating Waldman's concerns, Aug. 13, 1973.
100 **"Let's not get labeled"** Robert Pauley letter to Everett Barnhardt, Adolph Coors Company, July 1, 1974.
100 **In February 1974** Gould, "Coors Brews the News."
100 **By the spring, Coors seized** TVN board minutes, May 21, 1974.
100 **"I hate all those network people"** Baum, *Citizen Coors,* 113.
100 **In short order** Gould, "Coors Brews the News"; "Slimmed-Down TVN Says It's Alive and Well: Spokesman Talks of Expansion Despite Personnel Reductions," *Broadcasting,* Nov. 18, 1974.
100 **In July 1974, Ailes delivered** Minutes of TVN board meeting of July 23, 1974.
101 **four months later** *Variety,* "TVN Gets Shot for What Ailes It: St. John Return," Nov. 20, 1974.
101 **"He didn't know anything"** Author interview with CNN cofounder Reese Schonfeld.
101 **"He took on a role"** Author interview with Stephen Rosenfield.
101 ***"Ran 1968 Nixon campaign"*** Handwritten notes of Robert Pauley on an agenda for a July 23, 1974, Television News board of directors meeting.
101 **"Their politics"** Author interview with Stephen Rosenfield.
101 **"Roger Ailes has quickly given"** Report from Jack Wilson to the TVN board, Nov. 27, 1974.
101 **The week of Thanksgiving** Memo from Roger Ailes to Jack Wilson, Nov. 25, 1974.
101 **"Roger Ailes has suggested"** Memo from TVN cofounder Richard Perkin to Jack Wilson, Nov. 1974 (no day specified).
102 **a profile of Kelly Garrett** Gould, "Coors Brews the News."
102 **TVN Enterprises** In its Sept. 8, 1975, issue, *Broadcasting* ran a full-page ad with the title "TVN Enterprises Presents The Last Frontier." The ad identified TVN Enterprises as the distributor of the film and as a division of Television News Incorporated.
102 **Reese Schonfeld, TVN's vice president** Author interview with Reese Schonfeld.
102 **In the winter** Gould, "Coors Brews the News."
103 **In its first year, TVN** TVN financial statement, Dec. 30, 1973. See also handwritten notes of Bob Pauley from the Sept. 25, 1975, TVN board of of directors meeting.
103 **Western Union and NASA** "Satellite Launched by Western Union for Communication," *New York Times,* April 14, 1974.
103 **on January 9, 1975** Letter from Jack Wilson to Robert Pauley, Jan. 16, 1975.
103 **"I want to find out"** Gould, "Coors Brews the News."
104 **He talked with Art Rush** Roger Ailes report to TVN Board of Directors, June 2, 1975.
104 **Joyce Brothers** Memo from Roger Ailes to Jack Wilson, November 25, 1974.
104 **Paul Keyes** Roger Ailes report to TVN Board of Directors, June 2, 1975.
104 **Around this time** Report from Roger Ailes to TVN board, June 2, 1975.
104 **On his West Coast swing** Letter from Jack Wilson to Richard Nixon, June 7, 1975.
104 **Wilson hired Bruce Herschensohn** *Variety,* "Nixon Aide Joins TV News Agency," Feb. 19, 1975.
104 **$200-per-day** Bruce Herschensohn Private Papers, Pepperdine University.
104 **"It is not [Eric] Sevareid"** Ibid.
104 **From his apartment on Virginia Avenue** Ibid.

104 **"the disguise of neutrality"** Letter from Bruce Herschensohn to Jack Wilson, March 23, 1975.

104 **He proposed that TVN producers** Bruce Herschensohn's proposed script of Feb. 17, 1975.

104 **Herschensohn viewed his television proposal** Bruce Herschensohn Private Papers, Pepperdine University.

105 **On April 30** Bruce Herschensohn private papers, Pepperdine University.

106 **Anchor Bob Sellers** Author interview with former Fox News anchor Bob Sellers.

106 **The dish to receive** Schonfeld, *Me and Ted Against the World*, 40.

106 **at a choreographed rollout** Author interview with Reese Schonfeld.

106 **bicentennial film** Letter from Bruce Herschensohn to Jack Wilson, July 6, 1975.

106 **By September 1975** Handwritten notes of Bob Pauley from the Sept. 25, 1975, TVN board of directors meeting.

106 **After his father died** Author interview with Jack Wilson.

106 **During a board meeting** Notes of Robert Pauley on Sept. 25, 1975, TVN board of directors meeting.

106 **A few days later** TVN press release, Sept. 29, 1975.

106 **On October 3** Letter from Jack Wilson to Richard Nixon, Oct. 3, 1975.

107 **Ailes did not wait** Pauley's handwritten notes from TVN board meeting of Sept. 25, 1975. Ailes and John McCarty would have a longtime connection. McCarty's son, Michael, went on to own a pair of eponymous restaurants in Santa Monica, California, and Manhattan frequented by media heavyweights. Ailes was given the head table at Michael's New York outpost.

107 **"He believed all news"** Author interview with Barbara Pauley.

107 **Reese Schonfeld founded** Reese Schonfeld, *Me and Ted Against the World: The Unauthorized Founding of CNN* (New York: HarperCollins, 2001), 46.

107 **In 1976** Ibid., 13.

107 **In December 1976** Robert Goldberg and Gerald Jay Goldberg, *Citizen Turner: The Wild Rise of an American Tycoon* (New York: Harcourt Brace, 1995), 169.

107 **hired Schonfeld** Schonfeld, *Me and Ted Against the World*, 13–14.

107 **In the spring of 1975** Kermit Bloomgarden Papers, Wisconsin Historical Society.

107 **Arnaud d'Usseau** C. Gerald Fraser, "Arnaud d'Usseau, 73, Playwright, Screenplay Writer and Instructor," *New York Times*, Feb. 1, 1990.

107 **Ailes persuaded Coors** Letter from Roger Ailes to Joseph Coors, undated; letter from Roger Ailes to Kermit Bloomgarden, May 29, 1975. Ailes perhaps also turned to TVN as a source of funding for the Kennedy television special. Robert Pauley's handwritten notes include a reference to Ailes's wildlife documentary. "Kennedy show cost $120,000," Pauley wrote in April 1975, indicating that the company may have invested in it.

108 **a throng of reporters** Laurie Johnston, "Notes on People," *New York Times*, Sept. 3, 1975.

108 **"I hope his mom"** Author interview with Stephen Rosenfield.

108 **In November 2005** Matea Gold, "Fox News Displays a Green Side," *Los Angeles Times*, Nov. 12, 2005.

108 **"Those guys were absolutely convinced"** Author interview with Robert Kennedy Jr.

108 **A few months later** "Climatologist to Do Fox News Interview," *Richmond* (Virginia) *Times Dispatch*, May 20, 2006.

108 **"Roger believes"** Author interview with Robert Kennedy Jr. *Ionescapade* creator and director Robert Allan Ackerman echoed Kennedy's dislike of Fox News. In the fall of 2003, Bill O'Reilly and other prominent Republicans raised hell over a CBS miniseries about Ronald Reagan directed by Ackerman. The series had not yet aired, but portions of the script had leaked. "The right wing went completely ballistic," Ackerman said, recalling that executives at the network "were starting to

get all sorts of death threats." Under pressure, CBS CEO Les Moonves killed the series. As a compromise, a shortened version aired on CBS's cable channel Showtime. "I was so disgusted by it," Ackerman said. "We were forced to tell everyone it was put on the way we wanted it, but it wasn't true. That was it for me," he said. "I made one film after that."

108 **multiple campaigns** Author interview with Stephen Rosenfield. In an interview, Monks did not recall Ailes criticizing his campaign positions.

109 **"This guy has got to learn"** Author interview with Stephen Rosenfield.

109 **When Monks was campaigning** Ibid.

109 **During one town hall meeting** Ibid.

109 **Monks lost** Christian P. Potholm, *The Splendid Game: Maine Campaigns and Elections, 1940–2002* (Lanham, Md.: Lexington, 2004), 98.

110 **"Roger liked thirty-second"** Author interview with Stephen Rosenfield.

110 **One time Monks brought** Ibid.

110 **"psychological adjustment"** James C. Condon, "Coaching Executives on Stage Presence," *New York Times,* Feb. 6, 1977.

110 **He developed a $4,000 seminar** Ibid.

110 **Polaroid, Philip Morris, and Sperry** Ibid.

110 **In October 1983** "Articles of Incorporation, Ailes Business Communications, Inc.," Oct. 4, 1983. "Agreement and Plan of Merger of Ailes Business Communications Inc., a Pennsylvania Corporation with and into Ailes Communications, Inc., a Pennsylvania Corporation," March 22, 1985; "Certificate of Merger," July 5, 1985.

110 **He traveled to Rome** The name of the documentary was *Fellini: Wizards, Clowns and Honest Liars*. See John J. O'Connor, "TV Weekend," *New York Times,* Sept. 2, 1977.

110 **When he came back** Author interview with Stephen Rosenfield.

110 **On September 20, 1976** Krebs, "Kermit Bloomgarden, Producer of Many Outstanding Plays, Dead."

110 **About a year later** Author interview with Stephen Rosenfield.

111 ***Present Tense*** Richard Eder, "Stage: 'Present Tense' Out of Sequence," *New York Times,* Oct. 5, 1977.

111 **Garrett experienced limited success** Sharbutt, "Kelly Garrett Isn't 'Overnight' Success"; www.tonyawards.com/p/tonys_search.

111 **"When she didn't get"** Author interview with Paul Turnley.

111 **Garrett was devastated** Author interview with a friend of Kelly Garrett.

111 **Ailes tried to help** Liz Smith, "Sherrie Rollins Won't Follow Hubby to Perot," as printed in *The Blade,* Toledo, Ohio, June 12, 1992. Smith wrote: "When the White House is chasing, begging you to come back . . . (as I know is perfectly well the case with former political mastermind Roger Ailes, even though he denies it), and you prefer to stay in show biz and tout a singer you are handling, then it behooves all of us denizens of the night to check that singer out. So what has Kelly Garrett got that makes Roger Ailes so high on her talent? Well, I just answered my own question. . . . Kelly opens June 16 through the 27 at the Supper Club, and New York will get the chance to applaud her once again."

111 **In 2006, she moved** Tom Sharpe, "Kelly Garrett, 1944–2013: Acclaimed Singer Had Roots in New Mexico," *Santa Fe New Mexican,* Aug. 12, 2013.

111 **In 1977** Author interview with a friend of Roger Ailes from this period.

111 **He named Norma** Richard Eder, "Stage: 'Present Tense' Out of Sequence."

111 **"Roger made the people"** Author interview with Stephen Rosenfield.

111 **In 1976, eight years after** "Lunatics, Drunkards, Divorces, 1977–1978."

111 **She took possession** Indenture filed on March 3, 1977, in the Deed Book in the Recorder of Deeds Office, Media, Pennsylvania, Book 2604, page 1139; deed filed on July 18, 2007, in the Recorder of Deeds Office, Media, Pennsylvania, Instru-

ment Number 2007064022, Book/Page: RECORD-04156/2034. Although Marjorie Ailes never remarried, she had a longtime companion, Jim Jeffreys, a volunteer fireman and code enforcement officer in Media, Pennsylvania.

111 **"I've spent my life"** Author interview with Roger Ailes's first wife, Marjorie Ailes.

111 **In 1981, Ailes married Ferrer** Chafets, *Roger Ailes*, 42.

111 **She idolized her husband** Baer, "Roger Rabid."

111 **Shortly before** Author interview with Stephen Rosenfield. Rosenfield has written, directed, and produced numerous comedies and is director of the American Comedy Institute in New York City, http://www.comedyinstitute.com/.

## EIGHT: RISKY STRATEGY

112 **On January 31** Vincent Canby, "Movie Review: Screen: 'Power,' by Sidney Lumet," *New York Times*, Jan. 31, 1986.

112 **Richard Gere starred** David Denby, "Dressed for Success," *New York*, Feb. 17, 1986.

112 **When one client** Brian McNair, *Journalists in Film: Heroes and Villains* (Edinburgh: Edinburgh Press, 2010), 189.

112 **"Richard practically"** Author interview with Democratic political consultant Joel McCleary.

112 **1990 presidential election** Frederick Kempe, "Should Arias Return His Nobel? Since the Prize, Costa Rica's Leader Has Had Nothing but Trouble," *Washington Post*, Dec. 11, 1988.

112 **"You are paying me"** *Power,* directed by Sidney Lumet, Warner Home Video, 1986, 11:30 mark.

112 **"He wasn't trying"** Author interview with public opinion researcher V. Lance Tarrance Jr.

112 **Ailes's candidates** "Governor Hires New Yorker to Create Campaign Ads," *Los Angeles Times*, Nov. 14, 1985.

113 **D'Amato had stunned** Chafets, *Roger Ailes*, 40.

113 **Javits was staying in** Tom Buckley, "After Javits, the G.O.P. Turns Right with D'Amato," *New York Times Magazine*, Oct. 19, 1980.

113 **Elizabeth Holtzman** See, generally, Elizabeth Holtzman and Cynthia L. Cooper, *Who Said It Would Be Easy? One Woman's Life in the Political Arena* (New York: Arcade, 1996).

113 **"Jesus, nobody likes you"** Chafets, *Roger Ailes*, 40.

113 **In Ailes's first commercial** Ibid.

113 **Several weeks** Buckley, "After Javits, the G.O.P. Turns Right with D'Amato."

113 **But on election day** U.S. Government Printing Office, "Statistics of the Presidential and Congressional Election of November 4, 1980," April 15, 1981, http://clerk.house.gov/member_info/electionInfo/1980election.pdf.

113 **"In a less obvious"** Nicholas Lemann, "The Storcks," *Washington Post Magazine*, Dec. 7, 1980.

113 **The *Post* dubbed** Lemann, "The Storcks."

113 **D'Amato said** Chafets, *Roger Ailes*, 41.

113 **Larry McCarthy** McCarthy Hennings Whalen, Inc., Larry McCarthy biography, http://mhmediadc.com/larry-mccarthy.aspx, accessed Sept. 23, 2013.

113 **Jon Kraushar** Jon Kraushar & Associates, Inc., "Jon's Credentials," http://www.jonkraushar.net/jon-s-credentials.html, accessed Sept. 23, 2013.

113 **Kathy Ardleigh** Kathy Ardleigh biography, C-Span Video Library, available at http://www.c-spanvideo.org/kathyardleigh, accessed Oct. 30, 2013.

113 **Ken LaCorte** *Bloomberg Businessweek*, Ken LaCorte Executive Profile and Biography, http://investing.businessweek.com/research/stocks/private/person.asp?

personId=30252761&privcapId=4245059&previousCapId=4245059&previous Title=FOX%20News%20Network,%20L.L.C., accessed Oct. 30, 2013.

114 **"Whatever it takes"** Tom Mathews and Peter Goldman, *The Quest for the Presidency: The 1988 Campaign* (New York: Simon & Schuster, 1989), 331.

114 **After the D'Amato campaign** "Domestic News," United Press International, Jan. 1, 1981.

114 **On one occasion, Ailes punched a hole** Chafets, *Roger Ailes*, 216.

114 **"He got into"** Author interview with television producer Shelley Ross.

114 **"Roger was not"** Author interview with television personality, columnist, and businesswoman Rona Barrett.

114 **While interviewing** Author interviews with Randi Harrison and Chris Calhoun.

115 **Shelley Ross** Ken Auletta, "The Curious Rise of Network Television, and the Future of Network News," *New Yorker*, Aug. 8, 2005.

115 **"This is making"** Author interview with Shelley Ross.

115 **When asked** Author interview with David Brock.

115 **"He has worked"** Donald Baer, "Roger Rabid," *Manhattan Inc.*, Sept. 1989.

116 **In the summer of 1981** Ailes and Kraushar, *You Are the Message*, 2.

116 **"As our eyes"** Ibid.

116 **"Let me just tell you"** Author interview with Shelley Ross.

116 **The interview** Ailes and Kraushar, *You Are the Message*, 1.

116 **In November 1981** "David Letterman Gets Late-Night NBC Show," Associated Press, Nov. 9, 1981.

116 **Harrison "Jack" Schmitt** Eric M. Jones, "Apollo 17 Crew Information," NASA.gov, Nov. 1, 2005, http://www.hq.nasa.gov/alsj/a17/a17.crew.html.

116 **In 1976, Ailes had** Author interview with former astronaut and U.S. senator Harrison Schmitt.

116 **"We parked"** Ibid.

116 **He went on** U.S. Government Printing Office, "Statistics of the Presidential and Congressional Election of November 2, 1976," April 15, 1977, http://clerk.house.gov/member_info/electionInfo/1976election.pdf.

116 **But in the fall** Martin Schram, "Found: The Attraction of Detraction," *Washington Post*, Oct. 30, 1982.

117 **Bingaman won** U.S. Government Printing Office, "Statistics of the Congressional Election of November 2, 1982," May 5, 1983, http://clerk.house.gov/member_info/electionInfo/1982election.pdf.

117 **With two months to go** Author interview with V. Lance Tarrance Jr.

117 **"We were in"** Author interview with former George H. W. Bush campaign strategist Janet G. Mullins Grissom.

117 **As Ailes would tell it** Jane Mayer, "Who Let the Attack-Ad Dogs Out?," "News Desk" (blog), NewYorker.com, Feb. 15, 2012, http://www.newyorker.com/online/blogs/newsdesk/2012/02/roger-ailes-larry-mccarthy-dogs-ad.html.

117 **During a strategy meeting** Author interview with Janet G. Mullins Grissom.

117 **"There was Roger"** Ibid.

117 **Ailes dispatched** Mayer, "Who Let the Attack-Ad Dogs Out?"

117 ***"My job was"*** Pete Snyder, "Forget the Super Bowl: Which Political Ad Was the All-Time MVP?," "Campaign Trail" (blog), *Ad Age*, Feb. 7, 2012, http://adage.com/article/campaign-trail/political-ad-ailes-trippi-murphy-snyder-pick/232576/.

117 **"He called me"** Author interview with V. Lance Tarrance Jr.

117 **"They flicked us"** Author interview with Janet G. Mullins Grissom.

118 **"All the local"** Paul Taylor, "Senators Keep Guard Against Absenteeism; Nameplates Vanish After 'Committee Cameos,'" *Washington Post*, Feb. 11, 1986.

118 **McConnell squeezed** U.S. Government Printing Office, "Statistics of the Congressional Election of 1984."

118 **"We all know Roger"** Author interview with Janet G. Mullins Grissom.
118 **"The charge was baseless"** Marc Starr and Aric Press, "Gridlock on the Hill?," *Newsweek*, Election Extra edition, Nov./Dec. 1984.
118 **The ad, Mullins said** Author interview with Janet G. Mullins Grissom.
118 **Not long after it aired** Author interview with advertising executive Tom Messner.
118 **In early October** Author interview with member of the 1984 Ronald Reagan campaign for president Wally Carey.
118 **A few days earlier** Howell Raines, "Chance of Revival Seen for Mondale After TV Debate," *New York Times*, Oct. 9, 1984.
118 **"It was a disaster"** Author interview with Wally Carey.
118 **"When I arrived"** Ailes and Kraushar, *You Are the Message*, 20.
118 **"Reagan said"** Author interview with Wally Carey.
118 **Afterward, Ailes demanded** Ailes and Kraushar, *You Are the Message*, 21.
119 **As Ailes walked** Ibid., 23–24.
119 **At the second debate** Commission on Presidential Debates, "October 21, 1984, Debate Transcript," Oct. 21, 1984, http://www.debates.org/index.php?page=october-21-1984-debate-transcript.
119 **"Even he broke"** Ailes and Kraushar, *You Are the Message*, 25.
119 **"It's a question"** Martin Tolchin, "For Some, Low Road Is the Only Way to Go," *New York Times*, Oct. 28, 1984.
119 **In 1986, he produced** Raymond Coffey, "No Pulled Punches in Wisconsin," *Chicago Tribune*, Oct. 30, 1986.
119 **A few days before** Janet Bass, "Garvey Files Libel Suit Against Kasten," United Press International, Oct. 31, 1986.
119 **"There are limits"** "Candidate Sues Senator over TV Ad," Associated Press, Nov. 1, 1986.
119 **Kasten won** U.S. Government Printing Office, "Statistics of the Congressional Election of November 4, 1986," May 29, 1987, http://clerk.house.gov/member_info/electionInfo/1986election.pdf.
119 **Seven months later** Maralee Schwartz, "Sen. Kasten Settles Garvey Libel Suit," *Washington Post*, June 30, 1987.
119 **In October 1984** Author interview with Janet G. Mullins Grissom.
119 **"We had to restrain"** Ibid.
119 **During a strategy session** Lloyd Grove, "The Image Shaker: Roger Ailes, the Bush Team's Wily Media Man," *Washington Post*, June 20, 1988.
120 **"We used to joke"** Author interview with a former Ailes Communications employee.
120 **As the 1988** Mathews and Goldman, *The Quest for the Presidency*, 190.
120 **"Everybody tells me"** Miller Center, "Interview with Craig Fuller," University of Virginia, May 12, 2004, http://millercenter.org/president/bush/oralhistory/craig-fuller.
120 **He did not project** See, e.g., Mathews and Goldman, *The Quest for the Presidency*, 192; Richard Ben Cramer, *What It Takes: The Way to the White House* (New York: Vintage, 1993), 572.
120 **Martin Van Buren was the last** David Germain, "Bush First VP in 152 Years to Win White House," Associated Press, Nov. 9, 1988.
120 **"He didn't know how"** Author interview with George H. W. Bush's former chief of staff, Craig Fuller.
120 **"If you were a professional"** Miller Center, "Interview with Craig Fuller."
120 **Bush planned** Mathews and Goldman, *The Quest for the Presidency,* 193; author interview with Tom Messner.
120 **He took an apartment** Author interview with Tom Messner.
120 **huddled with Bush** Mathews and Goldman, *The Quest for the Presidency*, 193.
121 **"Why didn't you bail out?"** Cramer, *What It Takes*, 999.

121 **Ailes suggested a character** Mathews and Goldman, *The Quest for the Presidency*, 191.
121 **He taught Bush** Ibid., 193.
121 **"Don't *ever* wear that shirt"** Cramer, *What It Takes*, 568.
121 **"Roger was the only guy"** Author interview with political consultant Roger J. Stone Jr.
121 **As the Bush campaign structure** Mathews and Goldman, *The Quest for the Presidency*, 182.
121 **In addition to** Ibid., 192.
121 **"He had other business"** Miller Center, "Interview with Sigmund Rogich," University of Virginia, March 8–9, 2001, http://millercenter.org/president/bush/oralhistory/sigmund-rogich.
121 **This reality was confirmed** Cramer, *What It Takes*, 729.
121 **That morning** *Newsweek*, Oct. 19, 1987.
121 **The press response** Cramer, *What It Takes*, 730–31.
122 **"Ab-so-lute-ly no!"** Mathews and Goldman, *The Quest for the Presidency*, 198.
122 **A few days before** Author interview with Craig Fuller.
122 **Rather was planning** Matthews and Goldman, *The Quest for the Presidency*, 198.
122 **"I knew if we were"** Author interview with Craig Fuller.
122 **Ailes met with Bush** Ibid.
122 **"All they have to do"** Mathews and Goldman, *The Quest for the Presidency*, 199.
122 **Fuller proposed a zinger** Cramer, *What It Takes*, 852.
122 **Ailes loved Fuller's suggestion** Ibid.
122 **Ailes, reprising his role** Dickinson, "How Roger Ailes Built the Fox News Fear Factory."
123 **"I find this to be"** C-Span, "Dan Rather Interview of George Bush," C-Span Video Library, Jan. 25, 1988, http://www.c-spanvideo.org/program/Geo, accessed Sept. 24, 2013.
123 **"*Go! Go!*"** Dickinson, "How Roger Ailes Built the Fox News Fear Factory."
123 **"It's not fair"** C-Span, "Dan Rather Interview" (portion begins around 7:00).
123 **He got the time and place** Richard Stengel, "Bushwhacked! Dan Rather Sets Sparks Flying in a Showdown with the Vice President," *Time*, Feb. 8, 1988.
123 **"Well, I had my say"** Cramer, *What It Takes*, 853–54.
123 **The CBS switchboard** Stengel, "Bushwhacked!" At a breakfast at the 21 Club attended by Manhattan media and political leaders held shortly after the election, Ailes bumped into Dan Rather and practiced a bit of stagecraft. According to one attendee, Ailes hustled up to Rather as he was getting coffee at the buffet. "We oughta be seen having a conversation. Everyone will be surprised," Ailes said. He wanted people to think the two had made peace since Bush dismembered him. Rather, amused by the scheme, played along.
123 **On the campaign trail** Stengel, "Bushwhacked!"
123 **"Lee Atwater said"** Author interview with Craig Fuller.
123 **On February 8** "Republican Caucus History," *Des Moines Register*, http://caucuses.desmoinesregister.com/data/iowa-caucus/caucus-history-gop/.
124 **On Tuesday morning** Cramer, *What It Takes*, 882.
124 **"I said, look"** Author interview with Tom Messner.
124 **With laughably poor** Cramer, *What It Takes*, 889–90.
124 **Bush rejected it** Ibid.
124 **He called his wife** Ibid., 886.
124 **By Thursday** Ibid., 890.
124 **That night, Ailes played** Ibid., 888–89.
124 **George W. Bush** Ibid., 889.
124 **"The press is gonna say"** Ibid., 897.

124 **"This is your business"** Ibid.
124 **The campaign put big money** Ibid., 898.
124 **On Tuesday, February 16** E. J. Dionne, Jr., "Bush Overcomes Dole's Bid and Dukakis Is Easy Winner in New Hampshire Primaries," *New York Times*, Feb. 17, 1988.
125 **On primary night** Cramer, *What It Takes*, 902–3.
125 **"He responded with"** Author interview with Janet G. Mullins Grissom.
125 **Five weeks later** William M. Welch, "Dole Bows Out of Republican Race," Associated Press, March 29, 1988.
125 **On Thursday, May 26** Mathews and Goldman, *The Quest for the Presidency*, 299–300.
125 **The son of** Christopher B. Daly, "Dukakis: Son of Greek Immigrants Runs for White House," Associated Press, Feb. 2, 1988.
125 **His brand** Bob Drogin, "Dukakis Draws Heavy Crowds, Money, Press," *Los Angeles Times*, May 25, 1987.
125 **Ailes watched** Mathews and Goldman, *The Quest for the Presidency*, 300.
125 **"If you learned"** Ibid., 301.
125 **Ailes had consulted** Ibid., 360.
126 **At a campaign retreat** Cramer, *What It Takes*, 998–99.
126 **"We're gonna have to"** Author interview with a source familiar with the conversation.
126 **Polls showed** Cramer, *What It Takes*, 998.
126 **"Well, you guys"** Ibid., 999.
126 **On June 9** Ibid., 1010.
126 **"Michael Dukakis on crime"** Ibid., 1011.
126 **Ignoring the slick** Mathews and Goldman, *The Quest for the Presidency*, 362.
126 **Ailes also tapped** Author interviews with Tom Messner and Sig Rogich.
126 **While only fifteen** Paul Taylor, "Campaigns Take Aim Against Consultants; Incumbents' Tactic May Deter Later Attacks; Some See Other Motives," *Washington Post*, Feb. 15, 1990.
126 **To attack Dukakis** Miller Center, "Interview with Sigmund Rogich," University of Virginia, March 8–9, 2001, http://millercenter.org/president/bush/oralhistory/sigmund-rogich.
126 **The ad's centerpiece** Museum of the Moving Image, "The Living Room Candidate: Presidential Campaign Commercials 1952–2012," http://www.livingroomcandidate.org/commercials/1988.
126 **To hammer** Miller Center, "Interview with Sigmund Rogich"; author interview with Sig Rogich.
126 **The warning was** Mathews and Goldman, *The Quest for the Presidency*, 363.
127 **The proposed ad** Ibid., 361.
127 **Ailes told his team** Ibid., 362.
127 **"He didn't give"** Author interview with former Bush campaign spokesperson Sheila Tate.
127 **"Roger had an uncanny ability"** Author interview with former Secretary of State James Baker III.
127 **He called Dukakis** "Election '88: Waving the Bloody Shirt," *Newsweek*, Nov. 21, 1988.
127 **"You're the reason"** Mathews and Goldman, *The Quest for the Presidency*, 361.
127 **"Weekend Passes"** Museum of the Moving Image, http://www.livingroomcandidate.org/commercials/1988.
127 **In August, Ailes had boasted** Stengel, "The Man Behind the Message."
128 **And the Horton ad** Joe Conason, "Roger & He," *New Republic*, May 28, 1990.
128 **Roger Stone said that** Author interview with Roger Stone.

128 **"I know Roger very well"** Martin Schram, "The Making of Willie Horton," *New Republic*, May 28, 1990.
128 **"Roger detected"** Author interview with Sheila Tate.
128 **That night** Ibid.
128 **"That was his idea"** Ibid.
128 **In August** Stengel, "The Man Behind the Message."
128 **"He threatened to kill"** Author interview with Janet G. Mullins Grissom.
128 **Staffers noted** Author interview with Roger Stone.
128 **He told the press** Stengel, "The Man Behind the Message."
128 **His weight ballooned** Ibid.
129 **Craig Fuller recalled** Author interview with Craig Fuller.
129 **He was also known** Mathews and Goldman, *The Quest for the Presidency*, 191.
129 **Tom Messner recalled** Author interview with Tom Messner.
129 **"When he would have"** Author interview with Sig Rogich.
129 **Leaks sent Ailes** Author interviews with Sig Rogich and Tom Messner.
129 **A week and a half** Mathews and Goldman, *The Quest for the Presidency*, 422.
129 **"It was a hard ad"** Author interview with Janet G. Mullins Grissom.
129 **By mid-October,** Mathews and Goldman, *The Quest for the Presidency*, 422.
129 **From the time Dukakis** Ibid., 420.
129 **In the campaign's most memorable** Museum of the Moving Image, http://www.livingroomcandidate.org/commercials/1988.
130 **"I sat there mute"** Author interview with former Massachusetts governor and presidential candidate Michael Dukakis.
130 **"Wedge issues"** Author interview with Roger Stone.
130 **"Here's a man"** Author interview with Craig Fuller.
130 **In late October** Mathews and Goldman, *The Quest for the Presidency*, 398.
130 **Bush won** Ibid., 422.
130 **Ailes's marriage to Norma** Author interview with friends of Roger Ailes.
130 **"My wife has made the case"** Howard Fineman and Peter McKillop, "Roger Ailes: I Have to Take the Heat," *Newsweek*, Nov. 6, 1989.
130 **In 1983, Ailes's father** Author interview with Roger Ailes's brother, Robert Ailes Jr.
130 **"New York's master of"** Fineman and McKillop, "Roger Ailes: I Have to Take the Heat."
130 **"political terrorism"** Vlae Kershner, "Campaign Insider," *San Francisco Chronicle*, Oct. 10, 1990.
130 **He offered a $100,000 reward** Barbara Demick, "Bush Campaign Role in Ads Probed; New Light Cast on Willie Horton Flap," *Houston Chronicle*, Feb. 4, 1992.
130 **"TO IMPLY COLLUSION"** Conason, "Roger & He."
131 **In July 1989** Baer, "Roger Rabid."
131 **In the fall of 1989** Kerwin Swint, *Dark Genius: The Influential Career of Legendary Political Operative and Fox News Founder Roger Ailes* (New York: Sterling, 2008), 39.
131 **Ailes continued to stoke** "Good Night, Gracie," *Newsday Magazine*, Dec. 17, 1989.
131 **At another point** Howard Kurtz, "Giuliani Presses Dinkins's Connection to Jackson as Campaign Intensifies," *Washington Post*, Sept. 30, 1989.
131 **Jackson had called New York** Laurence McQuillan, United Press International, Feb. 27, 1984.
131 **Dinkins attacked** Swint, *Dark Genius*, 41.
131 **On the night of October 23** Vivienne Walt, "Ailes Faces Assault Complaint," *Newsday*, Oct. 26, 1989; Joe Klein, "Gandhi vs. Gumby: Can't Anybody Here Run This Town?," *New York*, Nov. 6, 1989.

131 **"We were screaming"** Author interview with activist Kathy Ottersten, who at the time and in news reports was known as Kevin Ottersten.
131 **At the time, Sergeant** Walt, "Ailes Faces Assault Complaint."
132 **"I attempted to file"** Author interview with Kathy Ottersten.
132 **On the Sunday before** Joe Klein, "Willie Ailes," *New York*, Dec. 4, 1989.
132 **Giuliani lost** Kenneth Jackson, Lisa Keller, and Nancy Flood, eds., *The Encyclopedia of New York City: Second Edition* (New Haven: Yale University Press, 2010), 511.
132 **Ailes's candidate** Peter Kerr, "The 1989 Elections: The Governor-Elect; Transition and Insurance Come First, Florio Says," *New York Times*, Nov. 9, 1989.
132 **In the fall of 1989** Fineman and McKillop, "Roger Ailes: I Have to Take the Heat."
132 **Lee Atwater's sudden diagnosis** Richard Benedetto, "Atwater Has a Benign Brain Tumor," *USA Today*, March 7, 1990.
132 **In May 1990** Charles R. Babcock, "Willie Horton Political Ads Become Issue in Ohio Race," *Washington Post*, May 26, 1990.
132 **the FEC was deadlocked** Demick, "Bush Campaign Role in Ads Probed."
132 **"I'm not the candidate"** Baer, "Roger Rabid."
132 **On Tuesday, October 9** Ed White, "Martin Media Adviser Calls Simon 'Slimy,' 'Weenie,'" Associated Press, Oct. 9, 1990.
132 **Martin lost** U.S. Government Printing Office, "Statistics of the Congressional Election of November 6, 1990," April 29, 1991, http://clerk.house.gov/member_info/electionInfo/1990election.pdf.
133 **In 1988** Ailes and Kraushar, *You Are the Message*.
133 **"When you control"** Ibid., 111.
133 **"You *can* learn"** Ibid., 112.
133 **In the summer of 1988** Californians Against Unfair Tax Increases, agreement with Ailes Communications Inc., July 1, 1988, http://legacy.library.ucsf.edu/tid/gri44a00, Bates no. 87699641.
133 **last at least for five years** Thomas Collamore, email conversation with Craig Fuller, June 29, 1994, http://legacy.library.ucsf.edu/tid/upq91a00/pdf, Bates. no. 2047915175A.
133 **His first assignment** "Tobacco Group on Hotseat for Failure to Honor Advertising Contract," Business Wire, Sept. 6, 1988.
133 **At the time, it represented** David S. Wilson, "2 Ballot Issues Raise Question: Is Smoking Becoming Taboo?," *New York Times*, Oct. 25, 1988.
133 **In one memo, Ailes wrote** Ailes Communications Inc., "Creative Strategy to Defeat the Tobacco Tax Initiative," June 29, 1988, http://legacy.library.ucsf.edu/tid/jsy44b00/pdf, Bates no. TI02450986.
133 **"We have no obligation"** Ibid., Bates no. TI02450989.
133 **One ad portrayed** Ailes Communications Inc., "Medical School," script, Aug. 30, 1988, available at http://legacy.library.ucsf.edu/tid/ljz54c00/pdf, Bates no. 87700232.
133 **One commercial portrayed** David S. Wilson, "2 Ballot Issues Raise Question: Is Smoking Becoming Taboo?," *New York Times*, Oct. 25, 1988.
134 **Prop 99 supporters'** Mark A. Stein, "Deception Seen in Anti-Cigarette Tax Ads," *Los Angeles Times*, Sept. 28, 1988.
134 **His biggest role** Ibid.
134 **In November 1988** "Final Election Vote Returns," *Los Angeles Times*, Nov. 9, 1988.
134 **"The antismoking zealots"** Andy Plattner, "Big Tobacco's Toughest Road: Invigorated Activists and Lawmakers Launch New Attacks on Smoking," *U.S. News & World Report*, April 17, 1989.
134 **In 1987, Reagan's FCC** Steve Rendall, "Rough Road to Liberal Talk Success: A Short History of Radio Bias," *Extra!*, Jan./Feb. 2007.
134 **More than seven million** Catherine Hinman, "Rush to Judgment: Radio Talk

Show Host Rush Limbaugh Has Opinions on Just About Everything, Including a Big One of Himself," *Orlando Sentinel*, June 15, 1991.

134 **In 1991, after bumping into each other** Chafets, *Roger Ailes*, 61–62.

134 **The GOP paid him** Baer, "Roger Rabid."

134 **In August 1990** Roger Ailes, letter to New Hampshire Governor John Sununu, Aug. 17, 1990, http://edge-cache.gawker.com/gawker/ailesfiles/ailes11.html, accessed Sept. 26, 2013.

134 **"In the field"** Rogers Ailes, letter to New Hampshire Governor John Sununu, Nov. 16, 1990, http://edge-cache.gawker.com/gawker/ailesfiles/ailes12.html, accessed Sept. 26, 2013.

135 **Bushworld put out feelers** Author interview with a member of the Bush campaign team.

135 **"He was thinking about"** Author interview with a source familiar with the conversation.

135 **On December 6, 1991** "Financial News," PR Newswire, Dec. 6, 1991.

135 **consulting for Paramount Television** See, generally, the Bradley Prizes, "2013 Recipients: Roger Ailes," Bradleyprizes.org, http://bradleyprizes.org/recipients/roger-ailes, accessed Oct. 22, 2013.

135 **At the 1992 Democratic convention** Author interview with Bob LaPorta.

135 **One writer who ran into** Author interview with an associate of Roger Ailes.

135 **In 1992, he lined up** Thomas Hardy, "Election-Year Board Games Try to Capture the Real Thing," *Chicago Tribune*, May 18, 1992.

135 **In August, he traveled** Harry Berkowitz, "GOP Pit Bull Roaming Convention; Adman Ailes Says He's There for Fun," *Newsday*, Aug. 20, 1992.

135 **To advance around the board** Golden Games, "Risky Strategy: The Game of Campaign Capers," board game, Jim Bear Enterprises, Inc., 1991.

135 **"Politics was a 20-year habit"** Berkowitz, "GOP Pit Bull Roaming Convention."

135 **"By that time"** Author interview with James Baker III.

136 **On the night of June 2** Paul D. Colford, *The Rush Limbaugh Story: The Unauthorized Biography* (New York: St. Martin's, 1993).

136 **Bill Clinton's campaign** Michael Kelly, "The 1992 Campaign: The Democrats: Clinton's Staff Sees Campaign as a Real War," *New York Times*, Aug. 11, 1992.

136 **During the 1988 GOP convention** Author interview with former NBC News producer Joe Angotti.

136 **In the spring of 1990** Naftali Bendavid, "GOP Campaign Adviser Tries Broadcasting," *Miami Herald*, May 18, 1990.

137 **"It was an oldies station"** Author interview with radio personality Greg Wyatt.

137 **Ailes came up with** Ibid.

137 **"It's just a fun thing"** Bendavid, "GOP Campaign Adviser Tries Broadcasting."

137 **"He wanted to do"** Author interview with Sig Rogich.

# ACT III

## NINE: AMERICA'S TALKING

141 **In early 1993** Author interview with former NBC chairman Robert Wright.

141 **he wanted to resign** Geraldine Fabrikant, "Ex-Consultant to Bush Named to Head NBC," *New York Times*, Aug. 31, 1993.

141 **After NBC launched** Bill Carter, "The Media Business: Television; NBC Walks into a Cable Minefield," *New York Times*, April 10, 1989. See also Geraldine Fab-

rikant, "Surprise Pact by G.E. Unit to Buy FNN," *New York Times,* Feb. 27, 1991; PR Newswire, "Court Approves CNBC's $154.3 Million Bid for FNN Media Business," May 9, 1991.

141 **"Al was a great guy"** Author interview with Robert Wright.

142 **"One of the things"** Ibid.

142 **But when Ailes's name** Author interview with CNBC producers.

142 **In interviews, he called** Liz Trotta, "Roger Ailes Still Has Snap in His Political Jabs," *Washington Times,* May 11, 1993.

142 **"He always craved"** Author interview with a former colleague of Roger Ailes.

142 **On July 8** Letter from Roger Ailes to former NBC Cable president Tom Rogers, July 8, 1993.

143 **On July 25** Ken Parish Perkins, "Exploring the Mystery of Comedy," *Dallas Morning News,* July 22, 1993.

143 **Later that week** Deirdre Donahue, "Chronicling Kennedy," *USA Today,* July 29, 1993. In early July, Ailes offered McGinniss three days of private media training to help him combat the negative press reaction to the book. McGinniss and Ailes had been out of touch for years, but the controversy over his Kennedy book brought them back together. McGinniss called his old friend to commiserate about the Kennedys' aggressive response to *The Last Brother*. McGinniss's personal publicist had quit on him, explaining that Caroline Kennedy, who was also a client, threatened to pull all of her business if she stuck with him. "I was calling Roger up, asking for sympathy. He was always bitching about the Kennedys playing dirty and the Kennedys doing this and Kennedys doing that," McGinniss recalled. "So I said, 'Boy, I just had an experience with the Kennedys.' Roger said, '*Well, fuck them*. You know what, here's what I can do.' He said, 'You can come into my studio for three days and we'll just work with the video cameras and the tape machines and I'll be the prick host asking you all these terrible questions, and you'll answer them and we'll sit there and I'll point out where your answers can be improved.' " McGinniss took Ailes up on his offer and camped out in Ailes's Park Avenue South office. The two ordered in sandwiches for lunch as they worked on his responses. "No interview came close to being as penetrating, as hostile, and as pointed as Roger's," McGinniss later recalled. "Roger could have been Mike Wallace plus Tom Snyder. If he had gotten into that business, he could have been the nastiest interviewer on television." When McGinniss offered to pay Ailes for his services or for dinner at Patsy's, Ailes declined. "I said, 'Roger, this is unbelievable of you.' He said, 'We can't let the Kennedys push you around.' Whether Simon & Schuster paid him, I don't know. It never came up between him and me. He said, 'I'm doing good right now, I'll pick up the check.' " Author interview with Joe McGinniss.

143 **on July 21** Daniel LeDuc, "Whitman Hires Ad Man Who Raised Ire with Willie Horton," *Philadelphia Inquirer,* July 21, 1993. See also Daniel LeDuc, "Controversial Ad Man Quits Whitman Camp," *Philadelphia Inquirer,* July 22, 1993.

143 **In an interview** Dan Balz, "Dispute over 'Horton' Ad Adds More Heat to Race for New Jersey Governor," *Washington Post,* Aug. 1, 1993.

143 **He tried reaching Whitman** Author interview with Carl Golden, a former press secretary to Governor Christine Todd Whitman.

144 **"Ailes went off"** Ibid.

144 **On the afternoon of July 27** Ailes Communications, "Ailes Labels Whitman 'Slick Christie' " (press release), July 27, 1993.

144 **Whitman's apology** Chris Conway, "GOP Ad Man Gets Apology," *Philadelphia Inquirer,* July 29, 1993; Jerry Gray, "A Republican Attacks Whitman, Too," *New York Times,* Aug. 1, 1993.

144 **He flew to Nantucket** Brock, "Roger Ailes Is Mad as Hell."

144 **"Roger had a really good relationship"** Author interview with a colleague of Roger Ailes.

144 **"I was all for it"** Author interview with former General Electric CEO Jack Welch.
144 **Ailes downplayed** Peter Johnson and Brian Donlon, "GOP Strategist Ailes Wooed to Run CNBC," *USA Today,* Aug. 16, 1993.
144 **three-year contract** Letter from Robert Wright to Roger Ailes, Aug. 23, 1993.
145 **"Tom's role was pushed back"** Author interview with Jack Welch.
145 **"Roger had enemies"** Ibid.
145 **When Wright made the announcement** Hass, "Embracing the Enemy."
145 **Ailes did not inspire** Author interview with a former CNBC staffer.
145 **"A lot of us were leery"** Author interview with former CNBC host Doug Ramsey.
145 **"Look, there's one way"** Author interview with a former CNBC producer.
145 **In a cost-cutting move** Linda Moss, "NBC's Cable Gambit Sends Out a Signal," *Crain's New York Business,* April 10, 1989.
145 **"We're going to knock"** Author interview with a former CNBC producer.
145 **He recruited** Author interview with a former CNBC staffer.
145 **"It used to be"** Author interview with a former CNBC senior producer.
145 **"He was there"** Author interview with Bob Wright.
145 **Early on, Ailes summoned** Author interview with a former CNBC anchor.
146 **"Some said it was vicious"** Author interview with a former CNBC executive.
146 **As a campaign operative** Richard Ben Cramer, *What It Takes: The Way to the White House* (New York: Open Road Integrated Media ebook, 2011), 565.
146 **presidential tie clip** David Lieberman, "Taking to New Stump: CNBC's Ailes Dares to Raise Cable Stakes," *USA Today,* April 28, 1994.
146 **Ailes became a regular** Author interview with Jack Welch. "He and Ebersol would come in together," Welch recalled. "They'd love to order cheeseburgers and French fries. That's part of Roger. He's the most entertaining person to hang out with. He's funny and quick."
146 **He attended parties** Hass, "Embracing the Enemy."
146 **Positioning himself** Author interview with a former CNBC anchor.
146 **To celebrate the marriage** Author interview with Jane Wallace, who attended the party.
146 **"My wife called it"** Author interview with a former CNBC host.
146 **"I'll never forget"** Author interview with a former CNBC executive.
146 **At GE budget meetings** Author interview with a former NBC executive.
146 **"I saw that"** Author interview with Robert Wright.
146 **Eight months into his run** David Lieberman, "Taking to New Stump/CNBC's Ailes Dares to Raise Cable Stakes," *USA Today,* April 28, 1994.
147 **"Markets were becoming a huge story"** Author interview with a former CNBC producer.
147 **Ailes thought CNBC** Lieberman, "Taking to New Stump."
147 **"The Dow plummets"** Rebecca Johnson, "The Correction, or Whatever It Is, Will Be Televised," *New Yorker,* April 18, 1994.
147 **"We talked about the feel"** Author interview with a former CNBC senior producer.
147 **"Chet was his father"** Author interview with former CNBC producer Glenn Meehan.
147 **Lingering over a scotch** Author interview with a former CNBC employee.
148 **Paul Rittenberg** Richard Linnett, "Media Mavens: Paul Rittenberg," *Advertising Age,* Sept. 29, 2003.
148 **David Zaslav** Biography of David Zaslav at Businessweek.com, http://investing.businessweek.com/research/stocks/people/person.asp?personId=612978&ticker=DISCA.
148 **Brian Lewis** Biography of Brian Lewis at http://view.fdu.edu/?id=1963.
148 **In the fall of 1993** Author interview with a person familiar with the matter.

148 **Jeanine Pirro** Jacques Steinberg, "Rancor in District Attorney's Race; Cherkasky-Pirro Campaign Pits Newcomer Against Veteran," *New York Times,* Oct. 19, 1993. In 2006, Ailes hired Pirro at Fox News, http://www.foxnews.com/on-air/personalities/jeanine-pirro/bio/#s=m-q.
148 **On his first day** Author interview with a former CNBC staffer.
148 **"She lived and breathed CNBC"** Author interview with a former CNBC producer.
148 **One weekend, Ailes came into** Author interview with a former CNBC staffer.
148 **"Roger demanded loyalty"** Author interview with a former CNBC producer.
148 **Her boss, Peter Sturtevant** See *Broadcasting & Cable,* Oct. 24, 1994, 63.
148 **In December, he made her** "Tilson's Talking," *Broadcasting & Cable,* Dec. 13, 1993.
148 **Producers would often see her** Author interview with a former CNBC producer.
149 **"I used to have lunch"** Author interview with a former CNBC producer.
149 **"As someone"** Jane Hall, "CNBC Chief No Stranger to the Tube," *Los Angeles Times,* Oct. 18, 1993.
149 **"I figure there are"** Frazier Moore, "Trying to Cure What Ailes You," Associated Press, Aug. 6, 1995.
149 **"His idea was"** Author interview with Robert Wright.
149 **"The first day"** Author interview with former A-T executive producer Renata Joy.
149 **The lineup** Joe Flint, *Daily Variety,* May 5, 1994.
150 **In late June 1994** NBC contract with Belmont Street Broadcasting, June 20, 1994.
150 **"He very much believed"** Author interview with former A-T producer Dennis Sullivan.
150 **"When you work with Roger"** Author interview with a former A-T assistant producer.
150 **"He's very good"** Author interview with Dennis Sullivan.
150 **"They were like a pep rally"** Author interview with a former A-T producer.
150 **At around 4:30** "Fire Knocks Out CNBC," *Boston Globe,* May 11, 1994.
150 **"Roger went back"** Author interview with a former CNBC staffer.
151 **In one early session** Author interview with a former CNBC staffer.
151 **"He called it"** Author interview with a former CNBC producer.
151 **"We'd get newspapers"** Author interview with Glenn Meehan.
151 **The network signed a deal** "America's Talking is nation's first interactive live television network—exclusive deal with Prodigy; Prodigy simultaneously begins chat for television interactivity," Business Wire, June 15, 1994.
151 **"They were struggling"** Author interview with former A-T producer Tony Morelli.
151 **During his first year** Hass, "Embracing the Enemy."
151 **he drew a $5,000-a-month** Email from former Philip Morris executive Thomas Collamore to Craig Fuller, http://legacy.library.ucsf.edu/tid/upq91a00/pdf.
152 **The goal, according to** Philip Morris internal document, http://legacy.library.ucsf.edu/tid/wnc97g00/pdf.
152 **He went after** Collins, *Crazy Like a Fox,* 19, citing Kurt Andersen as the source. Andersen's story, "Big Mouths," appeared in the Nov. 1, 1993, issue of *Time.*
152 **One day Peter Sturtevant got** Author interview with a former CNBC executive.
152 **Ailes called in to Don Imus's** Lois Romano, "The Reliable Source" (column), *Washington Post,* March 11, 1994.
153 **one was under investigation** David Johnston, "Clinton Associate Quits Justice Post as Pressure Rises," *New York Times,* March 15, 1994. Bernard Nussbaum was forced to resign in early March 1994. Webster Hubbell, who was under investigation at the time, resigned a week later.

153 **Like all the networks** Peter Johnson, "Ailes' Whitewater Jokes Don't Amuse White House," *USA Today,* March 15, 1994.
153 **Lewis launched** Mary Alma Welch, "Cable Exec's 'Joke' Bombs at White House; Remarks by Ailes 'Inappropriate,'" *Washington Post,* March 12, 1994.
153 **"Ailes wasn't joking"** Author interview with a former CNBC executive.
153 **"He had no right"** Author interview with former CNBC host Jane Wallace.
153 **Wallace quit** Joe Flint, "FX Talker Taps Wallace," *Daily Variety,* April 6, 1994.
153 **After the weekend** Peter Johnson, "Ailes' Whitewater Jokes Don't Amuse White House."
153 **"Tom's had a little trouble"** Collins, *Crazy Like a Fox,* 18, citing an interview Ailes gave to *Multichannel News* in May 1994.
154 **Rogers was furious** Author interview with a former CNBC executive.
154 **"Roger has a very large ego"** Author interview with Robert Wright.
154 **"Who are you loyal to?"** Author interview with a former senior executive at NBC.
154 **"I'm going to rip"** Author interview with a former CNBC executive.
154 **One day, the executive noticed** Ibid.
154 **"Ailes didn't trust David"** Author interview with a former staffer at America's Talking.
154 **Ailes asked Scott Ehrlich** Author interview with a person familiar with the matter.
154 **Rogers approached Peter Sturtevant** Author interview with a former CNBC executive.
154 **"Sturtevant, I don't want"** Ibid.
154 **She had cut off** Author interview with a person familiar with the matter.
154 **Sturtevant finally was transferred** J. Max Robins, "NBC Cable Ups Sturtevant, Reilly," *Daily Variety,* Oct. 4, 1994.
154 **While Ailes seemed happy** Author interview with a former CNBC executive.
154 **Ailes openly criticized** David Brock, "Roger Ailes Is Mad as Hell," *New York,* Nov. 17, 1997.
155 **In late 1994** Author interview with a former A-T producer. See also Alan Bash, "Vignettes Give Cable Networks Identity," *USA Today,* March 14, 1994.
155 **Modeled after** "The Fastest Soaps, Bar None," *Washington Post,* Feb. 5, 1995.
155 **"Roger ran his life"** Author interview with Glenn Meehan.
155 **"America is talking, but"** Author interview with a former senior NBC executive.
155 **Dennis Sullivan** Author interview with Dennis Sullivan.
155 **She grew up** Elizabeth Ailes's commencement speech for the Mount Saint Mary College class of 2012, YouTube, http://www.youtube.com/watch?v=LoTlCx7Kzxo.
156 **"I remember"** Author interview with a former CNBC producer.
156 **Others marveled** Author interview with a former CNBC producer.
156 **Glenn Meehan also noticed** Author interview with Glenn Meehan.
156 **Nancy Hass** Nancy Hass, "Embracing the Enemy: Roger Ailes," *New York Times Magazine,* Jan. 8, 1995.
156 **At first Ailes resisted** Author interview with a person familiar with the matter.
157 **Hass interviewed Welch** Ibid.
157 **"It was taken internally"** Author interview with a former America's Talking staffer.
157 **"Roger sees everyone"** Hass, "Embracing the Enemy."

## TEN: "A VERY, VERY DANGEROUS MAN"

158 **Five days** The following account is based on Ted Turner and Bill Burke, *Call Me Ted* (New York: Hachette Digital, 2008), 309–10. See also Skip Wollenberg, "Turner Broadcasting Breaks Off Talks with NBC," Associated Press, Jan. 16, 1995.

158 **The network's operating income** Charles Haddad, "Ready for a Rivalry," *Atlanta Journal and Constitution,* Dec. 24, 1995.
159 **One afternoon** Author interview with a former CNBC executive.
159 **Shortly afterward, Wright and Scanlon** Letter from Andy Friendly to Robert Wright and Ed Scanlon, March 13, 1995.
159 **CNBC's prime-time chief Andy Friendly confided** Ibid.
159 **Executives dubbed her** Author interview with a former CNBC staffer.
159 **On Monday, March 13** Letter from Andy Friendly to Robert Wright and Ed Scanlon, March 13, 1995.
160 **"When you get"** Author interview with Robert Wright.
160 **He took a job** King World, "CNBC's Andy Friendly Joins King World as Executive VP of Programming and Production" (press release), Oct. 2, 1995.
160 **In June 1995** Bill Carter, "CNN Officials to Propose a Business News Cable Service," *New York Times,* June 9, 1995.
160 **Ailes had tried** J. Max Robins, "The ABC's of Michael Jackson," *Variety,* June 26–July 9, 1995.
160 **He contemplated running attack ads** Joe Flint, "Brand Name Good for Biz," *Variety,* Dec. 11–Dec. 17, 1995.
160 **"At this point"** Robins, "The ABC's of Michael Jackson."
160 **Ailes told the press** Carter, "CNN Officials to Propose a Business News Cable Service."
161 **The negotiating window** Peter Johnson and Alan Bash, "Roger Ailes Ponders His Future with CNBC," *USA Today,* June 21, 1995.
161 **Nine days** Johnson and Bash, "Roger Ailes Ponders His Future with CNBC."
161 **On June 30, 1995** Letter from Robert Wright to Roger Ailes, June 30, 1995.
161 **"This is where"** Author interview with Robert Wright.
161 **In May 1995** Evan Ramstad, "Business News," Associated Press, May 16, 1995. See also Bradley Johnson, "Microsoft-NBC: A 'Virtual Corporation'; Details May Be Fuzzy but Packaging Is Loud as Companies Converge," *Advertising Age,* May 22, 1995.
161 **Tom Rogers started** Author interview with Robert Wright.
161 **Ailes was initially unaware** Swint, *Dark Genius,* 124–26. See also Collins, *Crazy Like a Fox,* 15, 18.
161 **"The reality"** Author interview with Robert Wright.
161 **"meltdown mode"** Collins, *Crazy Like a Fox,* 22.
161 **Norma had filed** Divorce case 309767-1994, Supreme Court of the State of New York, Justice Phyllis Gangel-Jacob.
162 **"The bubble broke"** Author interview with Robert Wright.
162 **At a company dinner** Brock, "Roger Ailes Is Mad as Hell."
162 **"a little fucking Jew prick"** Handwritten notes of Edward Scanlon following the alleged incident.
162 **On Saturday, September 30** Ibid.
162 **That night, Scanlon briefed** Ibid. Much of the following paragraph is based on Scanlon's notes.
162 **"Howard Ganz"** Author interview with Robert Wright.
162 **NBC gave Ganz** Typed notes of Proskauer partner Howard Ganz. Much of the account of Ganz's investigation detailed in subsequent paragraphs is based on these notes.
162 **A week into Ganz's inquiry** Letter from Jim Greiner to Roger Ailes, Oct. 10, 1995, forwarded to Edward Scanlon, Oct. 10, 1995.
163 **"Roger is really working"** Letter from Edward Scanlon to Howard Ganz, Oct. 10, 1995.
163 **Bob Wright later said** Author interview with Robert Wright.
163 **Friday, October 13** Letter from David Zaslav to Howard Ganz, Oct. 17, 1995.

164 **On October 17** Typed notes of Howard Ganz prior to meeting with Hon. Milton Mollen.

164 **When later asked** Author interview with Milton Mollen. In an author interview, Howard Ganz confirmed that he was brought in by NBC to handle the dispute between Ailes and Zaslav. In a follow-up email, Ganz said: "I did, however, review what remains of my files regarding the matter involving Roger Ailes and they do not add anything more to the recollection I had when I spoke with you." When I asked Tom Rogers about the events, he denied both being involved and that any incident ever occurred. "I am denying having gone to Scanlon," he said. A day after I spoke with Tom Rogers, David Zaslav returned my call, having previously declined to speak with me for the book. "Tom Rogers called me and told me what you're gonna lay out," Zaslav said. As I began to detail my reporting, Zaslav cut the conversation off. "I don't mean to be rude. I don't care about the context," he said. "It's your book. You are going to write the narrative you are going to write. I'm saying to you that Roger and I had a screaming match and we had it out with each other. The anti-Semitic remark: If you write it, it's false." Zaslav continued: "Roger and I had many arguments. If there were an HR investigation, it was because we were telling each other to go to hell. Gabe, I wish you luck with your book." He hung up the phone. After the conversation, I called his spokesperson and requested a follow-up conversation. Zaslav never responded to my request. Ed Scanlon and Richard Cotton declined to comment.

164 **NBC drafted** Internal NBC memo, Oct. 19, 1995.

165 **On October 20** Letter from Roger Ailes to Robert Wright, Oct. 20, 1995.

165 **But Ailes was getting reports** Memo from Brian Lewis to Roger Ailes, Oct. 18, 1995.

165 **Wednesday, October 25** Letter from David Zaslav to Edward Scanlon, Oct. 25, 1995.

166 **"It was a he-said"** Author interview with Robert Wright.

166 **At a staff meeting** Internal NBC memo, Oct. 30, 1995.

166 **On November 10** Employment agreements regarding Roger Ailes and David Zaslav, Nov. 10, 1995.

166 **"There was no apology"** Author interview with Milton Mollen.

166 **On November 21** "Communications Personals," *Communications Daily,* Nov. 21, 1995.

166 **One Ailes loyalist** Author interview with a former CNBC colleague of Ailes.

167 **In late November 1995** Collins, *Crazy Like a Fox,* 18.

167 **"It was very, very uncomfortable"** Ibid.

167 **"He said he would run it"** Author interview with Robert Wright.

167 **"I love competition"** Elizabeth Sanger, "Financial News Is Hot," *Newsday,* Dec. 3, 1995.

167 **On December 14** Collins, *Crazy Like a Fox,* 5–10, 17.

167 **On-screen, Bob Wright** CNBC/Dow Jones Business Video, "NBC Holds News Conference to Announce New 24-Hour News Channel" (transcript), Dec. 14, 1995.

167 **Microsoft was investing** Collins, *Crazy Like a Fox,* 9.

167 **The staggering $7.5 billion** Mark Landler, "Turner to Merge into Time Warner; a $7.5 Billion Deal," *New York Times,* Sept. 23, 1995.

168 **In early December** United Press International, "ABC to Launch 24-Hour Cable News Channel," Dec. 5, 1995.

168 **Speaking to a group** Associated Press, "Murdoch Planning All-News TV Network," Nov. 29, 1995.

168 **Just a few months earlier** Ken Auletta, "The Pirate," *New Yorker,* Nov. 13, 1995.

168 **A day after Murdoch's announcement** "Battle of the Cable Stars: Turner Unfazed by Murdoch All-News Network Challenge," *Los Angeles Times,* Times Wire Services, Nov. 30, 1995.

168 **"From CNN's earliest days"** Turner and Burke, *Call Me Ted,* 336.

168 **One reporter asked** CNBC/Dow Jones, "NBC Holds News Conference to Announce New 24-Hour News Channel."
168 ***"Fuck them"*** Collins, *Crazy Like a Fox,* 17.
168 **"I remember Dan Quayle"** Author interview with a former America's Talking producer.
168 ***Vanity Fair*** Marie Brenner, "Steve Forbes's Quixotic Presidential Quest," *Vanity Fair,* Jan. 1996.
168 **When *The Washington Post*** Howard Kurtz, "CNBC's Roger Ailes, Talking a Fine Line," *Washington Post,* Dec. 11, 1995.
168 **Ten days later** Liz Smith, "Roger's a Free Man," *Newsday,* Dec. 11, 1995.
169 **"We both realized"** Author interview with former General Electric chairman Jack Welch.
169 **On January 9** NBC separation agreement with Roger Ailes.
169 **A week later, dozens** Scott Williams, "Roger Ailes Out at CNBC," Associated Press, Jan. 18, 1996.
169 **"Now look"** Collins, *Crazy Like a Fox,* 21.
169 **"When Roger came out"** Collins, *Crazy Like a Fox,* 22.
170 **"It's an awkward day"** Ibid.
170 **What Wright did not say** Author interview with Robert Wright.
170 **Tom Rogers left** Richard Katz, "NBC's Rogers Takes Post as Primedia's CEO," *Variety.com,* Sept. 28, 1999, http://variety.com/1999/biz/news/nbc-s-rogers-takes-post-as-primedia-ceo-1117756095/. See also Michael Singer, "Tom Rogers Named New CEO of TiVo," *CNET News,* June 27, 2005, http://news.cnet.com/Tom-Rogers-named-new-CEO-of-TiVo/2100-1040_3-5764357.html.
170 **David Zaslav followed Rogers** Paula Bernstein, "Zaslav Is Wired to Replace Rogers as NBC Cable Chief," *Hollywood Reporter,* Oct. 5, 1999. See also Ana Campoy, "Discovery Communications Names David Zaslav CEO," *Marketwatch,* Nov. 16, 2006, http://www.marketwatch.com/story/discovery-communications-names-david-zaslav-ceo.
170 **In 2011** Christina Rexrode and Bernard Condon, "Typical CEO Made $9.6 Million Last Year, AP Study Finds," Associated Press, May 25, 2012.
170 **In the weeks before his departure** Author interview with former executives at CNBC.
170 **The New York *Daily News*** Richard Huff and Douglas Feiden, "Ailes Quits CNBC, Ch. 4 GM Steps In," New York *Daily News,* Jan. 19, 1996.
170 **Earlier that fall** Collins, *Crazy Like a Fox,* 22–23. See also Auletta, "Vox Fox."

## ELEVEN: THE AUSSIE AND THE MIDWESTERNER

171 **Less than two weeks after** Scott Williams, "Murdoch Names Ailes to Launch 24-Hour TV News Channel," Associated Press, Jan. 30, 1996. See also Bill Carter, "Murdoch Joins a Cable-TV Rush into the Crowded All-News Field," *New York Times,* Jan. 31, 1996; and *Washington Post,* "Ailes to Run Murdoch's New Network," Jan. 31, 1996. The *Times* reported that the channel was not yet named, while the *Post* said it was to be called the Fox All News Network or Fox News.
171 **But the tabloid saga** Author interviews with CNN executives, anchors, and producers.
171 **In a break from** Howard Kurtz, "The Little Network with Big Names," *Washington Post,* July 12, 1996. See also John Carmody, "The TV Column," *Washington Post,* Aug. 18, 1997.
171 **"The appetite for news"** Williams, "Murdoch Names Ailes to Launch 24-Hour TV News Channel."

171 **"entrepreneurial spirit"** Jane Hall, "Murdoch Will Launch 24-Hour News Channel," *Los Angeles Times,* Jan. 31, 1996.

172 **"We're not starting up"** Paavo Thabit, "Roger Ailes to Head Fox's New Venture," United Press International, Jan. 30, 1996.

172 **"I don't think people"** Richard Huff and Tom Lowry, "It's Roger and Rupert: Murdoch Taps Ailes to Head News Venture," New York *Daily News*, Jan. 31, 1996.

172 **Ailes said that it** Gary Levin, "Murdoch Makes News; Confirms Ailes Hire to New News Web," *Daily Variety,* Jan. 31, 1996.

172 **"I left politics"** Thabit, "Roger Ailes to Head Fox's New Venture."

172 **Murdoch's grandiosity** For Murdoch's career, see William Shawcross, *Murdoch: The Making of a Media Empire* (New York: Simon & Schuster, 1992); Thomas Kiernan, *Citizen Murdoch* (New York: Dodd, Mead, 1986); Michael Wolff, *Inside the Secret World of Rupert Murdoch: The Man Who Owns the News* (New York: Random House, 2008); Andrew Neil, *Full Disclosure: The Most Candid and Revealing Portrait of Rupert Murdoch Ever* (London: Macmillan, 1996); Ken Auletta, "The Pirate," *New Yorker,* Nov. 13, 1995.

173 **In Britain** William Shawcross, *Murdoch: The Making of a Media Empire* (New York: Simon & Schuster, 1992), 113, 128–29.

173 **in Australia** Jenny Hocking, "How Murdoch Wrote the Final Act in Gough Saga," *Melbourne* (Australia) *Sunday Age,* Aug. 26, 2012. See also Philip Dorling, "Getting Gough; Murdoch Files—'He Was a Partisan Political Player Working with Fraser,'" *Melbourne* (Australia) *Age,* Nov. 19, 2011.

173 **And in New York** Jennifer Preston, "Murdoch's Denials of Political Favors Hard to Swallow in New York," "City Room" (blog), *New York Times,* April 27, 2012, http://cityroom.blog.nytimes.com/2012/04/27/Murdochs-denials-of-political-favors-hard-to-swallow-in-New-York/. In an October 4, 2010, interview with the documentary filmmaker Neil Barsky, Koch recalled Murdoch's influence: "It was interesting how I found out. I was home. I usually left my house at 6:30 in the morning to get on my . . . political transportation, we called it the 'beastmobile,' it was a sort of a large camper, I don't even know what it . . . and it broke down in front of my house. So, the guy who was driving it called me to say 'Don't come down, I'll call you when it's ready.' So instead of leaving at 6:30, I'm still in the house at 7:00. The phone rings, and the voice said, 'Is Congressman Koch there?' and I, being somewhat suspicious, said, 'Who's calling?' And he said, 'Rupert.' And I thought to myself, 'I don't know any Rupert. Rupert's not a Jewish name, who could this be?' So, I said, 'Rupert who?' and he said, as I recall, 'Rupert Murdoch.' 'Oh yes, Rupert! How can I help?' 'Congressman, the *Post* will be endorsing you today in a front-page editorial and I hope that it helps you.' I said, 'Rupert, you've just elected me.' And that was the major conversation."

173 **"If you are an arch-conservative"** Shawcross, *Murdoch,* 208.

173 **In the spring of 1985** Reginald Stuart, "Murdoch, ABC Deals Approved," *New York Times,* Nov. 15, 1985.

173 **But for the deal** Shawcross, *Murdoch,* 212.

174 **NBC Entertainment president** Bill Carter, "By One Key Monetary Measure, Fox Could Push Past Both CBS and ABC This Fall," *New York Times,* March 31, 1997.

174 **A year before** Turner and Burke, *Call Me Ted,* 244–45.

174 **In 1992** Deborah Hastings, "Van Gordon Sauter Named President of Fox News," Associated Press, July 13, 1992.

174 **In 1994, Murdoch secured distribution** Edmund L. Andrews, "Fox TV Deal Seems to Face Few Official Barriers," *New York Times,* May 24, 1994.

174 **"The American press"** Thomas Kiernan, *Citizen Murdoch* (New York: Dodd, Mead, 1986), 145.

174 **When he shipped off** Shawcross, *Murdoch,* 38. On page 22 of *Citizen Murdoch,* Kiernan has the bust on a windowsill.
174 **When he was nineteen** Michael Wolff, *Inside the Secret World of Rupert Murdoch: The Man Who Owns the News* (New York: Random House, 2008), 21.
175 **John F. Kennedy** Kiernan, *Citizen Murdoch,* 75.
175 **Murdoch, though modest** John Menadue, *Things You Learn Along the Way* (Melbourne: David Lovell, 1999), 105, available at http://www.johnmenadue.com/book/Menadue.pdf.
175 **Cavan, his forty-thousand-acre estate** Michael Wolff, "The Secrets of His Succession," *Vanity Fair,* Dec. 2008. See also Menadue, *Things You Learn Along the Way,* 105.
175 **On the ski slopes** Andrew Neil, "Murdoch and Me," *Vanity Fair,* Dec. 1996.
175 **Murdoch's brush with bankruptcy** Shawcross, *Murdoch,* 350–70.
175 **"Murdoch loved"** Menadue, *Things You Learn Along the Way,* 97.
175 **Murdoch, for one, loathed** Neil, "Murdoch and Me."
175 **"You can say what"** Ibid.
176 **After Murdoch bought** Ruth Ryon, "Hot Property: Rupert Murdoch Buying Stein House," *Los Angeles Times,* June 15, 1986. See also Wolff, *Inside the Secret World of Rupert Murdoch,* 297.
176 **"They wouldn't recognize one"** Andrew Neil, *Full Disclosure: The Most Candid and Revealing Portrait of Rupert Murdoch Ever* (London: Macmillan, 1996), 162.
176 **"We will be the insurgents"** Federal News Service, National Press Club (transcript), Feb. 26, 1996.
176 **The most critical review** Bill Carter, "Murdoch Joins a Cable-TV Rush into the Crowded All-News Field," *New York Times,* Jan. 31, 1996.
177 **After reading the *Times* article** Collins, *Crazy Like a Fox,* 69.
177 **In March 1995** "Joseph F. Peyronnin Named President of Fox News," Associated Press, March 28, 1995.
177 **Peyronnin hired** Author interview with former Fox News staffers. See also "Fox News Picks Emily Rooney," *Pittsburgh Post-Gazette,* Sept. 6, 1995.
177 **In the fall of 1995** "Fox Hires Producer for Sunday Morning News Show," *Chicago Tribune,* Nov. 23, 1995.
177 **Eventually, Peyronnin** Scott Williams, "Fox News to Launch Sunday Show," Associated Press, April 3, 1996.
177 **"Mitch Stern was the enemy"** Author interview with Emily Rooney.
177 **Stern, whose performance** Author interview with a former CNBC executive.
178 **In December, they presented** Author interview with a former Fox News executive.
178 **"I've been trying"** Auletta, "Vox Fox."
179 **Some paid cash** Bill Carter, "Networks' New Cable Channels Get a Big Jump on the Competition," *New York Times,* March 14, 1994.
179 **At America's Talking** Bill Carter, "NBC Selling Microsoft a Stake in Cable Channel," *New York Times,* Dec. 14, 1995.
179 **Ailes took Peyronnin** Author interview with a person familiar with the matter.
179 **Peyronnin went home** Author interview with a person familiar with the matter.
180 **"We had no news gathering operation"** Collins, *Crazy Like a Fox,* 70.
180 **Ailes told Murdoch** Chafets, *Roger Ailes,* 70.
180 **In the end** Jessica Lee, "Two Experts Brought in to Polish Up the Speech," *USA Today,* Jan. 29, 1992. See also Burt Solomon, "Speechwriters' Soaring Rhetoric Flops with a Prosaic President," *National Journal,* May 30, 1992.
180 **On April 3** "Sunday News Program Scheduled by Fox," *New York Times,* April 4, 1996.
181 **On April 4** Joe Flint, "Fox Unveils 'News Sunday,'" *Daily Variety,* April 4, 1996.
181 ***Daily Variety* reported** Flint, "Fox Unveils 'News Sunday.'"

181 **"Roger is acutely aware"** Author interview with a former senior executive at Fox News.
181 **As Stern remembered it** Author interview with former Fox Television Stations president Mitchell Stern.
181 **Though Tony Snow leaned** Howard Kurtz, "Fox News's Snow to Become White House Press Secretary," *Washington Post,* April 26, 2006.
181 **Worried that other networks** John Carmody, "The TV Column," *Washington Post,* April 30, 1996.
181 **Only a quarter** John Carmody, "The TV Column," *Washington Post,* April 30, 1996.
181 **In a tough write-up** Ibid.
182 **Two weeks before** John Dempsey, "NBC Ups Zaslav to Distribution Prexy," *Daily Variety,* April 12, 1996.
182 **In Los Angeles** "Cyperspace; L.A. Hooks Up with 26,000 Cable Types," *Los Angeles Times,* April 29, 1996.
182 **He bragged** Chuck Taylor, "NBC-Microsoft Channel May Not Be Available Here," *Seattle Times,* April 30, 1996.
182 **Malone held stakes** Ken Auletta, "John Malone: Flying Solo," *New Yorker,* Feb. 7, 1994.
182 **"We are the only players"** Scott Hettrick, "MSNBC Awaits Word from TW," *Hollywood Reporter,* April 30, 1996.
182 **Andy Lack announced** "Bryant Gumbel to Join NBC Colleagues as a Host for Prime-Time Talk Program on MSNBC Cable," PR Newswire, April 29, 1996.
182 **"We're here persuading"** Taylor, "NBC-Microsoft Channel May Not Be Available Here."
182 **"I went into their booth"** Author interview with Richard Aurelio.
183 **"I'm not going to tell you"** Kim Masters and Bryan Burrough, "Cable Guys," *Vanity Fair,* Jan. 1997.
183 **"There's a ritual dance"** David Lieberman, "Ailes Tackles Toughest Assignment," *USA Today,* Sept. 23, 1996.
183 **In 1996** Richard Mahler, "Media Overload?," *Los Angeles Times,* March 3, 1996.
183 **Murdoch flipped the equation** Masters and Burrough, "Cable Guys."
183 **"We had to put something on the table"** Masters and Burrough, "Cable Guys."
183 **As one former Ailes colleague** Author interview with a former Fox News executive.
183 **Less than a month** Bill Carter, "ABC's All-News Cable Channel Is Shelved," *New York Times,* May 24, 1996.
183 **Ailes gloated** David Lieberman, "Cap Cities/ABC Cuts Cord on Cable News," *USA Today,* May 24, 1996.
183 **Dozens of CNBC and A-T executives** Author interview with a former Fox News executive. See also Brian Lewis, master's thesis, Fairleigh Dickinson University, Dec. 11, 1995, available at https://coolcat.fdu.edu/vwebv/holdingsInfo?bibId=442618.
184 **In all, eighty-two** Auletta, "Vox Fox."
184 **That spring** John Motavalli, "Fox vs. CNBC? Now That Would Be a Grudge Match," *New York Times,* March 6, 2003.
184 **"Our view"** Stephen Battaglio, "Peacock Unruffled by Fox News $10 Cable Bid," *Hollywood Reporter,* May 7, 1996.
184 **On Friday, May 31** Letter from attorney Justin Manus to NBC executive vice president for employee relations Edward Scanlon, May 31, 1996.
184 **Several days later** Letter from NBC general counsel Richard Cotton to Justin Manus, June 4, 1996.
184 **The system reached** "Time Warner Closes Merger with Cablevision Industries," PR Newswire, Jan. 4, 1996.

184 **In early June** Masters and Burrough, "Cable Guys."
185 **After the lunch** Letter from Rupert Murdoch to Gerald Levin, June 4, 1996.
185 **FTC chairman Robert Pitofsky** Mark Landler, "An Accord That Could Help Murdoch," *New York Times*, July 18, 1996.
185 **On the morning of June 24** Bill Carter, "TCI Reaches Deal with Fox to Carry All-News Channel," *New York Times*, June 25, 1996.
185 **"There's a huge diversity"** Ken Auletta, "John Malone: Flying Solo," *New Yorker*, Feb. 7, 1994.
185 **Ailes denied** Carter, "TCI Reaches Deal with Fox."
186 **As important, Malone** "Rumors Dog News Station Debut," *Bergen Record*, July 16, 1996. See also Elizabeth Sanger, "Cable News Sweepstakes; Time Warner, Fox in Negotiations as MSNBC Debuts," *Newsday*, July 16, 1996; and Hiawatha Bray, "Network Official Reveals Higher Level of Competition," *Boston Globe*, July 16, 1996.
186 **A few weeks after** Jeffrey Daniels, "Murdoch Has the Whole New World in His Hands," *Hollywood Reporter*, July 18, 1996.

## TWELVE: OCTOBER SURPRISE

187 **"People are going to be on television"** Collins, *Crazy Like a Fox*, 130–31.
187 **At 9:00 a.m.** "Television; Electronic Eye Candy Dominates Hip Debut," *Boston Herald*, July 16, 1996; MSNBC's On-Air Launch, 1996 07–15 (video), YouTube, http://www.youtube.com/watch?v=WSS2s-4PrNQ.
187 **Jodi Applegate** " '*Today*' Taps Applegate," *Daily Variety*, April 3, 1996.
188 **On the day of the launch** Jane Hall, "Upstarts Hope to Make News of Their Own," *Los Angeles Times*, July 15, 1996.
188 **"MSNBC," he had told *USA Today*** David Lieberman, "Malone, Murdoch Forge All-New Cable Deals," *USA Today*, June 25, 1996.
188 **As NBC took out** Gary Levin and John Dempsey, "MSNBC Clears 1st Hurdle at Bow," *Variety*, July 15, 1996–July 21, 1996.
188 **Ailes assigned Scott Ehrlich** Author interview with a former Fox News executive.
188 **"It was a no-brainer"** Author interview with Robert Ailes Jr.
188 **two days later, when MSNBC** David Hinckley, "Imus Gets to Don a High Profile on MSNBC," New York *Daily News*, July 18, 1996.
189 **On Thursday, July 18** Jonathan Storm, "TV Critics Get a Posh Peak at New Season. They're Plunked in Classic Cars. Serenaded by Sheryl Crow. It's All Part of the Selling of Shows," *Philadelphia Inquirer*, July 15, 1996.
189 **The assembled reporters received printouts** John Carmody, "The TV Column," *Washington Post*, July 19, 1996.
189 **"We're not going to consider"** Chuck Taylor, "Fall TV—Fox Will Jump into the 'Very Competitive' All-News Arena," *Seattle Times*, July 19, 1996.
189 **Gone was the hype** Williams, "Murdoch Names Ailes to Launch 24-Hour TV News Channel."
189 **"We have not claimed"** Richard Huff, "Aiming to Outfox CNN, MSNBC," New York *Daily News*, July 19, 1996.
189 **"If you couldn't give me"** Stephen Battaglio, "Fox News Net Will Debut Oct. 7," *Hollywood Reporter*, July 19, 1996.
189 **"It's a very competitive climate"** Ibid.
189 **Unlike MSNBC, which had** Peter Johnson, "NBC Spells Out Format for Cable News Channel," *USA Today*, April 18, 1996.
189 **"There is no status"** Greg Braxton, "Fox News Announces Oct. 7 Launch of Cable Channel," *Los Angeles Times*, July 19, 1996.
190 **"Roger is a political animal"** Author interview with a former Fox News producer.

190 **The construction of studio space** This paragraph is based on author interviews with Fox News executives.

190 **Bahman Samiian** See résumé at http://www.bahmansamiian.com/resume.pdf.

190 **"We had to do more"** Author interview with a former Fox News staffer.

190 **MSNBC had recently hired** Doug Nye, "Larry, Curly and Moe: 'Moidering the Competition for a Long Time,' " *Philadelphia Inquirer,* Aug. 9, 1996.

190 **"Well I know your background"** Lawrie Mifflin, "Media: Broadcasting; At the New Fox News Channel, the Buzzword Is Fairness, Separating News from Bias," *New York Times,* Oct. 7, 1996. The dialogue between Kennedy and Ailes was recounted by Ailes to Mifflin.

190 **Ailes and Chet Collier questioned** Author interview with a person familiar with the matter.

190 **Bob Reichblum** See résumé at http://www.linkedin.com/pub/bob-reichblum/0/788/880.

191 **Collier was a Massachusetts liberal** Author interview with a former Fox News staffer. See also Richard Goldstein, "Chester Collier, 80, Dies; Led Westminster Show," *New York Times,* Aug. 29, 2007.

191 **"Chet's idea"** Author interview with a former CNBC executive.

191 **The trade journal *Dog News*** Chester F. Collier (paid obituary), *New York Times,* Aug. 19, 2007.

191 **Throughout the spring and summer** Author interview with a former Fox News executive.

191 **"I'm not hiring talent"** Author interview with a former Fox News executive. See also Brock, "Roger Ailes Is Mad as Hell."

191 **$1 million line item** Author interview with a former Fox News producer.

191 **"I didn't understand"** Author interview with a former Fox News producer.

191 **"Viewers don't want"** Author interview with a former Fox News producer.

191 **"He hated anything"** Author interview with a former Fox News executive.

191 **Collier regularly rebuked** Author interview with Emily Rooney. See also Swint, *Dark Genius,* 164.

192 **"Chet told me"** Author interview with a former Fox News producer.

192 **John Moody** Suzan Revah, *American Journalism Review,* May 1996.

192 **He had spent a decade** See John Moody résumé at http://www.linkedin.com/pub/john-moody/10/ba2/729.

192 **a Cold War thriller** John Moody, *Moscow Magician* (New York: St. Martin's, 1991).

192 **A "first-class journalist"** Author interviews with two former *Time* staffers who worked with Moody.

192 **"There are a lot"** Author interview with former *Time* assistant managing editor Janice Simpson.

192 **One of the problems** Collins, *Crazy Like a Fox,* 73.

192 **Speaking with a reporter** Mifflin, "At the New Fox News Channel, the Buzzword Is Fairness, Separating News from Bias."

192 **As they spoke** Sella, "The Red-State Network."

192 **"When he first came in"** Author interview with a former Fox News producer.

192 **Emily Rooney could not believe** Author interview with Emily Rooney.

192 **"Collier hated Moody"** Author interview with a former Fox News executive.

193 **Moody "hated" Collier's talk show concepts** Author interview with a Fox News founding producer.

193 **In meetings, Ailes spoke** Author interviews with Fox News executives.

193 **"He made sure"** Author interview with a person close to Ailes.

193 **"So much of the success"** Author interview with a former senior Fox executive.

193 **Murdoch invested** Stephen Battaglio, "Long, Busy Day Planned for Fox News Channel," *Hollywood Reporter,* Sept. 5, 1996.

193 **A stable of twenty** John Carmody, "The TV Column," *Washington Post*, Sept. 5, 1996.

193 **Louis Aguirre** See biographical note at http://www.wsvn.com/newsteam/?id =DBM430.

193 **Jon Scott** See biographical note at http://www.foxnews.com/on-air/personalities/ jon-scott/bio/.

193 **Shepard Smith** "Entertainment Briefs," BPI Entertainment News Wire, Aug. 24, 1999.

193 **Wendell Goler** Carmody, "The TV Column," Sept. 5, 1996.

193 **Camera crews** Jon Lafayette, "'Fairness' Will Set Fox News Apart," *Electronic Media*, Sept. 9, 1996.

193 **In addition, the network** Ibid. See also *Warren's Cable Regulation Monitor*, Oct. 7, 1996.

193 **Neil Cavuto** Carmody, "The TV Column," Sept. 5, 1996. Many of the details in this paragraph about the prime-time lineup came from Carmody's article.

193 **provisionally titled** Ibid.

194 **The weeknight slate** Gary Levin, "Fox News Channel Sets Slate," *Daily Variety*, Sept. 11, 1996.

194 **Starting at 10:00 p.m.** Ibid.

194 **Weekend coverage** Battaglio, "Long, Busy Day Planned for Fox News Channel."

194 **"He had been in the business"** Marvin Kitman, *The Man Who Would Not Shut Up: The Rise of Bill O'Reilly* (New York: St. Martin's, 2007), 163.

194 **Schneider, probably the biggest name** Author interview with Mike Schneider.

194 **At a press conference** Lafayette, "'Fairness' Will Set Fox News Apart."

194 **"There isn't a shred"** Michael Burgi, "Not Banking on Anchors," *Mediaweek*, Sept. 16, 1996.

194 **"most television people are idiots"** Kitman, *The Man Who Would Not Shut Up*, 6.

194 **He knew viewers made** Ailes and Kraushar, *You Are the Message*, 3.

194 **"If I have any ability"** Collins, *Crazy Like a Fox,* 140.

194 **"None of us were news people"** Author interview with a former Fox News producer.

194 **Sharri Berg** Tom Junod, "Because They Hate Him and Want Him to Fail," *Esquire*, March 1, 2009.

195 **Janet Alshouse** Martin C. Evans, "Exec Switching Channel," *Newsday* (New York), Aug. 17, 1996.

195 **Bill Shine** "Fox News Channel Names Bill Shine Senior Vice President of Programming," Business Wire, Jan. 13, 2005.

195 **"I was not a fan"** Author interview with former Fox News staffer Jordan Kurzweil.

195 **"This was not the A-team"** Author interview with a former Fox News producer.

195 **Catherine Crier** Author interview with former Fox News anchor Catherine Crier.

195 **"We became the enemy"** Author interview with Emily Rooney.

195 **"It became very clear"** Author interview with a former Fox producer.

195 **"Joe had an open-door policy"** Author interview with former Fox News accountant Jay Ringelstein.

195 **"At most organizations"** Author interview with a former News Corp executive.

195 **Once at a News Corp seminar** Neil, "Murdoch and Me."

196 **"If you're good"** David Lieberman, "Ailes Tackles Toughest Assignment: Cable Channel Battles Budget, Clock, Rivals," *USA Today*, Sept. 23, 1996.

196 **At a September 4 news conference** Frazier Moore, "Fox News Channel: More Round-the-Clock News a Month Away," Associated Press, Sept. 4, 1996. See also Robin Dougherty, "Fox News Chairman: Cable Service Shooting for 'Balanced' Coverage," *Miami Herald*, Sept. 5, 1996; Gary Levin, "Fox News Channel Sets

Slate," *Variety*, Sept. 9–Sept. 15, 1996; and Lafayette, " 'Fairness' Will Set Fox News Apart."

195 **It was a play off** Auletta, "Vox Fox."

195 **In an interview that fall** Verne Gay, "The All-News Wars Heat Up," *Newsday*, Oct. 7, 1996.

195 **"Journalists are by and large intelligent"** Jon Lafayette, "Fox's Upstart All-News Cable Channel to Take High Ground, Says Chairman," *Crain's New York Business*, Sept. 16, 1996.

196 **"I have noticed"** Dougherty, "Fox News Chairman: Cable Service Shooting for 'Balanced' Coverage."

197 **Fox's three foreign bureaus** Mifflin, "At the New Fox News Channel, the Buzzword Is Fairness, Separating News from Bias."

197 **CNN's twenty** "Galaxy Latin America Announces Agreement with Turner Broadcasting," PR Newswire, July 9, 1996.

197 **The projected staff of five hundred** Lafayette, " 'Fairness' Will Set Fox News Apart."

197 **Even O'Reilly was disappointed** Kitman, *The Man Who Would Not Shut Up*, 169–70.

197 **In the end, Fox would** Peter Johnson, "Fox Treads into 24-Hour Cable News," *USA Today*, Oct. 7, 1996.

197 **The indoctrination began** Collins, *Crazy Like a Fox*, 79. Author interviews with persons present.

197 **"He put it out there"** Author interview with a former Fox News executive.

198 **He introduced** Collins, *Crazy Like a Fox*, 80.

198 **At the orientation** Author interview with Jay Ringelstein.

198 **"There was almost a sense"** Author interview with Mike Schneider.

198 **"I don't expect"** Mifflin, "At the New Fox News Channel, the Buzzword Is Fairness, Separating News from Bias."

198 **In one early session** Author interview with former Fox News producer Adam Sank. During his years at Fox, Sank remembered several incidents he experienced as being anti-gay. In the fall of 1998, when the torture and murder of gay University of Wyoming student Matthew Shepard sparked a national uproar, Moody told Fox producers that they should not play into the media narrative. "He was apoplectic about the coverage," Sank recalled. "He said, 'this is an insane amount of coverage that this story is getting. If this wasn't a slow news week, no one would be paying attention.' " Sank was upset by Moody's seeming indifference to the impact of the heinous crime. Months later, Sank was outraged when Bret Baier invoked Matthew Shepard during a report on a grisly Arkansas case, in which two gay men were accused of sexually abusing and murdering a thirteen-year-old boy. "Nobody except for extreme right-wing blogs was comparing it to Matthew Shepard," Sank said. "I wanted to leave my first day, but when this happened, I knew I had to just get out." In 2002, senior management criticized him for airing a segment about a gay pride parade in Los Angeles. "I immediately got word that the powers that be were displeased," he recalled. His boss pulled him into an editing room and told him that Ailes and Moody thought the piece was "not fair and balanced" and that he "should have known better [than] to run a piece like that." Sank left Fox News several weeks later.

198 **Pointing to an article** "Gay Zimbabweans Win Fight for Book-Fair Booth," *New York Times*, Aug. 2, 1996.

198 **"Maybe the words"** Gay, "The All-News Wars Heat Up."

198 **Fox News, the memos stated** Sella, "Red State Network."

199 **Though credit for the slogan** Author interview with advertising executive Tom Messner.

199 **To wit** Hass, "Embracing the Enemy."

199 **These friends of Roger** Author interview with a former Fox News executive.
199 **"I was creeped out"** Author interview with a former Fox News producer.
200 **It was not the mere fact** Author interview with a former Fox News executive.
200 **What they found** Author interview with Jordan Kurzweil and Fox News producers.
200 **"These guys were researching people"** Author interview with a former Fox News executive.
200 **"It was very Nixonian"** Author interview with a former Fox News senior producer.
200 **One source close to Ailes** Author interview with a colleague of Roger Ailes.
200 **According to broadcast consultant** Author interview with George Case.
200 **It was his theory** Author interview with a former Fox News executive.
200 **In memos to staff** Sella, "The Red-State Network."
200 **"Power is best wielded"** Author interview with broadcast consultant George Case.
200 **Scott Ehrlich confided** Author interview with a person familiar with the matter.
201 **Fox hosts now routinely** See, e.g., John Gibson, *The Big Story with John Gibson,* Fox News Channel, April 8, 2004; Bill O'Reilly, *The O'Reilly Factor,* Fox News Channel, Oct. 25, 2010.
201 **Early on, Mike Schneider** Author interview with Mike Schneider.
201 **"I consider myself a freedom fighter"** Grove, "The Image Shaker; Roger Ailes, the Bush Team's Wily Media Man."
201 **According to Dan Cooper** Dan Cooper, *Naked Launch: Creating Fox News* (New York: 4 LLC ebook, 2008). Also available at www.dancooper.tv/NakedLaunch.htm.
201 **Rudy Nazath,** Author interview with a person familiar with the design of the Fox News studios. Ailes has denied the story. See Jim VandeHei and Mike Allen, "Roger Ailes Unplugged," *Politico,* June 6, 2013, http://www.politico.com/story/2013/06/behind-the-curtain-ailes-unplugged-92386.html.
202 **"We hired Alan"** Author interview with a former Fox producer.
202 **"We thought he looked better"** Author interview with a former Fox producer.
202 **Bill O'Reilly was also** Kitman, *The Man Who Would Not Shut Up,* 170.
202 **With the launch just days away** Collins, *Crazy Like a Fox,* 81–82.
202 **That evening, the channel would host** Clifford J. Levy, "Lobbying at Murdoch Gala Ignited New York Cable Clash," *New York Times,* Oct. 13, 1996.
202 **He called a meeting** Collins, *Crazy Like a Fox,* 82. Author interview with George Case.
203 **A Time Warner spokesperson** Masters and Burrough, "Cable Guys."
203 **David Zaslav negotiated** Ibid.
203 **It was pouring rain** Masters and Burrough, "Cable Guys." See also Plaintiffs' Proposed Findings of Fact and Conclusions of Law, Oct. 25, 1996, *Time Warner Cable v. City of New York,* 96-cv-7736, U.S. District Court, Southern District of New York (Manhattan).
203 **He made numerous angry calls** Masters and Burrough, "Cable Guys."
203 **"Murdoch thought"** Ibid.
203 **Murdoch insisted** Masters and Burrough, "Cable Guys." See also deposition of former New York City deputy mayor Fran Reiter, *Time Warner Cable v. City of New York.*
203 **"If these guys want"** Masters and Burrough, "Cable Guys."

## THIRTEEN: THE RIGHT KIND OF FRIENDS

204 **News Corp's assault** Shawcross, *Murdoch,* 412.
204 **"You are *immoral*"** Oral argument by Clifford Thau, an outside attorney repre-

senting Fox News. *Fox News v. Time Warner,* 96-cv-4963, U.S. District Court, Eastern District of New York (Brooklyn).

204 **"He called me a lot of names"** Masters and Burrough, "Cable Guys."

204 **"What the hell happened?"** Ibid.

204 **"Chase, calm down"** Ibid.

204 **The launch of Fox News** Elizabeth Sanger, "Uphill Fight for Fox," *Newsday* (New York), Nov. 7, 1996.

204 **The first intimation** Masters and Burrough, "Cable Guys."

205 **They directed Dressler** Ibid.

205 **the FTC announced** Martin Crutsinger, "FTC Approves Time Warner's Acquisition of Turner," Associated Press, Sept. 12, 1996.

205 **On September 12** Martin Crutsinger, "FTC Approves Time Warner's Acquisition of Turner," Associated Press, Sept. 12, 1996.

205 **Richard Aurelio, the president** Author interview with Richard Aurelio, former president of Time Warner New York City Cable Group.

205 **In his negotiations** Affidavit of former Time Warner executive vice president of cable programming Fred Dressler, *Time Warner Cable v. City of New York,* 96-cv-7736, U.S. District Court, Southern District of New York (Manhattan).

205 **The financial terms** Letter from Rupert Murdoch to Gerald Levin, June 4, 1996.

205 **Of more immediate concern** Masters and Burrough, "Cable Guys."

205 **After John Malone's TCI announced** John Dempsey, "Spurned Cable Webs Revile TCI," *Variety,* Aug. 19–Aug. 25, 1996. See also Bill Carter, "Plan to Cut TV Channel Angers Women's Groups," *New York Times,* Sept. 14, 1996.

205 **During Dressler's negotiations** Masters and Burrough, "Cable Guys."

206 **In the mid-1980s** Ibid.

206 **In the press** Louise McElvogue, "After Rupert," *Guardian* (London), April 22, 1996. See also Paul Farhi, "Mogul Wrestling; In the War Between Murdoch and Turner, Similarity Breeds Contempt," *Washington Post,* Nov. 18, 1996.

206 **When Turner agreed** Dennis Wharton, "Murdoch Turns Tables on Turner," *Daily Variety,* Feb. 27, 1996.

206 **Murdoch listened** Masters and Burrough, "Cable Guys."

206 **George Pataki** Kiley Armstrong, "Cuomo's Defeat Could Mean Trouble for NYC Mayor," Associated Press, Nov. 9, 1994.

207 **Murdoch donated** Candace Sutton (editor), Back Page, *Sydney* (Australia) *Sun Herald,* Dec. 11, 1994. See also Louise Branson, "TV's Big Guns Fall Silent," *Scotsman,* Jan. 4, 1997.

207 **The New York cable franchise** Masters and Burrough, "Cable Guys."

207 **The paper had endorsed** *New York Post* (cover), Oct. 29, 1993, and Oct. 28, 1994.

207 **Murdoch even employed** Elisabeth Bumiller, "Clash of Careers for First Lady; Donna Hanover's 2 Roles Are Not Always Separate," *New York Times,* Dec.1, 1995.

207 **It was also** Peter Grant, "20 M for Rupe's Biz but Foes Rip City, State on News Corp. Deal," New York *Daily News,* June 20, 1996.

207 **Though he officially renounced politics** Ailes Communications, "Roger Ailes for Governor? Not!" (press release), Dec. 21, 1992.

207 **On the evening** Author interview with a person who was present at Ailes Communications headquarters on the evening of the 1992 presidential election.

207 **A month later** Maurice Carroll, "Giuliani's New Style on Display at Dinner," *New York Newsday,* Dec. 3, 1992.

207 **When Giuliani took office** Author interview with a person familiar with the matter.

208 **On Friday, September 20** Brock, "Roger Ailes Is Mad as Hell."

208 **The previous spring** Affidavit of former New York City deputy mayor Fran Reiter, *Time Warner Cable v. City of New York.*

208 **"Time Warner informed us"** Author interview with Fran Reiter. Much of the fol-

lowing account of Reiter's involvement in the negotiations comes from this interview.

208 **As part of its** News America project financing proposal, submitted to the New York City Industrial Development Agency in 1996.

208 **Privately, however** Author interview with Fran Reiter.

208 **In 1993, he had won** Beth J. Harpaz, "Giuliani Defeats Dinkins in Tight Race," Associated Press, Nov. 3, 1993.

209 **"Rudy was walking into a snake pit"** Ibid.

209 **On Thursday, September 26** Clifford J. Levy, "An Old Friend Called Giuliani, and New York's Cable Clash Was On," *New York Times,* Nov. 4, 1996.

209 **Meanwhile, uptown** David Lieberman, "Time Warner–Murdoch Feud Heats Up," *USA Today,* Sept. 27, 1996. See also Arthur Spiegelman, "Murdoch Pledges to Get Even with Turner," Reuters, published in *Toronto Financial Post,* Sept. 28, 1996; and Brett Thomas, "Turner Slams Murdoch," *Sydney Sun Herald,* Sept. 29, 1996.

209 **By Friday afternoon** Affidavit of Fran Reiter, *Time Warner Cable v. City of New York.*

210 **Over the weekend** Ibid. See also Levy, "An Old Friend Called Giuliani"; and David L. Lewis, Angela G. King, and Dean Chang, "TV Titans in Power Play," New York *Daily News,* Oct. 20, 1996.

210 **On Monday morning** Opinion of U.S. District Court Judge Denise Cote, Nov. 6, 1996, *Time Warner Cable v. City of New York,* http://www.nyls.edu/documents/media_center/the_media_center_library_u_s_cases/timewnyc.pdf.

210 **Aurelio left a message** Affidavit of Fran Reiter, *Time Warner Cable v. City of New York.*

210 **As they spoke by phone** Author interview with Fran Reiter. See also Lewis, King, and Chang, "TV Titans in Power Play."

211 **Aurelio was entering** Author interview with Richard Aurelio.

211 **On Tuesday, October 1** Plaintiffs' Proposed Findings of Fact and Conclusions of Law, Oct. 25, 1996, *Time Warner Cable v. City of New York.* See also Masters and Burrough, "Cable Guys."

211 **Later that day** Affidavit of Fran Reiter. See also Plaintiffs' Proposed Findings of Fact, *Time Warner Cable v. City of New York.*

212 **"When you're screwed over"** Elizabeth Lesly, "The Dumbest Show in Television," *Businessweek,* Oct. 20, 1996.

212 **That evening** Michele Greppi and Gregory Zuckerman, "24-Hour Channel's Toast of the Town," *New York Post,* Oct. 2, 1996. See also Clifford J. Levy, "Lobby at Murdoch Gala Ignited Cable Clash," *New York Times,* Oct. 13, 1996; Masters and Burrough, "Cable Guys."

212 **Giuliani called** Author interview with Richard Aurelio. See also Clifford J. Levy, "Murdoch Gets Pataki Support in Cable Fight," *New York Times,* Oct. 9, 1996.

212 **On Thursday, October 3** Letter from former Time Warner general counsel Peter Haje to Fran Reiter, Oct. 3, 1996, *Time Warner Cable v. City of New York.*

212 **Norman Sinel** Opinion of U.S. District Court Judge Denise Cote, Nov. 6, 1996, *Time Warner Cable v. City of New York.*

213 **Reiter's chief of staff** Letter from David Klasfeld, former chief of staff for Deputy Mayor Fran Reiter, to former Time Warner president Richard Parsons, Oct. 4, 1996, *Time Warner Cable v. City of New York.*

213 **"People who are out there"** Jane Hall, "How Fox News Plans to Challenge Cable's Giant," *Los Angeles Times,* Oct. 3, 1996.

213 **"I see no value"** Verne Gay, "The All-News Wars Heat Up," *Newsday* (New York), Oct. 7, 1996.

213 **Andy Lack told** Ed Bark, "Fox Joins the Hunt in TV News," *Dallas Morning News,* Oct. 6, 1996.

213 **Shortly before 6:00** Frazier Moore, "Fox News Channel Signs On—to Take On CNN and MSNBC," Associated Press, Oct. 7, 1996.
214 **In the control room** Moore, "Fox News Channel Signs On—To Take On CNN and MSNBC." See also Collins, *Crazy Like a Fox,* 82–83.
214 **For the opening day** Matt Roush, "Fox News Channel: Not Craft Enough," *USA Today,* Oct. 8, 1996. See also Erik Mink, "Fox News Channel's off to a Dizzying Start," New York *Daily News,* Oct. 8, 1996; Tom Shales, review, *Washington Post,* Oct. 12, 1996; Collins, *Crazy Like a Fox,* 138.
214 **In his second-floor office** Roger Ailes, "Roy H. Park Lecture," University of North Carolina, April 12, 2012, http://jomc.unc.edu/roger-ailes-park-lecture-april-12-2012-transcript.
214 **Unlike the executives** Author interview with a former Fox News executive.
214 **"He knew there were"** Author interview with Ed Rollins.
215 **Time Warner had previously agreed** Testimony of former New York City corporation counsel Paul Crotty, *Time Warner Cable v. City of New York.*
215 **"Good morning"** Testimony of Roger Ailes, Joint Public Hearing of the New York City Franchise and Review Committee (transcript), Oct. 7, 1996.
215 **Conspicuously missing** Matt Roush, "Fox News Channel: Not Crafty Enough," *USA Today,* Oct. 8, 1996.
215 **As evidence, Ailes** Sallie Hofmeister, "He May Be Working for Someone Else, But He's Still Ted Turner," *Los Angeles Times,* Sept. 24, 1996.
216 **He called Deputy Mayor** Michael O. Allen and David L. Lewis, "Rudy: Is Ted Fit for Cable?," New York *Daily News,* Oct. 20, 1996.
216 **On multiple occasions** Author interview with Richard Aurelio.
216 **Soon after speaking** Letter from Richard Parsons to David Klasfeld, Oct. 7, 1996, *Time Warner Cable v. City of New York.*
216 **Parsons publicly severed ties** David Firestone, "Time Warner Wins Order Keeping Fox off City Cable TV," *New York Times,* Oct. 12, 1996.
216 **On October 9** Complaint, *Fox News v. Time Warner,* 96-cv-4963, U.S. District Court, Eastern District of New York (Brooklyn).
216 **New York State attorney general** Jay Mathews, "Murdoch's News Channel Denied N.Y. Cable Outlet," *Washington Post,* Oct. 15, 1996.
216 **At once, Manhattan borough president** Letter from Ruth Messinger to former New York City Conflicts of Interest Board chairman Sheldon Oliensis, Oct. 8, 1996.
216 **The board would dismiss** Clifford J. Levy, "City Ethics Panel Rules for Giuliani in Time Warner Cable Case," *New York Times,* Oct. 22, 1996.
216 **"Disagree with me"** Levy, "Lobbying at Murdoch Gala Ignited New York Cable Clash."
217 **On October 9** Clifford J. Levy, "In Cable TV Fight, Mayor Plans to Put Fox Channel on a City Station," *New York Times,* Oct. 10, 1996.
217 **After receiving a tip** Masters and Burrough, "Cable Guys." See also affidavit of Richard Aurelio, *Time Warner Cable v. City of New York.*
217 **"We decided"** Author interview with Richard Aurelio.
217 **A few minutes later** Masters and Burrough, "Cable Guys."
217 **One of many** Amicus brief of Ruth Messinger, Mark Green, and Fernando Ferrer, *Time Warner Cable v. City of New York.*
217 **Ailes suffered the first** Firestone, "Time Warner Wins Order Keeping Fox off City Cable TV."
217 **Reiter told the lawyers** Affidavit of Fran Reiter, *Time Warner Cable v. City of New York.*
217 ***New York* magazine speculated** Beth Landman Keil and Deborah Mitchell, "Intelligencer" (column), *New York,* Nov. 11, 1996, http://books.google.com/books?id=NuECAAAAMBAJ&pg=PA15&dq=%22reiter%22+ailes+%22time+warner%22&hl=en&sa=X&ei=4-FbUtywH9PqkQf17IGgAg&ved

=oCEoQ6AEwAQ#v=onepage&q=%22reiter%22%20ailes%20%22time%20warner%22&f=false.

217 **Parsons was forced** Author interview with Richard Aurelio.

218 **Meanwhile, during** Testimony of Ted Turner, *Time Warner Cable v. City of New York.*

218 **On Monday, October 21** *New York Post,* Oct. 21, 1996.

218 **The immature taunts** I. J. Rosenberg, "World Series; Braves vs. Yankees; Braves Notebook; Cox Plays Pendleton Hunch," *Atlanta Journal and Constitution,* Oct. 22, 1996. See also Ellis Henican, "Ink-Stained; Tainted Coverage in Clash of Network Titans," *New York Newsday,* Oct. 23, 1996; Turner and Burke, *Call Me Ted,* 337.

218 **"I thought about killing him"** Masters and Burrough, "Cable Guys." See also Turner and Burke, *Call Me Ted,* 338.

218 **The three-day preliminary injunction hearing** Harry Berkowitz, "Media Blitz/ Time Warner, Fox Battle for New York Returns to Court. Big Cable Clash Has Big Egos," *Newsday* (New York), Oct. 28, 1996.

218 **The 106-page opinion** Opinion of U.S. District Court Judge Denise Cote, Nov. 6, 1996, *Time Warner Cable v. City of New York,* http://www.nyls.edu/user_files/1/3/4/30/84/85/114/136/timewnyc.pdf.

218 **"I used to say"** Author interview with Catherine Crier.

218 **Most Fox affiliates** Author interview with a former Fox News executive.

219 **Mike Schneider and Crier bickered** Author interview with a Fox News executive.

219 **"Chet Collier called us in"** Author interview with Emily Rooney.

# ACT IV

## FOURTEEN: ANTI-CLINTON NEWS NETWORK

223 **On a summer afternoon** Author interview with former Fox News correspondent David Shuster.

223 **McDougals' recent trial** R. H. Melton and Michael Haddigan, "Three Guilty in Arkansas Fraud Trial," *Washington Post,* May 29, 1996.

223 **the same year** Philip Weiss, "The Clinton Haters: Clinton Crazy," *New York Times,* Feb. 23, 1997. See also *Clinton Chronicles* on YouTube (video), http://www.youtube.com/watch?v=eLnZwwYlYPo.

224 **had subpoenaed Hillary Clinton** Alison Mitchell, "Hillary Clinton Is Subpoenaed to Testify Before a Grand Jury," *New York Times,* Jan. 23, 1996.

224 **"Why is this important?"** Author interview with David Shuster.

224 **the first lady** Hillary Clinton was never indicted.

224 **Two weeks after mailing** Author interview with David Shuster.

225 **"I remember Roger"** Author interview with former Fox News producer Adam Sank.

225 **It was *The New York Times*** Jeff Gerth and Stephen Engelberg, "U.S. Investigating Clinton's Links to Arkansas S. & L.," *New York Times,* Nov. 2, 1993.

225 **"Monica [Lewinsky] was a news"** Kinney Littlefield, "Reliable Sources," *Orange County Register,* May 9, 1999.

226 **"I was having the time"** Author interview with David Shuster.

226 **One of the things Shuster** Ibid.

226 **many of the suburban precincts** Alicia Mundy, "Washington: Is Anybody Out There?" *Mediaweek,* Feb. 3, 1997.

226 **Moody had gone to Washington** Collins, *Crazy Like a Fox,* 79.

227 **When Defense Secretary** David Bauder, "Fox News Channel Fuming Over Exclusion from Cohen Trip," Associated Press, Feb. 27, 1997.
227 **A few months later** John Carmody, "The TV Column," *Washington Post,* Sept. 8, 1997.
227 **in the spring of 1997** *Fox News v. Time Warner,* 96-cv-4963, U.S. District Court, Eastern District of New York (Brooklyn), judicial order, May 16, 1997. See also *Time Warner v. Bloomberg L.P.,* 96-9515, 96-9517, U.S. Court of Appeals for the Second Circuit, judicial order, July 3, 1997.
227 **But in mid-July** Lawrie Mifflin, "In the Murdoch-Levin Dispute, Money Talked," *New York Times,* July 28, 1997.
227 **Ailes was triumphant** Jon Lafayette, "New Pro: With New York Hurdle Crossed, Fox Hits Stride," *Electronic Media,* Sept. 15, 1997.
227 **once declared** David Brock, "Confessions of a Right-Wing Hit Man," *Esquire,* July 1997.
227 **In a bid to get** Author interview with David Brock.
227 **"Three people in the world"** Brock, "Roger Ailes Is Mad as Hell."
227 **His friend, gossip columnist** Liz Smith, "Valentine's Day Wedding," Los Angeles Times Syndicate, published in *Toledo Blade,* Dec. 23, 1997.
228 **On Sunday morning** Author interview with a senior Fox News Channel executive.
228 **Just past midnight** Matt Drudge, "Newsweek Kills Story on White House Intern," *Drudge Report,* Jan. 17, 1998, http://www.drudgereportarchives.com/data/2002/01/17/20020117_175502_ml.htm.
228 **"At the last minute"** Ibid.
228 **What should Fox put** Author interview with a senior Fox News Channel executive.
228 **In December, he met with** Stephen Battaglio, "Net Columnist Drudge Uploads Fox News Deal," BPI Entertainment News Wire, March 2, 1998.
228 **The thirty-one-year-old** See Matt Drudge, *Drudge Manifesto* (New York: New American Library, 2000).
228 **He relished beating the press pack** Todd S. Purdum, "It Was Something He Said," *New York Times*, Aug. 17, 1997.
228 **On August 11, 1997** *Blumenthal v. Drudge,* 992 F.Supp. 44 (D.C. Cir. 1998), complaint.
229 **Though Drudge pulled down the story** Ibid.
229 **"I don't give a damn"** Bruce Haring, "Matt Drudge's Maverick Journalism Jars Internet," *USA Today*, Aug. 14, 1997.
229 **"You better have multiple sources"** Author interview with a source familiar with the matter.
229 **Acting on Ailes's directive** Author interview with a senior Fox News Channel executive.
229 **Snow's co-anchor** Tony Snow and Mara Liasson, *Fox News Sunday,* Fox News Channel, Jan. 18, 1998.
229 **David Shuster was not surprised** Most of the details involving David Shuster are derived from author interviews with Shuster.
229 **The item revealed** Matt Drudge, "Former White House Intern Called; New Background Details Emerge," *Drudge Report*, Jan. 18, 1998, http://www.drudgereportarchives.com/data/2002/01/17/20020117_175502_ml.htm.
229 **At 6:00 p.m.** Matt Drudge, "Former White House Intern Denied Sex with President in Sworn Affidavit," *Drudge Report*, Jan. 19, 1998, http://www.drudgereportarchives.com/data/2002/01/17/20020117_175502_ml.htm.
230 **"They didn't want to play"** Author interview with a senior Fox producer.
230 **Linda Tripp** Josh Getlin and Marc Lacey, " 'Tell-All' Book Called Goal of Linda Tripp," *Los Angeles Times,* Jan. 25, 1998.
230 **"You ought to talk to Lucianne Goldberg"** Jeffrey Toobin, *A Vast Conspiracy:*

*The Real Story of the Sex Scandal That Nearly Brought Down a President* (New York: Touchstone, 1999), 100.

230 **"We were all part of"** Author interview with literary agent Lucianne Goldberg.

230 **"His message was"** Author interview with a participant on the call.

230 **"TONIGHT ON THE DRUDGE REPORT"** Matt Drudge, "Tonight on the Drudge Report: Controversy Swirls Around Tapes of Former White House Intern, as Starr Moves In," *Drudge Report*, Jan. 20, 1998, http://www.drudgereportarchives.com/data/2002/01/17/20020117_175502_ml.htm.

230 **"CLINTON ACCUSED OF URGING AIDE TO LIE"** Susan Schmidt, Peter Baker, and Toni Locy, "Clinton Accused of Urging Aide to Lie; Starr Probes Whether President Told Woman to Deny Alleged Affair to Jones's Lawyers," *Washington Post*, Jan. 21, 1998.

230 **"WASH POST SCREAMS INTERN STORY!"** Matt Drudge, "Wash Post Screams Intern Story," *Drudge Report*, Jan. 20, 1998, http://www.drudgereport archives.com/data/2002/01/17/20020117_175502_ml.htm.

231 **On Monday morning, January 26** President William J. Clinton, "Child Care," C-Span, Jan. 26, 1998 (relevant portion begins at 24:30), http://www.c-spanvideo.org/program/ChildCare4.

231 **For Ailes, who had watched** Author interview with a Fox staffer who was present.

231 **"Roger saw Clinton thumbing"** Author interview with a friend of Ailes.

231 **"Roger once said"** Author interview with a former Fox producer.

231 **"Roger thought it was amusing"** Author interview with Lucianne Goldberg.

231 **It was all eerily reminiscent** E. J. Dionne Jr., "Gary Hart: The Elusive Front-Runner," *New York Times*, May 3, 1987. See also Robin Toner, "Hart Drops Race for White House in a Defiant Mood," *New York Times*, May 9, 1987; E. J. Dionne Jr., "Courting Danger: The Fall of Gary Hart," *New York Times*, May 9, 1987.

232 **Ailes envisioned Hume's** Sarah Goldstein, "The Wire Q&A: Ted Koppel Remembers the Iran Hostage Crisis," "The Q" (blog), *GQ*, Nov. 3, 2009, http://www.gq.com/blogs/the-q/2009/11/the-wire-qa-ted-koppel-remembers-the-iran-hostage-crisis.html.

232 **"We're trying very hard"** John Higgins and Donna Petrozzello, "Fox Chases the News," *Broadcasting & Cable*, May 18, 1998.

233 **"The Clinton administration—they hated us!"** Marshall Sella, "The Red-State Network: How Fox News Conquered Bush Country—and Toppled CNN," *New York Times Magazine*, June 24, 2001.

233 **Launching Hume's newscast** "Around the Dial," *Boston Herald*, Jan. 28, 1998.

233 **"How did it happen?"** Bill O'Reilly, *The O'Reilly Report*, Fox News Channel, Oct. 7, 1996.

233 **"Few broadcasts take any chances these days"** Ibid.

233 **His career began in Scranton** "Bill O'Reilly's Bio," FoxNews.com, April 29, 2004, http://www.foxnews.com/story/0,2933,155,00.html.

233 **In 1982, he was called up to the Bigs** Kitman, *The Man Who Would Not Shut Up,* 100, 102, 124.

233 **"He would say"** Author interview with journalist, producer, and television host Emily Rooney.

233 **At six-four** Nicholas Lemann, "Fear Factor: Bill O'Reilly's Baroque Period," *New Yorker*, March 27, 2006.

233 **In one five-year period** Kitman, *The Man Who Would Not Shut Up,* 102–22 passim.

233 **"He was always in trouble"** Ibid., 163.

233 **In 1989, he bailed out** Ibid., 135–36.

234 **"I'm not sure"** Neil Swidey, "The Meanest Man on Television," *Boston Globe*, Dec. 1, 2002.

234 **One evening he told** Bill O'Reilly, "Two Year Anniversary Special," *The O'Reilly Report*, Fox News Channel, Dec. 29, 1998
234 **"It's important if the president of the United States"** Ibid.
234 **"You guys wanted him out since Day One"** Ibid.
234 **O'Reilly once remarked** Kitman, *The Man Who Would Not Shut Up,* 166.
234 **"It was very basic"** Ibid., 16.
234 **At prep school** Evan Thomas, "Life of O'Reilly," *Newsweek*, Feb. 11, 2001.
234 **At Marist College** Kitman, *The Man Who Would Not Shut Up,* 33–42 passim.
235 **"I could feel those rich girls"** Thomas, "Life of O'Reilly."
235 **"Bill O'Reilly is one"** Author interview with Robert Ailes.
235 **Disgraced former Clinton adviser** Richard L. Berke, "Call-Girl Story Costs President a Key Strategist," *New York Times*, Aug. 30, 1996.
235 **"What do you want me to say?"** Author interview with a former Fox producer.
235 **In March 1998** *Hannity & Colmes,* Fox News Channel, March 11, 1999.
235 **In April, Ailes hired** David Bauder, "Dick Morris Joins Fox, Kinsley Back on CNN," Associated Press, April 14, 1998.
235 **Several weeks later** Tim Goodman, "Fox News Hires Drudge—You Decide," *San Francisco Examiner*, July 23, 1998.
235 **"It'll be me, a hat"** Jennifer Weiner, "Foremost Internet Gossip Moves to TV," *Chicago Tribune*, June 20, 1998.
235 **"Raymond Chandler detective's office"** Ibid.
235 **To complete the picture** David Bauder, "Matt Drudge: Out from Behind the Laptop and onto TV," Associated Press, June 25, 1998.
235 **In July, Ailes hired** Weiner, "Foremost Internet Gossip Moves to TV."
236 **The new lineup premiered** "TV Ticker," *New York Post*, July 27, 1998.
236 **On the evening of August 17** Ted Koppel, "Bill Clinton Admits Affair," *Nightline*, ABC, Aug. 17, 1998, http://abcnews.go.com/Archives/video/bill-clinton-lewinksy-affair-1998-9533796.
236 **As Clinton's presidency** Josef Adalian and Richard Katz, "Presidents Day: Clinton Speech, TBS Pic Spike Cable Ratings," *Daily Variety*, Aug. 19, 1998.
236 **"It's all popping"** Matt Drudge, *Hannity & Colmes*, Fox News Channel, Aug. 17, 1998.
236 **"Which of the following"** *Fox News Sunday,* Fox News Channel, Feb. 1,1998.
236 **"What is President Clinton more thankful for"** *Special Report with Brit Hume,* Fox News Channel, Nov. 26, 1998.
236 **In April 1998** *Hannity & Colmes*, Fox News Channel, April 1, 1998.
236 **In another report** Rita Cosby, *Special Report with Brit Hume*, Fox News Channel, March 10, 1998.
236 **Some Fox viewers** Joe Muto, *An Atheist in the FOXhole: A Liberal's Eight-Year Odyssey Inside the Heart of the Right-Wing Media* (New York: Dutton, 2013), 26.
237 **David Shuster was no longer** Author interview with David Shuster.
237 **But Mort Kondracke** Mort Kondracke, *Special Report with Brit Hume*, Fox News Channel, Sept. 4, 1998.
237 **"There was initially"** Author interview with former Fox producer and media consultant Steve Hirsh.
237 **"We would hear"** Author interview with David Shuster.
237 **"I'm very interested in conflict resolution"** Ed Bark, "Fox Joins the Hunt in TV News," *Dallas Morning News*, Oct. 6, 1996.
238 **"He had admiration"** Author interview with a former Fox producer.
238 **Crier found the** Author interview with Catherine Crier.
238 **An Irish Catholic** Sean Hannity, *Let Freedom Ring: Winning the War of Liberty over Liberalism* (New York: HarperCollins, 2002), 47.
238 **Radio personalities like** Ibid.

238 **He tried college three times** Sean Hannity, *Hannity*, Fox News Channel, Oct. 4, 2013.

238 **By the late 1980s** Christopher H. Sterling, ed., *Biographical Encyclopedia of American Radio* (New York: Routledge, 2011), 164.

239 **In his spare time** Ibid.

239 **Though he was not a student** Marta Ulveaus, "Revisiting Sean Hannity: Audio/Podcast from KCSB's '50 Years of People Powered Radio,'" KCSB.org, Dec. 22, 2011, http://www.kcsb.org/blog/2011/12/22/revisiting-sean-hannity-audiopodcast/ (mp3 audio of the retrospective radio broadcast).

239 **In April 1989** Ibid.

239 **A Lutheran minister** Jean Latz Griffin, "McHenry Coroner's AIDS Warning Ripped," *Chicago Tribune*, March 13, 1987.

239 **He wrote that** See Gene Antonio, *The AIDS Cover-Up?: The Real and Alarming Facts About AIDS* (San Francisco: Ignatius, 1986), 71, 113.

239 **At the opening of** The complete archived audio of Sean Hannity's interview with Gene Antonio can be found at http://www.kcsb.org/blog/2011/12/22/revisiting-sean-hannity-audiopodcast/.

240 **Hannity played the victim** Steve Rendall, "An Aggressive Conservative vs. a 'Liberal to Be Determined,'" *Extra!*, Nov. 1, 2003.

240 **After applying for** Sterling, *Biographical Encyclopedia of American Radio*, 164.

240 **His bio** Rendall, "An Aggressive Conservative vs. a 'Liberal to Be Determined.'"

240 **In an interview** Peter Goodman, "Radio Waves: Out of Nowhere to No. 5 on the Charts," *Newsday*, July 12, 1999.

240 **Each morning, a producer** Author interview with a former Fox producer.

240 **"There was a real"** Author interview with a former Fox producer.

241 **"I had higher-ups"** Author interview with former Fox producer Rachel Katzman.

241 **"John Moody would call"** Author interview with former Fox producer Jordan Kurzweil.

241 ***"What is the crime"*** Author interview with a former Fox producer.

241 **"If you come out"** James Endrst, "Fox News Pursues Balance, Boldness; Nervy Network Elbows Way into Crowded Cable Lineup," *Hartford Courant*, Aug. 5, 1998.

241 **"There'd been four failures"** Marshall Sella, "The Red-State Network," *New York Times*, June 24, 2001.

241 **Two decades later** Alex Chadwick, *Morning Edition*, NPR, Feb. 7, 1995.

241 **Brian Lewis and the PR operation** Author interview with sources familiar with the matter.

242 **By the winter of 1999** Paula Bernstein, "Fox, MSNBC, CNN Score for Iowa Coverage," *Daily Variety*, Jan. 27, 2000.

242 **nine million more homes** Felicity Barringer, "Networks to Cover Primaries in Force," *New York Times*, March 7, 2000.

242 **But in February** Alison Mitchell, "The President's Acquittal: The Overview; Clinton Acquitted Decisively: No Majority for Either Charge," *New York Times*, Feb. 13, 1999.

242 **The news cycle was favoring** Author interview with a former Fox producer.

242 **During the conflict's opening days** Gary Levin, "War Is a Ratings Boost, to Second, for MSNBC," *USA Today*, April 6, 1999.

242 **One afternoon** Author interview with a Fox producer.

242 **In January 1999, Ailes poached** John Dempsey, "Fox Steals Zahn for News," *Daily Variety*, Jan. 22, 1999.

242 **He moved Zahn to 10:00** Jon Lafayette, "Shepard Smith's No Talking Head; 'Fox Report' Anchor Brings His Own Set of Rules to the Chair," *Electronic Media*, Oct. 25, 1999.

242 **"Put Shep in front"** Author interview with a former Fox producer.
242 **began dating Julia Rolle** Author interview with Julia Rolle's father, Gene Rolle.
242 **He was known to explode** Author interview with a former Fox producer.
242 **To produce his show** Author interviews with current and former Fox employees.
242 **On one of his early shows** Author interview with a Fox producer.
243 **In November 1999** "All TV," *Newark Star-Ledger*, Nov. 17, 1999.
243 **Drudge wanted** "This Morning," *The Hotline*, Nov. 17, 1999.
243 **The messy episode** Howard Kurtz, "The Going Gets Tough, and Matt Drudge Gets Going," *Washington Post*, Nov. 15, 1999; Gail Shister, "War of Words Continues Between Matt Drudge and Fox News Channel," *Philadelphia Inquirer*, Nov. 18, 1999.
243 **Drudge agreed to cancel** Paula Bernstein, "Fox News, Drudge Reach Accord as 'Net Wag Exits," *Daily Variety*, Nov. 19, 1999.
243 **"The network cannot live"** Shister, "War of Words Continues Between Matt Drudge and Fox News Channel."

## FIFTEEN: THE CALL

244 **As Americans made** John Ellis, "A Hard Day's Night," *Inside*, Dec. 26, 2000.
244 **A confidant of** Bill Carter, "Counting the Vote: The Fox Executive; Calling the Presidential Race, and Cousin George W.," *New York Times*, Nov. 14, 2000.
244 **In an hour** Ed Bark, "Fox Prepares for First Foray into Covering Election Night; Network's News Channel Will Conduct Bulk of Reporting," *Dallas Morning News*, June 30, 2000.
244 **For the conservatives** Ellis, "A Hard Day's Night."
244 **Democratic presidential candidate** Ibid.
244 **For weeks, the consensus** Marjorie Menzel, "Candidates Target Florida," *Florida Today*, Aug. 7, 2000.
244 **The electoral math was such** Ellis, "A Hard Day's Night."
244 **After the briefing** Ibid.
244 **In 1978, as his uncle** John Ellis, LinkedIn profile, www.linkedin.com/pub/john-ellis/5/ba2/5a7, accessed July 29, 2013.
245 **In 1993** John Ellis, "Thank You for Reading," *Boston Globe*, July 29, 1999.
245 **"Looking back over"** John Ellis, "Dangerous Lies," *Boston Globe*, May 27, 1999.
245 **"Loyalty supersedes candor"** John Ellis, "Why I Won't Write Any More About the 2000 Campaign," *Boston Globe*, July 3, 1999.
245 **Three weeks later** Ellis, "Thank You for Reading."
245 **"We at Fox News"** Roger Ailes, House of Representatives, Hearing Before the Committee on Energy and Commerce, 107th Congress, statement of Roger Ailes (Feb. 14, 2001).
245 **"I wouldn't worry about early numbers"** Ellis, "A Hard Day's Night."
245 **"I have no idea"** Ibid.
245 **Ailes was waiting** Ibid.
245 **before venturing over** Author interviews with former Fox executives and producers.
245 **"What's your gut say?"** Jane Mayer, "George W.'s Cousin," *New Yorker*, Nov. 20, 2000.
246 **While Ellis certainly possessed** Author interview with a former Ailes Communications staffer.
246 **"From what Ellis says"** David W. Moore, *How to Steal an Election* (New York: Nation Books, 2006), 58.
246 **They included** Patricia Sullivan, "Fox News Pollster John Gorman; Did Research

for Carter, McGovern," *Washington Post*, Feb. 18, 2008; Arnon Mishkin, LinkedIn .com profile, http://www.linkedin.com/pub/arnon-mishkin/1/359/515; author interview with statistician Cynthia Talkov.

246 **Fox News received** Alicia C. Shepard, "How They Blew It," *American Journalism Review*, Jan./Feb. 2001. See also Moore, *How to Steal an Election*, 31; Murray Dubin, "The Group Behind the Numbers: Voter News Service Does Exit Polls and Provides the Data to News Operations," *Philadelphia Inquirer*, Nov. 9, 2000.

246 **Although the networks** Moore, *How to Steal an Election*, 32.

246 **Cynthia Talkov** Ellis, "A Hard Day's Night"; author interview with Cynthia Talkov. See also Adam Clymer, "Warren J. Mitofsky, 71, Innovator Who Devised Exit Poll, Dies," *New York Times*, Sept. 4, 2006.

246 **"They didn't understand"** Author interview with Cynthia Talkov.

247 **As a last resort** Moore, *How to Steal an Election*, 52.

247 **"My God, you were right!"** Ibid., 53.

247 **Ellis, Edelman later recalled** Ibid.

247 **"I enjoy crunching numbers"** Author interview with Cynthia Talkov.

247 **"I was brought up"** Ibid.

247 **When Ellis stepped away** Moore, *How to Steal an Election*, 53; author interview with Cynthia Talkov.

247 **Talkov was incredulous** Author interview with Cynthia Talkov.

247 **When Ellis got back** Ibid.

247 **The new data stream** Ellis, "A Hard Day's Night."

247 **the state that had elected** Jane Prendergast, "Ohio's Ultra-Bellwethers: What Do They Foretell," *Cincinnati Enquirer*, July 22, 2012.

247 **At 7:50** Shepard, "How They Blew It."

247 **At 7:49** Bill Sammon, *At Any Cost: How Al Gore Tried to Steal the Election* (Washington, D.C.: Regnery, 2001), 36.

247 **"We're going to now project"** Tom Brokaw, *NBC Nightly News,* NBC, Nov. 7, 2000.

248 **Thirty-one seconds later** Linda Mason, Kathleen Frankovic, and Kathleen Hall Jamieson, "CBS News Coverage of Election Night 2000: Investigation, Analysis, Recommendations," report prepared for CBS News, Jan. 2001, 12.

248 **CNN echoed** Shepard, "How They Blew It."

248 **It was up to Moody** Ellis, "A Hard Day's Night"; author interview with a senior Fox executive.

248 **Ellis polled his team** Ellis, "A Hard Day's Night."

248 **At 7:52** Mason et al., "CBS News Coverage of Election Night 2000," 12.

248 **The polls had yet to close** Florida Division of Elections, "Reports by the Division of Elections," http://election.dos.state.fl.us/reports/.

248 **Bush's senior strategist** Evan Thomas, "What a Long, Strange Trip," *Newsweek*, Nov. 20, 2000; Jake Tapper, *Down & Dirty: The Plot to Steal the Presidency* (Boston: Little, Brown, 2001), 28.

248 **"Jeb, I'm sorry"** Ellis, "A Hard Day's Night."

248 **Ten minutes after** Mason et al., "CBS News Coverage of Election Night 2000," 12.

248 **Ailes sat in a plush** Author interview with a person who was present.

248 **At 9:00 p.m.** Ibid.

248 **Ellis was now virtually certain** Ellis, "A Hard Day's Night."

248 **"I think Americans oughta wait"** Tapper, *Down & Dirty*, 28.

248 **"Can you guys take a look"** Ellis, "A Hard Day's Night."

248 **A message flashed** Author interview with Cynthia Talkov.

248 **"We are canceling the vote"** Moore, *How to Steal an Election*, 36.

248 **It turned out that a VNS employee** Tapper, *Down & Dirty*, 30.

249 **The VNS screen showed** Ellis, "A Hard Day's Night."

249 **At 10:23** Mason et al., "CBS News Coverage of Election Night 2000," 12.
249 **In the Sports Suite** Author interview with a former Fox executive.
249 **Ellis later recalled** Ellis, "A Hard Day's Night."
249 **In a first-person account** Ibid.
249 **"What do you think?"** Ibid.
249 **"Any reason not to call Bush in Florida?"** Ibid.
249 **The analysts still wanted more time** Ibid.
249 **"John, based on these numbers"** Collins, *Crazy Like a Fox*, 147.
249 **Ailes, who had left Fox** Author interview with a former senior Fox executive.
249 **At 2:07 a.m.** Moore, *How to Steal an Election*, 41.
249 **Cynthia Talkov, who was sitting** Ibid., 58; author interview with Cynthia Talkov.
249 **Nor did he discuss** Moore, *How to Steal an Election*, 58; Ellis, "A Hard Day's Night." In an email, Ellis disputed Talkov's account, asserting he did check the "need/get" ratios. "You cannot run an election night decision desk without constantly and frantically checking the VNS monitors. That's pretty much all you do, all night. . . . Need/get is the sine qua non of calling elections. You don't call winners; you determine that one or the other of the candidates cannot win. When elections are close, that determination is arrived at by need/get. Everyone on an Election Night Decision Desk (any Election Night Decision Desk) works off of 'need/get.' "
249 **Around 2:10 a.m.** Author interview with Cynthia Talkov.
249 **"Jebbie says we got it!"** Moore, *How to Steal an Election*, 59.
249 **No other network** Mason et al., "CBS News Coverage of Election Night 2000," 12.
249 **This time, no one expressed objections** Moore, *How to Steal an Election*, 59.
249 **Talkov would later be haunted** Author interview with Cynthia Talkov.
249 **"At the time"** Ibid.
250 **"Let me introduce you"** Author interview with a person familiar with the matter.
250 **"We're gonna call it"** Author interview with a person familiar with the matter.
250 **At 2:16 a.m.** Brit Hume, *Special Report with Brit Hume*, Fox News Channel, Nov. 7, 2000; footage of Fox's coverage can be found on YouTube at http://www.youtube.com/watch?v=vJIGQyF2Yjo, accessed Aug. 13, 2013.
250 **Confusion reigned** Thomas, "What a Long, Strange Trip."
250 **"It's just Fox"** Tapper, *Down & Dirty*, 32.
250 **"Is this going to be"** Thomas, "What a Long, Strange Trip."
250 **At NBC News** Ibid., 72.
250 **Around midnight, Jack Welch** Author interview with a person present that evening.
250 **"Gotta go"** Ibid.
250 **Tom Brokaw made the announcement** Mason et al., "CBS News Coverage of Election Night 2000," 12.
250 **Twenty-two seconds** Ibid.
250 **"That's it"** Dan Rather, *CBS News Election Night*, CBS, Nov. 8, 2000.
250 **CNN called it** Mason et al., "CBS News Coverage of Election Night 2000," 12.
250 **Only the AP** Moore, *How to Steal an Election*, 83.
250 **Bush reveled in** Ellis, "A Hard Day's Night."
251 **At 2:48 a.m.** Moore, *How to Steal an Election*, 43.
251 **Twenty minutes later** Ibid., 43.
251 **Gore was already** Thomas, "What a Long, Strange Trip."
251 **Campaign aides frantically** Ibid.
251 **At 3:27 a.m.** Ellis, "A Hard Day's Night."
251 **"Florida—the Sec of State Web site"** Moore, *How to Steal an Election*, 44.
251 **Ellis called Moody over** Collins, *Crazy Like a Fox*, 148.
251 **"You gotta be kidding me"** Tapper, *Down & Dirty*, 37.

251 **"Gore unconceded"** Ellis, "A Hard Day's Night."
251 **At 3:57 a.m.** Mason et al., "CBS News Coverage of Election Night 2000," 12.
251 **Fox News, the first** Ibid.
251 **Brit Hume made** Ibid.
251 **Talkov was concerned** Author interview with Cynthia Talkov.
251 **For the next thirty-three days** See, e.g., Sean Hannity, *Hannity & Colmes*, Fox News Channel, Dec. 4, 2000 ("now there's an effort out there to delegitimize the Bush presidency, which is now inevitable."); Brit Hume, Mort Kondracke, Fred Barnes, Mara Liasson, *Special Report with Brit Hume*, Fox News Channel, Dec. 4, 2000; Sean Hannity, *Hannity & Colmes*, Fox News Channel, Nov. 26, 2000 ("At the end of the day, George W. Bush is the president-elect, right now," Anthony Weiner: "Have you ever said that Al Gore's trying to steal the election?" Sean Hannity: "He is.")
252 **"The day after the election"** Author interview with a senior Fox producer.
252 **"It won't be easy"** Brit Hume, *Special Report with Brit Hume*, Fox News Channel, Nov. 8, 2000.
252 **"There is a minor brouhaha"** Bill O'Reilly, *The O'Reilly Factor*, Fox News Channel, Nov. 8, 2000.
252 **"I think what's going on"** John Gibson, *The O'Reilly Factor*, Fox News Channel, Dec. 9, 2000.
252 **On November 26** Collins, *Crazy Like a Fox*, 156–57; Paula Zahn, *Special Report with Brit Hume*, Fox News Channel, Nov. 26, 2000.
252 **"If it hadn't been for Fox"** Howard Kurtz, "Doing Something Right, Fox News Sees Ratings Soar, Critics Sore," *Washington Post*, Feb. 5, 2001.
252 **In November 2000** Collins, *Crazy Like a Fox*, 158.
252 **David Shuster was** Much of the information in the following pages is taken from an author interview with broadcaster and journalist David Shuster.
253 **On Thursday, November 2** Alicia C. Shepard, "A Late-Breaking Campaign Skeleton," *American Journalism Review*, Dec. 2000.
253 **Carl Cameron broke it** Brit Hume, *Special Report with Brit Hume*, Fox News Channel, Nov. 2, 2000.
253 **"I knew it would hurt him"** Ken Auletta, "Vox Fox: How Roger Ailes and Fox News Are Changing Cable News," *New Yorker*, May 26, 2003.
253 **the reporter's source was a Democrat** Shepard, "A Late-Breaking Campaign Skeleton."
253 **On air, Tony Snow** Tony Snow, *Special Report with Brit Hume*, Fox News Network, Nov. 3, 2000.
254 **"I don't know whether"** Alan Colmes, *Hannity & Colmes*, Carl Cameron interview with George W. Bush, Fox News Channel, Nov. 4, 2000.
254 **The coverage reflected** Author interview with David Shuster.
254 **As the recount stalemated** Ibid.
254 **Shuster also clashed** Author interview with David Shuster.
254 **Bret Baier** "Bret Baier," Foxnews.com, http://www.foxnews.com/on-air/personalities/bret-baier/bio/; David Folkenflik, "Bret Baier: The Next Generation of Fox News Anchor," NPR.org, April 6, 2011, http://www.npr.org/2011/04/07/135176903/bret-baier-the-next-generation-of-fox-news-anchor.
254 **On Fox, Brit Hume** Brit Hume, *Special Report with Brit Hume*, Fox News Channel, Nov. 15, 2000.
254 **Shuster's time was running out** Author interview with David Shuster.
255 **He would leave the network** "First Bites," *Bulldog Reporter Business Media*, July 26, 2002.
255 **On November 9** Mayer, "George W.'s Cousin."
255 **"Jebbie'll be calling me"** Ibid.

255 **"It was just the three of us"** Ibid.
255 **Gore's campaign manager** Tapper, *Down & Dirty*, 69n.
255 **There were congressional hearings** Katharine Q. Seelye, "Congress Plans Study of Voting Processes and TV Coverage," *New York Times*, Feb. 9, 2001.
255 **Cynthia Talkov had become** Author interview with Cynthia Talkov.
255 **On Valentine's Day 2001** House of Representatives, 107th Congress, Hearing Before the Committee on Energy and Commerce, Feb. 14, 2001.
255 **Prior to the hearing** Author interview with former Associated Press CEO Lou Baccardi.
256 **"Obviously, through"** House of Representatives, Hearing Before the Committee on Energy and Commerce, prepared statement of Roger Ailes.
256 **"That one little moment"** Author interview with a senior Fox producer.

## SIXTEEN: HOLY WAR

257 **In a few hours** Author interview with attorney and political adviser John Coale, Van Susteren's spouse.
257 **Six days before** Lisa de Moraes, "CNN Nabs Paula Zahn from Miffed Fox News," *Washington Post*, Sept. 6, 2001.
257 **Before she left** Auletta, "Vox Fox."
257 **In March 2001** Allyson Lieberman, "The New King of Cable: WB Whiz Jamie Kellner Is Taking On His Biggest Challenge Yet: Turner's Empire," *New York Post*, March 11, 2001.
257 **"Give us six months"** Jim Rutenberg, "Hatfield vs. McCoy in TV Land," *New York Times*, Jan. 13, 2002.
257 **"Roger printed that quote"** Ibid.; author interview with a senior Fox News producer.
257 **"Who wouldn't want to be"** Author interview with former Fox News producer Anne Hartmayer.
258 **Kellner, whom *The New York Times*** Jim Rutenberg, "Mix, Patch, Promote and Lift; A Showman Speeds the Makeover of Ted Turner's Empire," *New York Times*, July 15, 2001.
258 **offered Zahn $2 million** de Moraes, "CNN Nabs Paula Zahn from Miffed Fox News."
258 **"She thought her career"** Collins, *Crazy Like a Fox*, 178.
258 **On Tuesday, August 28** The account of Fox's negotiations with Zahn can be found in ibid., 177–82.
258 **"He made it very clear"** Auletta, "Vox Fox."
258 **The following morning** Collins, *Crazy Like a Fox*, 180–81.
258 **The suit was later dismissed** Bill Carter, "Judge Dismisses Fox News Suit over Anchor's Defection to CNN," *New York Times*, March 26, 2002; Bill Carter, "Fox Loses Round in Its Suit over Anchor's Move to CNN," *New York Times*, May 1, 2003.
259 **"I don't pay for disloyalty"** Bill Carter, "Fox News Fires a Star Host over CNN Bid," *New York Times*, Sept. 6, 2001.
259 **Ailes said he was** Ibid.
259 **"I could have put"** Ibid.
259 **"The key to the whole thing"** Author interview with a senior Fox executive.
259 **Shortly after 9:00** Author interview with John Coale.
259 **"Oh my God"** The account of this meeting is based on author interview with a person in the room as well as the account in Scott Collins's book, *Crazy Like a Fox*, p. 161.

259 **Moody, sitting** Author interviews with senior Fox executives and producers.

259 **The producers sitting around** Author interviews with senior Fox executives and producers.

260 **"Welcome back to Fox News"** The descriptions of Fox's coverage of the day of 9/11 can be found here: http://www.youtube.com/playlist?list=PL3E8B2399764ABE7D.

260 **Jon Scott** "On Air Personalities," Foxnews.com, http://www.foxnews.com/on-air/personalities/jon-scott/bio/#s=r-z, accessed Sept. 3, 2013.

260 **"That means the second tower"** Author interview with a person familiar with the matter.

260 **"The country is at war"** Author interview with a person in the room.

260 **"Roger rallied"** Ibid.

260 **Barely twenty minutes** Kat Stoeffel, "Ticker Taped: The 9/11 News Crawl," "Our City Since" (blog), *New York Observer*, Sept. 11, 2011, http://observer.com/2011/09/ticker-taped-the-911-news-crawl/.

261 **"Day of Terror"** For video footage of this text, see http://www.youtube.com/watch?v=pNk6jOXRfwo.

261 **"A lot of guidance"** Author interview with a senior Fox executive.

261 **"They had this problem"** E. D. Donahey, "Terrorism Hits America," Fox News Channel, Sept. 12, 2001; video is available at https://www.youtube.com/watch?v=-1It_PsSENc.

262 **On the night of September 13** Bill O'Reilly, *The O'Reilly Factor*, Fox News Channel, Sept. 13, 2001; video is available at http://www.youtube.com/watch?v=GUQSY4C6CwE.

263 **"it was like a World War Two"** Author interview with a senior Fox producer.

263 **"I remember running"** Ibid.

263 **"What we say is"** Jim Rutenberg, "Fox Portrays a War of Good and Evil, and Many Applaud," *New York Times*, Dec. 3, 2001.

264 **"smoke out"** George W. Bush, "Remarks by the President Upon Arrival," press conference, South Lawn of the White House, Sept. 16, 2001, http://georgewbush-whitehouse.archives.gov/news/releases/2001/09/20010916-2.html.

264 **"dead or alive"** Brian Knowlton, " 'We're Going to Smoke Them Out': President Airs His Anger," *New York Times*, Sept. 19, 2001.

264 **In January 2002** Matt Kempner, "Fox News Bests CNN in Viewers; Broad-Based Monthly Win Is First Ever," *Atlanta Journal-Constitution*, Jan. 30, 2002.

264 **"He told me having a kid"** Author interview with former Fox News Channel anchor Bob Sellers.

264 **At the time** Alex Koppelman, "Did Fox News Chief Ailes Try to Protect Rudy Giuliani?," Salon.com, Nov. 16, 2007, http://www.salon.com/2007/11/16/ailes/.

264 **On the night of September 11** Author interview with a source with direct knowledge of the matter.

264 **Later, an internal** Leonard Levitt, "The NYPD: Indulging Mort and Roger," NYPDConfidential.com, April 9, 2012, http://nypdconfidential.com/columns/2012/120409.html, accessed Oct. 8, 2013.

264 **"After 9/11"** Author interview with a senior Fox employee.

264 **On the second floor** Ibid.

264 **About a year after the attacks** Jo Becker, "Murdoch, Ruler of a Vast Empire, Reaches Out for Even More," *New York Times*, June 25, 2007.

264 **"Roger said this insane thing"** Author interview with a person in the room.

265 **As the evening wound down** The information in the following paragraphs was obtained from author interviews with sources familiar with the incident.

265 **In London, Sam Chisholm** Mathew Horsman, "Sky: The Inside Story: Bowing Out to the Inevitable," *The Guardian*, Nov. 10, 1997.

265 **"On one level"** Author interview with an executive close to Ailes.

266 **"Don't ever fucking fire"** Ibid.
266 **"Rupert is not"** Author interview with a source close to the Murdoch family.

## SEVENTEEN: QUAGMIRE DOESN'T RATE

267 **"The only thing America"** Chafets, *Roger Ailes*, 97.
267 **"I wrote that letter"** Author interview with a senior Fox employee. When Bob Woodward revealed Ailes's memo to Bush in his 2002 book *Bush at War*, Ailes was defiant. He said there was not anything untoward about the head of a news organization offering a president military advice. Ailes defended it by complaining that CNN chief Rick Kaplan had been close to Bill Clinton in the 1990s, and he pointed out that Kaplan even bunked in the Lincoln Bedroom. "I'm not saying [Woodward] deliberately distorted it," Ailes told *The New York Times* on November 19, 2002. "But he's like Tom Clancy. They both make up a lot of stories, but Clancy does better research." When I spoke with Karl Rove's office, Rove declined to comment.
267 **That's why, he'd say** Hoover Institution, "Fox and More with Roger Ailes," interview, *Uncommon Knowledge with Peter Robinson*, Feb. 5, 2010; video available at http://www.hoover.org/multimedia/uncommon-knowledge/26681; transcript available at http://media.hoover.org/sites/default/files/documents/UK-Ailes-transcript.pdf.
267 **Rove made sure** Author interview with a senior Bush administration official.
267 **"Roger was the bigger figure"** Ibid.
267 **"Ailes would call Karl"** Ibid.
268 **"It focused on"** Ibid.
268 **Around the time** The information in this paragraph comes from author interview with a senior Bush administration official.
268 **"Roger was afraid"** Ibid.
268 **"Someone has to speak"** Author interview with a senior Fox producer.
268 **Three days after 9/11** Bill O'Reilly, *Special Report: America United*, Fox News Channel, Sept. 14, 2001.
268 **A year earlier, Mylroie** Ibid.; see also Laurie Mylroie, *Study of Revenge: Saddam Hussein's Unfinished War Against America* (Washington, D.C.: AEI Press, 2000).
268 **"the Neocons' favorite conspiracy theorist"** Peter Bergen, "Armchair Provocateur," *Washington Monthly*, Dec. 2003.
268 **"No," she said** O'Reilly, *Special Report: America United*, Sept. 14, 2001.
269 **Given the president's** Gallup, "Presidential Approval Ratings—George W. Bush," Nov. 2–4, 8–11, and 26–27, http://www.gallup.com/poll/116500/presidential-approval-ratings-george-bush.aspx.
269 **"Every story"** Author interview with a senior Fox producer.
269 **"From a marketing point of view"** "Quotation of the Day," *New York Times*, Sept. 7, 2002.
269 **Twice each day** Author interviews with senior Fox employees.
269 **"It's not easy"** Author interview with a senior Fox executive.
269 **In the network's early days** Author interviews with senior Fox executives.
269 **During George H. W. Bush's** David Q. Bates Jr. interview with James S. Young and George C. Edwards III, Miller Center at the University of Virginia, http://millercenter.org/president/bush/oralhistory/david-bates.
269 **"Fox never went"** Author interview with a senior Fox executive.
269 **"Roger is very good"** Author interview with a senior Fox producer.
270 **In the newsroom** Author interview with a senior Fox executive.
270 **"You can't say"** Author interview with a former Fox executive.
270 **Judy Laterza** Author interviews with senior Fox employees.

270 **"When Roger said something"** Author interviews with sources familiar with the matter.

270 **One producer joked** Author interview with a former senior Fox producer.

270 **Bill Shine** Information on Shine is from author interviews with current and former Fox News employees.

270 **"Call me"** Author interview with a senior Fox producer.

270 **As payback** Author interview with a senior Fox employee.

270 **Lewis had a nickname** Ibid.

270 **Like Fox's prime-time stars** John M. Higgins, "Shine Makes Fox News Glow," *Broadcasting & Cable*, Dec. 5, 2004.

271 **He was "a blue-collar"** Author interview with a former senior Fox producer.

271 **From his modest roots** Author interview with a former senior Fox producer.

271 **"We looked at them"** Author interview with a former Fox employee.

271 **"When Ashcroft was being confirmed"** Author interview with former Fox News producer Adam Sank.

271 **In October 2003** Tim Grieve, "Fox News: The Inside Story," Salon.com, Oct. 31, 2003, http://www.salon.com/2003/10/31/fox_20/.

271 **"People know who's"** Author interview with Bob Sellers.

271 **"Watch out for"** Author interview with former Fox producer Charles Reina.

271 **Adam Sank remembered** Author interview with Adam Sank.

271 **"Look, I know everything"** Author interview with a person familiar with the conversation.

272 **One executive called it** Author interview with a Fox executive.

272 **"She had rules"** Author interview with a former Fox producer.

272 **"She had no"** Author interview with a former senior Fox producer.

272 **Brian Lewis's department** The descriptions of Fox's media relations department are based on author interviews with current and former Fox News employees.

272 **"He would call"** Author interview with a senior Fox producer.

272 **"Am I a Republican?"** Author interview with Charles Reina.

273 **At the Fox News Christmas party** Dickinson, "How Roger Ailes Built the Fox News Fear Factory"; author interview with Charles Reina.

273 **As the administration** Information in this paragraph is derived from author interviews with a senior Fox executive.

273 **At the time** Auletta, "Vox Fox."

273 **When the war** Collins, *Crazy Like a Fox*, 189–90.

273 **Shortly after receiving** Author interviews with sources familiar with the matter.

273 **"Fox approached news"** Author interview with a former Fox producer.

274 **"I need a better Muslim!"** Author interview with a source who was present in the newsroom.

274 **"You're doing a service"** Author interview with a senior Fox producer.

274 **the United Nations** See, e.g., John Gibson, "Is United Nations Irrelevant in Today's World?," *The Big Story with John Gibson*, Fox News Channel, Feb. 19, 2003.

274 **France** See, e.g., Neil Cavuto, "Stock Market Surges as U.N. Continues to Debate Potential Iraq War," *Your World with Neil Cavuto*, Fox News Channel, March 13, 2003.

274 **Germany** See, e.g., John Gibson, "Three NATO Members Veto Plan to Defend Turkey in Case of Iraq War," *The Big Story with John Gibson*, Fox News Channel, Feb. 10, 2003.

274 **Al Jazeera** See, e.g., Bill O'Reilly, *The O'Reilly Factor*, analysis with Mansoor Ijaz, Nov. 12, 2002.

274 **"If they're going to get us"** Michael Starr, "Geraldo's Got a Gun . . . And Bin Laden in His Sights," *New York Post*, Dec. 4, 2001.

274 **In November 2001** Paula Bernstein, "Rivera Vaults to Fox News," *Daily Variety*, Nov. 2, 2001.

274 **"We walked over"** Sridhar Pappu, "Being Geraldo," *Atlantic*, June 2005.
274 **A week later** David Folkenflik, "War News from Rivera Seems off the Mark," *Baltimore Sun*, Dec. 12, 2001.
274 **He attributed the error** Mark Jurkowitz, "Rivera's Defense of His Shoddy Reporting Is Unconvincing," *Boston Globe*, Dec. 4, 2002; Folkenflik, "War News from Rivera Seems off the Mark."
274 **"Have *you* ever been shot at?"** Folkenflik, "War News from Rivera Seems off the Mark."
274 **When Dan Rather sat down** Auletta, "Vox Fox."
275 **"Nowhere in the"** Ibid.
275 **"Americans and, indeed"** Bill O'Reilly, *The O'Reilly Factor*, Fox News Channel, Feb. 26, 2003.
275 **When antiwar protesters** John M. Higgins, "Fox News Mocks Media Protesters," *Broadcasting & Cable*, March 31, 2003.
275 **Five days before** James Deaville, "Selling War: Television News Music and the Shaping of American Public Opinion," *Echo: A Music-Centered Journal* 8, no. 1 (Fall 2006), http://www.echo.ucla.edu/Volume8-Issue1/roundtable/deaville.html.
275 **"The other networks"** Peter Dobrin, "Media's War Music Carries a Message," *Philadelphia Inquirer*, March 30, 2003.
275 **After listening** Deaville, "Selling War."
275 **In one, a fighter jet** Deborah Lynn Jaramillo, *Ugly War, Pretty Package: How CNN and Fox News Made the Invasion of Iraq High Concept* (Bloomington: Indiana University Press, 2009), 156.
275 **The script for a thirty-second** Ibid., 181–82.
276 **Anchor Bob Sellers** Author interview with Bob Sellers.
276 **On March 20** Jaramillo, *Ugly War, Pretty Package*, 113.
276 **"The conservatives were not"** Author interview with a former Bush administration official.
276 ***The New York Times*'s Judith Miller** See, e.g., the following articles written by Miller for the *Times* in the months prior to the commencement of war: "U.S. Says Hussein Intensifies Quest for A-Bomb Parts" (with Michael R. Gordon, Sept. 8, 2002); "White House Lists Iraq Steps to Build Banned Weapons" (with Michael R. Gordon, Sept. 13, 2002); "Lab Suggests Qaeda Planned to Build Arms, Officials Say" (Sept. 14, 2002); "Defectors Bolster U.S. Case Against Iraq, Officials Say" (Jan. 24, 2003).
276 **Both CNN and MSNBC** Author interviews with executives from CNN and MSNBC.
276 **In the summer of 2001** John Bresnahan and Mark Preston, "CNN Chief Courts GOP," *Roll Call*, Aug. 6, 2001.
277 **He also wooed** Maureen Dowd, "CNN: Foxy or Outfoxed?," *New York Times*, Aug. 15, 2001.
277 **In October 2001** Howard Kurtz, "CNN Chief Orders 'Balance' in War News; Reporters Are Told to Remind Viewers Why U.S. Is Bombing," *Washington Post*, Oct. 31, 2001.
277 **"It was torture"** Author interview with television executive Phil Griffin.
277 **Prior to joining** Felix Gillette, "Phil Griffin Gets New Title: President of MSNBC," *New York Observer*, July 16, 2008.
277 **MSNBC was faltering** The accounts and quotations regarding MSNBC's struggle to compete with Fox News are derived from author interviews with MSNBC executives, and were first reported on by the author in "Chasing Fox: The Loud, Cartoonish Blood Sport That's Engorged MSNBC, Exhausted CNN—and Is Making Our Body Politic Delirious," *New York*, Oct. 11, 2010.
278 **On the day MSNBC** Auletta, "Vox Fox."
278 **After Andy Lack** Collins, *Crazy Like a Fox*, 130.

279 **After MSNBC anchor** See, e.g., "Good Morning Lowcountry," *Post and Courier* (Charleston, South Carolina), April 24, 2002.
279 **"Take her out"** Author interview with a Fox employee.
279 **"He was the oppo research guy"** Author interview with a Fox executive.
279 **One morning in late fall** Auletta, "Vox Fox."
279 **"You know who's"** Ibid.
279 **Doocy's producers** Ibid.
279 **"You wake up"** Ibid.
279 **"Are we going to continue"** Author interview with a person who was in the room.
280 **By early April** "Baghdad Under Heavy Bombing as US Troops Push In," *Agence France-Presse*, April 5, 2003.
280 **On the morning of** Author interview with a senior Fox executive.
280 **statue of Saddam Hussein** For a thorough look at the events of the April 9 removal of the Saddam Hussein statue, see Peter Maass, "The Toppling: How the Media Inflated a Minor Moment in a Long War," *New Yorker*, Jan. 10, 2011. Several of the quotations in this section are taken from that story, as well as from Jaramillo, *Ugly War, Pretty Package*, 197–200.
280 **As the scene on the ground** The information pertaining to the activity in the Fox newsroom during the flag-raising incident is from author interviews with current and former Fox News producers.
280 **"Get that flag going!"** Maass, "The Toppling."
281 **"My goose bumps"** Frank Rich, *The Greatest Story Ever Sold: The Decline and Fall of Truth From 9/11 to Katrina* (New York: Penguin, 2006), 83.
281 **"This transcends anything"** Maass, "The Toppling."
281 **"What better picture"** Author interview with a Fox producer.
281 **"Here we go!"** Jaramillo, *Ugly War, Pretty Package*, 199.
281 **" 'Jubilance' seems too mild"** David Asman, Fox News Channel, April 9, 2003; video available at http://www.youtube.com/watch?v=4uyttSrkW6Q.
281 **"The scenes of free Iraqis"** Maass, "The Toppling."
281 **Throughout the day** Rich, *The Greatest Story Ever Sold*, 84.
281 **"Now that the war"** John Gibson, *The Big Story with John Gibson*, Fox News Channel, April 16, 2003.
281 **Although thirteen** Sean Aday, John Cluverius, and Steven Livingston, "As Goes the Statue, So Goes the War: The Emergence of the Victory Frame in Television Coverage of the Iraq War," *Journal of Broadcasting & Electronic Media* 49, no. 3 (Sept. 2005): 326.
282 **"They had their ending"** Author interview with a former Fox producer.
282 **In September 2003** Author interview with a former senior Bush administration official.
282 **"I think he hid them"** Rich, *The Greatest Story Ever Sold*, 288.
282 **"signs of a return to normal"** Brit Hume, *Special Report with Brit Hume*, Fox News Channel, Oct. 9, 2003.
282 **One October 1 segment** Brit Hume, *Special Report with Brit Hume*, Fox News Channel, Oct. 1, 2003.
282 **When a Spanish diplomat** *Special Report with Brit Hume*, Fox News Channel, Oct. 9, 2003.
282 **"For a huge part"** Ibid.
282 **"Do not fall into"** Media Matters staff, "33 Internal FOX Editorial Memos Reviewed by *MMFA* Reveal FOX News Channel's Inner Workings," Media Matters for America, July 14, 2004, http://cloudfront.mediamatters.org/static/pdf/fox-memo_040604.pdf.
283 **"It was the same"** Author interview with a senior Fox producer.
283 **"[T]he pictures from Abu Graeb"** Media Matters staff, "33 Internal FOX Edito-

rial Memos Reviewed by *MMFA* Reveal FOX News Channel's Inner Workings," http://cloudfront.mediamatters.org/static/pdf/foxmemo_050504.pdf.

283 **In 2004, Fox even considered** Author interview with a former Bush administration official.

283 **Dan Senor** Jim Dwyer, "Bush Voice in Iraq Eyes U.S. Senate Run," *New York Times*, March 16, 2010.

283 **Senor turned down** Author interview with a former Bush administration official.

283 **In the fall of 2003** The account of Lewis's negotiations is taken from author interviews with sources familiar with the matter.

## EIGHTEEN: "WHAT ARE YOU GOING TO DO WITH ALL THIS POWER?"

285 **On Wednesday, August 4** Much of the detail in this section is taken from the author's interview with former substitute Fox host and Democratic politician Patrick Halpin.

285 **The August 4 edition** Sean Hannity, "Veterans Run Ad Against Kerry," *Hannity & Colmes*, Fox News Channel, Aug. 4, 2004.

286 **The spot opened** Swift Boat Veterans for Truth, "Any Questions?," 2004 political advertisement, available at http://archive.org/details/swb_anyquestions.

286 **The next day** "It's Not All Fair Game," editorial, *Los Angeles Times*, Aug. 6, 2004.

287 **On August 5** Brit Hume, "Political Headlines" and "All-Star Panel," *Special Report with Brit Hume*, Fox News Channel, Aug. 5, 2004.

287 **"I think this is awful"** Bill O'Reilly, "Unresolved Problem," *The O'Reilly Factor*, Fox News Channel, Aug. 5, 2004.

287 **"Cable news"** Auletta, "Vox Fox."

287 **Since Kerry locked up** For examples, see *On the Record with Greta Van Susteren*, Fox News Channel, Nov. 1, 2004 (Laura Ingraham: "A lot of people are going to get in there and realize they're aligning themselves, if they support Kerry, with the people of France"); *The Big Story with John Gibson*, Fox News Channel, Oct. 22, 2004 (John Gibson: "Kerry in the White House, speaking French to Chirac?").

287 **"There were subtle commands"** Author interview with a senior Fox producer.

287 **"He may be a Boston aristocrat"** Brit Hume, "All-Star Panel," *Special Report with Brit Hume*, Fox News Channel, April 6, 2004.

287 **"Kerry, starting to feel"** Media Matters staff, "33 Internal FOX Editorial Memos Reviewed by *MMFA* Reveal FOX News Channel's Inner Workings."

287 **"Ribbons or medals?"** Ibid.

287 **The week after** Sean Hannity, "Interview with John O'Neill," *Hannity & Colmes*, Fox News Channel, Aug. 10, 2004.

287 **"I read the book"** Ibid.

288 ***Unfit for Command* hit** "Hardcover Nonfiction," *New York Times*, Sept. 19, 2004, http://www.nytimes.com/2004/09/19/books/bestseller/0919besthard nonfiction.html; see also Robert Novak, "Did John Kerry Misrepresent Vietnam Record?," *Crossfire*, CNN, Aug. 12, 2004; Chris Matthews, interview with John O'Neill, *Hardball*, MSNBC, Aug. 12, 2004.

288 **"Heck, I know our group"** Author interview with author and lawyer John O'Neill.

288 **Fox News contributor Susan Estrich** Much of this section is based on author's interview with former Dukakis campaign manager and current analyst for Fox News Channel Susan Estrich.

288 **In '88, the Willie Horton ad** "The Race for the White House Notebook: Maker

of Horton Ad Sets Sights on Clinton," *Boston Globe*, March 31, 1992; author interview with Roger Stone.

288 **The Swift Boat attack** See, e.g., Evan Thomas, "All in the Family," *Newsweek*, Nov. 15, 2004.

288 **The spot mockingly** Asawin Suebsaeng, "A Political History of the Cicadas," Political Mojo" (blog), MotherJones.com, May 10, 2003, http://www.motherjones.com/mojo/2013/05/political-history-cicadas-ronald-reagan.

288 **"We want you to respond"** Author interview with Susan Estrich.

289 **As it happened** Sean Hannity, *Hannity & Colmes*, Fox News Channel, Aug. 5, 2004.

289 **When Estrich called** Evan Thomas, *Election 2004: How Bush Won and What You Can Expect in the Future* (New York: PublicAffairs, 2004), 121; author interview with Susan Estrich.

289 **"Wherever I went"** Author interview with Susan Estrich.

289 **Greta Van Susteren's husband** Mark Leibovich, "'C-List' Debate Spinners Stand Alone," *Washington Post*, Oct. 10, 2004.

289 **A few days before Hannity** The information in this section is taken from author's interview with John Coale.

289 **Kerry's campaign manager** Thomas, *Election 2004*, 125.

289 **By the time Kerry** Jim Rutenberg and Kate Zernike, "Going Negative: When It Works," *New York Times*, Aug. 22, 2004.

289 **After a tape** Dan Collins, "Kerry Camp Fumes at Fox Anchor," CBSNews.com, Feb. 11, 2009, http://www.cbsnews.com/2100-250_162-652595.html.

289 **John Sasso** Patrick Healy, "Angry over On-Air Remark, Adviser Threatens a Ban," *Boston Globe*, Oct. 31, 2004; author interview with a source who was present during the incident.

290 **On the night of** Michael Wolff, *The Man Who Owns the News: Inside the Secret World of Rupert Murdoch* (New York: Random House, 2008), 38.

290 **Fox called Ohio for Bush** Jacques Steinberg and David Carr, "Once Bitten, Twice Tempted, but No Call in Wee Hours," *New York Times*, Nov. 4, 2004.

290 **As the minutes ticked by** Ibid.; author interview with a senior Bush campaign official.

290 **Rove called Fox analyst** Steinberg and Carr, "Once Bitten, Twice Tempted, but No Call in Wee Hours."

290 **Dan Bartlett, at Bush high command** Author interview with a senior Bush administration official.

290 **"You know I wasn't"** Author interview with a Bush campaign official.

290 **After Bush's victory** Bill Ward, "Word Up," *Minneapolis Star Tribune*, Nov. 7, 2012.

290 **"Sean said"** Author interview with Patrick Halpin.

290 **Months later** James Dobson and Rick Santorum, *Hannity & Colmes*, Fox News Channel, March 18, 2005.

290 **"Go easy"** Author interview with Patrick Halpin.

290 **"Sean was pissed"** Ibid.

291 **Fox News was now** Jacques Steinberg, "Fox News, Media Elite," *New York Times*, Nov. 8, 2004.

291 **In July 2004** Robert Greenwald, *Outfoxed: Rupert Murdoch's War on Journalism*, Carolina Productions and MoveOn.org, film, July 13, 2004.

291 **a surprise hit** Pamela McClintock, " 'Outfoxed' Jumps over DVD Rivals on Amazon," *Daily Variety*, July 21, 2004.

291 **They watched on average** Stephen Battaglio, "New CNN Team Seeks a Long Run," *Daily News*, Sept. 16, 2003.

291 **When Ailes later decided** Howard Kurtz, "Fox News Launches Conservative Web Site Fox Nation," *Washington Post*, March 30, 2009.

291 **"Before Fox News"** Author interview with Democratic political consultant Robert Shrum.
291 **Given Ailes's audience** Michele Greppi, "Ratings Increase for Fox, Headline," *TelevisionWeek*, July 11, 2005.
292 **"It's stupid"** Author interview with John Coale.
292 **Connecting online** Jonathan Chait, "The Left's New Machine," *New Republic*, May 21, 2007.
292 **During a 2002 interview** Josh Benson, "Gore's TV War: He Lobs Salvo at Fox News," *New York Observer*, Dec. 2, 2002.
292 **And throughout the contentious** Howard Kurtz, "Reporters Shift Gears on the Dean Bus; Iowa Vote and Outburst Rewrite the Campaign Saga," *Washington Post*, Jan. 23, 2004.
292 **Dean's eventual ascension** Nancy Benac, "Dean and the Democrats: The Outsider Is In," Associated Press, Feb. 11, 2005.
292 **At a Democratic fundraiser** Author interview with John Coale.
292 **One morning in** This account is based on author interviews with sources with direct knowledge of the meeting.
293 **In the 1990s** See, e.g., David Brock, "His Cheatin' Heart," *American Spectator*, Jan. 1994.
293 **hailed as the Bob Woodward** David Brock, *Blinded by the Right: The Conscience of an Ex-Conservative* (New York: Crown, 2002), 191.
293 **The tactic** Eric Alterman, "Think Again: 'Working the Refs,' " *Center for American Progress*, May 26, 2005, http://www.americanprogress.org/issues/media/news/2005/05/26/1476/think-again-working-the-refs/.
293 **Other liberals** Michael Shear, "Soros Donates $1 Million to Media Matters," *New York Times*, Oct. 20, 2010.
293 **Media Matters launched** "Ex-Conservative Insider Brock Launches Progressive Research and Information Center; Group to Correct Conservative Misinformation," PR Newswire, May 3, 2004.
293 **A few months earlier** "Progressive Talk Radio Show Hits National Airwaves; Conservative Talk Meets Its Match with the Debut of The Ed Schultz Show," PR Newswire, Jan. 7, 2004.
294 **A member of the comedy elite** Al Franken, "Meet Al," AlFranken.com, http://www.alfranken.com/meet-al/.
294 **In 1996, he published** "Best Sellers," *New York Times*, March 3, 1996.
294 **For his follow-up** Al Franken, *Lies and the Lying Liars Who Tell Them* (New York: Penguin, 2003).
294 **By the spring** Matt Zoller Seitz, "O'Reilly Formula: It's All About Good vs. Evil," *Newark Star-Ledger*, May 11, 2003.
294 **Often his targets** Bill O'Reilly, "Back of the Book," *The O'Reilly Factor*, Fox News Channel, March 24, 2003.
294 **Or Hollywood** Bill O'Reilly, "Talking Points," *The O'Reilly Factor*, Fox News Channel, April 9, 2003.
294 **He hammered** Bill O'Reilly, "Talking Points," *The O'Reilly Factor*, Fox News Channel, Jan. 5, 2005.
294 **"We've changed the country"** Kitman, *The Man Who Would Not Shut Up*, 208.
294 **Through his various** Ibid., 185.
294 **"He sees O'Reilly"** Author interview with a senior Fox executive.
295 **One night, he called** Bill O'Reilly, "Interview with *Progressive Magazine*'s Matthew Rothschild," *The O'Reilly Factor*, Fox News Channel, May 19, 2003.
295 **On another program** Bill O'Reilly, "Top Story," *The O'Reilly Factor*, Fox News Channel, Aug. 27, 2002.
295 **"He's hyper-suspicious"** Author interview with a former O'Reilly producer.
295 **O'Reilly declared to a reporter** Kitman, *The Man Who Would Not Shut Up*, 217.

295 **"This has happened"** Ibid.
295 **During a February 2003** Bill O'Reilly, "Personal Stories," *The O'Reilly Factor*, Fox News Channel, Feb. 4, 2003.
295 **"Get the fuck"** Author interview with a former O'Reilly producer.
295 **After one taping** Author interviews with sources familiar with the incident.
295 **"I'm the big gun"** Kitman, *The Man Who Would Not Shut Up*, 232.
295 **His relationship with Sean Hannity** Author interviews with Patrick Halpin and senior Fox executives.
296 **"His was the only show"** Author interview with a former senior Fox executive.
296 **As Franken was putting** Bill O'Reilly, *Who's Looking Out for You?* (New York: Crown, 2003).
296 **"You're just going to give"** Kitman, *The Man Who Would Not Shut Up*, 226.
296 **The event** "BEA 2003: Al Franken, Molly Ivins, and Bill O'Reilly Panel Discussion," BookTV.org, C-Span2, http://www.booktv.org/Watch/3856/BEA+2003+Al+Franken+Molly+Ivins+Bill+OReilly+Panel+Discussion.aspx, accessed Sept. 19, 2013.
296 **"This is what he does"** Bill O'Reilly, "Profiting from Malice," Foxnews.com, June 3, 2003, http://www.foxnews.com/story/2003/06/03/profiting-from-malice/.
296 **He told Fox** Kitman, *The Man Who Would Not Shut Up*, 232; author interview with a senior Fox executive.
296 **On August 7** *Fox News Network, LLC v. Penguin Group (USA), Inc.*, 2003 W.L. 23281520 (2003), complaint, http://news.findlaw.com/hdocs/docs/ip/foxpenguin80703cmp.pdf, accessed Sept. 19, 2013.
296 **Penguin's outside counsel** Kitman, *The Man Who Would Not Shut Up*, 233.
297 **"Is Fox really claiming"** Ibid., 234.
297 **It was ironic** Ibid., 235.
297 **Penguin rushed *Lies*** Emily Eakin, "Among Best-Selling Authors the Daggers Are Out," *New York Times*, Oct. 5, 2003.
297 **"It's time to return"** "Fair or Not, Fox Drops Suit Against Franken," *Philadelphia Inquirer*, Aug. 26, 2003.
297 **He launched a show** Seth Sutel, "Franken, Garofalo to Take on Limbaugh on New Liberal Radio Network," *Associated Press*, March 10, 2004.
297 **"When somebody calls you"** Kitman, *The Man Who Would Not Shut Up*, 225.
297 **But in private** Author interviews with current and former Fox News executives.
297 **The letter was hand-delivered** The details of this letter can be found in Richard T. Pienciak, "How Covers Came Off the O'Reilly Fone Sex Scandal: Behind-the-Scenes Look at Her Harassment Rap," New York *Daily News*, Oct. 24, 2004.
297 **Morelli wrote** See *Fox News Network, LLC v. Mackris*, complaint (N.Y. Sup. Ct., 2004); also available at http://www.thesmokinggun.com/file/oreilly-female-aide-60m-extort-bid?page=0, accessed Oct. 30, 2013.
297 **He claimed** Robert Kolker, "Benedict Morelli Feels Your Pain," *New York*, March 13, 2000.
298 **Morelli's client** Kitman, *The Man Who Would Not Shut Up*, 249.
298 **"Dianne would often say"** Author interview with a former Fox producer.
298 **"Not my politics"** Author interview with a media talent agent.
298 **"The whole Fox culture"** Author interview with a former Fox producer.
298 **In their meeting** Pienciak, "How Covers Came Off the O'Reilly Fone Sex Scandal."
298 **The document stipulated** *Mackris v. O'Reilly*, verified complaint (N.Y. Sup. Ct., 2004); also available at http://www.thesmokinggun.com/file/oreilly-falafel-suit-turns-five?page=0. Many of the details in the following paragraphs are taken directly from this complaint.
298 **It wasn't just** Author interview with a former Fox producer.
299 **"She was a"** Author interview with a former Fox producer.

299 **Feeling underpaid** Heather Gilmore, "How 'Buddies' Andrea and Bill Entered Their Tailspin Zone," *New York Post*, Oct. 24, 2004.
300 **In one passage** Kitman, *The Man Who Would Not Shut Up*, 251.
300 **So was Murdoch** Author interview with a Murdoch adviser.
300 **Morelli continued to play hardball** Lloyd Grove and Adam Nichols, "Say O'Reilly Accuser Scoffed at 2M Offer," New York *Daily News*, Oct. 20, 2004.
300 **Morelli's refusal** Ibid., 257.
300 **There were unanswered questions** Author interviews with sources familiar with the matter.
300 **"When she was with"** Author interview with a former Fox producer.
301 **On the evening** Pienciak, "How Covers Came Off the O'Reilly Fone Sex Scandal."
301 **"If you don't resolve"** Ibid.
301 **"This is indeed"** Ibid.
301 **Green filed** Ibid.
301 **From the outset** Author interview with a source familiar with the matter.
301 **Except for a few** See Kitman, *The Man Who Would Not Shut Up*, 256.
301 **To gather dirt** "O'Reilly's Lawyer Explains the Extortion Suit Against Andrea Mackris," *The Abrams Report*, MSNBC, Oct. 21, 2004, http://www.nbcnews.com/id/6298207/ns/msnbc-the_abrams_report/t/oreillys-lawyer-explains-extortion-suit-against-andrea-mackris/#.UjzOEWQ60y8.
301 **"This could be"** *The Abrams Report*, MSNBC, Oct. 15, 2004.
301 **On October 15** Todd Venezia, " 'Flipping Out'—'Lunatic' O'Reilly Gal Went Nuts in Bar: Chef," *New York Post*, Oct. 15, 2004.
302 **A few days later** The details of the meeting with Paratore are derived from the author's interview with a source familiar with the incident.
302 **On October 19** Dareh Gregorian, " 'Boozy' Boast: Gal Said She'd Ruin O'Reilly: Bar Owner," *New York Post*, Oct. 19, 2004.
302 **O'Reilly's lawyer also** Ibid.
302 **On October 17** Paul H. B. Shin, "For Extortion, O'Reilly's Suit Might Not Fit," New York *Daily News*, Oct. 17, 2004.
302 **On October 20** Adam Nichols, "Her Dad Mad as Hell, Out to Whup O'Reilly," New York *Daily News*, Oct. 21, 2004.
302 **He told the paper** Pienciak, "How Covers Came Off the O'Reilly Fone Sex Scandal."
302 **Brian Lewis told people** Author interview with a source familiar with the matter.
302 **"Word came down"** Author interview with a source involved in the negotiations.
302 **The *Daily News* played** Derek Rose, George Rush, and Nancy Dillon, "Call Him Owe-Reilly! Multi-million Dollar Deal to End Sex-Harass Case," New York *Daily News*, Oct. 29, 2004.
302 **"This brutal ordeal"** Bill O'Reilly, "Talking Points Memo," *The O'Reilly Factor*, Fox News Channel, Oct. 28, 2004.
302 **Lewis was disappointed** Author interview with a source familiar with the matter.
302 **Ratings for the *Factor*** Sarah Rodman, "From the Hub to Hollywood: Sex Scandal Spins Up O'Reilly Ratings," *Boston Herald*, Oct. 30, 2004.
302 **On Monday** Ibid.
303 **"About a week"** Kitman, *The Man Who Would Not Shut Up*, 258.
303 **Chernin, who held** Author interviews with current and former News Corp executives.
303 **Chernin also fashioned himself** Wolff, *The Man Who Owns the News*, 45.
303 **Lachlan Murdoch** Details of Lachlan Murdoch's departure from News Corp come from author's interviews with current and former News Corp executives.
304 **As deputy COO** Steve Fishman, "The Boy Who Wouldn't Be King," *New York*, Sept. 19, 2005.

304 **In early 2005** Jim Finkle, "Can Peter Brennan Rekindle His 'Affair'?," *Broadcasting & Cable*, Jan. 9, 2005.
304 **Rejecting the show** Fishman, "The Boy Who Wouldn't Be King."
304 **"Do the show"** Ibid.
305 **"Rupert used to say"** Author interview with television executive Mitchell Stern.
305 **On Tuesday, July 26** Fishman, "The Boy Who Wouldn't Be King."
305 **"I have to do"** Ibid.
305 **Three days later** Sallie Hofmeister, "Murdoch's Heir Apparent Abruptly Resigns His Post," *Los Angeles Times*, July 30, 2005.
305 **"There was a thinking"** Author interview with Mitchell Stern.
305 **In the winter** David Bianculli, "A Revealing Docudrama: 'Pentagon Papers' Shows How Cable Outclasses Nets," New York *Daily News*, March 6, 2003.
305 **He called Peter Liguori** Author interviews with sources familiar with the conversation.
306 **Around this time** The details of this conversation were related to the author by a person with direct knowledge of the exchange.

# ACT V

## NINETEEN: SEARCHING FOR A NEW CAST

309 **On the evening of April 26** "The Reliable Source" (column), *Washington Post,* April 28, 2006.
309 **the newest addition to the Bush** Jennifer Loven, "Fox Host Tony Snow Named White House Spokesman," Associated Press, April 26, 2006.
309 **"Congratulations on your promotion"** George Rush and Joanna Rush Molloy, "As Rosie Joins, Star May Take a Dim 'View,'" New York *Daily News,* April 28, 2006.
309 **"Ten years ago"** "The Reliable Source" (column), *Washington Post,* April 28, 2006.
309 **More than 2,300** Desmond Butler, "Thousands Converge on Manhattan for Anti-War Demonstration," Associated Press, April 30, 2006.
310 **"Look at these people"** Author interview with a Fox executive.
310 **Fox lost about 15 percent** John Dempsey and Michael Learmonth, "Cable Basks in Originals' Success," *Variety*, Dec. 25–Dec. 31, 2006.
310 **Keith Olbermann** *Countdown,* MSNBC (transcript), Dec. 18, 2006.
310 **That year** MacKenzie Carpenter, "Anger Becomes Him," *Pittsburgh Post-Gazette,* Dec. 12, 2006.
310 **That summer** Helen Kennedy, "Hil and Rupert Dine on Sly," New York *Daily News,* July 18, 2006.
310 **Ailes told a reporter** Roger Ailes, "A Conversation with Roger Ailes," transcript of live interview conducted by Ken Auletta, S. I. Newhouse School of Public Communications, New York, March 31, 2005.
310 **Julia Angwin** Julia Angwin, "After Riding High with Fox News, Murdoch Aide Has Harder Slog," *Wall Street Journal,* Oct. 3, 2006.
311 **Fox's PR department** Author interview with a person familiar with the situation.
311 **Later that day** Joshua Chaffin and Aline van Duyn, "Interview with Rupert Murdoch and Roger Ailes," *Financial Times,* Oct. 6, 2006.
311 **At one point, Steve Doocy** Author interview with a person familiar with the situation.
311 **Ailes approached Angwin** Author interview with a person who attended the event.
311 **Peter Chernin expressed concern** Author interviews with News Corp executives.

312 **" 'We don't want to give' "** Author interview with former Fox Television Stations Inc. CEO Mitchell Stern.
312 **"He needs to know"** Author interview with a former News Corp executive.
312 **"I was watching CNN in 2004"** Author interview with a Fox employee in the room.
312 **The next day** David Bauder, "ABC Wins the Election-Night Ratings Race," Associated Press, Nov. 9, 2006.
312 **"We had the concern"** Author interview with a former Fox News executive.
312 **"Rush was kind of laughing"** Author interview with a friend of Rush Limbaugh.
312 **"We're in a challenging news cycle"** Chaffin and van Duyn, "Interview with Rupert Murdoch and Roger Ailes."
312 **"Roger said, 'Let me think' "** Author interview with Robert Ailes Jr.
313 **Moody told executives** Author interview with a former Fox News executive.
313 **"Roger is not a news guy"** Author interview with a former Fox producer.
313 **A Fox contributor recalled that Moody** Author interview with a friend of John Moody.
313 **"He was aghast"** Author interview with a person close to John Moody.
313 **"I look at John"** Author interview with former Fox News producer Adam Sank.
313 **But, in early 2006** Author interview with a person familiar with the situation.
313 **The MSNBC job** Bill Carter, "New MSNBC Managers," *New York Times,* June 13, 2006.
313 **Kim Hume, the Washington bureau chief** Author interview with a former staffer in the Washington, D.C., bureau of Fox News.
313 **Fox and several other outlets** Eric Deggans, "Circumstances Left Many in Media with Inaccurate Reports," *St. Petersburg Times,* Jan. 5, 2006. See also John MacDonald, "Media, You Failed Me," *Arizona Republic,* Jan. 8, 2006.
314 **In the fall of 2006** Author interview with a former *Mike Douglas* producer.
314 **the Los Angeles memorial** "Mike Douglas Tribute Scheduled Saturday," *Los Angeles Times,* Oct. 19, 2006.
314 **The following spring** Fox News, "Joel Cheatwood Named Vice President of Development for Fox News" (press release), Business Wire, April 5, 2007.
314 **"Roger would call him Helmet Head"** Author interview with a former colleague of Joel Cheatwood.
314 **And at CNN** Colby Hall, "Warning Shots? Glenn Beck to Poach Fox News Bigwig, Suggesting Big Plans," Mediaite.com, March 21, 2011, http://www.mediaite.com/tv/warning-shots-glenn-beck-to-poach-fox-news-bigwig-foreshadowing-big-plans-2/.
314 **Over the summer** Author interview with a former Fox News executive.
314 **"Roger likes things"** Author interview with a Fox News executive.
314 **"One person should not"** Author interview with a person familiar with the matter.
314 **The show typically had higher ratings** Paul J. Gough, "Larry King Hot Thanks to Hilton," *Hollywood Reporter,* June 29, 2007.
314 **While some observers** Brian Stelter, "Hannity to Go It Alone, Without Colmes," *New York Times,* Nov. 25, 2008.
314 **"Sean was bitter"** Author interview with a former Fox News executive.
314 **As the Iraq War** Author interview with a person familiar with the situation.
315 **"There were times"** Author interview with a former senior executive at Fox News.
315 **"Roger wanted the counterpoint"** Author interview with a former senior Fox executive.
315 **As a stopgap** Brian Stelter, "It's 'Hannity's America' Starting This Sunday," TVNewswer.com, Jan. 4, 2007.
315 **"I want you guys"** Author interview with a person familiar with the matter.

315 **In the fall of 2008** Brian Stelter, "One Half of 'Hannity & Colmes' Is Leaving," "Media Decoder" (blog), *New York Times,* Nov. 24, 2008, http://mediadecoder.blogs.nytimes.com/2008/11/24/one-half-of-hannity-colmes-is-leaving/.

316 **Katon Dawson** Author interview with former South Carolina Republican Party chairman Katon Dawson.

316 **On February 14** Ronald Reagan Presidential Library Foundation, "Reagan Presidential Library Foundation to Host GOP Presidential Candidates' Debate" (press release), Feb. 14, 2007, http://www.gwu.edu/~action/2008/primdeb08/reagan021407pr.html.

316 **moderated by MSNBC's Chris Matthews** Liz Sidoti, "Ten Republicans Meet Thursday in First GOP Presidential Debate," Associated Press, May 3, 2007.

316 **Frederick Ryan Jr.** Mike Allen, "Mitt's Moment," *Politico,* May 4, 2007, http://www.politico.com/news/stories/0507/3841.html.

316 **"Roger likes to win"** Author interview with *Politico* president Frederick Ryan Jr.

316 **Fox hosts** Fox News, *The Five* (transcript of May 3, 2012, broadcast), Finance Wire, May 3, 2012.

316 **On March 8** Erik Schelzig, "Fred Thompson for President?," Associated Press, March 10, 2007.

316 **A couple of months earlier** CNN, *Reliable Sources* (transcript), Jan. 21, 2007; John Gibson, *The Big Story,* Fox News Channel (transcript), Jan. 19, 2007.

316 **Robert Gibbs** Author interview with an adviser to President Barack Obama.

316 **On March 9** Ryan Grim, "Nevada Dems Nix Fox Debate," *Politico,* March 9, 2007.

317 **Around this time** Chafets, *Roger Ailes,* 27.

317 **On March 29** Fox News, "Fox News and the Congressional Black Caucus Institute Present Two Presidential Debates for the 2008 Campaign," Business Wire (press release), March 29, 2007.

317 **One week later** Kate Phillips, "D.N.C. Shuns Fox in Debate Schedule," The Caucus (blog), *New York Times,* April 5, 2007, http://thecaucus.blog.nytimes.com/2007/04/05/dnc-shuns-fox-in-debate-schedule.

317 **The next day** Kate Phillips, "Two Democrats Avoid Debate on Fox News," *New York Times,* April 10, 2007.

317 **Ailes called them** Author interview with a person familiar with the matter.

317 **In April** Russ Buettner, "In Fox News, Led by an Ally, Giuliani Finds a Friendly Stage," *New York Times,* Aug. 2, 2007.

317 **A study found** Alex Koppelman and Erin Renzas, "Rudy Giuliani's Ties to Fox News," *Salon,* Nov. 15, 2007, citing a study by *Hotline.*

317 **Judith Regan** Russ Buettner, "Ex-Publisher's Suit Plays a Giuliani-Kerik Angle," *New York Times,* Nov. 14, 2007.

318 **In 2006** Vanessa Grigoriadis, "Even Bitches Have Feelings," *New York,* Feb. 5, 2007.

318 **In 2002** Author interview with a person familiar with the matter.

318 **Regan told the press** Jonathan Bing, "The Write Stuff," *Daily Variety,* Dec. 18, 2002.

318 **Regan had even relocated** Edward Wyatt, "O. J. Simpson Writes a Book He'll Discuss on Fox TV," *New York Times,* Nov. 15, 2006.

318 **The whole thing** Josef Adalian, "O.J. to Tell How He'd Murder on Fox Spec," *Variety.com,* Nov. 14, 2006, http://variety.com/2006/scene/news/o-j-to-tell-how-he-d-murder-on-fox-spec-1117953915/.

318 **News Corp pulled the plug** Bill Carter and Edward Wyatt, "Under Pressure, News Corp. Pulls Simpson Project," *New York Times,* Nov. 21, 2006.

318 **Stories of her office rage** Grigoriadis, "Even Bitches Have Feelings."

318 **In December** Steven Zeitchik, "Regan Ousted from HarperCollins," *Variety.com,* Dec. 15, 2006, http://variety.com/2006/biz/news/regan-ousted-from-harpercollins

-1117955887/. See also Steven Zeitchik, "Regan's Fate Is Unwritten," *Daily Variety,* Dec. 18, 2006.

318 **Accounts soon leaked** Julie Bosman and Richard Siklos, "Fired Editor's Remarks Said to Have Provoked Murdoch," *New York Times,* Dec. 18, 2006. See also Josh Getlin, "Regan Was Fired After Slur, News Corp. Says," *Los Angeles Times,* Dec. 19, 2006.

319 **The complaint** Patricia Hurtado, "Publisher Regan Says News Corp. Fired Her to Protect Giuliani," *Bloomberg News,* Nov. 14, 2007. See also *Judith Regan v. HarperCollins Publishers LLC,* 603758/2007, New York State Supreme Court (Manhattan).

319 **Giuliani's disgraced former police commissioner** Jim Fitzgerald, "Bernard Kerik Pleads Not Guilty to Corruption Charges," Associated Press, Nov. 9, 2007.

319 **Regan would later allege** Russ Buettner, "Fox News Chief Is Said to Urge Lying in Inquiry," *New York Times,* Feb. 25, 2011. In February 2011, *The New York Times* broke the news that Regan had claimed in court papers that Ailes was the unnamed News Corp executive who had urged her to lie to investigators to protect Rudy Giuliani's presidential prospects. Blogs speculated that, now that Ailes's name was public, he opened himself up to being indicted on obstruction of justice charges. "Roger was really scared," a Fox executive said. "I knew because he just never talked about the news." News Corp defended him, informing the *Times* that the company had a letter from Regan stating that Ailes did not intend to influence her role in the investigation. When the scandal blew over without any indictment materializing, Ailes returned to his blustery self. He called the *Times* a "bunch of lying scum" during a speech.

319 **Susan Estrich** Author interview with a person familiar with the matter.

319 **Peter Johnson Sr.** Gabriel Sherman, "Meet Roger Ailes's Fox News Mouthpiece," *New York,* Oct. 25, 2012.

319 **"He's the talent"** Author interview with an executive involved in the negotiations with Judith Regan.

320 **"Susan acted as"** Author interview with a person involved in the negotiations.

320 **"It's embarrassing"** Author interview with a person familiar with the matter.

320 **"I need to know"** Author interview with a person involved in the negotiations.

320 **On January 25** Patricia Hurtado and Gillian Wee, "News Corp. Settles Suit by Judith Regan over Firing," *Bloomberg News,* Jan. 25, 2008. See also Bob Van Voris and Patricia Hurtado, "Regan Accused Lawyer Dreier of Disclosing Settlement," *Bloomberg News,* Dec. 10, 2008.

320 **He dropped out** Michael Powell and Michael Cooper, "Resurgent McCain Is Florida Victor; Giuliani Far Back," *New York Times,* Jan. 30, 2008.

320 **Years later** Author interview with Judith Regan.

320 **CNN's prime-time audience** Molly Willow, "TV Ratings Upset," *Columbus* (Ohio) *Dispatch,* Feb. 21, 2008. See also Anthony Crupi, "Turner Nets Defy Soft Market," *Mediaweek,* Nov. 6, 2008.

320 **Wolf Blitzer** Paul J. Gough, "In '08, Big Headlines for Everybody," *Hollywood Reporter,* Dec. 31, 2008.

320 **In the fall** Gabriel Sherman, "Chasing Fox," *New York,* Oct. 11, 2010.

321 **Griffin debuted a new tagline** Linda Moss, "MSNBC Votes to Boost Politics Coverage," *Multichannel News,* Oct. 8, 2007.

321 **"Roger felt that as Obama emerged"** Author interview with a person close to Roger Ailes.

321 **The day after Clinton roared** David Bauder, "Chris Matthews Says He Wronged Clinton by Tying Her Success to Husband's Infidelities," Associated Press, Jan. 18, 2008.

321 **At Clinton campaign headquarters** Author interview with a former campaign staffer for Hillary Clinton.

321 **On the evening of February 7** Howard Kurtz, "Chelsea Remark Earns MSNBC Correspondent a Suspension," *Washington Post,* Feb. 9, 2008.

321 **In early March** ABC News, *Nightline* (transcript), March 5, 2008.

321 **On March 19** John Cook, "The Anti-Obama Emails Roger Ailes Forwards to His Underlings," *Gawker,* April 19, 2012, http://gawker.com/5903082/the-anti+obama-emails-roger-ailes-forwards-to-his-underlings.

321 **O'Reilly and Hannity did segments** *The O'Reilly Factor,* Fox News Channel (transcript), March 19, 2008. See also *Hannity & Colmes,* Fox News Channel (transcript), March 19, 2008.

322 **Susan Estrich** Author interview with a person familiar with the situation.

322 **an attack by John Edwards** "Edwards Urges Fellow Democrats to Reject Murdoch's Money," *Washington Post,* Aug. 3, 2007.

322 **the company had paid Edwards** Nedra Pickler, "Murdoch's News Corp. Says Edwards Benefited from Book Deal with the Media Company," *Washington Post,* Aug. 3, 2007.

322 **In May** *The O'Reilly Factor,* Fox News Channel (transcript), May 1, 2008.

322 **"She made some kind of compact"** Author interview with former White House communications director Anita Dunn.

322 **Another senior Obama** Author interview with a senior adviser to President Barack Obama.

322 **After clinching** Michael Wolff, "Tuesdays with Rupert," *Vanity Fair,* Oct. 2008. See also Howard Kurtz, "Obama Met with News Executives," *Washington Post,* Sept. 3, 2008; author interview with Stephen Rosenfield, who recounted Ailes's description of the meeting.

323 **A few weeks later** Sherman, "The Elephant in the Green Room."

323 **Ailes responded** CQ Transcripts, "Senator Barack Obama Delivers Remarks at a Campaign Event" (transcript), July 2, 2008.

323 **He later said** Sherman, "The Elephant in the Green Room."

323 **"He doesn't have the charisma"** Author interview with a former Fox News executive.

323 **In January** "New York Post Endorses Obama for President, Snubs Home-Town Senator," Associated Press, Jan. 30, 2008.

324 **In a preview of** Wolff, "Tuesdays with Rupert."

324 **"Is this true?"** Gabriel Sherman, "The Raging Septuagenarian," *New York,* Feb. 28, 2010.

324 **Murdoch assured** Matea Gold, "Roger Ailes Extends Fox Deal," *Los Angeles Times,* Nov. 21, 2008.

324 **"That was the beginning"** Author interview with an adviser to Rupert Murdoch.

324 **"As Ginsberg was blowing up"** Author interview with a former Fox executive.

324 **Any speculation** "Post Endorses John McCain," *New York Post,* Sept. 8, 2008.

324 **Within the next year** Tim Arango, "An Adviser to Murdoch Is Leaving News Corp.," *New York Times,* Nov. 17, 2009.

324 **"Roger took credit"** Author interview with a Fox News executive.

324 **"She hit a home run"** Author interview with a person familiar with the matter.

324 **During Palin's speech** Anthony Crupi, "RNC Coverage Lifts Fox News Channel to Ratings Win," *Mediaweek,* Sept. 9, 2008.

325 **He was intensely interested** Sherman, "The Elephant in the Green Room."

325 **Ailes didn't know Walshe** Author interview with a person familiar with the situation.

325 **He called Suzanne Scott** Author interview with a person familiar with the matter.

325 **Ratings for his CNN** Robyn-Denise Yourse, "Arts Etc.; Tuning in to TV," *Washington Times,* Oct. 21, 2008. See also Brian Stelter, "For Conservative Radio, It's a New Dawn, Too," *New York Times,* Dec. 22, 2008.

325 **As they spoke** Author interview with a person familiar with the matter.
325 **Fox executives dubbed** Author interview with a person familiar with the matter.
325 **This was especially** Brian Stelter, "Fox's Brit Hume to Stop Anchoring 'Special Report' After Election," "Media Decoder" (blog), *New York Times,* July 15, 2008, http://mediadecoder.blogs.nytimes.com/2008/07/15/foxs-brit-hume-to-stop-anchoring-special-report-after-election/.
325 **On Thursday, October 16** "Glenn Beck Joins Fox News" (press release), Business Wire, Oct. 16, 2008.
326 **In late September, McCain had suspended** Michael Cooper, "For the Nominees, New Roles and New Risks," *New York Times,* Sept. 25, 2008.
326 **"He was so angry"** Author interview with a person familiar with the situation.
326 **Ailes told executives** Author interview with a person familiar with the matter.
326 **A few days before** Author interview with a person familiar with the matter.

# TWENTY: COMEBACK

327 **The week after Obama's 2008 election** William K. Alcorn, "Fox News Chairman Ailes Comes Home, Discusses Obama's Tasks," *Youngstown* (Ohio) *News,* Nov. 11, 2008.
327 **It was unseasonably cold** http://www.almanac.com/weather/history/OH/Warren/2013-11-11.
327 **The Aileses were in town** Author interview with Warren attorney Ned Gold. See also Alcorn, "Fox News Chairman Ailes Comes Home, Discusses Obama's Tasks."
328 **During one eighteen-day** Author interview with Michael O'Brien, former mayor of Warren, Ohio.
328 **The municipal government** Author interview with Mayor Michael O'Brien.
328 **They chatted for** Alcorn, "Fox News Chairman Ailes Comes Home, Discusses Obama's Tasks."
329 **"If you want a helping hand"** Larry Ringler, "Fox News Chief Returns to Warren," *Warren* (Ohio) *Tribune Chronicle*, Nov. 11, 2008.
329 **He liked to tell** Website of the Ailes Apprentice Program, Ailesapprentice.foxnews.com.
329 **"If every company did this"** Chris Ariens, "Roger Ailes on His Apprentices and His Legacy," *TVNewser*, Nov. 15, 2012.
329 **It was cold and damp** http://www.wunderground.com/history/airport/KYNG/2008/11/12/DailyHistory.html?req_city=Warren&req_state=OH&req_statename=Ohio.
329 **Hundreds of people** Author interview with Ned Gold.
329 **"You see that fountain pool"** Author interviews with Warren residents who attended the dedication of the veterans memorial.
329 **He told the audience that** Alcorn, "Fox News Chairman Ailes Comes Home, Discusses Obama's Tasks."
329 **Webster's life** Biography of Douglas Webster on website of A-4 Skyhawk Association, http://a4skyhawk.org/?q=3e/va56/webster-memorial.htm, accessed Nov. 15, 2013.
329 **Ailes went to** Alcorn, "Fox News Chairman Ailes Comes Home, Discusses Obama's Tasks."
329 **An hour later** Author interview with two Warren residents who were present at the country club lunch.
330 **"I grew up"** Junod, "Roger Ailes on Roger Ailes: The Interview Transcripts, Part 2."
330 **Ailes told the Monsmans** Author interview with Chris and Danella Monsman.

330 **Three years later** Brenda J. Linert, "Tribune Plans Year of Anniversary Events," *Warren* (Ohio) *Tribune Chronicle*, Oct. 16, 2011.

330 **"I left there in 1958"** Author conversation with Roger Ailes.

330 **"We are in a storm"** Author's transcript of speech given by Roger Ailes at the Kennedy Center, June 12, 2013.

331 **Rick Santelli** "Rick Santelli's Shout Heard 'Round the World," CNBC.com, Feb. 22, 2009, http://www.cnbc.com/id/29283701.

331 **prime-time ratings jumped** Daniel Frankel, "CNN: A Fall from Glory, or a Much Better Story?," *Variety,* April 13, 2009.

331 **Fox personalities** Michael Calderone, "Fox Teas Up a Tempest," *Politico*, April 15, 2009.

331 **"There would not have been"** Author interview with national Tea Party Express cofounder Sal Russo.

331 **In July 2008** Brian Stelter, "Fox's Brit Hume to Stop Anchoring 'Special Report' After Election," *New York Times*, July 15, 2008.

331 **Then, two weeks after** Chris Ariens, "David Rhodes Leaves Fox News for Bloomberg," *TVNewser* (blog), Nov. 19, 2008, http://www.mediabistro.com/tvnewser/david-rhodes-leaves-fox-news-for-bloomberg_b21839.

331 **Rhodes's brother, Ben** Mark Landler, "Worldly at 35, and Shaping Obama's Voice," *New York Times,* March 15, 2013.

331 **David, for his part** Author interview with a person familiar with the matter.

331 **He cringed when** David G. Savage, "Legal Challenges Have Slim Chances," *Chicago Tribune*, Dec. 8, 2008.

332 **a few months after Rhodes's departure** Michael Liedtke, "New Venture to Introduce Fees for Online News," Associated Press, April 15, 2009. John Moody would return to Fox News in June 2013 to serve as executive editor and executive VP.

332 **"They used to tell Roger no"** Author interview with a senior executive at Fox News.

332 **One Christmas** Author interviews with Fox News executives.

332 **Bill Sammon** John Eggerton, "Fox News Names New VP and Bureau Manager in Washington," *Broadcasting & Cable,* Feb. 26, 2009, http://www.broadcastingcable.com/article/179936-Fox_News_Names_New_VP_and_Bureau_Manager_in_Washington.php.

332 **Days after Obama's inauguration** Author interview with a former employee in the Washington, D.C., bureau of Fox News.

332 **Later, Sammon caused problems** Ben Dimiero, "Fox's Bill Sammon Problem," *Media Matters for America,* March 29, 2011, http://mediamatters.org/research/2011/03/29/foxs-bill-sammon-problem/178036.

333 **Moody's replacement** Fox News, "Michael Clemente Joins Fox News from ABC News," Business Wire (press release), Feb. 24, 2009.

333 **Early in his tenure** Author interviews with Fox News executives.

333 **The most potent** Richard Huff, "He's Beck Again, with Commentary, Not News," New York *Daily News,* Jan. 19, 2009.

333 **Within weeks** "Fox News's Mad, Apocalyptic, Tearful Rising Star," *New York Times,* March 29, 2009.

333 **Only Bill O'Reilly and Sean Hannity** Ibid.

333 **"You are probably the most"** Author interview with a person familiar with the matter.

333 **"I see your show"** Ibid.

333 **He conceived his program** Ibid.

333 **With the Dow plunging** http://finance.yahoo.com/echarts?s=%5Edji+interactive#symbol=%5Edji;range=20070101,20090918;compare=;indicator=volume;charttype=area;crosshair=on;ohlcvalues=0;logscale=off;source=undefined.

334 **He founded his own company** http://www.glennbeck.com/content/program/.

334 **In a break from Fox tradition** Glenn Beck hired Matthew Hiltzik, who had worked for Miramax. His firm, Hiltzik Strategies, represented such clients as Couric.

334 **The day after** "Fox Host Glenn Beck: Obama Is a Racist" (video), *Huffington Post*, Aug. 28, 2009.

334 **Ailes told his executives** Author interviews with a person familiar with the matter.

334 **"Glenn Beck expressed"** Chris Ariens, "FNC Responds to Glenn Beck Calling Pres. Obama a Racist," *Mediabistro*, July 28, 2009.

334 **The White House failed** *Glenn Beck*, Fox News Channel (transcript), Aug. 24, 2009.

334 **One day in the summer** Author interview with former White House adviser Van Jones. Much of the following information comes from interviews with Jones.

334 **Dan Pfeiffer** Author interview with a senior Obama adviser.

334 **Jones asked his chief of staff** Author interview with Van Jones.

335 **On September 1** Ibid.

335 **A YouTube video** Van Jones speech in Berkeley, video, Feb. 11, 2009, YouTube, http://www.youtube.com/watch?v=yt66eWnjoTo, accessed Nov. 12, 2013.

335 **Under pressure** Glenn Thrush, "Van Jones: A**hole Remark 'Inappropriate,' " "On Congress" (blog), *Politico*, Sept. 2, 2009, http://www.politico.com/blogs/glennthrush/0909/Van_Jones_Ahole_remark_inappropriate.html.

335 **The same week** Martin Kady II, "Pence Calls on Van Jones to Resign," "On Congress" (blog), *Politico*, Sept. 4, 2009, http://www.politico.com/blogs/glennthrush/0909/Pence_calls_on_Van_Jones_to_resign.html.

335 **On September 6** John M. Broder, "White House Official Resigns After Flood of G.O.P. Criticism," *New York Times*, Sept. 7, 2009.

335 **On the morning of September 10** *Special Report with Bret Baier*, Fox News Channel (transcript), Sept. 10, 2009.

335 **Andrew Breitbart** Author interview with Andrew Breitbart before his death in 2012.

335 **Breitbart thought it was a bombshell** Darryl Fears and Carol D. Leonnig, "The $1,300 Mission to Fell ACORN," *Washington Post*, Sept. 18, 2009.

335 **That summer** Patrick Gavin, "Obama Slams Fox News," *Politico*, June 16, 2009, http://www.politico.com/blogs/michaelcalderone/0609/Obama_slams_Fox_News.html.

336 **"We had anecdotal reports"** Author interview with Anita Dunn, former communications director for President Barack Obama.

336 **In meetings** Author interview with a Fox producer.

336 **What most alarmed** Howard Kurtz, "Unamplified, Beck's Voice Still Carries," *Washington Post*, Sept. 14, 2009.

336 **In an interview** *New York Times*, "Talk to the Times" (Q&A with Jill Abramson), Sept. 7, 2009.

336 **"The narrative"** Author interview with Anita Dunn.

336 **Dunn reached out** Sherman, "The Elephant in the Green Room."

336 **After conferring with Obama** Author interview with current and former administration officials.

336 **In mid-September** *The O'Reilly Factor*, Fox News Channel (transcript), Sept. 18, 2009. See also Jonathan Karl, "Obama, in Media Blitz, Snubs 'Whining' Fox," ABCNews.com, Sept. 19, 2009, http://abcnews.go.com/Politics/obamas-media-tour-include-fox-news/story?id=8621065.

336 **In early October** *Reliable Sources*, CNN (transcript), Oct. 11, 2009.

336 **in late October** *Reliable Sources*, CNN (transcript), Oct. 25, 2009.

336 **The move backfired** Steve Krakauer, "Tipping Point? White House Press Pool Stands Up for Fox News," *Mediaite*, Oct. 23, 2009, http://www.mediaite.com/tv/tipping-point-white-house-press-pool-stands-up-for-fox-news/.

336 **"He's a fierce competitor"** Joan Vennochi, "The Brains of the Bush Offensive; Strategist Roger Ailes Remade the Candidate," *Boston Globe,* Oct. 26, 1988.

337 **About a week before Dunn's** Sherman, "The Elephant in the Green Room."

337 **"He relished it"** Author interview with a senior producer.

337 **Another recalled** Author interview with a senior producer.

337 **One told news chief** Author interview with a Fox executive.

337 **"The D.C. bureau's job"** Author interview with a senior producer.

337 **On Friday, October 23** Author interview with people familiar with the matter.

337 **Clemente finally called Gibbs** Author interview with a Fox executive.

337 **In November** David Bauder, "Fox's Major Garrett Gets Obama Interview," Associated Press, Nov. 17, 2009.

337 **But Major Garrett had had enough** Howard Kurtz, "Major Garrett Leaves Behind Obama-Fox War; White House Correspondent Moves from Fox TV to Print at National Journal," *Washington Post,* Aug. 26, 2010.

337 **"Roger's thinking"** Author interview with a senior executive.

337 **"The way the business works"** Author interview with a former Fox News executive.

338 **In the months since** Frankel, "CNN: A Fall from Glory, or a Much Better Story?"

338 **The attacks were successful** *Esquire*, "Rupert Murdoch Has Potential," Oct. 1, 2008.

338 **O'Reilly was regularly crowned** Howard Kurtz, "Out and a Bout," *Washington Post*, Aug. 7, 2009. See also Kurtz, "Feud Fuels Bill O'Reilly's Blasts at GE," *Washington Post,* May 19, 2008; Keith Olbermann, *The Worst Person in the World: And 202 Strong Contenders* (Hoboken: John Wiley, 2006).

338 **Raising the stakes** See Kurtz, "Feud Fuels Bill O'Reilly's Blasts at GE," for each of O'Reilly's comments regarding Immelt, the incident with the GE logo, and O'Reilly's comments regarding Zucker.

339 **Ailes had warned Zucker** At the time it was reported that Roger Ailes threatened to use the *New York Post* to go after Jeff Zucker, Ailes denied it.

339 **Beth Comstock** Author interviews with a person familiar with the matter. See also Kurtz, "Out and About."

339 **The whole deal got blowtorched** Brian Stelter, "Voices from Above Silence a Cable TV Feud," *New York Times*, July 31, 2009.

339 **During his "Worst Persons" segment** Keith Olbermann, "Worst Persons" (transcript), *Countdown with Keith Olbermann,* MSNBC, Aug. 3, 2009.

339 **O'Reilly answered** Bill O'Reilly, "Talking Points Memo" (transcript), *The O'Reilly Factor,* Fox News, Aug. 5, 2009.

339 **He set up an anonymous** Author interview with a person familiar with the matter. Appearing on *Fox News Watch* the evening of April 26, 2008, Pinkerton mentioned a story he had read about on "a blog called the Cable Game," which pointed out that Reverend Jeremiah Wright had an enormous stake in Obama losing, given how often he'd said that white people are terrible. Pinkerton did not respond to requests for comment.

339 **"Is CNN on the Side"** "Is CNN on the Side of the Killers and Terrorists in Iraq?," *Cable Game* (defunct blog), Oct. 24, 2006; archived at http://web.archive.org/web/20061025010450/http://thecablegame.blogspot.com/.

339 **"David Brock Gets Caught!"** "David Brock Gets Caught! (Although Secretly, He Probably Loves Being Naughty and Nasty)," *Cable Game* (defunct blog), Sept. 28, 2007; archived at http://web.archive.org/web/20070929103305/http://thecablegame.blogspot.com/.

340 **He called Ailes** Author interview with a person familiar with the matter. When asked to comment, Klein wrote, "I'm not confirming I ever had that convo w Roger," adding: "I think a good executive quietly does what he or she needs to do

to protect the team and the brand. Roger enjoys the game and respects others who can play it."

340 **Cooper wouldn't announce** Andrew Sullivan, "Anderson Cooper: 'The Fact Is, I'm Gay,' " "The Dish" (blog), AndrewSullivan.com, July 2, 2012, http://dish.andrewsullivan.com/2012/07/02/anderson-cooper-the-fact-is-im-gay/.

340 **Klein did not last** Brian Stelter, "CNN Fires Executive Who Led Makeover," *New York Times*, Sept. 24, 2010.

340 **For Sarah Palin** Most of the information in the following paragraphs was originally reported in Gabriel Sherman, "The Revolution Will Be Commercialized," *New York*, May 3, 2010.

340 **Her sky-high approval ratings** Becky Bohrer, "Palin Center Stage in Politics, but What of 2012?," Associated Press, July 2, 2010.

340 **The worst was** Rachel D'Oro, "New Palin Defense Fund Uses Fighting Words," Associated Press, June 29, 2010.

340 **In November 2008** Matea Gold, "Palin to Talk with Van Susteren," *Los Angeles Times*, Nov. 8, 2008.

340 **Later, the Fox camera crew** Author interview with a person familiar with the situation.

341 **Conservative pundit** Scott Martelle, "The Book on Sarah Palin," *Los Angeles Times*, Nov. 12, 2009. See also author interview with Mary Matalin.

341 **with Alaska's strict ethics rules** Hillel Italie, "Palin Has Book Deal, Memoir to Come Next Year," Associated Press, May 13, 2009.

341 **On the morning of July 3** Rachel D'Oro, "Palin Resigning as Alaska Governor," Associated Press, July 3, 2009.

341 **Once she resigned** Sherman, "The Revolution Will Be Commercialized."

341 **in September 2009** Sherman, "The Elephant in the Green Room." See also Sherman, "The Revolution Will Be Commercialized."

341 **In January 2010** Jim Rutenberg, "Palin Joins Fox News Team," *New York Times*, Jan. 12, 2010. See also Sherman, "The Elephant in the Green Room."

342 **A Wall Street analyst** "The 35 Most Powerful People in Media," *Hollywood Reporter*, April 20, 2012.

342 **In 2009, Ailes earned** Carr and Arango, "A Fox Chief at the Pinnacle of Media and Politics."

342 **Ailes "predicted"** Author interview with a senior Fox producer.

342 **In the midterms** Quinn Bowman and Chris Amico, "Congress Loses Hundreds of Years of Experience—But Majority of Incumbents Stick Around," "The Rundown" (blog), *PBS NewsHour*, Nov. 5, 2010, http://www.pbs.org/newshour/rundown/2010/11/congress-loses-hundreds-of-years-of-experience---but-vast-majority-of-incumbents-stick-around.html.

342 **"I've never seen anyone build"** Author interview with a person familiar with the matter.

342 **Sean Hannity complained** Author interview with a person familiar with the matter.

342 **And it didn't help matters** Author interview with a person familiar with the matter.

342 **In March** Howard Kurtz, "The Beck Factor at Fox," *Washington Post*, March 15, 2010.

342 **Palin also ruffled** Sherman, "The Elephant in the Green Room."

342 **In the control room** Author interview with an employee of Fox News.

343 **Ailes began to doubt** Sherman, "The Elephant in the Green Room."

343 **her website had put the image** http://abcnews.go.com/Politics/sarah-palins-crosshairs-ad-focus-gabrielle-giffords-debate/story?id=12576437.

343 **"He thinks Palin is an idiot"** Author interview with a person familiar with the matter.

343 **Ailes also got an earful** Author interview with a person familiar with the matter.
343 **Christine "I'm not a witch" O'Donnell** Ashley Parker, "O'Donnell Ad Confronts Reports on Her Past," "The Caucus" (blog), *New York Times,* Oct. 4, 2010.
343 **"Why are you letting Palin"** Author interview with a person familiar with the matter.
344 **One afternoon** Author interview with a person familiar with the matter.

## TWENTY-ONE: TROUBLE ON MAIN STREET

345 **"All I ever wanted"** Peter Boyer, "Fox Among the Chickens," *New Yorker,* Jan. 31, 2011.
345 **Putnam County even had** See Putnam County Board of Elections, http://www.putnamcountyny.com/board-of-elections/election-results, accessed Nov. 15, 2013.
345 **From his mountaintop aerie** Chafets, *Roger Ailes,* 105.
345 **To the west** "Obstructed the Hudson: Chains Used for This Purpose During the Revolutionary War," *New York Times,* Feb. 17, 1895.
346 **To the north** "West Point Foundry Preserve Re-opens Oct. 19," *Philipstown.info,* Oct. 16, 2013, http://philipstown.info/2013/10/16/scenic-hudson-and-partners-celebrate-new-park-opening-at-historic-west-point-foundry-preserve/Across the river.
346 **The grand interior** Chafets, *Roger Ailes,* 105–6.
346 **They attended** Ibid., 175.
346 **Leonora Burton** Author interview with Cold Spring shop owner Leonora Burton.
346 **One was that** Boyer, "Fox Among the Chickens."
346 **Buying *The Putnam County News*** Brian Stelter, "Big-Time Cable News to Small-Town Paper," *New York Times,* July 14, 2008.
346 **Founded in the mid-nineteenth century** Boyer, "Fox Among the Chickens."
346 **In a one-room office** Ibid.
346 **"It covered the 4-H Club"** Author interview with investment adviser Elizabeth Anderson.
346 **Letters to the editor** Boyer, "Fox Among the Chickens."
346 **When citizens complained** Author interview with former *Putnam County News & Recorder* employees.
347 **In the 1960s** *Scenic Hudson Preservation Conference v. Federal Power Commission,* U.S. Court of Appeals, Second Circuit, Docket 29853.
347 **The ensuing legal battle** Kathleen Teltsch, "Hudson Group Seeking River Study Proposals," *New York Times,* Dec. 19, 1982.
347 **The landmark victory** Marist College, "Scenic Hudson Collection: Records Relating to the Storm King Case, 1963–1981," historical note, http://library.marist.edu/archives/shc/scenichudsoncollection.xml, accessed Nov. 13, 2013.
347 **In Philipstown, a host** See Open Space Institute, Hudson Highlands Land Trust.
347 **the Garrison Institute** Garrison Institute, "Mission and Vision," http://www.garrisoninstitute.org/about-us/mission-and-vision, accessed Nov. 13, 2013.
347 **One morning in July 2008** Author interviews with *Putnam County News & Recorder* employees.
347 **They could keep their jobs** Boyer, "Fox Among the Chickens."
347 **"The first one"** Author interview with journalist Michael Turton.
348 **In public** Stelter, "Big-Time Cable News to Small-Town Paper."
348 **"He said the community"** Author interview with Kevin Foley.
348 **campaign volunteer** Matthew Boyle, "A Force Behind Met Life's IPO," *PR Week,* July 26, 1999.

348 **Later that summer** Author interviews with former *Putnam County News & Recorder* employees.
348 **she didn't last** Maureen Hunt email to *Putnam County News & Recorder* staff, Oct. 31, 2008.
348 **Alison Rooney** Author interview with a former *Putnam County News & Recorder* employee.
348 **But that honeymoon ended** "Myth and Deception at Play in Maria Pia Marrella Exhibit at Garrison Art Center," *Putnam County News & Recorder,* March 4, 2009.
348 **After the release** Reverend Brian McSweeney, "A Degradation of the Religious Beliefs of the Catholic Church," *Putnam County News & Recorder,* March 11, 2009.
348 **A few weeks later** "PVHS TheatreWorks Presents a Musical," *Putnam County News & Recorder,* April 15, 2009.
349 **After the event** Draft of article submitted by Michael Turton on the October 2008 mock election at Haldane Middle School viewed by author.
349 **The headline had been changed** Michael Turton, "Mock Presidential Election Held at Haldane," *Putnam County News & Recorder,* Oct. 22, 2008.
349 **"I've been mulling"** Email from Michael Turton to Maureen Hunt and Brian O'Donnell.
349 **a series of accusatory emails** Email correspondence between Michael Turton, Beth Ailes, and Roger Ailes. Beth Ailes declined to be interviewed for this book.
350 **In February 2009** Author interview with a person familiar with the meeting.
350 **Lindsley came on** Author interview with former News Corp executive Martin Singerman.
350 **Lindsley jumped at the opportunity** Author interviews with acquaintances of Joe Lindsley. Lindsley declined to comment.
350 **"[Ailes] was said"** Author interview with Leonora Burton.
350 **"I don't think"** Author interview with Robert Ailes Jr.
351 **"A team of landscapers"** Leonora Burton, *Lament of an Expat: How I Discovered America and Tried to Mend It* (Bloomington, Ind.: AuthorHouse, 2013), 164–65.
351 **"He can live"** Author interview with a friend of Roger Ailes.
351 **"I'm not allowed"** Author interview with Robert Ailes Jr.
351 **As Lindsley began** Boyer, "Fox Among the Chickens."
351 **The unsigned attack** "Debt, Decisions, and Destiny" (editorial), *Putnam County News & Recorder,* May 13, 2009.
351 **Leonora Burton stopped selling the paper** Author interview with Leonora Burton.
351 **Elizabeth Anderson later decided** Author interview with Elizabeth Anderson.
352 **Lindsley relished the partisan combat** Author interviews with acquaintances of Joe Lindsley.
352 **James Borkowski** Author interview with attorney and former Putnam County town justice James Borkowski.
353 **Borkowski lost to Smith** Terence Corcoran, "Smith Easily Defeats McConville for 3rd Term as Putnam Sheriff," *Journal News* (Westchester County), Nov. 4, 2009.
353 **Richard Shea** See website for Richard Shea Construction, http://www.richardsheaconstruction.com/contact.
353 **"Jesus, wait a minute"** Junod, "Why Does Roger Ailes Hate America?"
354 **The first time Shea met Ailes** Carr and Arango, "A Fox Chief at the Pinnacle of Media and Politics."
354 **A few weeks later** Author interview with a person familiar with the matter. Richard Shea declined to comment.

354 **"You can't mention"** Author interview with a person familiar with the matter.

354 ***"You have no fucking idea"*** Author interview with a person familiar with the matter.

354 **Jeannette Yannitelli** Author interview with Putnam County resident Jeannette Yannitelli.

355 **Shortly before 7:30** "Residential Re-Zoning: Will Property Owners Weigh In?," *Putnam County News & Recorder,* April 7, 2010.

355 **"Let us observe"** Account of the meeting comes from "Zoning Workshop Draws Hundreds," *Putnam County News & Recorder,* April 14, 2010.

355 **An hour into the contentious meeting** Transcript provided by Cold Spring resident Susan Peehl.

355 **Ailes stood up and intervened** For footage of Ailes's remarks, see YouTube video of town hall meeting at Haldane High School on April 7, 2010 (video by Susan Peehl), http://www.youtube.com/watch?v=iqEErpyQWAs.

356 **Ailes loved to quote Washington** In an email from Mary Thompson, a research historian at the Fred W. Smith National Library for the Study of George Washington: "We'd love to know the source where you found this alleged quote, so that we can add it to our records on spurious George Washington quotes." The phrase "a violation of my property is a violation of my personhood" appears in L. William Countryman, *Dirt, Greed, & Sex: Sexual Ethics in the New Testament and Their Implications for Today* (Minneapolis: Fortress Press, 2007), p. 144, in a chapter on women and children as property.

357 **After the meeting concluded** Author interview with Philipstown board member Nancy Montgomery.

357 **Later, Ailes had his own version** Junod, "Roger Ailes on Roger Ailes: The Interview Transcripts, Part 2."

357 **In the fall of 2010** Author interview with two persons familiar with the meeting in Richard Shea's office. Shea declined to comment on the meeting.

357 **"It was ninety percent inaccurate"** Author interview with land use attorney Joel Russell.

358 **To that end** Liz Schevtchuk Armstrong, "Mystery Point Sold to Billionaire Philanthropist," *Philipstown.info,* June 22, 2013, http://philipstown.info/2013/06/22/mystery-point-sold-to-billionaire-philanthropist/.

358 **"I used to think"** Author interview with Philipstown supervisor Richard Shea.

358 **Putnam County resident Gordon Stewart** Author interview with Gordon Stewart.

359 **"He was an easy guy"** Author interview with Robert Ailes Jr.

359 **Shortly after Stewart** Author interview with Gordon Stewart. See also Annie Chesnut, "District Settles with School-Related Personnel," *Putnam County News & Recorder,* Dec. 17, 2008.

359 **In the fall of 2009** Author interviews with Gordon Stewart and Susan Peehl.

360 **When Ailes got wind** Boyer, "Fox Among the Chickens."

360 **But by the time** Author interview with Gordon Stewart.

360 **On Tuesday morning, July 6** Boyer, "Fox Among the Chickens."

360 **The following day** Author interview with Gordon Stewart.

361 **"There was no push"** Author interview with a former senior executive at Fox News.

361 **Ailes decided to sit** Author interview with Gordon Stewart.

361 **"They thought"** Author interview with former *Putnam County News & Recorder* reporter Liz Schevtchuk Armstrong.

361 **Alison Rooney noticed** Author interview with Gordon Stewart. Rooney declined to comment.

361 **"It was weird"** Author interview with a former *Putnam County News & Recorder* employee.

362 **Tucked between the articles** *Putnam County News & Recorder,* July 14, 2010, 10.
362 **T. J. Haley** The details of Haley's tenure at *The Putnam County News & Recorder* come from author interviews with acquaintances of Haley and people familiar with the matter. Haley declined to comment.
362 **The decor in the bathroom** Author interview with a person who visited the *Putnam County News & Recorder* office.
362 **Like Haley, Panny** See résumé of Carli-Rae Panny at www.carliraepanny.com/resume.html, accessed Nov. 13, 2013.
363 **"Anytime that anyone"** Author interview with a Putnam County politician. Leibell declined to comment.
363 **"Vinnie thought it was great"** Author interview with Putnam County legislator Sam Oliverio.
363 **They ran into each other** Author interview with an acquaintance of Vincent Leibell.
363 **Ailes spent months** Author interview with two Leibell family intimates.
363 **In the spring of 2010** Michael Brendan Dougherty, "Longtime Senator Has Staying Power," *Putnam County News & Recorder,* April 28, 2010.
363 **Some weeks after** Author interview with a person familiar with the matter.
364 **For years, there had been talk** Author interviews with Putnam County politicians.
364 **Sheriff Don Smith called** Author interview with Putnam County sheriff Don Smith.
364 **In June 2010** "FBI Probes Putnam," *Putnam County Courier,* June 3, 2010.
364 **"This was an ego fight"** Author interview with Sam Oliverio.
364 **Although Uncle Vinnie** Eric Gross, "Leibell Is New County Executive," *Putnam County News & Recorder,* Nov. 3, 2010.
364 **Then, on Monday morning** William K. Rashbaum and Nate Schweber, "Sidewalk Meeting for State Senator and Lawyer Leads to Guilty Plea," *New York Times,* Dec. 6, 2010. See also Ashley Parker, "Ex-Senator Gets 21-Month Prison Term in Tax Evasion Case," *New York Times,* May 13, 2011.
365 **Roger and Beth were trying** Author interview with two people familiar with the matter.
365 **Initially, the proximity** Author interviews with three people in whom Joe Lindsley confided.
365 **According to two** Author interview with senior executives at Fox News.
366 **"You going to talk"** Author interview with Gordon Stewart.
366 **But as Boyer** Peter J. Boyer, *Who Killed CBS? The Undoing of America's Number One Network* (New York: Random House, 1988).
366 **When Boyer showed up** Author interview with a person familiar with the matter.
366 **The *New Yorker* article** Boyer, "Fox Among the Chickens."
367 **Ailes was pleased** Author interview with Gordon Stewart. When asked to respond to criticism of his article by some residents of Philipstown, Boyer wrote in an email: "It's beginning to sound like you've decided on what you want to write, whatever the facts (you could, by the way, ask David Remnick what he thought of that piece, or Dwight Garner, book critic at the NYT who lives in Cold Spring) . . . C'mon, Gabe. Be a journalist. It's an honorable calling."
367 **Lindsley finally decided to resign** Author interviews with acquaintances of Joe Lindsley.
367 **Roger and Beth did not** Details of the former *Putnam County News & Recorder* reporters exit from the paper come from author interviews with people familiar with the matter.
367 **"They made it clear"** Author interview with Peter Boyer.
368 **In April 2011** John Cook and Hamilton Nolan, "Roger Ailes Caught Spying on the Reporters at His Small-Town Newspaper," *Gawker,* April 18, 2011, http://

gawker.com/5793012/roger-ailes-caught-spying-on-the-reporters-at-his-small +town-newspaper.

368 **"I hate everything"** Author interview with a person familiar with the matter.

369 **When Ailes walked into** Author interview with a former senior Fox producer.

369 **In the spring** Author interviews with people familiar with the former *Putnam County News & Recorder* reporters.

369 **On January 31** Jeremy W. Peters, "Newsweek and Daily Beast Hire Two More," "Media Decoder" (blog), *New York Times,* Jan. 31, 2011, mediadecoder.blogs .nytimes.com/2011/01/31/newsweek-daily-beast-hire-two-more/.

369 **On October 18** Christine Haghney and David Carr, "At Newsweek, Ending Print and a Blend of Two Styles," *"Media Decoder"* (blog), *New York Times,* Oct. 18, 2012.

369 **Boyer found a new job** Alexander C. Kaufman, "Fox News Hires Peter J. Boyer from Newsweek," *The Wrap,* Oct. 18, 2012, http://www.thewrap.com/media/ article/fox-news_names-prestigious_newsweek-writer-editor-61251. In an email, Boyer explained the details of his hiring at Fox News: "I hadn't known the Aileses before I wrote that *New Yorker* story, and I spent most of my time with Beth up there at her paper. I interviewed Roger by telephone, as I recollect. A couple of months after the story was published, I met Roger socially, and we got along quite well, and over the next year or so we had a couple of lunches, and had some laughs. By this time, I'd taken the leap to *Newsweek* with Tina whom Roger knew pretty well. In the spring of 2012, Roger mentioned the prospect of coming to Fox, and by summer, he had me over to meet with his news executives about coming to the channel and working with the doc[umentary] unit (I'd done a bunch of *Frontlines* over the years). I said, Hell, yes, and haven't looked back. It's been great fun."

## TWENTY-TWO: THE LAST CAMPAIGN

370 **On Monday afternoon, March 28** Sherman, "The Elephant in the Green Room."

370 **"You've got to be crazy"** Author interview with a person familiar with the meeting.

370 **"Let's make a deal"** Sherman, "The Elephant in the Green Room."

371 **In early 2009** Author interview with a person familiar with the matter.

371 **Things took a turn** Kate Zernike and Carl Hulse, "At the Lincoln Memorial, a Call for Religious Rebirth," *New York Times,* Aug. 29, 2010.

371 **"I'm going to D.C."** Author interview with a person familiar with the matter.

371 **Ailes praised Beck** Author interview with a person familiar with the matter.

371 **Brian Lewis** Author interview with a former Fox News producer.

371 **Beck, who had graced the covers** Lacey Rose, "Glenn Beck Inc.," *Forbes,* April 26, 2010; David von Drehle, "Mad Man: Is Glenn Beck Bad for America?," *Time,* Sept. 28, 2009; Mark Leibovich, "Being Glenn Beck," *New York Times Magazine,* Sept. 29, 2010.

371 **"Beck had his own"** Mercury Radio Arts employed Manhattan PR firm Hiltzik Strategies.

371 **Tensions continued** Steve Kraukauer, "Exclusive: Glenn Beck Launches 'News and Opinion' Website, The Blaze," *Mediaite,* Aug. 30, 2010, http://www.mediaite .com/online/exclusive-glenn-beck-launches-news-and-opinion-website-the-blaze -tonight/.

371 **Fox executives told** Author interview with a person familiar with the matter.

371 **At times, *The Blaze*** Emily Esfahani Smith, "Ends vs. Means: The Ethics of Undercover Journalism," *The Blaze,* March 9, 2011. See also Sherman, "The Elephant in the Green Room."

371 **Beck's company** Bill Carter, "Former Huffington Post Chief Is Hired to Run

Glenn Beck Site," *New York Times,* Jan. 6, 2011. See also David Bauder, "Glenn Beck's Fox Show Ending," Associated Press, April 7, 2011.

372 **Brian Lewis retaliated** Nellie Andreeva, "Glenn Beck's Exec Expected to Leave Fox News," *Deadline Hollywood,* March 21, 2011, http://www.deadline.com/2011/03/Glenn-Becks-exec-to-leave-fox-news/.

372 **Reporters began** Scott Collins and Melissa Maerz, "Fox Gives Beck Show the Boot," *Los Angeles Times,* April 7, 2011. See also Robert Quigley, "Advertisers Wimp Out: 'Boycott' Glenn Beck, but Stay on Fox News," *Mediaite,* Aug. 11, 2009, http://www.mediaite.com/tv/advertisers-wimp-out-boycott-glenn-beck-but-stay-on-fox-news/.

372 **On April 6** Collins and Maerz, "Fox Gives Beck's Show the Boot."

372 **When the Affordable** Author interview with a senior producer.

372 **In the summer of 2010** Sherman, "The Elephant in the Green Room."

373 **"I still like"** Jonathan Alter, *The Center Holds: Obama and His Enemies* (New York: Simon & Schuster, 2013), 179.

373 **In April 2011** Bob Woodward, "Fox Chief Proposed Petraeus Campaign," *Washington Post,* Dec. 4, 2012. See also "Petraeus in 2011 Fox News Interview: 'I'm Not Running for President' " (audio), *Washington Post,* Dec. 3, 2012, http://www.washingtonpost.com/posttv/lifestyle/style/petraeus-in-2011-fox-news-interview-im-not-running-for-president/2012/12/03/c0aa0c72-3d6d-11e2-a2d9-822f58ac9fd5_video.html. Ailes told Woodward that his outreach to Petraeus was "a joke." The day Woodward's article appeared, McFarland wrote a column on Foxnews.com taking the blame for the scandal. "I know now that Roger was joking, but at the time, I wasn't sure," she wrote. According to a close McFarland friend, she wrote it under pressure from Ailes after she was banned from Fox shows. Ailes's remark "was not a joke," the friend said. "She was devastated by it."

373 **"He adored Petraeus"** Author interview with a senior executive at Fox News. See also Jake Tapper, "MoveOn.org Ad Takes Aim at Petraeus," *ABCNews* (blog), Sept. 10, 2007, http://abcnews.go.com/Politics/Decision2008/Story?ID=3581727.

373 **Around this time** Author interview with a person familiar with the matter. A spokeswoman for the Kochs said that Charles Koch did not fly to New York. "A third party suggested a meeting but it was never scheduled," she said.

373 **"Listen, the premise"** Author conversation with Roger Ailes.

373 **In the winter of 2011** Author interview with a person familiar with the matter.

373 **The first Fox primary debate** Karen Tumulty, "Stage Set for First GOP Debate. So Where Are the Candidates?," *Washington Post,* May 5, 2011.

374 **"I still owe you one"** Author interview with a person familiar with the matter. See also Carr and Arango, "A Fox Chief at the Pinnacle of Media and Politics."

374 **The Ailes-backed conservative** Author interviews with Philipstown residents.

374 **Stewart even promised** Kevin E. Foley, "Readers Can Affect Forum Questions," *Philipstown.info,* Oct. 2, 2011.

374 **cover story** Murdock, "This Is the Most Powerful Man in News."

374 **That day, several** Author interview with a Putnam County resident.

374 **After Beth gave** Liz Schevtchuk Armstrong, "Shea and Erickson Clash on Dirt Roads, Zoning Stance, Governance and More," *Philipstown.info,* Oct. 26, 2011.

375 **Shea won decisively** Douglas Cunningham, "Election Day 2011," *Putnam County News & Recorder,* Nov. 9, 2011.

375 **Republicans referred to** Author interview with Republican officials.

375 **"It's like a town hall"** Jeff Zeleny, "The Up-Close-and-Personal Candidate? A Thing of the Past," *New York Times,* Dec. 1, 2011.

375 **In the last eight months** "The Fox Primary: 8 Months, 12 Candidates, 604 Appearances, 4644 Minutes," *Media Matters for America,* Feb. 27, 2012, http://mediamatters.org/blog/2012/02/27/the-fox-primary-8-months-12-candidates-604-appe/185876.

375 **"I'm sorry, we're only"** Author interview with a senior CNN producer.

375 **"He doesn't like green energy"** Author interview with a senior producer.

376 **"Governor Huckabee"** Michael D. Shear, "Huckabee a Candidate? Tune In at 8," *New York Times,* May 14, 2011.

376 **On the night of May 14** Jack Mirkinson, "Mike Huckabee Gets Mixed Ratings for Presidential Announcement," *Huffington Post*, May 17, 2011, http://www.huffingtonpost.com/2011/05/17/mike-huckabee-gets-mixed-_n_863073.html.

376 **Ailes, like any director** Gabriel Sherman, "Sarah Palin Got Scolded by a Furious Roger Ailes," *New York,* Nov. 21, 2011.

376 **In October, Sarah Palin** Michael D. Shear, "After Summer of Speculation, Palin Says She Won't Join the 2012 Race," *New York Times,* Oct. 6, 2011. See also: Sherman, "The Elephant in the Green Room."

376 **In a private conversation** Author interview with a person familiar with the conversation.

376 **Romney's shaky interview** "Interview with Mitt Romney" (transcript), *Finance Wire,* Nov. 29, 2011.

376 **Romney's campaign did not think** Author interview with a Romney adviser.

377 **When the cameras cut** Jack Mirkinson, "Mitt Romney Complained About Fox News Interview," *Huffington Post,* Dec. 1, 2011, http://www.huffingtonpost.com/2011/12/01/mitt-romney-fox-news-bret-baier_n_1122801.html.

377 **After receiving just** "Republican Primary Map" (interactive graphic), *New York Times,* http://elections.nytimes.com/2012/primaries/results, accessed Nov. 15, 2013.

377 **His springboard** CQ Transcriptions, Republican presidential debate (transcript), Jan. 16, 2012.

377 **Gingrich carried** "Republican Primary Map," *New York Times*.

377 **Stuart Stevens** Author interview with a senior Romney adviser.

377 **In one editorial meeting** Author interview with a senior Fox producer.

377 **Fox News was on track** Brian Stelter, "Fox News Is Set to Renew O'Reilly and Hannity Through 2016 Elections," "Media Decoder" (blog), *New York Times,* April 19, 2012, http://mediadecoder.blogs.nytimes.com/2012/04/19/fox-news-is-set-to-renew-oreilly-and-hannity-through-2016-elections/.

378 **"Listen, one out of every"** Howard Kurtz, "Roger's Reality Show," *Newsweek,* Sept. 25, 2011.

378 **In the fall of 2011** Author interviews with a person familiar with the matter. Fox also feuded with one of its own local Fox stations. In April 2010, a senior Fox News executive named David Winstrom sent a critical letter to Steve Smith, the chairman and CEO of Journal Communications, the parent company of the Fox broadcast affiliate in Naples, Florida. A reporter for the affiliate, Rob Koebel, had interviewed Ailes at Ave Maria Law School, the conservative Catholic institution funded by Domino's Pizza billionaire Tom Monaghan. Media Matters had posted the interview online. "The story your station produced and aired was forwarded to me," Winstrom wrote Smith. "I was surprised at the bias in the story. At Fox we understand when you're number 1 you need a thick skin because other news organizations are going to take shots at you. I was just surprised one of our own Fox affiliates would be taking the shots." The letter noted that Koebel had asked Ailes: "How do you defend [Fox News] from the critics especially when you have a lineup that includes Sarah Palin?" Winstrom informed Smith that he hadn't "discussed the interview with Roger" and added "he probably doesn't have any strong feelings one way or another about the clearly biased questions." But, Winstrom explained, "Fair & Balanced is not just a slogan. . . . The Fox News Channel has a strong following in Florida. We appreciate the south Florida viewers. I hope that your Fox station and our Fox News team can work at keeping those loyal viewers."

378 **"I'd give anything"** Chafets, *Roger Ailes,* 234.

378 **"I don't want the kid"** Sella, "Red-State Network."
378 **"He has common feelings"** Author interview with a close colleague of Roger Ailes.
378 **When Zachary was twelve** Author interview with a Dilenschneider Group employee.
378 **Around this time** Chafets, *Roger Ailes,* 235.
379 **In February 2012** Author interview with Gordon Stewart.
379 **That week** Liz Schevtchuk Armstrong, "Neighbors Object to Mega-Structure for Art Collection," *Philipstown.info,* Feb. 20, 2012, http://philipstown.info/2012/02/20/neighbors-object-to-mega-structure-for-art-collection/.
380 **Later that month** David Brock, Ari Rabin-Haft, and Media Matters for America, *The Fox Effect: How Roger Ailes Turned a Network into a Propaganda Machine* (New York: Random House, 2012).
380 **"He was obsessed"** Author interview with a Fox News contributor.
380 **In retaliation** "The Fox Effect: The Book That Terrifies Roger Ailes and Fox News," *Daily Kos,* Feb. 28, 2012, http://www.dailykos.com/story/2012/02/28/1069245/-The-Fox-Effect-The-Book-That-Terrifies-Roger-Ailes-And-Fox-News.
380 **On April 10** "Announcing Our Newest Hire: A Current Fox News Channel Employee," *Gawker,* April 10, 2012, http://gawker.com/5900710/announcing-our-newest-hire-a-current-fox-news-channel-employee.
380 **Within twenty-four hours** Joe Muto, "Hi Roger. It's Me, Joe: The Fox Mole," *Gawker,* April 11, 2012, http://gawker.com/5901228/hi-roger-its-me-joe-the-fox-mole.
380 **When Muto quickly landed** John Cook, "A Low Six-Figure Book Deal for the Fox Mole," *Gawker,* May 3, 2012, http://gawker.com/5907475/a-low-six+figure-book-deal-for-the-fox-mole.
380 **Jimmy Gildea** Chafets, *Roger Ailes,* 229.
380 **"I told them"** Sherman, "Roger Ailes Fired His PR Chief, and Now He's All Alone," "Daily Intel" (blog), *New York,* Aug. 20, 2013, http://nymag.com/daily/intelligencer/2013/08/roger-ailes-fired-his-pr-chief-now-all-alone.html.
380 **At 6:30 in the morning** Kat Stoeffel, "Fox Mole Joe Muto Says His Laptop Was Seized in Grand Larceny Investigation," *New York Observer,* April 25, 2012.
380 **A year later** David Bauder, "Joe Muto, Fox News Mole, Resurfaces with Book," Associated Press, June 3, 2013.
381 **"He likes to raise"** Author interview with a senior producer.
381 **While Fox reporters** Eric Bolling, *The Five,* Fox News Channel, Sept. 28, 2012.
381 **A few days before the election** Jeanette Steele and Nathan Max, "Families Differ on U.S. Response," *San Diego Union-Tribune,* Nov. 2, 2012.
381 **"ELECTION OFFICIALS"** Megyn Kelly, *America Live,* Fox News Channel, Nov. 5, 2012.
381 **Michael Clemente had** Author interview with a person familiar with the matter.
381 **So when Ailes wanted** Author interview with a person familiar with the matter.
382 **On the day before** *Fox & Friends,* Fox News Channel, Oct. 21, 2012.
382 **On the afternoon** Chafets, *Roger Ailes,* 240.
382 **Rove's Super PAC** Nicholas Confessore, "At 40, Steering a Vast Machine of G.O.P. Money," *New York Times,* July 22, 2012.
382 **"Hell, maybe Karl's right"** Chafets, *Roger Ailes,* 240.
382 **At 5:00 p.m.** Author interview with a person in the room.
382 **About an hour later** Chafets, *Roger Ailes,* 239–46.
383 **One Fox executive** Author interview with a person in the room.
383 **Downstairs** Sherman, "How Karl Rove Fought with Fox News over the Ohio Call."
383 **On air, Dick Morris** Don Frederick, "Dick Morris Stands His Ground," *Bloomberg News,* Nov. 5, 2012, http://go.bloomberg.com/political-capital/2012-11-05/dick-morris-stands-his-ground-romney-wins-maybe-by-landslide/.

383 **In private** Author interview with a person who attended the rehearsal.

384 **"You're a hero"** Author observation of Ailes at Bradley Prize ceremony, June 12, 2013.

384 **"When the mainstream media"** Paul Goldman and Mark J. Rozell, "Right-Wing Talk Shows Turned White House Blue," Reuters, April 11, 2013.

384 **Bill Shine sent** Sherman, "Fox News Puts Karl Rove on the Bench," "Daily Intel" (blog), *New York,* Dec. 4, 2012, http://nymag.com/daily/intelligencer/2012/12/fox-news-puts-karl-rove-on-the-bench.html.

384 **In February** Brian Stelter, "Fox News and Dick Morris Part Ways," "Media Decoder" (blog), *New York Times,* Feb. 6, 2013, http://mediadecoder.blogs.nytimes.com/2013/02/06/fox-news-and-dick-morris-part-ways/.

384 **The previous month** Brian Stelter, "Fox Says Its 3-Year Relationship with Palin Is Over," "Media Decoder" (blog), *New York Times,* Jan. 26, 2013, http://mediadecoder.blogs.nytimes.com/2013/01/25/fox-news-and-sarah-palin-part-ways/.

384 **In meetings** Author interview with a person familiar with the matter.

385 **A day after the shooting** Gabriel Sherman, "Fox News Spikes Pro-Gun Column; Writer Told Issue Is 'Too Sensitive,'" *New York,* Dec. 20, 2012.

385 **The reprieve ended** Noah Rothman, "*Fox & Friends:* Obama's Inauguration Happens to Be 'The Most Depressing Day of the Year,'" *Mediaite,* Jan. 21, 2013, http://www.mediaite.com/tv/fox-friends-obamas-inauguration-day-happens-to-be-the-the-most-depressing-day-of-the-year/.

385 **"This was an unyielding"** *Special Inauguration Coverage,* Fox News Channel, Jan. 21, 2013.

385 **"The GOP couldn't organize"** Author interview with a person familiar with the matter.

385 **At a speech** Roger Ailes, Roy H. Park Lecture at the University of North Carolina School of Journalism (transcript). April 12, 2013, http://jomc.unc.edu/roger-ailes-park-lecture-april-12-2012-transcript.

385 **When Ailes re-signed** Brian Stelter, "Roger Ailes Signs Up for Another 4 Years at Fox News," "Media Decoder" (blog), *New York Times,* Oct. 20, 2012. According to the journalist David Folkenflik's book *Murdoch's World: The Last of the Old Media Empires* (New York: PublicAffairs, 2013), Ailes was "obsessed" with David Zaslav's compensation. In 2012, Zaslav earned $36 million. Ailes considered leaving Fox News to join *Newsmax* with a salary of $25 million plus equity.

385 **He brought back** Joe Pompeo, "John Moody Returns to Roger Ailes, His Murdochian Wire Service in Tow," *Capital New York,* June 7, 2012, http://www.capitalnewyork.com/article/media/2012/06/6007210/john-moody-returns-roger-ailes-his-murdochian-wire-service-tow.

385 **Hannity, O'Reilly** Fox News, "Megyn Kelly to Move to Primetime on Fox News Channel," Business Wire (press release), July 2, 2013. See also Brian Stelter, "Kelly and Van Susteren Are Said to Re-Sign with Fox News," *New York Times,* May 8, 2013.

385 **Even Sarah Palin was rehired** Brian Stelter, "Palin Is Returning to Fox News, Months After They Parted Ways," *New York Times,* June 14, 2013.

385 **In October 2013** Mike Allen, "The New Fox News Prime-Time Lineup," *Politico,* Sept. 17, 2013, http://www.politico.com/blogs/media/2013/09/the-new-fox-news-primetime-lineup-172859.html.

386 **In June 2013** Amy Chozick, "Shareholders Approve Plan to Split News Corp.," *New York Times,* June 12, 2013. See also Chozick, "Cable Helps News Corp. Post Gains," *New York Times,* Feb. 7, 2013; Annlee Ellingson, "It's Official: 21st Century Fox and News Corp Split, with New Shares to Be Issued Monday," *L.A. Biz,* June 30, 2013; and Gina Hall, "21st Century Fox Finding Its Footing After the Split from News Corp," *L.A. Biz,* Aug. 7, 2013.

386 **The ratings** Katherine Fung and Jack Mirkinson, "Fox News Ratings: O'Reilly, Hannity See Huge Drop-Off in February Demo Numbers," *Huffington Post,* Feb. 26, 2013, http://www.huffingtonpost.com/2013/02/26/fox-news-ratings-february-oreilly-hannity_n_2768265.html.

386 **Ad revenue was also down** "News Corporation Reports Third Quarter Earnings Per Share of $1.22 on Net Income Attributable to Stockholders of $2.85 Billion," Business Wire, May 8, 2013.

386 **After a News Corp** Author interview with a person familiar with the matter.

386 **Ailes at times seemed** Author interview with a person familiar with the matter.

386 **The Fox Business Network** D. M. Levine, "Neil Cavuto Wants Your Business," *Adweek,* Feb. 7, 2012, http://www.adweek.com/news/technology/neil-cavuto-wants-your-business-137997.

387 **When Murdoch tapped** Author interview with a senior executive.

387 **Kevin Magee** Author interview with a senior executive.

387 **One night, the judge** Judge Andrew Napolitano, *Freedom Watch,* Fox Business Network, Nov. 11, 2011.

387 **A few weeks later** Frances Martel, "Judge Andrew Napolitano Signs Off from the Last Episode of *Freedom Watch,*" *Mediaite,* Feb. 13, 2012, http://www.mediaite.com/tv/watch-judge-napolitano-sign-off-from-the-last-episode-of-freedom-watch/.

387 **"If all the people"** Author interview with a senior executive.

387 **Shortly before** Author interview with a person in the room.

387 **In September 2009** Bio of Don Imus on Fox Business, www.foxbusiness.com/watch/anchors-reporters/don-imus-bio/.

388 **"Roger passed on her"** Author interview with a Fox executive.

388 **In November 2013** Bill Carter, "Maria Bartiromo to Leave CNBC for Fox Business," *New York Times,* Nov. 18, 2013.

388 **Executives noticed** Richard Pérez-Peña, "News Corp. Completes Takeover of Dow Jones," *New York Times,* Dec. 14, 2007; author interview with News Corp executives.

388 **In the fall of 2012** Author interview with a senior Fox executive.

389 **Rupert doesn't have** Author interview with a former senior News Corp executive.

389 **In one meeting** Author interview with a senior Fox executive.

389 **Top News Corp brass** Author interviews with News Corp executives. See also Alter, *The Center Holds,* 65.

389 **Ailes was more isolated** Author interview with a person close to Roger Ailes.

390 **On the afternoon** Author interview with a person familiar with the matter.

390 **On August 20** Bill Carter, "Fox News Confirms the Firing of a Top Executive Who Was Once Close to Ailes," *New York Times,* Aug. 20, 2013. See also Dylan Byers, "Roger Fires His 'Right Hand,'" *Politico*, Aug. 20, 2013, and Paul Bond and Matthew Belloni, "Top Roger Ailes Adviser Fired and Escorted from Fox News Building," *Hollywood Reporter,* Aug. 20, 2013.

390 **On August 27** J. K. Trotter, "Brian Lewis Speaks Out: Roger Ailes and Fox News Should Fear Him," *Gawker,* Aug. 27, 2013, http://gawker.com/brian-lewis-speaks-out-roger-ailes-and-fox-news-should-1208497354.

390 **In September, Burstein met** Author interview with a person familiar with the matter.

391 **A month before the 2012 election** Author interview with Joe McGinniss.

391 **A few days after** Author interview with Gordon Stewart, to whom Shea later described the meeting. Shea declined to comment on the matter.

391 **In June** Gabriel Sherman, "In Kennedy Center Speech, Roger Ailes Gets Wild," *New York,* June 13, 2013.

391 **His acceptance speech** Author's transcript of speech given by Ailes at the Kennedy Center, June 12, 2013.

391 **senior center** Catherine Garnsey, "Town Has Good News for Seniors," *Putnam County News & Recorder,* Aug. 7, 2013.

392 **"If I'm going to risk"** Eliza Gray, "Roger Ailes's Border War," *New Republic,* Feb. 22, 2013.

392 **Throughout his career** Chafets, *Roger Ailes,* 175.

392 **In June 2012** Sherman, "Roger Ailes, Upstate Press Baron, Is in a Newspaper War," "Daily Intel" (blog), *New York,* May 31, 2012, http://nymag.com/daily/intelligencer/2012/05/roger-ailes-is-in-an-upstate-newspaper-war.html.

392 **In March 2013** Kevin E. Foley, "Chamber Dinner to Honor 2013 Award Winners," *Philipstown.info,* March 13, 2013. See also Liz Schevtchuk Armstrong, "Chamber Hosts Record Crowd for Award Dinner," *Philipstown.info,* March 29, 2013.

392 **"Due to scheduling conflicts"** Annie Chesnut, "Elizabeth Ailes Clarifies Chamber Confusion," *Putnam County News & Recorder,* March 20, 2013.

392 **A few months later** Author interview with Gordon Stewart.

393 **When the *PCN&R*** Michael Turton, "Village Trustees Express Regret over July Fourth Ads," *Philipstown.info,* Aug. 3, 2013.

393 **a parody website** *The Pretend Putnam County News and Recorder,* ppcnr.com.

393 **"I have nothing"** Author interview with Gordon Stewart.

393 **Shea was up for reelection** Liz Schevtchuk Armstrong, "Philipstown Democrats Set Slate for Town Board Elections," *Philipstown.info,* May 31, 2013. See also Eric Gross, "Erickson Joins Leonard, Van Tassel in Town Race," *Putnam County News & Recorder,* July 7, 2013.

393 **Richard Shea won** Putnam County Board of Elections, http://www.putnamcountyny.com/board-of-elections/2013-elections/liveelectionresults/.

393 **"He doesn't want"** Author interview with a national Republican.

393 **"All progress is made"** Donald Baer, "Roger Rabid," *Manhattan Inc.,* Sept. 1989.

394 **"I don't care"** Chris Ariens, "Roger Ailes on His Apprentices and His Legacy," *TVNewser,* Nov. 15, 2012, http://www.mediabistro.com/tvnewser/roger-ailes-on-his-apprentices-and-his-legacy-i-dont-care-about-my-legacy-its-too-late_b155146.

394 **"Right now"** Chafets, *Roger Ailes,* 233.

394 **"Most of the media"** Author interview with Robert Ailes Jr.

394 **"I can't walk away"** Hoover Institution, "Fox and More with Roger Ailes" (video interview), *Uncommon Knowledge with Peter Robinson,* Feb. 5, 2010, http://www.hoover.org/multimedia/uncommon-knowledge/26681.

394 **Near the end of his book** Ailes and Kraushar, *You Are the Message,* 203–4.

395 **"If you can get the audience"** Ibid.

395 **He had two million** Rick Kissell, "MSNBC Continues Ratings Slide as CNN Surges over Summer," *Variety.com,* Aug. 21, 2013, http://www.variety.com/2013/tv/news/msnbc-continues-ratings-slide-as-cnn-surges-over-summer-1200585373/.

# SELECTED BIBLIOGRAPHY

## BOOKS

Ailes, Roger, and Jon Kraushar. *You Are the Message: Getting What You Want by Being Who You Are*. New York: Crown Business, 1988.

Alter, Jonathan. *The Center Holds: Obama and His Enemies*. New York: Simon & Schuster, 2013.

Auletta, Ken. *Media Man: Ted Turner's Improbable Empire*. New York: W. W. Norton, 2005.

———. *Three Blind Mice: How the TV Networks Lost Their Way*. New York: Random House, 1991.

Babiak, Paul, and Robert D. Hare. *Snakes in Suits: When Psychopaths Go to Work*. New York: HarperCollins e-books, 2009.

Barnouw, Erik. *Tube of Plenty: The Evolution of American Television*. New York: Oxford University, 1975.

Baum, Dan. *Citizen Coors: A Grand Family Saga of Business, Politics, and Beer*. New York: HarperCollins, 2000.

Bibb, Porter. *Ted Turner: It Ain't As Easy As It Looks: The Inside Story of the Billion-Dollar Donor*. Boulder, Colo.: Johnson, 1997.

Black, Conrad. *Richard M. Nixon: A Life in Full*. New York: PublicAffairs, 2007.

Blumenthal, Sidney. *The Clinton Wars*. New York: Farrar, Straus and Giroux, 2003.

Boyer, Peter J. *Who Killed CBS? The Undoing of America's Number One News Network*. New York: Random House, 1988.

Brinkley, Alan. *Voices of Protest: Huey Long, Father Coughlin, and the Great Depression*. New York: Vintage, 1983.

Brock, David. *Blinded by the Right: The Conscience of an Ex-Conservative*. New York: Random House, 2002.

Brock, David, Ari Rabin-Haft, and Media Matters for America. *The Fox Effect: How Roger Ailes Turned a Network into a Propaganda Machine*. New York: Random House, 2012.

Bruck, Connie. *Master of the Game: How Steve Ross Rode the Light Fantastic from Undertaker to Creator of the Largest Media Conglomerate in the World*. New York: Simon & Schuster, 1994.

Carter, Graydon, Bryan Burrough, Sarah Ellison, William Shawcross, and Michael Wolff. *Rupert Murdoch, the Master Mogul of Fleet Street: 24 Tales from the Pages of Vanity Fair* (New York: Vanity Fair ebook, 2011; New York: Penguin, 2013). All material for which this book is the source comes from the Kim Masters and Bryan Burrough article "Cable Guys," published in the Jan. 1997 issue of *Vanity Fair*.

Chafets, Zev. *Roger Ailes: Off Camera*. New York: Sentinel, 2013.

Colford, Paul D. *The Rush Limbaugh Story: The Unauthorized Biography*. New York: St. Martin's, 1993.

Collins, Scott. *Crazy Like a Fox: The Inside Story of How Fox News Beat CNN*. New York: Penguin, 2004.

Conason, Joe, and Gene Lyons. *The Hunting of the President: The Ten-Year Campaign to Destroy Bill and Hillary Clinton*. New York: St. Martin's, 2000.

Cramer, Richard Ben. *What It Takes: The Way to the White House*. New York: Open Road Media ebook, 2011.

Douglas, Mike. *Mike Douglas: My Story*. New York: Ballantine, 1979.

Douglas, Mike, Thomas Kelly, and Michael Heaton. *I'll Be Right Back: Memories of TV's Greatest Talk Show*. New York: Simon & Schuster, 2000.

Edwards, Lee. *The Power of Ideas: The Heritage Foundation at 25 Years*. Ottawa, Ill.: Jameson, 1997.

Ellroy, James. *American Tabloid*. New York: Vintage, 2001.

Evans, Harold. *Good Times, Bad Times*. New York: Open Road Media, 2011.

Evans, Rowland, and Robert Novak. *Nixon in the White House: The Frustration of Power*. New York: Random House, 1971.

Folkenflik, David. *Murdoch's World: The Last of the Old Media Empires* (New York: PublicAffairs, 2013).

Gabler, Neal. *Winchell: Gossip, Power and the Culture of Celebrity*. New York: Alfred A. Knopf, 1994.

Garment, Leonard. *Crazy Rhythm: From Brooklyn and Jazz to Nixon's White House, Watergate, and Beyond*. Cambridge, Mass.: Da Capo, 1997.

Gitlin, Todd. *The Sixties: Years of Hope, Days of Rage*. New York: Bantam, 1993.

Goldberg, Robert, and Gerald Jay Goldberg. *Citizen Turner: The Wild Rise of an American Tycoon*. New York: Harcourt Brace, 1995.

Goldman, Peter, Tom Mathews, and the *Newsweek* Special Election Team. *The Quest for the Presidency: The 1988 Campaign*. New York: Simon & Schuster, 1989.

Goldwater, Barry M. *The Conscience of a Conservative*. Shepherdsville, Ky.: Victor, 1960.

Gormley, Ken. *The Death of American Virtue: Clinton vs. Starr*. New York: Random House, 2010.

Halberstam, David. *The Fifties*. New York: Ballantine, 1994.

Haldeman, H. R. *The Haldeman Diaries: Inside the Nixon White House*. New York: Putnam, 1994.

Halperin, Mark, and John Harris. *The Way to Win: Taking the White House in 2008*. New York: Random House, 2006.

Harris, Harry. *Mike Douglas: The Private Life of the Public Legend*. New York: Award, 1976.

Harris, John F. *The Survivor: Bill Clinton in the White House*. New York: Random House, 2005.

Hendershot, Heather. *What's Fair on the Air? Cold War Right-Wing Broadcasting and the Public Interest*. Chicago: University of Chicago Press, 2011.

Hitchcock, A. B. C. *History of Shelby County, Ohio, and Representative Citizens*. Chicago: Richmond-Arnold, 1913.

Holtzman, Elizabeth, and Cynthia L. Cooper. *Who Said It Would Be Easy? One Woman's Life in the Political Arena*. New York: Arcade, 1996.

Isikoff, Michael. *Uncovering Clinton: A Reporter's Story*. New York: Random House, 1999.

Jamieson, Kathleen Hall, and Joseph N. Cappella. *Echo Chamber: Rush Limbaugh and the Conservative Media Establishment*. New York: Oxford University Press, 2008.

Jenkins, William D. *Steel Valley Klan: The Ku Klux Klan in Ohio's Mahoning Valley*. Kent, Ohio: Kent State University Press, 1990.

Kazan, Elia. *Elia Kazan: A Life*. New York: Alfred A. Knopf, 1988.

Kiernan, Thomas. *Citizen Murdoch*. New York: Dodd, Mead, 1986.

Kirk, Russell. *The Conservative Mind: From Burke to Eliot*. Washington, D.C.: Regnery, 1953.

Kitman, Marvin. *The Man Who Would Not Shut Up: The Rise of Bill O'Reilly*. New York: St. Martin's, 2007.

Kreskin, The Amazing. *Secrets of the Amazing Kreskin*. New York: Prometheus, 1991.

Kurtz, Howard. *The Fortune Tellers: Inside Wall Street's Game of Money, Media, and Manipulation*. New York: Free Press, 2000.

———. *Spin Cycle: How the White House and the Media Manipulate the News*. New York: Simon & Schuster, 1998.

Mahler, Jonathan. *Ladies and Gentlemen, The Bronx Is Burning: 1977, Baseball, Politics, and the Battle for the Soul of a City*. New York: Picador, 2006.

McGinniss, Joe. *Heroes*. New York: Simon & Schuster, 1976.

———. *The Selling of the President 1968: The Classic Account of the Packaging of a Candidate*. New York: Simon & Schuster, 1969.

McMahon, Ed, and David Fisher, *Laughing Out Loud: My Life and Good Times* (New York: Warner, 1998), e-book.

Menadue, John. *Things You Learn Along the Way*. Ringwood, Australia: David Lovell, 1999.

Moore, David. *How to Steal an Election: The Inside Story of How George*

*Bush's Brother and Fox Network Miscalled the 2000 Election and Changed the Course of History*. New York: Nation Books, 2006.

Munk, Nina. *Fools Rush In: Steve Case, Jerry Levin, and the Unmaking of AOL Time Warner*. New York: HarperCollins, 2004.

Neil, Andrew. *Full Disclosure: The Most Candid and Revealing Portrait of Rupert Murdoch Ever*. London: Macmillan, 1996.

Perlstein, Rick. *Nixonland: The Rise of a President and the Fracturing of America*. New York: Scribner, 2008.

Reagan, Ron. *My Father at 100: A Memoir*. New York: Viking, 2011.

Reeves, Richard. *President Nixon: Alone in the White House*. Simon & Schuster, 2001.

Safire, William. *Before the Fall: An Inside View of the Pre-Watergate White House*. New York: Doubleday, 1975.

Sammon, Bill. *At Any Cost: How Al Gore Tried to Steal the Election*. Washington, D.C.: Regnery, 2001.

Schonfeld, Reese. *Me and Ted Against the World: The Unauthorized Founding of CNN*. New York: HarperCollins, 2001.

Shawcross, William. *Murdoch: The Making of a Media Empire*. New York: Simon & Schuster, 1992.

Stephanopoulos, George. *All Too Human: A Political Education*. Boston: Little, Brown, 1999.

Stewart, James B. *Blood Sport: The President and His Adversaries*. New York: Simon & Schuster, 1996.

———. *Disney War*. New York: Simon & Schuster, 2005.

Suskin, Steven. *Second Act Trouble: Behind the Scenes at Broadway's Big Musical Bombs*. New York: Applause Theatre & Cinema, 2006.

Swaim, Don. *Radio Days*. Self-published at donswaim.com/WOUB.html, donswaim.com/WOUB2.html.

Swint, Kerwin. *Dark Genius: The Influential Career of Legendary Political Operative and Fox News Founder Roger Ailes*. New York: Sterling, 2008.

Tapper, Jake. *Down and Dirty: The Plot to Steal the Presidency*. Boston: Little, Brown, 2001.

Toobin, Jeffrey. *Too Close to Call: The Thirty-Six-Day Battle to Decide the 2000 Election*. New York: Random House, 2001.

———. *A Vast Conspiracy: The Real Story of the Sex Scandal That Nearly Brought Down a President*. New York: Simon & Schuster, 2000.

Turner, Ted, and Bill Burke. *Call Me Ted*. New York: Hachette Digital, 2008.

Welch, Jack, and John A. Byrne. *Jack: Straight from the Gut*. New York: Warner, 2001.

White, Theodore H. *The Making of the President 1968*. New York: HarperCollins, 1969.

Wiener, Robert. *Live from Baghdad: Making Journalism History Behind the Lines*. New York, St. Martin's, 1992.

Wills, Garry. *Nixon Agonistes: The Crisis of the Self-Made Man*. New York: Houghton Mifflin, 1969.

Wolff, Michael. *Inside the Secret World of Rupert Murdoch: The Man Who Owns the News*. New York: Random House, 2008.

Woodward, Bob. *The Agenda: Inside the Clinton White House*. New York: Simon & Schuster, 2005.

## PERIODICALS

Ailes, Melville D. "Pure Drinking Water." *Boston Daily Globe,* June 27, 1928.

"Ailes to Run Murdoch's New Network." *Washington Post,* Jan. 31, 1996.

Alcorn, William K. "Fox News Chairman Ailes Comes Home, Discusses Obama's Tasks." *Youngstown* (Ohio) *News,* Nov. 11, 2008.

———. "Webster Scholarship to Help City Youths." *Youngstown* (Ohio) *News,* July 3, 2006.

". . . And Now from Our Man in Bangkok." *TV Guide,* June 8, 1974.

Andrews, Edmund L. "F.C.C. Vote Gives Murdoch Big Victory on Ownership." *New York Times,* May 5, 1995.

———. "Fox TV Deal Seems to Face Few Official Barriers." *New York Times,* May 5, 1994.

———. "Mr. Murdoch Goes to Washington." *New York Times,* July 23, 1995.

Angwin, Julia. "After Riding High with Fox News, Murdoch Aide Has Harder Slog." *Wall Street Journal*, Oct. 3, 2006.

"Announcing Our Newest Hire: A Current Fox News Channel Employee." *Gawker,* April 10, 2012.

Auletta, Ken. "John Malone: Flying Solo." *New Yorker,* Feb. 7, 1994.

———. "The Lost Tycoon," *New Yorker,* April 23, 2001.

———. "The Pirate." *New Yorker,* Nov. 13, 1995.

———. "Promises, Promises: What Might the Wall Street Journal Become If Rupert Murdoch Owned It?" *New Yorker,* July 2, 2007.

———. "Vox Fox: How Roger Ailes and Fox News are Changing Cable News." *New Yorker,* May 26, 2003.

Baer, Donald. "Roger Rabid." *Manhattan Inc.,* Sept. 1989.

Barnes, Clive. "Stage: 'Mother Earth,' a Rock Revue." *New York Times,* Oct. 20, 1972.

Battaglio, Stephen. "Ailes the Cure for What Ails Fox News." *Hollywood Reporter,* Jan. 31, 1996.

———. "Bombing Spurs Fox News to First Special." *Hollywood Reporter,* April 21, 1995.

———. "Fox News Net Will Debut Oct. 7." *Hollywood Reporter,* July 19, 1996.

———. "Long, Busy Day Planned for Fox News Channel." *Hollywood Reporter,* Sept. 5, 1996.

Bauder, David. "Joe Muto, Fox News Mole, Resurfaces with Book." Associated Press, June 3, 2013.

Biddle, Frederic M. "What's Wrong with Ted-TV's Picture?" *Boston Globe,* July 16, 1995.

Bosman, Julie, and Richard Siklos. "Fired Editor's Remarks Said to Have Provoked Murdoch." *New York Times,* Dec. 18, 2006.

Bovsun, Mara. "The Case of Adolph Coors." New York *Daily News,* Sept. 13, 2009.

Bowers, Peter. "Revealed: Murdoch's Role in 1975." *Sydney Morning Herald,* Nov. 4, 1995.

Boyer, Peter J. "Fox Among the Chickens." *New Yorker,* Jan. 31, 2011.

———. "NBC Rules Out TBS Stake as Talks with Turner Fail." *New York Times,* Jan. 16, 1988.

Brenner, Marie. "Steve Forbes's Quixotic Presidential Quest." *Vanity Fair,* Jan. 1996.

Brock, David. "Roger Ailes Is Mad as Hell." *New York,* Sept. 17, 1997.

Brooks, Richard. "Neil Lacks Bite in the Big Apple TV War." *London Observer,* July 17, 1994.

Bruck, Connie. "A Mogul's Farewell." *New Yorker,* Oct. 18, 1993.

Buettner, Russ. "Ex-Publisher's Suit Plays a Giuliani-Kerik Angle." *New York Times,* Nov. 14, 2007.

———. "Fox News Chief Is Said to Urge Lying in Inquiry." *New York Times,* Feb. 25, 2011.

———. "In Fox News, Led by an Ally, Giuliani Finds a Friendly Stage." *New York Times,* Aug. 2, 2007.

Byers, Dylan. "Fox News Firing Tied to Ailes Book." *Politico,* Aug. 21, 2013.

———. "Tucker Carlson to Fox & Friends Weekends." *Politico,* March 27, 2013.

Carlson, Tucker, and Vince Coglianese. "Inside Media Matters: Source, Memos Reveal Erratic Behavior, Close Coordination with White House and News Organizations," *Daily Caller,* Feb. 12, 2012.

Carr, David, and Tim Arango. "A Fox Chief at the Pinnacle of Media and Politics." *New York Times,* Jan. 9, 2010.

Carter, Bill. "Fox News Confirms the Firing of a Top Executive Who Was Once Close to Ailes." *New York Times,* Aug. 20, 2013.

———. "The Media Business: Murdoch Joins a Cable-TV Rush Into the Crowded All-News Field." *New York Times,* Jan. 31, 1996.

———. "Networks' New Cable Channels Get a Big Jump on the Competition." *New York Times,* March 14, 1994.

———. "TCI Reaches Deal with Fox to Carry All-News Channel." *New York Times,* June 25, 1996.

Carter, Bill, and Edward Wyatt. "Under Pressure, News Corp. Pulls Simpson Project." *New York Times,* Nov. 21, 2006.

Cassidy, John. "Murdoch's Game: Will He Move Left in 2008?" *New Yorker,* Oct. 16, 2006.

Chaffin, Joshua, and Aline van Duyn. "Interview with Rupert Murdoch and Roger Ailes." *Financial Times,* Oct. 6, 2006.

"A Changing World Catches Up with Delphi, Shocks Valley." *Youngstown* (Ohio) *News,* Oct. 9, 2005.

Cook, John. "A Low Six-Figure Book Deal for the Fox Mole." *Gawker,* May 3, 2012.

Cook, John, and Hamilton Nolan. "Roger Ailes Caught Spying on the Reporters at His Small-Town Newspaper." *Gawker,* April 1, 2011.

"Coors Beer; Tastes Right." *Economist,* May 17, 1975.

Cornwell, Rupert. "Ed Koch: Brash and Feisty Politician Who Served Three Terms as Mayor of New York." *Independent* (London), Feb. 2, 2013.

———. "Noted New York Judge Starring in War of the Richardsons Saga." *Independent* (London), reprinted in *Vancouver Sun,* Aug. 10, 1995.

Coscarelli, Joe. "Roger Ailes Lied About the New York *Times* Being 'Lying Scum.'" *New York,* May 29, 2012.

Crutsinger, Martin. "FTC Approves Time Warner's Acquisition of Turner." Associated Press, Sept. 12, 1996.

Dana, Rebecca. "Good Night, ABC! TV Tabloid Empress Packs Up and Leaves." *New York Observer,* Dec. 11, 2006.

Davis, Stephen, and Ian Bailey. "The War on Wapping: Anatomy of a Pitched Battle." *Sunday Times* (London), Feb. 1, 1987.

Dickinson, Tim. "How Roger Ailes Built the Fox News Fear Factory." *Rolling Stone,* June 9, 2011.

Dorling, Philip. "Getting Gough; Murdoch Files." *Melbourne Age,* Nov. 29, 2011.

"Eckerd's Moves Hint Nixon's Fighting Kirk." Times Wire Services, *St. Petersburg Times,* Feb. 28, 1970.

Evans, Rowland, and Robert Novak. "Unilateral Withdrawal of 200,000 GIs Is Key to Nixon Strategy on Vietnam." *Washington Post,* April 11, 1969.

Fabrikant, Geraldine. "Ex-Consultant to Bush Named to CNBC." *New York Times,* Aug. 31, 1993.

———. "Walt Disney to Acquire ABC in $19 Billion Deal to Build a Giant for Entertainment." Media Business, *New York Times,* Aug. 1, 1995.

Farthi, Paul. "Mogul Wrestling; In the War Between Murdoch and Turner, Similarity Breeds Contempt." *Washington Post,* Nov. 18, 1996.

———. "No News Is Good News: CNN's Ratings Tumble as Events Fail to Capture the TV-Viewing Public's Attention." *Washington Post,* June 10, 1994.

Firestone, David. "Giulianis Earned $303,889." *New York Times,* April 13, 1996.

———. "Mayor's Family Income at All-Time High." *New York Times,* April 16, 1997.

———. "Time Warner Wins Order Keeping Fox off City Cable TV." *New York Times,* Oct. 12, 1996.

"The Fox Effect: The Book That Terrifies Roger Ailes and Fox News." *Daily Kos,* Feb. 28, 2012.

Gay, Verne. "The All-News Wars Heat Up." *Newsday,* Oct. 7, 1996.

Getlin, Josh. "Regan Was Fired After Slur, News Corp. Says." *Los Angeles Times,* Dec. 19, 2006.

Gold, Matea. "Fox News Displays a Green Side." *Los Angeles Times,* Nov. 12, 2005.

Gould, Stanhope. "Coors Brews the News." *Columbia Journalism Review,* Vol. 13, No. 6 (March/April 1975).

Grigoriadis, Vanessa. "Even Bitches Have Feelings." *New York,* Feb. 5, 2007.

Grim, Ryan. "Nevada Dems Nix Fox Debate." *Politico,* March 9, 2007.

Grove, Lloyd. "The Image Shaker; Roger Ailes, the Bush Team's Wily Media Man." *Washington Post,* June 20, 1988.

Hampson, Rick. "Diaries Put 'Love Judge' on Trial." Associated Press, published in *Memphis Commercial Appeal,* Aug. 9, 1995.

Hass, Nancy. "Embracing the Enemy: Roger Ailes." *New York Times Magazine,* Jan. 8, 1995.

Heller, Zoë. "Full Disclosure." *Granta,* Vol. 53 (Spring 1996).

Henry, Georgina. "Thatcher Knew of TV Merger Plans." *Guardian Weekly,* Jan. 18, 1990.

Hill, Gladwin. "Nixon Denounces Press as Biased." *New York Times,* Nov. 8, 1962.

Hocking, Jenny. "How Murdoch Wrote the Final Act in Gough Saga." *Melbourne Sunday Age,* Aug. 26, 2012.

Hofmeister, Sallie. "Changing Channels; Quirky Programming Whiz Puts Spin on USA Networks." *Los Angeles Times,* May 9, 1998.

Huff, Richard, and Douglas Feiden. "Ailes Quits CNBC, Ch. 4 GM Steps In." New York *Daily News,* Jan. 19, 1996.

Hunter, Marjorie. "Networks Chided on Election Role; Conservative Group Urges Strict Policing in Future." *New York Times,* Nov. 25, 1966.

Hurtado, Patricia. "Publisher Regan Says News Corp. Fired Her to Protect Giuliani." *Bloomberg News,* Nov. 14, 2007.

Hurtado, Patricia, and Gillian Wee. "News Corp. Settles Suit by Judith Regan over Firing." *Bloomberg News,* Jan. 25, 2008.

Isaacs, Stephen. "Coors Beer—and Politics—Move East." *Washington Post,* May 4, 1975.

Johnson, Bradley. "Microsoft-NBC: A 'Virtual Corporation'; Details May Be Fuzzy but Packaging Is Loud as Companies Converge." *Advertising Age,* May 22, 1995.

Johnson, Peter, and Alan Bash. "Roger Ailes Ponders His Future with CNBC." *USA Today,* June 21, 1995.

Junod, Tom. "Why Does Roger Ailes Hate America?" *Esquire,* Feb. 2011.

Kakutani, Michiko. "Thatcher Deciphers Her Indelible Mark on Britain." *New York Times,* Jan. 17, 1993.

Kempton, Murray. "Roger Ailes and the Autumn of His Vocational Discontent." *Newsday,* Nov. 8, 1989.

Kerr, Walter. "The Crazies Are Good to Listen To." *New York Times,* March 4, 1973.

Krebs, Albin. "Kermit Bloomgarden, Producer of Many Outstanding Plays, Dead." *New York Times,* Sept. 21, 1976.

Kurtz, Howard. "Chelsea Remark Earns MSNBC Correspondent a Suspension." *Washington Post,* Feb. 9, 2008.

———. "CNBC's Roger Ailes, Talking a Fine Line." *Washington Post,* Dec. 11, 1995.

——— "The Little Network with Big Names; Microsoft, NBC Boldly Venture into the Cable News Game." *Washington Post,* July 12, 1996.

———. "Obama Met with News Executives." *Washington Post,* Sept. 3, 2008.

Landler, Mark. "An Accord That Could Help Murdoch." *New York Times,* July 18, 1996.

Large, Arlen J. "Mr. Nixon on TV: 'Man in the Arena.'" *Wall Street Journal,* Oct. 1, 1969.

Laurent, Lawrence. "Virginia TV Gets School Film Contract." *Washington Post,* Oct. 4, 1969.

Leduc, Daniel. "Controversial Ad Man Quits Whitman Camp." *Philadelphia Inquirer,* July 22, 1993.

———. "Whitman Hires Ad Man Who Raised Ire with Willie Horton." *Philadelphia Inquirer,* July 21, 1993.

Lescaze, Lee. "Now Ailes Is Packaging Business Executives." *Washington Post,* July 30, 1977.

Lesly, Elizabeth. "The Dumbest Show in Television." *Businessweek,* Oct. 20, 1996.

Levy, Clifford J. "In Cable TV Fight, Mayor Plans to Put Fox Channel on a City Station." *New York Times,* Oct. 10, 1996.

———. "Lobbying at Murdoch Gala Ignited New York Cable Clash." *New York Times,* Oct. 13, 1996.

———. "An Old Friend Called Giuliani, and New York's Cable Clash Was On." *New York Times,* Nov. 4, 1996.

Lieberman, David. "Cap Cities/ABC Cuts Cord on Cable News." *USA Today,* May 24, 1996.

———. "Taking to New Stump: CNBC's Ailes Dares to Raise the Cable Stakes." *USA Today,* April 28, 1994.

———. "Time Warner–Murdoch Feud Heats Up." *USA Today,* Sept. 27, 1996.

Linert, Brenda J. "Tribune Plans Year of Anniversary Events." *Warren* (Ohio) *Tribune Chronicle,* Oct. 16, 2011.

Lippman, John. "Murdoch Fires President of Fox TV Unit." *Los Angeles Times,* June 22, 1992.

Lomartire, Paul. "A Night in Ted's Empire." *Palm Beach Post,* July 11, 1995.

Lowry, Brian. "New World Vision: Murdoch's News Corp. to Buy Broadcast Group." *New York Times,* July 18, 1996.

Mahler, Jonathan. "What Rupert Wrought." *New York,* April 11, 2005.

Margasak, Larry. "Democrats Question Gingrich's Ethics over Book Deal." Associated Press, Dec. 22, 1994.

Masters, Kim, and Bryan Burrough. "Cable Guys." *Vanity Fair,* Jan. 1997.

McGinniss, Joe. "The Resale of the President." *New York Times Magazine*, Sept. 3, 1972.

Moore, Frazier. "Fox News Channel: More Round-the-Clock News a Month Away." Associated Press, Sept. 4, 1996.

"Murdoch Planning All-News TV Network." Associated Press, Nov. 29, 1995.

Murdock, Deroy. "This Is the Most Powerful Man in News." *Newsmax*, Nov. 2011.

Muto, Joe. "Hi Roger. It's Me, Joe: The Fox Mole." *Gawker*, April 11, 2012.

Neil, Andrew. "Murdoch and Me." *Vanity Fair*, Dec. 1996.

"Nixon Aide Joins TV News Agency." *Variety*, Feb. 19, 1975.

"Nixon in New Hampshire. Granite State Saved Nixon's Political Life." *Manchester* (New Hampshire) *Union Leader*, April 23, 1994.

"Nixon's Roger Ailes." *Washington Post*, Feb. 13, 1972.

"Now, the Meat of the Kimba Wood Story; 'Love Judge' Returns to Bench for Spam Case." *Washington Post*, Aug. 11, 1995.

Nyhan, David. "Roger Ailes: He Doctors a Politician's TV Image." *Boston Globe*, May 3, 1970.

O'Brian, Jack. "Gal from Santa Fe." *Spartanburg* (South Carolina) *Herald*, July 26, 1974.

Painton, Priscilla. "The Taming of Ted Turner." *Time*, Jan. 6, 1992.

Pearson, Drew. "Fluoridation Battle Dividing New Canaan; DAR Leading Foe." *Sunday Herald* (Bridgeport, Ct.), April 2, 1948.

Peer, Elizabeth, with Philip S. Cook. "Foaming over Coors." *Newsweek*, Sept. 22, 1975.

Pierce, Scott D. "Fox News Chief Ailes Is Certainly Arrogant." *Salt Lake City Deseret News*, July 31, 1996.

Preston, Jennifer. "Murdoch's Denials of Political Favors Hard to Swallow in New York." "City Room" (blog), *New York Times*, April 27, 2012.

Prodigy and CNBC. "America's Talking Is Nation's First Interactive Live Television Network." Press release. *Business Wire*, June 15, 1994.

Purdum, Todd S. "Amid the Shouts, Dinkins Remains Calm." *New York Times*, Oct. 26, 1989.

Rashbaum, William K., and Nate Schweber. "Sidewalk Meeting for State Senator and Lawyer Leads to Guilty Plea." *New York Times*, Dec. 6, 2010.

Rexrode, Christina, and Bernard Condon. "Typical CEO Made $9.6 Million Last Year, AP Study Finds." Associated Press, May 25, 2012.

Ringler, Larry. "Fox News Chief Returns to Warren." *Warren* (Ohio) *Tribune Chronicle*, Nov. 11, 2008.

Robins, J. Max. "The ABC's of Michael Jackson." *Variety*, June 26–July 9, 1995.

"Roger Ailes Still Has Snap in His Political Jabs," *Washington Times*, May 11, 1993.

Rosenstiel, Tom. "The Myth of CNN." *New Republic*, Aug. 22, 1994.

Safire, William. "Citizen of the World." *New York Times*, May 16, 1985.

Sanger, David. "U.S. Confirms It Lost an H-Bomb Off Japan in '65." *New York Times*, May 9, 1989.

Sanger, Elizabeth. "Financial News Is Hot." *Newsday,* Dec. 3, 1995.

Seelye, Katharine. "Murdoch, Joined by Lobbyist, Talked of Regulatory Problem at Meeting with Gingrich." *New York Times,* Jan. 15, 1995.

Sella, Marshall. "The Red-State Network." *New York Times Magazine,* June 24, 2001.

Sellers, Patricia. "Gone with the Wind." *Fortune,* May 26, 2003.

Shafer, Jack. "Fox News 1.0." *Slate,* June 5, 2008.

Sharbutt, Jay. "Kelly Garrett Isn't 'Overnight' Success," Associated Press, published in *Pittsburgh Post-Gazette,* July 1, 1974.

Sherman, Gabriel. "Chasing Fox." *New York,* Oct. 11, 2010.

———. "The Elephant in the Green Room." *New York,* May 22, 2011.

———. "Fox News Spikes Pro-Gun Column; Writer Told Issue Is 'Too Sensitive.'" *New York,* Dec. 20, 2012.

———. "How Karl Rove Fought with Fox News over the Ohio Call." *New York,* Nov. 7, 2012.

———. "In Kennedy Center Speech, Roger Ailes Gets Wild." *New York,* June 13, 2013.

———. "Meet Roger Ailes's Fox News Mouthpiece." *New York,* Oct. 25, 2012.

———. "Sarah Palin Got Scolded by a Furious Roger Ailes." *New York,* Nov. 21, 2011.

Smith, Liz. "Roger's a Free Man." *Newsday,* Dec. 11, 1995.

Stelter, Brian. "Big-Time Cable News to Small-Town Paper." *New York Times,* July 14, 2008.

———. "Fox News and Dick Morris Part Ways." "Media Decoder" (blog), *New York Times,* Feb. 6, 2013.

———. "Fox News Is Set to Renew O'Reilly and Hannity Through 2016 Elections." "Media Decoder" (blog), *New York Times,* April 19, 2012.

———. "Fox Says Its 3-Year Relationship with Palin Is Over." "Media Decoder" (blog), *New York Times,* Jan. 26, 2013.

———. "Fox's Brit Hume to Stop Anchoring 'Special Report' After Election." *New York Times,* July 15, 2008.

———. "Hannity to Go It Alone, Without Colmes." *New York Times,* Nov. 25, 2008.

———. "Kelly and Van Susteren Are Said to Re-Sign with Fox News." "Media Decoder" (blog), *New York Times,* May 8, 2013.

———. "Palin Is Returning to Fox News, Months After They Parted Ways." *New York Times,* June 14, 2013.

———. "Robert Pauley, Former Head of ABC Radio, Dies at 85." *New York Times,* May 13, 2009.

———. "Roger Ailes Signs Up for Another 4 Years at Fox News." "Media Decoder" (blog), *New York Times,* Oct. 20, 2012.

Stoeffel, Kat. "Fox Mole Joe Muto Says His Laptop Was Seized in Grand Larceny Investigation." *New York Observer,* April 25, 2012.

Sullivan, Patricia. "A Father of Modern Conservative Movement." Obituaries, *Washington Post,* Dec. 19, 2008.

Swift, Pamela. "Keeping Up with Youth." *Modesto Bee,* April 28, 1974.

Taylor, Carol. "History: Students for a Democratic Society Was Top 1968 Story in Boulder." *Boulder Daily Camera,* Oct. 11, 2011.

Television News, Inc. "New Television News Service for U.S. Broadcasters Announced." Press release. Shaw Elliott Public Relations, Jan. 22, 1975.

Thomas, Bob. "Both Critics and Audience Like 'Mother Earth' Stage Musical." Associated Press, published in *Daytona Beach Morning Journal,* Aug. 25, 1971.

Thompson, Howard. " 'Ionescopade' Shifts to the Cherry Lane." *New York Times,* July 28, 1973.

Turton, Michael. "Mock Presidential Election Held at Haldane." *Putnam County News & Recorder,* Oct. 22, 2008.

———. "Village Trustees Express Regret over July Fourth Ads." *Philipstown .info,* Aug. 3, 2013.

"TVN Gets Shot for What Ailes It: St. John Return." *Variety,* Nov. 20, 1974.

"Typical CEO Made $9.6 Million Last Year, AP Study Finds." Associated Press, May 25, 2012.

"Valentine's Day Wedding." Los Angeles Times Syndicate, published in *Toledo Blade,* Dec. 23, 1997.

VandeHei, Jim, and Mike Allen. "Roger Ailes Unplugged." *Politico,* June 6, 2013.

Van Gelder, Lawrence. "Officials Deny Murdoch Link to Book Pact for Gingrich." *New York Times,* Dec. 24, 1994.

Van Voris, Bob, and Patricia Hurtado. "Regan Accused Lawyer Dreier of Disclosing Settlement." *Bloomberg News,* Dec. 10, 2008.

Vaughan, Kevin. "Adolph Coors' Murder: Notorious Killer's Quiet End." *Denver Post,* Aug. 30, 2009.

Weinraub, Bernard. "Strip Show Flops at Fox: Murdoch Ousts Official." *New York Times,* June 23, 1992.

Weiss, Murray. "Son of Sam's Reign of Fear—Siege by a Murderous Madman." *New York Post,* July 23, 2007.

Welch, Mary Alma. "Cable Exec's 'Joke' Bombs at White House; Remarks by Ailes 'Inappropriate.' " *Washington Post,* March 12, 1994.

Wenner, Jann S. "Obama in Command: The Rolling Stone Interview." *Rolling Stone,* Oct. 14, 2010.

Wharton, Dennis. "NAACP Decries Fox's TV Station Ownership." *Daily Variety,* Nov. 23, 1993.

Williams, Scott. "Murdoch Names Ailes to Launch 24-Hour TV News Channel." Associated Press, Jan. 30, 1996.

Wilson, Earl. "Snakes Alive! Patrice Munsel Has Pet Boa." *Milwaukee Sentinel,* June 24, 1974.

Windeler, Robert. "Nixon's Television Aide Says Candidate 'Is Not a Child of TV.' " *New York Times,* Oct. 9, 1968.

Winter, Jana. "Former Fox News Employee Pleads Guilty in 'Mole' Case." Foxnews.com, May 9, 2013.

Witt, Linda. "Reclusive Joe Coors Peddles Beer and a Tough Right-Wing Line." *People,* July 7, 1975.

Wolff, Michael. "The Secrets of His Succession." *Vanity Fair,* Dec. 2008.

———. "The Trouble with Judith." *Vanity Fair,* March 2007.

———. "Tuesdays with Rupert." *Vanity Fair,* Oct. 2008.

Wollenberg, Skip. "CNBC Corners Wealthy Audience." Associated Press, Jan. 2, 1992.

———. "Turner Broadcasting Breaks Off Talks with NBC." Associated Press, Jan. 15, 1995.

Woodward, Bob. "Fox Chief Proposed Petraeus Campaign." *Washington Post,* Dec. 4, 2012.

Zeitchik, Steven. "Regan Ousted from HarperCollins." *Variety,* Dec. 15, 2006.

## TRANSCRIPTS, TAPES, AND PRIVATE PAPERS

Ailes, Elizabeth. Commencement speech, Mount Saint Mary College, Class of 2012. May 19, 2012. http://www.youtube.com/watch?v=LoTlCx7Kzxo.

Ailes, Roger. Roy H. Park Lecture at the University of North Carolina School of Journalism (transcript). April 12, 2013, http://jomc.unc.edu/roger-ailes-park-lecture-april-12-2012-transcript.

Bloomgarden, Kermit. Private papers, Wisconsin Historical Society.

CNBC/Dow Jones Business Video. "NBC Holds News Conference to Announce New 24-Hour News Channel." Transcript of news conference, Dec. 14, 1995.

Federal News Service. Transcript of remarks by Rupert Murdoch at National Press Club, Feb. 26, 1996.

Federal News Service. Transcript of remarks by Ted Turner at National Press Club, Sept. 27, 1994.

Herschensohn, Bruce. Private papers, Pepperdine University Library.

Pauley, Robert. Private papers, courtesy of Pauley's family.

Rourke, Jack. Letters, courtesy Martha Rourke.

# INDEX

## ABOUT THE AUTHOR

GABRIEL SHERMAN is a contributing editor at *New York* magazine. His journalism has appeared in *The New York Times, The New Republic, The New York Observer,* and *GQ,* among other publications. He has served as a commentator on National Public Radio, CNN, Fox News, MSNBC's *Morning Joe,* NBC's *Today* show, and ABC's *World News.* Since 2012, he has been a Bernard L. Schwartz Fellow at the New America Foundation. He lives in New York City with his wife, Jennifer Stahl. This is his first book.

theloudestvoiceintheroom.com